TAKING SIDES

Clashing Views in

World History, Volume 2

D0218590

TAKING SIDES

Clashing Views in

World History, Volume 2

SECOND EDITION, EXPANDED

Selected, Edited, and with Introductions by

Joseph R. Mitchell
Howard Community College

and

Helen Buss Mitchell
Howard Community College

**McGraw-Hill
Higher Education**

Boston   Burr Ridge, IL   Dubuque, IA   New York   San Francisco   St. Louis
Bangkok   Bogotá   Caracas   Kuala Lumpur   Lisbon   London   Madrid   Mexico City
Milan   Montreal   New Delhi   Santiago   Seoul   Singapore   Sydney   Taipei   Toronto

TAKING SIDES: CLASHING VIEWS IN WORLD HISTORY, VOLUME 2,
SECOND EDITION, EXPANDED

 This book is printed on recycled, acid-free paper containing
10% postconsumer waste.

1 2 3 4 5 6 7 8 9 0 DOC/DOC 0 9 8 7

MHID: 0-07-351517-5
ISBN: 978-0-07-351517-5
ISSN:1538-716X

Managing Editor: *Larry Loeppke*
Production Manager: *Faye Schilling*
Senior Developmental Editor: *Susan Brusch*
Editorial Assistant: *Nancy Meissner*
Production Service Assistant: *Rita Hingtgen*
Permissions Coordinator: *Lori Church*
Senior Marketing Manager: *Julie Keck*
Marketing Communications Specialist: *Mary Klein*
Marketing Coordinator: *Alice Link*
Project Manager: *Jane Mohr*
Design Specialist: *Tara McDermott*
Senior Administrative Assistant: *DeAnna Dausener*
Senior Operations Manager: *Pat Koch Krieger*
Cover Graphics: *Maggie Lytle*

Compositor: ICC Macmillan Inc.
Cover Image: Corbis/Royalty Free

Library of Congress Cataloging-in-Publication Data

Main entry under title:
    Taking sides: clashing views in world history, volume 2/selected, edited, and with introductions
    by Joseph R. Mitchell and Helen Buss Mitchell.—2nd ed.

    Includes bibliographical references.
    1. World History. 2. History, modern. I. Mitchell, Joseph R., ed. II. Helen,
    Buss, ed. III. Series

909

Preface

In *Taking Sides: Clashing Views in World History, Volume 2*, we identify the issues that are typically covered in the teaching of world history, using scholarly and readable sources that argue these issues. We have taken care to choose issues that will make this volume multicultural, gender based, and reflective of current historical scholarship. We frame these issues with preview and follow-up sections that are user-friendly for both teachers and students. Students who use this volume should come away with a greater understanding and appreciation of the value of studying history as well as enhanced skills in critical thinking.

Plan of the book   This book is made up of 20 issues that argue pertinent topics in the study of world history. Each issue has an issue *introduction*, which sets the stage for the debate as it is argued in the yes and no selections that follow. Each issue concludes with a *postscript* that makes some final observations and points the way to other questions related to the issue. In reading the issue and forming your own opinions, you should not feel confined to adopt one or the other of the positions presented. There are positions in between the given views or totally outside them, and the *suggestions for further reading* that appear in each issue postscript should help you to find resources to continue your study of the subject. We have also provided Internet site addresses (URLs) in the *On the Internet* page that accompanies each part opener. At the back of the book is a listing of all the *contributors to this volume*, which will give you information on the historians and commentators whose views are debated here.

Using the book   Care has been taken to provide issues that are in various ways related. They could be used to: (a) compare/contrast those with like content; (b) show relationships between and among some topics across time, geographic, and cultural boundaries; (c) make connections between past historical events and their contemporary relevance. For example, Issues 1 and 9 analyze the effects of two revolutions—one economic (Industrial), one political (Russian)—on the lives of women. Issues 2 and 4 deal with the effects of revolution on nineteenth-century France and Japan respectively. Issues 3, 5, and 6 cover nineteenth-century British imperialism and its effects on colonial populations in Ireland, Africa, and Asia. Issue 4 and 11 trace the rise to power of Japan during the 19th-century Meiji Restoration and its fall from grace during World War II. Issues 4 and 6 analyze the different responses of Japan and China to Western imperialism. Issues 7, 8, 10, and 11 cover the causes of war and its horrendous consequences. Issues 13, 14, 15, and 18 deal with important questions facing much of the non-Western world in this postcolonial era. Finally, Issues 15, 16 and 17 explore conflict and disintegration in Rwanda, Yugoslavia, and Afghanistan, looking in the last case for possible positive outcomes. Issue 19 treats the issue of European union influence on world affairs, and finally, Issue 20 explores a policy of liberal imperialism for the United States.

A word to the instructor   An *Instructor's Manual With Test Questions* (multiple choice and essay) is available through the publisher for the instructor using *Taking Sides* in the classroom. A general guidebook, *Using Taking Sides in the Classroom*, which discusses methods and techniques for integrating the pro-con approach into any classroom setting, is also available. An online version of *Using Taking Sides in the Classroom* and a correspondence service for *Taking Sides* adopters can be found at http://www.mhcls.com/usingts/.

   Taking Sides: Clashing Views in World History is only one title in the Taking-Sides series. If you are interested in seeing the table of contents for any of the other titles, please visit the Taking Sides Web site at http://www.mhcls.com/takingsides/.

Acknowledgments   We would like to thank Larry Madaras of Howard Community College—fellow teacher, good friend, coeditor of *Taking Sides: Clashing Views on Controversial Issues in American History*, and editor of *Taking Sides: Clashing Views on Controversial Issues in American History Since 1945*—for his past and present assistance in making our work possible. Special acknowledgment also goes to David Stebenne of Ohio State University—friend, scholar, teacher, and author of *Arthur J. Goldberg: New Deal Liberal* (Oxford University Press, 1996)—for his suggestions and advice. Thanks also go out to the library staffs of Howard County, Maryland; University of Maryland, College Park; University of Maryland, Baltimore County (UMBC); and Howard Community College—particularly Ela Ciborowski, who secured interlibrary loans.

   At McGraw-Hill/Contemporary Learning Series, a debt of gratitude is owed to list manager Larry Loeppke and developmental editor Susan Brusch, who guided us through the publishing process and gave encouraging words and positive feedback when they were needed most.

A final word   We would appreciate any questions, comments, or suggestions regarding our work, especially which issues work best in your classroom and which issues you never use. Please contact us at joemitch@bigjar.com. We promise a quick response.

Joseph R. Mitchell
Howard Community College

Helen Buss Mitchell
Howard Community College

Contents In Brief

Contents

Christine Kinealy, fellow of the University of Liverpool, argues that the British government's response to the Irish potato famine was deliberately inadequate. The British government's "hidden agenda" of long-term economic, social, and agrarian reform was accelerated by the famine, and mass emigration was a consequence of these changes. Historian Hasia R. Diner documents large-scale emigration both before and after the Irish potato famine. Diner credits the Irish people with learning from their famine experiences that the reliance of the poor on the potato and the excessive subdivision of the land within families were no longer in their own best interests.

Historian Andrew Gordon states that the Meiji Restoration created fundamental changes in Japanese society, thus meriting the term "revolution." Historian W.G. Beasley argues that when compared with other revolutions like the French and Russian, the Meiji Restoration did not constitute a revolution in the classical sense.

Lance E. Davis and Robert Huttenback state that, although statistics prove that British imperialism was not a profitable venture, it was supported by an economic elite that was able to promote and derive profits from it. Professor John M. MacKenzie argues that the motivation for British imperialism was multicausal and that most of the causes can be found in the general anxiety crisis permeating British society in the late nineteenth century.

Professor Paul A. Cohen contends that while anti-foreign and anti-Christian attitudes played a role in the start of the Boxer rebellion, a more immediate cause was a severe drought and its impact on Chinese society. Historian Henrietta Harrison concedes that while the Boxers were motivated by more than one factor, opposition to Christian missionary activity was at the core of their rebellion.

PART 2 THE EARLY TWENTIETH CENTURY   123

Issue 7. Were German Militarism and Diplomacy Responsible for World War I?   124

YES: **V.R. Berghahn,** from *Imperial Germany, 1871–1914: Economic, Society, Culture, and Politics* (Berghahn Books, 1994)   *126*

NO: **Samuel R. Williamson, Jr.,** from "The Origins of the War," in Hew Strachan, ed., *The Oxford Illustrated History of the First World War* (Oxford University Press, 1998)   *135*

History professor V.R. Berghahn states that, although all of Europe's major powers played a part in the onset of World War I, recent evidence still indicates that Germany's role in the process was the main factor responsible for the conflict. History professor Samuel R. Williamson, Jr., argues that the factors and conditions that led to the First World War were a shared responsibility and that no one nation could be blamed for its genesis.

Issue 8. Was the Treaty of Versailles Responsible for World War II?   145

YES: **Derek Aldcroft,** from "The Versailles Legacy," *History Review* (December 1997)   *147*

NO: **Mark Mazower,** from "Two Cheers for Versailles," *History Today* (July 1997)   *155*

Historian Derek Aldcroft states that a combination of the flaws present in the post-war Versailles Treaty and the resultant actions and inactions of European statesmen created a climate that paved the way for World War II. Historian Mark Mazower finds that while the Treaty of Versailles contained weaknesses, it failed due to the lack of enforcement of its principles by a generation of European leaders.

Issue 9. Did the Bolshevik Revolution Improve the Lives of Soviet Women?   163

YES: **Richard Stites,** from "Women and the Revolutionary Process in Russia," in Renate Bridenthal, Claudia Koontz, and Susan M. Stuard, eds., *Becoming Visible: Women in European History,* 2nd. ed. (Houghton Mifflin, 1987)   *165*

NO: **Lesley A. Rimmel,** from "The Baba and the Comrade: Gender and Politics in Soviet Russia," *The Women's Review of Books* (September 1998)   *173*

History professor Richard Stites argues that, in the early years of the Bolshevik Revolution, the Zhenotdel, or Women's Department, helped many working women take the first steps toward emancipation. Russian scholar Lesley A. Rimmel finds that the Russian Revolution remains unfinished for women, who were mobilized as producers and reproducers for a male political agenda.

Political science professor Daniel J. Goldhagen states that due to the nature of German society in the twentieth century—with its endemic, virulent antisemitism—thousands of ordinary German citizens became willing participants in the implementation of Holocaust horrors. Holocaust historian Christopher R. Browning argues that Goldhagen's thesis is too simplistic, and that a multicausal approach must be used to determine why ordinary German citizens willingly participated in the Holocaust.

Herbert Bix offers proof that Emperor Hirohito should be held responsible for Japan's World War II actions. Historian Stephen S. Large argues that Emperor Hirohito's lack of real political power to effect change absolves him from any direct responsibility for World War II.

Historian John Lewis Gaddis states that after more than half a century of cold war scholarship, Joseph Stalin still deserves most of the responsibility for the onset of the cold war. Historian Martin J. Sherwin counters that the origins of the cold war can be found in World War II diplomacy involving the use of the atomic bomb, and he places much of the blame for the cold war on the shoulders of Franklin D. Roosevelt, Harry S. Truman, and Winston Churchill.

Philosophy professor A.T. Nuyen maintains that the basic tenets of classical capitalism are perfectly compatible with the key elements of Chinese philosophy. Management professor Jack Scarborough contrasts the Western heritage of democracy, rationality, and individualism with Confucian values of harmony, filial loyalty, and legalism. Based on his comparison, Scarborough finds that Chinese Confucianism is incompatible with Western capitalism.

Professor of Middle Eastern studies John L. Esposito sees the Iranian Revolution against Western-inspired modernization and Egypt's "holy war" against Israel as examples of the Islamic quest for a more authentic society and culture, which challenges a stable world order. Professor of international relations Sharif Shuja identifies the rise of Islamic movements as resistance to Western domination rather than a threat to the West as such and traces Western fears of a monolithic Islamic entity to the errors of an "Orientalist" mindset.

Alison Des Forges states that ethnic hatred between Hutus and Tutsis in Rwanda was primarily responsible for the Rwandan Genocide of 1994. René Lemarchand admits that ethnic rivalries played a role in the catastrophe, but the ability of the Hutus to engage in "planned annihilation" free of any local or international restraint was a more important factor.

Career diplomat Warren Zimmerman, the United States' last ambassador to Yugoslavia, argues that the republic's ethnic leaders, especially Slobodan Milosevic, bear primary responsibility for the nation's demise. Political science professor Steven Majstorovic contends that while manipulation by elite ethnic leaders played a role in the disintegration of Yugoslavia, the fragile ethnic divisions, formed by memory and myth, also played an important role in the country's demise.

World policy analyst Anatol Lieven states that dated United States cold war policies and despair-inducing political, economic, and social conditions have contributed to the rise of radical Islamists, some of whom were responsible for the September 11, 2001, attacks. International relations specialist Mark Juergensmeyer contends that the roots of the September 11, 2001, attacks lie in the radical views of the terrorists, especially the symbolism of cosmic war and the battle between good and evil.

International Afghan advocate for refugee women Sima Wali documents the pivotal roles Afghan women have played in rebuilding their communities, praises their courage in denouncing warlords, and calls for their full participation in the newly formed constitutional government. Journalist Noy Thrupkaew argues that dissension among women's groups in Afghanistan and the high profile of the Western-backed Revolutionary Association of the Women of Afghanistan (RAWA) are hampering progress; a more unified and moderate approach is needed.

Political science and international studies professor Mitchell P. Smith argues that the European Union excels in the use of soft power to achieve desired outcomes at minimal cost, by avoiding the use of military force and sharing the burden of enforcement with others. Efstathios T. Fakiolas, Strategy and SouthEast European Affairs Analyst, contends that Europe's failure to achieve European "Union-hood" seriously hampers its effectiveness in the global community.

Foreign policy author and commentator Max Boot argues that the United States should continue its policy of liberal imperialism in the twenty-first century because it represents the best alternative to insure permanent world peace. Author and professor Immanuel Wallerstein argues that U.S. foreign policy has created major problems and that the United States should cease aggressive actions, preventing further damage at home and abroad.

Introduction

The Study of World History

Joseph R. Mitchell
Helen Buss Mitchell

What Is History?

History is a dialogue between the past and the present. As we respond to events in our own time and place, we bring the concerns of the present to our study of the past. What seems important to us, where we turn our attention, how we approach a study of the past—all these are rooted in the present. It has been said that where you stand determines what you see. This is especially the case with history. If we stand within the Western tradition exclusively, we may be tempted to see its story as the only story or the only one worth telling. And whose perspective we take is also critical. From the point of view of the rich and powerful, the events of history take one shape; through the lens of the poor and powerless, the same events can appear quite different. If we take women, or non-Western cultures, or the ordinary person as our starting point, the story of the past may present us with a series of surprises.

Tools of the Historian

Much of the raw material of history consists of written sources. Original sources—from a period contemporary with the events or ideas described—are called *primary sources*. These may include documents of all kinds, including official records as well as personal letters and diaries. The writings of historians reflecting on the past are called *secondary sources*. It is important to keep in mind that primary sources may not automatically be assumed to be free from bias. Each contains historical and personal perspectives. Their principal limitation, however, is that they record what people considered noteworthy about their own age and not necessarily what would most interest us today. As the concerns of the present evolve, the questions we bring to our study of the past will also change. Much of what you read in this book will reflect differences in focus between one historian and another. As Edward Hallett Carr points out, the historian constructs a working model that enables him or her to understand the past. It would be a great mistake to confuse this working model with a photocopy.

Traditional History

Only recently has history considered itself a social science and striven for a kind of scientific accuracy in speaking about the past. For much of human history, until perhaps the beginning of the twentieth century, history was considered a branch of literature rather than a kind of science. It was concerned first of all with narrative, with the telling of a compelling story, and its focus was on the fascinating characters whose lives shaped and defined the past.

Biography, the recounting of the life and times of a powerful man, was regarded as one of the most reliable windows on the past. The so-called "great man" was credited with shaping and defining his own time. As a result, studying Emperor Hirohito of Japan (see Issue 11) or Soviet Premier Josef Stalin (see Issue 12) was assumed to offer one of the most reliable keys to unlocking a specific historical time period.

And, traditional history looked relatively uncritically at the great men from the past. Military heroes, for example, were lauded for their conquests with little or no focus on the carnage that made those conquests possible. Another unspoken assumption was the dominance and superiority of the West as the creator and bearer of human civilization. Divine power was sometimes seen as directing or, at least, approving the actions of powerful nations and men.

The traditional areas of focus for the historian have been political, diplomatic, and constitutional. Political history considers how power has been organized and enforced by the state within human societies. Diplomatic history looks at what has influenced the power struggles between states as they continually struggled for dominance. Constitutional history examines the evolution of national states, with special attention to who rules and who or what confers the right to rule. These questions continue to intrigue historians as Issues 4 (about reasons for the Meiji Restoration in Japan) and 7 (concerning German militarism and World War I) illustrate. Ethnic conflict in Rwanda and Yugoslavia (Issues 15 and 16), as well as war in Afghanistan (Issue 18) reflect contemporary conflicts and concerns.

A related domain has been that of intellectual history or the history of ideas—in the fields of politics, economics, sociology, theology, and science. Taking this approach to its widest scope, one might explore the intellectual climate of an age, such as the age of Imperialism, the rise of Communism, the period of the Cold War, or the dominance of Capitalism. This question has become complicated by the psychological insights of Sigmund Freud. Are we really motivated primarily by our primal, internal drives no matter how high minded we might wish to appear? And, especially since the economic theories of Karl Marx have become widely known, the influence of both ideas and economic forces on individuals and civilizations has been widely explored. As an example, Issue 5 on the motivation for British Imperialism asks which was more prominent: economic factors or national anxiety?

Revisionism

However, history is not a once-and-for-all enterprise. Each generation formulates its own questions and brings new tools to the study of the past resulting in a process called *revisionism*. Much of what you will read in this book is a product of revisionism as historians reinterpret the past in the light of the present. One generation values revolutions, the next focuses on their terrible costs. One generation assumes that great men shape the events of history, the next looks to the lives of ordinary people to illuminate the past. There is no final answer, but where we stand will determine which interpretation seems more compelling to us. Issues 11 and 12 introduce the tension between traditional and revisionist interpretations of Hirohito and Stalin.

As new tools of analysis become available, our ability to understand the past improves. Bringing events into clearer focus can change the meaning we assign to them. Many of the selections in this book reflect new attitudes and new insights made possible by the tools that historians have borrowed from the other social sciences. For instance, studies of climate and its historical consequences can shed new light on what motivates people to act as they do. To explore this question, see Issue 6 on the Boxer Rebellion in China. Were the disaffected motivated primarily by anti-religious feelings or left with nothing meaningful to do by the drought?

Presentism

While we stand in the present, we must be wary of what historians call *presentism*, that is, reading the values of the present back into the past. If we live in a culture that values individualism and prizes competition, we may be tempted to see these values as good even in a culture that preferred communalism and cooperation. And, we may miss a key component of an ancient civilization because it does not match what we currently consider worthwhile. We cannot and should not avoid our own questions and struggles. They will inform our study of the past; and yet, they must not warp our vision. Ideally, historians engage in a continual dialogue in which the concerns but not the values of the present are explored through a study of the past.

At the same time, though, we might bring the moral standards of the present to bear on the past. Cultural relativism, pioneered in the field of anthropology, made us sensitive to the many and varied ways in which civilizations define what is "normal" and what is "moral." So, we remain appropriately reluctant to judge individuals from other times and places by our standards since they were or are, in fact, behaving perfectly normally and morally by the standards of their own time and place. However, from the perspective of the present, we do not hesitate to condemn slaveholding, genocide, or even the hidden costs of revolutions. Issue 2, for instance, explores whether or not the French Revolution could be said to be worth its human costs. And, Issues 15, 16, and 18 examine the devastation caused by contemporary ethnic hatred and war.

Changing Historiographical Focuses

All cultures are vulnerable to the narrow mindedness created by *ethnocentrism*—the belief that my culture is superior to all others. From inside a particular culture, certain practices may seem normative—that is, we may assume that all humans or all rational humans must behave the way we do or hold the attitudes we hold. When we meet a culture that sees the world differently from ourselves, we may be tempted to write them off as inferior or primitive. As an alternative to ethnocentrism, we might want to enter the worldview of another and see what we can learn from expanding our perspective. These issues will offer you many opportunities to try this thought experiment.

Stepping outside the Western tradition has allowed historians to take a more globocentric view of world events. Accusing their predecessors of Eurocentrism, some historians have adopted an Afrocentric view of world history that emphasizes Africa's seminal role in cultural evolution. Within the Western tradition, women have challenged the male-dominated perspective that studied war but ignored family. Including additional perspectives complicates our interpretation of past events but permits a fuller picture to emerge. We must be wary of *universalism*—assuming, for example, that patriarchy has always existed or that being a woman was the same for every woman no matter what her historical circumstances. What similarities exist between women swept up in the European Industrial Revolution (Issue 1) and Afghan women seeking liberation from oppression (Issue 18)? Are there ways in which changing circumstances offer new possibilities for both groups of women? And, in what ways are their lives and circumstances profoundly different? If cultures other than the West have been dominant in the past, what did the world look like under those circumstances? Issues 14 and 17 examine Islamic revivalism and its yearning for Islam's "Golden Age."

Social History

Some historians have moved beyond political, diplomatic, and constitutional history to explore economics and demographics as well as to study social processes. Moving from a focus on nations and rulers to a close examination of forces that can be studied analytically has opened up the realms of business and the family to the historian. Proponents of the so-called new social history rejected what they called history from the top down. Instead of the great man whose influence shaped his age, they looked to the lives of ordinary people and called what they were doing history from the bottom up. The previous generation of historians had sometimes acted as if only the influential had a role in shaping history. Social history assumes that all people are capable of acting as historical agents rather than being passive victims to whom history happens. With this shift in attitude, the lives of slaves, workers, women of all kinds, and children, too, become worthy subjects of historical investigation.

Because the poor and powerless seldom leave written records, other methods must be used to understand their lives. Applying the methods of social scientists to their own discipline, historians have broadened and deepened their field of study. Archaeological evidence, DNA analysis, the tools of paleoanthropology, computer analysis of demographic data—all these have allowed the voiceless to speak across centuries. Fossil evidence, for instance, and the analysis of mitochondrial DNA—the structures within cells we inherit only from our mothers—may each be employed, sometimes with strikingly different results, to trace the migrations of pre-literate peoples. And, oral history can expand the number and variety of voices we "hear."

What historians call *material culture* reveals the everyday lives of people by analyzing what they discarded as well as the monuments and other material objects they intended to leave as markers of their civilizations. And, the high speed comparative functions of computers have allowed the historian to ana-lyze vast quantities of data and look for demographic trends. As an example, Issue 1 examines a rise in illegitimacy rates in industrializing Europe and the questions it raises about changes in attitude or circumstances. Other demo-graphic questions include: How old are people when they marry for the first time, have a child, or die? Only with the expanded life expectancy made pos-sible by the modern world has it been possible for people to see their chil-dren's children—to become grandparents. If we study weather patterns and learn that certain years were periods of drought, we can imagine ourselves into the lives of those living under drought conditions. Would disaffected young men with nothing meaningful to occupy their labor turn to protest? Issue 6 on the Boxer Rebellion explores this question.

Race, Class, and Gender

The experience of being a historical subject is never monolithic. That is, each of us has a gender, a race, a social class, an ethnic identity, a religion (even if it is atheism or agnosticism), an age, and a variety of other markers that color our experiences. At times, the most important factor may be my gender and what happens may be more or less the same for all members of a particular gender. Under other circumstances, however, race may be predominant. Being a member of a racial minority or of a powerful racial majority may lead to very different experiences of the same event. At other times social class may determine how an event is experienced; the rich may have one story to tell, the poor another. And, other factors, such as religion or ethnic identity, even age, can become the most significant piece of a person's identity especially if prejudice or favoritism is involved. Historians try always to take into account how race, class, and gender (as well as a host of other factors) intersect in the life of a historical subject. Issue 9 examines the lives of Bolshevik women who discovered that the revolution they hoped would benefit their gender was first and foremost devoted to issues of class. And, Issue 18 considers what possibilities exist for Afghan women in a post-Taliban world.

Issues Involved in Historical Interpretation

Often historians will agree on what happened but disagree about why or how something occurred. Sometimes the question is: Were internal or external causes more responsible? Both may have contributed to an event but one or the other may have played the more significant role. Looking at differing evi-dence may lead historians to varying interpretations. A related question is: Was it the circumstances that changed or only the attitudes of those who experienced them? Issue 1 debates the cause for a rise in illegitimacy rates. Was the capitalist industrial revolution responsible for changing young women's attitudes in a more sexually permissive environment? Or, did they retain traditional attitudes but find the external circumstances dramatically altered? Issue 8 questions the role of the Treat of Versailles in powerfully affecting the attitudes of defeated nations.

Periodization

Even more basically, the student of the past must wonder whether the turning points that shape the chapters in our history books are the same for all historical subjects? The process of marking turning points is known as *periodization*. It is the more or less artificial creation of periods that chunk history into manageable segments by identifying forks in the road that took people and events in a new direction. Using an expanded perspective, we may learn that the traditional turning points hold for men but not for women or reflect the experiences of one ethnic group but not another. And, if periodization schemes conflict, which one should we use? Were there sharp breaks at the periods we designate The Renaissance, the Scientific Revolution, or the Industrial Revolution? If there were, did women and men experience these breaks identically?

It is also important to keep in mind that people living at a particular moment in history are not aware of labels that later historians will attach to their experience. People who lived during the Middle Ages were surely not aware of living in the middle of something. Only much after the fact were we able to call a later age the Renaissance. To those who lived during what we call the Middle Ages or the Renaissance, marriage, childbirth, work, weather, sickness, and death were the real concerns, just as they are for us. Our own age will certainly be characterized by future historians in ways that might surprise and shock us. As we study the past, it is helpful to keep in mind that some of our assumptions are rooted in a traditional periodization that is now being challenged.

Continuity or Discontinuity?

A related question concerns the connection or lack of connection between one event or set of events and another. When we look at the historical past, we must ask ourselves whether we are seeing continuity or discontinuity. In other words, is the event we are studying part of a normal process of evolution or does it represent a break from a traditional pattern. Questions of continuity vs. discontinuity are the fundamental ones on which the larger issue of periodization rests. The first issue in this volume explores whether the Industrial Revolution took the lives of workers in wholly new directions or whether traditional behaviors continued, albeit in a radically different context?

Sometimes events may appear continuous from the point of view of one group and discontinuous from the point of view of another. Suppose that factory owners found their world and worldview shifting dramatically, whereas the lives and perspectives of workers went on more or less as they had before. When this is the case, whose experience should we privilege? Is one group's experience more historically significant than another's—and how should we decide?

Issues 15 and 16 examine the eruption of longstanding ethnic hatreds. In Rwanda and Yugoslavia, was there a tipping point that took events in a violent, new direction? Or, did centuries of simmering resentment and mistrust finally reach a boiling point? In an earlier century, we might want to ask whether the Meiji Restoration in Japan, discussed in Issue 4, was truly revolutionary—are we looking at more continuity or radical discontinuity? And, in Issue 13, is modern capitalism continuous with traditional capitalism or does the modern version represent such a strong discontinuity with its historical past that Confucian values appear incompatible with it?

The Power of Ideas

Can ideas change the course of history? People have sometimes been willing to die for what they believe in and revolutions have certainly been fought, at least in part, over ideas? Some historians believe that studying the clash of ideas or the predominance of one idea or set of ideas offers the best key to understanding the past. Issue 3 looks at how much British policy decisions during the Irish potato famine of the mid-nineteenth century were justified by prevailing ideas—such as those of laissez-faire capitalism and the contrast between the deserving and the undeserving poor. Issues 18 and 14 explore what ideas are powering war in Afghanistan and Iraq and fueling Islamic revivalism.

What do you think? Do ideas shape world events? Would devotion to a political or religious cause lead you to challenge the status quo? Or, would economic conditions be more likely to send you to the streets? Historians differ in ranking the importance of various factors in influencing the past. Do people challenge the power structure because they feel politically powerless, or because they are hungry, or because of the power of ideas?

The Timeliness of Historical Issues

When we read the newspaper, check in at an online website, or listen to the evening news, there are a confusing number of present day political, economic, religious, and military clashes that can be understood only by looking at their historical contexts. The role of the United States in world events, the perennial conflicts in the Middle East, the horror and enigma of the Holocaust (see Issue 10), the nature and future of terrorism (see Issue 17), the threat posed by religious revivalism (see Issue 14), the question of whether ancient ethnic hatred can ever be quenched (see Issues 15 and 16)—these concerns of the global village have roots in the past. Understanding the origins of conflicts gives us the possibility of envisioning their solutions. The issues in this book will help you think through the problems facing our world and give you the tools to make an informed decision about what you think is the best course of action.

In a democracy, an informed citizenry is the bedrock on which a government stands. If we do not understand the past, the present will be a puzzle to us and the future may seem out of our control. Seeing how and why historians disagree can help us determine what the critical issues are and where informed interpreters part company. This, at least, is the basis for forming our own judgments and acting upon them. Looking critically at clashing views also hones our analytic skills and makes us thoughtful readers of all our textbooks as well as magazines and newspapers.

Why Study World History?

You may be wondering why this book deals with world history rather than exclusively with Western Civilization. At times the West has felt its power and dominance in the world made only its own story worth studying. History, we are sometimes told, is written by the winners. For the Chinese, the Greeks, the Ottoman Turks and many other victors of the past, the stories of other civilizations seemed irrelevant, unimportant, not nearly as valuable as their own triumphal saga. The Chinese considered their Middle Kingdom the center of the world; the Greeks labeled all others barbarians; and the Ottoman Turks expected never to lose their position of dominance. From our perspective in the present these stories form a tapestry. No one thread or pattern tells the tale and all seem equally necessary for a complete picture of the past to emerge.

Any single story—even that of a military and economic superpower—is insufficient to explain the scope of human history at a given moment in time. Our story is especially interesting to us and you will find issues specific to Western Civilization in this book. However, as we are learning, our story achieves its fullest meaning only when it is told in concert with those of other civilizations who share an increasingly interconnected planet with us. As communications systems shrink the Earth into a global village, we may be ignoring the rest of the world at our own peril. At the very least the study of civilizations other than our own can alert us to events that may have worldwide implications. And, as we are beginning to learn, no story happens in isolation. The history of the West can perhaps be accurately told only within a global context that takes into account the actions and reactions of other civilizations as they share the world stage with the West. As you read the issues that concern non-Western civilizations, stay alert for what you can learn about your own.

Your textbook may take a global focus or it may be restricted to the study of Western Civilization. In either case, the readings in this book will enrich your understanding of how the peoples of the world have understood themselves and their relationships with others. As we become a more clearly multicultural society, we have an additional reason for studying about other civilizations that have blended with our own through immigration. Perhaps the biggest challenge for an increasingly diverse United States of America is to understand its own role in world affairs and its relationship with other countries, which may have different histories, value systems, and goals.

On the Internet . . .

Industrial Revolution

Background on the Industrial Revolution, including topics such as the agricultural revolution, techonological change since 1700, electric power, transportation, communications, and changing social patterns.

```
http://mars.acnet.wnec.edu/~grempel/courses/wc2/
             lectures/industrialrev.html
```

Liberty, Equality, Fraternity: Exploring the French Revolution

Features 12 topical essays, 250 images, 350 text documents, 11 songs, 13 maps, a timeline, and a glossary.

```
http://chnm.gmu.edu/revolution/
```

The Irish Potato Famine

Collection of short essays on how the potato came to Ireland and became the staple crop, the nature of the blight that caused the famine, and the effects and death and emigration. Contains links and a map.

```
http://collections.ic.gc.ca/potato/
           history/ireland.asp
```

Schauwecker's Guide to Japan: Meiji Period, 1868–1912

Part of a larger site on the history of Japan, Schauwecker's Guide to Japan: Meiji Period, 1868–1912, contains a brief article. If considered with the many links contained within it, this section presents a detailed account of history during the Meiji period.

```
http://www.japan-guide.com/e/e2139.html
```

History of Imperialism

The History of Imperialism Web site contains six pages of links to all sorts of information, including articles, definitions, timelines, maps, political cartoons, study questions, and book resources—all nicely organized for easy use.

```
http://members.aol.com/TeacherNet/World.html
```

The Boxer Rebellion of 1900

Contains background on the Qing Dynasty, maps and photos of China, the text of John Hay's First Open Door Note, and a concise history of China, as well as essays on spheres of influence and the secret society known as Fists of Righteous Harmony.

```
http://www.smplanet.com/imperialism/fists.html
```

PART 1

The Modern World

*T*his section traces the development of capitalism and democracy and the influence that they had on the modern world. It also covers the rise of nationalism and how countries were affected by it in both positive and negative ways, including the change brought about by various types of revolutions and their effects.

- Did the Industrial Revolution Lead to a Sexual Revolution?

- Was the French Revolution Worth Its Human Costs?

- Did British Policy Decisions Cause the Mass Emigration and Land Reforms That Followed the Irish Potato Famine?

- Did the Meiji Restoration Constitute a Revolution in Nineteenth-Century Japan?

- Were Economic Factors Primarily Responsible for British Imperialism?

- Was China's Boxer Rebellion Caused by Environmental Factors?

ISSUE 1

Did the Industrial Revolution Lead to a Sexual Revolution?

YES: Edward Shorter, from "Female Emancipation, Birth Control, and Fertility in European History," *The American Historical Review* (June 1973)

NO: Louise A. Tilly, Joan W. Scott, and Miriam Cohen, from "Women's Work and European Fertility Patterns," *Journal of Interdisciplinary History* (Winter 1976)

ISSUE SUMMARY

YES: Historian Edward Shorter argues that employment opportunities outside the home that opened up with industrialization led to a rise in the illegitimacy rate, which he attributes to the sexual emancipation of unmarried, working-class women.

NO: Historians Louise A. Tilly, Joan W. Scott, and Miriam Cohen counter that unmarried women worked to meet an economic need, not to gain personal freedom, and they attribute the rise in illegitimacy rates to broken marriage promises and the absence of traditional support from family, community, and the church.

Historians agree that between 1750 and 1850, the illegitimacy rate rose across Europe. In many of the European countries this time period coincides with industrialization. Did the arrival of capitalism change the living and working habits of unmarried women and introduce new attitudes that made them more interested in sex? When the result is agreed upon, what matters most is the evidence offered to explain the cause.

In the selection that follows, Edward Shorter asserts that a nineteenth-century sexual revolution that had its roots in industrial capitalism occurred. In his view the market economy, with its values of self-interest and competitiveness, changed the value system of the proletarian subculture—the young men and women working for wages in industrializing countries. Earning their own money, says Shorter, gave these workers the means to live independently. Young women in particular, he argues, declared their independence from family control, struck out in pursuit of personal freedom, and began to enjoy sex as a way of finding individual self-fulfillment. The predictable result was a rise in illegitimacy rates.

Louise A. Tilly, Joan W. Scott, and Miriam Cohen, in reply, fault Shorter for offering little or no hard evidence for his hypothesis. Citing the work of other historians, they assert that family interest rather than self-interest led women to work. Women moved very slowly into industrial work, and, even by the end of the period (1850), most women who were employed were doing domestic service, dressmaking, laundering, and tailoring, not factory work. Many women earned far too little to permit them to live independently. Those who did probably kept the traditional assumption that premarital intercourse with an intended bridegroom would be followed by marriage. Tilly, Scott, and Cohen argue that what changed was not the attitudes but the external context. In the absence of traditional pressures, young men moved on to other work or better opportunities, leaving the women they had impregnated behind.

As you read these two conflicting interpretations, look for the explanation offered by each selection and, most important, at what evidence is offered to support the interpretation. It may seem logical to assume that an increase in rates of illegitimacy must be due to a sexual revolution. But is that the only or the best explanation that existing information can support? There is a real temptation to use our "common sense" to fill in the gaps, but the historian insists on evidence.

For centuries history was written exclusively from the point of view of the rich, the powerful, and the literate. For some, understanding the "great man"—Alexander the Great, Julius Caesar, and Napoleon, for example—was the key to understanding the age in which he lived. This is often called history "from the top down." Many scholars, however, have begun to uncover the lives of the poor, the powerless, and the illiterate—what some call history "from the bottom up." Borrowing the methods of the social sciences, such as archaeology, anthropology, sociology, and psychology, and using quantitative analyses of economic and demographic data, historians are trying to fill in the missing pieces of the past. The selections in this issue take on the challenge of assessing the motives of people who left few, if any, written records. Since we cannot read their diaries and letters, we must use the evidence that we do have about the lives these women led and attempt to imagine how they might have seen the world.

In this issue, the chief question concerns continuity versus discontinuity. What changed? What remained the same? Did the attitudes of working women change as they entered the capitalist labor force, as Shorter states? And did these attitudes lead them to pursue personal pleasures such as sex, which, in the absence of birth control, resulted in higher rates of illegitimacy? Or, as Tilly, Scott, and Cohen argue, did the attitudes stay the same (premarital sex, as usual, in the context of courtship and with the expectation of marriage), while the context changed, leaving women pregnant and with no expectation of marriage?

N. Abramovitz and
Guilio A. De Leo

 **YES**

Female Emancipation, Birth Control, and Fertility in European History

The conventional wisdom about female emancipation is that it originated among upper-class women in the mid-nineteenth century, surfacing first in tandem with the movement for emancipation of the slaves, then moving forward independently as the suffrage movement. While this account may be substantially correct as involves women's participation in national political life, it is, in my opinion, inapplicable to family history. I suggest that the position of women within the family underwent a radical shift starting late in the eighteenth century; furthermore, the change progressed from young and lowly women to older women of higher status. The logic of this chronology sees involvement in the economy of the market place as the principal motor of emancipation.

What exactly is meant by "female emancipation"? General statements about the position of women within early modern European families are uncertain in the extreme because, at the same time, so many impressions of individual famous women are to be found in the literature and so little is known in a systematic, quantitative way about the cultural rules and norms of women in the popular classes. Yet one might fairly characterize the situation of most women as one of subordination. In the first place, both young men and women were subordinated to the authority of their parents, so that parental intervention in the mating market customarily replaced romantic love in bringing young couples together. In the second place, both social ideology and the force of events conspired to make the husband supreme over the woman in the household, his obligation being merely to respect her, hers, however, to serve and obey him. In most matters of sex, economics, or family authority the woman was expected to do the husband's bidding. Clearly individual exceptions existed, yet the rule seems to have been powerlessness and dependency for the woman.

Thus female emancipation involves, quite simply, the replacement of this subordination with independence. In the nineteenth and twentieth centuries married women acquired for themselves first, practical leverage on household political power, and second, a family ideology stressing their own rights to sexual gratification and emotional autonomy. And unmarried women became increasingly convinced of the impropriety of family and community restraints upon social and sexual relations, so that they came to ignore the strictures of both parents and community in order to gratify their own per-

From Edward Shorter, "Female Emancipation, Birth Control, and Fertility in European History," *The American Historical Review*, vol. 78, no. 3 (June 1973). Copyright © 1973 by The American Historical Association. Reprinted by permission. Notes omitted.

sonal needs. Therefore women's emancipation at the popular level means disregarding outside controls upon personal freedom of action and sexuality for the sake of individual self-fulfillment.

What evidence exists that the years 1750–1850 saw a movement toward female emancipation among the popular classes? We are, alas, at the beginning of the investigation rather than the end, and so I can merely anticipate the findings of future research. Yet even within the existing literature strong hints may be found that crucial changes in the status and authority of women were under way after 1750 and that these changes were linked in some way to economic modernization. The search for evidence may be aided by considering the nature of the change in the relationship between married woman and husband as well as that between the young, unmarried woman and parental and communal authority. To demonstrate that there is in fact an *explicandum*, let us briefly review some previous findings on these questions.

Least studied to date has been the family life and authority relationships of lower-class women in the years before 1900. Save for tiny pinpricks of information here and there the subject is uncharted, yet those studies that exist converge to demonstrate a radical upheaval in popular family life in the wake of capitalism. Neil Smelser, in a classic study of the British cotton industry, describes "the reversal of traditional age and sex roles as wives and children went to the factory." Industrial growth fragmented the customary "family economy" by making individual producers of its separate members. And, for the children at least, independence accompanied wage labor. Peter Stearns has recently reviewed the German literature, finding toward the end of the nineteenth century (a period inconveniently late for the case I wish to present here) "recognition of greater independence for the woman.... There is suggested here a new sentiment within the family, the possibility of greater affection for the children, who were not underfoot all the time, and greater sensuality and equality in the relationship between man and wife." And Rudolf Braun, in his sensitive reconstruction of life among cottage and factory workers in the Zurich highlands, notes massive shifts in family patterns, starting with the eighteenth century. While Braun is silent on specific changes in the relationships between married men and women, he pulls back the canvas for a brief instant to reveal, for example, women forgetting how to cook. Why, Braun asks, were ready-made foods in such great demand in factory towns?

> It was not merely the pressure to eat at the workplace that accelerated the demand for prepared dishes, nor the lack of time at home, but also the woman factory worker's lack of skill in cooking. Bound to the machine and the factory since earliest childhood, she inadequately learned the arts of cooking and homemaking. We have seen these complaints since the woman cottage workers of the *ancien régime*, but with factory workers they become even more urgent.

One can imagine that the authority patterns among traditional petit-bourgeois families were as different from those of worker couples out on the frontier of economic advance as night is from day.

Evidence is more abundant that young unmarried women were rebelling against parental and social authority in the period from 1750 to 1850. To draw upon my own research, I noted in early nineteenth-century Bavaria an absolute squall of outrage from middle-class observers of popular life, seated for the most part in lower levels of the governmental bureaucracy, about a new spirit of independence among young women in agricultural labor and domestic service. Through this chorus of complaints ran the themes of escape and experimentation, of throwing off old superordinates and codes, and of, in general, what a much later generation of emancipators was to call "liberation."

There was the theme of escape from old jobs. Young women wanted, when possible, to forsake domestic service for employment that would safeguard personal independence. The unpopularity of service may be seen in the cries about ashortage ofrural labor (*Dienstbotenmangel*) that became a constant theme in social criticism from the mid-eighteenth century onward. Or, to take another sort of example, Munich's police chief noted in 1815:

> It is sad, and most difficult for the police to prevent, that so many young girls leave service when they grow tired of waiting on people and under one pretext or another take a room somewhere, living from their own industry. But they do little real work and let themselves be supported by boyfriends; they become pregnant and then are abandoned.

And there was the theme of escape from old residences. Young women wanted to live alone, in their own quarters and away from the oppressive supervision of either parents or employers. In the late 1830s the indignant provincial government of Wurzburg observed:

> In our province the so-called practice of *Eigenzimmern* is quite customary, according to which the deflorated daughter leaves the parental house and rents a room elsewhere, not necessarily to avoid the reproaches of the parents for her misdeeds, but in order to move more freely, to accommodate the visit of the boyfriend [*Zuhälter*] and with him to live in concubinage [*wilde Ehe*].

On the matter of escape from old personal styles, let Joseph Maria Johann Nepomuck Freiherr von Frauenberg, archbishop of Bamberg, speak:

> A most detrimental alteration in the character of the female gender [has taken place]. Earlier, women distinguished themselves through their soft, withdrawn, modest, and chaste being, while nowadays they take part in all public entertainments, indeed providing some, set the tone [*den Ton angeben*], and so have entirely departed from their natural situation. Thus has female morality disappeared.

The archbishop noted this development had occurred principally in the cities. There were other complaints about how female servants and hired hands would squander their entire wages in buying expeditions to the cities, returning to the farm with clothes alien to native folkways. Still other laments were voiced about feminine indifference to pastoral authority and about newly grasping, calculating female attitudes to wage matters. All these threads led back in the opinion of contemporaries—and rightly so I think—to sexuality and thus ultimately to fertility: "In the countryside a young girl who has preserved her virgin purity until age twenty is exceptional, and moreover encounters even among her girlfriends no recognition."

Perhaps Bavaria was not typical of the rest of Europe, though I believe that it was, for within its frontiers the kingdom harbored a remarkable diversity of social and economic arrangements. Perhaps, even more serious for the case I wish to make, male complaints about "moral breakdown" among young women reflected sooner the beholder's own libidinal preoccupations than a change in objective social conditions. Perhaps, too, nostalgia is close to being a historical constant, so that most men who search their own memories invariably see behind the outlines of a gray, disorganized present the golden harmony of an idealized past. Yet in this case I doubt it. And I suspect that future research will verify that this particular set of social critics at this particular point in time—the years 1800–40—were onto something. The objective order of the real world was in fact changing, and a shift in the position of women was moving the ground directly from under the feet of these "patriarchs."

◦◦◦

These changes in the mentalities and sexual comportment of women may ultimately be linked to a variety of changes in economic structure that one might summarize under the label "capitalism." Three salients of industrial advance mattered to fertility, and two of the three made more of a difference to women than to men....

First, capitalism meant the formation of a proletarian subculture. Large numbers of people who had in common the fact that they were wage laborers found themselves living together in the same communities. Because the material conditions of their lives differentiated them clearly from the surrounding social order of small proprietors, these newly aggregated workers in both agriculture and industry began to develop their own rules for doing cultural business, which is, after all, the essence of a subculture. A way of life specific to the working classes began to elaborate itself within the large farm areas of modernizing agriculture, upon the upland slopes where the putting out of textiles and nail manufacture was thriving, and within the newly blossoming industrial cities themselves.

The subculture would sooner or later matter to fertility by providing alternative sets of rules for sexual comportment, target family sizes, and new techniques for contraception and abortion. But subcultures are especially important in the area of legitimation of behavior about which the individual might otherwise feel uneasy. It is now common knowledge that the charter culture of traditional Europe had internalized within young people a host of restraints against intercourse. So that if before 1750 there was relatively little premarital intercourse, it was not necessarily because external supervision was totalitarian in its strictness but because most people within the culture shared the belief that premarital sex was wrong. When in later years sex before marriage became commonplace, it was because a new generation of sexually active young men and women felt their behavior was socially accepted, at least by their peers. The point is that if an individual is going to bend the operating rules of the dominant culture, he must feel that members of his own group, whose good opinion he treasures, will support his venturesomeness.

The proletarian subculture was, of course, indulgent of eroticism. Yet this particular indulgence must not be attributed without further argument to the industrial origins of the subculture. The fact that a subculture exists does not automatically mean that its specific operating rules must be libertine. Indeed many subcultures with quite repressive sexual values have flourished in the past, such as the colonies of nineteenth-century pietists in the United States. Some additional aspect of industrialism must therefore be adduced to explain the expressly permissive sexual content of the European proletarian subculture.

The second important dimension of capitalism lay in the mentality of the market place. In the eighteenth and early nineteenth centuries the market economy encroached steadily at the cost of the moral economy, and the values of individual self-interest and competitiveness that people learned in the market were soon transferred to other areas of life. It was this process of the transfer of values that gave the proletarian subculture its libertine moral caste.

The years after 1750 saw the intrusion of the principles of the market place into popular life. In early modern Europe trade in foodstuffs and in most nonagricultural products was tightly regulated by communal and corporate bodies, so that the Continent was fragmented into countless tiny local markets, kept through a complot of regulation and poor transportation as hermetically sealed compartments. Of course long-distance trade existed, yet most of the labor force was involved in local production along noncapitalistic lines. German political economists made a classic distinction between *Export-* and *Lokalgewerbe*, and most of the population lived from the latter. Then late in the eighteenth century these locally administered economies began to be engulfed by free markets of vast territorial scope. The struggle over free trade in grain in France has been often told; the losing battle of German guilds against pack pedlars, retail merchandise shops, unlicensed competitors, and the Customs Union is similarly familiar. Everywhere the moral economy regulated by the village fathers lost out to free competition regulated only by the invisible hand of the price mechanism.

Contact with these new labor markets was the most direct source of personal autonomy. As women became immersed in the market, they learned its values. I have elsewhere suggested that capitalism's mental habits of maximizing one's self-interest and sacrificing community goals to individual profit transfer easily to other thought processes. It seems a plausible proposition that people assimilate in the market place an integrated, coherent set of values about social behavior and personal independence and that these values quickly inform the noneconomic realms of individual mentalities. If this logic holds true, we may identify exposure to the market place as a prime source of female emancipation, for women who learned autonomy and maximization of self-interest in the economy would quickly stumble upon these concepts within the family as well. Men would also have learned these values, but then it was men who had traditionally been the dominant sex; a more sensitive attunement to questions of individuality left men, if anything, less able to defend themselves against the demands for autonomy of their wives and daughters. The moral authority of traditional society was of a piece; the same communitarian principles that held together the moral economy also maintained the authoritarian family. And they crumbled together as well.

Thus a second crucial consequence of capitalism for women came in the area of personal values: an unwillingness to accept the dictates of superordinates and a new readiness to experiment with personal freedom and gratification. The reader should at this point bear in mind that we have to juggle simultaneously three different effects of capitalism: the first dimension of subculture weakened traditional moral taboos and destroyed internalized antisexual values; the second dimension, which we have just considered, quickened interest in intercourse as an aspect of personality development; and the third dimension of capitalism, to which we now turn, removed many of the external controls upon female sexual emancipation.

This last principal salient of industrial advance worked in the interest of women by modifying with wage labor the balance of power in the family. Paid employment meant that women would bring a distinct, quantifiable contribution to the family's resources, and accordingly would probably be entitled to a greater voice in the disposal of these resources. As many sociologists of the family have noted, the wife's (or daughter's) influence within the conjugal unit is a direct function of the status she enjoys in the outside world and of the resources she is able to import from that world into the family circle. Richard F. Tomasson has convincingly explained the historical development and the present-day international singularity of the Swedish family with such an approach, arguing also that, "Where females have greater equality and are subject to less occupational and social differentiation, the premarital sex codes will be more permissive than where the female's status is completely or primarily dependent on the status of her husband." Altogether, capitalism entailed a quite material source of female independence and autonomy, increasing vastly the leverage formerly obtained from customary, dependent, unpaid, "women's work."

Popular involvement in the market economy started with the young and the poor and ended with the older and more prosperous. It was the most marginal whom capitalism could first detach from their traditional economic moorings, and so in the eighteenth century the young members of the proletarian classes that population growth had been creating went first to the cottage looms and spinning wheels. Thereafter ever more prosperous groups of the traditional economy found themselves pulled into the flux of the market, so that by the late nineteenth century even the most isolated sectors of the old middle class had been plunged into price competition and profit rationality. Immersion in the market progressed by stages.

Early in the eighteenth century the putting-out system began its conquest of the countryside, drawing in the landless poor. Then, in the course of the century agricultural capitalism began to encroach upon traditional subsistence and manorial farming, recruiting from among the landless and especially from the youth, for often unmarried laborers would live in the farmer's house, or newly married couples in nearby cottages. Next came migration to the newly rising factories and mills. The timing varied from one region to another, but normally it was the youth whom the fresh modern sector pulled from small farms and craft shops into factories.

In the nineteenth century industrial growth created a prosperous new middle class of administrators and clerks, of technicians and professionals. Because these people had often to endure long delays before marriage, women entered their childbearing periods at relatively advanced ages and largely abstained from intercourse beforehand. Finally, in the nineteenth century capitalism tore at the heart of the traditional old middle class itself, rather than merely at the supernumary poor. Across the Continent the masters of craft shops had to accommodate themselves to industrial capitalism, either by servicing the new factories or by going to work in them. And the depopulation of the countryside on the threshold of the twentieth century is an oft-told tale. It was frequently as mature men and women that these families were forced out of the traditional sector, of which they had constituted the backbone.

Thus the market started with the youngest and lowliest on the age-status spectrum and concluded with the most established and mature. It was also in this order that, I suggest, the spirit of female emancipation spread, from young and poor to well to do and middle-aged.

꘎◉꘎

How, precisely, did these massive shifts in economic structure, culture, and individual mentalities affect either marital or nonmarital fertility? The linkages between emancipation and the increase in illegitimacy seem crisp and strong; those between capitalism and marital fertility are largely artifacts.

For the unmarried woman capitalism meant personal freedom, which meant in turn sexual freedom. The young woman could withstand parental sanctions against her sexual and emotional independence because the modern sector promised employment, economic self-sufficiency, and if need be, migration from home to another town. Such independence meant often, as we have seen, a paramour and therewith, in the absence of birth control, illegitimacy.

NO

Louise A. Tilly, Joan W. Scott,
and Miriam Cohen

Women's Work and European Fertility Patterns

According to [Edward] Shorter, a change in fertility rates can only mean a change in sexual practices, which has to mean a change in attitudes, particularly of women. The sequence must be linear and direct. As Shorter argues:

> It seems a plausible proposition that people assimilate in the market place an integrated, coherent set of values about social behavior and personal independence and that these values quickly inform the noneconomic realm of individual mentalities. If this logic holds true, we may identify exposure to the market place as a prime source of female emancipation.

This statement, as its language clearly reveals, is based on a claim of reasoning, not on evidence. Shorter offers nothing to prove that more women worked in the capitalist marketplace in this period. He merely assumes that they did. Similarly, he assumes that women at the end of the eighteenth century had different family roles and attitudes from their predecessors. And he assumes as well that changes in work opportunities immediately changed values. Ideas, in his opinion, instantly reflect one's current economic experience. Shorter employs a mechanistic notion of "value transfer" to explain the influence of changes in occupational structure on changes in collective mentalities: "In the eighteenth and early nineteenth centuries the market economy encroached steadily at the cost of the moral economy, and the values of individual self-interest and competitiveness that people learned in the market were soon transferred to other areas of life."

For Shorter, sexual behavior echoes market behavior at every point. "Emancipated" women gained a sense of autonomy at work that the subordinate and powerless women of pre-industrial society had lacked. That work, created by capitalist economic development, necessarily fostered values of individualism in those who participated in it, and individualism was expressed in part by a new desire for sexual gratification. Young women working outside the home, Shorter insists, were by definition rebelling against parental authority. Indeed, they sought work in order to gain the independence and individual fulfillment that could not be attained at home. It follows, in Shorter's logic, that sexual behavior, too, must have been defiant of parental restraint. As the market econ-

Excerpted from Louise A. Tilly, Joan W. Scott, and Miriam Cohen, "Women's Work and European Fertility Patterns," *Journal of Interdisciplinary History*, vol. 6, no. 3 (Winter 1976), pp. 447-476. Copyright © 1976 by The Massachusetts Institute of Technology and the editors of the *Journal of Interdisciplinary History*. Reprinted by permission of MIT Press Journals. Notes omitted.

omy spread there arose a new, libertine, proletarian subculture "indulgent of eroticism." Once married, the independent young working women engaged in frequent intercourse because they and their husbands took greater pleasure in sex. Female "emancipation" thus began among the young and poor. In the absence of birth control, the sexual gratification of single working girls increased the illegitimate birthrate; that of married women (who worked or had worked) inflated the legitimate birthrate. In this fashion Shorter answers a central question of European historical demography. The fertility increase in the late eighteenth century was simply the result of the "emancipation," occupational and sexual, of working-class women....

It is now time to examine the historical evidence that Shorter neglected on women's role in pre-industrial society; on the effects of industrialization on women's work and on their attitudes; and on the motives which sent young girls out into the "marketplace" at the end of the eighteenth and beginning of the nineteenth century. None of the evidence that we have found supports Shorter's argument in any way. Women were not powerless in "traditional" families; they played important economic roles which gave them a good deal of power within the family. Industrialization did not significantly modernize women's work in the period when fertility rates rose; in fact, the vast majority of working women did not work in factories, but at customary women's jobs. Women usually became wage earners during the early phases of industrialization not to rebel against their parents or declare independence from their husbands, but to augment family finances. Indeed, women in this period must be studied in their family settings, for the constraints of family membership greatly affected their opportunities for individual autonomy. No change in attitude, then, increased the numbers of children whom working women bore. Rather, old attitudes and customary behavior interacted with greatly changed circumstances—particularly in the composition of populations—and led to increased illegitimate fertility.

Women eventually shed many outdated priorities, and by the end of the nineteenth century some working women had clearly adopted "modern" life styles. But these changes involved a more gradual and complex adaptation than Shorter implies. The important point, however, is that the years around 1790 were not a watershed in the history of women's economic emancipation—despite the fact that the locus of women's work began to move outside the home. These *were* the crucial years for the increases in fertility in Europe. All of the evidence is not in, by any means; what we offer, however, indicates that in this period, women of the popular classes simply were not searching for freedom or experiencing emancipation. The explanation for changed fertility patterns lies elsewhere.

Women's Place in "Traditional" Families

In the pre-industrial family, the household was organized as a family or domestic economy. Men, women, and children worked at tasks which were differentiated by age and sex, but the work of all was necessary for survival. Artisans' wives assisted their husbands in their work as weavers, bakers, shoemakers, or tailors. Certain work, like weaving, whether carried on in the city or the country, needed the cooperation of all family members. Children and women did the spinning and carding; men ran the looms. Wives also managed many aspects of the household, including family finances. In less prosperous urban families, women did paid work which was often an extension of their household chores: They sewed and made lace; they also took odd jobs as carters, laundresses, and street cleaners.

Unmarried women also became servants. Resourcefulness was characteristic of poor women: When they could not find work which would enable them to contribute to the family income, they begged, stole, or became prostitutes. Hufton's work on the Parisian poor in the eighteenth century and Forrest's work on Bordeaux both describe the crucial economic contribution of urban working-class women and the consequent central role which these women played in their families.

In the country, the landowning peasant's family was also the unit of productive activity. The members of the family worked together, again at sex-differentiated tasks. Children—boys and girls—were sent to other farms as servants when their help was not needed at home. Their activity, nonetheless, contributed to the well-being of the family. They sent their earnings home, or, if they were not paid wages, their absence at least relieved the family of the burden of feeding and boarding them. Women's responsibilities included care of the house, barnyard, and dairy. They managed to bring in small net profits from marketing of poultry and dairy products and from work in rural domestic industry. Management of the household and, particularly, of finances led to a central role for women in these families. An observer in rural Brittany during the nineteenth century reported that the wife and mother of the family made "the important decisions, buying a field, selling a cow, a lawsuit against a neighbor, choice of future son-in-law."For rural families who did not own land, women's work was even more vital: From agricultural work, spinning, or petty trading, they contributed their share to the family wage—the only economic resource of the landless family.

In city and country, among propertied and propertyless, women of the popular classes had a vital economic role which gave them a recognized and powerful position within the household. It is impossible to guess what sort of sexual relations were practiced under these circumstances. We *can* say, however, that women in these families were neither dependent nor powerless. Hence, it is impossible to accept Shorter's attempt to derive women's supposed sexual subordination from their place in the pre-industrial household.

Why Women Worked

Shorter attributes the work of women outside the home after 1750, particularly that of young, single women, to a change in outlook: a new desire for independence from parental restraints. He argues that since seeking work was an individualistic rebellion against traditionalism, sexual behavior, too, reflected a defiance of parental authority. The facts are that daughters of the popular classes were most often sent into service or to work in the city by their families.

Their work represented a continuation of practices customary in the family economy. When resources were scarce or mouths at home too numerous, children customarily sought work outside, generally with family approval.

Industrialization and urbanization created new problems for rural families but generated new opportunities as well. In most cases, families strategically adapted their established practices to the new context. Thus, daughters sent out to work went farther away from home than had been customary. Most still defined their work in the family interest. Sometimes arrangements for direct payment in money or foodstuffs were made between a girl's parents and her employer. In other cases, the girls themselves regularly sent money home. Commentators observed that the girls considered this a normal arrangement—part of their obligation to the family.

In some cases the conditions of migration for young working girls emphasized their ties to family in many ways limited their independence. In Italy and France, factory dormitories housed female workers, and nuns regulated their behavior and social lives. In the needle trades in British cities, enterprising women with a little capital turned their homes into lodging houses for pieceworkers in their employ. Of course, these institutions permitted employers to control their employees by limiting their mobility and regulating their behavior. The point is not that they were beneficient practices, but that young girls lived in households which permitted them limited autonomy. Domestic service, the largest single occupation for women, was also the most traditional and most protective of young girls. They would be sent from one household to another and thus be given security. Châtelain argues that domestic service was a safe form of migration in France for young girls from the country. They had places to live, families, food, and lodgings and had no need to fend for themselves in the unknown big city as soon as they arrived. It is true that servants often longed to leave their places, and that they resented the exploitation of their mistresses (and the advances of their masters). But that does not change the fact that, initially, their migration was sponsored by a set of traditional institutions which limited their individual freedom.

In fact, individual freedom did not seem to be at issue for the daughters of either the landed or the landless, although clearly their experiences differed. It seems likely that peasant families maintained closer ties with their daughters, even when the girls worked in distant cities. The family interest in the farm (the property that was the birthright of the lineage and not of any individual) was a powerful influence on individual behavior. Thus, farm girls working as domestics continued to send money home. Married daughters working as domestics in Norwegian cities sent their children home to be raised on the farm by grandparents. But even when ties of this sort were not maintained, it was seldom from rebellious motives. Braun describes the late eighteenth-century situation of peasants in the hinterland of Zurich. These peasants were willing to divide their holdings for their children because of new work opportunities in cottage industry. These young people married earlier than they would have if the farm had been held undivided, and they quickly established their own families. Braun suggests that the young workers soon lost touch with their parents. The process, as he describes it, however, was not rebellion; rather, the young people went into cottage industry to lessen the burden that they represented for the family. These motives were welcomed and encouraged by the parents. Family bonds were stretched and broken, but that was a consequence, not a cause, of the new opportunities for work.

Similarly, among urban artisans, older values informed the adaptation to a new organization of work and to technological change. Initially, artisans as well as their political spokesmen insisted that the old values of association and cooperation could continue to characterize their work relationships in the new industrial society. Artisan subculture in cities during the early stages of industrialization was not characterized by an individualistic, self-seeking ideology, as Thompson, Hufton, Forrest, Soboul, Gossez, and others have clearly shown. With no evidence that urban artisans adopted the values of the marketplace at work, Shorter's deduction about a "libertine proletarian sub-culture" has neither factual nor logical validity. It seems more likely that arti-san families, like peasant families, sent their wives and daughters to work to help bolster their shaky economic situation. These women undoubtedly joined the ranks of the unskilled who had always constituted the urban female work force. Wives and daughters of the unskilled and propertyless had worked for centuries at service and manufacturing jobs in cities. In the nine-teenth century there were more of them because the proportions of unskilled propertyless workers increased.

Eighteenth- and early nineteenth-century cities grew primarily by migration. The urban working class was thus constantly renewed and enlarged by a stream of rural migrants. Agricultural change drove rural laborers and peasants cityward at the end of the eighteenth century, and technological change drove many artisans and their families into the ranks of the unskilled. Women worked outside the home because they had to. Changed attitudes did not propel them into the labor force. Family interest and not self-interest was the underlying motive for their work.

Women's Work

What happened in the mid-eighteenth century with the spread of capitalism, the growth of markets, and industrialization? Did these economic changes bring new work experiences for women, with the consequences which Shorter describes? Did women, earning money in the capitalist marketplace, find a new sense of self that expressed itself in increased sexual activity? In examin-ing the historical evidence for the effects on women's work of industrializa-tion and urbanization, we find that the location of women's work did change—more young women worked outside the home and in large cities than ever before. But they were recruited from the same groups which had always sent women to work.

The female labor force of nineteenth-century Europe, like that of seven-teenth- and eighteenth-century Europe, consisted primarily of the daughters of the popular classes and, secondarily of their wives. The present state of our knowledge makes it difficult to specify precisely the groups within the work-ing classes from which nineteenth-century women wage earners came. It is clear, however, that changes in the organization of work must have driven the daughters and wives of craftsmen out of the family shop. Similarly, population growth (a result of declining mortality and younger age at marriage due to opportunities for work in cottage industry) created a surplus of hands within the urban household andonthe family farm. Womeninthese families always had been expected to work. Increasingly, they were sent away from home to earn their portion of the family wage.

Shorter's notion that the development of modern capitalism brought new kinds of opportunities to working-class women as early as the middle of the eighteenth century is wrong. There was a very important change in the location of work from rural homes to cities, but this did not revolutionize the nature of the work that most women did. Throughout the nineteenth century, most women worked at traditional occupations. By the end of the century, factory employment was still minimal....

Shorter is also incorrect in his assumption that the working woman was able to live independently of her family because she had the economic means to do so. Evidence for British working women indicates that this was not the case. Throughout the nineteenth century, British working women's wages were considered supplementary incomes—supplementary, that is, to the wages of other family members. It was assumed by employers that women, unlike men, were not responsible for earning their own living. Female wages were always far lower than male. In the Lancashire cotton mills in 1833, where female wages were the highest in the country, females aged 16–21 earned 7/3.5 weekly, while males earned 10/3. Even larger differentials obtained among older workers. In London in the 1880s, there was a similar differential between the average earnings of the sexes: 72 percent of the males in the bookbinding industry earned over 30/– weekly; 42.5 percent of women made less than 12/–.Inprecious metals, clocks, and watch manufacturing, 83.5 percent of the males earned 30/– or more weekly; females earned 9–12/–. Women in small clothing workshops earned 10–12/– weekly, while women engaged in outwork in the clothing trades made only 4/– a week. In Birmingham, in 1900, the average weekly wage for working women less than age 21 was 10/–, for men 18/–.Women's work throughout this period, as in the eighteenth century, was for the most part unskilled. Occupations were often seasonal and irregular, leaving women without work for many months during the year. Is it possible that there were many single women who could enjoy a life of independence when the majority could not even afford to live adequately on their personal wages? ...

Women's work from 1750 to 1850 (and much later) did not provide an experience of emancipation. Work was hard and poorly paid and, for the most part, it did not represent a change from traditional female occupations. Those women who traveled to cities did find themselves free of some traditional village and family restraints. But, as we shall see, the absence of these restraints was more often burdensome than liberating. Young women with inadequate wages and unstable jobs found themselves caught in a cycle of poverty which increased their vulnerability. Having lost one family, many sought to create another.

The Origins of Increased Illegitimacy

The compositional change which increased the numbers of unskilled, propertyless workers in both rural and urban areas and raised their proportion in urban populations also contributed to an increase in rates of illegitimacy. Women in this group of the population always had contributed the most illegitimate births. An increase in the number of women in this group, therefore, meant a greater incidence of illegitimacy.

A recent article by Laslett and Oosterveen speaks directly to Shorter's speculations: "The assumption that illegitimacy figures directly reflect the prevalence of sexual intercourse outside marriage, which seems to be made whenever such figures are used to show that beliefs, attitudes and interests have changed in some particular way, can be shown to be very shaky in its foundations." Using data from Colyton, collected and analyzed by E. A. Wrigley, they argue that one important component in the incidence of illegitimacy is the existence of illegitimacy-prone families, which bring forth bastards generation after generation. Nevertheless, they warn, "this projected sub-society never produced all the bastards, all the bastard-bearers."

The women who bore illegitimate children were not pursuing sexual pleasure, as Shorter would have us believe. Most expected to get married, but the circumstances of their lives—propertylessness, poverty, large-scale geographic mobility, occupational instability, and the absence of traditional social protection—prevented the fulfillment of this expectation. A number of pressures impelled young working girls to find mates. One was the loneliness and isolation of work in the city. Another was economic need: Wages were low and employment for women, unstable. The logical move for a single girl far from her family would be to find a husband with whom she might re-establish a family economy. Yet another pressure was the desire to escape the confines of domestic service, an occupation which more and more young women were entering.

Could not this desire to establish a family be what the domestic servants, described by the Munich police chief in 1815, sought? No quest for pleasure is inherent in the fact that "so many young girls leave service.... But they do little real work and let themselves be supported by boyfriends; they become pregnant and then are abandoned." It seems a sad and distorted version of an older family form, but an attempt at it, nevertheless. Recent work has shown, in fact, that for many French servants in the nineteenth century, this kind of transfer to urban life and an urban husband was often successful.

Was it a search for sexual fulfillment that prompted young women to become "engaged" to young men and then sleep with them in the expectation that marriage would follow? Not at all. In rural and urban areas premarital sexual relationships were common. What Shorter interprets as sexual libertinism, as evidence of an individualistic desire for sexual pleasure, is more likely an expression of the traditional wish to marry. The attempt to reconstitute the family economy in the context of economic deprivation and geographic mobility produced unstable and stable "free unions."

... The central point here is that no major change in values or mentality was necessary to create these cases of illegitimacy. Rather, older expectations operating in a changed context yielded unanticipated (and often unhappy) results.... Women's work in the late eighteenth and early nineteenth centuries was not "liberating" in any sense. Most women stayed in established occupations. They were so poorly paid that economic independence was precluded. Furthermore, whether married or single, most women often entered the labor force in the service of the family interest. The evidence available points to several causes for illegitimacy, none related to the "emancipation" of women: economic need, causing women to seek work far from the protection of their families; occupational instability of men which led to *mariages manqués* (sexual intercourse following a promise of marriage which was never fulfilled). Finally, analysis of the effects of population growth on propertied peasants and artisans seems to show that the bifurcation of marriage and property arrangements began to change the nature of marriage arrangements for propertyless people.

POSTSCRIPT

Did the Industrial Revolution Lead to a Sexual Revolution?

In the world of the "great man," women, racial and ethnic minorities, and the poor are nearly invisible. They appear as passive participants in the historical drama; it is as if history happens to them. Revisionist historians, however, insist that even the apparently powerless have the potential to act as agents of historical change rather than as passive victims. Both Shorter and Tilly et al. assume that working-class, European women in the years between 1750 and 1850 made decisions and acted upon them. For reasons that may never be completely clear, there was a rise in illegitimacy rates, evidence that more babies than in the past were being born outside of marriage. What changed? A higher illegitimacy rate can mean that more sexual activity is taking place, but it can also mean that fewer unmarried, pregnant women are marrying.

To help you to make your own decision, you may wish to consider the evidence offered in the following books and essays. For a Marxist interpretation, see Friedrich Engels, *The Origin of the Family, Private Property and the State* (International Publishers, 1972). Ivy Pinchbeck, in *Women Workers and the Industrial Revolution, 1750–1850* (F. Cass, 1969), argues that occupational changes played a significant role in women's legal and political emancipation. Rudolf Braun, in "The Impact of Cottage Industry on an Agricultural Population," in David Landes, ed., *The Rise of Capitalism* (Macmillan, 1966), describes an economic system in rural Switzerland in which the daughters in a family learned to spin and weave, contributing their earnings to the family economic unit as a matter of course. Olwen Hufton makes a similar point about the Parisian poor in the eighteenth century in "Women in Revolution, 1789–1796," *Past and Present* (vol. 53, 1971) and about a broader segment of the population in "Women and the Family Economy in Eighteenth-Century France," *French Historical Studies* (vol. 9, 1975). Whether or not young working women kept their own wages and had enough money to support an independent lifestyle is a key historiographic question. For more work by this issue's authors, students may wish to read "Women's Work and the Family in Nineteenth-Century Europe," *Comparative Studies in Society and History* (vol. 17, 1975) and *Women, Work, and Family* (Holt, Rinehart & Winston, 1978) by Scott and Tilly. Essays by Shorter include "Illegitimacy, Sexual Revolution and Social Change in Modern Europe," *Journal of Interdisciplinary History* (vol. 2, 1971) and "Sexual Change and Illegitimacy: The European Experience," in Robert J. Bezucha, ed., *Modern European Social History* (D. C. Heath, 1972).

ISSUE 2

Was the French Revolution Worth Its Human Costs?

YES: Peter Kropotkin, from *The Great French Revolution, 1789-1793,* trans. N. F. Dryhurst (Schocken Books, 1971)

NO: *The Economist* staff writer, from "The French Revolution: Bliss Was It In That Dawn?" *The Economist* (December 24, 1988)

ISSUE SUMMARY

YES: Peter Kropotkin (1842–1921), a Russian prince, revolutionary, and anarchist, argues that the French Revolution eradicated both serfdom and absolutism and paved the way for France's future democratic development.

NO: An article in *The Economist* argues that the French Revolution "culminated in the guillotine and the substitution of the state for the sovereignty of the nation," leaving behind negative legacies to the modern world.

Few historical events have created the emotional responses and concomitant debates as has the French Revolution. Taking advantage of one of the largest bodies of historical data gathered, historians of the past two centuries have analyzed, synthesized, and evaluated every facet of this seminal event in the history of the Western world.

From this scholarship has come a myriad of important questions regarding the political, economic, social, religious, cultural, and intellectual aspects of the Revolution—questions involving causation, behavior, outcomes, and assessments. Each generation of historians has taken the work of its predecessors and used it to shape an understanding of the Revolution that emanates from the uncovering of new sources of information, the creation of new tools to assist in the process, and the development of new schools of historical thought, which attempt to give a more contemporary, relevant slant to this important event. As a result of this historiographical process, many major questions regarding the French Revolution have been raised, and plausible answers given.

One of the most important questions that this French Revolution scholarship has raised—a double-edged one that is both elemental and significant—

is: What were its outcomes, and were they worth the human cost that was paid to achieve them?

The debate began before anyone knew what course the Revolution would take. In a 1790 treatise entitled *Reflections on the Revolution in France*, English statesman Edmund Burke (1729–1797) uncannily predicted the future course of the Revolution and its catastrophic consequences for both France and Europe. He also argued in favor of a slow, evolutionary style of political change that was taking place in his own country, rather than the spasmodic one that was beginning to envelop France. Burke's message was clear: The Revolution in France will be costly and counterproductive.

A year later, the French Revolution gained an articulate defender in the person of Thomas Paine (1737–1809), an English-born American citizen. In *Common Sense* (1776), a stirring call-to-arms to the American colonists to throw off the yoke of English oppression, Paine acquired a reputation as a foe of tyrannical government and a strong supporter of human freedom and equality. In Part I of his political pamphlet *The Rights of Man*, Paine argued that revolution was necessary to purge civilization of those elements that stood in the way of democratic reform. According to Paine, no price was too high to pay for the realization of those cherished goals.

As generations passed, the basic question debated by Burke and Paine faded into the background as historians began to explore other fertile areas of historical research. There was either a general acceptance of the French Revolution's importance in changing the course of history or a quiet acquiescence to its outcomes, regardless of the consequences.

Peter Alexeievich Kropotkin (1842–1921) was an early historical defender of the French Revolution. Obviously influenced by his radical, anarchistic background and his desire to see all people freed from the yoke of oppression, his view of the Revolution was somewhat simplistic and uncritical. Coming from a nineteenth century environment where revolutions were commonplace—and were viewed by many as an inevitable part of political evolution—his opinions on the French Revolution were representative for his time, and for generations to come.

Of all the books written about the French Revolution in recent years, none has been as popular as Simon Schama's *Citizens: a Chronicle of the French Revolution*. Published in the midst of the Revolution's bicentennial celebration, the book aroused much controversy for many reasons; among them was Schama's view that the French Revolution was not worth its human costs. Seeing violence as an endemic part of the revolutionary process, Schama also stated that the Revolution produced few of the tangible results it had promised. This book encouraged others to question the nature and consquences of the French Revolution

An excerpt from Kropotkin's book and an article from *The Economist* written on the eve of the 200th anniversary of the French Revolution provide not only opposing viewpoints on whether or not the French Revolution was worth its human costs, but also a clear example of how different eras can have different values, which can affect how the past is interpreted.

Peter Kropotkin  **YES**

The Great French Revolution, 1789–1793

When one sees that terrible and powerful Convention wrecking itself in 1794–1795, that proud and strong Republic disappearing, and France, after the demoralising *régime* of the Directory, falling under the military yoke of a Bonaparte, one is impelled to ask: "What was the good of the Revolution if the nation had to fall back again under despotism?" In the course of the nineteenth century, this question has been constantly put, and the timid and conservative have worn it threadbare as an argument against revolutions in general.

... Those who have seen in the Revolution only a change in the Government, those who are ignorant of its economic as well as its educational work, those alone could put such a question.

The France we see during the last days of the eighteenth century, at the moment of the *coup d'état* on the 18th Brumaire, is not the France that existed before 1789. Would it have been possible for the old France, wretchedly poor and with a third of her population suffering yearly from dearth, to have maintained the Napoleonic Wars, coming so soon after the terrible wars of the Republic between 1792 and 1799, when all Europe was attacking her?

The fact is, that a new France had been constituted since 1792–1793. Scarcity still prevailed in many of the departments, and its full horrors were felt especially after the *coup d'état* of Thermidor, when the maximum price for all foodstuffs was abolished. There were still some departments which did not produce enough wheat to feed themselves, and as the war went on, and all means of transport were requisitioned for its supplies, there was scarcity in those departments. But everything tends to prove that France was even then producing much more of the necessaries of life of every kind than in 1789.

Never was there in France such energetic ploughing, Michelet tells us, as in 1792, when the peasant was ploughing the lands he had taken back from the lords, the convents, the churches, and was goading his oxen to the cry of *"Allons Prusse! Allons Autriche!"* Never had there been so much clearing of lands—even royalist writers admit this—as during those years of revolution. The first good harvest, in 1794, brought relief to two-thirds of France—at least in the villages, for all this time the towns were threatened with scarcity of food. Not that it was scarce in France as a whole, or that the *sans-culotte* municipalities neglected to take measures to feed those who could not find employment, but from the fact that all beasts of burden not actually used in tillage were requisitioned to carry food and ammunition to the fourteen armies of the Republic. In those days

From Peter Kropotkin, *The Great French Revolution*, 1789–1793, trans. N. F. Dryhurst (Schocken Books, 1971).

there were no railways, and all but the main roads were in the state they are to this day in Russia—well-nigh impassable.

A new France was born during those four years of revolution. For the first time in centuries the peasant ate his fill, straightened his back and dared to speak out. Read the detailed reports concerning the return of Louis XVI. to Paris, when he was brought back a prisoner from Varennes, in June 1791, by the peasants, and say: "Could such a thing, such an interest in the public welfare, such a devotion to it, and such an independence of judgment and action have been possible before 1789?" A new nation had been born in the meantime, just as we see today a new nation coming into life in Russia and in Turkey.

It was owing to this new birth that France was able to maintain her wars under the Republic and Napoleon, and to carry the principles of the Great Revolution into Switzerland, Italy, Spain, Belgium, Holland, Germany, and even to the borders of Russia. And when, after all those wars, after having mentally followed the French armies as far as Egypt and Moscow, we expect to find France in 1815 reduced to an appalling misery and her lands laid waste, we find, instead, that even in its eastern portions and in the Jura, the country is much more prosperous than it was at the time when Pétion, pointing out to Louis XVI. the luxuriant banks of the Marne, asked him if there was anywhere in the world a kingdom more beautiful than the one the King had not wished to keep.

The self-contained energy was such in villages regenerated by the Revolution, that in a few years France became a country of well-to-do peasants, and her enemies soon discovered that in spite of all the blood she had shed and the losses she had sustained, France, in respect of her *productivity*, was the richest country in Europe. Her wealth, indeed, is not drawn from the Indies or from her foreign commerce: it comes from her own soil, from her love of the soil, from her own skill and industry. She is the richest country, because of the subdivision of her wealth, and she is still richer because of the possibilities she offers for the future.

Such was the effect of the Revolution. And if the casual observer sees in Napoleonic France only a love of glory, the historian realises that even the wars France waged at that period were undertaken to secure the fruits of the Revolution—to keep the lands that had been retaken from the lords, the priests and the rich, and the liberties that had been won from despotism and the Court. If France was willing in those years to bleed herself to death, merely to prevent the Germans, the English, and the Russians from forcing a Louis XVIII. upon her, it was because she did not want the return of the emigrant nobles to mean that the *ci-devants* would take back the lands which had been watered already with the peasant's sweat, and the liberties which had been sanctified with the patriots' blood. And France fought so well for twenty-three years, that when she was compelled at last to admit the Bourbons, it was she who imposed conditions on them. The Bourbons might reign, but the lands were to be kept by those who had taken them from the feudal lords, so that even during the White Terror of the Bourbons they dared not touch those lands. The old régime could not be re-established.

This is what is gained by making a Revolution.

There are other things to be pointed out. In the history of all nations a time comes when fundamental changes are bound to take place in the whole of the national life. Royal despotism and feudalism were dying in 1789; it was impossible to keep them alive; they had to go.

But then, two ways were opened out before France: reform or revolution.

At such times there is always a moment when reform is still possible; but if advantage has not been taken of that moment, if an obstinate resistance has been opposed to the requirements of the new life, up to the point when blood has flowed in the streets, as it flowed on July 14, 1789, then there must be a Revolution. And once the Revolution has begun, it must necessarily develop to its conclusions—that is to say, to the highest point it is capable of attaining—were it only temporarily, being given a certain condition of the public mind at this particular moment.

If we represent the slow progress of a period of evolution by a line drawn on paper, we shall see this line gradually though slowly rising. Then there comes a Revolution, and the line makes a sudden leap upwards. In England the line would be represented as rising to the Puritan Republic of Cromwell; in France it rises to the *Sans-culotte* Republic of 1793. However, at this height progress cannot be maintained; all the hostile forces league together against it, and the Republic goes down. Our line, after having reached that height, drops. Reaction follows. For the political life of France the line drops very low indeed, but by degrees it rises again, and when peace is restored in 1815 in France, and in 1688 in England—both countries are found to have attained a level much higher than they were on prior to their Revolutions.

After that, evolution is resumed: our line again begins to rise slowly: but, besides taking place on a very much higher level, the rising of the line will in nearly every case be also much more rapid than before the period of disturbance.

This is a law of human progress, and also a law of individual progress. The more recent history of France confirms this very law by showing how it was necessary to pass through the Commune to arrive at the Third Republic.

The work of the French Revolution is not confined merely to what it obtained and what was retained of it in France. It is to be found also in the principles bequeathed by it to the succeeding century—in the line of direction it marked out for the future.

A reform is always a compromise with the past, but the progress accomplished by revolution is always a promise of future progress. If the Great French Revolution was the summing up of a century's evolution, it also marked out in its turn the programme of evolution to be accomplished in the course of the nineteenth century.

It is a law in the world's history that the period of a hundred or a hundred and thirty years, more or less, which passes between two great revolutions, receives its character from the revolution in which this period began. The nations endeavour to realise in their institutions the inheritance bequeathed to them by the last revolution. All that this last could not yet put into practice, all the great thoughts which were thrown into circulation during the turmoil, and which the revolution either could not or did not know how to apply, all the attempts at sociological reconstruction, which were born during the revolution, will go to make up the substance of evolution during the epoch that follows the revolution, with the addition of those new ideas to which this evolution will give birth, when trying to put into practice the programme marked out by the last upheaval. Then, a new revolution will be brought about in some other nation, and this nation in its turn will set the problems for the following century. Such has hitherto been the trend of history.

Two great conquests, in fact, characterise the century which has passed since 1789–1793. Both owe their origin to the French Revolution, which had carried on the work of the English Revolution while enlarging and invigorating it with all the progress that had been made since the English middle classes beheaded their King and transferred his power to the Parliament. These two great triumphs are: the abolition of serfdom and the abolition of absolutism, by which personal liberties have been conferred upon the individual, undreamt of by the serf of the lord and the subject of the absolute king, while at the same time they have brought about the development of the middle classes and the capitalist *régime*.

These two achievements represent the principal work of the nineteenth century, begun in France in 1789 and slowly spread over Europe in the course of that century.

The work of enfranchisement, begun by the French peasants in 1789, was continued in Spain, Italy, Switzerland, Germany, and Austria by the armies of the *sans-culottes*. Unfortunately, this work hardly penetrated into Poland and did not reach Russia at all.

The abolition of serfdom in Europe would have been already completed in the first half of the nineteenth century if the French *bourgeoisie*, coming into power in 1794 over the dead bodies of Anarchists, Cordeliers, and Jacobins, had not checked the revolutionary impulse, restored monarchy, and handed over France to the imperial juggler, the first Napoleon. This ex-*sans-culotte*, now a general of the *sans-culottes*, speedily began to prop up aristocracy; but the impulsion had been given, the institution of serfdom had already received a mortal blow. It was abolished in Spain and Italy in spite of the temporary triumph of reaction. It was closely pressed in Germany after 1811, and disappeared in that country definitively in 1848. In 1861, Russia was compelled to emancipate her serfs, and the war of 1878 put an end to serfdom in the Balkan peninsula.

The cycle is now complete. The right of the lord over the person of the peasant no longer exists in Europe, even in those countries where the feudal dues have still to be redeemed.

This fact is not sufficiently appreciated by historians. Absorbed as they are in political questions, they do not perceive the importance of the abolition of serfdom, which is, however, the essential feature of the nineteenth century. The rivalries between nations and the wars resulting from them, the policies of the Great Powers which occupy so much of the historian's attention, have all sprung from that one great fact—the abolition of serfdom and the development of the wage-system which has taken its place.

The French peasant, in revolting a hundred and twenty years ago against the lord who made him beat the ponds lest croaking frogs should disturb his master's sleep, has thus freed the peasants of all Europe. In four years, by burning the documents which registered his subjection, by setting fire to the chateaux, and by executing the owners of them who refused to recognise his rights as a human being, the French peasant so stirred up all Europe that it is today altogether free from the degradation of serfdom.

On the other hand, the abolition of absolute power has also taken a little over a hundred years to make the tour of Europe. Attacked in England in 1648, and vanquished in France in 1789, royal authority based on divine right is no longer exercised save in Russia, but there, too, it is at its last gasp. Even the little Balkan States and Turkey have now their representative assemblies, and Russia is entering the same cycle.

In this respect the Revolution of 1789–1793 has also accomplished its work. Equality before the law and representative government have now their place in almost all the codes of Europe. In theory, at least, the law makes no distinctions between men, and every one has the right to participate, more or less, in the government.

◦⟨◉⟩◦

The absolute monarch—master of his subjects—and the lord—master of the soil and the peasants, by right of birth—have both disappeared. The middle classes now govern Europe.

But at the same time the Great Revolution has bequeathed to us some other principles of an infinitely higher import; the principles of communism. We have seen how all through the Great Revolution the communist idea kept coming to the front, and how after the fall of the Girondins numerous attempts and sometimes great attempts were make in this direction. Fourierism descends in a direct line from L'Ange on one side and from Chalier on the other. Babeuf is the direct descendant of ideas which stirred the masses to enthusiasm in 1793; he, Buonarotti, and Sylvain Maréchal have only systematised them a little or even merely put them into literary form. But the secret societies organized by Babeuf and Buonarotti were the origin of the *communistes matérialistes* secret societies through which Blanqui and Barb'es conspired under the *bourgeois* monarchy of Louis-Philippe. Later on, in 1866, the International Working Men's Association appeared in the direct line of descent from these societies. As to "socialism" we know now that this term came into vogue to avoid the term "communism," which at one time was dangerous because the secret communist societies became societies for action, and were rigorously suppressed by the *bourgeoisie* then in power.

There is, therefore, a direct filiation from the *Enragés* of 1793 and the Babeuf conspiracy of 1795 to the International Working Men's Association of 1866–1878.

There is also a direct descent of ideas. Up till now, modern socialism has added absolutely nothing to the ideas which were circulating among the French people between 1789 and 1794 and which it was tried to put into practice in the Year II. of the Republic. Modern socialism has only systematised those ideas and found arguments in their favour, either by turning against the middle-class economists certain of their own definitions, or by generalising certain facts noticed in the development of industrial capitalism, in the course of the nineteenth century.

But I permit myself to maintain also that, however vague it may have been, however little support it endeavoured to draw from arguments dressed in a scientific garb, and however little use it made of the pseudo-scientific slang of the middle-class economists, the popular communism of the first two years of the Republic saw clearer, and went much deeper in its analyses, than modern socialism.

First of all, it was communism in the consumption of the necessaries of life—not in production only; it was the communalisation and the nationalisation of what economists know as consumption—to which the stern republicans of 1793 turned, above all, their attention, when they tried to establish their stores of grain and provisions in every commune, when they set on foot a gigantic inquiry to find and fix the true value of the objects of prime and secondary necessity, and when they inspired Robespierre to declare that *only the superfluity of food stuffs should become articles of commerce, and that what was necessary belonged to all.*

Born out of the pressing necessities of those troublous years, the communism of 1793, with its affirmation of the right of all to sustenance and to the land for its production, its denial of the right of any one to hold more land than he and his family could cultivate—that is, more than a farm of 120 acres—and its attempt to communalise all trade and industry—this communism went straighter to the heart of things than all the minimum programmes of our own time, and even all the maximum preambles of such programmes.

In any case, what we learn today from the study of the Great Revolution is, that it was the source of origin of all the present communist, anarchist, and socialist conceptions. We have but badly understood our common mother, but now we have found her again in the midst of the *sans-culottes*, and we see what we have to learn from her.

Humanity advances by stages and these stages have been marked for several hundred years by great revolutions. After the Netherlands came England with her revolution in 1648–1657, and then it was the turn of France. Each great revolution has in it, besides, something special and original. England and France both abolished royal absolutism. But in doing so England was chiefly interested in the personal rights of the individual, particularly in matters of religion, as well as the local rights of every parish and every community. As to France, she turned her chief attention to the land question, and in striking a mortal blow at the feudal system she struck also at the great fortunes, and sent forth into the world the idea of nationalising the soil, and of socialising commerce and the chief industries.

Which of the nations will take upon herself the terrible but glorious task of the next great revolution? One may have thought for a time that it would be Russia. But if she should push her revolution further than the mere limitation of the imperial power; if she touches the land question in a revolutionary spirit—how far will she go? Will she know how to avoid the mistake made by the French Assemblies, and will she socialise the land and give it only to those who want to cultivate it with their own hands? We know not: any answer to this question would belong to the domain of prophecy.

The one thing certain is, that whatsoever nation enters on the path of revolution in our own day, it will be heir to all our forefathers have done in France. The blood they shed was shed for humanity—the sufferings they endured were borne for the entire human race; their struggles, the ideas they gave to the world, the shock of those ideas, are all included in the heritage of mankind. All have borne fruit and will bear more, still finer, as we advance towards those wide horizons opening out before us, where, like some great beacon to point the way, flame the words—LIBERTY, EQUALITY, FRATERNITY.

The French Revolution: Bliss Was It In That Dawn?

Historians have always been the supreme street-sweepers and organisers of the past; revolutions are fascinating because they are so untidy. The Marxist historical filofax dictated that the bourgeois revolution of 1789 in France led to repeated revolutionary outbursts in nineteenth-century Europe. Bourgeois gave way to proletarian revolution in France in June 1848 and March 1871. The French experience gave birth to a world-wide socialist and communist movement witnessed first in the Paris Commune of 1871, then in the October revolution of 1917 in Russia, in China in 1949 and subsequently in a range of states from Cuba to Ethiopia. This Marxist model of revolution was marketed by France's academic historical hierarchy until recent years. It carried such conviction that a scrap of a Communard red flag was taken up to the moon by a Russian expedition.

But the Marxist-socialist millenarian vision of man on an escalator of progress—from the triumph of an industrial bourgeoisie in France in 1789 towards a classless society—was dismembered by the experience of "socialism" in action from the Stalinist purges of the 1930s onwards. From the 1950s historians in Britain and France, led by Alfred Cobban, revealed that even the Marxist model of 1789 itself was misconceived. The revolution delayed, rather than accelerated, the rise of an industrial middle class in France. 1789 was just an attempt by a traditional office-holding and professional bourgeoisie to hold on to their position in society and advance their claims to be consulted in a more modern and rational political framework.

The stature of 1789 has also been reduced by stressing the "Atlantic" impetus to revolution. Chronologically and spritually, the American revolution stole the show, and in Europe's response the French experience was only one element. What then was left of 1789 as an example to the world? Apparently little enough. After all, Alexis de Tocqueville had begun the undressing of Marianne in the 1850s when he noted that the much-vaunted administrative and other institutional restructuring of the years of revolution and of Napoleon were part of a continuum begun under the ancien regime.

In the early 1980s, when the French socialist government realised that decorum would dictate the celebration of a bicentenary, senior French academics travelled the world to arouse interest in the event. The British were astounded to discover that they were expected to celebrate the impact of 1789 on these islands, and the French recoiled in disbelief at the claim by the Britiish that they might dare to celebrate what happened in France. In a recent survey of the importance of the revolution, the president of the official 1789 committee admitted that 1789 has meaning for other countries today only where a link is discerned with their own history. Thus Australia, currently recalling its own birth as a nation, finds an echo in 1789 as the birth of nation-state France. The big controversial ideological claims have gone.

What remains? Politics and political culture, which are once more respectable areas for study by historians of 1789. Foreigners may delight in recalling the embarrassingly prolonged moments of bloody conflict during the Terror and of the substitution of the military dictatorship of Napoleon for the will o' the wisp of political freedom in 1799; but the French are now remembering the positive achievements of 1789, and the rest of the world might do likewise.

The 1790s were uniquely and uncomfortably for the French a decade of political experiment and radical institutional change. France's many European neighbours that were absorbed into the Consulate and Empire witnessed, to varying degrees, a similar reshaping of administrative, judicial and other institutions, together with the introduction of the new French codes covering all aspects of law. Napoleon governed an Empire larger than any since the Roman one. The map of pre-revolutionary Europe could never be rewritten. Many of the new institutions and codes were retained after Napoleon's fall, even though the idea of 1789 was anathema to conservatives in the first half of the nineteenth century.

It used to be claimed that subsequent revolutionary liberal and national movements in these territories were directly inspired by the French example, however illogical it might appear. It has been suggested that the experience of the revolutionary years in Italy and Germany threw up a new bourgeois ruling elite, an echo of the Marxist analysis of 1789 in France. But empirical investigation into the Napoleonic Empire in recent years has shown that the revolution did no more to create a middle-class elite outside France than in and that the rationalisation of government began before the French armies arrived.

To appreciate the significance of 1789 for other peoples, yet another idol of the past must be challenged—Tocqueville. It was politically convenient and expedient for his theories to stress the continuity of *ancien régime* and revolution; but today, with 1789 stripped of the weight of its formerly assumed social and economic content, it is the huge scope of both the political experiment and the institutional innovation that is more striking. The *ancien régime* may have fiddled with the notions of the philosophes on rational government, but the revolutionaries in France created the institutional framework of a modern state, which France retains in essence today and which was to be a model for others.

The political heritage of 1789 was ambiguous, to put the matter politely. But the setting-up of a constiutional monarchy in 1814 (although it had echoes of the British system) launched a French brand of constitutionalism much copied in nineteenth-century Europe. The ideals of the revolution as expressed in the "Declaration of the Rights of Man and the Citizen" may have been swamped by political limitations; but a statement was made by the French, as by the Americans before them, which has a validity that should not be ignored today.

The myth of a Marxist 1789 will be long a-dying among more nostalgic socialists, but the growing gap between rich and poor in all societies will perhaps create the groundswell for new forms of social upheaval in which the ideas of Babeuf and others in the 1790s may find a new audience. Peasants and artisans who fought in the 1790s were trying to hold on to old forms of communal organisation which offered them some protection from misery. Newly privatised modern states risk creating similar dispossessed elements. At present 1789 may be regarded in France and the world as a toothless model—but for how much longer?

Writers' Block

One of the curious facts of literary history is the almost complete absence of outstanding works of literature in France during the revolution and for the following two decades. Mention of 1789 is more likely to bring to mind works that immediately precede the revolution and which are commonly thought to herald its arrival. There is a disquieting *fin de siècle* spirit in, for example, Lados's novel "Les Liaisons dangereuses" and Beaumarchais's play' "Le Mariage de Figaro".

The turbulent period from 1789 to 1794 conjures up deeds and images rather than words: the figure of the young Andre Chenier about to be guillotined (his revolutionary poems were not known until 1819), the marquis de Sade being released by the revolutionaries from prison (not the Bastille but the asylum at Charenton), and a host of amigres like Chateaubriand and Madame de Stael, off to discover more exotic vistas in America and Germany. The most "memorable" products of the revolution are the patriotic songs, the often tiresome pamphlets and the hectoring speeches: the Marseillaise (its composer thereby escaping complete oblivion), Marat's vitriolic journalism, Saint just's impassioned rhetoric. The same frantic activity is to be seen in the theatre of the day—1,000 plays in ten years, hardly one of any merit.

Paradoxically, it was not until the restoration of the monarchy that the revolution began to make a serious impact on French literature. This kind of delayed effect was foreseen by Diderot some 20 years before the revolution; he looked forward to a time when poets might be born again, a time which would come only after a period of cataclysmic events. In the 1820s Stendhal corroborates this view, offering an explanation. He pointed out that between 1792 and 1800 Frenchmen were simply preoccupied with the defence of their territory; and that from 1800 to 1814 the censorship of the Napoleonic régime did not allow the revolution to extend itself to literature.

Stendhal himself is a perfect example of this delayed literary renewal. His novels are full of the sense that what has happened in his time is an extension, under the impetus of the French revolution, of democratic feeling and a more realistic way of looking at the world. The hero of "Le Rouge et le Noir",

Julien Sorel, combines a peasant realism with an inspired revolutionary romanticism. This upstart who falls in love with and seduces (but with a purity of feeling) women far above his own station cannot be confused with the philandering Don Juan of ancien régime literature. A reversal of social circumstances has taken place. There are new dreams of happiness on an altogether more egalitarian basis than ever before.

The issue of emancipation from the past is one taken up by English writers in the early years of the revolution. "Bliss was it in that dawn to be alive", as Wordsworth wrote of the fall of the Bastille. After the Terror and the revolutionary wars, many of the same generation of poets were disenchanted. Only Blake and Shelley remained staunch supporters. For Shelley, the revolution was "the master theme of the epoch in which we live". For Blake, it was a portent of the Apocalypse. A similar messianism glows in the poetry of his German contemporaries, Holderlin and Schiller, with their images of fire and sun, dawn and spring.

For others, once the first wave of enthusiasm had passed, the revolution introduced egalitarianism into literature. Hazlitt writes of Wordsworth's "levelling Muse" which "proceeds on a principle of equality". The revolution unleashed common human hopes. At the same time, the common man—and all that was ordinary—became infused with grandeur. This is what lies behind such apparent simplicities as Wordsworth's "Simon Lee", where the poet assists an old man trying to sever a tree-root in the wastes of the moors. But the levelling and unleashing could go too far; for Carlyle, writing later, the revolution represents the tyranny of "King Mob", the ultimate outburst of destructive fury.

In France the revolution continued to reverberate throughout the nineteenth century and beyond. Above all, the events of 1789 were felt to be unfinished business. They had given rise to certain expectations and these had not been fulfilled. In 1830, 1848 and 1870 complacency was again broken by outbursts of discontent. In the writings of the time, fantastic visions of a better world are continually being juxtaposed with bitter disillusionment. Musset's "Lorenzaccio" ends with the counter-productive murder of a tyrant; Vigny's "Chatterton", with capitalism sacrificing both poet and proletariat. Baudelaire, in spite of his kinship with the downtrodden, retreats into the same type of political defeatism.

Romantic idealism is finally cut to pieces by Flaubert's 'L'Education sentimentale' in which the revolutionaries ofthe 1840s are viewed with caustic scepticism, as they dream of glorious times and model themselves on Saint Just, Danton, Marat or Robespierre. Yet the myth of violence, disorder and even stupidity associated with the revolution is never so strong as to efface the legend of fraternity and equality. A strain of heroic endeavour pervades the work of more than one nineteenth-century writer. The revolutionary masses ("the people") are celebrated in Michelet's history, and they are still there in Zola's "Germinal".

It has been said that revolutions in France never repeat themselves: every one since 1789 has been made by different groups of dissidents. But literature does not see it that way. Each surge of protest finds an expression that harks back to the drama of the revolution. It is true that the students of 1968 did not dance the carmagnole; but in the same decade Peter Brook's "Marat/Sade" and Ariane Mnouchkine's "1789" played to packed houses in Paris, London and New York. "Is the French revolution still worth talking about?" wrote Pieter Geyl in a famous article in 1956. The answer lies with the authors who continue to draw inspiration from it.

Popular Myths

The revolutionaries believed that art should have a dual purpose: to instill patriotic and republican feelings into Frenchmen, and to strike fear into their enemies. On both counts, Jacques-Louis David was the outstanding painter of the revolution.

A contemporary pamphleteer declared that David's "Oath of the Horatii", exhibited at the salon of 1785, "had inflamed more souls for liberty than the best books." It was the painting's moral message that struck home: the swearing of an oath by the three Horatii before their father to defend republican Rome against its enemies. In the background the swooning womenfolk symbolise the gentler family feelings that have been sacrificed to public duty. It is easy to see why this work was understood after 1789 to indict an effete monarchy; harder to understand why such an exemplum virtutis, more suited to the mores of the revolutionaries than of the monarchy, should have been executed by one of the King's own painters and purchased for the royal collection.

At least part of the answer lies in the monarchy's attempt, through its minister for the arts, the comte d'Angiviller, to swim with the incipient republican tide. The painting, which was one of many harbingers of the revolution, would soon become its talisman. It was re-exhibited frequently during the revolution, when it was protected by David's pupils in the uniform of the National Guard. The work was also to reach a still wider audience by being re-enacted as a tableau on the stage, that influential school of contemporary patriotism. David was commissioned too by the National Convention to draw cartoons for use as propaganda against the Republic's enemies abroad; in his robustly scatological "Le Gouvemement anglois"....

Artistic propaganda, pushed by the French revolutionaries further than ever before, achieved expression in what was virtually a new art form, the revolutionary festival. In place of the staid processions of Church and monarchy or the innocent gambolling of peasants round their May Trees, the festivals featured the people as active agents of a cause which was their own. They brought together all the main art forms—architecture, sculpture, painting, music, singing, dancing and dress. Royalists affected to scorn them, but that in itself was testimony to their effectiveness. Most contemporary observers were deeply impressed by the vast and orderly crowds, by their commitment, and not least by the beauty of the dream-like processions, conjured up by contemporary imaginations from the antique, with the women draped in the flowing white robes de, signed—once again—by David.

If David's art and the revolutionary festivals tended to show the revolution from above, the grass-roots version is to be seen in popular paintings and prints. It would be hard to find a clearer example of popular art than Cholat's "Fall of the Bastille". In view of the faulty perspective and childlike draughts-manship, it is not surprising to discover that Cholat was not an artist by pro-fession at all, but a wine-seller. He explains in a pamphlet, where he shows himself no more expert with the pen than with the brush, that he had felt impelled to depict the events as they had really happened. That "reality" is, of course, distorted by the charged imagination of a patriotic revolutionary; the Bastille is known to have surrendered with scarcely a struggle, still less one involving the siege of heroic dimensions depicted here. Yet it was precisely the myths created by Cholat and other popular artists that were to efface often humdrum realities and to endow the revolution with so much of its continu-ing appeal to oppressed peoples everywhere....

Goya's "Third of May" (1809) marks both an end and a new beginning for the art of the French revolution. An end, because the automata-like sol-diers of the French firing squad show what had happened to the ideals of the revolution after France and much of Europe had fallen under the military dic-tatorship of Bonaparte. The new beginning is manifest in the farouche defi-ance of the insurgent with outstretched arms, as he kneels supported by his suffering compatriots. The revolutionaries, having first sought their champi-ons among the privileged heroes of antiquity, had finally entrusted their cause to the oppressed peoples of their own time.

Women's Travails

On October 3 1789 a group of women took up flails and marched to Versailles. Ostensibly their purpose was to secure cheaper bread and a better supply of it to the Paris market. But the movement took on a new dimension. It ended with the King, "the chief baker", and his family accompanying the women and the National Guard back to the capital. The isolation of Louis XVI in the court of Versailles was ended; he was exposed to the demands of a critical city. No more significant journee was enacted in the annals of the revolution.

Astonished Victorian historians could not believe that women could achieve so much. They tried to insist that the participants were men "dressed up as women", but the working women of Paris knew exactly what they had achieved. The march on Versailles converted them at a blow into revolutionar-ies in their own right and architects of a new order.

These women were the wives of artisans whose incomes invariably lagged behind prices. They believed they had the right to defend the consumer interests of their families. And as legatees of an old West European tradition of direct female action in the market place, they also believed themselves endowed with the power to riot with impunity if they respected one rule: the sanctity of property. In the absence of their husbands, whose job it was to restrain them, justice would not pursue them.

This heady glimpse of power was almost unique. Few of the great revolu-tionary journies, such as the fall of the Bastille or the attacks on the Tuileries in 1792, involved many women. After October 1789 the most conspicuous intrusion of women en masse was in the great riots of Germinal and Prairial of the year III (April–June 1795) when the women of the poor quartiers of Paris again demonstrated tumultuously before the Convention to secure bread at a controlled price. This final act of the people's revolution was a dismal failure. After the fall of Robespierre, the politicians did not cede to the demands of Paris. Rather, they proceeded to strip the working populace of its weaponry, including the great cannon of the Faubourg Saint Antoine. The housewives of the quartier were particularly reluctant to give up the cannon, sensing it was the last vestige of their power.

The maitresse is Revolution was without doubt the Parisian sans culotte's wife. Like him, she believed in popular sovereignty to guarantee the people's interests: chiefly, controlled food prices, a war on hoarders and death to traitors at home and abroad. Apparently indifferent to whether or not women might exercise the vote, her job—as she saw it—was to make sure that the policies of the Terror worked. While her husband laboured to support the family and her son fought for the Republic at the front, she sat before the guillotine knitting stockings for the war effort and watching the execution of traitors. She imagined she dwelt in the middle of a vast conspiracy orchestrated by Pitt and Cobourg, aristocrats and fanatical priests, which threatened at any moment to undermine her revolution.

She had little contact, if any, with the women's clubs which emerged in Paris and some of the larger cities and which, with perhaps one exception, had an overtly bourgeois recruitment. The Societe Fratemelle des Patriotes de l'un et l'autre Sexe, for example, under the direction of Olympe de Gouges and Theroigne de Mericourt, demanded citizenship for middle-class women. When war came in the spring of 1792, de Mericourt, to the delight of caricaturists, exhorted women to form legions of Amazons to defend the revolution. By taking up arms, she argued, women demonstrated their right to citizenship.

This was something less than a new dawn in the struggle for women's rights. The women of the bourgeois clubs were, like Mary Wollstonecraft, terrified of the masses. They hoped for recognition from the Legislative Assembly and from the Girondist politicians in particular; association with the latter meant that they were loathed by the women of the Paris quartiers. On May 25 1793 de Maricourt narrowly avoided being lynched by a group of Parisian working women. Six months later de Gouges was guillotined amid popular derision. Once the Jacobins had consolidated their hold, all the women's clubs were closed down. The Comite de Salut Public did not want extremely radical women calling for an acceleration of the Terror. Jacobins believed such women should stay at home.

In provincial France the scene was quite different. Women's attitudes to revolution varied considerably according to class, place and local circumstances. The revolution brought downturn in luxury-textile production, in which thousands were employed; the war brought food shortages; and the doctrinaire religious policies of successive revolutionary governments were locally enforced by over-zealous, over-ambitious patriots. In the provinces, it was the campaign to "de-Christianise" France that most enraged women. Priest-sheltering and clandestine masses were organised mostly by spinsters.

In the aftermath of Thermidor, when freedom of worship was allowed as long as it used no "exterior signs", it was women who forced priests out of hiding to serve their churches. They threw out the revolutionary calendar, reinstated Sunday and religious festivals and hence reconstructed much of the framework of life as it had been. Napoleon in the Concordat had only to recognise a fait accompli.

The French revolution is a goldmine for historians of women, but no golden age. In Paris, some women were agents of change. In the provinces, more were guardians of tradition. Still denied citizenship and certainly far from liberated, they nonetheless played as large a part as they could.

What Price Liberty?

The French naturally see their revolution as the great founding act of modern political culture. In their view it provided the model for the process of revolution; it explored the principles central to modern political concepts; its institutional experiments left a framework for others to build on. As liberal and democratic thought and practice emerged in continental Europe—especially in the German, Italian and Spanish lands occupied under Napoleon—it was the revolution that informed them.

Of course, the English-speaking world does not see things in this light. Indeed, this is one of the main sources of the endless misunderstandings between Anglo-Saxons and the French. The English and the Americans had already had their revolutions. The celebrated debate between Edmund Burke and Thomas Paine over revolutions and the rights of man was conducted almost entirely in terms of English practices and values. Burke did not understand the French (even those who opposed the revolution). Poor Tom Paine was completely at sea when he was elected to the French Convention assembly in 1792.

What cut the revolutionaries off from any common ground with England was their repudiation of history. The debate about historic rights and the constitution in France foundered in early 1789 on the competing claims of the three Estates and in the quagmire of privilege. The revolutionaries escaped from the impasse by preaching a new beginning, upon new first principles. The completeness of their repudiation of the past henceforth distinguished them from the reformers.

From the often contradictory messages of the eighteenth-century philosophers, the revolutionaries had picked out at least one principle. That was universalism—the idea that something is true only if it is universally so. This meant for them that there was only one set of principles upon which a society could be constructed and governed; and this sense of a single correct and permanent solution was part of the reason that the revolutionaries did terrible things to each other and their fellow citizens.

The "Declaration of the Rights of Man and the Citizen" in 1789 was the first theoretical expression of this perceived universal truth. The first article has echoes of Rousseau: "Men are born and remain free and equal in rights". Here, of course, uniformity was the essence of universality. Indeed, it was the most striking characteristic of the revolutionaries' practical work—uniformity of laws, institutions and, for a time, the political behaviour of the population.

Yet the declaration left much unsaid. What was the nature of "liberty" and "rights"? How could those notions be expressed and defended? And how could they be reconciled with that other awkward concept, the sovereignty of the nation? In a nation of men uniformly free and exactly equal in rights, no one part could exercise sovereignty for or over the other. Rousseau had solved the problem with the General Will: the emergence of a single purpose expressing the indivisibility of a society of equal men. Yet even he recognised that, in a large society, it could not work. Hence one of the revolutionaries' greatest legacies to nineteenth-century European liberalism: the idea of representation.

Representation resolved the issue by stating that, although sovereignty could be neither divided nor delegated, the power to represent it could be delegated. Political activity therefore became a function, not a right. The imprescriptable rights, in which all men were equal, were essentially civil rights—with each member of the sovereign nation equally represented, but not necessarily choosing or being a representative.

In the early years this meant in practice a property-owners' paradise, with a tax-defined electorate and an even more restricted qualification for deputy. It was war which brought this edifice crashing down: first in 1792, with the destruction of the monarchy and then in 1793 with the Terror. Yet failure was also inherent in the idea. The reason monarchy had disappeared was because a monarch's possession of some ill-defined portion of sovereignty was incompatible with the singleness of the sovereign nation.

More than that, Jacobin radicals and popular militants alike pointed up the absurdity of replacing an aristocracy of birth with an aristocracy of wealth. Political rights were not separable from other rights. Besides, the social right to protection included protection from poverty, hunger, exploitation and ignorance. This was what republic, as opposed to monarchy, meant. And here lay the foundation of another powerful tradition for the next 200 years.

Yet, unlike popular militants, Jacobins did not see political rights in terms of direct democracy. On the contrary, La Republique une et indivisible was the true political form of the indivisible sovereign nation. It was expressed in the increasingly centralised government of the committee of the Convention. Of course, this centralisation and the coercive measures that went with it to constitute the Terror were made imperative by war. Yet there was more than that to Jacobinism and the Terror. The Jacobins were the last of the revolutionaries to try to build a new society from first principles. Faced with the failure of the French to be regenerated by revolution, they tried to exclude from society the irredeemable and instil in the others what Robespierre called virtue—the civic virtue of men who devoted themselves not to their own interests, but to the public good.

The revolution's high ideal of a regenerated man in a regenerated society culminated in the guillotine and the substitution of the state for the sovereignty of the nation. This tragedy also was not without import for the next 200 years.

POSTSCRIPT

Was the French Revolution Worth Its Human Costs?

The bicentennial celebration of France's revolution in 1989 was somewhat muted in nature. While credit for it was duly given, in the background was a sense of caution and concern, perhaps brought on by reminders of the Revolution's violent dark side, which had been noted by some historians and commentators. It certainly bore little resemblance to our own bicentennial celebration on July 4, 1976.

The most controversial feature of the French Revolution was the infamous Reign of Terror, and it is a subject that all toilers in the garden of the Revolution have to explain. The horrors of the twentieth century (some committed in the name of revolution) demand that the Terror gets the fullest treatment possible. Only then can the question as to whether or not the Revolution was worth its human cost be answered.

Issue 4 in this volume contains an analysis of Japan's ninteenth century Meiji Restoration, and whether it was a revolution in the classical sense. To examine this question, we suggest a comparison of the Meiji movement with other revolutions (including the French) by using the model established by Crane Brinton in *The Anatomy of Revolution* (Random House, 1966). A comparison of the Meiji Japan and French revolutionary experiences would be a tool that could be used to learn about the nature of revolutions.

To list all of the major sources on the French Revolution is daunting, but two general accounts, readable and perfect for the beginning student would be, William Doyle, *The Oxford History of the French Revolution* (Oxford University Press, 1989), and Donald M.G. Sutherland, *France, 1879–1815: Revolution and Counter-Revolution* (Oxford University Press, 1986). As always, much can be learned from Alexis de Tocqueville, whose *The Old Regime and the French Revolution*, first published in the 1850s, could be a useful starting point for a study of the causes and effects of the French Revolution from one of that century's keenest observers.

Finally, two films whose visuals would provide an understanding of the French Revolution would be "La Nuit de Varennes," for its study of the chaotic nature of French Revolutionary society before the Reign of Terror, and "Danton, for the horror that the Terror would become.

ISSUE 3

Did British Policy Decisions Cause the Mass Emigration and Land Reforms That Followed the Irish Potato Famine?

YES: Christine Kinealy, from *This Great Calamity: The Irish Famine 1845–52* (Roberts Rinehart, 1995)

NO: Hasia R. Diner, from *Erin's Daughters in America: Irish Immigrant Women in the Nineteenth Century* (Johns Hopkins University Press, 1983)

ISSUE SUMMARY

YES: Christine Kinealy, fellow of the University of Liverpool, argues that the British government's response to the Irish potato famine was deliberately inadequate. The British government's "hidden agenda" of long-term economic, social, and agrarian reform was accelerated by the famine, and mass emigration was a consequence of these changes.

NO: Historian Hasia R. Diner documents large-scale emigration both before and after the Irish potato famine. Diner credits the Irish people with learning from their famine experiences that the reliance of the poor on the potato and the excessive subdivision of land within families were no longer in their own best interests.

Beginning in 1845 a fungal disease repeatedly struck the potato crop of Ireland and was not eradicated until the early 1850s. The failure of the potato harvest in a country with a population of eight million people caused the death of approximately one million and the emigration of another million. On the eve of the famine, two-thirds of the population earned their living by working the land—for the most part land that they did not own. Still, Ireland was able to feed its own people and also to export food to feed two million Britons. During these years, Ireland was part of the United Kingdom, which also included England and Scotland.

Initially the British government responded to the failure of the Irish potato crop by purchasing and storing Indian corn from America, which it later sold to those who could afford to buy it. Unwilling to offer handouts, the British government provided subsidy only to those who entered the workhouses. As the crisis deepened, the government undertook public works projects, such as road and pier construction, to offer the poor a means to earn money. Ultimately it set up a network of soup kitchens.

By 1847, however, the British government transferred responsibility for Ireland's poor to Ireland itself, insisting that outside aid would be available only after local resources were exhausted or if it could be demonstrated that without outside aid people would die. As the blight continued, British aid was provided to the manufacturing districts in the north of England, which were undergoing an economic slump, but not to the Irish.

Prosperous counties in Ireland were less dependent on the potato crop and resented being held exclusively responsible for the financial bailout of the poorest of their neighbors. If Ireland is truly part of the United Kingdom, they argued, all of the United Kingdom should be equally responsible for alleviating the suffering of any of its members.

However, prevailing stereotypes frequently contrasted the "deserving" poor—industrious factory workers in England's manufacturing centers—with the "undeserving" poor—notably the Irish, who were believed to be lazy and without ambition. How much of a role did these prejudices, which appeared regularly in cartoons and print descriptions, play in the neglect that allowed a million people to die and forced another million to emigrate?

Laissez-faire (literally, to leave alone) economic principles, pioneered by British philosopher Adam Smith and others, contend that government should stay out of the regulation of the economy. Without outside manipulation, this theory suggests, the "hidden hand" of economic forces, such as supply and demand, will regulate the economy efficiently. The prevalence of this theory and others concerning the "undeserving" status of the Irish gave the British government solid justification for withholding economic aid to Ireland.

Christine Kinealy faults British government policies for exploiting the chaos of the famine in order to implement what she calls a "hidden agenda." Seeing the failure of the potato crop as a golden opportunity to force conversion of the Irish economy to a more commercial system of agriculture, the British government, Kinealy explains, was able to rid itself of "non-productive elements." These included landless laborers and apathetic landlords. The million Irish who emigrated, along with the million who died, improved the demographics and facilitated modernization of the Irish economy—but at a terrible cost.

Hasia R. Diner sees more continuity than discontinuity in emigration patterns. While the famine may have accelerated this process, the Irish had been moving to other parts of the British Empire and to the United States in large numbers at least since the late eighteenth century. Calling the famine the "great convincer," Diner attributes changes in agricultural diversity, land inheritance patterns, and marriage practices to the Irish people themselves, acting on their own behalf as agents of historical change.

Christine Kinealy

 **YES**

This Great Calamity:
The Irish Famine 1845–52

The Famine that affected Ireland from 1845 to 1852 has become an integral part of folk legend. In the popular imagination, the Famine is associated with nationwide suffering, initially triggered by the potato blight, compounded by years of misrule and consolidated by the inadequate response of the British government and Irish landlords alike. The resultant large-scale emigration took the tragedy of the Famine beyond the shores of Ireland to an international stage. Recent scholarly studies of the Famine have attempted to move away from this traditional view. In doing so, a sanitised alternative has emerged that has endeavoured to remove the patina of blame from the authorities involved in providing relief, while minimising the suffering of those who were most directly affected by the loss of the potato crop.

Several specific issues need to be addressed in order to evaluate the varying responses of those in power. At a broad level there are three questions. First, what relief measures were implemented? Second, what were the determinants of the measures that were introduced? Third, and most significantly, how effective were they?

These questions are fundamental to an understanding of the Famine. There is still a widespread view that the Famine relief measures were inadequate. Much of the blame is laid at the door of the British government, and to a lesser degree, Irish landlords. Is this an unfair assessment, especially when seen in the context of the perceived role of government in the middle of the nineteenth century?

Early in the nineteenth century, Ireland was widely regarded as a poor country, dominated by a stagnant subsistence agriculture based substantially upon the ubiquitous potato. On the eve of the Famine, the Irish economy supported a population in excess of eight million people which was large by European standards and represented a sizeable portion of the United Kingdom population as a whole—the population of England and Wales at the same period was approximately sixteen million, and of Scotland, under three million. On the eve of the Famine, the economy of Ireland supported its own population and supplied food for a further two million mouths in Britain. Ireland, therefore, should have been a significant consideration in any social or economic policies that affected the United Kingdom as a whole.

The onset of the Famine was unexpected although partial crop failures and food shortages were not unusual. In 1845, therefore, the potato blight, regardless of the lack of understanding of either its origins or an antidote, was not regarded with undue alarm. Although approximately 50 per cent of the main subsistence crop failed in 1845-6, the consequence of the resultant shortages was not famine, nor did emigration or mortality increase substantially. The role played by the government, local landlords, clerics, and various relief officials was significant in achieving this outcome. The second, more widespread, blight of 1846 marked the real beginning of the Famine. Ominously, the impact of the shortages was apparent in the period immediately following the harvest. Inevitably also, the people undergoing a second year of shortages were far less resilient than they had been twelve months earlier. The government responded to this potentially more serious situation by reducing its involvement in the import of food into the country and by making relief more difficult to obtain.

The distress that followed the 1847 harvest was caused by a small crop and economic dislocation rather than the widespread appearance of blight. The government again changed its relief policy in an attempt to force local resources to support the starving poor within their district. The government professed a belief that this policy was necessary to ensure that a burden which it chose to regard as essentially local should not be forced upon the national finances. This policy underpinned the actions of the government for the remainder of the Famine. The relief of famine was regarded essentially as a local responsibility rather than a national one, let alone an imperial obligation. The special relationship between the constituent parts of the United Kingdom forged by the Act of Union appeared not to extend to periods of shortage and famine.

To what extent was a famine or other disaster inevitable when viewed within the context of the general, and some would say increasing, poverty of Ireland? This assumption of Irish poverty, which underpinned political prescription during the Famine, perhaps owed more to distantly derived dogmas than to the reality. For example, a number of recent studies have suggested that height is a reliable indicator of 'nutritional status' (that is, 'the balance of nutritional intake with growth, work, and the defeat of disease'). Surveys of nineteenth-century British military records indicate that Irish recruits were taller than recruits from the rest of the United Kingdom. This implies a sustained nutritional advantage within Ireland. Also, it is now widely accepted that Ireland's pre-Famine economy was more diverse, vibrant, dynamic and responsive to change than has traditionally been depicted. In contrast to this situation, recent quantitative studies of the British economy have reassessed the impact of industrialisation in the first half of the nineteenth century and concluded that, throughout this period, Britain's economic growth remained 'painfully slow'....

The slump of 1847 was a sharp reminder to the government of the problems on its own doorstep. During the autumn of 1847, news of Irish distress vied increasingly for column space in the English newspapers with stories of hardship, unemployment and bankruptcies in England, notably in Lancashire, the flagship of industrial Britain. Poverty and distress, therefore, were not confined to Ireland but were also evident in one of the wealthiest parts of the

British Empire. The demands of the Irish poor were now in direct competition with the demands of the urban poor within Britain. An obvious comparison was drawn between the distress of the feckless Irish peasants and their irresponsible and greedy landlords, with the distress of the hard-working factory operatives and the enterprising entrepreneurs upon whom, it was believed, much of the success of the British Empire rested. Since the reign of Elizabeth I, Poor Law philosophy had drawn a distinction between the 'deserving' and the 'undeserving' poor. The English factory operatives, unemployed through no fault of their own, were regarded as deserving poor; it was apparent that the Irish peasants could be regarded with equal justification as falling into the latter category.

A hardening attitude to Irish distress was illustrated by the response to appeals for additional assistance as a third year of shortages became inevitable. An early indication of a resistant official response occurred in October 1847, when a group of Catholic bishops and archbishops appealed to the government for an increase in official aid. They were informed, in a widely published response, that such a request was unreasonable, particularly as it implied that:

> the means for this relief should be exacted by the government from classes all struggling with difficulties, and at a moment when in England trade and credit are disastrously low, with the immediate prospect of hundreds of thousands being thrown out of employment or being as destitute of the means of existence as the poorest peasant in Ireland.

An appeal for funds in the form of a second 'Queen's Letter' was also published in October 1847 and read out in all churches throughout England. It elicited more criticism than cash.

The government remained committed to the policy of forcing Ireland to depend on its own resources as far as possible, chiefly through the mechanism of the Poor Law. Within the domestic economy, however, the government did depart from its declared *laissez faire* policy and intervened to allow the terms of the 1844 Bank Charter Act to be relaxed in order to aid the industrial sector. By the end of 1847, the financial crisis in Britain was over and a period of prosperity was under way. The Great Exhibition of 1851 was a triumphant demonstration of Britain's international industrial and economic supremacy. In the same year, in a different part of the United Kingdom, the west of Ireland, a portion of the population was about to confront a seventh consecutive year of famine and shortages.

The contribution of outside charitable bodies was mostly confined to the early years of the Famine. By 1847, most of these sources had dried up or, as in the case of the Quakers, they had decided to use their remaining funds to concentrate on long-term improvements rather than immediate relief. Significantly, the Quakers' men on the ground who toured the west of Ireland in the winter of 1846-7 were critical both of absentee landlords and the policies pursued by the British government alike. The British Relief Association, which remained operative after 1847, allowed its funds to be allocated through the medium of the Treasury. This was not without problems. Count Strzelecki, the Association's local agent, fought a hard battle with the Treasury to ensure that a successful scheme to feed schoolchildren was continued, regardless of the disapproval of [Charles] Trevelyan.

A fundamental policy position of government, enforced rigorously throughout the Famine, as noted earlier, was the determination to make local resources support local distress. The Irish landlords were singled out continually as a group that needed to be reminded of, and occasionally coerced into, undertaking their duties to the poor. Following the 1845 blight, however, the money contributed voluntarily by the landlords and other subscribers was the highest amount ever raised. Regardless of this achievement, the Irish contribution was represented as derisory and the landlords increasingly targeted as the object of public opprobrium. Irish landlords undoubtedly provided an easy and obvious scapegoat both as a cause of, and as contributors to, the Famine. This was a view taken both by their contemporaries and by some later historians....

To what extent, however, can any individual group, organisation or state body be blamed for the degree of suffering that resulted from successive years of potato blight? Would the outcome of the years of shortages and suffering have been different if the response of the authorities, various charitable organisations, and other key individuals to successive years of blight had been different?

There is no doubt that the part played by the government was pivotal within the whole relief endeavour. Was it, however, within the remit of the government—either ideologically or financially—to provide sufficient relief to keep suffering, emigration, and mortality to a minimum level? The policies of the government, and the way in which it perceived its role, are crucial to an understanding of the Famine years. The changing perceptions and strategies of the British government determined the type of relief provided and the methods and timing of its allocation. The role played by the Treasury, both in implementing the various relief policies and in advising the government, was critical. Charles Wood, the Chancellor of the Exchequer, together with his colleague, Charles Trevelyan, represented a school of economic orthodoxy which advocated both non-intervention and fiscal rectitude. A populist version of their views found a wider audience in the columns of *The Times* and the cartoons of *Punch*. It was also supported in the learned contributions to the *Edinburgh Review* and the fledgling *Economist*. In the wake of the financial and monetary crisis of 1847, the demand for retrenchment was also welcomed by a politically influential industrial middle class. The Treasury, in effect, became not only the guardian of the relief purse, but—mainly due to the energetic and prolonged involvement of Charles Trevelyan—was increasingly deferred to by members of the government as the oracle of all wisdom regarding Ireland. Although no one person can be blamed for the deficiencies of the relief policies, Trevelyan perhaps more than any other individual represented a system of response which increasingly was a mixture of minimal relief, punitive qualifying criteria, and social reform.

The Treasury's agenda for Irish relief went far beyond the mere allocation of government funds. Its imprint was evident throughout both the public and private sectors. Not only did it arbitrate on the crucial issue of who deserved to be given financial support and how much they should receive, but increasingly it attempted to control the day-to-day administration of relief. No other organisation played such a sustained role or showed such an obvious interest in the affairs of Ireland. The government, which was in the midst of a foreign crisis, an economic depression, and a year of revolutions and uprisings in Europe which extended both to Britain and Ireland, was no doubt glad to be able to allow the Treasury to shoulder such a large portion of the Irish relief burden. Also, despite evidence to the contrary, many officials, including even the well-informed Trevelyan, publicly declared the Famine to be over in 1848. The problems of Ireland, therefore, were necessarily a low priority to a government at the centre of a large and still expanding Empire. However, by allowing the Treasury to play such a pivotal role in the provision of relief, it was perhaps inevitable that the need to 'balance the books'—an excellent objective in Treasury terms—should at times overshadow the need to provide adequate relief. By using the Treasury in such a capacity, its role far exceeded that of guardian of the public purse and extended both to influencing public policy and, even more significantly, to final arbitrator in the provision of relief....

The Famine was a disaster of major proportions, even allowing for an inevitable statistical uncertainty on its estimated effect on mortality. Yet the Famine occurred in a country which, despite concurrent economic problems, was at the centre of a still-growing empire and was an integral part of the acknowledged workshop of the world. There can be no doubt that despite a short-term cyclical depression, the combined resources of the United Kingdom could either completely or much more substantially have removed the consequences of consecutive years of potato blight in Ireland. This remains true even if one accepts Trevelyan's proud assertion that no government had done more to support its poor than Britain had done during the Famine years. The statement implies that not only was enough done to help the suffering people in Ireland, but that it was accompanied by a generosity that patently is not borne out by the evidence. To have fed in excess of three million people in the summer of 1847 was a worthy and notable achievement. It also dispels the frequent assertion that the British government did not possess the administrative capability to feed such a large number of starving people. But if the measure of success is judged by the crudest yet most telling of all measures—that of mortality—the British government failed a large portion of the population in terms of humanitarian criteria.

In this context, Trevelyan's comment reveals the separateness of Ireland from the rest of the United Kingdom. His perception mocked the precepts of the Act of Union. It should not, however, be forgotten that the government and the Treasury had to provide a system of relief that would satisfy both parliamentary and public opinion. If measured by this criterion alone—accepting, however, the individual criticisms of the opposition party—the relief measures were undoubtedly regarded as successful, and to some, even over-generous.

The policies of the government increasingly specified criteria that disallowed external assistance until distress was considerable and evident. The leitmotif of relief provided by the central government throughout the course of the Famine was that assistance would be provided only when it—or, in fact, its agent, the Treasury—was satisfied that local resources were exhausted, or that if aid was not provided, the distressed people would die. By implementing a policy which insisted that local resources must be exhausted before an external agency would intervene, and pursuing this policy vigorously despite local advice to the contrary, the government made suffering an unavoidable consequence of the various relief systems which it introduced. The suffering was exacerbated by the frequent delays in the provision of relief even after it had been granted and by the small quantity of relief provided, which was also of low nutritional value. By treating the Famine as, in essence, a local problem requiring a local response, the government was, in fact, penalising those areas which had the fewest resources to meet the distress.

The government response to the Famine was cautious, measured and frequently parsimonious, both with regard to immediate need and in relation to the long-term welfare of that portion of the population whose livelihood had been wiped out by successive years of potato blight. Nor could the government pretend ignorance of the nature and extent of human tragedy that unfolded in Ireland following the appearance of blight. The Irish Executive and the Poor Law Commissioners sent regular, detailed reports of conditions within the localities and increasingly requested that even more extensive relief be provided. In addition, Trevelyan employed his own independent sources of information on local conditions, by-passing the existing official sources of the Lord Lieutenant. This information revealed the extent of deprivation caused by the Famine. It also showed the regional variations arising from the loss of the potato crop; and it exposed the inability of some areas to compensate for such losses from their own internal resources. There was no shortage of detailed and up-to-date information. What was crucial was the way in which the government used this information.

While it was evident that the government had to do something to help alleviate the suffering, the particular nature of the actual response, especially following 1846, suggests a more covert agenda and motivation. As the Famine progressed, it became apparent that the government was using its information not merely to help it formulate its relief policies but also as an opportunity to facilitate various long-desired changes within Ireland. These included population control and the consolidation of property through a variety of means, including emigration, the elimination of small holdings, and the sale of large but bankrupt estates. This was a pervasive and powerful 'hidden agenda'. The government measured the success of its relief policies by the changes which were brought about in Ireland rather than by the quality of relief provided *per se*. The public declaration of the Census Commissioners in the Report of the 1851 Census, which stated that Ireland had benefited from the changes brought about by the Famine, is a clear example of this....

The response of [Whig leader Lord John] Russell's government to the Famine combined opportunism, arrogance and cynicism, deployed in such a way as to facilitate the long-standing ambition to secure a reform of Ireland's economy. In the midst of dealing with a famine in Ireland, increasing reference was made to the need to restructure agriculture in Ireland from the top to the bottom. This had been the ambition of a succession of governments prior to 1845, but the Famine provided a real opportunity to bring about such a purpose both quickly and, most importantly, cheaply.

In the early decades of the nineteenth century, for example, state-sponsored emigration had been recommended by select committees, social theorists and government advisors alike, all of whom agreed that it would be beneficial to Ireland; but the government had refused to involve itself in the additional expenditure that an active pursuit of this policy would involve. The Famine, however, gave the impetus to emigration to flourish, without imposing an additional financial burden on the government. It, therefore, provided opportunities for change. The Whig administration, through legislation such as the Quarter-Acre Clause and the Encumbered Estates Acts, ensured that such opportunities were not wasted.

If the potato blight had been confined to 1845, its impact would have been insignificant and it would have been remembered only as one of the many intermittent subsistence crises which affected Ireland and all agricultural societies. Even though over half of the crop was lost through blight in 1845, the increase in excess mortality and emigration was insignificant. In 1845-6, as had so clearly been demonstrated in the subsistence crisis of 1782-4, if the political and social will existed, a subsistence crisis did not necessarily have to become a famine.

In the 1840s, the policy of the British government was shaped by a prevailing economic dogma, inspired by a particular interpretation of free market economics. The champions of this philosophy were Adam Smith and his successors such as Nassau Senior and Harriet Martineau. In the context of providing poor relief in Ireland, this influential philosophy decreed that ultimately such relief was damaging and that genuine improvements could be achieved only through self-help. In its more extreme form, the principles embodied in this dogma denied any government responsibility for the alleviation of distress. Proponents of such theories even managed to suggest that during periods of extraordinary distress it could be better for those affected not to have access to extraneous relief lest the self-righting mechanisms of the economic system—the allegedly ubiquitous yet truly imperceptible 'invisible hand'—became ensnared by unwarranted interference. The outcome of a slavish adherence to these self-adjusting mechanisms would inevitably be human suffering. Yet this appeared to be of little consequence to those who worshipped at the altar of *laissez faire*. Short-term suffering appeared to be a small price to be paid for long-term improvement, especially if the theoreticians did not have to participate directly in the experiment.

Despite the fashionable adherence to these theories at the time of the Famine, they were only one of the many influences upon political decision-making. It is clear that such theoretical dogma could be dismissed when prevailing pressures demanded: the intervention by the government in the autumn of 1847 to alleviate the impact of a slump in the manufacturing districts of England providing a concurrent example. The philosophy of non-interference was in practice employed selectively and pragmatically. Its content and application changed as the government considered necessary. Within the Whig government itself, there existed differences of opinion regarding the level of financial intervention in Ireland. Significantly, those who favoured a minimalist approach, spearheaded by the men at the Treasury, were in the ascendant. Nevertheless, during the crucial period in the provision of Famine relief, that is, after the complete devastation of the potato crop in 1846, there is no doubt that this economic theory had powerful public support and, more significantly, enjoyed a popular appeal among many of the ruling elite, particularly those most directly responsible for determining the extent and means of providing relief.

From the perspective of a political response to the Famine, the most substantial deviation from the purist theories of free market economics came about in Ireland itself. This deviation was motivated by the less than purist desire to seek a major reform of the Irish economy, especially in the 'potato economy' districts in the west. In these areas, the free market clearly had failed to deliver spontaneously the desired result, particularly in terms of larger, more efficient holdings, and the British government chose to use the Famine as a means of facilitating and imposing their own reforms. The Famine provided a unique opportunity to bring about long-term structural changes in Ireland's agrarian sector.

During the latter part of the Famine, notably following the transfer of relief to local responsibility through the mechanism of the Poor Law in the autumn of 1847, a 'hidden agenda' of reform is increasingly apparent. Much of this was covert. The government and its agents were not willing to admit openly that the suffering of many people in Ireland, and the consequent high levels of mortality and emigration, was being employed to achieve other purposes. The government was able to use the chaos caused by the Famine to facilitate a number of social and economic changes. In particular, it took the opportunity to bring about a more commercial system of farming within Ireland which no longer would offer refuge to a variety of non-productive elements—whether they were landless labourers or apathetic landlords. If, due to its ultimate aim, this policy could be judged as altruistic, its implementation, based on the prevailing view of the Irish, cannot be. Irish peasants, feckless and indolent as they were perceived to be, were judged less 'worthy' to receive relief than their counterparts in Britain. One consequence of this perception occurred in 1846 when Ireland was not allowed to receive imports of food until supplies had been delivered to Scotland first....

In conclusion, therefore, the response of the British government to the Famine was inadequate in terms of humanitarian criteria and, increasingly after 1847, systematically and deliberately so. The localised shortages that followed the blight of 1845 were adequately dealt with but, as the shortages became more widespread, the government retrenched. With the short-lived exception of the soup kitchens, access to relief—or even more importantly, access to food—became more restricted. That the response illustrated a view of Ireland and its people as distant and marginal is hard to deny. What, perhaps, is more surprising is that a group of officials and their non-elected advisors were able to dominate government policy to such a great extent. This relatively small group of people, taking advantage of a passive establishment, and public opinion which was opposed to further financial aid for Ireland, were able to manipulate a theory of free enterprise, thus allowing a massive social injustice to be perpetrated within a part of the United Kingdom. There was no shortage of resources to avoid the tragedy of a Famine. Within Ireland itself, there were substantial resources of food which, had the political will existed, could have been diverted, even as a short-term measure, to supply a starving people. Instead, the government pursued the objective of economic, social and agrarian reform as a long-term aim, although the price paid for this ultimately elusive goal was privation, disease, emigration, mortality and an enduring legacy of disenchantment.

Hasia R. Diner

Where They Came From

If poverty, persecution, and violence seem to have been eternal elements of Irish life, changes in the economic and social structure nonetheless did occur.... Historians love watersheds: dramatic incidents that set off one epoch from another; major upheavals that loom as signposts along the historic path. The Great Famine of the late 1840s has generally been considered the event in Irish history which sent shock waves throughout Irish society, whose reverberations could be felt around the world, in Boston, London, Toronto, Sydney, and Melbourne, and whose intensity lasted over a century. Nothing remained the same after the devastation of the Famine. The harrowing memory of the starvation, disease, and destruction that engulfed Ireland after the potato blights of 1845–49 altered all relationships; the footing between landlord and tenant changed, as did that between priest and parishioner. The ruler and the ruled shifted ground as they faced each other. Entire classes of people disappeared. The Famine signaled the demise of the Irish cottier class, that landless mass on the lowest stratum of the social structure.

Sheer numbers also confirm the brutal impact of the Famine. After the four years of continuous blight on the potato crop, the Irish staff of life, at least one million people had vanished. Some were felled by starvation, typhus, and dysentery. In the same year three million were reduced to charity. Others fled the Emerald Isle. The Famine's shadow seems to have left no one untouched. The memory of the starvation and what was considered the inaction of the British (some saw it as pure malice) would, over the course of the next century, become a major weapon of nationalist propaganda. Irish journalists, poets, novelists, and playwrights would constantly cull the maudlin scenes of those years for pathetic and gripping material. Father Theobald Matthew, who led Ireland's highly popular temperance movement in the 1870s, invoked such wrenching scenes in sermon after sermon:

> There, admist the chilling damp of a dismal hovel see yon famine-stricken fellow-creature; see him extended on his scanty bed of rotten straw; see his once manly frame, that labour had strengthened with vigour, shrunk to a skeleton; see his once ruddy complexion, the gift of temperance, changed by hunger and concomitant disease to a shallow ghastly hue. See him extend his yellow withering arm for assistance; hear how he cries out in agony for food, for since yesterday he has not even moistened his lips!

Diner, Hasia R., ERIN'S DAUGHTERS IN AMERICA: IRISH IMMIGRANT WOMEN IN THE NINETEENTH CENTURY, pp. 2–10. Copyright © 1983 by The John Hopkins University Press. Reprinted with permission of The John Hopkins University Press. Notes omitted.

> Who could forget the vision of a strange and fearful sight like what
> we read of in beleaguered cities; its streets crowded with gaunt wanderers,
> sauntering to and from with hopeless air and hunger-struck look—a mob of
> starved, almost naked women around the poor-house clamoring for soup
> tickets.

People around the world gasped at the horrors of the Famine. Relief poured in. Generous Americans collected money to send food to Ireland's starving millions. American magazine readers were fed a constant diet of grim details about "a widow with two children who for a week had eaten nothing but cabbage.... Another woman with two children, and not far from being confined again, stated that during the last week they had existed upon two quarts of meal and two heads of cabbage ... famine was written in the faces of this woman and her children."

Intimate relationships between men and women, husbands and wives, parents and children, brothers and sisters, were not exempted from this massive restructuring of life. The qualities of personal ties and social bonds were swept away by the Famine's blast. The 1851 Census of Ireland surveyed the ruin of the countryside and lamented that

> the closest ties of kinship were dissolved; the most ancient and long cher-
> ished usages of the people were disregarded; the once proverbial gaiety and
> lightheartedness of the peasant people seemed to have vanished com-
> pletely, and village merriment or marriage festival was no longer heard or
> seen throughout the regions desolated by the intensity and extent of the
> Famine....

❧❦❧

The watershed approach does have its pitfalls. Few of the changes that occurred after the cataclysm were totally unrelated to the nature of the earlier society. The great upheaval merely accentuated trends that had begun earlier and accelerated forces unleashed in more tranquil and stable times. For example, the great upsurge in religiosity that occurred in post-Famine Ireland, the devotional revolution with its tremendous growth in both the number and the power of the clergy, swept a society that was religiously oriented to begin with. Religion had been a powerful political identity for a long time, and the priest, the *soggarth aroon*, had long held a cherished place in the hearts of the masses.

So, too, the trends in Irish demography—a constantly decreasing population with late and infrequent marriage and high rates of celibacy, a social environment of gender segregation and reluctant sexuality, the concomitant ethic of intense gender animosity—had roots that reached far back into Irish folk life and characterized some classes in the pre-Famine structure. Yet after the Famine these elements came to be synonymous with all of Irish culture and these trends became the norm of Irish behavior. Similarly, the Famine did not cause the massive emigrations. For one thing, the Famine of the late 1840s was not the first to ravage Ireland in modern times. In 1800, 1807, 1816, 1822, and

1839 massive crop failures and wide-ranging epidemics had shaken up the rural Irish. Immigration had in fact begun before the Famine and it continued well afterwards. At least seven hundred thousand people abandoned the thirty-two counties of Ireland between 1825 and 1844. As early as 1841 a half million Irish-born men and women had decided to settle permanently in England and Scotland, while in the same year over ten thousand new arrivals to the port of Boston listed Ireland as their birthplace. In the 1831–41 decade a half million Irish emigrated. Long after the Great Famine had become a memory and a closed chapter of Ireland's sorrowful history, twentieth-century Ireland continued to send its young men and women around the world, making people Ireland's chief export.

❧◆❧

The legacy of the Famine as it shaped emigration to the United States, and particularly as it stimulated a massive female exodus, involved a demographic transition and an alteration in family relations much more subtle than millions of individuals merely fleeing their native land. Drawing upon older Irish traditions and social trends associated with the more stable classes in pre-Famine society, Ireland became a country that held out fewer and fewer attractions to women. By the last decades of the nineteenth century many young women had no reason to remain in the agricultural towns of Catholic Ireland. They had no realistic chances for marriage or employment. For Irish women to attain either, they had to turn their backs on the land of their birth.

Ireland became the Western world's most dramatic and stark example of a demographic pattern associated with the shift from traditional to modern societies. Ireland led the world by the 1870s as the nation with the latest age of marriage. Irish men and women decided more frequently than men and women elsewhere to eschew marriage and live out their lives in a single state. Ireland was, in fact, one of the only countries in Europe to enter the twentieth century unconcerned about overpopulation, because decades earlier it had achieved more than "zero population growth." This, however, had not always been the case. Before the Great Famine, more likely than not an Irish peasant or laborer married young. Until the decade of the Famine Irish population figures had risen with alarming rapidity. Ireland's mushrooming—perhaps, more appropriately, exploding—population had, in fact, provided Thomas Malthus with his gloomiest example of the improvidence of the poor and the inexorable cycle whereby population grew far out of proportion to resources.

A large and controversial body of demographic literature has attempted to explain how this happened. The issues in the analysis of Irish population trends are clouded by the difficulty of obtaining accurate statistics on just how many births and deaths occurred in any given year before 1864, when compulsory registration of nationwide vital statistics was enacted. The first official head count of any kind was made in 1821, and that of 1841 is considered the first that approached reliability. Generally, it is accepted by demographers and historians that the 1821 Census counted fewer people than actually existed, whereas the 1831 count overstated the number. Despite the technical problems of portraying Irish demographic movement, scholars and commentators on the Irish scene have sought to come to terms with the ways in which the population changed and why. The impact of the Great Famine is central to this endeavor, and from it we can begin to discern the nature of women's lives in Irish society.

On the eve of the Famine, over eight million people inhabited Ireland. Fifty years later the same island had been home to fewer than three million. This tremendous growth occurred without any industrialization or increase in economic opportunities and without any influx of foreigners. In fact, this staggering proliferation occurred while emigration had already become an established part of life. Over four hundred thousand Irish-born men and women lived in Great Britain in 1841, whereas between 1780 and 1845 more than one million Irish had made their way to the United States and Canada. Thus, despite a continuous stream of Irish leaving Ireland in this same half century, the rate of population increase constituted a major demographic revolution.

One strand of analysis which attempts to explain Irish population dynamics focuses on diet—on the impact of the lowly potato on mortality and fertility trends. The potato culture, which gradually came to characterize all Ireland, triggered a constant and seemingly unending process by which the land was broken into smaller and smaller holdings. Widespread was "the general practice with farmers to divide their land into portions, which were given to their children as they got married. The last married frequently got his father's cabin along with his portion of the ground, and there the parents liked to stop feeling attached to the place where they spent their lives." The fleshy tuber could be grown anywhere, even on the most miniscule of plots, and contained just enough nutrients to sustain the life of the poor.

As the Irish had become potato-eaters by the end of the eighteenth century, they also had become early marriers. The poor, in particular, saw no reason not to marry spontaneously, that is, without protracted negotiations between families, and certainly without the aid of a matchmaker. Young men and women married when they wanted, and since they could always grow potatoes, a family of hungry mouths was not a burden. A priest from Mayo generalized to the Commission of Inquiry on the Irish Poor in 1836 that "small holders are induced to marry by feeling that their condition cannot be made worse, or rather, they know they can lose nothing, and they promise themselves some pleasure in the society of a wife." This testimony typified the statements that were offered by the clerics and laymen alike to the commission, to the Devon Commission, which met in 1841, and to other, similar bodies. One man in County Galway confessed in 1835, "if I had been a blanket to cover her, I would marry the woman I liked; and if I should get potatoes enough to put into my children's mouths, I would be as happy and content as any man." Similarly, very few Irish men and women did not marry. The nature of the economy and the social structure left very little room for the unattached adult. Within marriage, fertility was high. There was no incentive for, or seeming interest in, contraception of any kind as there was in France at the same time. Some scholars even argue that, by providing a cheap and easily cultivated source of nutrition, the potato improved the health of women and gradually led to heightened fertility.

Even before the Famine this pattern of early and improvident marriage characterized the depressed peasants—the cottiers and the poor laborers—much more than any other class. Townspeople, tradesmen, and farmers with more than a potato plot demonstrated greater reticence about marriage. For those with hope of economic stability and with aspirations for a more "middle-class" kind of existence improvident marriage could spell disaster. Marrying too young meant the expense of feeding and clothing a family too soon. Marrying too young was clearly associated with the reckless behavior of the poor, who inched closer and closer to doom as they subdivided and resubdivided their possessions.

A County Kilkenny observer noted that "those who are a grade above the cottier are more cautious as to marriage, and it is chiefly among small farmers that you will find bachelors." Similarly, in County Limerick one could have found "a greater proportionate number of unmarried men amongst the farmers and tradesmen than amongst the lowest classes of agricultural labourers." This same phenomenon could be plotted geographically. In the wealthier and more fertile East, which supported the cultivation of grains as well as potatoes, people generally married later than in the poverty-stricken West, which was home for the most destitute of laborers and cottiers. Thus, even in the early nineteenth-century, when Irish population grew rapidly, the growth was clustered in the bottom classes.

The late- and nonmarriers of "higher" social status in Irish society provided the link between the pre- and post-Famine eras of Irish history. They undermine the more dramatic interpretation that sees the Famine as the central and defining event in Ireland's development. It is in part because of these more prosperous farmers that the rapid population growth had actually begun to slacken by 1821, and the 1831 Census registered a marked increase in the number of nonmarried adults. What the Famine did accomplish was to dramatically universalize trends that were already in operation. This happened in a number of ways. In the first place, the Famine could claim grim responsibility for the almost total elimination of the cottier class. Second, the memory of the Famine impressed the British lawmakers enough in the succeeding decades to enact legislation that outlawed subdivision and other practices associated with pre-Famine agriculture, thus transforming most Irish men into holders of small, although viable, farms.

The Famine might also be seen as the great convincer. It demonstrated to all the folly of agrarian practices that defined a postage-stamp-size piece of land as enough just because it brought forth potatoes. Irish agriculture was going to have to become much more diversified, and though potatoes could remain a central dish on the Irish family's table, that same farm family would also have to produce a cash crop as well as butter, eggs, and other dairy products for markets. The Famine also demonstrated to Irish parents that no one prospered if they cut up their holdings into equal portions for all their sons. An inheritance came to be the entire holding or nothing. Similarly, the Famine also convinced Irish men and women that early marriage was reckless marriage; that nonmarriage was an option, too. As the Irish changed their marriage patterns, they basically adapted the behavior of the more economically stable elements in the society, convinced that the devastation and destruction of the late 1840s had in part been caused by irrational, carefree marriage and family practices that failed to treat conjugal life as a fundamentally economic enterprise.

⋅◈⋅

Whereas before the Famine commentators on Irish life—Catholic clergymen, economists, and British officials alike—lamented the reckless marriage patterns that seemed to accompany the Irish descent into poverty and destitution, after the Famine concern mounted that the Irish in Ireland were increasingly uninterested in remaining at home, marrying, and reproducing themselves. In 1902 one writer mourned, "In saying all this we are fully alive to the sadness of seeing a grand old race disappear as it were, off the face of the earth." Richard J. Kelly in 1904 shared this pessimism with readers of the *New Ireland Review* and chided the experts. "Economists, so-called, read lessons to us on our over-population and improvident early marriages and, as they said, consequent wretchedness. But they can no longer, with any regard for truth say so now, with a smaller population, lower marriage and a lower birth rate than most countries in Europe." Descriptions of Irish life in the last decades of the century all stressed the gloom of decay, the moribund quiet of a society in decline, although perhaps a decline accompanied by increasing prosperity. A magistrate of County Meath saw his home as

> one of the most melancholy counties I know. This grass grown road, over which seemingly little, if any, traffic passes, is a type of solitude everywhere found. Tillage there is none; but in its stead one vast expanse of pasture land extends. Human habitations are rarer than the bare walls of roofless cottages. Where once a population dwelt, and as consequence, see how lonely and untrodden are these roads.

Census figures painfully recorded the dwindling of Irish numbers. In the fifty years between 1841 and 1891, Ireland lost 3,470,374 residents, plummeting from the pre-Famine population of 8,175,124 in 1841 to 4,704,750 in 1891. Constant migration picked off many of these Irish men and women, but migration could not alone be blamed. The decline in Irish population stemmed most fundamentally from a change in family life and a major demographic shift. There were, to be sure, bad harvests in the last half of the nineteenth century which took their toll, somewhat reminiscent of the Famine, but they lacked the bite of the 1840s devastation.

The bulk of the late-nineteenth-century population decline occurred in the rural areas, siphoning off the residents of farm regions much more rapidly than residents of towns. Ireland was becoming somewhat less overwhelmingly rural in the last half of the century. In 1841 only 17 percent of the population was urban; by 1891 over one-quarter of all the Irish could be found in cities like Dublin and Cork. Even the urban population of the country slumped, however, falling from over a million city dwellers in 1841 to eight hundred thousand in 1891. Only Dublin grew in that same time period, but that growth was hardly dramatic and clearly indicated the stagnation of Irish population and the absence of any industrial development or commercial rejuvenation to draw discontented farm people into the cities. Ireland had basically become a nogrowth nation. It had no urban-industrial attractions to stimulate a massive internal movement. It had in fact become a nation characterized by late and reluctant marriage as well as by a massive voluntary exodus.

In the early 1840s, before the Famine shocked and convinced the Irish out of impoverished, although perhaps comfortable, ways, the rate of marriage was 7.0–8.0 per thousand per year. It bore a close resemblance to the rate of marriage throughout Europe. From 1868, four years after compulsory registration of vital statistics, to 1870 the rate of marriage spiraled down to 5.1 per thousand and then fell to 4.0 in the years 1881–90. Clearly, in any given year or span of years during the second half of the century fewer Irish men and women were setting up families than in years past. Many were merely deferring, that is, they were marrying later than they might have in earlier periods. In 1864, for example, 18.1 percent of all women who married were under twenty-one. In 1911 only 5.3 percent entered marriage by that age. Similarly, in 1864 71.1 percent of all wives in a first marriage were under twenty-five; in 1911 only 51.1 percent were similarly situated. But Ireland also came to be the home of large numbers of men and women who just chose not to marry or who were unable to. In 1861, 11 percent of all men in Ireland sixty-five or over were permanent bachelors; in 1926 that figure had risen to 26 percent. Again using 1841, or the last pre-Famine census, as the point of contrast, the percentage of women age twenty-five to thirty-four who were single in Ireland went from 28 percent to 39 percent in 1851. It did not change in 1891. Although fewer Irish women continued to be unmarried as they approached old age, among women forty-five to fifty-four the number of singles also increased from 12 percent in 1841 to 17 percent in 1891. Figures for men were significantly higher in both age categories, in all years. No longer did Irish society live under the specter of the impetuous young rushing off emotionally to marry and set up homes.

Not surprisingly, this matrimonial trend occurred in tandem with yet another development that characterized post-Famine Irish society. Parents increasingly became reluctant to subdivide their land among heirs, and Ireland as a whole came to have fewer and fewer holdings. In 1841, for example, there were 691,000 holdings in all of Ireland, the largest percentage being the smallest holdings, one to five acres. In 1861, 568,000 estates were primarily of the five- to fifteen-acre size, whereas in 1891 the number of holdings declined to 469,000, most of them over thirty acres. Evictions certainly help account for this trend toward land accretion. The poorest could no longer hold onto their tiny plots, and consolidation in Ireland became the basic trend. The cottiers were gone and increasingly the middling Irish farmer had control of a reasonably viable piece of land, which was to be used for pasture-farming, not for tillage.

These middling Irish farmers either had survived the Famine themselves or their parents had witnessed the harrowing devastation, commonly attributed to the wrath of God, or to the heartlessness of the Saxon ruler, or, importantly, to the impetuous romanticism of the poor. The middling Irish farmers were *not* going to err again. They were not going to find themselves in the same position as had the Irish in the 1840s. To ensure their continuous survival without want and destitution they finally sought to shake off the yoke of British rule. To ensure their continued survival with a degree of material comfort and security they sought to establish families that enhanced their economic needs. Land and the economic security it brought became obsessions with the Irish. A folk proverb suggested, "Let any man go down to hell and open an Irish man's heart ... the first thing writ across it was land."

Whereas there is no agreement in sight for the lively and sparring scholarly debate over the cause of the pre-Famine population growth, there is unanimity as to the nature of post-Famine marriage: what it was and why it developed into a more discriminate and rationalized institution. Marriages were based now on economic calculation with parents figuring and weighing the financial benefits and liabilities of their children's marital futures. Land would not be divided. An estate would pass intact and undisturbed from one generation to another. Therefore, only one member of the family's younger generation could hope to inherit the land. No systematic or established pattern developed which designated that single heir. Primogeniture was not the rule, nor was the younger son the immediately designated heir. Who inherited the land became the decision of father and mother and they made that decision as late in their lives as possible. Parents held onto control of their fields until well into old age. (Interestingly, Ireland had among Europe's most impressive statistics on longevity.) At the same time they tenaciously held onto control of their children's futures.

POSTSCRIPT

Did British Policy Decisions Cause the Mass Emigration and Land Reforms That Followed the Irish Potato Famine?

Ireland's leading economist, Cormac O'Grada, studies famine folklore, the limitations of medical science, the selection of who would emigrate (many through landlord-funded programs) and who would not, and even the role of the weather in intensifying the famine in *Black '47 and Beyond: The Great Irish Famine in History, Economy, and Memory* (Princeton University Press, 1999). This interdisciplinary work looks at stories and songs that suggest what it was like to live during famine times, explores the impact of famine-related diseases on the city of Dublin, and follows one group of emigrants to New York City's Sixth Ward. *Emigrants and Exiles: Ireland and the Irish Exodus to North America* (Oxford University Press, 1985) by Kerby A. Miller documents both pre-and post-famine exoduses and explores the traditional Irish Catholic worldview that led the Irish to regard themselves as involuntary "exiles."

The Great Irish Famine, edited by Cathal Poirteir and produced in association with Irish Television (Radio Telefis Eireann), has an especially interesting essay by Peter Gray on "Ideology and the Famine," which explores anti-Irish prejudice, the influence of economic theories on British policy, and the reality of political considerations. Two television series have explored this topic: *The Great Famine*, produced by Arts & Entertainment Television Networks (A&E) and *Ireland: A History*, produced by the British Broadcasting Company and Radio Telefis Eireann (BBC/RTE). Accompanying the latter is a well-illustrated book of the same title by Robert Kee (Abacus, Little, Brown & Company, 2001). A similar "you are there" feeling is available in *Famine Diary* (Irish Academic Press, 1999) by Brendan O'Cathaoir, author of *The Irish Times* column of the same name. It features unabridged accounts from newspapers, official correspondence, and diaries.

The 150th anniversary of the beginning of the potato famine has sparked a scholarly reassessment of the traditional interpretation that focused on nationwide suffering, years of misrule, and inadequate responses from both the British government and Irish landlords. Revisionist interpretations have tended to minimize the degree of suffering and are reluctant to blame the authorities for the crisis. Works such as the Yes-side selection by Kinealy are, in part, a response to what can be viewed as a "sanitized" version of the potato famine that trivializes the catastrophe and fails to acknowledge its causes.

ISSUE 4

Did the Meiji Restoration Constitute a Revolution in Nineteenth-Century Japan?

YES: Andrew Gordon, from *A Modern History of Japan: From Tokugawa Times to the Present* (Oxford University Press, 2003)

NO: W.G. Beasley, from *The Meiji Restoration* (Stanford University Press, 1972)

ISSUE SUMMARY

YES: Historian Andrew Gordon states that the Meiji Restoration created fundamental changes in Japanese society, thus meriting the term "revolution."

NO: Historian W.G. Beasley argues that when compared with other revolutions like the French and Russian, the Meiji Restoration did not constitute a revolution in the classical sense.

In 1603, the Japanese closed themselves off from the rest of the world. Fearful of Western economic and religious influences, which could corrupt their traditions and mores, they banned foreign contacts and meted out severe punishments (including death) to any who violated the ban. Part of this process was the outlawing of Christianity as a recognized religion in Japan. This self-imposed exile would last for more than 250 years.

The decision to isolate was made by Tokugawa Shogunate (1603–1868), Japan's ruling power during that period. Since the feudal period of Japanese history, the country had been ruled by *shoguns*, who were hereditary leaders. Like dynastic rulers anywhere, their right to rule lasted as long as their ability to maintain control, and they could always be replaced by another leader who could then establish his family's rule over the country. Thus, for most of the second millennium, Japan was ruled by successive shogunates: Kamakura (1192–1333), Ashikaga (1335–1673), and Tokugawa (1603–1868). During this time, civil wars became prevalent, as there was no shortage of ambitious men to test the waters of political supremacy.

The shoguns were assisted in their rule by *daimyo*, feudal lords who sometimes posed threats to their masters. The *samurai*, Japan's legendary warrior class, provided the power base for any shogun (For more information of the samurai, see Volume I, Issue 12 of this series.) Under this system, the Japanese emperor, whose office dated back to the fifth century C.E., had been reduced to an isolated figurehead. With the modern world casting covetous eyes around the globe, many wondered how long Japan's self-imposed exile would last, and whether it would end by outside force or national choice.

In 1853, U.S. Commodore Matthew Perry arrived in Tokyo, seeking and receiving a treaty from the Japanese government. Although its terms were not seriously detrimental to Japanese hegemony, it did start a trend that resulted in similar treaties with other foreign nations. In Japan, these actions had the dual effect of forcing the Japanese to consider what they could do to limit further Western intervention and causing the rise of nationalist sentiment against foreign elements. This resulted in an overthrow of the Tokugawa shogunate by an alliance of feudal lords and samurai in 1866, which returned the emperor to a position of authority in the new Japanese government. The new emperor took the name *Meiji* (enlightened government), and since that time, the period in Japanese history from 1868 to 1912 has been known in the West as the Meiji Restoration. Thus began Japan's modern history.

The transformation of Japan seemed to be profound; no part of Japanese life escaped the winds of change. Although those who overthrew the Tokugawa government had no set plan—and many of them had diametrically opposed goals and objectives—change was the order of the day. Some of the most important results of Meiji rule were the growth of Japan's industrial and military power, presumably accomplished to counterbalance Western power in Asia. This was done under the aegis of a highly centralized government that featured a "top down" power structure. Under such a system, a premium was placed on nationalism as a unifying force. Some of the Meiji-made decisions were to have a positive impact on Japan's modernization; others, such as imperialism, were to have drastic consequences for the nation and its people.

Some basic questions about the Meiji Restoration concern the nature of the movement. How much and what type of change did it effect? Was it revolutionary? How does it compare to its French and Russian counterparts? A problem facing one who attempts to answer those questions lies in definition, and in this case, an accurate translation of words. The Japanese word to describe the Meiji movement is "Ishin," which may be closer in meaning to "renovation" than the Western-translated "restoration." Keep this in mind as we assess the revolutionary nature of the Meiji restoration through the work of Andrew Gordon and W.G. Beasley, who present complementary, yet differing opinions on the subject. The former refers to the Meiji Restoration and its reforms as "breathtaking and fully meriting the term revolution." The latter agrees that the Meiji Restoration was revolutionary, but argues that it "lacked the avowed social purpose that gives the 'great' revolutions of history a certain common character."

Andrew Gordon

 **YES**

A Modern History of Japan: From Tokugawa Times to the Present

The Samurai Revolution

The "restoration" of the young Emperor Meiji in 1867–68 was little more than a coup d'état. A relatively small band of insurgents had toppled the Tokugawa bakufu. They stated their intent to restore direct imperial rule, but this was not likely to occur. Strong emperors who exercised power directly had been exceptional in Japanese history. Political contenders at the time feared that the rebels from Satsuma and Chōshū would simply form a new bakufu and use the name of the emperor to rule from a narrow base of power. After all, beyond the political upheaval in Kyoto and Edo, little had changed. The islands of Japan were still divided into nearly two hundred relatively autonomous domains. Each maintained its own treasury and army. The samurai were still receiving stipends, which they viewed as a hereditary birthright. The daily life of the countryside and cities had gone through some tumult. But the scattered peasant rebellions were short-lived.

However, if we compare this situation of 1868 in any aspect—political, economic, social, cultural—to that of just a decade later, the changes are breathtaking and fully merit the term *revolution*. Of course, no society ever totally severs itself from its past, and Japan was no exception. But the range and depth of change were astonishing to observers at the time. It remains so when looking back after 150 years. One of the most insightful contemporaneous observers was a British scholar named Basil Hall Chamberlain. He lived in Japan for over thirty years beginning in 1873. In 1891, he wrote:

> To have lived through the transition stage of modern Japan makes a man feel preternaturally old; for here he is in modern times, with the air full of talk about bicycles and bacilli and "spheres of influence," and yet he can himself distinctly remember the Middle Ages. The dear old Samurai who first initiated the present writer into the mysteries of the Japanese language, wore a queue and two swords. This relic of feudalism now sleeps in Nirvana.
>
> His modern successor, fairly fluent in English, and dressed in a serviceable suit of dittos, might almost be European, save for a certain obliqueness of the eyes and scantiness of beard. Old things pass away between a night and a morning.

Although Chamberlain here stresses how unusually swiftly the events of this "transition stage" unfolded, his writing also suggests that Japan's transition was part of a broader global shift. And indeed, the revolution that began in the 1860s was a Japanese variation on a global theme of modern revolution. Changes that took place in societies around the world in the nineteenth and twentieth centuries also unfolded in Japan.

Although sharing much with a global history of modernizing societies, the Japanese revolution did take place through a process that differed from the revolutions in Europe of the late eighteenth and the nineteenth centuries. In Europe, members of newly powerful classes, especially the urban bourgeoisie, challenged and sometimes overturned the privileges of long-entrenched aristocrats. By contrast, in Japan of the Meiji era it was members of the elite of the old regime, the samurai, who spearheaded the attack on the old order. Their role has led many historians to describe Japan in the nineteenth century as undergoing a "revolution from above" or an "aristocratic revolution."

In the twentieth century, other modernizing revolutions also unfolded through a process in which members of elite groups undermined their own well-established positions while they restructured the political order. The Japanese mode of modern revolution was not unique. Rather, it contrasted with earlier Western revolutions and resembled some later ones. This sort of elite-led revolution took place in Japan because of particular features of the samurai class, both weaknesses and strengths. On the negative side, change was possible because the samurai were not a securely landed elite. They were essentially salaried employees of their lords. Although this status was hereditary, it was less rooted in property than a European-style feudal estate, a Chinese gentry holding, or a Korean aristocratic status (*yangban*). The samurai had less to lose than elites in such societies. They were hard-pressed to protect their privilege as hereditary government employees once the new rulers decided to revoke it. Some did protest the actions of their former comrades bitterly, but others were either unable or unwilling to resist. On the positive side, many of the activists in the restoration movement had already developed a commitment to serving and building a realm that went beyond the narrow confines of a single domain. This emerging national consciousness offered a compelling reason for many to accept programs of far-reaching change.

Programs Of Nationalist Revolution

The leaders of the new Meiji government in 1868 were thrilled at the ease and speed with which they overcame the Tokugawa. They remained insulted by the unequal and coerced foreign presence and worried about the prospect of continued foreign encroachment. They were simultaneously fearful of resistance from domestic opponents. Domain armies remained in place, after all. Some had considerable stocks of Western arms.

The Meiji revolutionaries were motivated by fear of these challenges. They were also moved by their own sense of the ongoing problems of the Tokugawa order: military and economic weakness, political fragmentation, and a social hierarchy that failed to recognize men of talent. Propelled by both fear and discontent with the old regime, they generated an ambitious agenda, through a process of trial and error, aiming to build a new sort of national power.

Political Unification and Central Bureaucracy

Their first dramatic step was to abolish all the daimyō domains, thus dismantling a political order in place for 260 years. By 1868, almost immediately after the restorationist coup, top leaders of the new provisional government such as Kido Kō n of Chō shū and Saigō Takamori of Satsuma decided that the politically fragmented system of domains had to be overhauled. They acted with careful tactics and reached their goal in just three years. One British observer marvelled at this and other changes in 1872: "[F]our years ago we were still in the middle ages—we have leapt at a bound into the nineteenth century—out of poetry into plain useful prose."

The move toward an integrated national polity began in March 1869. The new government convinced key daimyō of prestige and power, especially those of Satsuma, Chō shū, Tosa, and Hizen, to voluntarily surrender their lands back to the emperor. As the patrons of many of the coup planners, these men were guaranteed respect and a voice in the new order if they wished. In fact, they were all quickly reappointed as domain governors with handsome salaries. Nonetheless, the "return of lands" established the principle that all lands and people were subject to the emperor's rule. By early 1870, all daimyō had formally returned their lands and taken appointments as governors of their domains, but they retained significant autonomy, as in the past.

Preparing the ground for the complete abolition of the daimyō domains, the Meiji reformers worked to place domain governments in sympathetic hands. They pressed the daimyō to appoint men of talent and often modest rank to key adminstrative posts. Such people would be likely to welcome further reform. Kido Kō in and other top officials in the Meiji government also won support of powerholders in many domains, both daimyō and their followers, by promising them posts in the new central government. They backed such persuasion by threat of force, creating an imperial army primarily from Satsuma and Chō shū samurai. It was untested, but it was stronger than any single domain's forces or any likely combination of forces.

Having bought off potential opposition leaders and built support in key domains with these measures, the government in August 1871 had the emperor announce that all domains were immediately abolished. They were replaced with "prefectures" whose governors were appointed from the center. This was much more than a renaming of domains into prefectures. It was a stunning change, with immediate visible consequences. The central government would now collect taxes from domain lands. The daimyō were ordered to move to Tokyo. Many castles were dismantled. Within just three months, the number of political units was consolidated dramatically, from 280 domains to 72 prefectures. Most of the new governors were not former daimyō. They were middling samurai from the insurgent domains now controlling the government.

This decree was accompanied by a large payoff to the daimyō themselves. They were granted permanent yearly salaries equivalent to roughly 10 percent of their former domain's annual tax revenue. Daimyō were simultaneously relieved of all the costs of governing. Most were quite content to take early retirement on such generous terms. Thus, within the short span of three years, a political order in existence for over two and a half centuries simply disappeared. The Tokugawa bakufu, on the one hand, and the hundreds of semi-autonomous domains on the other, no longer existed.

Simultaneously, of course, the Meiji leaders had to erect a new national political structure to govern these domains turned prefectures. For several years they groped in this direction, experimenting with a confusing variety of political forms. They bolstered their claim as restorationists by labeling these first government offices with ancient Chinese terms used by the Japanese court in the Heian period (794–1192). In early 1868, the Sat-Chō rebels and court officials placed themselves atop a provisional government to rule in the name of emperor. Later that year they established the Council of State as the highest political authority and monopolized its highest posts. The organization of this council was revised in 1869 and again in 1871. Later in 1871 it was replaced by a tripartite set of ministries of the Center, Left, and Right, further subdivided into various functional ministries (Finance, Foreign Affairs, Public Works, Home Affairs).

This format proved relatively effective. It persisted until 1885, when the Meiji leaders inaugurated a cabinet system modeled explicitly along European lines. At the head of this government was a prime minister. He presided over a cabinet that ran the bureaucratic agencies—the several ministries—of the Japanese state. This structure was codified in the Meiji constitution of 1889, discussed in detail later in this chapter. Although this constitution provided for a deliberative assembly (the Diet), state ministers were responsible not to the Diet but to the emperor.

In the early Meiji years, the ministerial staff was recruited mainly by personal connections from the ranks of Satsuma and Chōshū samurai and their allies. But the government rather quickly moved toward a more impersonal, merit-based mode of recruitment. In 1887 it began a system of civil service examinations. From this point on, performance on this exam became the primary qualification for service in the prestigious ranks of the ministries of the Japanese imperial state.

The creation of this bureaucratic state was a step of great importance in the history of modern Japan. The Meiji rulers inherited a Tokugawa legacy of bureaucratic rule by civilianized samurai. They extended its reach by eliminating domains. They deepened its reach by replacing the clumsy Tokugawa administrative machinery of overlapping jurisdictions with functional ministries with clearly defined responsibilities. They bolstered its legitimacy by putting the meritocratic ideals of the Tokugawa system into practice. And finally, they elevated its prestige by defining the bureaucratic mission as one of service to the emperor. They gave the state a greater legitimacy and power than it had ever held in the past.

Eliminating the Status System

The second great change of early Meiji was even more remarkable. It was achieved at greater cost. By 1876, less than a decade after the restoration coup, the economic privileges of the samurai were wiped out entirely. The coup leaders expropriated an entire social class, the semi-aristocratic elite from which they came. They met some stiff, violent resistance, but they managed to overcome it. This remarkable change amounted to a social revolution.

The government moved to expropriate the samurai primarily for financial reasons. The government reduced samurai stipends when it abolished the domains, but in the mid-1870s these payouts still consumed a huge chunk—roughly half—of state revenues. The new rulers had other uses in mind for this money. They believed that the samurai gave back relatively little value for their high costs. Their ranks included many talented people sitting idle. Their time-honored military skills, focused on swords and archery, were useless. Thus the samurai's stipends were basically welfare for the well-born.

This case for expropriating the samurai was clear enough to government leaders soon after the restoration. But taking this step was a major undertaking. It took nearly a decade and enraged many former samurai. In particular, many of those who had supported the restoration drive, but remained in their domains after 1868, felt betrayed by their former comrades now running the Meiji government. The latter moved in small steps first, as they had with domain abolition. In 1869 they reduced the large number of samurai ranks to two, upper samurai (*shizoku*) and lower samurai (*sotsu*). In 1872 a large portion of the lower samurai were reclassified as commoners (*heimin*), although they retained their stipends for the moment.

In 1873, the government announced that stipends would be taxed. The next year it announced a voluntary program to convert stipends to bonds. The right to a stipend could be traded for an interest-bearing bond with a face value of five to fourteen years of income (in general, the lower the stipend, the higher the multiple). The bond would pay interest ranging from 5 to 7 percent, with smaller bonds paying higher rates. The income stream from all but the most generous bonds was a good bit lower than the annual stipend. Few samurai volunteered for this program.

The government made this program compulsory in 1876: All stipends were converted to bonds. In contrast to the well-compensated daimyō, many samurai suffered significant losses. Their annual incomes fell by anywhere from 10 to 75 percent. They further lost pride and prestige: The right to wear swords was denied to all but solidiers and policemen.

The elimination of samurai privilege allowed the new regime to redirect financial and human resources alike and was part of a larger transformation of society from a system of fixed statuses to a more fluid, merit-based social order. The other side to the abolition of samurai privilege was the end to formal restrictions on the rest of the population. At least in theory, this constituted social liberation. In 1870, all nonsamurai were classified in legal terms as commoners (*heimin*). With some important gender-based exceptions noted later, the restrictions of the Tokugawa era on modes of travel, dress, and hairstyle were eliminated. Restrictions on occupation were abolished. The government ended legal discrimination against the hereditary outcaste groups of Tokugawa times such as *eta* and *hinin*. These terms came to be considered slurs and were replaced in official language by the label *burakumin* (literally, "village people," in reference to their segregated villages). The descendants of these outcastes, however, continued to face prejudice and discrimination.

Some commoners fared well. Not surprisingly, many of those with education and money, in particular the landowners, moneylenders, and petty manufacturers at the upper levels of rural society, thrived in the more open social order of the Meiji era. Others, especially those with weak claims to farmland, lived in desperate poverty. They depended on the unreliable benevolence of landlords to survive illness, crop failures, or price declines. Although the samurai lost their income and social privilege, they were educated and ambitious. Many landed on their feet. Others invested their bonds in new businesses and failed miserably. Still others took up arms against the new government or joined political movements on behalf of a parliament and constitution.

The literature of the Meiji period offers one window into the excitement, the opportunities, and the risks of this era of change. One example is this comment by the narrator of *Footprints in the Snow*, a vibrant and widely read novel set in the 1880s and written in 1901 by Tokutomi Roka:

> The race will go to the swift, not the empty-headed! The real testing-time in politics will come after the Diet gets going in 1890—and in everything, not only politics: the further Japan advances on the world stage, the more opportunities for the really able!

The Conscript Army

Even before the samurai were fully dispossessed, the Meiji leaders decided they had to renovate the military from the bottom up. Key figures from Chōshū were deeply impressed at the superior performance of their mixed farmer-samurai militias in the restoration wars. These men—Kido Kōin, Ōmura Masujirō, and Yamagata Aritomo—argued forcefully for a conscript army drawn from the entire population. Their views were controversial, to say the least. In October 1869 a group of samurai in Kyoto, outraged at the conscript proposal, assassinated Ōmura. And among top government figures, the Satsuma men saw things differently from the Chōshū clique. They came from a domain where nearly one-fourth of the population had been samurai. They feared arming ignorant and potentially rebellious commoners. They wanted to ensure a major role for samurai in the new Meiji order. The champion of this position was Ōkubo Toshimichi, who ranked with Kido as one of the two most powerful leaders in the first decade of the Meiji era. At first he prevailed, with the support of Iwakura Tomomi, the most important court noble in the Meiji government. In April 1871 the government created an imperial army of just under ten thousand samurai recruited from the restoration forces.

The conservative military leadership seemed to be in control, but their ascendance was short-lived. Yamagata Aritomo returned from a trip to Europe fully convinced that mass conscription was the key not only to building military strength but also to disciplining a loyal populace. By 1873 his arguments had prevailed. The government decreed a system of universal conscription. Beginning at the age of twenty, all males were obligated to give three years of active service and four years on reserve status.

The draft was not popular. The 1873 decree noted several exemptions, for household heads, criminals, the physically unfit, students and teachers in many prescribed schools, and government officials. It also allowed people to buy their way out for a huge fee of 270 yen. This sum represented more than the annual wage of a common laborer. Large numbers of people sought to qualify for exemption or somehow scrape together the buyout fee. The army had trouble meeting the quotas for what the government itself labeled a "blood tax" (following European terminology). In 1873–74 angry crowds attacked and destroyed numerous registration centers in sixteen riots; nearly 100,000 people were arrested and punished.

As this resistance makes clear, the strong discipline and fierce loyalty shown by Japanese soldiers in later decades were by no means timeless traditional elements of Japan's "national character." Such resistance also took place in Europe and in the United States, where large anti-draft riots erupted during the Civil War. In Japan as elsewhere, a patriotic spirit that could induce willing military service—a key element of modern nationalism—had to be drummed into the masses of people over several decades. Japan's army passed its first major test when it put down a large samurai rebellion in 1877. An imperial rescript of 1882 addressed to soldiers and sailors enjoined youths to serve the emperor with loyalty and valor. Teachers and texts in the new public school system echoed the message. The navy was built up in the 1880s and 1890s. By the mid-1890s, Japan's military was strong enough to move from the task of keeping order at home to that of imposing its will overseas. Military service came to be accepted as the patriotic obligation of Japanese men by most recruits and their families.

Compulsory Education

Parallel to its program of military reform, the Meiji government instituted a new system of education with remarkable speed. With grand language, in 1872 it declared four years of elementary education to be compulsory for all children, boys and girls: "In a village there shall be no house without learning, and in a house, no individual without learning." This important step reflected the new leaders' understanding of the sources of Western power. Observation of European and American societies convinced leaders such as Kido Kō in that mass schooling, like mass conscription, was a fundamental source of the economic and military power of the West. Their initial models were primarily American and French, and the 1872 decree established a system of elementary and middle schools and national universities. At the outset, the government announced that schools were to encourage practical learning as well as independent thinking. By this means commoners would find their own way to serve the state.

Mass compulsory education was a bold initiative, and a risky one for the government. Tokugawa thinkers such as Aizawa Yasushi had complained endlessly of the "stupid commoners" who would easily be tricked by demagogic Christian missionaries into betraying the authorities, even the emperor. Such attitudes could have led the Meiji leaders to hold back from imparting literacy and potentially subversive "enlightenment" to imperial subjects who were expected to follow orders. The Meiji leadership consciously took this risk. They concluded that an ignorant populace would be a greater danger to their projects to build political and economic power. They also developed rather different views of the value of learning for girls and boys. The former were expected to learn the skills needed for future domestic roles as wives and mothers as well as loyal subjects of the emperor. The latter were expected to take their knowledge into a wider public realm of endeavor in the cause of building the nation.

Reactions to compulsory education were mixed. The era's literature conveys the excitement of many young men at the opportunity to better themselves and serve their country, if possible in the new capital of Tokyo. In *Footprints in the Snow*, Tokutomi also evoked the enthusiasm for learning of the early 1880s:

> About the end of August a letter came from Matsumura with a tremendous piece of news. "Tremendous news." For us boys, in those days, these words could have only one meaning: Matsumura was leaving next month, to study in the capital—in Tokyo! You could feel his excitement in the hardly legible scrawl; his handwriting was none too firm at the best of times, but this! The characters fairly danced their way down the page in a kind of dishevelled ecstasy.

Not everyone was so happy at the obligation to attend school and the opportunity to graduate. The elementary schools were to be financed by a 10 percent local surcharge to the national property tax. In the 1870s angry taxpayers reacted to compulsory schooling as they had to the draft: They rioted. Crowds of people destroyed at least two thousand schools, usually by setting them afire. This represented close to one-tenth of the total number of schools. The passive resistance of simply not going to school was even more widespread. Rates of attendance for school-age boys and girls stood at 25 to 50 percent of the eligible population for the first decade of the new system.

But eventually, as with serving in the military, attending school became a well-accepted obligation of the emperor's subjects. By the end of the nineteenth century, rates of elementary school attendance reached levels of 90 percent or more. By 1905, 98 percent of school-age boys and 93 percent of girls were attending elementary schools as the law required. As compulsory education took root, the idea that one's life course—at least that of young men—should be open at the outset and should reflect one's talent and efforts became one of Japan's most fundamental and widely held social values. In Tokugawa Japan, a major tension set the merit ideal—that men of talent should hold office—against the hereditary status system. The Meiji social revolution resolved this ideological tension clearly in favor of merit.

The Monarch at the Center

Finally, one of the most portentous new departures of the revolutionary years of early Meiji was the decision to put the emperor at the very center of the political order. The restoration activists carried out their coup in the name of the Meiji emperor. But once in power, they held no consensus on what to do with him. The populace was not particularly committed to the emperor as a political symbol. Nor was the emperor an impressive young man, whether in court garb or in Western military uniform.

After the emperor's triumphal progress from Kyoto to Edo in 1868, the early Meiji government struggled to decide where to locate a permanent capital. Some officials supported moving the capital permanently to Edo (renamed Tokyo, or Eastern capital), some wished to send the emperor and capital back to Kyoto, and still others spoke of establishing two capitals. Not until 1889 was the decision for Tokyo made permanent. The government called the emperor's Tokyo residence a "temporary court" until that year, when it officially renamed it the "Imperial Palace."

Over these same two decades, as the capital moved, the image of the monarchy was transformed as well. The government heaped more and more symbolic weight upon the emperor and empress. The empress and her retinue adopted Western clothes in the 1880s as part of the effort to project an image of the monarchy as a modern institution. The emperor also underwent a striking metamorphosis to become the symbol of a modern monarch. The contrast between his earlier portraits and the famous portrait prepared by an Italian artist in 1888 best illustrates this dramatic change. The painting was subsequently photographed and enshrined in schools throughout the nation. It has defined the Meiji emperor's image ever since.

At the same time, the constitution greatly elevated the emperor's legal and cultural authority. From the 1880s through the 1930s, the imperial institution became an all-too-powerful unifying force. It served as a touchstone for personal, social, and national identity. It came to link individuals to immediate communities of family, workplace, and neighborhood—and beyond that to the imagined community of nation and empire.

Building A Rich Country

The Meiji leaders, especially those who traveled abroad, were profoundly impressed with the energies unleashed by industrial capitalism. Manufacturing and trade seemed as important a source of European national power as did battleships and cannons. Economic strength, in fact, appeared to be the base that supported the military superstructure of European states. Kido Kō in was typical of his colleagues in the new government. While traveling in the United States and Europe in 1872 he filled his diary with references to the "astonishing," the "indescribable," or the "magnificent" achievements of Western architecture, education, and industry.

Motivated by such awestruck views of Western learning and industry, government leaders undertook numerous steps to realize the foremost Meiji slogan of building a "rich country, strong army" (*fukoku kyō hei*). Some initia-

tives were indirect measures to build the infrastructure of an industrial economy. Others were direct measures to construct and operate mines and
factories as government projects.

The most important economic reform of the 1870s was the new tax system. The new Meiji government began its life in poverty. It drew revenue
from a narrow base of former Tokugawa lands and borrowed funds from some
of the major Osaka merchant houses. When it replaced autonomous domains
with centrally managed prefectures in 1871, it inherited the huge obligation of
samurai stipends and daimyō pensions, but it also gained the opportunity to
draw taxes from all the former domains. In 1873, the government announced
a new national land tax designed by Ōkubo Toshimichi. It was intended to
stabilize state revenues at a level roughly comparable to the sum total of
bakufu and domain taxes.

The significance of the new tax system went beyond securing revenue. It
changed the economic relationship of individual landowners to the state and
to each other. In the Tokugawa system, land ownership had been decided by
custom in villages. Revenues were collected in lump sums from villages, not
from individuals. There was no state-supervised system of title deeds or land
registration and no officially sanctioned market in the purchase and sale of
land. In addition, taxes were based on assessed yield, not assessed value. They
were usually collected in kind (in rice). This meant that the government and
not the taxpayer stood to lose (or gain) from fluctuating commodity prices: If
the price of rice fell, so did government revenue. ...

For more than a century, historians have been arguing over how to describe
the profound changes of the first decades of the Meiji era. Early historians
typically used the French and other European revolutions since the late eighteenth century as their model, describing the changes set in motion by the
Meiji restoration as an incomplete or distorted revolution. If one accepts the
premise that France in the 1790s furnishes the paradigm for a true revolution,
then the changes in Japan indeed were not "complete." If one argues that the
untrammeled ascendance of a capitalist bourgeoisie that attacks and defeats
an aristocratic old regime is the essence of modern revolution, Japan's
changes do appear "distorted." After all, it was a faction of the samurai "aristocracy" more than an emerging class of bourgeois capitalists that imposed
the Meiji changes.

Even in recent years, many historians, both in Japan and outside it, have
explicitly or implicitly understood the history of the Meiji era and the early
twentieth century from this sort of comparative perspective. But such an
analysis is not helpful. It arbitrarily imposes a Eurocentric model onto world
history and does not make sufficient effort to understand the history of other
places on their own terms.

The great changes of the Meiji era constituted a sort of modern "revolution from above" because they were imposed by members of the hereditary
samurai elite of the old regime. But until 1868, many of these leaders had

been frustrated, insecure, and ambitious men in the middle to lower ranks of the samurai class. They held greater privilege than the mass of the population, but to call them aristocratic revolutionaries from above and leave it at that is misleading. It leaves us with an image of men who were cosseted in privilege and then gave it up. It was precisely their intermediate status and their insecure salaried position, coupled with their sense of frustrated ambition and entitlement to rule, that account for the revolutionary energy of the Meiji insurgents and their far-reaching program of reform. This was a revolution of a frustrated subelite.

In addition to avoiding Eurocentric comparisons, it is crucial to recognize that the Meiji revolution, like modern revolutions the world over, was an ongoing, turbulent process. Public schools, the new tax system, and the draft were imposed upon an often defiant population. The unequal treaties remained extremely controversial. Beginning with the birth of the new Meiji regime, the question of who would participate, and on what terms, was of the greatest importance to a quickly expanding public. The Meiji revolution had changed much but settled little.

NO

W. G. Beasley

The Meiji Restoration

Introduction

During the middle decades of the nineteenth century China and Japan both faced pressure from an intrusive, expanding West. This entailed, first, a political and military danger, manifested in two Anglo-Chinese wars and in the use of force on many other occasions, threatening their independence; and second, a challenge to their traditional culture from one that was alien in many of its fundamental concepts, as well as superior in technology and science. Emotionally and intellectually, Chinese and Japanese reacted to the threat in similar ways: with simple hostility, with manifestations of cultural chauvinism, with a grudging recognition of their own inferiority in "wealth and power." Yet they differed greatly in the kind of actions that this response induced. In China, the Confucian order proved strong enough to inhibit change, whether in polity or ideas, thereby bringing about a union of conservatism at home with concession abroad that led eventually to dynastic decline and an age of revolutions. In Japan, men succeeded in "using the barbarian to control the barbarian" so as to initiate policies that produced a "modern" state, powerful enough in the end to meet the West on equal terms. Hence Japan, unlike China, moved to empire and industry, not poverty and civil war.

The Meiji Restoration is at the heart of this contrast, since it was the process by which Japan acquired a leadership committed to reform and able to enforce it. For Japan, therefore, the Restoration has something of the significance that the English Revolution has for England or the French Revolution for France; it is the point from which modern history can be said to begin. For this reason it has been much studied. Equally, it has been the subject of enduring controversy, for its significance—and thus the way in which it is to be explained—has changed with every change of attitude toward the society that it brought into being....

Conclusions

The history of the Meiji Restoration ... is relevant to a number of themes that are important not only for Japan. In part it was a response to the nineteenth-century expansion of the West in Asia. Hence studying it raises questions about the nature of imperialism and nationalism and of their relationship to change in the modern world. Equally, the Restoration was at least in some respects a revolution. One must therefore ask, what kind of revolution was it? How does it compare with other great political upheavals in other parts of the world at other times? And are the features that mark it off from them idiosyncratically Japanese, or do they arise from the fact and nature of the West's involvement? Finally, since the Restoration is the historical starting point for the modernization of Japan, a process that is highly significant for theories of economic growth, it poses yet another question, to wit: How far is a radical restructuring of society a necessary condition—and not merely a consequence—of the transformation of a pre-modern into a modern economy.

Clearly, though the example of Japan is an element in the discussion of all these matters, it is not necessarily a decisive one. Therefore a [selection] like this, which approaches the Restoration from inside, as it were, that is, as a part of Japanese history, ought not to offer itself as providing answers that are universally valid. What it *can* do, what these closing remarks are intended to do, is to present its conclusions in such a way that others might be able to use them to these ends. As a preliminary to this, it might be helpful to recapitulate the story in a rather more generalized form than was possible when setting out the detailed narrative.

⁓◉⁓

Under the Tokugawa, Japanese society was gradually modified by economic change in such a way as to bring about by the nineteenth century a disjunction between contemporary reality and the inherited ideal. This was manifested in a number of phenomena for which the traditional order had no place: samurai whose debts turned them into ambitious office-holders or impoverished umbrella-makers; farmers abandoning subsistence agriculture to become commercial producers and rural entrepreneurs or laborers and quasi-tenants; and city merchants enjoying feudal patronage in a kind of symbiosis with authority or escaping into an urban subculture of their own.

Because these things happened at different speeds in different areas, they disturbed the balance of power between the Bakufu [or "tent government" because soldiers lived in tents] and the domains, which had depended originally on a carefully calculated distribution of land. Because they happened at all, they produced social upheaval: a blurring of status distinctions, stimulating samurai unrest; and economic disruption, provoking peasant revolt. These were reflected in turn in a "what-is-wrong-with-the-world" literature and attempts at "reform," the latter seeking either to reconstitute an ideal past (a restoration of feudal authority and its agrarian base) or to exploit commercial growth for the benefit of the ruling class (if at some cost to its ethos). One result was to give more samurai a degree of participation in active politics than hitherto. Another was to make the concept of "reform" familiar and to prompt a feeling that society was in danger of destruction from within.

Yet the country's social and political institutions proved to be remarkably durable: eroded but far from demolished, they did not seem in 1850 to be on the point of being swept away. Not least, this was because the system of institutional checks and balances coupled with deliberate regional fragmentation that had been devised to restrain the anticipated disaffection of samurai and feudal lords proved capable also of imposing controls on the new "men of substance" who might have challenged the established order from outside the samurai class. Accordingly, most of these men sought their opportunities of advancement through conformity, not revolution, acquiring status by purchase or marriage, but remaining politically passive.

It was into this situation that there were injected the West's demand for trade relations in the years 1853–58, leading to "unequal" treaties. The manner in which the treaties were obtained, that is, by gunboat diplomacy, was as important as their content, for it helped to produce in Japan an upsurge of emotion greater than any that had been aroused by domestic issues. Its importance was not merely that the blow to Japanese pride led to a call for "action" (not necessarily of any specific kind); it was also that this was a "national" dishonor in the sense that it could be felt in all areas and at all levels in Japanese society. It thereby helped to break down the regional and social fragmentation that had been one of the foundations of Tokugawa power.

Moreover, the humiliation at the hands of the West precipitated struggle and controversy. The struggle arose when men questioned the efficiency of the country's leaders, especially their ability to defend Japan; and it brought to the surface many of the latent divisions in the national polity by asking, if only implicitly, who their replacements should be in case they failed. The controversy concerned both short-term diplomatic issues and long-term cultural ones, but it had a single, central thread: the extent to which Japan must abandon custom in order to save herself, first in the context of technology, or particular institutional devices to serve particular ends, and then, more generally, in the context of radical changes in society, such as industrialization had induced in the countries of the West....

❧

History offers many different examples of the kind of motivating force that is capable of overcoming inertia and the bonds of tradition: imperial ambition, religious faith, the pursuit of social justice, the aspirations of a newly emergent class. For Japan in the nineteenth century, nationalism had this function. Again and again in the documents of the years we have been considering there are phrases that put policy of every kind—economic and political, as well as diplomatic—into the context of the "national" interest, justifying proposals on the grounds that they would "restore our national strength" or "make the imperial dignity resound beyond the seas." What is more, most of the major political crises centered on the question of Japan's relations with the outside world: that of 1858, when the signing of the treaties became linked with the question of the Tokugawa succession; that of 1863–64, when the fate of the "men of spirit" was decided against a background of foreign bombardment; that of 1873, when the debate about Korea brought into the open a struggle about priorities at home. Throughout, Japanese opinion was moving from a consciousness of foreign threat to an awareness of national identity, expressed in demands for unity and independence.

The contrast with China underlines the extraordinary speed and thoroughness of Japan's response. Despite widespread anti-foreign feeling among gentry and officials, Chinese continued to behave, at least until the end of the nineteenth century, as a people defending a civilization that was threatened, not a nation defending a country that was under attack. Long before then, the Japanese, subscribing to a more articulate and sophisticated version of the Restoration's search for "wealth and strength," had found in nationalism a means of reconciling the conflict between cultural tradition and imperative circumstance.

The "liberal" constitutional movement was heavily influenced by that new-found nationalism. "The one object of my life is to extend Japan's national power," Fukuzawa Yukichi wrote in 1882. "Compared with considerations of the country's strength, the matter of internal government and into whose hands it falls is of no importance at all. Even if the government be autocratic in name and form, I shall be satisfied with it if it is strong enough to strengthen the country." This is Fukuzawa the nationalist overcoming Fukuzawa the liberal, if only temporarily.

Taking a wider framework, the newspaper *Nihon* celebrated the announcement of the Meiji Constitution in 1889 by urging that a limit be set to the adoption of foreign ways. It had no desire "to revive a narrow xenophobia," *Nihon* declared, for "we recognize the excellence of Western civilization. We value the Western theories of rights, liberty and equality.... Above all, we esteem Western science, economics and industry." Nevertheless, it continued, these things "ought not to be adopted simply because they are Western; they ought to be adopted only if they can contribute to Japan's welfare." In Tokyo in 1889 this was a conservative warning not to go too fast or too far. In contemporary Peking it would have been reformist.

One is bound to ask, why did Japan evolve in a generation a nationalism that in China came much more slowly and with much less effect, given that both countries had long traditions of political and cultural unity? Difference of size was a factor, of course. In Japan, which was smaller and had a very long coastline, the presence of the foreigners and their ships was evident to a higher percentage of the population, making the danger from them easier to believe and act on. China was not only larger, but more varied—in spoken language, social patterns, types of crop—so that there were great practical obstacles to imposing administrative and economic unity in the nationalist sense, just as there were in India and the Ottoman Empire, for example. China did not lend herself very readily to being made into a "country," Japan did.

In addition to all this, however, there are historical differences between the two that have a particular relevance to the study of the Meiji Restoration. One is Japan's relative freedom of cultural choice: she was less bound than China to a single view of her society and her place in the world. Japan had already imported elements of Chinese civilization, which coexisted with others that were her own; thus to adopt a part of Europe's civilization was not to damage an entity that was whole and unique, but to add a third possibility to an existing two, one of which was in any case "foreign." For instance, medicine was a Chinese science in pre-modern Japan, using many Chinese drugs, hence accepting a Western alternative was not so very shocking. Warfare, the samurai's trade, was studied in a Chinese classic text (albeit embodied in a thoroughly Japanese mystique) and was conducted with the help of a seventeenth-century "Dutch" technology. There was nothing in this to inhibit following alien models. As Rutherford Alcock noted of the Japanese when he first became acquainted with them, "they have little of the stupid conceit of the Chinese, which leads them to ignore or deny the superiority of foreign things."

It was the same with political institutions. No educated Japanese of the Tokugawa period could fail to be aware that the political structure of his country differed from that of China, which the philosophers he read upheld as an ideal. His country had a Shogun as well as an Emperor; it was administered through a feudal system, not a bureaucratic one. This helped to heighten his sense of Japaneseness, which was an element in nationalism, but it also made him aware that substantial variations could exist within the limits of what was known and acceptable.

In other words, in abolishing the Bakufu, reasserting the Emperor's authority, and instituting a centralized bureaucratic state, the Japanese could see themselves as making a fresh set of choices among the variables that their history already contained, however much they reinterpreted them. Hence renovation (ishin) could be coupled with restoration (fukko) in a manner that causes the least offense. This was especially so because of the nature and ethos of the ruling class. In China, civil officials held office by virtue of being Confucian, that is, as exemplars of a structure of belief on which their whole society was founded. To tamper with part of that structure was to undermine the whole, weakening their power. This was not so in Japan. The samurai, it is true, had accepted the Confucian ethic and some of the bureaucratic habits that went with it. He did not depend on these, however, to validate his rule. As a feudal lord or retainer, his position rested on birth, on inheritable status received as a reward for past military prowess. His code, Bushidō, though it coexisted with Confucianism, emphasized different virtues, the specifically military ones. Accordingly, he did not feel a need to accept or reject Confucianism as a whole. He could employ it—as Meiji society did—in the context of personal and family behavior while turning to other concepts for his political and economic life: nationalist ones, which could be given a Shintō coloring; or Western ones, explaining the new phenomena of industry and commerce. And the fact that the new amalgam was not a conspicuously logical one worried him less because of the equal irrationality of the old.

Finally, one must note the significance of Japan's having entered this phase of her history, unlike China, under a *military* ruling class. This relates to nationalism to the extent that soldiers were more inclined to think of defending a territory than defending a system of ideas, more of defending country than culture. It also relates to modernization, since it contributed to the identification of agreed priorities, where individuals had a multiplicity of views. Indeed, it may well be that a military habit of mind, variously applied, was the samurai's most important contribution to Meiji society—and hence, to the making of the modern Japanese state.

What has been said [earlier] amounts to an assertion that nationalism had a double function in Japan in the twenty years after 1853: first, that it provided a motive compelling men to act; second, that it shaped their aims and priorities. Unhappily, this pleasingly simple explanation of what took place is incomplete. Side by side with the story of nationalism and the foreign threat, there is another, that of social change; and in turning to it, we move from a discussion of men's purposes to a discussion of the circumstance in which they found themselves. It was from the interaction of the two that history was made.

...[H]ow, then, are we to set political struggle and social change in relation to each other? I would suggest, as follows:

1. The class composition of the politically active minority in late-Tokugawa Japan already reflected the results of economic change in that it did not accord with the *formal* allocation of authority in society: a few daimyo, a few upper samurai, a good many middle samurai, a much larger number of lower samurai and "men of substance" from outside the samurai class. Proportionately, this corresponds fairly well with the number of men within each of these groups. Yet no Japanese of the time would have been prepared to argue that participation in decision-making should be proportional to numbers in this way; traditionally, it should have been almost entirely the prerogative of lords and senior retainers. Departure from traditional norms in this respect therefore suggests that at the *beginning* of the period with which we have dealt, the outlines of a new ruling class were emerging from within the old. It was *within* this class that most of the crucial debates took place.

2. In the various proposals for curing the country's ills after the conclusion of the treaties, there was usually an element of class or group interest, though not necessarily a dominant one. Bakufu and feudal lords, despite their rivalries, both sought to defend Japan without much disturbing its society; by promoting "men of talent," the middle samurai meant principally themselves; and the "men of spirit," despite an inability for the most part to get away from feudal terminology, clearly envisaged that the success of their plans would bring them a status they did not already have. Thus the defeat of kō bu-gattai, "unity of Court and Bakufu," and of kinnō, "serving the Emperor," were defeats for socially conservative and politically radical formulations of reform, respectively, as well as for particular ideas about how Japan could best be defended from the foreigner.

3. The men who emerged as leaders in succession to the reforming lords and dissident samurai, mostly after 1864, were realists, pragmatists, bureaucrat-politicians whose social origins matched their role: that is, they were nearly all middle or lower samurai, not high enough in the feudal hierarchy to be bent on preserving it, nor excluded from it to the point of wanting above all to break it down. Moreover, they were convinced that national defense required national unity. Accordingly, they believed as much in conciliation as

reform, and so began to bring together the components of what was a social, as well as a political, alliance. Edo intransigents and rebellious peasants they would not tolerate, because both were obstacles to order and unity in their different ways. But the rest could all find a place: Court nobles, feudal lords, samurai, landlords, influential merchants, even servants of the Shogun in the end. To belong, one needed only to subscribe to the national objectives, as the inner group defined them.

4. Victory over the Tokugawa made these men responsible for government, that is, for implementing on a national scale the policies that would bring Japan "wealth and strength." In much of what they then did they acted still as samurai-bureaucrats trained in Confucian ideas: manipulating the Emperor as they had their lords; caring for the people's welfare, subject to the tax needs of the state; framing an education system that contributed to good order and to the citizen's skills. Concepts of government and its functions did not change as much from Tokugawa to Meiji as the emphasis on modernization sometimes makes us think. Yet some of the differences were vital. Since feudalism contributed nothing to efficiency and was an obstacle to military strength, it had to go. Equally, since land tax was an essential resource and defining it involved the recognition of what had happened in the village, landlords got confirmation of their landed rights. Indirectly, they also obtained an extension of their economic opportunities. In fact, though the purpose of it all was not to change society, but rather to identify the least degree of social adjustment that would make possible fukō kukyohei—a militarily strong Japan rich enough to sustain a position of independence in the world—the application of these policies produced something very different from the Japan of twenty years before. For the minimal change, once identified, proved to be substantial. Consciously, there was an attack on samurai privilege; but consequentially this made possible the emergence into a position of influence of a new class, the well-to-do commoners whose power had until then been only latent.

5. Several factors came together to ensure that the society which emerged at the end of these years would be a capitalist one. Some of the long-term trends in the Tokugawa period were already moving in that direction, providing a basis on which to build. They were given a stimulus by contact with the capitalist West, initially through the effects of foreign trade, then because of the nature of the advice Japan received and the models she studied; the Western solutions that were applied to Japanese problems were inevitably those of the contemporary industrial state. Development was also given a particular direction by the nature of the policies that were devised for the promotion of national strength—the encouragement of industrial and commercial growth, coupled with an unusual degree of government intervention in the country's economy—so that Japan's transition from the "centralized feudalism" of Tokugawa days was to a similarly centralized form of capitalism. This resolved one Tokugawa anomaly, that of merchant wealth, by bringing the entrepreneur, like the landlord, into the dominant class and giving him a means to fulfill his aspirations legally. It left another, that of peasant

unrest, aside. In the short term the second issue was settled by force; but as the pressures on the cultivator increased with the growth of industry it re-emerged to become a problem of the twentieth century in a different form.

Does all this amount to a revolution? Perhaps to ask the question is to invite an argument about the meaning of words, since the reader is likely to have and to apply criteria of his own in finding an answer. Nevertheless, there are a number of points that can be made by way of a final gloss on what has been said [earlier]. For example, the Bakufu had some of the classic characteristics of an ancien régime; it had grave financial problems; it tried unsuccessfully to effect reform; it was indecisive and ineffective at the end in suppressing opposition; and for a variety of reasons it lost the confidence of a considerable segment of the ruling class. Also, those who overthrew it included men of many social origins (but not the lowest); they were generally of some respectability and experience; and they produced what might well be called "a dictatorship in commission." One could even argue that Restoration politics moved through appropriate stages of moderation and extremism before eventually bringing about, not "a brand-new ruling class," but "a kind of amalgamation, in which the enterprising, adaptable or lucky individuals of the old privileged classes [were] for most practical purposes tied up with those individuals of the old submerged classes, who, probably through the same gifts, were able to rise."

There are other tests, too. There was a considerable shift in the locus of political power, which was downwards by pre-Restoration standards. Broadly speaking, there was—if one takes a long enough time base—a change from feudalism to capitalism as the organizing principle of Japanese society. There was even an application of force to politics to bring about these things, or at least to bring about some of the specific decisions that went to make them up.

Yet despite it all, I am reluctant to call the Restoration a revolution in the full meaning of the term. In part, this is because what happened in Japan lacked the avowed social purpose that gives the "great" revolutions of history a certain common character. But it is also because of the nature of the society to which the Restoration gave rise, in which "feudal" and "capitalist" elements worked together in a symbiosis dedicated to acquiring national strength. The political movement that brought this society into being cannot properly be called "bourgeois" in view of the dominant role samurai played in it and the power they retained when it was done. It was certainly not "peasant," given the fate of peasant revolt. Nor was it "absolutist" or "rightist," if that is to imply that the primary stimulus was a fear of popular unrest. What then is left, when none of these standard categories satisfactorily apply? Only to call it a nationalist revolution, perhaps, thereby giving recognition to the nature of the emotions that above all brought it about.

POSTSCRIPT

Did the Meiji Restoration Constitute a Revolution in Nineteenth-Century Japan?

An interesting question raised by this issue is the nature and meaning of the term "revolution." The criteria used would have an impact on the debate. A good starting point to begin this issue would be a brief exploration of the term "revolution," with comparisons made with other noted world revolutions. In *The Anatomy of Revolution*, rev. ed. (Random House, 1966), Crane Brinton (1898–1966) presents an interesting model for studying the nature of revolutions and uses the English, American, French, and Russian ones as case studies. From his data, Brinton drew the following conclusions regarding the revolutionary process:

1. The countries were generally prosperous prior to the revolution; however, government machinery was clearly inefficient. Discontent was strongly felt by those wealthy citizens who felt restrained by the titled aristocracy who contributed little to the country's well-being. The intellectuals eventually transferred their loyalty from the ruling monarchy to the discontents.
2. The revolutions generally passed through three phases: (a) the moderate stage where reformers who overthrew the monarchy and now controlled the government worked to gradually solve the country's problems in a moderate, non-violent way; they are opposed by the extremists who argue for immediate change, if necessary, through violent means; (b) the radical phase in which the extremists take control of the government, get rid of the moderates, and begin a radical restructuring of society; they are assisted by the people who demand a strong central government to bring stability at home and provide the military forces to deal with foreign countries who oppose their revolution; (c) the counter-revolutionary phase in which the tyranny of the extremists is overthrown by a coalition of forces who desire an end to the violence and a return to a peaceful, secure society.
3. Results: While the revolution brings many changes to the country, it ends with a government that is similar to the one in place before the revolution.

Sources of modern Japanese history abound. A general reference work would be, *The Cambridge History of Japan*, vol. 5: *The Nineteenth Century*, Marius B. Jansen, ed. (Cambridge University Press, 1989). W.G. Beasley's *The Rise of Modern Japan* (St. Martin's Press, 1995) is a readable volume, written by someone who has contributed much to an enlightened understanding of Japan and its history. Some specific sources on the Meiji era would be, Carol

Gluck, *Japan's Modern Myths: Ideology in the Late Meiji Period* (Princeton University Press, 1985); Kenneth B. Pyle, *The New Generation in Meiji Japan, 1885-1895* (Stanford University Press, 1969); and two works by W.G. Beasley, *The Meiji Restoration* (Stanford University Press, 1972) and *Japanese Imperialism, 1894–1945* (Oxford University Press, 1987), which concentrates on late Meiji diplomacy and its influence on Japan's future twentieth-century course. A specialized study is *Japan in Transition: From Tokugawa to Meiji,* Marius Jansen and Gilbert Rozman, eds. (Princeton University Press, 1986), which contains scholarly essays on related aspects of Japanese history during this important time period.

ISSUE 5

Were Economic Factors Primarily Responsible for British Imperialism?

YES: Lance E. Davis and Robert A. Huttenback, from *Mammon and the Pursuit of Empire: The Economics of British Imperialism*, abridged ed. (Cambridge University Press, 1988)

NO: John M. MacKenzie, from *The Partition of Africa, 1880–1900: And European Imperialism in the Nineteenth Century* (Methuen & Co., 1983)

ISSUE SUMMARY

YES: Professor Lance E. Davis and Robert A. Huttenback state that, although statistics prove that British imperialism was not a profitable venture, it was supported by an economic elite that was able to promote and derive profits from it.

NO: Professor John M. MacKenzie argues that the motivation for British imperialism was multicausal and that most of the causes can be found in the general anxiety crisis permeating British society in the late nineteenth century.

From the earliest stages of history, civilizations have extended beyond their boundaries to conquer neighboring peoples. Historians use the term *empire* to describe this process of domination and what results from it. It is easy to chronicle human history as a series of eras in which one or more civilizations display dominance and maintain it until they are conquered by a more powerful force. With the development of nation-states in the early modern period, the nation replaced the civilization. But the process of conquest and dominance continued; perhaps there were more players in the game, but things didn't change very much.

The term *imperial* is used to characterize this empire building. Derived from the Latin *imperium* (command), it denotes the process by which a group of people extend their control over a larger area. For example, when the small Roman republic extended its control over vast territories, it assumed the title *Imperium Romanum*.

The last half of the nineteenth century is considered to be imperialism's apex. During that era European nations (and ultimately the United States) began to extend their influence over the non-Western world. The results were swift and decisive; within a generation there were few areas in Asia and Africa that were free from European intrusion. The mad scramble for colonies had begun.

Why did Western nations begin this process of domination? Historians have offered many reasons, among them the development of global capitalism, nationalistic imperialism, religious missionary zeal, reflections and demands of popular culture, strategic protection for national interests, and new technology. Despite the fact that modern imperialism is little more than a century old, it has received much attention from historians due to its far-reaching consequences.

Because nineteenth-century imperialism accompanied the rapid rise and development of capitalism, historians first saw the two as symbiotic. The West expanded to procure raw materials, establish foreign markets for domestically produced goods, and provide additional sources for investment capital. In 1902 Englishman John A. Hobson was the first to state this viewpoint. Russian Vladimir Lenin took the argument one step further. Borrowing Karl Marx's idea that capitalism must expand to survive, Lenin saw imperialism as capitalism's last spasm before the Communist revolution would bring it to an end.

This economic interpretation of imperialism held sway for many years until newer examinations began to uncover other possibilities. The national rivalries that led to World War I caused some historians to see imperialism as an example of nationalism gone mad, with Western nations using the acquisition of colonies as manifestations of national pride. Other historians saw strategic territories as an excuse for the acquisition of overseas territories. Once some were acquired, others were needed to protect and defend them. Heaven forbid that a rival nation be in a position to endanger one's colonial possessions!

In recent years historians have developed several new theses for the growth of nineteenth-century imperialism. Some point out the effect of the masses on its development, offering countless examples from popular culture as proof. Others show how the cultural images of non-Western peoples in Western literature and music (which are usually untrue and condescending) have created a "white man's burden" mentality that has both promoted and justified imperialism. Finally, there are those who stress the role of the military and diplomatic corps that led businesspeople, missionaries, and others down the primrose path of imperial conquest.

In the following selections, Lance E. Davis and Robert A. Huttenback investigate the profitability of nineteenth-century imperialism. They contend that, while on the whole the system did not pay for itself, an elite group did profit immeasurably and used its influence to promote it. Therefore, the authors propose an up-to-date use of economics as a factor in imperialist development. While not disagreeing with them, John M. MacKenzie finds all of the many causes of nineteenth-century imperialism rooted in a Europe strongly influenced by a crisis/anxiety mentality.

Lance E. Davis and
Robert A. Huttenback

 **YES**

Imperium Economicum: In Retrospect

M. K. Gandhi, an unlikely imperialist, once wrote, "Though Empires have gone and fallen, this Empire perhaps may be an exception." That opinion was based on the conviction that the British Empire was "not founded on material but on spiritual foundations." The future Mahatma was no more correct than the rhetoricians who saw the Empire as the expression of Britannia's divine mission. "Wherever her [Britain's] sovereignty has gone," one writer averred, "two blades of grass have grown where one grew before. Her flag wherever it has advanced has benefited the country over which it floats; and has carried with it civilization, the Christian religion, order, justice and prosperity." Other observers were not so certain. In response to Betsy Prig's comment, " ... ain't it lovely to see 'ow Britannia improved her position, since Benjy picked up the dropt threads of England's imperial tradition." Clio, less sure, in an 1878 issue of *Punch* replied: "Fine phrases and flatulent figures (sez she) are the charlatan's tools."

This book is essentially about the "flatulent figures" and the often eloquent message they carried. However difficult it may be to disentangle figures and messages, it is possible to measure one aspect of the Empire: its costs and its revenue. Even [Benjamin] Disraeli, the great avatar of Britain's conquering might, in a brief incarnation as Chancellor of the Exchequer, referred to "Those wretched colonies ..." as "a mill stone around our neck." A few years later, Karl Marx, an observer of a different political stripe, filed a supportive brief in the *New York Daily Tribune* in which he wondered whether "this dominion [India] does not threaten to cost quite as much as it can ever to expected to come to."

For whatever reason, Empire to many Britons seemed not only politically desirable but hypnotically alluring. Disraeli, despite his earlier reservations, thundered: "... no Minister in this country will do his duty who neglects the opportunity of reconstructing as much as possible of our colonial empire...." So potent was the message that the ordinarily archliberal [William] Gladstone was forced to dissemble and to protest: " ... Gentlemen, while we are opposed to imperialism we are devoted to empire." While he proclaimed that "nothing will induce me to submit to these colonial annexations," he nevertheless ordered the bombardment of Alexandria and the virtual annexation of Egypt. To conclude that Disraeli had suddenly discovered that Empire was costless is wrong. He merely felt that other considerations were of greater importance than cost effectiveness. Even in the Crystal Palace Speech, he admitted that: "

... It has been proved to us that we have lost money on our colonies. It has been shown with precise, with mathematical demonstration, that there never was a jewel in the Crown of England that was so costly as the possession of India." ...

No one can sanely argue that there were not British politicians dedicated to maintaining and expanding the Empire, nor that there were not business-men who recognized that such policies might redound to their profit. It may well have been that both groups increased in size after the mid-1880s as increasing political and economic competition from the continental powers and the United States exacerbated the rising protectionist sentiment both in the newly competitive nations and in the Dominions. [Joseph] Chamberlain, himself, bought Canadian Pacific Railroad bonds and lost £50,000 in an ill-fated attempt to grow sisal in the Bahamas. Nevertheless, Lenin went too far when he concluded that, "leading British bourgeois politicians fully appreci-ated the connection between what might be called purely economic and the political–social roots of imperialism."

Few of the nineteenth-century proponents and critics of Empire thought that the enterprise was without expense. Adderley had railed against the colo-nies' refusal to pay their just share of expenses; and Marx doubted that the Empire would ever carry its own financial weight. Disraeli, even as he pro-posed further imperial expansions, acknowledged that the Empire was costly and that India was a particularly expensive undertaking. Chamberlain, although he looked at imperial expenditures as potentially profitable invest-ments, admitted that they required money; and Hicks-Beach at the Treasury had threatened his resignation when presented with the estimated expenses of one of the Colonial Secretary's development schemes. For those, like Cham-berlain, who argued that the Empire was good business for the British, impe-rial costs had still to be offset against private profits in any calculation of social gain: a point Marx had recognized as early as 1858. Even if the claim was only that the Empire was good for a few but not for the many, the ques-tion still remains: How much did it cost the many to enrich the few?

Both Marx and Adderley emphasized the major, but not the only, ele-ment in the British subsidy to the imperial investor. The former, in reference to India, had pointed to "the military and naval expenses made by the people of England on Indian account," and the latter, speaking of a British colony, to the exemption "in purse and person from the cost of its own defense." Despite the widespread recognition of the absurdity of the situation—an appreciation that had already in 1861 led to the creation of a Parliamentary select committee—there is no evidence that circumstances were significantly better in 1914 than they had been in that earlier year....

The failure of a long succession of governments to distribute the defense burden between home and Empire in some more equitable fashion lay rooted in history, in the law, in the bureaucratic mire, and in the pressing nature of defense requirements. The colonies with responsible government argued that they did not have to contribute, the dependent Empire said that it could not afford to pay, and hence who but the British taxpayer was left to redress the balance?...

Nor was the peculiar inequity in the distribution of the burden a figment in the minds of British politicians. The expenditure figures suggest that, if anything, the magnitude of the problem was understated. On average, in the late nineteenth and early twentieth centuries, the cost of British defense was about two and a half times as great as that borne by the citizens of a typical developed country and almost twice that of the French and Germans. The denizens of the colonies with responsible government meanwhile assumed a fiscal responsibility only a quarter that of the resident of a foreign developed country; and in the dependent colonies, the impost was less than one-quarter of that demanded from inhabitants of underdeveloped nations....

Although defense was the largest single component in the total imperial subsidy, it was by no means the only one. De facto and de jure guarantees made it possible for Empire governments to borrow at rates much below those available to non-Empire nations. The gains were not spread evenly over the Empire but, given the actual level of borrowing, the differentials meant that the residents of the colonies with responsible government saved about 10 percent of their tax bill and those of the dependent Empire about one-half that amount.

The British government also provided regular administrative subsidies to the dependent colonies and a substantial additional amount of direct support on an irregular basis. At times, those latter awards were relatively small. (Newfoundland, for example, received a grant of £260 in 1906 to help offset the effects of a severe depression in the fishing industry.) At other times, however, they were not. The Gold Coast received more than £400,000 in 1900, and the Ugandan railroad cost the British taxpayer almost £9 million between 1896 and 1914.

The fact that the sun never set on the Empire may well have provided vicarious pleasure to many inhabitants of the home islands; however, the global dispersion of Dominions and colonies did present serious problems of administration and control. To help provide the links necessary to hold the Empire together, the government found it necessary to subsidize both telegraphs and steamship lines. The British, for example, paid a quarter of a million pounds to help finance a cable connection between Australia and Canada; and, even in the 1860s, Empire shipping subsidies were running over a million pounds a year.

Finally, the British government founded and underwrote the operations of the Crown Agents. This organization acted as the marketing agency for the sale of colonial securities and as the purchasing agent for colonial supplies. Acting as an effective monopolist in the market for colonial issues and as an monopsonist in the market for the supplies bought by those colonial governments, the Agents obtained very fortuitous marketing arrangements for bond issues and equally favorable prices for the goods and services destined for their colonial customers.

It is difficult to measure precisely the total cost to the British of the non-defense component of the imperial subsidy, but it appears unlikely to have been less than one-fifth of the defense subsidy and it may have been twice that. Although the actual amount of Empire investment is unknown, the best estimates indicate that it amounted on average to about £17–8 per capita in prices of 1913. As has been noted, the defense subsidy alone amounted to at least 10 shillings and 10 pence per year for every British man, woman, and child and it could have been as high as 12 shillings and 10 pence, more than 20 percent of national savings. The minimum figure suggests that private Empire returns would have to have been reduced by more than 3 percent to provide a true estimate of the social returns, even if the nondefense components of the subsidy were zero. At the other extreme, assuming the larger defense figure and a very generous £.20 for the nondefense component, the adjustment would be almost 5 percent. Even the lower charge is sufficient to reduce Empire returns below levels that could have been earned at home or in the foreign sector after the mid-1880s.

The British as a whole certainly did not benefit economically from the Empire. On the other hand, individual investors did. In the Empire itself, the level of benefits depended upon whom one asked and how one calculated. For the colonies of white settlement the answer is unambiguous: They paid for little and received a great deal. In the dependent Empire the white settlers, such as there were, almost certainly gained as well. As far as the indigenous population was concerned, while they received a market basket of government commodities at truly wholesale prices, there is no evidence to suggest that, had they been given a free choice, they would have bought the particular commodities offered, even at the bargain-basement rates.

It is clear that imperial exactions placed on the British taxpayer enabled the colonists and residents of the Dominions and the dependent Empire to pay fewer taxes and to devote a substantial proportion of the taxes they did pay to a variety of projects that did not include defense. The Empire was a political system, and it should have been possible to align the pattern of colonial expenditures so as to increase the level of support for business and to guarantee that the revenues required to command those resources were charged not to those businesses but to the taxpayers at large.

The potential for government subsidization is vast, and such subsidies can take as many forms as Joseph's coat had colors. Some, involving nothing but the manipulation of political decisions, are difficult to discover even at the time and probably impossible to uncover a century later. Many subsidies, however, involve government expenditures, and for those, the government budget provides a paper trail that can be followed. It is possible to measure the impact of government policy on expenditures on law and justice (costs incurred in part at least to maintain property rights and enforce contracts), public works (the real capital component of social overhead investment), science and human capital (the nontraditional component), and direct business support.

Whether it is the total package or its individual components that is analyzed, the pattern is the same. Great Britain spent somewhat more than other developed countries, but hardly more than that nation's advanced state of development would suggest. The same is not true for the colonies whether dependent or blessed with responsible government. On average the latter group of colonies spent at levels about twice those prevailing in Britain. The formerspent at rates not much different from those at home; but that figure is remarkable given the fraction of a colony's total expenditures that were involved, the relative state of development of the colonies in question, and the amounts spent by countries in the underdeveloped world....

In general, the colonial Empire provides strong evidence for the belief that government was attuned to the interest of business and willing to divert resources to ends that the business community would have found profitable. That behavior is, however, not necessarily evidence that the British used the political process to distort the allocation of governmental resources. Expenditures that benefited business were greatest in the colonies with responsible government, where even the British government, let alone British business-men, had almost no influence. They were next highest in the dependent colonies, where the British did have a very substantial voice in policy making but not a total monopoly. Moreover, within that set, expenditures tended to be larger in those colonies with some local participation in political decision making and smaller in those with little or no consultation. Finally, expenditures were lowest in India, where British influence was strongest and where there were no representative institutions at the national level.

Perhaps the explanation for this ordering lies not with the British but with the local business community. Those merchants and manufacturers may have been quite willing and able to bend the structure of government expenditures to their own benefit. If that is correct, except in India, where financial crisis and the threat of famine overrode all other considerations, they appear to have been successful. It cannot be denied, however, that the policies adopted, perhaps under local business pressure, served the interest of the British investor as well as his colonial cousin.

In the late nineteenth century the London capital market acted as a con-duit for the greatest international movement of private capital in the history of the world. Nevertheless, most of the flow of funds that passed through the stock exchange was not destined for the Empire. Of the almost £5-billion total, less than 70 percent passed out of Britain and almost two-thirds of that amount went to Europe and other parts of the world not pledging fealty to the House of Hanover. The largest single recipient was the United States, but a not-insubstantial portion (more than a quarter) was directed to the underdevel-oped but politically independent countries of South America. In fact these Latin countries received substantially more than all the funds destined for the dependent Empire. Although the Empire as a whole absorbed nearly a quarter of the total, two-thirds of that amount went to the colonies of white settle-ment; and those colonies were, at least in matters economic, not likely objects for British exploitation. They were colonies that, since the middle of the nine-teenth century, had begun pursuing a strongly protectionist policy—one aimed explicitly at British manufacturers and traders.

If Britain itself absorbed 30 percent of the total, if the nations over which the British exercised no political control drew an additional 45, and if the colonies over which its control was, at best, limited took an additional 16: Less than £1 in 10 remained for all of India and for colonies such as St. Kitts, the Bahamas, the Falklands, the Gold Coast, Malta, and Hong Kong, which had few representative institutions. Certainly, the amount of finance that was directed to the dependent Empire was substantial enough (it averaged more than £8 million per year) to ensure that some Englishmen could have become rich, but it appears doubtful (unless the "exploitative" profit rate was higher than even Lenin dreamed) that the total was sufficient—even if there were no offsetting social costs—to make the "average" British subject substantially better off.

Perhaps profits were very high, or possibly the dependent Empire was good business for the few but not for the many. In either case, financial flows were not evenly distributed across the world or across the industrial map. Of the £415 million received by India and the colonies of the dependent Empire, Asia received 65 percent (India alone, 56) and Africa an additional 19 percent. In India that investment was largely associated with railroads and, to a lesser extent, government finance. In the dependent colonies the relative concentrations of British investment were in the agriculture and extractive industries, in finance (the financial, land, and development companies) and in government. Just how profitable were these investments?

Although the measure of "the" rate of return is only approximate, the general outlines confirm the individual industry comparisons. Questions of timing and level are still open, but it would take a massive reversal of the evidence to alter the general conclusions. If the standard is domestic earnings, it appears that in the years before 1885 Empire returns were substantially higher. While some of the observed differences may reflect the small size of the sample and the mix of firms included in the study, it would be very difficult to argue that colonial profits were any less than domestic, and they were almost certainly substantially higher. In the case of the returns on manufacturing and commercial investments, for example, Empire returns through 1880 were one and one-quarter of domestic—and that measure is the most favorable for the home economy. Over time, the advantage eroded, and for the last half of the period Empire returns were substantially below those available at home. There was, however, some recovery in Empire earnings after the turn of the century, and in the last decade before the War they may well have equaled domestic.

As Marx had predicted, profits were falling; however, they were declining more rapidly in the Empire than in the foreign sector and faster there than in the domestic. It is, of course, not the trend but the home–Empire differential that is important for the Hobson–Lenin argument [This argument, created by John A. Hobson and Vladmir Lenin, states that capitalism by nature must expand to survive. Imperialism is necessary to ensure this expansion.] In the same way that it is difficult to deny that the Empire was *relatively* very profitable in the earlier years, it is even more difficult to conclude that profits in the colonies were substantially above those at home in the later ones.

The explanation of the trends in relative returns can in large measure be traced to two phenomena. First, early entrants into new markets and regions had distinct advantages. To the extent that property rights were well defined and enforced they may have been able to acquire the potentially most profitable lands at bargain prices. Secondly, they frequently had an initial monopoly position that allowed them to exploit those new opportunities until, in

[Joseph] Schumpeter's terms, the "herd like movement" of the imitative entrepreneurs undercut their profits....

While some stockholders clearly benefited from the imperial connection, the evidence indicates that probably at no time, and certainly not after the 1870s, were Empire profits sufficient to underwrite *British* prosperity. However, for the shareholders in the agricultural and extractive and the public utility sectors (and perhaps others as well), where competition was blunted or enforced property rights pushed potential competitors onto inferior lands, the Empire was important, and it was profitable. One can readily conclude that there should have been some economic imperialists. How many and who they were is a different matter....

A separation of investors into businessmen and elites (peers, gentlemen, financiers, and the like) indicates that, place of residence aside, businessmen were less likely to invest in foreign securities than were their elite counterparts. Moreover, they were *far* less inclined to invest in Empire than foreign enterprise; and among all businessmen, only merchants displayed any significant willingness to invest beyond the seas. In the Empire the elites were most willing to invest in commercial banks; in financial, land, and development companies; in iron, coal, and steel firms; and in the public utilities. To the extent that they entrusted their resources to the Empire at all, businessmen tended to put their funds to work in the private sector—competitive and less in need of government charters or licenses—industries, in short, much less dependent on political control.

The geographic distribution of shareholder "tastes" indicates that there were two very different groups of investors: those who lived in London, and others, who made their homes in the provinces. A typical Londoner's portfolio was composed of about one-quarter domestic, one-third foreign, and two-fifths Empire shares. Outside the metropolis, the portfolio was more than one-half domestic and contained less than one-quarter each of foreign and Empire shares. Within London, those who gave the City as their address preferred Empire to domestic securities, but much preferred foreign to Empire. Beyond the Wall, however, London investors appeared largely indifferent between home and foreign issues, but displayed a very strong preference for Empire over both. The London connection was particularly well illustrated in the case of South African gold mines, and even [Cecil] Rhodes turned to metropolitan investors when he needed further capital.

Further exploration of the "two-England" hypothesis indicates that Empire investors in London were drawn from a different socioeconomic background than were the Empire investors who lived outside the capital. While London elites do not appear to have behaved substantially differently than their provincial counterparts, London businessmen acted very differently than their confreres residing elsewhere. London merchants, manufacturers, professionals, and managers all invested far less frequently in home and far more frequently in Empire activities. On average, London businessmen were only one-fifth as likely to invest in domestic securities as those businessmen who lived in places like Sheffield or Manchester, but they were half again as inclined to put their resources to work in the Empire.

Overall, Empire investors tended to be drawn from two groups: elites, wherever they lived, and businessmen (particularly, in terms of numbers, merchants) who resided in London. The attractiveness of the Empire seemed to decline almost exponentially the farther one traveled north from the City. In terms of the socioeconomic background of its participants, the British capital market was clearly two markets, and it is from one of those segments, the segment populated by elites and London businessmen, that the most strident Empire support could have been expected to come.

Finally, to the extent that the Empire investments were less profitable than home and foreign alternatives, it would have been expected that the elites, while continuing to rally political support for the Empire, would gradually have attempted to divest themselves of those securities and to reinvest their assets in other more viable enterprises. Although the data do not permit an exact test of this hypothesis, they do allow a less precise examination. If the firm sample is split at 1890 and the two parts compared, the ratio of elite to business investors is substantially lower in the second period. The decline, however, is not related to a rise in business holdings (in fact, they fell as well), but to an increase in the Other owners—including women, children, and retirees....

If the residents of the dependent Empire spent little on taxes, the British, as we have already seen, spent a great deal. Even the citizens of the colonies with responsible government, who chose to tax themselves more heavily than they might have, were largely freed of defense costs and thus able to devote the vast bulk of their resources to more directly productive ends. In the United Kingdom, however, the real tax level increased by about two-thirds over the half-century in question, and as a fraction of per capita national income it rose by about one-sixth. In England the tax structure historically had depended very heavily on consumption taxes, and it was certainly regressive. As the second half of the century wore on, however, regressivity declined as customs and excises were replaced by increases in the income and inheritance taxes. The latter sources together had produced only about one-quarter of the total when Disraeli first became prime minister but had risen to account for more than £2 in 5 by the election of 1911. Over the same period, consumption taxes had declined from more than three-fifths to less than one-half of all the imposts. Over Gladstone's protests, the income tax had "lost its terrifying character" and by the mid-1890s, again despite Gladstone's reservations, death duties had begun to bite.

Even with the very regressive tax structure of the 1860s, between three-fifths and two-thirds of British taxes were paid by the middle and upper classes. Given the increasing reliance on income and inheritance taxes, it seems reasonable to conclude that this proportion did not decline and may have risen as the century wore on. Of more direct interest, the fraction that fell on the middle class was probably close to two and a half times the amount paid by the upper class. It is hardly surprising that the Gladstonian Liberals opposed higher taxes while the upper classes found that, if the resources gained by tax increases could be used for "productive purposes," they would not only countenance but support such levies. The middle class bore far more than its share of the imperial subsidy and, as is so apparent in an enumeration of their investments, they did not share equally in its benefits. The profits of Empire accrued largely to the upper class.

When it came to the formulation and execution of official policy toward the Empire, the responsibility, of course, rested fundamentally with Parliament and particularly the House of Commons. It was a quintessentially patrician legislative body, dominated by the elite classes, business, and the professions. The members had attended the ancient universities and the major public schools and they were "club men" with a vengeance. It is this homogeneity that makes it difficult to explain individual political behavior. In general, on imperial issues Liberals deviated more from established party positions than Conservatives and university-educated Liberals were particularly anti-imperial. The safeness of a member's seat, his club memberships, his profession, his level of education, and the district from which he was elected seem to provide very little help in explaining his voting behavior. On the fundamental question of the degree to which economic self-interest affected a House member's voting behavior on imperial issues, no intimate connection appears to exist between the two, although further research may prove otherwise.

Parliament, much as any other democratic legislative body, was subject to considerable outside pressure. Individual companies, the chambers of commerce, the trade associations, and a fluctuating array of usually short-lived commercial coalitions all tried to influence the course of events. Although not usually successful in the foreign arena, in the colonies with responsible government, and in the dependent colonies, because of long-established British disinclination to interfere on behalf of private businessmen, they were more effective in the case of India—the cotton tariffs being a case in point. Tariffs in the self-governing colonies attracted considerable attention from the various pressure groups, but constitutional inhibitions and lack of Parliamentary sympathy precluded the implementation of the desired policy. Even in the dependent colonies, the Crown Agents actively sought foreign bids when they felt domestic ones were excessive.

Much, no doubt, remains to be said concerning the relationship between Empire and economics. But perhaps, when all is said and done, Cecil Rhodes came closest to summing the whole thing up when he said, not totally in jest, that imperialism was nothing more than philanthropy plus 5 percent! But philanthropy for whom? It appears that imperialism can best be viewed as a mechanism for transferring income from the middle to the upper classes. Because of the technology of the imperial machine, the process involved some transfer of those resources to the colonies; however, it is not obvious that either India or the dependent colonies would have chosen to accept that imperial subsidy had they been given the opportunity to object. The Elites and the colonies with responsible government were clear winners; the middle class, certainly, and the dependent Empire, probably, were losers. A strange kind of philanthropy— socialism for the rich, capitalism for the poor.

NO

John M. MacKenzie

The Partition of Africa: 1880–1900

We have been witnesses of one of the most remarkable episodes in the history of the world.

So wrote Sir John Scott Keltie in the opening sentence of his book *The Partition of Africa*, published in 1893. Keltie and his contemporaries were enthralled by the statistics of that 'most remarkable episode'. More than 10 million square miles of African territory and over 100 million African people had fallen to European rule in the space of little more than a decade. The concluding acts of the Partition were yet to come in the late 1890s and in the years immediately preceding the first world war, but in Keltie's time the map of Africa was already beginning to look like its modern counterpart. In the middle of the century the European cartographer saw Africa as a continent of blank spaces where the principal physical features—rivers, lakes, mountains—were gradually being filled in by European exploration. In the late 1880s and early 1890s maps of Africa in school atlases were revised every year, for political boundaries and various colourings for the different empires were now the rage.

Since the publication of Keltie's book, writers and historians have conducted an energetic debate on the causes of the Partition of Africa, culminating in a veritable flood of books and articles in the last twenty years. This enduring interest is perhaps not surprising. The Scramble for Africa (as the Partition is sometimes more luridly known) was the most dramatic instance of the partition of the world by Europe and America in the late nineteenth century. It inaugurated a great revolution in the relationship between European and African peoples, and it sent out political, economic and social shockwaves, which continue to be felt in Africa to this day. Africans naturally find the Partition a distasteful event, yet they are prepared to defend the artificial boundaries established by it to the point of war if necessary. The modern challenge to Africa remains the struggle to consolidate and develop the national and economic units carved out by Europeans in the Partition period, and so knowledge of the Partition is fundamental to an understanding of contemporary Africa.

This [selection] is concerned, however, with one great problem. What were the causes of the Partition of Africa and why did it occur when it did? Why was it that, after several centuries of nibbling at the edges of Africa, Europeans suddenly rushed in to establish direct military and political control over almost the entire continent? Why did European politicians who had tra-

From John M. MacKenzie, *The Partition of Africa, 1880–1900: And European Imperialism in the Nineteenth Century* (Methuen & Company Ltd., 1983). Copyright © 1983 by John M. MacKenzie. Reprinted by permission of the author.

93

ditionally resisted the extension of empire in Africa become caught up in a hectic demarcation of territory?...

Interpretation

... [T]he Partition was not a sudden and wholly unpremeditated affair. 'Creeping partition' had been going on in Africa for some time. The French had already conceived grand designs in the 1870s, and commercial pressures had been exerted on the British from the same period. Nevertheless, the speed with which the Partition was finally accomplished, after more than 300 years of European coastal activity, and the comprehensiveness of the land grab do suggest that this was a new and dramatic phase. Historians have elaborated and debated many different theories to explain the events of the 1880s and 1890s.

These interpretations have overlaid each other, and it is perhaps helpful to divide them into categories to bring some order to a very complex process of theorizing. It has become customary to divide explanations into metropolitan and peripheral, economic and non-economic. Metropolitan interpretations are those which seek to explain the Scramble in terms of developments in Europe, while peripheral ones look to events in Africa itself. The economic–non-economic categories cut across the metropolitan–peripheral ones, so that there are some metropolitan and some peripheral explanations which are also economic and some which are not.

Metropolitan

Capitalist Imperialism
The first explanation offered for the Partition in the early years of this century saw the European grab for Africa as arising from an inherent problem in capitalism. To maintain their capacity for growth capitalist economies had repeatedly to find new outlets for investment. In the late nineteenth century, the capitalist economies entered upon a particularly difficult period. Rates of return on capital invested at home were falling, and so capitalists believed that surplus capital had to be exported. Further, this interpretation suggests that the power to dispose of capital was falling into fewer hands, particularly large banking interests. Those who disposed of such capital desired that it should be protected, and imperialism was therefore the policy of a small, highly influential capitalist group.

Certainly this was a period of considerable capital exports from Europe, and such exports played an important role in the development of Europe's relationship with the world as a whole, but this explanation seems to offer little help for the Partition of Africa. Significant amounts of capital were exported to South Africa, but Africa generally remained the continent receiving less investment than any other right up to the first world war. Moreover, the development of great capitalist combines and concentrated banking interests did not occur until after the Partition had been accomplished.

Markets

The second metropolitan explanation is also economic. This suggests that European capitalist economies had encountered not so much a crisis of excess capital as a crisis of excess competition and production. Germany and the United States were industrializing rapidly, and France and Italy were also attempting to produce their industrial response. The British experience showed that industrialism necessarily involved global specialization. The industrial state had to maintain itself through an exchange of foodstuffs and raw materials for industrial goods. No industrial state could be self-sufficient, and to survive it had to export. New industrial states had to find new markets or encroach on those of existing exporters. Colonies could offer assured markets, particularly if the European state's relationship with them was protected by tariffs which would keep competitors out.

In addition, the capitalist economies seemed to have moved into a period of depression between the 1870s and 1890s. There were downturns in trading activity in the decade preceding the Scramble and again in the 1880s and 1890s when the Scramble was at its height. These difficulties caused alarm to industrialists and merchants throughout Europe. Italy, Germany and France responded with new tariffs in 1878, 1879 and 1881 respectively, and that compounded alarm in Britain, where the Government was still wedded to free trade. It is true that protectionist policies did not come fully to fruition until the 1890s, but the anxiety was there at the earlier period. Some indication of the alarm in Britain can be secured from the Royal Commission appointed to enquire into the Depression of Trade and Industry in 1885-6. Chambers of Commerce and Trades Societies, representing both employers and labour, were circularized as to the reasons for the depression, and their suggestions for the measures that could be taken to alleviate it. Many commented on foreign competition and tariffs, and several urged the opening of new markets, for example in Africa, and the consolidation of trading relations with colonies.

Again this market explanation, though much used at the time as an argument that colonial expansion should be undertaken, is limited in the African case. Africa's population was small, and the opportunities for marketing industrial goods were slight. But hopes are invariably more potent than reality.

Raw Materials

If markets are one end of the industrial chain, raw materials are the other. The early phase of the industrial revolution depended on iron and coal which were available in Europe, and on cotton which had to be supplied by the United States and later by India and Egypt. But by the late nineteenth century other raw materials were beginning to be important. Vegetable oils were used in the manufacture of soaps and industrial lubricants. The large firm of Lever Brothers on Merseyside built its power mainly on west African palm oil, and Liverpool was the port most closely connected with the west African trade. Rubber had become important for insulation of the new electrical and telegraph wires and for tyres. Until the rubber plantations were developed in Malaya at the beginning of this century, rubber was only collected in the wild in South America and in Africa....

It was recognized too that the new industrial age would emphasize base metals like copper. Copper deposits were well known in Africa, for Africans had exploited them for hundreds of years, and in many places had used copper as a currency. If base metals were to become more important, gold retained the fascination it had held for Europeans for many centuries. All industrial states had placed their currencies on the gold standard in the nineteenth century in order to stabilize them, and were building up reserves of gold to underpin these currencies. Gold had therefore become, even more than before, a source of power and stability for the western economic system. Some of the older sources of gold were beginning to decline in significance, so no state could allow a vital source of gold like the Transvaal to fall into the hands of a protectionist rival.

There was, therefore, much discussion of Africa as a source of raw materials, and the continent was likely to be more significant as a supplier than as a market. But raw materials had been extracted from Africa for many years without the need for political controls. The mere existence of raw materials does not fully explain why Europe felt it necessary to partition the continent, although there can be no doubt that the pace was quickening, and the fears and hopes were intensifying at this period.

Statesmen's Imperialism

This political and diplomatic explanation sees the Partition as part of European statesmen's power-play. Statesmen used overseas territories as bargaining counters in a global game of diplomacy, as a safety valve for European nationalist tensions. This idea has always been suggested most forcibly with reference to Bismarck, who has been seen by some as actually precipitating the Scramble in order to secure his diplomatic ends in Europe, namely the isolation of France. It is a view which is no longer fashionable, for it smacks too much of the influence of 'great men' upon history, and the forces at work in Africa were much too powerful and complex to be controlled or manipulated by single political figures. Even before Leopold and Bismarck took a hand, some form of Partition was gathering momentum.

However, the last acts of the Partition in north Africa do seem to have rather more diplomatic content. Britain had the most considerable economic interests in Morocco, but she allowed France to have a free run there. Even so France did not declare a protectorate over Morocco (partitioning it with Spain) until threatened by Germany in the Moroccan crises of 1905 and 1911.

Imperialism and Nationalism

This is the argument that the Partition of Africa occurred as a by-product of the friction created by new aggressive nationalisms in Europe rubbing against old-established centralized states and imperial powers. Both Germany and Italy were newly united states in this period. Both had to satisfy strongly nationalist demands within them; both sought to use colonial policies to reconcile internal tensions. Italy was already dreaming of recreating the Roman empire in the 1870s and turned her attention to Tunis, the historic Carthage. Both Germany and Italy made grabs for territory in 1884 and 1885. Neither seemed to base its claim on strong existing commercial rights. In both coun-tries there were powerful colonial propaganda groups at work looking to empire as a means whereby the new nation states could come of age. More-over in Germany, with its liberal franchise, a colonial policy seemed to be a popular one. It has even been said that Bismarck staged his colonial advances on several fronts in 1884 as an electioneering stunt for the election that took place in Germany late that year.

If Germany and Italy represented the aggressive force of new national-isms, Britain and France represented the defensiveness of the old. For France after all, the German empire had been proclaimed in the aftermath of the humiliation of the Franco-Prussian War of 1870–1, in which France lost Alsace-Lorraine. A forward French policy dated from the 1870s. Defeat forced France to look outwards. Colonies, it has been suggested, were a balm for French wounded pride. The British on the other hand had been accustomed to secure their commercial ends without competition from other powers. Some-times they had been forced to annex territory in the mid-nineteenth century, but generally they had avoided it. The British had preferred to work through informal empire, and British politicians were reluctant to translate that into formal control unless some very important national interest demanded it. From 1880 the British were forced to do so repeatedly to protect their interests from the new aggressive nationalisms and the revived imperial vision of France.

Popular Imperialism

It has also been argued that the new nationalisms were not just a matter for statesmen and colonial pressure groups; they also satisfied popular psycholog-ical needs. European peoples (and no state was immune from this) developed an aggressive xenophobia in order to define sharply their national identity and national ambition. In Britain this came to be known as jingoism, a term significantly coined from a music-hall song at the time of the Congress of Ber-lin of 1878, an international conference which had an important bearing on the Partition. Popular culture, as expressed in the theatre and popular songs, took on a strongly nationalist and patriotic tone, and this inevitably became bound up with at least the protection, if not the extension of empire. Indeed, it became a great age of propaganda. The expansion of education led to a con-siderable increase in literacy, and this was exploited by colonial pressure groups, the army, the navy and above all the missions.

The missions were very important in propagating imperial ideas. Mis-sion societies, which had appeared in all denominations and in all European countries in the nineteenth century, became convinced of their divine mis-sion to convert the world, to save other people from what they saw to be 'bar-barism' and 'savagery'. To achieve this, they required both money and recruits, and they set about opening people's pockets and minds through every public-ity technique available to them. Notable missionaries became heroes, and books by them or about them became best-sellers. These and other popular works propagated racial ideas which seemed at one and the same time both to explain and to justify European technical and military superiority in the world.

It has sometimes been objected that 'popular imperialism' was a result of the Partition and other imperial advances of the age, not a cause. But popular imperialism does seem to have its roots in the 1870s and imperial events did raise popular outcries.... Thus popular opinion certainly seems to have been significant by the 1890s when politicians were confirming the more tentative moves (the chartering of companies, for example) of the 1880s. These are all British examples, but 'jingoism' was just as evident in the rest of Europe.

Electoral behaviour is of course the best index of popular opinion. We have already seen that Bismarck may well have been responding to electoral pressures in 1884. In Britain, there can be no doubt that colonial discontents contributed to the fall of Gladstone in 1885, and when he formed his fourth ministry in 1892 the Liberal Party had developed a strongly imperialist complexion. His successor, Rosebery, was almost indistinguishable from any Conservative imperialist. Even the Labour movement had imperial elements within it: some Labour leaders accepted the idea that the possession of empire was important to the interests of the working classes, or that it was an inevitable obligation which had to be fulfilled in as ethical a manner as was possible. To attack the possession of colonies seemed to be unpatriotic, and therefore electorally dangerous.

Feudal Atavism

Another social explanation is one that sees imperialism as the policy of the surviving feudal elements of European society, military castes which sought new employment and the continuation of their influence. In France, imperial attitudes were largely forged in the military establishments of Algeria. Both the German and Italian empires had a strongly military flavour, administrators being usually military men rather than civilians. Empire provided them with a source of power removed from domestic politics. Even in the British empire, where the principle of civilian rule was firmly established, the army found an opportunity for employment, and an excuse for growth. In all the empires, colonial revenues could be used to pay for a proportion of the army, a technique long used by the British in India.

Technology

Another explanation, at least for the timing of the Partition, is one which highlights the importance of technology. This suggests that railways, steamships, the telegraph, and medical advances were crucial to the Partition, which could not have been achieved without them....

Clearly, such technical advances did not create imperialism in Africa, but they did produce the vital conditions that rendered its extension more readily possible. Moreover, such technical achievements seemed to emphasize the cultural gap between Europe and Africa which was important in the popular thinking of the period.

Peripheral

Strategic and Egyptocentric

Perhaps the first and most influential peripheral explanation is that which relates the entire Partition to the crisis in Egypt and the two routes to India.... The British invaded Egypt in 1882. The French, having apparently lost their former influence in Egypt, now looked for compensation elsewhere and this provoked Anglo-French rivalries in west Africa.

The vital point about this interpretation is that the British went into Egypt not to protect the bondholders, but for strategic reasons, to protect the Suez Canal and the crucial route to India. Similarly, British interest in the Cape was strategic, to protect the Cape route to the East and the important Royal Navy base at Simon's Bay. The British could not permit any other power to achieve an interior preponderance which might threaten the Cape, and it was this that drew them into the interior. The Partition in east Africa was bound up with the strategic concern with the Nile. The British believed that their position in Egypt was only secure if they commanded the entire Nile system. To keep theFrench from the upper Nile they needed a convenient route from the east coast. It was this consideration that lay behind the retention of Uganda and the decision to build the east African railway. According to this view, the Partition of Africa is no more than a giant footnote to the British Indian empire. This interpretation had great influence for some time, but it can now be discounted. French advances were not necessarily related to Egypt. The complex interaction of peripheral and metropolitan forces, for example in south Africa, renders such a single-cause interpretation untenable....

The General Crisis

Finally, there is an interpretation which we can perhaps describe as 'global'. It seems to combine aspects of several of the interpretations.... This suggests that there was a 'general crisis' in the relations between European and non-European peoples at this time, a general crisis induced by the European efforts to create a fully integrated world economy. Industrial Europe required a highly specialized world, in which some areas would produce food for its industrial proletariat, others would produce raw materials for the industrial process, and the entire world would constitute a market for industrial goods. But to achieve this Europe needed to recast the world in its own image, to create the same infrastructures and similar institutions that would permit resources to be exploited and trade to be conducted. By the end of the nineteenth century it was apparent that Europe required a greater degree of coercion to press forward this process, coercion that could only be effected by direct imperial rule. In some areas people were resisting the new dispensation, and in consequence new military and political techniques were required to supplement the purely economic relationship.

This explanation is attractive because it appears to subsume metropolitan and peripheral elements, social and military strains, the widening of the technological gap, and the heightened tensions of the period under one umbrella thesis associated with a particular stage of economic development in the world. But there are some problems with it too. There were crises in some areas of the world, notably China, Siam, Persia and the Gulf, which did not lead to the imposition of direct political controls. But even more significantly from our point of view, there were large areas of Africa, on the face of it much less important economically than the Asian regions just mentioned, where no immediate crisis seemed to have occurred, and yet where political controls were established.

Conclusion

We must now attempt to draw from this complex set of explanations some answers to the question posed at the beginning of the [selection]. Why did the European powers cease their long-standing process of nibbling at Africa and suddenly seize huge chunks of the continent?

There are a number of theses that we can reject straightaway. It seems to have had little to do with the export of capital. The 'great man' explanation simply will not do, for statesmen were largely reacting to the growing pressures and a climate of opinion which they found difficult to oppose. Napoleon III may have had ambitions in the 1850s; Leopold II had personal pretensions by the 1870s; individual Germans like Nachtigal and Peters hoped that Germany would institute an imperial policy; Mackinnon, Goldie and Rhodes all developed, to varying degrees, a passionate interest in the extension of British rule. But none of these was able to achieve his ambitions until the necessary forces came together. Finally, the Egyptocentric and strategic thesis is no longer convincing except as a powerful expression of one motivation of one European country. French decisions to advance in west Africa were made ahead of the British invasion of Egypt. French and Italian rivalries in north Africa, for example over Tunisia, and new German ambitions cannot be related to it. And in southern Africa developments were much too complex to be linked solely to the route to India.

Other 'explanations' are not really explanations at all. Public opinion, technology and African initiatives cannot explain the Partition, but they can demonstrate that the convergence of forces was now such that a partition was more likely to take place. Indeed, one of the remarkable things about the 1870s and 1880s was that so many developments in the realm of ideas, in missionary activity, in propaganda, in the technical and military gap between Europe and the rest of the world did seem to converge. A set of background conditions made the partition much easier to accomplish.

Why then were the crucial decisions made against the background of these conditions? One thing does now seem to be clear, and that is that we cannot be satisfied with an explanation which is wholly European or solely peripheral. Very important lines of force were developed from the periphery, but the thinking of people in Europe was also vital. Despite the creeping imperialism of the British and the French in west Africa, or the creeping partition of southern Africa by Dutch and English settlers, wholesale extensions of territory were resisted for a time. Both Goldie and Mackinnon had their pleas for a recognition of their concessions and the provision of charters rejected at first. Yet a few years later they were accepted. This is not to say that they simply went into cold storage until statesmen decided to use them. It is to say that the tensions, anxieties and pressures had not yet reached the necessary pitch. If there was a convergence of background conditions, there also had to be a conjunction of economic, social and political tensions between metropolis and periphery.

The Scramble for Africa seems to have emerged from a combination of exaggerated hope and over-heated anxiety. The economic conditions of the day, the trough between the first industrial revolution of coal, cotton and iron, and the second of electricity, copper, steel; the appearance of new industrial states protecting themselves with tariffs; the decline in some commodity prices; and the heightened commercial competition everywhere produced all the alarms associated with the transition from one economic system to another. At the same time there were many publicists concerned to argue that Africa was a tropical treasure house, capable of producing plantation crops, base and precious metals, as well as other valuable commodities like rubber and ivory. Verney Lovett Cameron, who had been sent to find Livingstone, published just such an ecstatic account in his *Across Africa* in 1877. Many others wrote in similar vein. The growth in the palm oil trade, the buoyant prices of rubber and ivory, the discovery of diamonds and then of gold, all seemed to confirm this view. Africa could solve some of the problems of the age. A state which missed out on these opportunities might be imperilled in the future. These hopes and anxieties took some time to foment fully, but by the mid-1880s they were ready to blow the lid off the politicians' restraint. Politicians do not so much act as react to the forces round about them.

An influential generation was seized by this combination of exaggerated fear and overpowering ambition. Although it is difficult to see a small group of finance capitalists influencing governments to do their bidding, there was nevertheless a rather more extensive and powerful élite at work. In London, Paris and Berlin, commercial, shipping, geographical, intellectual and official figures did come together to press for imperial advance. Although politicians, particularly in Britain, liked to claim that no official actions were taken to further the interests of individual investors and economic concerns, in fact they were. The London élite was closely connected by ties of education, social life and marriage. Some officials in the Foreign and Colonial Offices developed close connections with the capitalist concerns and furthered their ends from a growing conviction of the need for British expansion. Ex-ministers joined the boards of companies, and colonial administrators were often rewarded with directorships of companies whose ends they had furthered when in office. This was not a conspiracy; it was merely the normal operations of such an élite group converted to a dominant idea.

There was, moreover, something irrational about the Partition—as reflected in the grandiose ambitions of figures like Leopold, Rhodes, Peters, even Mackinnon—which deeply disturbed the rational minds of politicians like Salisbury and Bismarck. In many respects the Scramble was not so much a reaction to events that had already taken place as to events it was feared might take place. It was less the result of a 'general crisis' than a symptom of the anxieties that a general crisis was on the way.

There was much that was chimerical about the Partition, and in many parts of Africa it produced disappointing results. South Africa remained the world's most important source of gold, yet by 1910 the British had abdicated political control there. Central Africa was to be one of the western world's most important sources of copper, but this was not fully exploited until the years before the second world war. In some places European coercion upon Africans to produce agricultural raw materials or to go out to work produced large-scale revolts. Railway lines often failed to pay, and administrations invariably required subsidies from the mother countries. Some of the resources of Africa, such as the oil of Nigeria, were scarcely even discovered during the imperial period.

In retrospect, Keltie's opening sentence takes on a new significance. Not only was the speed of Europe's grab for Africa a most remarkable episode, so was the speed of Europe's withdrawal. Many Africans were born before the Partition occurred, and were still alive when Europe departed in the early 1960s. By that time Africa had perhaps been recast in Europe's image, with recognizable national boundaries, an infrastructure of sorts, and relatively similar institutions. But was that what the original Scramblers really intended?

POSTSCRIPT

Were Economic Factors Primarily Responsible for British Imperialism?

No historian who has researched nineteenth-century imperialism will discount any of the factors—economic, political, social, strategic, religious, cultural—that influenced its development. Rather, their work concentrates on discovering which ingredients were either more or less important than others. History seldom provides monocausal explanations for events and movements.

Because nineteenth-century imperialism had such far-reaching consequences, ties can be made between it and several issues in this volume. Issue 7 deals with China's Boxer Rebellion, which some have seen as a manifestation of anti-imperialism. Issue 15 explores the causes of modern Africa's problems, some of which can be attributed to imperialism. Less directly it can be related to Issue 14, which deals with the growth of Islamic revivalism.

Works related to modern imperialism have been numerous and significant. Two important studies of economic factors and imperialism are John A. Hobson, *Imperialism: A Study* (1902) and Vladimir Lenin (Ulyanov), *Imperialism: The Highest Stage of Capitalism* (1916).

A seminal book in the study of nineteenth-century imperialism is Ronald Robinson, John Gallagher, and Alice Denny, *Africa and the Victorians: The Climax of Imperialism* (Doubleday, 1968), which argues that British imperialism's main impetus came from national security and diplomatic rivalry sources. A work of ancillary value is Daniel R. Headrick, *Tools of Empire: Technology and European Imperialism* (Oxford University Press, 1981), which relates technology to the entire process of imperialism.

Exploring the relationship between culture and imperialism has been a timely topic, and the work in this field has been dominated by Edward Said. His *Culture and Imperialism* (Alfred A. Knopf, 1993) shows how nineteenth-century Western misperceptions of non-Westerners in cultural venues such as literature and grand opera played a role in imperialism's development. On a lighter side (culturally speaking), MacKenzie's edited volume *Imperialism and Popular Culture* (St. Martin's Press, 1989) relates the fascination of the masses with exotic people and places and sees it as a motivating factor in imperialism's maturation.

Because many of the world's contemporary problems can be traced to the effects of imperialism on indigenous peoples, it would be remiss not to include some sources that deal with this subject. Eric Wolf's *Europe and the People Without History* (University of California Press, 1997) explores the topic as does David S. Landes's *The Wealth and Poverty of Nations: Why Some Are So Rich and Some So Poor* (W. W. Norton, 1998), which has provoked interesting responses from its reviewers.

ISSUE 6

Was China's Boxer Rebellion Caused by Environmental Factors?

YES: Paul A. Cohen, from *History in Three Keys: The Boxers as Event, Experience, and Myth* (Columbia University Press, 1997)

NO: Henrietta Harrison, from "Justice on Behalf of Heaven: The Boxer Movement," *History Today* (September 2000)

ISSUE SUMMARY

YES: Professor Paul A. Cohen contends that while antiforeign and anti-Christian attitudes played a role in the start of the Boxer rebellion, a more immediate cause was a severe drought and its impact on Chinese society.

NO: Historian Henrietta Harrison concedes that while the Boxers were motivated by more than a single factor, opposition to Christian missionary activity was at the core of their rebellion.

I ssue 5 of this volume examines the causes of imperialism, by which the West attempted to extend its influence over the peoples of the non-Western world. This issue provides a case study of the opposition that resulted from imperialism in China: the Boxer rebellion (1898–1900).

Western domination of Asia and Africa took different forms. The establishment of colonialism, which brought direct Western rule to much of Asia and Africa, was the most prevalent. In China, however, geographic size and a large population made this impossible. European nations established "spheres of influence," recognized zones of China that were controlled and exploited by various Western nations. In these areas, China's rule was in name only.

Accompanying those coming to Asia for economic gains were missionaries who came to gain converts for evangelical Christianity. In China, with so many souls to save, this missionary zeal was a powerful force, and to many Chinese, a particularly odious one.

What made this domination of China possible was the weakened nature of the Chinese government. The Manchu dynasty and its Empress Dowager Tsu

Hsi appeared to be powerless to stop this Western tidal wave sweeping over the country. When the Chinese did fight back, they were soundly defeated.

During the late 1830s the Chinese government made an attempt control the Western commerce within its borders, especially the opium traded by the British. The latter went to war to guarantee their right to sell the drug in China and won. As a result, the Chinese were forced to grant trade concessions, and a pattern of subservience was established. Any Western nation interested in trade with China would now demand the same deal the British received. In 1857 Britain and France went to war to force China to grant further diplomatic and commercial concessions, and once again the Chinese government was made to accede to their demands.

By the turn of the century, a seemingly intolerable situation became worse, made so by more Western nations becoming involved in Chinese affairs, their increasing demands for further concessions from the Chinese, and the large number of Christian missionaries who had entered China since 1860. These conditions were exacerbated by the Sino-Japanese War (1894–1895), which China lost. The war resulted in the signing of another humiliating treaty. The Chinese government not only seemed powerless to stop Western encroachment; it could not stop the encroachment of one of its Asian neighbors. If China's government was powerless, it was reasoned, perhaps some of China's citizens would have to fight to win back control of their country and bring an end to Western imperialism within its borders. The Boxers were a product of such conditions and concerns.

The Boxer rebellion had its roots in the economically depressed Shandong province, made so by a devastating drought that not only caused massive starvation but brought its people to a psychological breaking point. Many young people turned to secret societies to vent their anger and disillusionment. Eventually they coalesced into a group known as the "Fists of Righteous Harmony." Because its members practiced martial arts, the term *Boxer* was applied to the movement by Westerners. It is a misnomer, which has endured to this day.

The movement began with sporadic attacks in the countryside, aimed primarily at Western missionaries and Chinese converts to Christianity. As the movement grew and its influence spread to some of China's urban centers, many wondered what Tsu Hsi would do. She was under intense pressure from Western officials to suppress the insurrection. But she also recognized in the Boxers a useful tool in fighting against Western influences and restoring Manchu hegemony in China. After a period of fence-straddling, she decided to openly support the Boxer cause. Thus, when the rebellion was suppressed by Western forces, she had to bear responsibility for their actions.

What motivated the Boxers to act as they did seems a simple enough question to answer—they were fighting to rid their country of the "foreign devils" who were causing it irreparable damage. However, some recent scholarship on the subject points to the severe drought and its psychological impact on Chinese society as an overriding factor. In the following selections, Paul A. Cohen stresses the latter, while Henrietta Harrison emphasizes the former.

Paul A. Cohen

 **YES**

Drought and the Foreign Presence

Drought, Anxiety, and the Spread of the Boxer Movement

Prayer, ... even when offered up by the most powerful people in the realm, does not always work. And, as a drought continues and people become more and more desperate, restlessness, anxiety, and ultimately panic easily set in. To imagine how profound the panic can be among impoverished farmers and poor city folk living in a society with little in the way of a "safety net," it is illuminating to look at the reactions of the newly unemployed in California in the early stages of the recession that began in the latter half of 1990. "The hardest thing," observed the part owner of a small marketing company in Huntington Beach that had recently gone out of business, "is to see how panicked people are.... Right now, I don't have a dime. I'm worried about buying things like sugar. I'm that close to losing my home. Now is when the nerve systems are really going." A young film editor from Hollywood, noting the "prevailing air of uncertainty," expressed a lack of confidence "about the future."

Uncertainty about the future governs virtually all phases of human experience. But it does not always produce anxiety. For anxiety to result, the uncertainty must bear on an aspect of life that is of vital importance: a child's safety, one's performance in a play or a sporting event, the fate of a loved one engaged in combat, the time frame of one's own mortality, the security and dependability of one's livelihood. It was the last-named area of uncertainty that was shared by Californians in 1990 and Chinese farmers in North China almost a century earlier. Different societies, however, are differentially susceptible to the effects of natural or social disasters, and in the case of the drought of 1899–1900 in China (or that of 1899 in western India), because of the absence of a well-functioning crisis support system, it was much more a matter of life and death.

A wide range of sources, including gazetteers, diaries, official memorials, oral history accounts, and the reports of foreigners, indicate a direct link between the spread and intensification of the Boxer movement, beginning in late 1899, and growing popular nervousness, anxiety, unemployment, and hunger occasioned by drought. As early as October 1899, Luella Miner [American Board of Commissioners for Foreign Missions] (ABCFM) identified drought as one cause of growing Boxer-related unrest in northwestern Shandong. In the Beijing area, where for many months very little rain had fallen and the wheat seedlings had completely withered, popular feeling was described as unsettled and volatile, owing to drought-induced hunger, and from late April 1900 contagious diseases began to break out with increasing frequency and seriousness. In other parts of Zhili it was much the same. American legation secretary W. E. Bainbridge, noting that during the preceding year "there had been insufficient rain" and that "the entire province was on the verge of famine," concluded that conditions were "peculiarly favorable to its [the Boxer uprising's] friendly reception.... As Spring advanced and early Summer approached with no rains to aid the crops, the excitement ... reached a fever heat." From Zhuozhou, just southwest of Beijing, apprehensions were expressed in early June that, if it did not rain soon, it would become increasingly difficult to control the thousands of Boxers who had gathered in the area. A gentry manager of a *baojia* [local level mutual security system] bureau just west of Tianjin reported that in the spring of 1900 young farmers idled by the drought often took up boxing because they had nothing else to do with their time. The relationship among drought, idleness, and augmented Boxer activity found blunt corroboration in the testimony of a former Boxer from the Tianjin area: "*Gengzi* [1900] was a drought year and there was nothing to do, so we began to practice Yihe Boxing."...

Drought conditions in large areas of Shanxi had by summer 1900 become, if anything, even worse than in Zhili. In many places there had been no rain at all since winter. Farmers were without work. The prices of wheat and rice had shot up. Hunger was widespread and popular anxiety at a high pitch. A missionary report stated that the "organization of the Boxer societies spread rapidly throughout the province when so many were idle because of the drouth." The gazetteers of Qinyuan, Quwo, Lin, Jie, Linjin, Xiangning, and Yuci counties all connected the first emergence of the Boxers in mid- or late June to the protracted drought in their areas. Moreover, it was alleged that famine victims regularly joined in when the Boxers stirred up trouble.

I do not at all want to suggest that the expansion of the Boxer movement in the spring and summer of 1900 was due to drought alone. Within a given area, the official stance toward the Boxers, pro (as in Shanxi) or con (as in Shandong), played a role of perhaps equivalent weight. Nevertheless, drought—and the range of emotions associated with it—was a factor of crucial importance. It is significant, in this connection, that in a number of instances when rain fell to interrupt the drought and possibly bring it to an end, Boxers (as well as Big Sword Society members) dropped everything and returned to their fields. Esherick observes that when "a substantial penetrating rain" fell in early April along the Zhili-Shandong border, peasants went home to plant their spring crops, "quieting things down considerably." After being defeated by the foreign forces in Tianjin during a torrential downpour on July 4, fleeing Boxers are reported to have said to one another: "It's raining. We can return home and till the soil. What use is it for us to suffer like this?" The following day, accordingly, most of them dispersed.

Oral history accounts from Shandong tell a similar story. In late June 1900, during the drought in the western part of the province, a Big Sword Society leader from Zhili named Han Guniang (Miss Han) was invited to a Big

Sword gathering at the hemp market at Longgu, just west of the Juye county seat. Rumored to be a Red Lantern with extraordinary magical powers—it was said that, in addition to being able to withstand swords and spears, "when she mounted a bench it turned into a horse, when she straddled a piece of rope it turned into a dragon, and when she sat on a mat it turned into a cloud on which she could fly"—Han Guniang took charge of food distribution. Within a short time, upwards of a thousand people joined her Big Swords. The grain she handed out had been seized from the supplies of rich families. "After two or threedays,"one account continues, "therewas abig downpour.The next day there were no Big Swords anywhere in sight. They were all gone. The reason these people had come in the first place was to get something to eat. As soon as it rained, they all went back to tend their crops."

Lin Dunkui, who has made a special study of the role of natural disasters in the history of the Boxers, concludes that "from the time of the first outbreak of the Big Sword Society right up to the high tide of the Boxer movement, a sizable number of peasants were prompted to take part in these movements mainly by the weather."...

The Boxer Construction of the Drought

What is fascinating is the degree to which contemporary Chinese—non-Boxers as well as Boxers—also viewed everything that happened in the world, including whether it rained or not, as being in the control of Heaven or "the gods." Indeed, although the Chinese construction of reality differed greatly in specifics from that of the missionaries, in a number of broad respects it formed almost a mirror image of the missionaries' construction. Where the missionaries saw themselves as representatives of the Lord, sometimes describing themselves as "God's soldiers" and often believing quite literally that they had been called by Jesus Christ to go to China to labor for that country's salvation, in jingles repeated and notices circulated throughout North China in 1900 the Boxers were often portrayed, in comparably salvific (as well as martial) terms, as "spirit soldiers"(*shenbing*) sent down from Heaven to carry out a divine mission or, which amounted to the same thing, as mortals whose bodies had been possessed by spirits (thereby rendering them divine) for the identical purpose.

Again, where the missionaries constructed the Boxer movement as a satanic force, whose capacity for evil knew no bounds, the Boxers (and, one presumes, millions of Chinese who were not active participants in the movement) saw the missionaries, and by extension all other foreigners (as well, of course, as Chinese Christians and other Chinese who in one way or another had been tainted by foreign contact), as the root source of evil in their world, the immediate reason for the anger of the gods. The explanation of the drought found in Boxer notices was embedded in a full-blown religious structuring of reality; the notices also provided participants in the movement with a clear program of action designed to mollify the gods and restore the cosmic balance. Such notices began to be widely circulated at least as early as the beginning of 1900. (It is doubtful that one would encounter drought-related notices much before this date, as it was probably not until the late months of 1899 that people in North China began to experience the protracted dry weather as a "drought.") In February of this year the Tianjin agent of the American Bible Society reported the following text to have been "posted everywhere" in North China: "On account of the Protestant and Catholic religions the Buddhist gods are oppressed, and our sages thrust into the background. The Law of Buddha is no longer respected, and the Five Relationships are disregarded. The anger of Heaven and Earth has been aroused and the timely rain has consequently been withheld from us. But Heaven is now sending down eight millions of spiritual soldiers to extirpate these foreign religions, and when this has been done there will be a timely rain."...

Boxer Motives: Anti-Imperialism, Antiforeignism, or Anxiety Over Drought?

The crisis remedy proposed by the Boxers in 1900 reveals a close kinship to that described by [Norman] Cohn for the millenarian movement of 1420. In one placard after another, the Chinese people are enjoined to kill off all for-eigners and native Chinese contaminated by foreigners or foreign influence. Only after this process of physical elimination of every trace of the foreign from China has been completed will the gods be appeased and permit the rains once again to fall.

What is peculiar here and needs somehow to be accounted for is why at this particular moment in Chinese history there was such an extreme response to the foreign presence. Chinese had often shown a tendency, during times of military or cultural threat, to lapse into a form of racial thinking that catego-rized outsiders as fundamentally different and called for their expulsion, and this tendency had been greatly magnified in the nineteenth century with the appearance of "physically discontinuous" Westerners, who also happened to be carriers of a symbolic universe that diverged radically from the Chinese and, directly and indirectly, challenged the validity of the Chinese cultural world. From the early 1800s, people who had had contacts of any sort with Westerners were regularly referred to as "Chinese traitors" (Hanjian). More specifically, there had been efforts prior to the Boxer era to link natural disas-ters (as well as the failure of Chinese prayers to relieve them) with the pres-ence of Christians. And of course there had been no end of anti-Christian and antiforeign incidents in China in the decades leading up to 1900. Never before, however, had there been a movement like the Boxers, uncompromis-ingly dedicated to the stamping out of foreign influence and backed, all the evidence indicates, by the broadest popular support. How do we explain this?

The reasons are without doubt very complex. Chinese historians, insist-ing upon the "anti-imperialist and patriotic" (fandi aiguo) character of the Boxer movement, tend to assign primary responsibility to the intensification of foreign imperialism in the last years of the nineteenth century. My own view is that the vocabulary of anti-imperialism is so deeply colored by twenti-eth-century Chinese political concerns and agendas that it gets in the way of the search for a more accurate, credible reading of the Boxer experience. This is not to deny that imperialism was a fact of life in China at the turn of the century or that it formed an important part of the setting within which the Boxer movement unfolded. It was only one causal agency among several, however, and its gravity relative to other causal forces varied considerably from place to place and over time. Furthermore, action taken against the more tangible reflections of imperialism—missionaries and Chinese Christians, railways, telegraphs, foreign armies, and the rest—could, when it occurred, derive from a range of possible motives; it need not have been inspired by either "patriotism" or "anti-imperialism." To superimpose this vocabulary on the Boxer movement, therefore, is to risk radical oversimplification of the complicated and diverse motives impelling the Boxers to behave as they did.

...We have hundreds of samples of Boxer writing—handbills, wall notices, charms, slogans, jingles, and the like. And even though most if not all of these may be assumed to have been composed by Boxer leaders or elite Chinese sympathetic to the Boxer cause rather than by rank-and-file participants in the movement, there is, as argued earlier, little doubt that they incorporate values and beliefs widely shared among the Boxers in general, not to mention millions of Chinese who witnessed and often supported, but were not directly engaged in, the activities of the Boxer movement. Still, as crucially important as these materials are in establishing the mindset of the Boxers, they fall well short of supplying the kind of intimate tracking of experience that we get, say, from the memoir literature of participants in the Cultural Revolution or the heresy trial testimony of the sixteenth-century Italian miller Menocchio or the letters, journals, and even poems composed by British soldiers in the trenches in World War I. In fact, it was not until after 1949 that elderly survivors of the Boxer uprising, mainly in western Shandong and Tianjin and other parts of Hebei (Zhili) province, were finally given a chance to describe more or less in their own words their experiences at the turn of the century. As useful as these oral history materials can sometimes be, however, their value is circumscribed by the advanced age of the respondents, the remoteness in time of the events under discussion, the political and ideological constraints built into the environment within which the interviewing was conducted, the specific questions the interviewers posed, and the editorial process by which the resulting responses were structured.

Consequently, in attempting to get at the range of motives that impelled the Boxers to attack foreigners, foreign-made objects, and foreign-influenced Chinese, we are regularly faced with the necessity of inferring these motives from Boxer actions, of reading back, as it were, from behavior to intent. This is one of the more dangerous kinds of business in which historians must unfortunately all too often engage, as it presents us with an open invitation to discern in the experience of the past the values, thought patterns, and psychological orientations that make the greatest sense to us in our own day.

Although on a macrohistorical level we hear much of the intensification of foreign imperialism that took place in China in the years following the Sino-Japanese War of 1894, it is arguable that, unlike drought, a conspicuously growing foreign presence was not, in 1899–1900, the common experience of the vast majority of Chinese inhabiting the North China plain. Whether we train our sights on expanded communities of native Christians or the growth in strength of the Catholic and Protestant missionary bodies or the construction of railways and telegraphs or the intrusion of foreign armies, the experience of direct confrontation with the foreign or foreign-influenced remained, for those living away from large urban centers, a sporadic and highly localized one in these years. Despite a substantial increase in the numbers of Protestant and Catholic converts in China as a whole in the 1890s—from approximately 37,000 Protestants in 1889 to 85,000 in 1900, and from about 500,000 to over 700,000 Catholics between 1890 and 1900—there were still, in 1899–1900, large stretches of North China that had Christian communities of negligible size or none at all. Similarly, in the case of both the Catholic and Protestant missionary efforts in the empire, although impressive growth occurred in the last decade of the century, this growth was far more in evidence in certain areas—the greatly expanded Catholic presence in southern Shandong, for example—than in others. Again, as of 1899–1900, the only railway lines that had been completed in North China were the Beijing-Baoding line, the Beijing-Tianjin line, and the line extending northeastward from Tianjin, through Tangshan, into Manchuria. And, leaving out the military activities of the Russians in Manchuria, foreign troop movements in the Boxer summer were largely confined to Tianjin and Beijing, their immediately surrounding areas, and the corridor connecting these two cities (although in the months following the lifting of the siege of the legations, ... punitive expeditions were carried out in other parts of Zhili and in eastern Shanxi).

In other words, despite an overall expansion in the opportunities for direct contact with foreigners, foreign-influenced Chinese, and foreign technology in the last years of the century, these opportunities were not evenly distributed throughout North China. Furthermore, there is the curious circumstance—curious, at least, if one interprets the behavior of the Boxers as having been guided in significant measure by anti-imperialist impulses—that the areas where the impact of imperialism was greatest often did not coincide with those areas in which the Boxers were most active. This was especially true in Shandong, where the arenas of greatest foreign economic activity—the eastern and southern coasts—were conspicuously free of Boxer involvement and where approximately half of the missionized areas also were left untouched by the Boxers. Mark Elvin, who includes southern Zhili as well as Shandong within his purview, is so struck by the weakness of the link between "Boxerism and the religious and foreign irritant usually supposed to have caused it" that he questions whether it can serve as "a convincing sufficient explanation" of the movement's origins.

I am not particularly concerned here with the origins of the Boxer movement. I do, however, believe that there is room for a fresh understanding of the range of motives that lay behind what was perhaps the Boxers' most distinctive and defining characteristic: their antiforeignism. The reality of Boxer antiforeignism—and the antiforeignism of many millions of Boxer supporters and sympathizers—is not at issue. What is at issue is the underlying meaning of this antiforeignism. Was it a reflection of simple hatred of foreigners owing to their foreignness? Or did it result from anger over specific foreign actions? Or did it spring from fear and anxiety and the need for a credible explanation for the problems—above all, drought—occasioning this fear and anxiety?

My own view is that antiforeignism, in the sense of fear and hatred of outsiders, was there all along in China in latent form, but that it needed some disturbance in the external environment, a rearrangement of the overall balance of forces within a community or a geographical area, to become activated. Chinese antiforeignism thus functioned in much the same way as fear of witchcraft in late seventeenth-century Salem or anti-Semitism in 1930s Germany. In each of these instances outsiders—Westerners in China, people accused of being witches in Salem, Jews in Germany—lived more or less uneventfully within their respective communities when times were "normal." But when something happened to create an "abnormal" situation—economic insecurity in Germany, apprehension concerning the enormous economic and social forces transforming New England in the late 1600s, anxiety over drought in turn-of-the-century North China—and people sought in desperation to address their grievances and allay their insecurities, outsiders became especially vulnerable.

The specific circumstances favoring outbreaks of antiforeignism in North China in 1899–1900 varied from place to place. In Shandong, escalating Boxer anti-Christian activity in late 1899 resulted (under foreign pressure) in the replacement as governor of Yuxian, who had followed a policy of leniency toward the Boxers, with Yuan Shikai, who, after the killing of the British missionary S. M. Brooks on December 31, pursued an increasingly strong policy of suppression. In Zhili province, especially in the Beijing and Tianjin areas and the corridor connecting the two, there was a relatively high level of exposure to the full range of foreign influences and, from the winter of 1899–1900, to rapidly growing numbers of Boxers. In Shanxi, where there were no significant manifestations of foreign influence apart from the missionaries and native Christians, there was a governor (Yuxian having been transferred there in March) who was deeply antiforeign and pro-Boxer.

Although the precise mix of factors was thus variable, the drought was shared in common throughout the North China plain. It was this factor, more than any other, in my judgment, that accounted for the explosive growth both of the Boxer movement and of popular support for it in the spring and summer months of 1900. Missionary reports and oral history accounts occasionally used the term "famine" to describe conditions in North China at the time. This was, for the most part, a loose usage; severe famine did not appear until the early months of 1901, mainly in Shanxi and Shaanxi. The evidence is overwhelming, on the other hand, that *fear* of famine, with all its attendant bewilderment and terror, was extremely widespread. As has often been the case in other agricultural societies, moreover, the uncertainty, anxiety, and increasingly serious food deprivation accompanying the Chinese drought—the *delírio de fome* or "madness of hunger," in the arresting formulation of Nancy Scheper-Hughes—seem to have inclined people to be receptive to extreme explanations and to act in extreme ways. The year 1900 was not a normal one in China. The menace of inopportune death was everywhere. And, as can be seen in the periodic eruptions of mass hysteria and the apparent readiness of many members of society to give credence to the most spectacular religious and magical claims of the Boxers, there was a strong disposition on the part of the population to depart from normal patterns of behavior.

Henrietta Harrison

Justice on Behalf of Heaven

On the fifth day of the seventh month of the twenty-sixth year of the Guangxu Emperor, Liu Dapeng, a tutor and diarist, stood at the door of his family home in the village of Chiqiao in Shanxi province and watched an army of a thousand Boxers pass through. Liu was a brave man; some forty years later during the Second World War he was to stand on the roof of that same house watching the bombs falling from Japanese planes on his neighbours' houses. When the Boxers passed through, most of the other villagers had fled to the hills or were hiding behind the locked doors of their houses in fear that the Boxer forces would loot and extort money and goods. Liu himself had taken leave from his job as a private tutor in a grand house some twenty or thirty miles away and come home to look after his mother, wife and children because of the crisis. At the head of the Boxers came a young man known as Third Prince, who Liu guessed was less than twenty years old. Two banners before him proclaimed 'Bring justice on behalf of Heaven!' and 'Support the Qing! Destroy the foreign!' Then came rank after rank of men marching down the narrow street that ran through the centre of the village. There were men of all ages, but Liu reckoned that at least two-thirds were not yet adults. All of them wore red belts and red cloths tied around their heads. They marched in an orderly fashion, divided into companies and brigades, and did not, after all, do any damage in the village.

Liu's attitude to the Boxers was divided. On the one hand he approved of their loyalty to the Qing dynasty and their opposition to the expansion of foreign power in China. He was particularly supportive of their campaign against the local Catholics, whom he perceived as having sold out to the foreigners. On the other hand, he was dubious about the movement's religious elements and particularly concerned about the threat they posed to law and order. While he approved of the provincial governor's efforts to force Catholics to renounce their religion, he found it hard to condone the murder of travellers suspected of poisoning wells, let alone pitched battles between Catholic villages and Boxer forces. Liu's feelings, in this respect, were typical of the time and were shared across a wide social spectrum. Indeed, it was just such conflicting attitudes at court that allowed the Boxer movement to spread on such a wide scale. Although events in the northern coastal province of Shandong where the Boxer movement originated are better known, some of the worst violence in the uprising took place in the adjoining Shanxi province, witnessed by Liu.

The Boxers' opposition in the foreign powers and especially to Christianity struck a chord with many Chinese and drew widespread support. China's defeat by Japan in the war over Korea in 1894 was a turning point in perceptions of the foreign threat. The country's perception of itself as the Middle Kingdom, a central realm of civilisation surrounded by tributary states, and by savages and barbarians beyond that, had been affirmed by Korea, which had conducted an elaborate tributary relationship with China. The loss of Korea, moreover, brought with it humiliating defeat by the Japanese, hitherto often dismissively referred to as 'dwarf pirates'. In the Treaty of Shimonoseki, which concluded the war, China not only agreed to Korean independence, but ceded Taiwan to Japan and gave the Japanese the same treaty rights as those of Westerners. These were the events that roused Sun Yat-sen, later China's first President, to plan his first revolutionary uprising. But it was not only members of China's tiny reformist elite who were concerned at this outcome. The news was carried across the country and was talked about by the farmers in Chiqiao village, all of whom, Liu reported, opposed the terms of the treaty. Li Hongzhang, who had been the chief negotiator on the Chinese side, became extremely unpopular, with rumours circulating in the countryside that he had married his son to the daughter of the Japanese emperor, and satirical rhymes attacking him for selling his country. It is important to remember that, though often condemned as ignorant, superstitious and xenophobic, the Boxers were acting in an environment where China's changing international situation was widely known and resented.

Popular opposition to foreign power was confirmed in Shanxi when news came through in the summer of 1900 that the government had declared war on the foreign powers. Liu heard that governors had been ordered to kill collaborators, that is to say Christians, and to arrest any foreigners and execute them if they planned to make trouble or plotted with the Christians. Shanxi's governor, Yu Xian, was said to be delighted at the news and immediately sent soldiers to round up those foreigners residing in the province and bring them to the provincial capital. Less than a month later some forty unfortunate foreigners were formally executed outside the provincial government building. The Chinese leaders of the Catholic community were ordered to renounce their faith and one who refused was executed. It was thus clear that the government declaration of war on the foreign powers included not only foreign civilians but also Catholic villagers. When the Boxers marched through the countryside carrying banners that said 'Restore the Qing! Destroy the foreign!' their claims that they were loyal forces obeying the orders of the dynasty were hard to deny.

Catholics were seen as potential collaborators in a war with the foreign powers because Christianity had been introduced into China by foreign missionaries. Indeed the right for Christian missionaries to reside in the interior had repeatedly been the object of treaty negotiations between the Qing dynasty and the foreign powers. In Shanxi, the Protestant missionaries had only a handful of converts, but Catholicism was firmly rooted in many rural areas and had been widespread since the eighteenth century. The heart of the problem lay in the contradictions between Christianity and the belief system that underlay the structures of the state. In the villages—where the Boxers operated—the problems of integrating Christianity in the imperial state were focused around the issue of temple festivals and opera performances. Temple festivals were funded by contributions from all members of the local community. In addition to a market they included sacrifices to the deity in whose honour the festival was held and often theatrical performances on a stage facing the temple. Wealthy villages would hire a travelling opera company who would perform for three to five days. Poorer villages might only have a puppet theatre for a single day. The festival performances were intended for the deity but were also a source of entertainment. Friends and relations came from miles around to see the operas, meet and chat, while the market drew large crowds. The funds raised to pay for the opera, meanwhile, also provided a working budget for such village level local government as existed. They might, for example, be used to pay for the dredging of dikes for a communal irrigation system or a law suit against a neighbouring village. Christians, however, refused to pay the levies on the grounds that they would be used to support idolatrous practices.

By refusing to contribute to the festivals, Shanxi Catholics were excluding themselves from the local community. At the same time locals were aware that allowing Christians to opt out of paying taxes made Christianity, which was generally seen as a heterodox religion, a financially advantageous option for the poor, who often turned out to enjoy the festivities even if they had not helped to pay for them. As a result, the 1890s saw an increasing number of legal cases being brought by village leaders against recalcitrant Catholics. The Catholics were able to fight these suits because the foreign consuls, backed by the threat of arms, negotiated with the central government for the right of Christians not to pay for religious practices in which they did not believe. Both the village leaders and the magistrates, however, saw the cases as resting on matters of loyalty and obedience to the state rather than on religious toleration. An extract (translated by Roger Thompson) from one magistrate's interrogation of a Catholic named Yang accused of refusing to pay village levies gives a sense of the way in which Christians were seen as alienating themselves from the state:

Magistrate: You are a person of what country?

Yang: I am a person of the Qing.

Magistrate: If you are a person of the Qing dynasty then why are you following the foreign devils and their seditious religion? You didn't pay your opera money when requested by the village and you were beaten. But how can you dare to bring a suit? Don't you know why Zuo Zongtang went to Beijing? In order to kill—to exterminate—the foreign devils. You certainly ought to pay the opera subscription. If you don't you won't be allowed to live in the land of the Qing. You'll have to leave for a foreign country.

Liu Dapeng, watching the Boxers pass his front door on their way to join an attack on Catholic villages, shared this view. In his opinion:

When the foreign barbarians preach their religion, they say they are urging men to do good, but in fact they are disrupting our government, creating turmoil in our system, destroying our customs, and deceiving our people; that is to say that they want to turn the people of China into barbarians.

The issue of Catholic refusal to participate in the religious practices of the local community became particularly powerful and problematic in the summer of 1900 because of the fear of drought. Drought was a constant threat to the North China Plain, where farmers rely on rain falling at precisely the right times of year. In Shanxi many remembered with fear the great famine of the 1870s when in Chiqiao one in ten of the population died, and in parts of the south of the province the death toll was worse still. Drought like this was widely seen as divine punishment for immorality and people reacted with ritual and prayer. In Chiqiao men went with bare heads and bare feet to a spring high up in the mountains to pray for rain. The villages through which they passed set up altars in front of their homes laid out with candles, cakes, branches of willow and dragons' heads carved from gourds. As the procession passed through the village the men would repeat the words 'Amitabha Buddha' and the onlookers knelt and used the willow branches to scatter water on them. For three days the men stayed at the temple beside the spring, eating only thin gruel and praying constantly for rain. Such rituals were commonplace throughout northern China in times of drought and were believed to require the sincere participation of the whole community in order to be effective. Catholic refusal to participate in the rituals needed to save the local community from famine accentuated an already problematic relationship.

The conflict between Catholics and villagers meant that the Boxers could be seen as representing and embodying the community even as they attacked and burned their neighbours' homes. With their banners 'Bring justice on behalf of Heaven!' and 'Support the Qing! Destroy the foreign!', they claimed to uphold the moral and social order where the dynasty, because of foreign pressure, was unable to do so. As Liu Dapeng put it, 'the court could not kill the Christians and the officials dared not kill them, so the Boxers killed them.'

However, the people of Chiqiao village, which had no Catholic families at all, nevertheless fled in panic when they heard the Boxers were approaching the village. Doubts lingered about the beliefs and rituals of the Boxers, and about their violence. People expected that boxing, or martial arts, techniques would be learned from a teacher over many years, but these were mostly young boys with hardly any training. Liu Dapeng went to see them practising at a large temple near Chiqiao. They set up sticks of incense and kowtowed to them. Then they stood facing southeast, put their hands in a certain position and recited an invocation to several deities. Immediately they fell on the floor, as if asleep. Then, as the crowds of spectators gathered, their hands and feet began to move and slowly they stood up and began a kind of dance sometimes with weapons, all the time keeping their eyes closed. Although their expressions were terrifying, they somehow looked as if they were drunk. After keeping up these strange movements for a while they fell to the ground again, and eventually awoke. Later they said that they did not remember what they had done while they were in the trance. When one of the onlookers asked what would happen if they had to face guns, they replied that Heaven was angry and had sent them as soldiers to warn the people. This was the 'spirit possession' that was central to the Boxer movement. Spirit possession by semi-professional mediums is a feature of Chinese folk-religious practice, but mass spirit possession of this sort was, as Liu commented, very strange indeed.

But the strangeness of Boxer claims was not limited to spirit possession. As at other times when drought threatened, bizarre rumours were rife. In Shanxi it was said that the wives of the foreign missionaries stood naked on the roofs of their houses fanning back the winds that would have brought rain. Other rumours concerned the Catholics, who were said to be poisoning village water supplies. Western power, and particularly science, was considered to border on black magic in the eyes of much of the population. The same black magic was also attributed to the Chinese Catholics. Rumours spread through Shanxi that Catholics had painted blood on doorways, and where they had done this the entire family would go mad within seven days. The Boxers claimed to have the power to oppose this Catholic magic and Liu saw people washing the blood off their doors with urine as the Boxers instructed. Strange stories told of full-scale battles between the Catholic and the Boxer magic. In a large town near Chiqiao there was a panic one night that the Catholics had come and many of the townspeople went to guard the city walls. When they were there they heard a huge noise like tens of thousands of people attacking and then suddenly a green hand as big as a cartwheel appeared in the air. The local Boxer leader pointed at it and there was a crash of thunder and rain began to fall. He explained that the green hand had been a form of Catholic magic and he had destroyed it. Outside the city wall the villagers saw the lights, heard strange noises and fled from their homes in panic to hide in the fields. It is clear that such stories were widely believed at the time, and yet there was always an underlying distrust. The next morning, when the villagers cautiously emerged from their hiding places, they realised that there had been no Catholic army and no battle. The fear of drought inevitably gave rise to rumours, but many, including Liu, were not wholly convinced by the magical claims of the Boxers.

Distrust of the Boxers' spiritual powers was increased by a growing reali-sation of the threat they posed to law and order. This began with the murder of people accused of poisoning wells. Most of these were not even Catholics, but were accused of being in their pay. Magistrates, unsure of how to respond to the movement, failed to investigate the crimes and Boxer confidence grew. Large groups of men assembled and began to fight their Catholic neighbours. The army of men that Liu saw marching through his village had gone out to a nearby village which had a sizable Catholic population. The Catholics had hired men from another province to protect them and had withdrawn to their solidly-built stone church. The Boxers besieged the church and the battle lasted for six days. More than thirty of the mercenaries were killed before the church fell. A few of the Catholics survived the seige and escaped, but the rest were massacred and the church burned.

Magistrates' failure to act in the face of such disorder was due to the weakness and indecision of the central government, which vacillated between support for the Boxers and fear of the foreign powers. For more than fifty years the foreign threat had been at the centre of factional divisions within the court. At the heart of this debate was the question of whether a modern, well-equipped army or popular feeling should be more important in withstanding the foreign powers. The leaders of the bureaucracy were examined and trained in Confucian thought and for many of them it was an article of faith that victory in battle would bethe result of thepeople'ssupport.Onthe othersidestood afaction, many of whom were drawn from the Manchu ruling ethnic group, who had accepted the strength of the European powers and believed that it was necessary to approach them cautiously until such time as China had built up the technical expertise to face them. The radical Confucians saw the growth of the Boxer movement as a sign that the people were at last aroused to fight the foreigners. Putting their trust in this, they were prepared to overlook the folk-religious aspects of the movement, which were clearly at odds with Confucian rationalism, and also the inevitable threat to law and order that would arise if the people were allowed to bear arms outside state control. With the support of the ruling Empress Dowager the court declared war on the foreign powers. However, the more cautious modernisers, many of whom had power bases in the southern provinces, believed that China was still unable to defeat the foreign powers; the governors general of the southern provinces refused to enter the war. Instead they drew up private agreements with the foreign powers, giving protection to foreigners and Christians in return for a promise that the foreigners would not invade. Although the Confucian radicals had won at court the central government was not strong enough to control the regions. The result was indecision and a series of conflicting orders. The Qing army never really engaged with the foreign troops, but country magistrates dared not arrest the Boxers, and thus appeared to be encouraging the movement to spread.

The debate over whether the Boxers should be seen as loyal and patriotic enforcers of the moral order or superstitious and xenophobic peasants has remained at the heart of Chinese perceptions of the uprising. In the early years of the twentieth century the modernisers, who had added a desire for the adoption of Western culture to their Qing predecessors' perception of the need for Western technology, continued to criticise the movement. Indeed, for this group in the 1910s and 20s, the failure of the uprising to solve China's problems by driving out the foreigners was symbolic of the failure of China's encounters with the West. The Boxers embodied what the modernisers saw as the very national characteristics that had led to China's international weakness. They were depicted as ignorant and conservative, a group whose folly and credulous belief that they could be saved from bullets by reciting magic rhymes had ultimately led to the imposition of the huge Boxer Indemnity that sunk the nation in the burden of debt.

However, from the 1920s onwards, a new generation of historians and politicians began to rewrite history in terms of China's resistance to Western imperialism, rather than of its development towards modernity. The events of

1900 came to be known, as they are in China today, not as the Boxer Uprising but as the invasion of the Eight Allied Armies, thus shifting the focus from the Boxers themselves to the foreign response. In addition, the Communists took over the mantle of the radical Confucians in their belief in the centrality of mass popular movements as the foundation of resistance to foreign powers. During the Cultural Revolution in the 1960s the Boxers were depicted as heroic, anti-imperialist fighters while the threat they posed to law and order was reconstructed as rebellious opposition to the forces of feudalism. The mass spirit possession and other elements of folk religion at the centre of the movement were completely ignored. The story of the Boxers was rewritten as one of peasant rebellion against foreign imperialism.

Since the 1980s there has been renewed interest in the Boxers. Chinese social historians are beginning to integrate popular folk religion and mass spirit possession into their interpretations of the movement. However, the ambivalence between interpretations of the Boxers as patriots or a superstitious and disorderly rabble has continued to form the framework of the argument. The ambivalence of contemporaries who observed the Boxers and which in many ways created the movement as a national phenomenon has continued to inform Chinese interpretations of the uprising.

POSTSCRIPT

Was China's Boxer Rebellion Caused by Environmental Factors?

Many problems arise when current interpretations of the Boxer uprising as a historical movement are attempted. One concerns motivation, the subject covered in this issue. Another concerns how the Boxers themselves should be viewed. Were they, as Harrison expresses it, "loyal and patriotic enforcers of the moral order or superstitious and xenophobic peasants"? Finally, as Cohen points out, an important question is, How do we separate Boxer myth from Boxer reality? All of these questions form the basis of all historical inquiry and answers to them must be sought.

Complicating matters is China's status today as a communist nation, adhering to a strict Marxist interpretation of history. There is strong pressure in such a society to fit historical events into this predetermined historical theory, and sometimes the truth can be lost within that process. But even as China's needs change, so does its history. According to Harrison, during the cultural revolution of the 1960s, "The story of the Boxers was rewritten as one of peasant rebellion against foreign imperialism," different from previous Chinese interpretations of the movement. See Hu Sheng's *From the Opium War to the May Fourth Movement*, 2 vols. (Foreign Language Press, 1991) for an analysis of the major events in Chinese history from 1840 to 1920 from a Marxist perspective.

Joseph W. Eshrick's *The Origins of the Boxer Uprising* (University of California Press, 1987) was an important modern work that encouraged others to pursue the Boxers-as-history movement. Cohen's *History in Three Keys: The Boxers as Event, Experience, and Myth* (Columbia University Press, 1997) is an interesting companion, and when combined with Sheng's work mentioned earlier, provides the reader with three different points of view on the Boxer uprising.

The centenary anniversary of the Boxer uprising has produced a number of interesting articles on the subject. R. G. Tiedemann's "Baptism of Fire: China's Christians and the Boxer Uprising of 1900," *International Bulletin of Missionary Research* (January 2000) views the rebellion as a "tragic anomaly" in China's relationship with Christian missionaries. Robert Bickers, in "Chinese Burns Britain in China, 1842–1900," *History Today* (August 2000), places the blame for the Boxer rebellion squarely on the shoulders of British and European imperialism.

Finally, for a more popularly written account of the Boxer uprising, see Diane Preston, *The Boxer Rebellion: The Dramatic Story of China's War on Foreigners That Shook the World in the Summer of 1900* (Walker & Company, 2000).

German Responsibility for the Outbreak of the War

Despite its title, this lengthy, essay-based Web site finds plenty of blame to go around. Its scope extends beyond the war to include its effect on the post-war decades. Also includes a World War I document archive.

```
http://www.colby.edu/personal/r/rmscheck/GermanyC1.html
```

The Treaty of Versailles

This site contains extensive background on the Treaty of Versailles, beginning with the attitude toward Germany of the "Big Three," the actual terms of the teaty, Germany's reaction to the treaty, the consequences of Versailles, and other peace settlements with Austria, Hungary, Bulgaria, and Turkey. Exam questions on the peace settlement are included.

```
http://www.historylearningsite.co.uk/
treaty_of_versailles.htm
```

Marxist Writers: Alexandra Kollontai (1872–1952)

Devoted to the early Soviet Union's most powerful women, this site contains a biographical sketch and more than 30 links to her most important writings and actions.

```
http://www.marxists.org/archive/kollonta/
```

Holocaust Learning Center

This Web site, the creation of the Washington-based United States Holocaust Memorial Museum and provides multilinked connections to the subject; useful for both novice and experienced hands.

```
http://www.ushmm.org
```

The American Experience: Douglas MacArthur

PBS site on the life of the man who accepted the Japanese surrender in 1945, governed Japan during the immediate post-war years, conducted the Tokyo war crimes trial, and decided that Emperor Hirohito would not be held responsible for World War II.

```
http://www.pbs.org/wgbh/amex/macarthur/peopleevents/
pandeAMEX97.html
```

Cold War International History Project

Contains a document library of materials related to all aspects of the Cold War, many of them of Soviet Union origin. Organized around 15 different Cold War–related topics.

```
http://cwihp.si.edu/cwihplib.nsf?OpenDatabase&
Start=1&Count=30&Expand=15
```

PART 2

The Early Twentieth Century

T his section covers the first half of the creative, chaotic twentieth century, which was marked by great technological improvements and two disastrous world wars. The events of the twentieth century prove that societies in every century face the same problems. However, as the world becomes more technologically sophisticated, the stakes seem to get higher.

- Were German Militarism and Diplomacy Responsible for World War I?

- Was the Treaty of Versailles Responsible for World War II?

- Did the Bolshevik Revolution Improve the Lives of Soviet Women?

- Was German "Eliminationist Antisemitism" Responsible for the Holocaust?

- Should Japanese Emperor Hirohito Have Been Held Responsible for Japan's World War II Actions?

- Was Stalin Responsible for the Cold War?

ISSUE 7

Were German Militarism and Diplomacy Responsible for World War I?

YES: V. R. Berghahn, from *Imperial Germany, 1871–1914: Economy, Society, Culture, and Politics* (Berghahn Books, 1994)

NO: Samuel R. Williamson, Jr., from "The Origins of the War," in Hew Strachan, ed., *The Oxford Illustrated History of the First World War* (Oxford University Press, 1998)

ISSUE SUMMARY

YES: History professor V. R. Berghahn states that, although all of Europe's major powers played a part in the onset of World War I, recent evidence still indicates that Germany's role in the process was the main factor responsible for the conflict.

NO: History professor Samuel R. Williamson, Jr., argues that the factors and conditions that led to the First World War were a shared responsibility and that no one nation can be blamed for its genesis.

One could argue that the First World War was the twentieth century's most cataclysmic event. It was responsible for the destruction of four major empires (Turkish, Russian, Austrian, and German), was tied inexorably to the rise of fascism and communism, and caused more death and carnage than any event up to that time. It also created an age of anxiety and alienation that shook the foundations of the Western artistic, musical, philosophical, and literary worlds. No wonder it has attracted the attention of countless historians, who have scrutinized every aspect in search of lessons that can be derived from it.

The major historical questions to answer are why it occurred and who was responsible for it—a daunting task yet an important one if we are to learn any lessons from the mistakes of the past. Historians have identified four major long-range causes of the war: nationalism, militarism, imperialism, and the alliance system. But these causes only partly answer why in August 1914, after a Serbian nationalist assassinated Archduke Franz Ferdinand of Austria-Hungary, Europe divided into two armed camps—the Allied Governments (England, France, and Russia, and later, Italy) and the Central Powers

(Germany, Austria-Hungary, and the Ottoman Empire)—and engaged in a conflict that would involve most European countries and spread to the rest of the world.

Important as these factors are, they fail to include the human factor in the equation. To what extent were the aims and policies of the major powers, which were formulated by individuals acting on behalf of national states, responsible for the war? Is there enough culpability to go around? Or was one nation and its policymakers responsible for the onset of the Great War? Of course, the Treaty of Versailles, which brought an end to the war, answered the question of responsibility. In the now-famous Article 231, Germany and her allies were held accountable for the war and all concomitant damages since the war was imposed on the Allied and Associated Governments "by the aggression of Germany and her Allies." Little or no historical investigation went into making this decision; it was simply a case of winners dictating terms to losers.

The first to write of the war were the diplomats, politicians, and military leaders who tried to distance themselves from responsibility for what they allowed to happen and offered explanations for their actions suited to their country's needs and interests. Historian Sidney Bradshaw Fay was the first to offer an unbiased interpretation of the war's onset. In a monumental two-volume work, *Before Sarajevo: The Origins of the World War and After Sarajevo: The Ori-gins of the World War* (The Macmillan Company, 1928), he states that liability has to be shared by all involved parties. To find Germany and her allies solely responsible for it, "in view of the evidence now available, is historically unsound" (vol. 2, p. 558).

Unfortunately, the influence of Fay's work was minimized by the effects of the worldwide economic depression and the fast-approaching Second World War. The historiography of the First World War was temporarily put on hold. It was reopened after 1945 with some surprising results.

In 1961 German historian Fritz Fischer's *Germany's Aims in the First World War* (W. W. Norton, 1967) ignited the debate. While believing that no nation involved in the war was blameless, Fischer found primary culpability in the expansionist, militarist policies of the German government. The book sparked a national controversy that later moved into the international arena. Thus, two works published more than 30 years apart established the framework of the debate.

Recent historical scholarship seems to balance both sides of the World War I historical pendulum. V. R. Berghahn, working within the framework of Germany's economy, society, culture, and politics from 1871 to 1914, holds Germany primarily responsible for the war. Samuel R. Williamson, Jr., sees the onset of World War I as a condition of joint responsibility.

V. R. Berghahn

 **YES**

The Crisis of July 1914 and Conclusions

In the afternoon of August 1, 1914, when the German ultimatum to Russia to revoke the Tsarist mobilization order of the previous day had expired, Wilhelm II telephoned [Chief of the General Staff Helmuth von] Moltke, [Reich Chancellor Theobald von] Bethmann Hollweg, [Admiral Alfred von] Tirpitz, and Prussian War Minister Erich von Falkenhayn to come without delay to the Imperial Palace to witness the Kaiser's signing of the German mobilization order that was to activate the Schlieffen Plan and the German invasion of Luxemburg, Belgium, and France. It was a decision that made a world war inevitable.

The meeting took place at 5 p.m. When the monarch had signed the fateful document, he shook Falkenhayn's hand and tears came to both men's eyes. However, the group had barely dispersed when it was unexpectedly recalled. According to the later report of the Prussian War Minister, "a strange telegram had just been received from Ambassador Lichnowsky" in London, announcing that he had been mandated by the British government "to ask whether we would pledge not to enter French territory if England guaranteed France's neutrality in our conflict with Russia." A bitter dispute apparently ensued between Bethmann Hollweg, who wanted to explore this offer, and Moltke, whose only concern by then was not to upset the meticulously prepared timetable for mobilization. The Chief of the General Staff lost the argument for the moment. The Kaiser ordered Foreign Secretary Gottlieb von Jagow to draft a reply to Lichnowsky, while Moltke telephoned the Army Command at Trier ordering the Sixteenth Division to stop its advance into Luxemburg. As Falkenhayn recorded the scene, Moltke was by now "a broken man" because to him the Kaiser's decision was yet another proof that the monarch "continued to hope for peace." Moltke was so distraught that Falkenhayn had to comfort him, while the latter did not believe for one moment "that the telegram [would] change anything about the horrendous drama that began at 5 p.m." Lichnowsky's reply arrived shortly before midnight, detailing the British condition that Belgium's border must remain untouched by the Germans. Knowing that German strategic planning made this impossible, Moltke now pressed Wilhelm II to order the occupation of Luxemburg as a first step to the German invasion of Belgium and France. This time he won; World War I had definitely begun.

After many years of dispute among historians about who was responsible for the outbreak of war in August 1914 in which German scholars either blamed the Triple Entente for what had happened or argued that all powers had simultaneously slithered into the abyss, the ... Fischer controversy [a controversy involving historian Frite Fischer's theory of the origin of World War I] produced a result that is now widely accepted in the international community of experts on the immediate origins of the war—it was the men gathered at the Imperial Palace in Berlin who pushed Europe over the brink. These men during the week prior to August 1 had, together with the "hawks" in Vienna, deliberately exacerbated the crisis, although they were in the best position to de-escalate and defuse it. There is also a broad consensus that during that crucial week major conflicts occurred between the civilian leadership in Berlin around Bethmann Hollweg, who was still looking for diplomatic ways out of the impasse, and the military leadership around Moltke, who now pushed for a violent settling of accounts with the Triple Entente. In the end Bethmann lost, and his defeat opened the door to the issuing of the German mobilization order on August 1.

In pursuing this course, the German decision-makers knew that the earlier Russian mobilization order did not have the same significance as the German one. Thus the Reich Chancellor informed the Prussian War Ministry on July 30, that "although the Russian mobilization has been declared, her mobilization measures cannot be compared with those of the states of Western Europe." He added that St. Petersburg did not "intend to wage war, but has only been forced to take these measures because of Austria" and her mobilization. These insights did not prevent the German leadership from using the Russian moves for their purposes by creating a defensive mood in the German public without which the proposed mobilization of the German armed forces might well have come to grief. The population was in no mood to support an aggressive war. On the contrary, there had been peace demonstrations in various cities when, following the Austrian ultimatum to Serbia on 23 July, suspicions arose that Berlin and Vienna were preparing for a war on the Balkans. The Reich government responded to this threat by calling on several leaders on the right wing of the SPD [Social Democratic Party] executive and confidentially apprising them of Russia's allegedly aggressive intentions. Convinced of the entirely defensive nature of Germany's policy, the leaders of the working-class movement quickly reversed their line: the demonstrations stopped and the socialist press began to write about the Russian danger.

It is against the background of these domestic factors that a remark by Bethmann may be better understood. "I need," the Reich Chancellor is reported to have said to Albert Ballin, the Hamburg shipping magnate, "my declaration of war for reasons of internal politics." What he meant by this is further elucidated by other surviving comments. Thus Admiral von Müller, the Chief of the Naval Cabinet, noted in his diary as early as July 27 that "the tenor of our policy [is] to remain calm to allow Russia to put herself in the wrong, but then not to shrink from war if it [is] inevitable." On the same day, the Reich Chancellor told the Kaiser that "at all events Russia must ruthlessly be put in the wrong." Moltke explained the meaning of this statement to his Austro-Hungarian counterpart, Franz Conrad von Hoetzendorff, on July 30: "War [must] not be declared on Russia, but [we must] wait for Russia to attack." And when a day later this turned out to be the sequence of events,

Müller was full of praise. "The morning papers," he recorded in his diary on August 1, "reprint the speeches made by the Kaiser and the Reich Chancellor to an enthusiastic crowd in front of the Schloss and the Chancellor's palace. Brilliant mood. The government has succeeded very well in making us appear as the attacked."

While there is little doubt about the last days of peace and about who ended them, scholarly debate has continued over the motives of the Kaiser and his advisors. In order to clarify these, we have to move back in time to the beginning of July 1914. Fritz Fischer has argued in his *Griff nach der Welt-macht* and in *War of Illusions* that the Reich government seized the assassination of Archduke Ferdinand and his wife at Sarajevo on June 28 as the opportunity to bring about a major war. He asserted that Bethmann, in unison with the military leadership hoped to achieve by force the breakthrough to world power status which German diplomacy had failed to obtain by peaceful means in previous years. However, today most experts would accept another interpretation that was put forward by Konrad Jarausch and others and captured by a chapter heading in Jarausch's biography of Bethmann: "The Illusion of Limited War." In this interpretation, Berlin was originally motivated by more modest objectives than those inferred by Fischer. Worried by the volatile situation on the Balkans and anxious to stabilize the deteriorating position of the multinational Austro-Hungarian Empire (Germany's only reliable ally, then under the strong centrifugal pressure of Slav independence movements), Berlin pushed for a strategy of local war in order to help the Habsburgs in the southeast. Initially, Vienna was not even sure whether to exploit, in order to stabilize its position in power politics, the assassination crisis and the sympathies that the death of the heir to the throne had generated internationally. Emperor Franz Joseph and his civilian advisors wanted to wait for the outcome of a government investigation to see how far Serbia was behind the Sarajevo murders before deciding on a possible punitive move against Belgrade. Only the Chief of the General Staff Conrad advocated an immediate strike against the Serbs at this point. Uncertain of Berlin's response, Franz Joseph sent Count Alexander von Hoyos to see the German Kaiser, who then issued his notorious "blank check." With it the Reich government gave its unconditional support to whatever action Vienna would decide to take against Belgrade.

What did Wilhelm II and his advisors expect to be the consequences of such an action? Was it merely the pretext for starting a major war? Or did Berlin hope that theconflict between Austria-Hungary and Serbia would remain limited? The trouble with answering this question is that we do not possess a firsthand account of the Kaiser's "blank check" meeting with Hoyos and of the monarch's words and assumptions on that occasion. Jarausch and others have developed the view that Bethmann persuaded Wilhelm II and the German military to adopt a limited war strategy which later turned out to be illusory. They have based their argument to a considerable extent on the diaries of Kurt Riezler, Bethmann's private secretary, who was in close contact with his superior during the crucial July days. As he recorded on July 11, it was the Reich Chancellor's plan to obtain "a quick fait accompli" in the Balkans. Thereafter he proposed to make "friendly overtures toward the Entente Powers" in the hope that in this way "the shock" to the international system could be absorbed. Two days earlier Bethmann had expressed the view that "in case of warlike complications between Austria and Serbia, he and Jagow believed that it would be possible to localize the conflagration." But according to Riezler the Reich Chancellor also realized that "an action against Serbia [could] result in a world war." To this extent, his strategy was a "leap into the dark" which he nevertheless considered it as his "gravest duty" to take in light of the desperate situation of the two Central European monarchies.

A localization of the conflict since the risks of a major war seemed remote—this is how Bethmann Hollweg appears to have approached the post-Sarajevo situation. It was only in subsequent weeks, when Vienna took much longer than anticipated to mobilize against Serbia—and above all when it became clear that the other great powers and Russia in particular would not condone a humiliation of Belgrade—that the Reich Chancellor and his advisors became quite frantic and unsure of their ability to manage the unfolding conflict. In its panic, the German Foreign Ministry proposed all sorts of hopelessly unrealistic moves and otherwise tried to cling to its original design. Thus on 16 July, Bethmann wrote to Count Siegfried von Roedern that "in case of an Austro-Serbian conflict the main question is to isolate this dispute." On the following day the Saxon chargé d'affaires to Berlin was informed that "one expects a localization of the conflict since England is absolutely peaceable and France as well as Russia likewise do not feel inclined toward war." On 18 July, Jagow reiterated that "we wish to localize [a] potential conflict between Austria and Serbia." And another three days later the Reich Chancellor instructed his ambassadors in St. Petersburg, Paris, and London that "we urgently desire a localization of the conflict; any intervention by another power will, in view of the divergent alliance commitments, lead to incalculable consequences."

The problem with Bethmann's limited war concept was that by this time it had become more doubtful than ever that it could be sustained. Another problem is that Jarausch's main source, the Riezler diaries, have come under a cloud since the Berlin historian Bernd Sösemann discovered that, for the July days, they were written on different paper and attached to the diary as a loose-leaf collection. This has led Sösemann to believe that Riezler "reworked" his original notes after World War I. Without going into the details of these charges and the defense and explanations that Karl Dietrich Erdmann, the editor of the diaries, has provided, their doubtful authenticity would seem to preclude continued reliance on this source unless other documents from early July corroborate the localization hypothesis. This would seem to indicate at the same time that the strategy was not just discussed and adopted in the Bethmann Circle, but by the entire German leadership, including the Kaiser and the military. Several such sources have survived. Thus on July 5, the Kaiser's adjutant general, Count Hans von Plessen, entered in his diary that he had been ordered to come to the New Palace at Potsdam in the late afternoon of that day to be told about the Hoyos mission and Francis Joseph's letter to Wilhelm II. Falkenhayn, Bethmann, and the Chief of the Military Cabinet Moritz von Lyncker were also present. According to Plessen, the view predominated that "the sooner the Austrians move against Serbia the better and that the Russians—though Serbia's friends—would not come in. H.M.'s departure on his Norwegian cruise is supposed to go ahead undisturbed."

Falkenhayn's report about the same meeting to Moltke, who was on vacation, had a similar tone. Neither of the two letters which the Kaiser had received from Vienna, both of which painted "a very gloomy picture of the general situation of a Dual Monarchy as a result of Pan-Slav agitations," spoke "of the need for war"; "rather both expound 'energetic' political action such as conclusion of a treaty with Bulgaria, for which they would like to be certain of the support of the Germain Reich." Falkenhayn added that Bethmann "appears to have as little faith as I do that the Austrian government is really in earnest, even though the language is undeniably more resolute than in the past." Consequently he expected it to be "a long time before the treaty with Bulgaria is concluded." Moltke's "stay at Spa will therefore scarcely need to be curtailed," although Falkenhayn thought it "advisable to inform you of the gravity of the situation so that anything untoward which could, after all, occur at any time, should not find you wholly unprepared."

Another account of the "blank check" meeting on July 5 comes from Captain Albert Hopman of the Reich Navy Office. On the following day he reported to Tirpitz, who was vacationing in Switzerland, that Admiral Eduard von Capelle, Tirpitz's deputy, was "ordered this morning to go to the New Palace at Potsdam" where Wilhelm II briefed him on the previous day's events. Again the Kaiser said that he had backed Vienna in its demand "for the most far-reaching satisfaction" and, should this not be granted, for military action against Serbia. Hopman's report continued: "H.M. does not consider an intervention by Russia to back up Serbia likely, because the Tsar would not wish to support the regicides and because Russia is at the moment totally unprepared militarily and financially. The same applied to France, especially with respect to finance. H.M. did not mention Britain." Accordingly, he had "let Emperor Franz Joseph know that he could rely on him." The Kaiser believed "that the situation would clear up again after a week owing to Serbia's backing down, but he nevertheless considers it necessary to be prepared for a different outcome." With this in mind, Wilhelm II had "had a word yesterday with the Reich Chancellor, the Chief of the General Staff, the War Minister, and the Deputy Chief of the Admiralty Staff" although "measures which are likely to arouse political attention or to cause special expenditures are to be avoided for the time being." Hopman concluded by saying that "H.M., who, as Excellency von Capelle says, made a perfectly calm, determined impression on him, has left for Kiel this morning to go aboard his yacht for his Scandinavian cruise." That Moltke, clearly a key player in any German planning, had also correctly understood the message that he had received from Berlin and approved of the localization strategy is evidenced by his comment: "Austria must beat the Serbs and then make peace quickly, demanding an Austro-Serbian alliance as the sole condition. Just as Prussia did with Austria in 1866."

If, in the face of this evidence, we accept that Berlin adopted a limited war strategy at the beginning of July which turned out later on to have been badly miscalculated, the next question to be answered is: Why did the Kaiser and his advisors fall for "the illusion of limited war"? To understand this and the pressures on them to take action, we must consider the deep pessimism by which they had become affected and which also pervades the Riezler diaries.

In his account of the origins of World War I, James Joll, after a comprehensive survey of various interpretations, ultimately identified "the mood of 1914" as the crucial factor behind Europe's descent into catastrophe. Although he admits that this mood can "only be assessed approximately and impressionistically" and that it "differed from country to country or from class to class," he nevertheless comes to the conclusion that "at each level there was a willingness to risk or to accept war as a solution to a whole range of problems, political, social, international, to say nothing of war as apparently the only way of resisting a direct physical threat." In his view, it is therefore "in an investigation of the mentalities of the rulers of Europe and their subjects that the explanation of the causes of the war will ultimately lie." There is much substance in this perspective on the origins of the war, but it may require further sociological differentiation with regard to the supposedly pervasive pessimistic sense that a cataclysm was inevitable. As in other countries, there were also many groups in German society that were not affected by the gloomsters and, indeed, had hopes and expectations of a better future. They adhered to the view that things could be transformed and improved. After all, over the past two decades the country had seen a period of unprecedented growth and prosperity. German technology, science, and education, as well as the welfare and health care systems, were studied and copied in other parts of the world. There was a vibrant cultural life at all levels, and even large parts of the working-class movement, notwithstanding the hardships and inequalities to which it was exposed, shared a sense of achievement that spurred many of its members to do even better. As the urbanization, industrialization, and secularization of society unfolded, German society, according to the optimists, had become more diverse, modern, colorful, complex, and sophisticated.

However, these attitudes were not universally held. There were other groups that had meanwhile been overcome by a growing feeling that the *Kaiserreich* was on a slippery downhill slope. Some intellectuals, as we have seen, spoke of the fragmentation and disintegration of the well-ordered bourgeois world of the nineteenth century. Their artistic productions reflected a deep cultural pessimism, a mood that was distinctly postmodern. Some of them even went so far as to view war as the only way of the malaise into which modern civilization was said to have maneuvered itself. Only a "bath of steel," they believed, would produce the necessary and comprehensive rejuvenation. If these views had been those of no more than a few fringe groups, their diagnoses of decadence and decline would have remained of little significance. The point is that they were shared, albeit with different arguments, by influential elite groups who were active in the realm of politics. The latter may have had no more than an inkling of the artistic discourse that was pushing beyond modernism, but they, too, assumed that things were on the verge of collapse, especially in the sphere of politics. Here nothing seemed to be working anymore.

The sense of crisis in the final years was most tangible in the field of foreign policy. The monarch and his civilian and military advisors along with many others felt encircled by the Triple Entente. Over the years and certainly after the conclusion of the Franco-British Entente Cordiale in 1904 and the Anglo-Russian accord of 1907 they had convinced themselves that Britain, France, and Russia were bent on throttling the two Central Powers. While the Anglo-German naval arms race had gone into reverse due to Tirpitz's inability to sustain it financially, the military competition on land reached new heights in 1913 after the ratification of massive army bills in Germany, France, and Russia.

However, by then tensions on the European continent were fueled by more than political and military rivalries. [I]n the early 1890s Germany finally abandoned Bismarck's attempts to separate traditional diplomacy from commercial policy. Reich Chancellor Caprivi had aligned the two before Bülow expanded the use of trade as an instrument of German foreign policy following the Tsarist defeat in the Far East at the hands of the Japanese in 1904 and the subsequent revolution of 1905. By 1913 a dramatic change of fortunes had taken place. Russian agriculture had been hit hard by Bülow's protectionism after 1902, and now it looked as if St. Petersburg was about to turn the tables on Berlin. As the correspondent of *Kölnische Zeitung* reported from Russia on March 2, 1914, by the fall of 1917 the country's economic difficulties would be overcome, thanks in no small degree to further French loans. With Germany's commercial treaties coming up for renewal in 1916, the Tsar was expected to do to the Reich what Bülow had done to the Romanov Empire in earlier years. Accordingly an article published in April 1914 in Deutscher Aussenhandel warned that "it hardly requires any mention that in view of the high-grade political tension between the two countries any conflict in the field of commercial policy implies a serious test of peace."

What, in the eyes of Germany's leadership, made the specter of a Russo-German trade war around 1916 so terrifying was that this was also the time when the French and Russian rearmament programs would be completed. Not surprisingly, this realization added the powerful Army leadership to the ranks of German pessimists. Given the precarious strategic position of the two Central European monarchies, the thought that the Tsarist army was to reach its greatest strength in 1916 triggered bouts of depression, especially in Moltke, the Chief of the General Staff, and Conrad, his Austro-Hungarian counterpart. By March 1914 the latter's worries had become so great that he wondered aloud to the head of his Operations Department, Colonel Joseph Metzger, "if one should wait until France and Russia [are] prepared to invade us jointly or if it [is] more desirable to settle the inevitable conflict at an earlier date. Moreover, the Slav question [is] becoming more and more difficult and dangerous for us."

A few weeks later Conrad met with Moltke at Karlsbad, where they shared their general sense of despair and confirmed each other in the view that time was running out. Moltke added that "to wait any longer [means] a diminishing of our chances; [for] as far as manpower is concerned, one cannot enter into a competition with Russia." Back in Berlin, Moltke spoke to

Jagow about his meeting at Karlsbad, with the latter recording that the Chief of the General Staff was "seriously worried" about "the prospects of the future." Russia would have "completed her armaments in two or three years time," and "the military superiority of our enemies would be so great then that he did not know how we might cope with them." Accordingly Moltke felt that "there was no alternative to waging a preventive war in order to defeat the enemy as long as we could still more or less pass the test." He left it to Jagow "to gear our policy to an early unleashing of war." That Russia had become something of an obsession not just for the generals, but also for the civilian leadership, can be gauged from a remark by Bethmann, as he cast his eyes across his estate northeast of Berlin. It would not be worth it, he is reported to have said, to plant trees there when in a few years' time the Russians would be coming anyway.

However serious Germany's international situation may have been, the Reich Chancellor and his colleagues were no less aware of the simultaneous difficulties on the domestic front. Surveying the state of the Prusso-German political system in early 1914, it was impossible to avoid the impression that it was out of joint. The Kaiser's prestige was rapidly evaporating.... The government was unable to forge lasting alliances and compromises with the parties of the Right and the center—the only political forces that a monarchical Reich Chancellor could contemplate as potential partners for the passage of legislation. Meanwhile the "revolutionary" Social Democrats were on the rise and had become the largest party in the Reichstag. The next statutory elections were to be held in 1916/17 and no one knew how large the leftist parties would then become. Faced with these problems and fearful of a repetition of the 1913 tax compromise between the parties of the center and the SPD, Bethmann had virtually given up governing. The state machinery was kept going by executive decrees that did not require legislative approval. At the same time the debt crisis continued. Worse, since 1910 there had been massive strike movements, first against the Prussian three-class voting system and later for better wages and working conditions. While the integration of minorities ran into growing trouble, reflecting problems of alienation among larger sections of the population who felt left behind and were now looking for convenient scapegoats, the working class became increasingly critical of the monarchy's incapacity to reform itself. Even parts of the women's movement had begun to refuse the place they had been assigned in the traditional order. So the situation appeared to be one of increasing polarization, and the major compromises that were needed to resolve accumulating problems at home and abroad were nowhere in sight. Even increased police repression and censorship was no longer viable.

Even if it is argued, with the benefit of hindsight, that all this did not in effect amount to a serious crisis, in the minds of many loyal monarchists and their leaders it certainly had begun to look like one. Perceptions are important here because they shaped the determination for future action and compelled those who held the levers of power to act "before it was too late." With the possibilities of compromise seemingly exhausted and the Kaiser and his advisors running out of options that were not checkmated by other political forces, there was merely one arena left in which they still had unrestricted freedom of action. It is also the arena where the broad structural picture that has been offered in previous chapters links up with the more finely textured analysis put forward in the present one. [T]he Reich Constitution gave the monarch and his advisors the exclusive right to decide whether the country would go to war or stay at peace. It was this prerogative that was now to be used in the expectation that a war would result in a restabilization of Germany's and Austria-Hungary's international and domestic situation. The question was, what kind of war would achieve this objective? From all we know and have said about the early response to the assassinations of Sarajevo, this was not the moment to unleash a world war with its incalculable risks. The conservatives in Berlin and Vienna were not that extremist. They expected that war would lead to a major breakthrough in the Balkans and would stabilize the Austria-Hungarian Empire against Serb nationalism. If Moltke's above-mentioned reference to Prussia's victory over Austria in 1866 is any guide, memories of that war may indeed have played a role in German calculations. After all, the Prusso-Austrian had been a limited war in Central Europe, and it had the added benefit of solving the stalemate in Prussian domestic politics, in the wake of the constitutional conflict. Bismarck's "splendid" victory not only produced, after a snap election, a conservative majority in the Prussian Diet that enabled him to overcome the legislative deadlock that had existed since 1862, but it also "proved" that such "shocks" to the international system could be absorbed without further crisis.

And so the Kaiser and his advisors encouraged Vienna to launch a limited war in the Balkans. Their expectations that the war would remain limited turned out to be completely wrong. The Kaiser and his entourage, who under the Reich Constitution at that brief moment held the fate of millions in their hands, were not prepared to beat a retreat and to avoid a world war. The consequences of that total war and the turmoil it caused in all spheres of life were enormous. The world had been turned upside down.

NO

Samuel R. Williamson, Jr.

The Origins of the War

Sarajevo

Košutnjak Park, Belgrade, mid-May 1914: Gavrilo Princip fires his revolver at an oak tree, training for his part in the plot. Those practice rounds were the first shots of what would become the First World War. Princip, a Bosnian Serb student, wanted to murder Archduke Franz Ferdinand, heir to the Habsburg throne, when the latter visited the Bosnian capital of Sarajevo. Princip had become involved with a Serbian terrorist group—the Black Hand. Directed by the head of Serbian military intelligence, Colonel Dragutin Dimitrijević (nick-named Apis, 'the Bull'), the Black Hand advocated violence in the creation of a Greater Serbia. For Princip and Apis, this meant ending Austria-Hungary's rule over Bosnia-Hercegovina through any means possible.

Princip proved an apt pupil. If his co-conspirators flinched or failed on Sunday, 28 June 1914, he did not. Thanks to confusion in the archduke's entourage after an initial bomb attack, the young Bosnian Serb discovered the official touring car stopped within 6 feet of his location. Princip fired two quick shots. Within minutes the archduke and his wife Sophie were dead in Sarajevo.

Exactly one month later, on 28 July, Austria-Hungary declared war on Serbia. What began as the third Balkan war would, within a week, become the First World War. Why did the murders unleash first a local and then a wider war? What were the longer-term, the mid-range, and the tactical issues that brought Europe into conflict? What follows is a summary of current historical thinking about the July crisis, while also suggesting some different perspectives on the much studied origins of the First World War....

Vienna's Response to the Assassination

The Serbian terrorist plot had succeeded. But that very success also threatened [Serbian Prime Minister Nikolai] Pašić's civilian government. Already at odds with Apis and his Black Hand associates, Pašić now found himself compromised by his own earlier failure to investigate allegations about the secret society. In early June 1914, the minister had heard vague rumours of an assassination plot. He even sought to make inquiries, only to have Apis stonewall him about details. Whether Belgrade actually sought to alert Vienna about the plot remains uncertain. In any event, once the murders occurred, the premier could not admit his prior knowledge nor allow any Austro-Hungarian action that might unravel the details of the conspiracy. Not only would any compromise threaten his political position, it could lead Apis and his army associates to attempt a coup or worse.

After 28 June Pašić tried, without much success, to moderate the Serbian press's glee over the archduke's death. He also sought to appear conciliatory and gracious towards Vienna. But he knew that the Habsburg authorities believed that Princip had ties to Belgrade. He only hoped that the Habsburg investigators could not make a direct, incontrovertible connection to Apis and others.

Pašić resolved early, moreover, that he would not allow any Habsburg infringement of Serbian sovereignty or any commission that would implicate him or the military authorities. If he made any concession, his political opponents would attack and he might expose himself and the other civilian ministers to unacceptable personal risks. Thus Serbia's policy throughout the July crisis would be apparently conciliatory, deftly evasive, and ultimately intractable. It did not require, as the inter-war historians believed, the Russian government to stiffen the Serbian position. Once confronted with the fact of Sarajevo, the Serbian leadership charted its own course, one which guaranteed a definitive confrontation with Vienna.

The deaths of Franz Ferdinand and Sophie stunned the Habsburg leadership. While there were only modest public shows of sympathy, limited by the court's calculation to play down the funeral, all of the senior leaders wanted some action against Belgrade. None doubted that Serbia bore responsibility for the attacks. The 84-year-old emperor, Franz Joseph, returned hurriedly to Vienna from his hunting lodge at Bad Ischl. Over the next six days to 4 July 1914, all of the Habsburg leaders met in pairs and threes to discuss the monarchy's reaction to the deaths and to assess the extensive political unrest in Bosnia-Hercegovina in the wake of the assassinations. Nor could the discussions ignore the earlier tensions of 1912 and 1913 when the monarchy had three times nearly gone to war with Serbia and/or Montenegro. Each time militant diplomacy had prevailed and each time Russia had accepted the outcome.

The most aggressive of the Habsburg leaders, indeed the single individual probably most responsible for the war in 1914, was General Franz Conrad von H¨otzendorf, chief of the Austro-Hungarian general staff. In the previous crises he had called for war against Serbia more than fifty times. He constantly lamented that the monarchy had not attacked Serbia in 1908 when the odds would have been far better. In the July crisis Conrad would argue vehemently and repeatedly that the time for a final reckoning had come. His cries for war in 1912 and 1913 had been checked by Archduke Franz Ferdinand and the foreign minister, Leopold Berchtold. Now, with the archduke gone and Berchtold converted to a policy of action, all of the civilian leaders, except the Hungarian prime minister István Tisza, wanted to resolve the Serbian issue. To retain international credibility the monarchy had to show that there were limits beyond which the south Slav movement could not go without repercussions.

The Habsburg resolve intensified with reports from Sarajevo that indicated that the trail of conspiracy did indeed lead back to at least one minor Serbian official in Belgrade. While the evidence in 1914 never constituted a 'smoking gun', the officials correctly surmised that the Serbian government must have tolerated and possibly assisted in the planning of the deed. Given this evidence, the Habsburg leaders soon focused on three options: a severe diplomatic humiliation of Serbia; quick, decisive military action against Serbia; or a diplomatic ultimatum that, if rejected, would be followed by military action. Pressed by Conrad and the military leadership, by 3 July even Franz Joseph had agreed on the need for stern action, including the possibility of war. Only one leader resisted a military solution: István Tisza. Yet his consent was absolutely required for any military action. Tisza preferred the diplomatic option and wanted assurances of German support before the government made a final decision. His resistance to any quick military action effectively foreclosed that option, leaving either the diplomatic one or the diplomatic/military combination. Not surprisingly, those anxious for military action shifted to the latter alternative.

The Austro-Hungarian foreign minister, Berchtold, made the next move on 4 July, sending his belligerent subordinate Alexander Hoyos to Berlin to seek a pledge of German support. Armed with a personal letter from Franz Joseph to Wilhelm II and a long memorandum on the need for resolute action against Serbia, Hoyos got a cordial reception. The Germans fully understood Vienna's intentions: the Habsburg leadership wanted a military reckoning with Belgrade. The German leadership (for reasons to be explored later) agreed to the Habsburg request, fully realizing that it might mean a general war with Russia as Serbia's protector.

With assurances of German support, the leaders in Vienna met on 7 July to formulate their plan. General Conrad gave confident assessments of military success and the civilian ministers attempted to persuade Tisza to accept a belligerent approach. At the same time the preliminary diplomatic manoeuvres were planned. Finally on 13–14 July Hungarian Prime Minister Tisza accepted strong action and possible war with Serbia. He did so largely because of new fears that a possible Serbian-Romanian alignment would threaten Magyar over-lordship of the 3 million Romanians living in Transylvania. Drafts of the ultimatum, meanwhile, were prepared in Vienna. Deception tactics to lull the rest of Europe were arranged and some military leaves were cancelled.

But there remained a major problem: when to deliver the ultimatum? The long-scheduled French state visit to Russia of President Raymond Poincaré and Premier René Viviani from 20 July to 23 July thoroughly complicated the delivery of the ultimatum. Berchtold, understandably, did not want to hand over the demands while the French leaders were still in St Petersburg. Yet to avoid that possibility meant a further delay until late afternoon, 23 July. At that point the forty-eight-hour ultimatum, with its demands that clearly could not be met, would be delivered in Belgrade.

Germany's decision of 5–6 July to assure full support to Vienna ranks among the most discussed issues in modern European history. A strong, belligerent German response came as no surprise. After all, Wilhelm II and Franz Ferdinand had just visited each other, were close ideologically, and had since 1900 developed a strong personal friendship. Chancellor Theobald von Bethmann Hollweg, moreover, believed that Berlin must show Vienna that Germany supported its most loyal ally. Far more controversial is whether the civilian leaders in Berlin, pressured by the German military, viewed the Sarajevo murders as a 'heaven-sent' opportunity to launch a preventive war against Russia. This interpretation points to increasing German apprehension about a Russian military colossus, allegedly to achieve peak strength in 1917. And Russo-German military relations were in early 1914 certainly at their worst in decades. Nor did Kaiser Wilhelm II's military advisers urge any modicum of restraint on Vienna, unlike previous Balkans episodes. An increasingly competitive European military environment now spilled over into the July crisis.

However explained, the German leadership reached a rare degree of consensus: it would support Vienna in a showdown with Serbia. Thus the German kaiser and chancellor gave formal assurances (the so-called 'blank cheque') to Vienna. From that moment, Austria-Hungary proceeded to exploit this decision and to march toward war with Serbia. Berlin would find itself—for better or worse—at the mercy of its reliable ally as the next stages of the crisis unfolded.

The Austrian Ultimatum to Serbia

For two weeks and more Berlin waited, first for the Habsburg leadership to make its final decisions and then for their implementation. During this time the German kaiser sailed in the North Sea and the German military and naval high command, confident of their own arrangements, took leaves at various German spas. Bethmann Hollweg, meanwhile, fretted over the lengthy delays in Vienna. He also began to fear the consequences of the 'calculated risk' and his 'leap into the dark' for German foreign policy. But his moody retrospection brought no changes in his determination to back Vienna; he only wished the Habsburg monarchy would act soon and decisively.

By Monday 20 July, Europe buzzed with rumours of a pending Habsburg *démarche* in Belgrade. While the Irish Question continued to dominate British political concerns and the French public focused on the Caillaux murder trial, Vienna moved to act against Belgrade. Remarkably, no Triple Entente power directly challenged Berchtold before 23 July, and the foreign minister for his part remained inconspicuous. Then, as instructed, at 6 p.m. on 23 July Wladimir Giesl, the Habsburg minister in Belgrade, delivered the ultimatum to the Serbian foreign ministry. Sir Edward Grey, the British foreign secretary, would immediately brand it as 'the most formidable document ever addressed by one State to another that was independent'.

With its forty-eight-hour deadline, the ultimatum demanded a series of Serbian concessions and a commission to investigate the plot. Pašić, away from Belgrade on an election campaign tour, returned to draft the response. This reply conceded some points but was wholly unyielding on Vienna's key demand, which would have allowed the Austrians to discover Pašić's and his government's general complicity in the murders.

News of the Habsburg ultimatum struck Europe with as much force as the Sarajevo murders. If the public did not immediately recognize the dangers to the peace, the European diplomats (and their military and naval associates) did. The most significant, immediate, and dangerous response came not from the Germans, but from the Russians. Upon learning of the ultimatum, Foreign Minister Serge Sazonov declared war inevitable. His actions thereafter did much to ensure a general European war.

At a meeting of the Council of State on 24 July, even before the Serbians responded, Sazonov and others pressed for strong Russian support for Serbia. Fearful of losing Russian leadership of the pan-Slavic movement, he urged resolute behaviour. His senior military leaders backed this view, even though Russia's military reforms were still incomplete. The recently concluded French state visit had given the Russians new confidence that Paris would support Russia if war came.

At Sazonov's urgings, the Council agreed, with the tsar approving the next day, to initiate various military measures preparing for partial or full mobilization. The Council agreed further to partial mobilization as a possible deterrent to stop Austria-Hungary from attacking the Serbs. These Russian military measures were among the very first of the entire July crisis; their impact would be profound. The measures were not only extensive, they abutted German as well as Austrian territory. Not surprisingly, the Russian actions would be interpreted by German military intelligence as tantamount to some form of mobilization. No other actions in the crisis, beyond Vienna's resolute determination for war, were so provocative or disturbing as Russia's preliminary steps of enhanced border security and the recall of certain troops.

Elsewhere, Sir Edward Grey sought desperately to repeat his 1912 role as peacemaker in the Balkans. He failed. He could not get Vienna to extend the forty-eight-hour deadline. Thus at 6 p.m. on 25 July, Giesl glanced at the Serbian reply, deemed it insufficient, broke diplomatic relations, and left immediately for nearby Habsburg territory. The crisis had escalated to a new, more dangerous level.

Grey did not, however, desist in his efforts for peace. He now tried to initiate a set of four-power discussions to ease the mounting crisis. Yet he could never get St Petersburg or Berlin to accept the same proposal for some type of mediation or diplomatic discussions. A partial reason for his failure came from Berlin's two continuing assumptions: that Britain might ultimately stand aside and that Russia would eventually be deterred by Germany's strong, unequivocal support of Vienna.

Each of Grey's international efforts, ironically, alarmed Berchtold. He now became determined to press for a declaration of war, thus thwarting any intervention in the local conflict. In fact, the Habsburg foreign minister had trouble getting General Conrad's reluctant agreement to a declaration of war on Tuesday 28 July. This declaration, followed by some desultory gunfire between Serbian and Austro-Hungarian troops that night, would thoroughly inflame the situation. The Serbs naturally magnified the gunfire incident into a larger Austrian attack. This in turn meant that the Russians would use the casual shooting to justify still stronger support for Serbia and to initiate still more far-reaching military measures of their own.

By 28 July every European state had taken some military and/or naval precautions. The French recalled some frontier troops, the Germans did the same, and the Austro-Hungarians began their mobilization against the Serbs. In Britain, Winston Churchill, First Lord of the Admiralty, secured cabinet approval to keep the British fleet intact after it had completed manoeuvres. Then on the night of 29 July he ordered the naval vessels to proceed through the English Channel to their North Sea battle stations. It could be argued that thanks to Churchill Britain became the first power prepared to protect its vital interests in a European war.

Grey still searched for a solution. But his efforts were severely hampered by the continuing impact of the Irish Question and the deep divisions within the cabinet over any policy that appeared to align Britain too closely with France. Throughout the last week of July, Grey tried repeatedly to gain cabinet consent to threaten Germany with British intervention. The radicals in the cabinet refused. They wanted no British participation in a continental war.

Grey now turned his attention to the possible fate of Belgium and Britain's venerable treaty commitments to protect Belgian neutrality. As he did so, the German diplomats committed a massive blunder by attempting to win British neutrality with an assurance that Belgium and France would revert to the status quo ante after a war. Not only did Grey brusquely reject this crude bribery, he turned it back against Berlin. On 31 July, with cabinet approval, Grey asked Paris and Berlin to guarantee Belgium's status. France did so at once; the Germans did not. Grey had scored an important moral and tactical victory.

In St Petersburg, meanwhile, decisions were taken, rescinded, then taken again that assured that the peace would not be kept. By 28 July Sazonov had concluded that a partial mobilization against Austria-Hungary would never deter Vienna. Indeed his own generals argued that a partial step would complicate a general mobilization. Sazonov therefore got the generals' support for full mobilization. He then won the tsar's approval only to see Nicholas II hesitate after receiving a message from his cousin, Kaiser Wilhelm II. The co-called 'Willy-Nicky' telegrams came to nothing, however. On 30 July the tsar ordered general mobilization, with a clear recognition that Germany would probably respond and that a German attack would be aimed at Russia's French ally.

The Russian general mobilization resolved a number of problems for the German high command. First, it meant that no negotiations, including the proposal for an Austrian 'Halt in Belgrade', would come to anything. Second, it allowed Berlin to declare a 'defensive war' of protection against an aggressive Russia, a tactic that immeasurably aided Bethmann Hollweg's efforts to achieve domestic consensus. And, third, it meant that the chancellor could no longer resist General Helmuth von Moltke's demands for German mobilization and the implementation of German war plans. Alone of the great powers, mobilization for Germany equalled war; Bethmann Hollweg realized this. Yet once the German mobilization began, the chancellor lost effective control of the situation.

At 7 p.m. on Saturday, 1 August 1914, Germany declared war on Russia. The next day German forces invaded Luxembourg. Later that night Germany demanded that Belgium allow German troops to march through the neutral state on their way to France. The Belgian cabinet met and concluded that it would resist the German attack.

In France general mobilization began. But the French government, ever anxious to secure British intervention, kept French forces 6 miles away from the French border. In London Paul Cambon, the French ambassador, importuned the British government to uphold the unwritten moral and military obligations of the Anglo-French *entente*. Still, even on Saturday 1 August, the British cabinet refused to agree to any commitment to France. Then on Sunday 2 August, Grey finally won cabinet approval for two significant steps: Britain would protect France's northern coasts against any German naval attack and London would demand that Germany renounce any intention of attacking Belgium. Britain had edged closer to war.

On Monday 3 August, the British cabinet reviewed the outline of Grey's speech to parliament that afternoon. His peroration, remarkable for its candour and its disingenuousness about the secret Anglo-French military and naval arrangements, left no doubt that London would intervene to preserve the balance of power against Germany; that it would defend Belgium and France; and that it would go to war if Germany failed to stop the offensive in the west. This last demand, sent from London to Berlin on 4 August, would be rejected. At 11 p.m. (GMT) on 4 August 1914 Britain and Germany were at war.

With the declarations of war the focus shifted to the elaborate prearranged mobilization plans of the great powers. For the naval forces the issues were relatively straightforward: prepare for the great naval battle, impose or thwart a policy of naval blockade, protect your coast lines, and keep the shipping lanes open. For the continental armies, the stakes were far greater. If an army were defeated, the war might well be over. Committed to offensive strategies, dependent on the hope that any war would be short, and reliant on the implementation of their carefully developed plans, the general staffs believed they had prepared for almost every possible contingency.

In each country the war plans contained elaborate mobilization schedules which the generals wanted to put into action at the earliest possible moment. While mobilization raised the risks of war, in only two cases did it absolutely guarantee a generalized engagement: (1) if Russia mobilized, Germany would do so and move at once to attack Belgium and France; (2) if Germany mobilized without Russian provocation, the results were the same. Any full Russian mobilization would trigger a complete German response and, for Germany, mobilization meant war. Very few, if any, civilian leaders fully comprehended these fateful interconnections and even the military planners were uncertain about them.

The German war plans in 1914 were simple, dangerous, and exceptionally mechanical. To overcome the threat of being trapped in a two-front war between France and Russia, Germany would attack first in the west, violating Belgian neutrality in a massive sweeping movement that would envelop and then crush the French forces. Once the French were defeated, the Germans would redeploy their main forces against Russia and with Austro-Hungarian help conclude the war. The Russian war plans sought to provide immediate assistance to France and thereby disrupt the expected German attack in the west. The Russians would attack German troops in East Prussia, while other Russian forces moved southward into Galicia against the Habsburg armies. But to achieve their goals the Russians had to mobilize immediately, hence their escalatory decisions early in the crisis, with fateful consequences for the peace of Europe.

The Italians, it should be noted, took some preliminary measures in August 1914 but deferred general mobilization until later. Otherwise Rome took no further action to intervene. Rather the Italian government soon became involved in an elaborate bargaining game over its entry into the fray. Not until April 1915 would this last of the major pre-war allies enter into the fighting, not on the side of their former allies but in opposition with the Triple Entente.

The Process of Escalation

By 10 August 1914 Europe was at war. What had started as the third Balkan war had rapidly become the First World War. How can one assess responsibility for these events? Who caused it? What could have been done differently to have prevented it? Such questions have troubled generations of historians since 1914. There are no clear answers. But the following observations may put the questions into context. The alliance/*entente* system created linking mechanisms that allowed the control of a state's strategic destiny to pass into a broader arena, one which the individual government could manage but not always totally control. Most specifically, this meant that any Russo-German quarrel would see France involved because of the very nature of Germany's offensive war plans. Until 1914 the alliance/*entente* partners had disagreed just enough among themselves to conceal the true impact of the alliance arrangements.

The legacy of Germany's bombastic behaviour, so characteristic of much of German *Weltpolitik* and *Europolitik* after 1898, also meant that Berlin was thoroughly mistrusted. Its behaviour created a tone, indeed an edginess, that introduced fear into the international system, since only for Germany did mobilization equal war. Ironically, and not all historians agree, the German policy in 1914 may have been less provocative than earlier. But that summer Berlin paid the price for its earlier aggressiveness.

Serbia allowed a terrorist act to proceed, then sought to evade the consequences of its action. It would gain, after 1918, the most from the war with the creation of the Yugoslav state. Paradoxically, however, the very ethnic rivalries that brought Austria-Hungary to collapse would also plague the new state and its post-1945 successor.

Austria-Hungary feared the threat posed by the emergence of the south Slavs as a political force. But the Dual Monarchy could not reform itself sufficiently to blunt the challenge. With the death of the Archduke Franz Ferdinand, who had always favoured peace, the monarchy lost the one person who could check the ambitions of General Conrad and mute the fears of the civilians. While harsh, Ottokar Czernin's epitaph has a certain truth to it: 'We were compelled to die; we could only choose the manner of our death and we have chosen the most terrible.'

Germany believed that it must support its Danubian ally. This in turn influenced Berlin's position towards Russia and France. Without German backing, Vienna would probably have hesitated to been more conciliatory toward Belgrade. But, anxious to support Vienna and possibly to detach Russia from the Triple Entente, Berlin would risk a continental war to achieve its short- and long-term objectives. Berlin and Vienna bear more responsibility for starting the crisis and then making it very hard to control.

Nevertheless, the Russians must also share some significant responsibility for the final outcome. St Petersburg's unwavering support of Serbia, its unwillingness to negotiate with Berlin and Vienna, and then its precipitate preparatory military measures escalated the crisis beyond control. Russia's general mobilization on 30 July guaranteed disaster.

Those Russian decisions would in turn confront the French with the full ramifications of their alliance with Russia. Despite French expectations, the alliance with Russia had in fact become less salvation for Paris and more assuredly doom. France became the victim in the Russo-German fight. Throughout the crisis French leaders could only hope to convince Russia to be careful and simultaneously work to ensure that Britain came to their assistance. Paris failed in the first requirement and succeeded in the second.

The decisions of August 1914 did not come easily for the British government. Grey could not rush the sharply divided cabinet. The decade-old *entente* ties to the French were vague and unwritten and had a history of deception and deviousness. Nor did the vicious political atmosphere created by Ireland help. Grey desperately hoped that the threat of British intervention would deter Germany; it did not. Could Grey have done more? Probably not, given the British political system and the precarious hold the Liberal Party had on power. Only a large standing British army would have deterred Germany, and that prospect, despite some recent assertions, simply did not exist.

In July 1914 one or two key decisions taken differently might well have seen the war averted. As it was, the July crisis became a model of escalation and inadvertent consequences. The expectation of a short war, the ideology of offensive warfare, and continuing faith in war as an instrument of policy: all would soon prove illusory and wishful. The cold, hard, unyielding reality of modern warfare soon replaced the romantic, dashing legends of the popular press. The élite decision-makers (monarchs, civilian ministers, admirals, and generals) had started the war; the larger public would die in it and, ultimately, finish it.

POSTSCRIPT

Were German Militarism and Diplomacy Responsible for World War I?

Recent events in the former Yugoslavia may have spurred interest in World War I—the first time that the Balkan powder keg exploded into the world's consciousness. Yugoslavia was created after that war, and some see its recent problems as a failure of the Versailles settlement.

Regardless of the truth of this assumption, it is certainly true that the last decade has seen the publication (and republication) of a number of important works on the Great War, including books by both authors in this issue: Berghahn's *Germany and the Approach of War in 1914* (St. Martin's Press, 1993) and Williamson's *Austria-Hungary and the Origins of the First World War* (St. Martin's Press, 1991). David G. Hermann's *The Arming of Europe and the Making of World War I* (Princeton University Press, 1996) concentrates on the size and strength of land armies and their role in the genesis of the war, a subject that has been neglected by historians who have emphasized naval buildup.

Many recent books on World War I have either been written by English historians or have concentrated on England's role in the war. Edward E. McCullough's *How the First World War Began: The Triple Entente and the Coming of the Great War of 1914–1918* (Black Rose Books, 1999) is a revisionist work that sees the creation of the Triple Entente as a prime force in the causes of the First World War. Comparing the condition of Germany today to England, France, and Russia, McCullough questions not only the folly of the war but notes its counterproductive results.

In *The Pity of War* (Basic Books, 1999), Scottish historian Niall Ferguson takes the revisionist viewpoint to a higher level. Arguing that the First World War was not inevitable, he asserts that the British declaration of war turned a continental conflict into a world war. He further argues that not only was Britain's participation in the war a colossal error, but it was counterproductive to the interests of the British nation and its people. He finds proof in the causes and results of World War II and the present condition of Great Britain.

Eminent English military historian John Keegan's *The First World War* (Alfred A. Knopf, 1999) may well prove to be one of the most widely read and influential volumes on the Great War. A general work written with skill, scholarship, and readability, it is strongly recommended. *World War I: A History* (Oxford University Press, 1998), edited by Hew Strachan, contains 23 chapters, each written by a different historian, that cover the war from origins to memory and everything in between. William Jannen's *The Lions of July: Prelude to War, 1914* (Presidio Press, 1997) is an extremely readable account of Europe's last month of peace as its statesmen and military men blundered into war.

ISSUE 8

Was the Treaty of Versailles Responsible for World War II?

YES: Derek Aldcroft, from "The Versailles Legacy," *History Review* (December 1997)

NO: Mark Mazower, from "Two Cheers for Versailles," *History Today* (July 1997)

ISSUE SUMMARY

YES: Historian Derek Aldcroft states that a combination of the flaws present in the post-war Versailles Treaty and the resultant actions and inactions of European statesmen created a climate that paved the way for World War II.

NO: Historian Mark Mazower finds that while the Treaty of Versailles contained weaknesses, it failed due to a lack of enforcement of its principles by a generation of European leaders.

T he previous issue covered the causes of World War I and who was responsible for it. The war lasted 4 years, and the loss of lives, property, and psychological well-being was staggering. Even before the war's end, statesmen were already making plans for the peace that would follow. Not surprisingly, there were differences of opinion as to what shape that peace would take.

For the European Allied Powers—mainly England, France, and Italy—the answer was simple; Germany and its allies must be held accountable for their belligerence. This would include: responsibility for the war, severe reduction in military forces to prevent future conflicts, substantial reparation payments to its victims, and substantial losses in territory and resources. This would eventually result in the end of old empires and the subsequent creation of many new nations. Having suffered so much doing the war, getting even and preventing future wars was all the Allied Powers could imagine coming out of the peace process.

The United States, also an Allied Power, had a different peace plan to offer. Entering the war in 1917, its sacrifices in life and property were minimal compared with those of its European allies. This allowed President Woodrow Wilson to propose a different type of peace. Describing it as "a peace without victory," Wilson urged his fellow allies to pursue a peace plan that would anger no nation, thus preventing future wars through its just settlement of the present one.

The cornerstone of Wilson's plan was the creation of an international congress of nations that would meet regularly in order to insure the absence of war and the continuance of peace. This was a radical proposal, the likes of which the world had never seen.

When the war ended in 1918, the allied nations convened in Paris to draw up the new peace plan; the defeated Central Powers were not invited. The Paris Peace Conference would be dominated by four men: English Prime Minister David Lloyd George, French Premier Georges Clemenceau, Italian Prime Minister Vittorio Orlando, and U.S. President Woodrow Wilson. The world's future was in their hands.

The peace process was marked by disagreements, debates, and eventual compromises. In the end, the Treaty of Versailles was a compromised document that satisfied no one. And within a generation of its passage, the world's nations were at war again, repeating the mistakes of their elders.

Was the Treaty of Versailles responsible for World War II? Two historians offer differing opinions on this question. Derek Aldcroft contends that the treaty left major unresolved issues and left Germany bitter and resentful. The failures of the post-war leaders to deal with these issues exacerbated an already volatile situation. Mark Mazower offers a qualified endorsement of the Versailles Treaty, stating that it did a credible job and created a model world order under which Europe lives today.

Derek Aldcroft **YES**

The Versailles Legacy

Both Sir Edward Grey and Maynard Keynes were remarkably perceptive about Europe's future in the aftermath of war. On the eve of hostilities the former commented: 'The lamps are going out all over Europe; we shall not see them lit again in our lifetime'. Keynes, in his vitriolic denunciation of the peace settlement with Germany, wrote as follows: 'The Treaty includes no provisions for the economic rehabilitation of Europe—nothing to make the defeated Central Empires into good neighbours, nothing to stabilise the new States of Europe, nothing to reclaim Russia; nor does it promote in any way a compact of economic solidarity amongst the Allies themselves; no arrangement was reached at Paris for restoring the disordered finances of France and Italy, or to adjust the systems of the Old World and the New.'

The war itself seriously weakened Europe both economically and politically and she never fully recaptured her former glory before a second conflagration occurred. However, while hostilities undoubtedly caused serious damage to the economic landscape, we shall argue here that it was what came afterwards that ultimately determined the fate of the Continent. It was primarily the actions of statesmen and policy-makers in the 1920s which were to blame for Europe's weakened state and which left her vulnerable to external shocks and exposed to internal collapse. The manner in which this happened can be illustrated by reference to the response to a number of key issues thrown up by the war and which failed to be resolved satisfactorily. These include (1) the reshaping of Europe; (2) the treatment of Germany; (3) relief and reconstruction; (4)international monetary stabilisation; and (5) the leadership issue.

New states for old empires

Old Empires collapsed and fledgling states took their place in one of the biggest exercises in the reshaping of the boundaries of Europe ever undertaken. Even without a war there would no doubt have been some important changes in the map of Europe, since the Austro-Hungarian, Romanov and Turkish Empires were near the point of extinction. Hostilities speeded up the process and allowed nationalist groups to lay claim to territories out of which emerged several new or reconstituted states, many of which were confirmed by the allied powers in the post-war settlement. The main problem was that in giving free reign to ethnic claims the European map came to resemble a patchwork mosaic which had no real coherence and which shattered the balance of power

From *History Today*, December 1997, pp. 8-13. Copyright © 1997 by History Today, Ltd. Reprinted by permission. References omitted.

that had prevailed in the nineteenth century. The collapse of the Austro-Hungarian Empire, which had once been the bulwark between East and West, played into German hands since it left the way open for Germany, once she had recovered from the war, to further her aims of finding living space in the East. A serious vacuum emerged in Central/East Europe which the new states could never fill. With the partial exception of Czechoslovakia, which had done well out of the peace settlement, the new states were weak in every sense of the word. They were very backward economically, they lacked experience in parliamentary institutions, their administrations were poor and open to corruption, and despite the good intentions of the peacemakers they contained an assortment of different nationalities and religions, which inevitably gave rise to political and social tensions, while nationalist sentiments were rife. Even more significant was that most of them contained pockets of Germans anxious to unite with the mother country.

Thus by the early 1920s the European political and economic landscape had become decidedly fragmented and this effectively provided the breeding ground for the Second World War. Newman has no doubts about the crucial role of the region in determining the future distribution of power within Europe and ultimately the fate of the Continent. The new and reconstituted states, he says, were 'extremely weak reeds to place in the path of Germany, and they possessed few features that could lead to any hope of their being anything else but satellites ... of Germany, Hitler or no Hitler.' The question is why Germany became the predator nation.

The Path to German Hegemony in Europe

In theory any one of a number of European powers could conceivably have filled the vacuum in East/Central Europe: the possible contenders were Britain, France, Russia (Soviet Union), Italy and Germany. Britain ruled herself out since she regarded Europe with somewhat benign indifference and in any case her imperial interests took precedence. France was too weak to play an effective role despite her machinations in the region. Russia had her own internal problems after the Bolshevik revolution in 1917, while Italy, much as Mussolini would have loved to pose as a world leader, was a non-starter. This left Germany and Germany had the resources, the motives and the ambition to lay claim to the East.

Though Germany lost the war and had to pay the price of a transgressor, she could by no means be written off as a great power. The country still had enormous potential and in fact emerged from the war as the strongest power on the continent. The collapse of the Austro-Hungarian Empire and the nationality principle in peacemaking served to strengthen her hand in Europe. For the first time the way was clear to gain space in the East.

The terms of the Versailles peace settlement provided the resolve to further her ambitions since it saddled Germany with what seemed to be iniquitous penalties. She lost significant amounts of territory and resources in Europe (including West Prussia which especially rankled) and overseas, she was saddled with a huge bill for reparations and a war guilt clause, while security provisions entailed demilitarisation and allied occupation of key zones in Germany.

This harsh treatment was no doubt understandable from the Allied point of view, especially by the French who had every reason to fear the worst if Germany was not successfully contained. Whether a more moderate settlement would have ensured a more compliant loser is a moot point. However, the fact is that the damage had been done and Germany harboured a burning resentment against the victors and was determined to secure revenge for such ignominious treatment by whittling down the original demands made upon her.

The crucial issue proved to be the reparations burden. Not only did it have important long-term political implications, but it provided the test case for demonstrating that Germany was not prepared to accept the treaty provisions without protest. Once she had achieved some measure of relaxation on this issue, it was only a matter of time before she gained other concessions.

The final reparations bill was presented in May 1921 in the famous London Schedule. It was a heavy but not an impossible burden, though there is still much debate on this issue. Prior to the final tally Germany had been making interim payments equivalent to some 10 per cent of her national income. However, the precise figures are less important than the fact that Germany perceived the burden to be unreal. Failing to secure any relief by verbal argument, the German government resorted to the printing press to prove their incapacity to pay, the results of which were one of the most spectacular inflations in history.

From the longer-term point of view it is the political consequences of the debacle that are the most significant, rather than the fact that Germany gained some concessions in the revised payment schedules under the Dawes Plan of 1924. The inflationary experience probably contributed more to the disintegration of democracy in Germany than any other factor. By destroying the savings of many middle class citizens, it effectively undermined the bourgeois political consensus of Weimar Germany. In particular, the subsequent failure to implement a fair and equitable system of compensation for creditors who had borne the burden of inflation left many people extremely embittered and disenchanted with the Weimar regime, thereby resulting in 'a fundamental breakdown of voter identification with the traditional parties of bourgeois centre and right'. This led to the emergence of splinter parties composed of interest groups, shifting voter preferences and political instability. Ultimately it was the extreme right which became the major beneficiary of the alienated middle groups who were the chief losers from inflation. Estimates suggest that members of the Mittelstand (which included the bulk of the former creditors) accounted for a very substantial part of the Nazi Party's electoral support.

The Reconstruction Fiasco

Curiously, the Allied powers, having carved up Europe to almost no one's satisfaction, did little to ensure the viability of the new configuration. It was recognised that German recovery was important for the future prosperity of

Europe, though initially the Allies did their best to suppress it. It was also recognised, especially by the French, that security was equally important but
again little was done to secure it. However, arguably the most urgent task initially was that of ensuring the viability of the smaller and weaker states.

Apart from famine and relief deliveries in the immediate post-war
period, which proved totally inadequate, there was never any serious attempt
to plan the reconstruction of Europe. The United States had no desire to get
embroiled in European affairs on a permanent basis, while Allied cooperation
disintegrated soon after the ending of hostilities, partly because of Anglo-
American rivalry. Hence relief aid, most of which came from the United States,
was sharply curtailed after the summer of 1919. To make matters worse, the
sharp boom in commodity prices of 1919–20, followed by deflationary policies in the Anglo-Saxon countries, added to the difficulties of war-torn
Europe.

Thus the new states of Europe were left to fend for themselves and desperate conditions called forth desperate remedies, including trade control,
inflation and currency depreciation. Inflationary financing of budgetary defi-
cits became a convenient way of easing the task of reconstruction in the short-
term, since it gave a boost to economic activity and employment which was
paid for by a tax on people's cash balances. Whether the benefits outweighed
the costs is a debatable point given the fact that when stabilisation finally
occurred employment and output were checked, while many creditors lost
their savings. It is significant that by the mid-1920s industrial output in many
countries was still well below the 1913 level, while the one country that
showed solid advance was Czechoslovakia, which had stabilised her currency
and eliminated inflation at an early date.

Moreover, the drastic measures did little to solve the fundamental economic problems of the successor states and in fact they may well have weakened their political viability. The League of Nations in one of its later reports
explained how the economic and social fabric of many countries was allowed
to rot away and when it was finally faced, it had ceased to be a general problem of transition and reconstruction and had become a problem of cutting
the gangrene out of the most affected areas. Reconstruction in fact had to start
afresh once stabilisation was achieved and this time it was dependent on private foreign lending. This in turn added to the instability of the region: growing debt burdens at a time of weakening commodity prices eventually spelled
disaster in the early 1930s.

The International Monetary System

International currency matters exercised the minds of statesmen continually during the 1920s and beyond. The pre-war gold standard, on which so much faith had
been placed, disintegrated during the war and there was no plan to devise a new
system as occurred in the closing stages of the Second World War. Once wartime
control was removed most currencies depreciated sharply against the dollar, now
the strongest currency unit, and for the next few years the exchanges in Europe
'danced and jumped with tireless and spasmodic energy.'

On one point there was fairly universal agreement: that stabilisation of exchanges and a return to the gold standard were essential for trade revival and world prosperity. Yet despite several resolutions to this effect at international conferences in the early 1920s, no plan for coordinated action ever materialised. The result was that countries stabilised their currencies and returned to gold as and when it best suited them and largely without reference to the relative changes in costs and prices that had occurred since the war began. Inevitably therefore, restoration was a piecemeal affair with countries stabilising their exchanges throughout the decade at different dates and at different parities relative to pre-war rates. Britain, the Netherlands, Switzerland and the Scandinavian countries regained their pre-war parities, Austria, Germany, Hungary, Poland and Russia introduced new currency units after the old ones had become worthless through hyper-inflation, France, Belgium and Italy stabilised at one quarter to one fifth of their pre-war values, while other countries adopted even more devalued rates.

What materialised was a largely unworkable system of exchange rates, since so few were in equilibrium from the start. As the League of Nations commented: 'The piecemeal and haphazard manner of international monetary reconstruction sowed the seeds of subsequent disintegration. It was partly because of the lack of proper co-ordination during the stabilization period of the Twenties that the system broke down in the Thirties'. The pre-war parity countries had overvalued currencies, as did Italy, while France and Belgium had undervalued rates. No fixed exchange rate system can work satisfactorily when currencies are seriously misaligned; the essential feature of the pre-war system was that rates of exchange, among the major countries at least, were for the most part in equilibrium. Moreover, under the pre-war system there was a fair degree of harmony in rates of development and costs and price structures between countries, so that few really serious pressures emerged. This balance no longer prevailed post-war, due to the differential impact of war on European economies and the distortions caused by inflation and inter-country debts, among other things.

There were other factors making for a less effective international monetary system. The dispersion of leadership among three main financial centres (London, New York and Paris, whereas before 1914 Britain's hegemonic role had been important in orchestrating the system) was one important factor. In addition, failure to abide by the rules of the game, the increasing reluctance of countries to sacrifice domestic stability on the altar of the exchanges, and the greater volume and volatility of short-term capital movements between financial centres, all added to the problem.

The resurrected gold standard was not of course the prime cause of the great depression of the early 1930s. But, once begun, the links forged by the fixed exchange rate mechanism helped to transmit recessionary forces from one country to another. Some countries removed the constraint by going off gold and devaluing at an early date, but this only made things worse for the countries remaining on gold. Initially many countries were reluctant to abandon it for fear of the inflationary consequences, with recollections of the first half of the 1920s close to hand, and this in turn conditioned their policy reaction to the depression. In fact it was those countries which avoided inflation and returned to gold at the pre-war parity that were less averse to breaking the links with this system. Britain's departure in September 1931 effectively spelled the beginning of the end of the gold standard since many other countries followed suit, culminating in America's departure in 1933. By then only a few diehard countries such as France, Belgium, the Netherlands and Switzerland clung to gold, but they were forced to relinquish it by the middle of the decade.

The Leadership Issue and the Role of the United States

The European settlement as it emerged in the course of the 1920s had two main defects: it did not satisfy anyone, and it lacked firm leadership. France, Germany and Italy, for different reasons, were extremely disgruntled—France over compensation and the security issue, Germany because of the harsh treatment inflicted on her by the victors, and Italy as a result of unfulfilled promises of territory for joining the war. None of these countries was willing to promote the European cause. The remnants of the Austro-Hungarian Empire and the new and reconstituted states each in their turn had their grievances, all of which led to fragmentation rather than unity. This left Russia and Britain. The former, not having been invited to the Paris Peace Conference, was not particularly happy with the territorial arrangements arising from the peace settlement; but in any case her exclusion policy and domestic problems precluded her from playing a European role of any significance. And even when she did at a later date it took the form of clandestine communist infiltration into East European countries. Britain, the one country which might have been in a position to take an active role, was more concerned with her imperial connections, which meant that she preferred to view the affairs of Europe with benign indifference when it suited her to do so. The independence of the new states was welcomed so long as it did not involve active intervention. The attitude was summed up by the British Foreign Secretary (Simon) in a communication to the Prime Minister (MacDonald) in July 1934 over the question of Austria: 'Our policy is quite clear. We must keep out of trouble in Central Europe at all costs.... There are circumstances in which Italy might move troops into Austria. There are no circumstances in which we would ever dream of doing so'. In fact a year later Simon was of the view that the ramshackle regime was only worth tolerating 'for fear of meeting something worse.'

The result of this fissiparous tendency, in contrast to the situation after 1945, was that competitive national sovereignties dominated the scene in the 1920s to such an extent that there was little prospect of achieving unity and stability in Europe.

The question is why did America not take over the European mantle and reshape the destiny of Europe as she was to do after the Second World War? America's entry into the war and Woodrow Wilson's grandiose designs for Europe initially augured well for the future. Yet the United States was subsequently to play a very equivocal role in the affairs of Europe. She refused to ratify the Versailles Treaty, failed to endorse the League of Nations, abandoned the relief of Europe with almost indecent haste, and rejected proposals to link reparations and interallied war debts. Moreover, though America professed a belief in the importance of European recovery, her own economic policy often ran counter to the interests of European countries, for example on matters of tariffs, immigration, overseas lending and monetary policy. It is true that her attitude towards Germany was more lenient than that of either Britain or France, but this only served to antagonise the French since it offered little in the way of security against a recalcitrant Germany.

America's isolationist approach towards Europe has to be seen within the context of her domestic politics. The United States had entered the war reluctantly in April 1917. After the conclusion of hostilities there was a wave of revulsion against war and military activity, together with an unwillingness to get involved in the affairs of other countries which might lead to further conflict. This largely explains why the United States found herself in such a low state of military preparedness at the outbreak of the Second World War. The United States also felt remote from the European scene, both geographically and politically, and her own domestic interests were affected only marginally by what happened in Europe. Unlike the situation after the Second World War, America did not perceive any immediate power threat from Europe, and though European recovery was regarded as intrinsically important it was never seen as crucial to her own well-being. Thus, when it suited her own needs, the United States could afford to turn a blind eye to the problems of Europe, especially as these seemed likely to entail direct involvement in the affairs of that continent. America's refusal to assume a hegemonic role had several unfortunate consequences. It meant first of all, that certain aspects of the post-war settlement, such as reparations and territorial rights, emerged as international issues. Secondly, it left Europe stranded in the early and later 1920s when American credits ceased to flow. For a time private benefaction in the form of international lending emerged to fill the gap, but over which there was little control. As Hogan comments: 'The toothless loan control programme left the American government with no way to ensure that capital exports really contributed to recovery' Thirdly, it robbed Europe of the leadership it so badly needed in the 1920s, especially with regard to currency stabilisation. Finally, the absence of US backing meant that the League of Nations played a diminutive role in the affairs of Europe. Apart from its work in rescuing several countries on the point of disintegration, perhaps its most lasting contribution was the large number of papers and documents it produced for the benefit of later historians.

Conclusion

Clearing up after a major war is always a messy business. Unfortunately the Allied statesmen did not do a very good job in the aftermath of the First World War. Had the Allied powers made a more concerted effort to provide for the reconstruction and stability of Europe, things might have turned out differently. As it was Europe remained in a fragile state both politically and economically and hence was unable to withstand later shocks. The Allies themselves were divided on many issues and it was all too easy therefore for nations to plough their own furrow with little regard for the greater good of Europe as a whole. Sovereignty rights and national issues counted for more than the sum of the parts. As Ross noted, 'There were few good Europeans'.

NO

Mark Mazower

Two Cheers For Versailles

Some suggest that Versailles was based on principles inconsistently applied. The charge is obviously true. The right of national self-determination was granted at Germany's expense, and the Anschluss with Austria, which Social Democrats in Vienna wanted in 1918, was prevented by the Great Powers and only achieved after the Nazis broke the League of Nations system and marched in twenty years later. But international affairs are not a matter of logic alone, and the principle of consistency must be matched against considerations of power politics or geography. National self-determination could never have been applied across the board; the basic issue is whether a better principle existed for the re-ordering of Europe.

More serious an accusation is that the peace settlement was not so much inconsistent as ineffective: it was based upon an inaccurate appraisal of the European balance of power and deprived of the means of its own defence by American withdrawal and British indifference. At Paris the Great Powers ignored the fact that the almost simultaneous collapse of Germany and Russia had produced an anomalous situation in eastern Europe. The French, who of all the Great Powers felt most immediately threatened, thought the only safe-guard of their own security—if the League was not to be equipped with an army of its own—was alliance with grateful clients like the Baltic states, Poland, Czechoslovakia, Romania and Yugoslavia. But it should have been obvious that the newly independent states formed there would be unable alone to ensure stability in the region once these two Great Powers reasserted themselves. The Treaty of Brest Litovsk of early 1918 had shown what intentions the Germans of the Kaiserreich harboured in that area; after 1939, Hitler's New Order pushed the principle of German (and Russian) hegemony one brutal stage further. But this is less an argument against the Versailles settlement itself than against the refusal of the Great Powers who sponsored it to back it up with armed force before 1939.

Thirdly, it is often felt that the whole approach to Germany after the Treaty was flawed. The enemy was humiliated but not crushed, burdened by reparations yet unopposed when it rearmed and marched into the Rhineland. It is true that the contrast is striking with the policies pursued towards Germany after the Second World War when long-term economic assistance was provided and by governments not the markets, and when the Bundeswehr was quickly incorporated within west European defence arrangements. But the

From *History Today*, vol. 49, issue 7, July 1999, pp. 8-14. Copyright © 1999 by History Today, Ltd. Reprinted by permission.

economic problem after 1919 was not so much reparations as the shaky structure of international lending and, in particular, the shock of the world depression. The Allies were helped to learn from the mistakes of the inter-war era by the Cold War, which divided Germany, and made Europe's German problem a question of reunification rather than of territorial expansion and revanche in the East.

Finally, there is the accusation common to conservatives and Communists alike that the Versailles peace settlement was overly ideological. For some, it was an extension of nineteenth-century liberal moralising, a combination of British utilitarianism and American idealism—a basically philosophical approach to the world which lacked realism or understanding of the political passions which animated people in Europe.

Alternatively, it was—behind the veil of noble sentiments—an anti-Communist crusade whose liberalism masked a fundamentally reactionary and deeply conservative goal: the containment, if not the crushing, of Bolshevism. Outflanked gradually by other more determined and forceful anti-Communist movements of the right, European liberals lost their enthusiasm for defending the Versailles order and sat back to watch fascism take over the task of saving Europe from red revolution.

One question, however, confronts the critics of Versailles: what were the alternatives? It was not, after all, as if the Powers had willed this new liberal order of independent, democratic nation-states into existence. They had certainly not been fighting the Great War to this end. On the contrary, as late as 1918 most Entente diplomats still favoured the preservation of the old empires in central Europe in the interests of continental stability. Of course, after 1919 the conflicts and tensions produced by the new states of the region made many people nostalgic for what the Austrian writer Stefan Zweig, looking back to the Habsburg era, called 'the world of yesterday'. Fragmentation since the war seemed to have harmed the region both politically and economically, especially once the world depression forced countries into an impoverished self-sufficiency.

Yet it was a rare blend of nostalgia and realpolitik which lay behind much of the antipathy to Versailles. The makers of America's new role in Europe after 1945, for example, who had grown up looking closely at these problems, held Versailles responsible for the instability of interwar Europe. Adolf Berle, Roosevelt's assistant secretary of state between 1938 and 1944, believed that French generals had been responsible for breaking up the Austro-Hungarian Empire and wanted some kind of reconstitution of that entity to ward off the Russians. Hitler, he advised the president on the eve of Munich, was perhaps 'the only instrument capable of re-establishing a race and economic unit which can survive and leave Europe in balance.'

George Kennan, a younger man but more influential than Berle in defining the Cold War policy of containment, took a very similar view in the late 1930s. In his despatches from Prague he wrote:

It is generally agreed that the breakup of the limited degree of unity which the Habsburg Empire represented was unfortunate for all concerned. Other forces are now at work which are struggling to create a new form of unity.... To these forces Czechoslovakia has been tragically slow in adjusting herself....   The adjustment—and this is the main thing—has now come.

It did not take long for someone as astute as Kennan to realise that the Nazi New Order was not going to stabilise central Europe in the way the Habsburgs had done. But the reason for this, in his mind, was not the apparently obvious one that Hitler's whole upbringing had turned him into a German nationalist critic of the Austro-Hungarian monarchy. It was, rather, what Kennan conceived as the excessively democratic character of Hitler's Germany and the limited involvement of Germany's aristocracy in the Third Reich. More aristocratic government was Kennan's answer to Europe's problems. It is hard to imagine a more far-fetched or unrealistic approach—the Habsburgs were marginalised between the wars even by Hungary's reactionary regent Admiral Horthy, and the most successful Habsburg aristocrat of that era was the bizarre and premature proponent of European union, Count Coudenhove-Kalergi. Perhaps only an American conservative intellectual like Kennan could have taken the prospect of a Habsburg restoration seriously. European conservatives, closer to the ground, had fewer illusions. 'The Vienna to Versailles period has run its course,' wrote the historian Lewis Namier in February 1940.

Whatever the weaknesses of the system created in 1919, a return to previous forms is impossible. They have been broken, and broken for good.

It was not aristocrats that had kept the old empires together but dynastic loyalty, and this had vanished. If dynasticism no longer offered an alternative principle to the Versailles order, then what of the rival ideologies of right and left? This was where root-and-branch critics of Versailles had to bite the bullet. Most anti-Communists between the wars had no difficulty in swallowing the idea of an authoritarian revision of the Versailles settlement. What made them hesitate was a quite different proposition; the reality of life under the Nazi New Order. The difference between a right tolerable to most conservatives and an extreme and ideological fascism was that, for instance, between King Alexander's royal dictatorship in Yugoslavia, and Ante Pavelic's genocidal Ustase state in Croatia, or between King Carol's Romania and that of the Iron Guard, with its bloody pogroms, in the winter of 1940–41. Above all, the New Order was based on the idea of German racial superiority, and few anti-Communists could stomach this once they saw what it meant in terms of practical politics.

If one agreed with Namier that 'no system can possibly be maintained on the European Continent east of the Rhine which has not the support either of Germany or of Russia,' then the only ideological alternative to Nazism was Communism, or more precisely the extension of Russian rule westwards into Europe. Just as Versailles's critics on the right had seen Germany's move east after 1933 as confirmation of their own prejudices, so critics on the left similarly interpreted the course of events after 1943 as a happy necessity. Historians like E.H. Carr saw this as realism replacing the idealism of Versailles. It was apparently not felt to be realistic to point out that all the historical evidence pointed to the unpopularity of Communism among the majority of the populations who now had to endure it. In only one country in central Europe,

Hungary, had a Bolshevik regime held power for any length of time before 1945, and that still brief experience—the Bela Kun regime of 1919—had only confirmed how unpropitious the soil was for such experiments. Today we are unlikely to see Communism as an attractive alternative to the principles embodied in the Versailles order: yesterday's 'realism' looks riddled with its own form of wishful thinking.

One of the reasons Bela Kun fell from power in 1919 was that he had not understood the strength of Hungarian nationalist feeling. So long as it had appeared to Hungarians that Bolshevik Russia might help them get back their traditional lands, they were prepared to tolerate Kun. But once it appeared that the Allies would not let this happen, Kun lost any popularity he had once enjoyed and he was easily defeated. The power of nationalism was the chief force to emerge from the First World War in Europe, and was the main political factor facing the architects of a new postwar settlement. From our perspective at the century's end, it hardly looks as though fascism and Communism were able to handle European nationalism better than the peacemakers at Versailles. Hitler's New Order proceeded by ignoring all nationalisms except the German, and lost Europe in consequence. Communism believed that eventually nationalist antipathies would vanish, subsumed within an internationalist struggle: but time ran out for the Communists before this happened. If we want to find guidance in the past for how to tackle the problems of nationalism that remain in Europe, we cannot do better than return to the diplomats who gathered in Paris eighty years ago.

In the Bukovina (a former province of the Habsburg empire), Paris seemed very far away in the spring of 1919. But events were occurring there which help us chart the trajectory of antisemitic violence from the unorganised pogroms of the nineteenth century to the more systematic population engineering of the twentieth. A manifesto was posted up in the village of Kamenestie, written in Romanian:

> Order to all the Jews in the village.
> Those Jews who are still in the village are asked to go to the city or somewhere else. You can leave in good condition [sic] and without fear in ten days. It will be made unbearable for those who stay beyond the limit.

Throughout the little villages of the Bukovina, pogroms were taking place in late 1918. 'Following the example of the neighbouring villages,' runs an account from Petroutz,

> The peasants decided to drive the Jews out of this place. On the night of November 17th, they attacked the Jewish families Hermann, Feller and Schubert, broke doors and windows and took away everything they found. A scroll of the Law was torn to pieces by the marauders. After the robbery they burned everything that remained. All three families fled to Suczawa.

The Jews were the chief targets of ethnic violence in the Bukovina, as they were elsewhere in eastern Europe, in Galicia for instance, or in Lithuania. But the war of nationalities could not be reduced to antisemitism: Poles were fighting with Ukrainians, Germans and Lithuanians. Across much of Europe there fell, a double shadow: ethnic as well as class war. Bolshevism was contained by a combination of land reform, reformist social democracy and the military defeat of the Red Army in the Russo-Polish war. But the nationalist enmities and suspicions which exploded into violence as the First World War ended, and which generated casualties on such a scale that some historians have compared them with the violence which erupted under Nazi rule after 1941, these proved harder to tackle.

Ethnic civil war emphasised in the most unmistakable way that the peacemakers in Paris were not sketching their maps on a tabula rasa. On the contrary, they were as much responding to circumstances as shaping them. East European critics of Great Power arrogance often forget today how far the Versailles settlement was brought into being, not by the Powers, but by local nationalist elites and their supporters. New nations were pressing their claims on paper, in the streets and by force of arms, as the war approached an end. Serb, Croat and Slovene delegates issued the Corfu Declaration in July 1917 and declared the new tripartite Yugoslav nation 'a worthy member of the new Community of Nations.'

The Provisional People's Government of the Polish Republic proclaimed 'the authority of Polish democracy' in its November 1918 manifesto. The Czech National Committee seized power in Prague as early as October 28th of the same year in the name of the infant Czechoslovak state. Much of the subsequent fighting from the Baltic to the Balkans was designed to conquer as much territory as possible for the new states, to see off rival claimants and to settle scores with Jews, Germans, Muslims and other hated, despised or feared peoples. Between 1920 and 1923, the Treaty of Sèvres was signed, scrapped and replaced by the Treaty of Lausanne as the struggle between Greece and Turkey shifted first one way then the other, culminating eventually in the forced population exchange of some two million people.

It is to the credit of the Versailles peacemakers that they confronted the problem of ethnic violence head on. They were aware of the chief defect of the Wilsonian principle of national self-determination—namely that if it was interpreted territorially and not merely as a grant of cultural autonomy, then on its own it ruled out either an equitable or a geographically coherent settlement of the problems of central and eastern Europe. No one, after all, was proposing to give the Kashubians, the Polesians, the Pomaks, or any of the other small ethnic groups of the region a state of their own. They, and several other larger peoples like the Jews, the Ukrainians and the Macedonians, would remain under the rule of others. In other words, the creation—or better, the recognition—of nation-states at Versailles was accompanied by its inescapable shadow, the problem of minorities.

Fearful in particular that Poland's appetite for territory might destabilise the whole area, the Powers obliged the reluctant Poles to sign a treaty granting the country's very sizeable minority population certain rights. The Polish treaty formed the basis for a series of similar treaties imposed in 1919 and 1920 upon most of the states of central and eastern Europe. The result was that for the first time an international organisation—the League of Nations—assumed the right to intervene in a member state's internal affairs on behalf of minority populations.

This right, however, was very limited and scarcely used at all by the League. Most countries feared doing away with the idea that a state was sovereign within its own borders, and even the Great Powers who had sponsored the Minority Rights Treaties trod warily. They had resisted calls to universalise the regime of minority rights on the grounds that 'the League cannot assume to guarantee good government in this matter throughout the world'. By 1929 they were very reluctant to act at all against member states accused of rights violations. British foreign secretary Austen Chamberlain warned that,

> We have not reached such a degree of solidarity in international affairs that any of us welcome even the most friendly intervention in what we consider to be our domestic affairs.

This attitude discouraged the most dynamic lobbyists for Europe's minorities, the Germans and the Jews. Until 1933, they worked together in the European Congress of Nationalities to try to give the Minorities Treaties teeth. Thereafter their paths diverged. But Hitler's rise to power can be seen in the context of the failure of the League to protect Europe's minorities. Where the League's rather timid use of international law had failed, the Nazis used force; their 'solution' involved forced population transfer, resettlement and ultimately genocide. And after 1944 many of these instruments were turned on the Germans themselves as they were driven out of Poland and the former Habsburg lands.

Yet we should not write off the peacemakers of Versailles too quickly. Despite the horrors of the 1940s, which virtually eliminated both the Jews and the Germans from much of eastern Europe, many minorities remained across the region. However, instead of building on the League's tentative efforts to construct an international regime of minority rights, the architects of the post-war order enshrined in the United Nations deliberately retreated from the problem and tried to dress up its reluctance to deal with it with meaningless persiflage about 'human rights'. As a result, when issues of minority rights came to the fore after the collapse of Communism in eastern Europe in the decade after 1989, most obviously in the context of the disintegration of Yugoslavia, the international community possessed no coherent strategy for tackling the problem.

The consequences have been all too visible in Bosnia and Kosovo. The United Nations was less equipped to tackle the fundamental problem of minority rights than its predecessor, the League, had been. It delivered food and tried to keep the peace without a clear doctrine of what kind of peace it should keep. The contrast between the self-confident and articulate liberal universalism of the 1920s and the post-modern evasions of the 1990s was all too conspicuous. In Kosovo, too, the contrast with the Versailles generation does not flatter our own times. NATO intervention in Kosovo could, as articulated somewhat optimistically by Tony Blair, be interpreted as marking a new doctrine of foreign affairs, according to which state sovereignty may be overridden to prevent massive violations of minority rights. Yet, NATO's attacks on the Serbs, in the absence of any UN mandate, do not indicate any great confidence in international law and institutions. The United States, which has been leading the charge, is, after all, opposed to the creation of an International Criminal Court. If inter-war Europe suffered because international guarantees were never acted upon, we may suffer in the 1990s through military action taken without any reference to international law at all, the late twentieth-century equivalent of gunboat diplomacy handled by a post-Holocaust generation of politicians.

The very least, then, that we can say for Versailles is that it recognised and articulated the major problems for European stability at that time. What was more, there was no palatable alternative to the nation-state then, or since. Where the peace was found wanting between the wars was in the will to uphold it. Today NATO is turning itself into the kind of force which the peacemakers of 1919 lacked. But do its political masters have a clear grasp of what kind of Europe they wish to defend? They could do worse than cast their eyes back to the work of their predecessors eighty years ago. ...

POSTSCRIPT

Was the Treaty of Versailles Responsible for World War II?

Europe's history has been marked by post-war treaties that have placed their stamp upon the generations that followed: the Peace of Augsburg (1555), which temporarily ended the continent's religious wars; the Peace of Utrecht in 1713, which stopped French King Louis XIV's domination of Europe; the 1815 Congress of Vienna, which brought an end to Napoleon's domination of Europe and established a new continental governing order; and the Treaty of Versailles, which marked the end of the First World War. One thing that these all had in common was that the peace they brought was only temporary. What was responsible for these failures? Was it weaknesses inherent in the peace processes, or was it the greed of nation states acting in their own self-interests that killed the peace in these instances? Some comparative research into these attempts at peace might produce worthwhile information.

Traditionally, it was easy to speak ill of the Treaty of Versailles. Making Germany eager for revenge, paving the way for Adolf Hitler's rise to power, creating inconsistent boundary lines drawn up by uninformed statesmen—all have been cited as evidence of the peace conference's weaknesses. And we now know what resulted from them.

But is it the treaty that was at fault, or was it the actions and inactions of a generation of European who were not up to the task of enforcing the treaty's provisions? It created a League of Nations for such actions, but the League proved incapable of using it for that avowed purpose. Sometimes institutions fail; sometimes individuals fail; oftentimes both are responsible for the failures that occur.

For sources on the Treaty of Versailles, see John Maynard Keynes, *The Economic Consequences of the Peace* (Vintage Classics, 1995), written by a man who was a member of the British delegation to the Paris Peace Conference, but eventually resigned to show his disgust and disapproval for its process and results. His book is a classic in the field. More recently, Manfred F. Boemeke, Gerald D. Feldman, and Elizabeth Glaser, eds., *The Treaty of Versailles: A Reassessment After 75 Years* (Cambridge University Press, 1998), provides a more balanced account of the Treaty of Versailles' strengths and weaknesses.

ISSUE 9

Did the Bolshevik Revolution Improve the Lives of Soviet Women?

YES: Richard Stites, from "Women and the Revolutionary Process in Russia," in Renate Bridenthal, Claudia Koontz, and Susan M. Stuard, eds., *Becoming Visible: Women in European History,* 2nd ed. (Houghton Mifflin, 1987)

NO: Lesley A. Rimmel, from "The Baba and the Comrade: Gender and Politics in Revolutionary Russia," *The Women's Review of Books* (September 1998)

ISSUE SUMMARY

YES: History professor Richard Stites argues that, in the early years of the Bolshevik Revolution, the Zhenotdel, or Women's Department, helped many working women take the first steps toward emancipation.

NO: Russian scholar Lesley A. Rimmel finds that the Russian Revolution remains unfinished for women, who were mobilized as producers and reproducers for a male political agenda.

Compared with life under the czars, life for women after the Bolshevik Revolution was characterized by greater variety and freedom. The Romanov dynasty had ruled Russia for 300 years and the Orthodox Church had been entrenched for a much longer period. Both had reinforced a world of patriarchal authority, class structure, and patterns of deference. Although the revolution overthrew the power of both church and monarch, the new communist state had a power and authority of its own. Between 1917 and 1920, Soviet women received equal rights in education and marriage, including the choice to change or keep their own names and the opportunity to own property; the rights to vote and hold public office; access to no-fault divorce, common-law marriage, and maternity benefits; workplace protection; and access to unrestricted abortion. They were the first women to gain these rights—ahead of women in France, England, and the United States—but the question is whether or not these legal rights translated into improvements in their day-to-day lives.

A feminist movement had developed in urban areas as early as the 1905 workers' revolution, and women joined men in leading strikes and protest demonstrations. By the time of the Bolshevik Revolution in 1917, however, the goals of the leadership were primarily economic, and feminism was dismissed as bourgeois or middle class. In a workers' revolution, women and men were to be equal. Housework and childcare were to be provided collectively, and the family, like the monarchy, was to be replaced with something new. In theory, women would become workers and gain access to economic independence, which would provide them the basis for equality within marriage.

German philosopher Karl Marx had argued that the family reflects the economic system in society. Under capitalism, the bourgeois family exists to reproduce workers and consumers; it exploits women by unfairly burdening them with full responsibility for housework and childcare. If similarly exploited workers—what Marx called the proletariat—overthrew the capitalist system that allowed factory owners to grow rich from their workers' labor, Marx believed that the family would undergo an equally dramatic transformation. In this scenario, no one would be "owned" by anyone else. Prostitution would disappear, and, as the state took responsibility for childrearing and education, women would be free to work and become economically self-sufficient. People would then be free to marry for love or sexual attraction rather than for economic considerations.

V.I. Lenin, who emerged as leader and architect of the new order, was committed to women's rights. First and foremost, however, he was committed to a socialist revolution. When the struggle to make abstract legal changes "real" in women's lives came into conflict with the goals of the revolution, there was no question in Lenin's mind about which would have to be sacrificed. In this early period, a fascinating group of women briefly held highly visible leadership positions and had the chance to put their ideas into practice, at least during the first decade. Alexandra Kollontai was one of the most articulate and effective leaders of the Zhenotdel, or Women's Department of the Communist Party, whose purpose between 1919 and 1930 was to educate and mobilize the women of the Soviet state to participate fully in the revolution.

In the following selections, Richard Stites focuses on what he calls the "idealistic foreground" of the Revolution—the part that is so often overlooked. Although poverty, cynicism, bureaucratic resistance, rural superstition, and urban blight ultimately thwarted many early dreams of reformers such as Alexandra Kollontai; bold efforts undertaken by the Zhenotdel and experiments in sexual equality raised the consciousness of women and men. A brief glimpse of what might be possible in a stable society kept the dreams and experiments alive—at least for a time, Stites concludes.

Lesley A. Rimmel uses the contrasting images of the baba—an ignorant peasant women—and the comrade—a full-fledged human and citizen—to describe how Russian women were targeted as workers in a class revolution while gender roles remained firmly in place. Rimmel sees the long-delayed gender goals, articulated during the Russian Revolution, including the right of women to define comradeship on their own terms, as, finally, being addressed in contemporary Russia.

Richard Stites

 **YES**

Women and the Revolutionary Process in Russia

Before the Revolution

Russian society before 1917 was a world of patriarchal power, deferential ritual, clear authority patterns, and visible hierarchy with stratified social classes or estates. At the pinnacle of the state, the tsar-emperor (called *batyushka* or little father by the common folk), considered Russia as a family estate or patrimony and his subjects as children—virtuous, obedient, and loyal. The imperial bureaucratic order of ranks, chanceries, uniforms, and rigidly ordered parades constituted a visual celebration of authoritarianism. To subjects of all classes of the empire, every official building—with its geography of guarded entrances, pass booths, waiting areas, office gates—represented authority, inequality, and the demand for deference. Far from the capital and the towns, in the vastness of rural Russia, a simpler absolutism prevailed in the village cabins where the male head of household wielded domestic power that contrasted sharply with the more or less egalitarian land distribution customs of the village community. The Russian Orthodox Church reinforced values of obedience and subordination at every level in its liturgical idiom, its symbols, its organization, and its political ethos of support for a conservative order. The women dwelling within this ancient authoritarian world felt the additional weight of male power and suffered from the sexual division of labor and open inequality between the sexes....

Women who chose not to challenge the regime and its entire patriarchal structure but who nonetheless wished to improve the lot of women organized the Russian feminist movement (ca. 1860–1917). Feminist women shared the class background (largely gentry) of the nihilists and radicals, but did not call for the destruction of the existing social system. They worked for women's rights—not for the rights of peasants or workers, and not on behalf of a socialist vision. In the four decades or so after 1860 feminists agitated, with considerable success, for permission to form legal societies, engage in charity work, and open university level and medical courses for women. These courses produced impressive numbers of physicians, teachers, lawyers, and engineers. At the dawn of the twentieth century, feminists turned their attention to the national suffrage issue and continued to press for and win reforms in the status of women in the realm of property rights, divorce, freedom of movement, and other matters that primarily affected women of the gentry and the professional classes of Russia. From 1905 to 1917, no fewer than four feminist parties struggled unsuccessfully in the political arena. Thus all women (and millions of men) remained without representation in the central government. Russian feminism, in the words of its most eloquent historian, was "a movement for women's civil and political equality, whose supporters trusted that a better world could be created without resort to violence, and a constitutional solution be found to Russia's ills." ...

Political Parties

The political parties of the late imperial Russia reacted to the question of women's rights in much the same way as their counterparts in Western Europe—their views on this issue being a litmus test for their outlook on social change and mass interests. Those on the right displayed outright hostility to any kind of feminist platform, identifying legitimate politics with the male sex and proclaiming as their program Faith, Tsar, and Fatherland. The liberal parties in the center—the Kadets, or Constitutional Democrats, most prominent among them—initially wavered on the question of votes for women in the Duma but by 1906 supported the more moderate of the feminist parties. The socialists—like the Populists earlier and like their counterparts in Western Europe—proclaimed support for women's equality, including political equality, maternity protection, and equal economic rights.

The socialist parties also included women activists at many levels, some of whom would become prominent political figures during the Revolution of 1917. Of the three major socialist parties—Socialist Revolutionary, Social Democrat-Menshevik, and Social Democrat-Bolshevik—the first eventually became the largest and most variegated. Heirs to the Populist tradition of the nineteenth century, the Socialist Revolutionaries continued to focus on peasant agrarian socialism and an alliance of the "social trinity": peasant, worker, and intelligentsia. Loose in organization and weak in theory, the Socialist Revolutionary party periodically fell back upon terror as its main weapon. Its best-known women were Ekaterina Breshko-Breshkovskaya (1844–1934), a veteran Populist of the 1870s who tried in the 1905 period to promote a theory of "agrarian terror" that included assaults on landlords in the countryside; and Maria Spiridonova (1886–?), a young schoolteacher who achieved fame first by her assassination of a general in 1906 and then in 1917 as the leader of the Left Socialist Revolutionary party. The Socialist Revolutionaries—like the Anarchist groups—could deploy a large number of female terrorists, but women played a minimal role in the organizational and theoretical work of the party.

The Marxists (Social Democrats) had split into Mensheviks and Bolsheviks in 1903. Both enrolled large numbers of women but in neither did many women rise to leadership positions. Among the Mensheviks, Vera Zasulich was the best-known woman (her fame arose from an attempted assassination she had performed in the 1870s) but her political influence remained strictly secondary. The most important activist women among the Bolsheviks—Roza Zemlyachka and Elena Stasova—were tough organizers, but not leaders or theoreticians. In all the socialist parties the leadership remained in the hands of men, men who spent most of the years from 1905 to 1917 in the émigré centers of Western Europe. Two of the best-known Bolshevik women, Nadezhda Krupskaya (Lenin's wife) and Inessa Armand (their friend), made their mark as loyal assistants of the party leader, Lenin, in the emigration years.

The presence of women in the major socialist parties did not advance the cause of women's rights in Russia. Less than ten percent of the delegates to Socialist Revolutionary conferences in the peak years from 1905 to 1908 were women; the percentages were even lower in Marxist and Social Democratic parties. Even if more women had risen to the top of these organizations, however, the picture would not have changed. Women constituted one-third of the Executive Committee of the People's Will of the 1870s, for example, yet those women displayed almost no interest in the issue of women's rights as such. The same mood prevailed in the generation of 1905; revolutionary women put what they called the "common cause" above what they saw as lesser issues. Vera Zasulich, when asked to help in forming a women workers' club, refused.

The most notable exception, Alexandra Kollontai, had to fight on many fronts when she set about combining the advocacy of women's rights with socialism: against her feminist competitors, against indifference in her own party (she was at first a Menshevik and later a Bolshevik), and against the prevailing opinion of the conservative society. Kollontai, a general's daughter, had come to a feminist consciousness through personal experience—the conflict of work and family. Like many European socialist women, particularly Clara Zetkin, Kollontai believed that women had special problems that Marxist programs did not sufficiently address. She opposed the feminists as bourgeois; she believed that women workers should rally to the proletarian banner; but she also insisted that working women needed their own self-awareness—as workers and as women. Out of this set of beliefs arose the Proletarian Women's Movement.

In the years from 1905 to 1908 Kollontai fought to create a socialist-feminist movement in order to win away proletarian women of St. Petersburg from the feminists who were trying to organize them into an "all-women's" movement. For three years, Kollontai and a few associates agitated among the factory women, taught them Marxism, and attempted to show them that their principal enemy was the bourgeoisie, not men. In this struggle, Kollontai opposed the bourgeois (as she perceived it) program of the feminists with her own vision of socialist feminism—a combination of gender and class awareness, a recognition of the double exploitation of working-class women (as workers and as women), and an honest facing of the issue of abusive proletarian husbands and insensitive socialist males. Although Kollontai exaggerated the selfish class character of Russian feminists, she did in fact go beyond them and beyond her own comrades in the socialist movement in trying to draw attention to these issues. Police harassment in 1908 forced her to leave the country, and during her years in Western Europe Kollontai deepened her understanding of the woman question through study and personal experience.

The Eve of Revolution

On the eve of war and revolution, the woman question in tsarist society remained a public issue. Thousands of women graduates of universities had entered professional life; hundreds languished in jail or in Siberia for their chosen profession as revolutionaries. The female terrorist was the Russian counterpart to the British suffragette—but far more violent. Organized feminists continued to agitate for important reforms in the status of women and won considerable legislative victories in legal, educational, and property rights—though mainly for women of the middle and upper classes. The female work force continued to grow and to feel the rigors of industrial life and of relative neglect by the rest of society. With the revival of the militant labor movement around 1912, Mensheviks and Bolsheviks alike reactivated their efforts to organize women workers. International Women's Day, established in Europe in 1910, was celebrated by adherents of both factions for the first time on Russian soil in 1913, and a newspaper, *The Woman Worker*, was established in 1914. During World War I much of the machinery for organizing women workers was smashed by the authorities and many leaders were arrested before the monarchy itself fell a victim to the same war.

The Revolutionary Era

After three winters of bitter fighting, bloody losses, and patent mismanagement of the war, widespread discontent and hatred of the regime found a focus. In February 1917, cold and hungry women of the capital (renamed Petrograd) rioted, beginning an uprising that led to the collapse of the Romanov dynasty within a week. With the men at the front and the women left behind as workers, breadwinners, and heads of households, the women of the lower classes perceived food shortages and related deprivations as a menace to their very existence and to their roles as women. They struck, demonstrated, rioted, and appealed to the class solidarity of garrison troops to persuade the troops not to fire upon them. When the tsar abdicated, the revolutionary parties linked up with the masses of women. A band of energetic Bolshevik women organizers—including Kollontai—created a network of agitation that was effective in spite of tactical squabbles and the enormous problems of communication in the midst of a major revolt. This network produced mass female demonstrations on behalf of Bolshevik issues, organized women in factories, and enlisted others in political, paramedical, and paramilitary work. Bolshevik leadership and dynamism in this arena proved vastly superior to that of the other radical parties, and Bolshevik hostility to the now-revived feminist movement was active and unambiguous. Out of this year of struggle and organization in many cities emerged the symbolically important "presence" of women in the October Revolution as well as the foundations of a post-revolutionary women's movement.

The Bolsheviks took power on October 25 (November 7 in the modern calendar), 1917, and established a Soviet socialist regime; in 1918 they moved the capital to Moscow, issued a constitution that was the framework for the world's first socialist state, and made peace with Germany. The first years of the new regime were marked by ruthless political struggle on all sides, a bloody and cruel civil war, intervention in that war by foreign troops on behalf of the anti-Bolshevik forces, and a deepening of the extraordinary economic hardship set off by war and revolution and made inevitable by the very backwardness of the country.

How, in this time of dreadful calamity, did the Bolshevik regime perceive the issue—historically always seen as marginal by all governments—of the emancipation of women? What did they do about it? The answers are very complicated; any assessment of their response depends upon how one views revolution in general and the Bolshevik Revolution in particular, and upon one's expectations from an insurgent, culture-changing government that sets out to remake the face of one of the largest countries in the world.

The men and women in the Bolshevik party displayed the contradictions inherent in all forceful agents of social and cultural change: practicality combined with vision, the imperatives of survival combined with the dream of transformation. The party's leader, V. I. Lenin, as both a Marxist and a Russian revolutionary, committed himself and his party to the educational, economic, legal, and political liberation of women; to the interchangeability of gender roles in a future under communism; and to special protection for woman as childbearer and nurturing mother. In addition, Lenin possessed an almost compulsive hatred of the domestic enslavement of women to mindless household work which he called "barbarously unproductive, petty, nerve-wracking, stultifying and crushing drudgery." Lenin's male and female colleagues shared his opinions on these major issues and framed their laws and policies accordingly. Most important, they endorsed the creation of a special women's organization to oversee the realization of these programs in Soviet society. Women did not play a major role in the upper reaches of the party hierarchy; and indeed hostility toward the expenditure of time on women's issues persisted in the party at various levels. This was an inheritance of the twenty years of underground life of party struggle, of the military mentality of Bolshevism that hardened during the Civil War, and of the upsurge within the party of people holding "traditional" patriarchal views of the female sex. In spite of these obvious weaknesses, it is astonishing what the Bolshevik regime proclaimed and actually carried out in the early years of Soviet power.

In a series of decrees, codes, electoral laws, and land reforms, the Bolsheviks proclaimed an across-the-board equality of the sexes—the first regime in history ever to do so. All institutions of learning were opened to women and girls. Women attained equal status in marriage—including the right to change or retain their own names—divorce, family, and inheritance and equal rights in litigation and the ownership of property. By separating church and state, the Bolsheviks legally invalidated all canonical and theological restrictions on the role of women in modern life—a sweeping and drastic measure in a land wrapped in the constraining meshes of traditional faiths, particularly Russian Orthodoxy and Islam. In 1920 the Bolsheviks legalized abortion. On the other hand, prostitution (legally licensed under the old regime) was made illegal. Taken together, these measures offered a structure for equality between the sexes unprecedented in history. The Bolsheviks offered a process as well: the organizations that helped overthrow the old order would help to erect the new one; art, culture, symbol, and mythic vision would reinforce the values of sexual equality.

The organizational form of women's liberation in the first decade of the Bolshevik (now renamed Communist) regime was the Women's Department of the Communist Party (1919–1930), known by its Russian abbreviation Zhenotdel. Founded as an arm of the party rather than as an independent feminist organization, Zhenotdel—led by Inessa Armand and Alexandra Kollontai in the early years—worked to transform the new revolutionary laws into reality through education, mobilization, and social work. Understaffed and hampered by a small budget, Zhenotdel went into the factory neighborhoods, the villages, and the remote provinces of the new Soviet state to bring the message of the Revolution to the female population. Instructors and trainees from among workers and peasant women addressed the practical concerns of women. In the towns they monitored factory conditions and fought against female unemployment and prostitution. In the countryside they opened literacy classes and explained the new laws. In the Muslim regions they opposed humiliating customs and attitudes. Everywhere they counselled women about divorce and women's rights—and tied all such lessons to political instruction about the values and aims of the regime. Activated by Zhenotdel, women virtually untouched by political culture entered into the local administrative process. Most crucial of all, the activists of Zhenotdel learned the rudiments of organizing and modernizing and taught themselves the meaning of social revolution.

Bolshevism contained vision as well as social policy. In societies wracked by poverty and dislocation, social vision—utopian or otherwise—plays a key role in capturing the sentiment of people, particularly the literate and the already engaged. Speculation about the future of sexual relations often helped to reinforce the process of working for improving such relations in the present. The most active and articulate Bolshevik woman activist, Kollontai, gave special attention to a program of communist sexual relations and communal "family" life. In regard to the first, Kollontai vigorously defended woman's need for independence and a separate income. This in turn would give her the dignity and strength needed for an equal and open love-sex relationship and would enhance the pleasure and quality of sexual intercourse. As to the second, she believed in a "marriage" unfettered by economic dependence or responsibility for children. The latter were to be cared for in communal facilities to which parents had easy access. Kollontai believed in parenthood—her ideal in fact for all humans—and in regular contact between parents and children. The material life of the children, however, was to be the responsibility of the local "collective" of work or residence. Housekeeping was to be no more than an "industrial" task like any other, handled by specialists—never the domain of a wife (or husband) alone.

Some of the more daring aspects of Kollontai's sexual theories fell victim to misinterpretation in the 1920s. Hers was an overall vision of equality in life, work, and love that matched the utopian visions of the science fiction writers and revolutionary town planners and architects who were the major futuristic thinkers in this decade of experiment. In the 1920s about 200 science fiction titles appeared, many of them outlining a future world of perfection characterized by social justice and ultramodern technology. Such utopian pictures almost invariably revealed a unified, urbanized globe bathed in peace, harmony, and affluent communist civilization inhabited by a near-androgynous population with genderless names and unisex costumes. Sexual tensions no longer tormented the human race, women worked as equals to men in a machine-run economy of universal participation and communist distribution, and healthy children thrived in colonies.

Architects and town planners of the 1920s and early 1930s designed living spaces as "social condensers"—communal buildings that would shape the collective consciousness of their inhabitants. Although the projects varied in scope, size, and density, almost all of the architectural planning of that period provided for private rooms for single persons and couples, easy divorce by changing rooms, communal care for children, communal cooking and dining, and an environment of male-female cooperation in household tasks. Some of these communal homes actually were built; others remained in the blueprint stage. As a whole, visionary architecture and town planning of that period attested to the central importance of woman's new role as an independent and equal member of society.

The ultimate experiments in sexual equality—the rural and urban communes of the 1920s—put communalism (the complete and equal sharing of lives, partly inspired by [Nicholas] Chernyshevsky) into practice wherever space could be found. Thousands in the countryside and hundreds in the cities joined to share goods, money, books, land, and property of every sort. Members of these collectives rotated work, apportioned income equally, and pooled all resources. Sexual equality worked better in the workers' and student communes of the cities than in the countryside, where the sexual division of labor often prevailed: women took over the big communal kitchens while men labored together in the fields. In the town communes, students and workers made sexual equality a mandatory condition. In these "living utopias," males learned how to cook and iron and wash floors under the guidance of women so that all could take their turns at housework on a strictly rotational basis. In some of the more rigorous communes, love and friendship were declared indivisible—cliques and romantic pairing were outlawed as violations of the collective principle. Tensions and flaring tempers beset many of these communes all through the 1920s; but they persisted as "laboratories of revolution" where communism could be practiced and lived day to day.

This part of the picture of women's liberation—the idealistic foreground—deserves emphasis because it is so often overlooked in assessments of the Revolution. Endemic misery and material poverty hampered these experiments, and cynicism and indifference made mockeries of the dreams, but the experiments and dreams persisted. Life for women—and men—was very difficult in the early years after the Revolution. The rural world presented a vast terrain of disease and superstition, suspicious peasants, archaic tools, and ancient agronomical technique. Towns were filled with unemployed women, deserted and abandoned children, criminals and organized gangs, and conspicuously wealthy businessmen. These last comprised a class created by the introduction of Lenin's New Economic Policy in 1921, which allowed a mixed economy, a limited arena of capitalism and hired labor with enclaves of privileged specialists, government leaders, and foreigners. Women were hit very hard by all of this. About 70 percent of the initial job cutbacks that occurred periodically during this period affected women. Between 70,000 and 100,000 women in de facto marriages with men possessed none of the financial security or legal protection that might have vouchsafed them with registered marriage.

NO

Lesley A. Rimmel

The Baba and the Comrade: Gender and Politics in Revolutionary Russia

During the nearly two years that I lived in Palo Alto, California, I translated several grant proposals from Russian into English for the Global Fund for Women, based nearby. As a long-time student of the USSR and Russia, I was fascinated to see how even in the farthest reaches of the former Soviet Union, women had organized on their own behalf and were writing to this explicitly feminist foundation for support. While all of the groups understandably focused on the need to counter the detrimental effects of recent economic changes on women, how they understood "feminism," and women's "nature" and role in society, varied considerably. This is not surprising, as the idea of gender is contentious in most societies. But what is most encouraging is that in Russia and the Newly Independent States, the issue of gender itself is being seriously grappled with for the first time. As these ... books ... indicate, women in Soviet times were defined as "the same as" or "different from" men according to the current needs of the regime, with gender-specific or gender-neutral policies then applied as the particular situation (war, peace, labor shortages) warranted. Only recently have post-Soviet women begun the difficult but necessary work of claiming agency and making themselves their own first priority.

These ... books— ... written or edited by scholars of distinction—diverge in their approaches and intended audiences. The one that addresses the earliest period of Communist Russia, Elizabeth A. Wood's long-awaited and richly documented *The Baba and the Comrade*, is also the most explicitly scholarly. Nonscholars should not be put off, however, for the book is clearly written and organized, and mostly free of jargon.

The Baba and the Comrade takes as its central theme the question that confronted Bolshevik (after 1918, Communist) activists: were women and men the same or different? Could a baba, generally defined as an ignorant peasant woman, become a comrade, a full-fledged human and citizen? Wood notes how reluctant the Bolsheviks were to target women separately in their propaganda and organizing efforts; only the competition with feminist groups and other socialist parties forced them to do so in the last years before the February and October 1917 revolutions and for several years thereafter.

From *The Women's Review of Books*, vol. 15, no. 12, September 1998. Copyright © 1998 by Lesley A. Rimmel. Reprinted by permission. Notes omitted.

The dilemma for the Communists was that their revolution was to be class-based, and "any special efforts on behalf of women threatened [the revolution's] class nature." Nadezhda Krupskaia, partner and wife of Bolshevik leader Lenin and usually a stalwart defender of women's interests, illustrated this reluctance (and some typical Communist condescension) in a draft editorial for the party paper Rabotnitsa ("Woman Worker") in 1913:

> The "woman question" for male and female workers is a question [of] how to draw the backward masses of women workers into organization, how best to explain to them their interests, how best to make them into comrades in the general struggle. Solidarity among the male and female workers, a general cause, general goals, a general path to that goal—that is the solution to the "woman" question in the workingclass environment.... The journal Rabotnitsa will strive to explain to unconscious women workers their interests, to show them the commonality of their interests with the interests of the whole working class.

Yet, for practical and historical reasons, women, who were less literate than men and who were charged with all household and childcare duties, in addition to whatever work they might have outside the home, could not be reached by Communist activists as easily as men. Many women could not or would not attend meetings with men, nor would they speak out with men present. But the Communists needed to appeal to women in order to mobilize their support (especially during the crucial years of the civil war, from 1918 to 1920). And if the backward baba was not made to support the new regime, then she might hinder the revolution and even become a source of counter-revolution (defined in practice as any opposition to Bolshevik policy). And as women would be raising the next generation, it was critical that they understand and support the new order. The spectre of the baba who would harm the revolution if not won over became the justification for focusing activism on women separately.

Wood concentrates on the period from 1918 to 1923, when woman-centered activism was most pronounced, but she begins by placing Communist ideas and stereotypes about women and reform in their Russian historical perspective. Beginning in the late [seventeenth] century under Tsar Peter I, who attempted to orient Russia to the West, women were viewed as surrogates for the backwardness of Russia; integrating them into male society would be a step toward "civilizing" Russia and turning women into human beings. The Bolsheviks basically continued in this vein, giving the tsarist interpretation a Marxist gloss. On the one hand, the Communist regime enacted legislation mandating sexual equality, with the only "special treatment" being pregnancy and maternity leaves for women in the workplace. On the other hand, the culture's traditional gender essentialism remained, to be resurrected when needed.

This dialectic of gender became evident during the civil war, when the Communists appealed to women's supposedly inherent traits as caregivers and homemakers to take on work as nurses and inspectors, to use their "sharp eyes and tender hearts" to care for wounded soldiers and root out any corruption or misdeeds. At the same time, local women's sections of the Communist Party were established, as well as a national organization, the Women's Department of the Party, the Zhenotdel.

Theoretically, the women's sections were to be "transmission belts" (a favorite Bolshevik metaphor) for bringing party policy to ordinary women. They did indeed function this way. However, as the civil war gave way to the era of the New Economic Policy, a time of some economic privatization with greater political centralization (somewhat like the situation of China today, and economically similar to present-day Russia), many women lost their jobs and their health benefits, and the women's sections began lobbying the government on women's behalf. Labor and enterprise leaders, seeing women more as mothers than as workers, were unsympathetic, and the state continued to curtail its "social programs." Zhenotdel activists countered by bringing out the threat of the baba: the NEP was forcing women into "domestic slavery" or prostitution in order to survive (a not untrue contention), and in their regression from comrade to baba, they would take men down with them.

If there was any regression, however, it was on the part of the government in general and men in particular, who by 1923–24 feared not that women would be a drag on the revolution, but that the housework would not get done. Women's section activists, whose political and material support from authorities was being cut, strove to assure men of the party that female comrades would not desert their posts—at the stove. Thus Bolshevik backlash against gender transformation began long before Stalinist family values became institutionalized in the 1930 and 1940s—a time often referred to as the "Great Retreat."

Wood's convincing work is a welcome addition to the growing literature on the gender-role traditionalism the Communists reinstitutionalized with their revolution. Women's opportunities—and workload—may have increased after 1917, but the culture's scepticism about women's "essential nature" did not. For those of us who for years have attempted to point this out (and were vilified, by some on both the Right and the Left, for doing so), Wood's readable narrative and copious examples bring further validation.

How did women in the Soviet Union negotiate their country's contradictory gender expectations? Mostly, it seems, they ignored them and concentrated on survival. Historian Barbara Alpern Engel and demographer and feminist activist Anastasia Posadskaya-Vanderbeck have collected eight interviews with women whose only commonality was (with one exception) that they were born before the Bolshevik Revolution, and survived to see the USSR's demise. The title of their book, *A Revolution of Their Own*, is [somewhat misleading], since it seems to imply that women actually got "their" revolution. In fact, as their stories indicate, most of these women did not benefit from the revolution, and for many the Soviet experience was a largely negative one.

Most interesting, however, is that neither the women's experiences nor their attitudes can be predicted from their backgrounds—a clear retort to the Communists' near obsession with people's "social origins." The interviews took place not just in Moscow but in Siberia and in Ekaterinburg in the Urals; the women themselves were born in a variety of places. While the eight are not a representative sample demographically, their experiences are varied enough to make for a rich and provocative portrait of a generation that lived through one of history's greatest dramas.

Each chapter consists of a thorough introduction to the woman being interviewed, complete with a description of the physical setting, followed by a portion of the interview (edited for length and variety), including abbreviated versions of Posadskaya's questions. The latter reveal Posadskaya's ability to prod the woman being interviewed—for example, on their views on abortion, which was not a topic these women normally discussed. (One area where Posadskaya did not prod was that of lesbian rights, which may have been an issue for one of the women.) Sometimes the questions illuminate more about Posadskaya and her generation's concerns than about her interviewees': when she asks Anna Dubova about who decided how the family income would be spent in the 1930s, Dubova responds, almost with surprise, "we had so little money, there was nothing to decide."

Neither family background nor individual efforts can totally explain each woman's fate or her orientation toward the Communist regime. Among those interviewed, the women with peasant backgrounds shared little except unpromising beginnings. Elena Ponomarenko was the youngest of seventeen siblings (from the same mother), and could rarely attend school because she did not have shoes and had to work. But joining the party gave her life structure and helped her to get a start in journalism, for which she repaid the regime with her consistent loyalty, even to the point of defending the Terror and leaving her dying mother to go on an assignment. Irina Kniazeva, on the other hand, knew nothing but hardship in her peasant life, from the father and husbands who mistreated her, the constant hard labor that was never rewarded, and even the burden of "sin" she carried for years for having stolen a handful of grain to feed her children during the famine of the early 1930s. Reading this woman's words, and seeing her careworn face (each interview includes pictures of the women, usually at various stages of their lives), I was moved to tears.

All the stories are dramatic and even novelistic—Communist activist Sofia Pavlova's nighttime escapes on horseback during the civil war, Ponomarenko fighting off wolves in her travels, Vera Malakhova's experience as a front line doctor during World War Two—and it's no wonder that they can be disdainful of today's younger generation and its seeming worship of luxury. Nearly all the women had difficult family lives—drunken and abusive husbands, wonderful but brief relationships with lovers or second husbands who suddenly disappeared in one of the convulsions of the Stalin era, and long periods of single motherhood in conditions of extreme poverty.

In fact, as Engel and Posadskaya observe, "the 'new Soviet family' essentially consisted of a mother who 'saved the children,' [...] raising one or two by herself, often with the help of her own mother or a nurse but with no evident support, financial or otherwise, from the government." (At the end of World War Two there were 26 million more women than men in the Soviet Union.) Some of these women had to renounce their families of origin in order merely to survive, while others found it necessary to marry men of "correct" backgrounds so as to "lose" their pasts—or even just to gain a place to live. But no amount of "family values" legislation, which the Stalin regime provided in abundance during the 1930s and 1940s, could overcome the problems of hunger, crowded housing, fatigue and policies that separated people from their loved ones and mined "family" happiness for so many.

What did give meaning to most of these women's lives was a love of work. Only a few of them, when prodded, complained about limited opportunities for women; but even party loyalist Pavlova had to admit that women could not get any farther than she had, as head of a department of the Communist Party's Central Committee (its second-highest decision-making body): "There was a ceiling. It's the tenacity of tradition, and unfortunately, to this day, we haven't broken its hold. I don't know how long it will take to overcome it." Under the personal, economic and political conditions that these women lived through, however, their survival and the survival of (most of) their children seems nothing short of miraculous—they were truly "heroes of their own lives," to use Linda Gordon's phrase.

> That these women tend to downplay any long-suppressed resentment at limitations they experienced because of their sex—the overt discrimination and the practical obstacles engendered by single motherhood and poverty—is probably because class-based discrimination affected them more deeply, for better or for worse....

Russian history is full of ironies, and nothing is more ironic than the fact that women's freedom to discuss and protest their situation arrived in the late 1980s and early 1990s, just as most women's lives really began to worsen. The contradictions of gender essentialism that were never really addressed by the Soviet Union bore fruit. Because, for example, parental leave and childcare had been associated with women only, women were and are the ones most likely to be fired as workplaces have to cut costs. With gender roles at home never questioned, and with housework being so extraordinarily time-consuming in Russia (which does not have enough well-supplied, conveniently located shops or labor-saving devices), women, with no more "reserved seats" (few as they were) in government bodies, are at a disadvantage in trying to compete as political players. Old-fashioned male chauvinism also plays a part in keeping women out of politics, and out of business as well.

Not all of this is new; the Communist Party and other powerful institutions had long been affirmative action programs for sons of party leaders. But along with the new opportunities of the post-Soviet era have come new obstacles for Russian women.

Yet the women in this book seem equal to the challenge. The larger groups they founded or reorganized all have Soviet roots, in some cases quite strong ones. One of the best-known is the Center for Gender Studies, the Soviet Union's first center for research on women, and its sister umbrella group, the Independent Women's Forum, which organized the first country-wide, independent gathering for women's groups. The Center and the Forum have been very successful in publicizing their critiques of Russian society. They are less involved in politicking to get women into positions of power, although their members often serve as consultants to government bodies. Although the Center is associated with the venerable Academy of Sciences, it has been outspoken in its feminism, as has its founding director, Anastasia Posadskaya-Vanderbeck.

Posadskaya early on found the Soviet system to be sexist and hypocritical, once she saw underqualified but well-connected men getting into academic programs for which she was rejected although she had passed the exams. She comes across in this book as less comfortable being interviewed than being the interviewer; she calls herself a "reluctant activist," saying she would have preferred to be a full-time scholar, but felt impelled to fight for women to "have their own voice, to speak independently, to speak not from a position of class or of one-half the population, which has been rescued by somebody else, but to set up their own agenda."...

What, then, has women's activism accomplished? There is not a lot of information here on specific achievements, and those interested will have to do further research elsewhere. What clearly has been achieved, however, has been a revolution of consciousness. Although Women's Activism leaves us with questions about the future of feminism in Russia—indeed, the future of Russia itself is always a big question—it also leaves us with hope. While some women have chosen to become active in far-left or far-right splinter groups in the belief that resurrecting the old Stalinism or traditional patriarchalism will restore some imagined women's paradise (although it should be noted that it was the post-Soviet Communists who first organized around women's disproportionate unemployment), there is no going back for Russian women. Too many now know their history, or are being forced to acknowledge it.

The challenges are truly daunting, especially with regard to women's economic situation, to which the growth in sex trafficking of Russian and other women from the Newly Independent States provides eloquent testimony. But activists won't get fooled again; there will be no more "mobiliz[ing] women's support for men's political agendas," for women to be only "producers and reproducers" for the state. There may be few babas left, but "comradeship" will be defined on women's terms. And then women will truly have a revolution of their own....

POSTSCRIPT

Did the Bolshevik Revolution Improve the Lives of Soviet Women?

It is one of history's ironies that, with the stroke of a pen, Soviet women were granted all the legal and political rights that women in Britain and the United States were struggling to achieve. Having won the rights to vote and hold public office, Soviet women struggled to translate those paper rights into improved lives for themselves and their children. It has been a conviction of Western feminism that legal and political equality pave the way for full emancipation of women. The Soviet case raises interesting questions about the confusion that arises when there are conflicting revolutions. Real political power belongs to those who can assure that the goals of their revolution receive first priority. It was the socialist revolution, not women's emancipation, that the party leadership worked to achieve.

Popular accounts of the Russian Revolution may be found in John Reed's *Ten Days That Shook the World* (Penguin, 1977) and Louise Bryant's *Mirrors of Moscow* (Hyperion Press, 1973). The story of Reed and Bryant, two Americans who find themselves eyewitnesses to the Bolshevik Revolution, is captured in the film "Reds." Another film covering the same period is "Doctor Zhivago," which is based on the book of the same title by Boris Pasternak (1958). For Lenin's views on women, one of the best sources is his book *The Emancipation of Women* (International Publishers, 1972). *The Unknown Lenin: From the Secret Archives*, edited by the eminent Russian historian Richard Pipes (Yale University Press, 1996) dips into the secret archives and brands Lenin a ruthless and manipulative leader. Robert McNeal's *Bride of the Revolution* (University of Michigan Press, 1972) focuses on the fascinating marriage and revolutionary relationship between Lenin and Bolshevik propagandist Nadezhda Krupskaya. And Sheila Fitzpatrick, in *The Russian Revolution* (Oxford University Press, 1982) surveys the critical 1917–1932 period with special emphasis on the work of Zhenotdel. For essays on the lives of women during this period, students may want to see *Women in Soviet Society,* edited by Gail Lapidus (University of California Press, 1978) and *Women in Russia,* edited by D. Atkinson, A. Dallin, and G. Lapidus (Stanford University Press, 1977), which grew out of a 1975 conference that was held at Stanford University titled "Women in Russia." The fascinating character Alexandra Kollontai, who died at 80, may be explored through her own writings in *Selected Writings* (W.W. Norton, 1972), *The Autobiography of a Sexually Emancipated Communist Woman* (Schocken Books, 1975), *Red Love* (Hyperion Press, 1990), and *Love of Worker Bees* (Academy of Chicago Press, 1978). Books about Kollontai include *Bolshevik Feminist* by Barbara Clements (Indiana University Press,

1979). Some recent scholarship on Bolshevik women includes: Elizabeth A. Wood's *The Baba and the Comrade: Gender and Politics in Revolutionary Russia* (Indiana Universtiy Press, 1997); Barbara Evans Clements's *Bolshevik Women* (Cambridge University Press, 1997); Anna Hillyar and Jane McDermid's *Revolutionary Women in Russia, 1870–1917: A Study in Collective Biography* (Manchester University Press, 2000); and Choi Chatterjee's *Celebrating Women: Gender, Festival Culture, and Bolshevik Ideology, 1910–1939* (University of Pittsburgh Press, 2002).

ISSUE 10

Was German "Eliminationist Antisemitism" Responsible for the Holocaust?

YES: Daniel Jonah Goldhagen, from "The Paradigm Challenged," *Tikkun* (May–June 1998)

NO: Christopher R. Browning, from "Ordinary Germans or Ordinary Men? A Reply to the Critics," in Michael Berenbaum and Abraham J. Peck, eds., *The Holocaust and History: The Known, the Unknown, the Disputed, and the Reexamined* (Indiana University Press, 1998)

ISSUE SUMMARY

YES: Political science professor Daniel Goldhagen states that due to the nature of German society in the twentieth century—with its endemic, virulent antisemitism—thousands of ordinary German citizens became willing participants in the implementation of Holocaust horrors.

NO: Holocaust historian Christopher R. Browning argues that Goldhagen's thesis is too simplistic and that a multicausal approach must be used to determine why ordinary German citizens willingly participated in the Holocaust.

Few historical events engender stronger emotional responses than the Nazi-directed Holocaust of World War II, in which millions of Jews were systematically exterminated as part of a ghastly plan for a diabolical new world order. Since its occurrence, many scholarly works have been written in an attempt to answer the questions that this "crime against humanity" has raised: What historical factors were responsible for it? How did people and nations allow it to roll toward its final destructive consequences? What lessons did it teach us about human nature? Could something like this happen again? Who bears the responsibility for it?

Much of Holocaust scholarship has concentrated on European anti-semitism as a major factor in the cause of the event itself and as a major reason why little was done to stop it. Some scholars have emphasized the schizophrenic nature of post–World War I politics, which they say allowed demagogic madmen to weave their magic web around an unsuspecting public. Others have stressed the violent nature of the twentieth-century world (especially after the Great War), which created an immunity-against-brutality temperament that made the Holocaust possible. And, of course, the major blame has been placed on Adolf Hitler and his Nazi henchmen for the initiation, design, and implementation of the Holocaust.

But just how unsuspecting was this public? Most people have long ago dismissed (as did the Nuremberg War Crimes Tribunal) the "I was only following orders" argument that so many who actively participated in Holocaust horrors have used. Others who were not directly involved have cited the hopelessness of opposition and the fear of reprisal to explain their acquiescence. But as we have been made witness to countless trials for war crimes in the last 50 years, some have wondered whether or not a larger segment of the population in those Nazi-controlled countries was involved in the Holocaust's worst aspects.

Daniel Jonah Goldhagen was not the first scholar to investigate this subject, but his 1996 book *Hitler's Willing Executioners: Ordinary Germans and the Holocaust* (Vintage Books, 1996), has raised the issue to a new level and has created a maelstrom of controversy within the historical profession. Using recently discovered sources of information and tools of analysis newly available to social scientists, Goldhagen takes a fresh look at why and how the Holocaust occurred through an analysis of three related subjects: "the perpetrators of the Holocaust, German antisemitism, and the nature of German society during the Nazi period." Central to his thesis is the concept of "eliminationist antisemitism" (his own phrase), which turned "ordinary Germans" into "Hitler's willing executioners." Goldhagen's conclusions are a stinging indictment of large numbers of average German citizens, who he claims willingly participated in the Holocaust's worst aspects, including police battalion killing squads, work camps, and death marches.

Goldhagen's work has received much public praise, including a National Book Critics nomination for nonfiction book of the year. But it has also had its share of critics, many of them Holocaust scholars. Some have found his work to be one-sided, inflammatory, and too narrow in its focus. One of Goldhagen's most persistent critics has been Christopher R. Browning. In the second selection, Browning states that antisemitism may have been widespread in pre-Nazi Germany, but it was not the major ideology of most German citizens. According to Browning, there are a variety of factors that were responsible for making ordinary Germans into willing killers. Goldhagen is critical of Browning's conclusions, and his critique can be found in "The Evil of Banality," *The New Republic* (July 13 and 20, 1992). Browning published a rejoinder to Goldhagen's critique as an afterword to the second edition of *Ordinary Men: Reserve Police Battalion and the Final Solution in Poland* (HarperPerennial, 1998).

Two articles written by these scholars form the basis of this issue's debate.

Daniel Jonah Goldhagen

 **YES**

The Paradigm Challenged

Imagine a history of American slavery whose authors assert that the testimony of slaves should not be used and where the practice is not to use it, where there is no extensive investigation of whites' conceptions of the enslaved Africans, where it is said that the whites were unwilling slave holders and that few non-slave owning southern whites supported the institutions of slavery, where it is said that those enslaving and routinely brutalizing the slaves were not at all influenced by their conceptions of the victims, where the precept and practice is not to describe the full extent and character of the slave holders' brutality, where it is said furthermore that African American scholars today are suspect because they are African American and the motivation is imputed to them of writing about slavery solely for monetary or political gain or psychological gratification. Imagine what our understanding of American slavery would look like, how skewed it would be, if even only some of these positions prevailed. We would wonder how slavery ever could have existed.

When writing about the Holocaust, many scholars and commentators routinely adopt positions analogous to one or several of these examples. Indeed, some of these positions are a never justified, seemingly unquestioned norm among those who write about the Holocaust. These positions would seem curious—methodologically, substantively, and interpretively—even absurd, if put forward about slavery or about other genocides or mass slaughters such as those in Rwanda or Bosnia. Yet when asserted about the Holocaust, barely an eyebrow is raised. The question naturally arises as to why such manifestly false positions have been frequently adopted? Why until recently were almost no studies, especially no systematic studies, of the perpetrators—namely of those who killed Jews, guarded the camps and ghettos, and deported them to their deaths—to be found among the tens of thousands of books written about the Holocaust, despite the wealth of evidence that had long been available?

The heretofore hegemonic paradigm about the Holocaust has rendered them puppet-like actors, mere pawns whose inner world need not be investigated. It denies the moral agency and assent of the perpetrators and holds that they were compelled to act by forces external to them, such as terror, bureaucratic strictures and modes of behaving, the logic of the system, or social psychological pressure. For a long time, this paradigm diverted attention away from the perpetrators because its logic of external compulsion meant that the perpetrators' internal lives (their beliefs and values) and anything that was

From *Tikkun*, vol.13, no.3, May-June 1998. Copyright © 1998 by Tikkun. Reprinted by permission.

sociohistorically particular to them (that they were members of a deeply anti-Semitic political culture) did not influence their actions and that, therefore, the study of them would not contribute much to explaining the Holocaust. The problems with this view and its construction can be indicated by comparing it to the hypothetical, fanciful rendering of slavery above.

The perpetrators are finally being discussed extensively, even if the number of empirical studies remains small. Yet in the last couple of years, a phalanx of scholars and commentators have adopted positions which would make the perpetrators of the Holocaust the only perpetrators of genocide who believed that their victims did not deserve to die, indeed that their victims were innocent. This strange view seems still stranger given that many of the German perpetrators knew explicitly that they had a choice not to kill, and that no German perpetrator was ever killed, sent to a concentration camp, jailed, or punished in any serious way for refusing to kill Jews. That it was possible for many perpetrators to avoid killing Jews, and that some of them availed themselves of this possibility, became known already at the Nuremberg Trials. The related, stunning fact that not a single German perpetrator was ever seriously punished for refusing to kill Jews has been known since 1967 when the jurist Herbert Jager published his pioneering study, Crime Under Totalitarian Domination. (I treated both the general issue and presented the case of one man who refused to kill in "The 'Cowardly' Executioner: On Disobedience in the SS" in 1985). Yet this latter fact has remained unmentioned in virtually every work written on the perpetration of the Holocaust since Jager first established it.

Why would Martin Broszat, Raul Hilberg, Eberhard Jackel, Hans Mommsen and other scholars who wish to explain the Holocaust not discuss these fundamental facts extensively or incorporate their significance into the explanations and interpretations which they put forward? Is it of so little import—that men and women who knew that they could avoid killing children would choose to destroy them anyway—that it is not even worth mentioning this information? Acknowledging these facts would have shaken the foundations of the paradigm to which many scholars are wedded, namely that the perpetrators were compelled by external forces to act against their will. This crucial omission of evidence, for which no justification has been offered, has for decades skewed non-experts' and the public's understanding of the Holocaust.

Similarly, when these writers depict and analyze the events of the Holocaust and particularly when they analyze the motives of the perpetrators, they rarely, if ever, use the testimony of the victims, neither their letters, diaries, memoirs, nor oral testimonies. That is not to say this testimony is never used; certainly, it is used by those writing about the lives and plight of the victims, and by scholars like Yehuda Bauer, Saul Friedlander, and Israel Gutman. But when constructing interpretations of the perpetrators of the Holocaust, it has been the unspoken practice of so many scholars to all but ignore, and certainly not to use systematically, victims' accounts of the perpetrators' actions and the victims' understanding of perpetrators' attitudes towards them. With the sometime exception of a quotation or two from Primo Levi (or some other particularly distinguished memoirist), one searches such authors' works in vain for the instances where they use such evidence seriously or even at all.

Some authors explicitly declare that victim testimony is of little value and an impediment to understanding. Raul Hilberg, who is one of the principal exponents of the conventional paradigm and practice and who often speaks authoritatively for those who are in his school, has written roughly seven pages on survivor testimony in his recent memoir, *The Politics of Memory*, which are highly distorting and almost thoroughly disparaging. He makes not a single positive statement about the victims' testimony as a historical source, except when it shows Jews in a bad light. Even though Hilberg acknowledges in passing, in a strikingly critical vein, that the survivors' "principal subjects are deportations, concentration camps, death camps, escapes, hiding, and partisan fighting"—precisely those themes relevant to learning about and analyzing the perpetrators—his practice and that of those who follow him suggests that they believe that there is little evidentiary or interpretive value in all this testimony.

This widespread devaluation of the testimony of the Jewish victims is peculiar. I know of no other historical or contemporary instance about which it is said that the victims of genocidal onslaughts, sustained violence, or brutality have little of value to tell us about those who victimized and brutalized them. I know of no other crime (e.g., assault, kidnapping), no instance of large scale brutal domination (e.g., slavery, serfdom), no genocide (e.g., Rwanda, Cambodia), nor any other historical instance in which the victims—in the case of the Holocaust a group of eyewitnesses numbering in the millions—are said, as a class, to have little or nothing to tell us about the deeds and attitudes of the men and women who victimized them and whose murderousness and brutalities against others they witnessed. And not only is their testimony silently ignored by many and explicitly devalued by some but it is also sometimes deprecated by writers like Istvan Deak, who began a review of several books on the Holocaust in *The New York Review of Books* (June 26, 1997) by presenting a caricature of and an attack on survivors' memoirs. He goes so far as to say that "an accurate record of the Holocaust has been endangered, in my opinion, by the uncritical endorsement, often by well-known Jewish writers or public figures, of virtually any survivor's account or related writings." How have the survivors' writings "endangered.... an accurate record of the Holocaust"? Except to say (correctly) that personal details may be inaccurate or embellished, Deak does not justify his sweeping condemnation.

The invaluable importance of survivor testimony is attested by the crucial, indeed, indispensable part that the survivors have played in the trials of thousands of perpetrators in the Federal Republic of Germany. Many of these trials could not have been held without survivor testimony. The judgment in the most famous of these trials, that of a contingent of guards and administrators of Auschwitz held in 1963, states: "Apart from scattered and not very informative documents, the court had to rely exclusively on witness testimony to help it reconstruct the acts of the defendants." One thousand three hundred witnesses (among them former guards) gave testimony for that trial.

The Germans' documentation of the killing institutions and operations never record the details of the hundreds or thousands of perpetrators' many actions. Typically, the documents contain, at most, the bare logistics and results of killing operations. So an entire killing operation that might have lasted a full day will appear in a document with nothing more than one line stating that on a given date, the German unit "resettled" (a euphemism) or "shot" some number of Jews.

The accounts of survivors afford a more transparent, more spacious window to the Nazi inferno than the often beclouded and distorting postwar testimonies of the perpetrators who, in order to escape punishment, frequently lie. (Still, some of the perpetrators are surprisingly forthcoming, especially about other perpetrators, and many unwittingly reveal a great deal. Such testimony is invaluable and should be used.) Who would expect to learn from the perpetrators or from contemporaneous German documents a full and accurate account of the texture and details of the Holocaust, of the daily living and dying, of the treatment of the prisoners by the German overlords, including their frequent gratuitous brutality, of the social life of the inmates, their thoughts and feelings, their suffering and their agony? Where can we more fully learn about the character of the perpetrators' actions—the degree to which the perpetrators tortured, brutalized, beat, degraded, and mocked the victims—about the perpetrators' demeanor and attitudes, about whether they acted zealously or reluctantly, about whether they expressed hatred for the victims, and gain insight into the perpetrators' willingness and motivation?

The answer is obvious: from the victims.

Could accurate histories of the Jewish ghettos and of the concentration camps be written without the accounts of the survivors contained in their depositions and memoirs? A perusal of three great books, H. G. Adler's *Theresienstadt, 1941–1945*, Israel Gutman's *The Jews of Warsaw 1939–1943*, and Hermann Langbein's panoramic analysis of Auschwitz, People in Auschwitz, shows that the authors have drawn heavily on the accounts of survivors. Are these historical works thereby vitiated? Do they imperil the accuracy of the historical record?

A comparison with the historiography of the Soviet Gulag is instructive. Its scholars do not cast aspersion on the memoirs and accounts of former inmates, whose narratives are indispensable. Aleksandr Solzhenitsyn writes in his Preface to The Gulag Archipelago: "This book could never have been created by one person alone. In addition to what I myself was able to take away from the Archipelago—on the skin of my back, and with my eyes and ears— material for this book was given me in reports, memoirs, and letters by 227 witnesses ... this is our common, collective monument to all those who were tortured and murdered." Evidence of the kind that Hilberg, Deak, Christopher, Browning, and others dismiss, explicitly or tacitly, as unreliable and inessential forms the foundation of Solzhenitsyn's magisterial work. Would Deak argue that Solzhenitsyn has "endangered.... an accurate record" of the Gulag? Or are only survivors of the Holocaust and those who find great value in their testimony prone to such "endangerment"?

It is not because this witness testimony is meager, imprecise, or devoid of insight that it has been ignored. It includes hundreds of memorial volumes, each one containing compilations from survivors of one destroyed Jewish community after another detailing their fates; depositions of many thousands of survivors in the trials of the perpetrators from one camp, killing unit, and ghetto after another; vast amounts of oral testimony; and thousands of memoirs. It would be hard to imagine an instance of mass slaughter, violence, or brutality that would be documented by a greater abundance of rich, detailed, often highly literate testimony that contains penetrating analyses of the events and of the people who perpetrated them. This makes the disparagement of the victims' testimony and its paltry use that much more surprising and indefensible.

Victims' accounts belie the conventional paradigm and the attendant scholarly theories about the perpetrators that have held sway, namely that the perpetrators either explicitly disapproved or at least did not approve of the mass slaughter of Jews and of other victims. The victims know differently. They have testified so again and again. If the proponents of these explanations had incorporated the voices of the victims into their own writings, then they would have undercut immediately and devastatingly their own theories, and the conventional paradigm.

The omission of the survivors' accounts has obscured, among many other aspects of the Holocaust, one of its constituent features. Scholars' failure to use victim accounts has thus, to use Deak's phraseology, "endangered" "an accurate record": the perpetrators' virtually boundless cruelty towards the Jews has been all but ignored by those who purport to explain the perpetrators' actions. If, as many authors do, one relies principally on highly partial and often unrevealing contemporaneous German documents, then, of course, one will not find frequent and detailed recitations of Germans' routine torturing of Jews. These authors construct a distorted portrait of the Holocaust in which the perpetrators' brutality—so frequent, inventive, and willful—is minimized, blurred, or absent. Consequently, it is not surprising that those few authors adhering to the conventional paradigm who do at least say something in passing about the sources of the German perpetrators' brutality to the Jews do not deem the perpetrators to have been moved by hatred of their victims.

Hilberg, for instance, in *Perpetrators, Vicitims, Bystanders*, puts forward the notion that the German perpetrators' brutality was "most often" an "expression of impatience" with the pace of killing operations. Browning's related view, in *Ordinary Men*, is that the perpetrators' brutality was utilitarian, the consequence of a pragmatic need to be brutal when they were under "pressure" "in terms of manpower ... to get the job done," like rounding up Jews for deportation. When not under such pressure, in Browning's view, they were cruel when under the sway of cruel officers but seemingly not at other times. Hilberg and Browning have failed to present evidence which supports what are ultimately little more than speculations. (How does Hilberg know that they were impatient? He never says. And is the torture of defenseless people, including children, the invariable result of impatience, as Hilberg's quick and casual manner of presenting his speculation suggests?) But that is the least of their problems. Hilberg and Browning's empirical claims are falsified by evidence of the perpetrators' widespread, non-utilitarian cruelty in all manner of circumstances, even when they were not undermanned, even when they were not impatient, even when they were not undertaking killing operations at all.

For example: although the Germans of Police Battalion 101, during one of the ghetto roundups and deportations in Miedzyrzec, Poland, degraded and tortured Jews in the most gratuitous, willful manner, their deeds are entirely absent from their testimony and, therefore, also from Browning's analysis of the killing operation. The accounts of survivors tell a different, more accurate, and more revealing story Survivors are adamant that the Germans' cruelty that day was anything but instrumental. It was wanton, at times turning into sadistic sport. At the marketplace the Jews, who had been forced to squat for hours, were "mocked" (khoyzek gemacht) and "kicked," and some of the Germans organized "a game" (shpil) of "tossing apples and whoever was struck by the apple was then killed." This sport was continued at the railway station, with empty liquor bottles. "Bottles were tossed over Jewish heads and whoever was struck by a bottle was dragged out of the crowd and beaten murderously amid roaring laughter. Then some of those who were thus mangled (tseharget) were shot." Afterwards, the Germans loaded the dead together with the living onto freight cars bound for Treblinka. One photograph documenting the final stage of what may be this deportation has survived.

Small wonder that in the eyes of the victims—but not in the self-serving testimony of the perpetrators, in contemporaneous German documents, or in Browning's book—these ordinary Germans appeared not as mere murderers, certainly not as reluctant killers dragged to their task against their inner opposition to genocide, but as "two-legged beasts" filled with "bloodthirstiness." (Browning claims that from survivors "we learn nothing about" Police Battalion 101 or, for that matter, about itinerant units in general.) Germans' cruelty towards Jews, as the victims (and also some of the perpetrators after the war) reveal, was voluntary, widespread, sustained, inventive, and gleeful. Such gratuitous cruelty could have been produced only by people who approved of what they were doing.

The vast corpus of the victims' testimony substantiates the conclusion that ordinary Germans degraded, brutalized, and killed Jews willingly because of their hatred of Jews. So profound and near universal was the anti-Semitism during the Nazi period that to the Jewish victims it appeared as if its hold on Germans could be captured and conveyed only in organic terms. As Chaim Kaplan, the trenchant observer and diarist of the Warsaw ghetto, concluded: "A poison of diseased hatred permeates the blood of the Nazis." Once activated, the Germans' profound hatred of Jews, which had in the 1930s by necessity lain relatively dormant, so possessed them, that it appeared to have exuded from their every pore. Kaplan observed many Germans from September 1939 until March 1940 when he penned his evaluation derived from their actions and words:

The gigantic catastrophe which has descended on Polish Jewry has no parallel, even in the darkest periods of Jewish history. First, in the depth of hatred. This is not just hatred whose source is in a party platform, and which was invented for political purposes. It is a hatred of emotion, whose source is some psychopathic malady. In its outward manifestations it functions as physiological hatred, which imagines the object of hatred to be unclean in body, a leper who has no place within the camp.

The [German] masses have absorbed this sort of qualitative hatred.... They have absorbed their masters' teachings in a concrete, corporeal form. The Jew is filthy; the Jew is a swindler and an evildoer; the Jew is the enemy of Germany, who undermines its existence; the Jew was the prime mover in the Versailles Treaty, which reduced Germany to nothing; the Jew is Satan, who sows dissension between one nation and another, arousing them to bloodshed in order to profit from their destruction. These are easily understood concepts whose effect in day-to-day life can be felt immediately.

Significantly, this characterization is based on the words and acts of Germans—of SS men, policemen, soldiers, administrators, and those working in the economy—before the formal genocidal program of systematic killing had begun. It is the masses, the ordinary Germans, not the Nazi ideologues and theoreticians, whom Kaplan exposes. The causal link between the Germans' beliefs and actions is palpable, so that the Jews feel the effect of their "concepts" "in day-to-day life." In the more than two-and-a-half years of subsequent concentrated observation of the Germans in Warsaw, Kaplan saw no reason to alter this evaluation, an evaluation confirmed by a German police official, who states plainly that those serving alongside him in the Cracow region of Poland "were, with a few exceptions, quite happy to take part in shootings of Jews. They had a ball!" Their killing was motivated by "great hatred against the Jews; it was revenge...." The revenge was not for any real harm that the Jews had visited upon Germans, but for the figmental harms for which the perpetrators believed, in their anti-Semitically-inflamed minds, the Jews were responsible.

Effectively extinguishing the voices of the victims, and sometimes suggesting that they do little more than glorify themselves, is not only indefensible methodologically but also a deep affront to survivors. Most victims want to do nothing more than convey what the perpetrators did to them, their families, and to others. Victims of such crimes can never gain full restitution for their losses and suffering. What they generally seem to want is to have the truth be told, particularly so that the perpetrators will acknowledge their crimes. Survivors often express bewilderment that their experience has been generally ignored by the scholarship that treats the perpetration of the Holocaust. Many survivors have told me that they are thankful for my book, *Hitler's Willing Executioners* and for its detailed analysis of the German perpetrators, including their gleeful cruelty and brutality, which the survivors attest was almost always voluntary. They say my interpretation of the Holocaust accords with what they and so many others witnessed and experienced.

A new way of approaching the study of the Holocaust is implicit in much of the unparalleled, widespread public discussion about various aspects of the

Holocaust that has been taking place for the last two years. The old paradigm consists of abstract, faceless structures and institutions (bureaucracy, the greatly exaggerated "terror apparatus" that was supposedly directed at ordinary Germans, the SS, the Nazi Party, the gas chambers) and allegedly irresistible external forces (totalitarian terror, the exigencies of war, social psychological pressure). This paradigm effaces the human actors and their capacity to judge what they were doing and to make moral choices. It is ahistorical. All of this implies that any people from any era with any set of beliefs about Jews (even non-anti-Semites) would have acted in exactly the same manner as the perpetrators, with the same brutality, zeal, and Mephistophelean laughter. This is being challenged by a view that recognizes that the Holocaust was brought about by human beings who had beliefs about what they were doing, beliefs which they developed within a highly specific historical context, and who made many choices about how to act within the institutions in which they worked and which brought them to their tasks in the first place. The human beings are finally at the center of the discussion. The heretofore dominant question of "What compelled them to act against their will?" is being replaced by the question of "Why did these people choose to act in the ways that they did?"

As a result, powerful myths are crumbling: the myth that the Swiss or the Swedes acted as they did only because of the German threat; the myth that the peoples in different occupied countries did not do more to thwart the Germans or less to help in the killing of the Jews merely because of their fear of the occupying Germans; the official Allied governmental myths that they could not reasonably have attempted to do much more to save the victims; the myth that those who procured Jewish property, including art, generally did so innocently; the myth that the perpetrators, by and large, disapproved of what they were doing but were coerced, were being blindly obedient, or were pressured to act as they did; and the three related myths that the German people more broadly (all the exceptions notwithstanding) did not know that their countrymen were killing Jews en masse, did not support the Nazi regime even though its many brutal policies (forced sterilization, so-called "euthanasia," the violent persecution of the Jews and others, the reintroduction of slavery into the European continent) were widely known, and did not approve of the general eliminationist persecution of the Jews.

Not surprisingly, many people who have either been comforted by such views or whose careers have been made by adopting positions that buttress them, and who find the new, powerful challenges to these views to be politically undesirable or personally threatening, are extremely unhappy and have let that be known. The frequent response is to attack, often in the most vitriolic and unprincipled ways, the messengers—whether they be scholars, institutions like the Hamburg Institute for Social Research which produced the exhibit, "War of Extermination: The Crime of the Wehrmacht, 1941–1944" that has been traveling around Germany, the World Jewish Congress for forcing the issue of Swiss gold onto the agenda, or the witnesses, namely Jewish survivors, whose testimony has always been a devastating threat to many of the myths.

It would be beneficial if certain basics could become widely accepted which the crumbling paradigm has obscured. They include:

1. The discarding of the caricature of individual Germans as having had no views of their own about the rightness of what they or their countrymen were doing, which included slaughtering children. We need to know how these views were distributed among Germans, and how they, singly or in interaction with other factors, influenced Germans' actions during these years. The same applies to the peoples of other countries, those where the Germans found many willing helpers and those where the populace worked to thwart (sometimes successfully) the program of extermination.

2. The rejection of the myth that the large scale, mass killing of Jews remained unknown to the broader German public. Germans themselves are becoming more candid: twenty-seven percent of those who were at least fourteen years old at the end of the war now admit that they knew of the extermination of the Jews when it was taking place. (The survey which determined this stunning new finding, which the chief pollster of the German wire service, dpa, says is still clearly a substantial underreporting of the real figure, was conducted for the German television network ZdF in September 1996. Yet in the flood of articles written about the Holocaust since then, I have seen no mention of this finding, perhaps because it explodes a central element of the conventional paradigm—even though the survey's results were announced and discussed on German national television during a panel discussion on the Holocaust and reported by the dpa.)

3. The acknowledgment that Germans who were not members of specifically targeted groups (Jews; Gays; the Sinti and Roma peoples, who are commonly known as gypsies; the mentally infirm; the Communist and Social Democratic leadership) were not so terrorized as the totalitarian terror model posits. The enormous amount of dissent and opposition that Germans expressed against so many policies of the regime and the regime's responsiveness to public sentiment and action makes this clear. So a new understanding of the relationship between state power, regime policy, and popular consent needs to be worked out. The comparative question of why Germans expressed different degrees of dissent and opposition to different policies, yet virtually no principled dissent against the eliminationist persecution of the Jews, becomes central. More generally, all models that posit that irresistible external forces compelled people—Germans, French, Poles, Swiss, or the Allies—to act as they did need to be replaced by views that acknowledge the existence of human agency. If the vast majority of the German people had genuinely been opposed to the radical eliminationist persecution of the Jews, then Hitler would have never been able to pursue it as he did.

4. The adoption of a comparative perspective on genocide, so that those who study the Holocaust do not adopt methodological practices or causal claims that are at odds with how we study and what we know of other analogous phenomena. All available evidence (contemporaneous documents and the testimony of perpetrators, victims, and bystanders) that is not rendered suspect according to

clearly articulated, standard social scientific principles is to be used. Regarding the use of the testimony of Jewish survivors, for example, the reasons given for excluding it must be defensible if one changed the word "Jews" to Tutsis, Bosnians, Cambodians, Armenians, the victims of the Gulag, or enslaved Blacks in the American South. The methods of the social sciences present rules regarding research design and the structure of inference, including when generalization is allowed and even required. A major research project might be undertaken using all available evidence to catalogue what is known of the backgrounds, actions, and attitudes of every perpetrator in every ghetto, camp, and other institution of killing—those who victimized Jews and non-Jews—so that a general portrait and systematic analysis of them can be composed.

5. The recognition that the Holocaust had both universal and particular elements. Its universal aspect is that all people have the capacity to dehumanize groups of others so intensely that their hatred can impel them to commit genocide. Its particular aspect is that such views do not come to exist in equal measure in every society about every group, and when they do, it is not every society that has a state which mobilizes those who hold such views in a program of mass annihilation. The universal capacity to hate does not mean that all people actually do hate and hate all others in the same way, or that all hatreds will motivate people to treat the object of their aggression similarly. Real existing hatreds, as opposed to the capacity to hate, are primarily socially constructed and historically particular.

The Holocaust is not "beyond human comprehension." In principle, it is as explicable as every other genocide. No one says that the Rwandan or Cambodian genocide cannot be explained. What so many people simply do not want to accept is that the victims of the Holocaust have a great deal to tell us about their victimizers (no less than do the victims in Rwanda and Bosnia); and that the German perpetrators were like the perpetrators of other mass slaughters: the vast majority of these Germans were also willing executioners. That people automatically accept these facts about non-Jewish victims of genocide and about African or Asian perpetrators but not about Jews and "civilized" white Christian Europeans respectively is disturbing. Does anyone think for a moment that the Turkish, Hutu, or Serbian perpetrators did not believe that slaughtering Armenians, Tutsis, or Muslims was right? Does anyone for a moment believe that the testimony of these genocides' victims should not be used extensively in order to learn about the texture of the genocides, including the attitudes of the perpetrators? Indeed, in the Armenian genocide, in Bosnia, Cambodia, Rwanda, and other instances of mass slaughter, such testimony is eagerly used by scholars and has provided the principal knowledge of the perpetrators' deeds and attitudes....

NO

Christopher R. Browning

Ordinary Germans or Ordinary Men?
A Reply to the Critics

In the spring of 1992, I published a book entitled *Ordinary Men*, the case studyofareservepolicebattalion from Hamburgthatbecame the chiefunit for killing Jews in the northern Lublin district of the General Government. In general, the book has been quite well-received, but it has not been without its critics in both the United States and Israel. While these critics have accepted the narrative presentation in the book that reveals the mode of operation and degree of choice within the battalion, they have objected to my use of sources, my portrayal of the perpetrators (particularly their motives and mindset) and, above all, the conclusions that I draw—the crux of which is summed up in the title *Ordinary Men*. As one friendly but critical letter-writer suggested, "Might not a preferable title ... possibly have been Ordinary Germans?"

The argument of my critics for German singularity rests above all upon their assertion of a unique and particular German antisemitism. The letter-writer cited above argued that "cultural conditioning" shaped "specifically German behavioral modes." He continued, hypothesizing that "even many decidedly non-Nazi Germans ... were so accustomed to the thought that Jews are less human than Germans, that they were capable of mass murder." Non-Germans in the same situation as the men of Reserve Police Battalion 101, he implies, would have behaved quite differently.

Daniel Goldhagen, the most severe critic of what he called my "essentially situational" explanation, put the matter more pointedly. The "Germans' singular and deeply rooted, racist anti-Semitism" was not "a common social psychological phenomenon" that can be analyzed in terms of "mere" negative racial stereotypes, as I had so "tepidly" done. "The men of Reserve Police Battalion 101 were not ordinary 'men,' but ordinary members of an extraordinary culture, the culture of Nazi Germany, which was possessed of a hallucinatory, lethal view of the Jews." Thus, ordinary Germans were "believers in the justice of the murder of the Jews." In their "inflamed imaginations," destruction of the Jews "was a redemptive act."

The issue raised here, namely the appropriate balance of situational, cultural, and ideological factors in explaining the behavior of Holocaust killers, is an important—indeed central—subject that merits further exploration. I would like to approach this issue along two lines of inquiry. First, what has the bulk of recent scholarship concluded about the nature, intensity, and alleged singularity of antisemitism within the German population at large? Second, what light can comparisons between German and non-German killers of Jews in the Holocaust shed on the issue of "specifically German behavioral modes"?

Let us turn to the first line of inquiry, namely the nature and intensity of antisemitism within Nazi Germany. Perhaps the most ardent advocate of an interpretation emphasizing the singularity and centrality of German antisemitism was Lucy S. Dawidowicz. In her book *The War against the Jews*, she argued that

> generations of anti-Semitism had prepared the Germans to accept Hitler as their redeemer.... Of the conglomerate social, economic, and political appeals that the NSDAP [National Socialist German Workers Party] directed at the German people, its racial doctrine was the most attractive.... Out of the whole corpus of racial teachings, the anti-Jewish doctrine had the greatest dynamic potency.... The insecurities of post–World War I Germany and the anxieties they produced provided an emotional milieu in which irrationality and hysteria became routine and illusions became transformed into delusions. The delusional disorder assumed mass proportions.... In modern Germany the mass psychosis of anti-Semitism deranged a whole people.

A large number of other scholars, however, have not shared this view. Three scholars in particular—Ian Kershaw, Otto Dov Kulka, and David Bankier—have devoted a significant portion of their scholarly lives to examining German popular attitudes toward National Socialism, antisemitism, and the Holocaust. While there are differences of emphasis, tone, and interpretation among them, the degree of consensus on the basic issues is impressive.

While Kulka and Bankier do not pick up the story until 1933, Kershaw argues that prior to the *Machtergreifung*, antisemitism was not a major factor in attracting support for Hitler and the Nazis. He cites Peter Merkl's study of the "old fighters," in which only about one-seventh of Merkl's sample considered antisemitism their most salient concern and even fewer were classified by Merkl as "strong ideological antisemites." Moreover, in the electoral breakthrough phase of 1929–1933, and indeed up to 1939, Hitler rarely spoke in public about the Jewish question. This reticence stood in stark contrast to the Hitler speeches of the early 1920s, in which his obsession with and hatred of the Jews was vented openly and repeatedly. Kershaw concludes that "antisemitism cannot ... be allocated a decisive role in bringing Hitler to power, though ... it did not do anything to hinder his rapidly growing popularity."

For the 1933–1939 period, all three historians characterize German popular response to antisemitism by two dichotomies. The first is a distinction between a minority of party activists, for whom antisemitism was an urgent priority, and the bulk of the German population, for whom it was not. Party activists clamored and pressed, often in violent and rowdy ways, for intensified persecution. The antisemitic measures of the regime, though often criticized as too mild by the radicals, served an integrating function within

Hitler's movement: they helped to keep the momentum and enthusiasm of the party activists alive. Despite Hitler's pragmatic caution in public, most of these radicals correctly sensed that he was with them in spirit.

The second dichotomy characterizes the reaction of the general population to the antisemitic clamor of the movement and the antisemitic measures of the regime. The vast majority accepted the legal measures of the regime, which ended emancipation and drove Jews from public positions in 1933, socially ostracized the Jews in 1935, and completed the expropriation of their property in 1938–1939. Yet this same majority was critical of the hooliganistic violence of party radicals toward the same German Jews whose legal persecution they approved. The boycott of 1933, the vandalistic outbreaks of 1935, and above all the Kristallnacht pogrom of November 1938 produced a negative response among the German population. Bankier and Kulka emphasize the pragmatic concerns behind this negative response: destruction of property, foreign policy complications, damage to Germany's image, and general lawlessness offensive to societal notions of decorum. In Kershaw's opinion, the idea that the population discounted virtually any moral dimension is "a far too sweeping generalization." Nonetheless, these historians agree that a gulf had opened up between the Jewish minority and the general population. The latter, while they were not mobilized around strident and violent antisemitism, were increasingly "apathetic," "passive," and "indifferent" to the fate of the former. Antisemitic measures—if carried out in an orderly and legal manner—were widely accepted for two main reasons: such measures sustained the hope of curbing the violence most Germans found so distasteful, and most Germans ultimately agreed with the goal of limiting, and even ending, the role of Jews in German society.

The records of the war years upon which Kulka, Bankier, and Kershaw based their studies were sparser and more ambiguous. Accordingly, the difference in interpretation is greater. Kulka and Bankier deduce a more specific awareness of the Final Solution among the German people than does Kershaw. Kershaw and Bankier advocate a more critical and less literal reading of the SD [security service] reports than does Kulka. Kershaw sees a general "retreat into the private sphere" as the basis for widespread indifference and apathy toward Nazi Jewish policy. Kulka sees a greater internalization of Nazi antisemitism among the population at large, particularly concerning the acceptance of a solution to the Jewish Question through some unspecified kind of "elimination," and accordingly prefers the term "passive" or "objective complicity" over "indifference." Bankier emphasizes a greater sense of guilt and shame among Germans, widespread denial and repression, and a growing fear concerning the consequences of impending defeat and a commensurate rejection of the regime's antisemitic propaganda. But these differences are matters of nuance, degree, and diction. Fundamentally, the three scholars agree far more than they differ.

Above all, they agree that the fanatical antisemitism of the party "true believers" was not identical to the antisemitic attitudes of the general population and that the antisemitic priorities and genocidal commitment of the regime were not shared by ordinary Germans. Kershaw concludes that while

> the depersonalization of the Jew had been the real success story of Nazi propaganda and policy ... the "Jewish question" was of no more than minimal interest to the vast majority of Germans during the war years.... Popular opinion, largely indifferent and infused with a latent anti-Jewish feeling ... provided the climate within which spiralling Nazi aggression towards the Jews could take place unchallenged. But it did not provoke the radicalization in the first place.

Kershaw summarized his position in the memorable phrase that "the road to Auschwitz was built by hatred, but paved with indifference."...

The general conclusions of Kershaw, Kulka, and Bankier—based on years of research and a wide array of empirical evidence—stand in stark contrast to the Dawidowicz/Goldhagen image of the entire German population "deranged" by a delusional mass psychosis and in the grips of a "hallucinatory, lethal view of the Jews." If "ordinary Germans" shared the same "latent," "traditional," or even "deep-seated" antisemitism that was widespread in European society but not the "fanatical" or "radical" antisemitism of Hitler, the Nazi leadership, and the party "true believers," then the behavior of the "ordinary Germans" of Reserve Police Battalion 101 cannot be explained by a singular German antisemitism that makes them different from other "ordinary men."

My characterization of the depersonalizing and dehumanizing antisemitism of the men of Reserve Police Battalion 101, which Goldhagen finds too "tepid," places them in the mainstream of German society as described by Kershaw, Kulka, and Bankier, distinct from an ideologically driven Nazi leadership. The implications of my study are that the existence of widespread negative racial stereotyping in a society—in no way unique to Nazi Germany—can provide fanatical regimes not only the freedom of action to pursue genocide (as both Kershaw and Kulka conclude) but also an ample supply of executioners.

In regard to the centrality of antisemitic motivation, it should be noted that German executioners were capable of killing millions of non-Jews targeted by the Nazi regime. Beginning in 1939, systematic and large-scale mass murder was initiated against the German handicapped and Polish intelligentsia. More than three million Soviet prisoners of war perished from hunger, exposure, disease, and outright execution—two-thirds of them in the first nine months after the launching of Barbarossa but before the death camps of Operation Reinhard had even opened. Tens of thousands fell victim to horrendous reprisal measures. Additionally, the Nazi regime included Gypsies in their genocidal assault. Clearly, something more than singular German antisemitism is needed to explain perpetrator behavior when the regime could find executioners to murder millions of non-Jewish victims.

Let us follow another approach to this issue as well by examining the behavior of non-German killing units in the Ukraine and Belorussia, which carried out killing actions quite similar to those performed by Reserve Police Battalion 101. I will not be looking at those elements that enthusiastically carried out the initial murderous pogroms in the summer of 1941—often at German instigation—and were then frequently formed into full-time auxiliaries of the Einsatzgruppen for the subsequent large-scale systematic massacres. The zealous followers of Jonas Klimaitis in Lithuania or Viktors Arajs in Latvia, who eagerly rushed to help the invading Germans kill communists and Jews, are not appropriate counterparts of Reserve Police Battalion 101 for the purpose of cross-cultural comparison.

Instead, I will examine the rural police units in Belorussia and the Ukraine, which did not really take shape until 1942, when they participated in the "second wave" of killing on Soviet territory. Like the men of Reserve Police Battalion 101 in Poland, these policemen provided the essential manpower for the "mopping-up" killings of Jews in small towns and villages and for the "Jew hunts" that relentlessly tracked down escapees....

In summary, the precinct-level Ukrainian police were first organized by the military administration in 1941. They were vastly expanded under the Order Police in 1942, whom they outnumbered in precinct service by at least a 10 to 1 ratio. The local police joined for numerous reasons, including pay, food for their families, release from POW camps, and especially a family exemption from deportation to forced labor in Germany. Although the Germans had difficulty recruiting as many Ukrainian police as they wanted, the Ukrainian police nonetheless numbered in the tens of thousands and constituted a major manpower source for the "second wave" of the Final Solution that swept through the Ukraine in 1942.

There is scant documentation from the precinct level on the day-to-day participation of the auxiliary police in the mass murder of Jews. From the Ukraine one series of police reports survives, from which we can see that the local Schutzm¨anner and their supervising German Gendarmerie performed precisely the same duties as Reserve Police Battalion 101 in Poland, with one exception—there were no deportations to death camps, only shooting actions....

The Gendarmerie outpost in Mir, in Belorussia ... reported the results of its killing activities to headquarters in Baranoviche. Its commander noted that "560 Jews were shot in the Jewish action carried out in Mir" on August 13, 1942.... Around Mir the Jew hunt continued. On September 29, 1942, a "patrol of the Mir Schutzmannschaft" found in the forest six Jews, who "had fled the previous Jewish action." They were shot on the spot. Six weeks later a forest keeper discovered a Jewish bunker. He led a patrol of three German gendarmes and sixty Schutzmänner to the site. Five Jews, including the former head of the Judenrat of Mir, were hauled from the bunker and shot. "The food"—including 100 kilos of potatoes—"as well as the tattered clothing were given to the Mir Schutzmannschaft."

In short, the role in the Final Solution of the precinct-level police recruited on Soviet territory seems scarcely distinguishable from that of German reserve police in Poland. The precinct-level Schutzm¨anner were not the eager pogromists and collaborators of mid-summer 1941, just as the German reserve police were not career SS and policemen but post–1939 conscripts. The role and behavior of the Ukrainian and Belorussian auxiliary police in carrying out the Final Solution do not lend support to the notion of "specifically German behavioral modes."

I would like to look into the particular case of the German Gendarmerie in Mir and their Belorussian auxiliaries in greater detail because this case pertains to a further criticism of my book, my alleged misuse of German sources and nonuse of Jewish sources. It has been suggested on the one hand that I was much too gullible and methodologically uncritical in my acceptance of German testimony, particularly that which I cited in support of my portrayal of a differentiated reaction by the perpetrators and a dramatic transformation in character of many of the policemen over time. I argued that most of the men were upset by the initial killing action, and that over time a considerable minority of the men became enthusiastic and zealous volunteers for the firing squads and Jew hunts; that the largest group within the battalion did not seek opportunities to kill but nonetheless routinely contributed to the murder operations in many ways with increasing numbness and callousness; and that a not insignificant minority remained nonshooters while still participating in cordons and roundups. On the other hand, both Goldhagen and a number of my Israeli colleagues have chided me for not using Jewish sources. If I had been more critical of my German sources and more inclusive in my use of Jewish sources, a more reliable image of a uniform and pervasive bestiality, sadism, and even "jocularity," "boyish joy," and "relish" on the part of the perpetrators would have resulted, they suggest.

After working with these German court testimony records for more than twenty years, I would readily concede that the vast bulk of it is pervasively mendacious and apologetic, especially concerning the motivation and attitude of the perpetrators. It was precisely on the basis of my previous experience with German court testimony, however, that I judged the court testimonies of Reserve Police Battalion 101 to be qualitatively different. The roster of the unit survived, more than 40 percent of the battalion members (most of them rank and file reservists rather than officers) were interrogated, and two able and persistent investigating attorneys spent five years carefully questioning the witnesses.

The resulting testimony provides a unique body of evidence that permits us to answer important questions for which previous court records did not provide adequate information. A historian would be wrong to lump this body of evidence together indiscriminately with other court records. Admittedly, these are subjective judgments on my part, and other honest and able historians could reach other conclusions. My critics' dismissal of my use of this particular German testimony as gullible and methodologically unsound, without giving due attention to the special character of these records, ought to be noted, however.

As for the nonuse of Jewish sources, I would make several observations. First, Jewish testimony was indispensable to my study in establishing the chronology for the fall of 1942. What became a blur of events for the perpetrators remained quite distinct days of horror for the victims. Also, while survivor testimony may be extremely valuable in many regards, it does not illuminate the internal dynamics of an itinerant killing unit. It would be difficult for the victim of such a unit to provide testimony concerning the various levels of participation of different perpetrators and any change in their character over time. Where long-term contact between victims and perpetrators did occur, survivors are able to and in fact do differentiate on such issues. Such long-term contactdid not occur in the situations that I examined, however. The testimony of survivors and even Polish bystanders of a massacre or ghetto-clearing action by a unit such as Reserve Police Battalion 101 would inevitably focus on the brutality, sadism, and horror of the perpetrator unit, with little differentiation among its individual members. It would indeed support the conclusions of my critics concerning the uniform and enthusiastic behavior of the perpetrators, but that does not make those conclusions correct....

A remarkable testimony has recently been published by Nechama Tec in her book about Oswald Rufeisen. It is especially valuable because Rufeisen observed the internal workings of the Mir Gendarmerie post as a translator for the German sergeant in charge. Since some of Rufeisen's testimony so strikingly confirms the dynamics within the reserve police that I portrayed based on perpetrator testimony, I will quote it at length. Tec reports that, according to Rufeisen, there was:

> a visible difference in the Germans' participation in anti-Jewish and anti-partisan moves. A selected few Germans, three out of thirteen, consistently abstained from becoming a part of all anti-Jewish expeditions.... No one seemed to bother them. No one talked about their absences. It was as if they had a right to abstain.

Among these middle-aged gendarmes too old to be sent to the front, Rufeisen noted the presence of enthusiastic and sadistic killers, including the second-incommand, Karl Schultz, who was described as "a beast in the form of a man." "Not all the gendarmes, however, were as enthusiastic about murdering Jews as Schultz," Tec notes. Concerning the policemen's attitude toward killing Jews, she quotes Rufeisen directly:

> It was clear that there were differences in their outlooks. I think that the whole business of anti-Jewish moves, the business of Jewish extermination they considered unclean. The operations against the partisans were not in the same category. For them a confrontation with partisans was a battle, a military move. But a move against the Jews was something they might have experienced as "dirty." I have the impression that they felt that it would be better not to discuss the matter.

This is hardly the image of men uniformly possessed of a "lethal, hallucinatory view of the Jews" who viewed their killing of Jews as "a redemptive act."

Finally, I would like to look at a third example of crosscultural comparison that is very suggestive: the Luxembourgers. Reserve Police Battalion 101 was composed almost entirely of Germans from the Hamburg region, including some men from Bremen, Bremerhaven, and Wilhelmshaven, as well as a few Holsteiners from Rendsburg who felt like relative outsiders. In addition, the battalion included a contingent of young men from Luxembourg, which had been annexed to the Third Reich in 1940. The presence of the Luxembourgers in Reserve Police Battalion 101 offers the historian the unusual opportunity for a "controlled experiment" to measure the impact of the same situational factors upon men of differing cultural and ethnic background.

The problem is the scarcity of testimony. Only one German witness described the participation of the Luxembourgers in the battalion's activities in any detail. According to this witness, the Luxembourgers belonged to Lieutenant Buchmann's platoon in first company and were particularly active in the roundups before the first massacre at Józéfow. This was a period in late June and early July 1942 when the trains were not running to Belzec, and Jews in the southern Lublin district were being concentrated temporarily in transit ghettos such as Piaski and Izbica. On the night before the initial massacre at Józéfow, Lieutenant Buchmann was the sole officer who said he could not order his men to shoot unarmed women and children, and who asked for a different assignment. He was designated responsible for taking the work Jews to Lublin and, according to the witness, the Luxembourgers under his command provided the guard. Hence they did not participate in the massacre.

Thereafter Lieutenant Buchmann continued to refuse participation in any Jewish action. However, those in his platoon, including the Luxembourgers, were not exempted. Under the command of the first sergeant, who was a "110% Nazi" and real "go-getter," the Luxembourgers in particular became quite involved. According to the witness, the company captain took considerable care in the selection of personnel for assignments. "In general the older men remained behind," he noted. In contrast, "*the Luxembourgers were in fact present at every action* [emphasis mine]. With these people it was a matter of career police officials from the state of Luxembourg, who were all young men in their twenties." Despite their absence at Józéfow, it would appear that the Luxembourgers became the shock-troops of first company simply because of their younger age and greater police experience and training, the absence of "specifically German behavioral modes" and a singular German antisemitism notwithstanding....

I will conclude briefly. If the studies of Kershaw, Kulka, and Bankier are valid and most Germans did not share the fanatical antisemitism of Adolf Hitler and the hardcore Nazis, then an argument based on a singular German antisemitism to explain the murderous actions of low-level perpetrators does not hold up. If the Nazi regime could find executioners for millions of non-Jewish victims, the centrality of antisemitism as the crucial motive of the German perpetrators is also called into question. If tens of thousands of local policemen in Belorussia and the Ukraine—taken as needed by the Germans, who were desperate for help and offered a variety of inducements—basically performed the same duties and behaved in the same way as their German counterparts in Poland, then the argument of "specifically German behavioral modes" likewise fails. Finally, if Luxembourgers in Reserve Police Battalion 101 did not behave differently from their German comrades, then the immediate situational factors to which I gave considerable attention in the conclusion of my book must be given even greater weight. The preponderance of evidence suggests that in trying to understand the vast majority of the perpetrators, we are dealing not with "ordinary Germans" but rather with "ordinary men."

POSTSCRIPT

Was German "Eliminationist Antisemitism" Responsible for the Holocaust?

Both in the United States and Germany, the publicity engendered by Goldhagen's book has been overwhelming. Because of its seemingly anti-German message, the book has been surprisingly well received in Germany, and a book tour there was attended by largely enthusiastic audiences. However, when the book was translated into German, its title was translated as *Hitler's Willing Executors,* which gives quite a different slant to the book's thesis. Some have accused Goldhagen and his publisher of changing the German title in order to increase sales in Germany, adding their complaints to those who claimed that Goldhagen's original title was intentionally inflammatory.

Many critical articles and reviews of *Hitler's Willing Executioners* have appeared—and Goldhagen has rebutted many of them in print. A most important one appeared in the *New Republic* (December 23, 1996) and is noteworthy because of the length, breadth, and depth of Goldhagen's response to his critics. It would provide a fitting and informative conclusion to this issue.

Needless to say, there have been so many books written about the Holocaust that to single out a few for mention can be a precarious operation. But a few general sources that should be consulted would be Raul Hilberg, *The Destruction of the European Jews* (Holmes & Meier, 1985); Yehuda Bauer, *A History of the Holocaust* (Franklin Watts, 1982); and Martin Gilbert, *The Holocaust: A History of the Jews of Europe During the Second World War* (Owl Books, 1987). Michael Marrus's, *The Holocaust in History* (Meridian Books, 1987) serves as one of the Holocaust's most thorough historiographical studies. Ron Rosenbaum's *Explaining Hitler* (Random House, 1998) provides an interesting and accessible look at Holocaust historiography, as the journalist/author interviews and writes about the world's leading Holocaust scholars and their works. For neophytes, this might be a good place to start. Also, the journal *Holocaust and Genocide Studies* always provides interesting and thought-provoking articles on the subject.

Lastly, a book of essays critiquing Goldhagen's work is *Hyping the Holocaust: Scholars Answer Goldhagen* (Cummings and Hathaway, 1997), which provides ample criticism of Goldhagen's scholarship. Finally, *Unwilling Germans? The Goldhagen Debate,* Robert R. Shandley, ed. (University of Minnesota Press, 1998), offers a large sampling of German reaction to *Hitler's Willing Executioners.*

ISSUE 11

Should Japanese Emperor Hirohito Have Been Held Responsible for Japan's World War II Actions?

YES: Herbert Bix, from "Emperor Hirohito's War," *History Today* (December 1999)

NO: Stephen S. Large, from *Emperor Hirohito and Showa Japan: A Political Biography* (Routledge, 1992)

ISSUE SUMMARY

YES: Herbert Bix offers proof that Emperor Hirohito should be held responsible for Japan's World War II actions.

NO: Historian Stephen S. Large argues that Emperor Hirohito's lack of real political power to affect change absolves him from any direct responsibility for World War II.

On August 15, 1945, Emperor Hirohito spoke to the Japanese people by way of a radio broadcast. It was the first time that many Japanese citizens had heard the voice of a man who was considered by many as descending from the gods. His message asked them to give up the war that Japan had provoked in Asia and ultimately expanded into a world-wide conflict. The word "surrender" was not used in his speech, but it was clear to all that Japan had lost the war.

Few Japanese, including Hirohito, knew what lay in store for their country. The emperor felt that there was a possibility that he would be deposed and perhaps even tried as a war criminal. These prospects forced him to seriously consider abdication as an alternative.

Six weeks later, Hirohito had a face-to-face meeting with General Douglas MacArthur, commander of Allied forces in Asia and soon-to-be Governor of Occupied Japan. Hirohito was informed that he would not be removed from office, nor tried as a war criminal, and would be allowed to remain as emperor, although he would have to renounce his claim to divine origins. All this was welcome news to a man whose fate was clearly in the hands of a general representing the U.S. government. To say that the emperor experienced a sense of relief would be an understatement.

Until his death in 1989, Hirohito was a model world citizen and the unofficial leader who presided over Japan's remarkable postwar recovery. His goodwill trip to the United States in 1975 was viewed by many as a symbolic end to World War II animosities held by both countries. Japan was a staunch, wealthy ally, and many Americans seemed willing to forgive and forget.

Hirohito's death also caused a historical reassessment of his career. which included a new look at his role in the planning and execution of Japan's war plans. Prior to this, it had been said that Hirohito was a constitutional monarch who possessed little political power, and even as emperor, he could have done little to control those who made the decisions for war. Some writers, however, looking at the question from a new perspective and with more sources of information available to them, began to draw a different picture of Hirohito. This emperor not only knew what Japan was doing during the pre-war period, but actively participated in it, never speaking out against the war that was to come. Rather than viewing Hirohito as an innocent bystander, some now viewed him as an unindicted co-conspirator.

These writers seriously questioned the efficacy of MacArthur's (and the U.S. government's) decision to absolve Hirohito from all responsibility. They saw the decision as one of many American policies (our strong postwar support for West Germany was another) designed to create potential allies in the free world's struggle with world communism. They also felt that if Japanese military and civilian leaders had been tried and found guilty of war crimes in 1946–1947—and many were even sentenced to death for their actions—absolving Hirohito from all responsibility was an unconscionable act.

Some have gone so far as to declare that a deliberate "cover-up" of Hirohito's participation in the war's planning and prosecution had occurred. To many, this was corroborated by a 1989 British Broadcasting Corporation–produced film entitled "Hirohito: Behind the Myth," and televised in this country by WGBH, the Public Broadcasting System's (PBS) Boston affiliate.

Although some were willing to give some credibility to the program's findings, a storm of protest arose from many influential American supporters of Japan and Hirohito, who saw it not only filled with errors, but as a deliberate attempt to sully the reputation of its subject. To those who welcomed the program's content, this response was part of another attempt to keep the truth hidden from the American people. This difference of opinion regarding Hirohito and his responsibility for the war frames the focus of this issue.

In our first selection, Herbert Bix states recent evidence proves that Emperor Hirohito should have been held responsible for Japan's World War II actions. Steven S. Large argues that Japan's constitutional monarchy-based political system offered Hirohito few opportunities to actively oppose the Japanese plans for war, and that other factors within the country also gravitated against any decisive actions that he could have taken to prevent the war.

Herbert Bix

 **YES**

Emperor Hirohito's War

Since the death of the Showa Emperor Hirohito in January 1989, new historical documents have focused public attention on the leadership role that he and his innermost circle of advisers played in the Japanese political process both during and after the Second World War. These new materials, and others published over the course of the 1980s, furnish a fresh starting point for situating the Showa emperor in the history of the twentieth century. They help to delineate more clearly key elements of Emperor Hirohito's character, while exposing certain myths pertaining to his innocence in starting the Pacific War, and his heroism in ending it. They also raise questions about his position in the post-war state, where he was supposed to be a powerless 'symbol', completely devoid of any political role.

The emperor's death lifted a taboo on discussing his role in history and in 1990 alone six 'insider' diaries and memoirs of considerable historical value appeared. Two of them—the diaries of Makino Nobuaki, the emperor's Grand Chamberlain and Privy Seal from 1925 to 1935, and Nara Takeji, his chief military aide-de-camp—reveal the emperor during his first political crises in 1928 and 1931–33. They show his permissive attitude toward the military elite from the very start of its rise to power; and also show that, with the exception of the Genro Saionji Kinmochi (whose influence relative to Makino declined after 1929), the emperor and his most important political advisers were never strong supporters of party cabinets.

The era of 'Taisho democracy' (First World War to 1926) had coincided with the physical and mental inability of Hirohito's father to exercise his power under the Meiji Constitution. That situation, which had been public knowledge ever since the First World War, facilitated a decline in the power and prestige of the throne, making possible the rise of 'Taisho democracy'. In 1926 when Emperor Hirohito ascended the throne and the 'Showa era' began, a major concern among ruling circles was how to implant in the people the authority of Emperor Hirohito. It was, therefore, not entirely accidental that the period that witnessed the decline and end of the era of political party governments—1928 to 1931—was also the period in which the young emperor and his close advisers, Makino Nobuaki, Suzuki Kantaro and Nara Taketsugu, were most pre-occupied with reasserting the power and prestige of the throne, and establishing the 'imperial will' as distinct from the policy of the government.

Sokkin nisshi, Kinoshita Michio, another diary revealing the emperor in the early post-war period, was kept by Kinoshita Michio, a Tokyo University

From *History Today*, vol. 41, issue 12, December 1991, pp. 12-19. Copyright © 1991 by History Today, Ltd. Reprinted by permission.

Law School graduate, who in 1924 became Crown Prince Hirohito's private secretary and chamberlain. Kinoshita's record covers the period from his appointment as Vice Grand Chamberlain in October 1945 until his resignation in June 1946. He has much to say about developments in the making of the post-war Japanese state, including the emperor's role in the emergence of a new 'give and take' relationship with the United States. Here one finds the emperor's defence of his wartime prime minister Tojo Hideki's discussions of the emperor's thoughts on the designation and arrest of war criminal suspects, and entries dealing with the making of the emperor's famous 'declaration of humanity', issued as an imperial rescript to the Japanese nation on January 1st, 1946.

According to Kinoshita seven people participated directly in the drafting process of the declaration, including the emperor. The Americans took the initiative and approved the original draft, believing that they were getting the emperor to participate directly in the debunking of emperor ideology. But Hirohito wanted to get across a different message: namely, that the monarchy had always been compatible with democracy. And his revisions ensured that the primary message of the rescript was not so much the disavowal of his alleged divinity but the idea that the democratisation of Japanese society marked a continuation of ideals inscribed in the Five Article 'Charter Oath' of the Meiji Restoration. In its reaffirmation of the past, and failure to explicitly repudiate the old wartime ideology of the divine origins of the imperial line, the 'Declaration of Humanity' had some of the same mendacious qualities as the emperor's famous August 15th, 1945, surrender broadcast, which cast his acceptance of the Potsdam Proclamation in the form of a unilateral assertion of imperial will.

Kinoshita is also helpful in explaining how the emperor and his entourage prepared for the Tokyo war crimes trials, and how American policy makers in Tokyo and Washington assisted the Japanese 'moderates' in transforming him from the symbol of Japanese militarism to the emblem of its new found pacifism. Kinoshita does not focus on the Japanese people who were the targets of this propaganda effort, but he was writing in that critical period when a gap had opened between the monarchy and the people, which the court, with General Headquarters co-operation, was attempting to close by promoting a new image of the emperor as a great pacifist. The emperor's periodic tours of local areas, which began in February 1946 and continued until 1954, were part of that effort. When historians examine Japan's road to war with the peoples of Asia and the West, they will not be able to ignore the issues of the emperor, the 'palace groups' and the 'emperor system'; nor will they be able any longer to treat the emperor in the post-war period as a completely non-political figure. The discovery of new historical materials have made it possible to put them all back into the picture. Doing this, however, will involve taking account of the emperor in his capacity as supreme military commander.

A recent Japanese language study of the Showa Emperor's war leadership, by Yamada Akira, gives new insight into the role of the emperor as commander-in-chief. In standard, authoritative historical accounts, such as Robert Butow's *Japan's Decision to Surrender* (1954) the wartime emperor is depicted as 'a bystander watching with interest the turmoil of political activity taking place around him but never interfering no matter how personally concerned for the outcome he might be'. However, this 'bystander' image of a constitutional monarch robotised and kept in the dark by the military, is a travesty. It is far more accurate to see Emperor Hirohito at the height of his political powers as an inconsistent wielder of sovereign power who did not want war with the United States and Britain but, by the late 1930s, moved squarely into the camp of the 'renovationist' group who were tending toward an ever expanding war in Asia.

By October 1941, as Konoe Fumimaro and his chief cabinet secretary, Tomita Kenji, have suggested, a major factor in Prime Minister Konoe's resignation, which paved the way for the war cabinet of General Tojo Hideki, was the emperor's own increasing inclination toward war. Less than seven weeks after he had bestowed the mandate of prime minister on Army Minister Tojo, Emperor Hirohito sanctioned the Japanese attack on Pearl Harbor. Thereafter, as the nation's supreme commander-in-chief, he frequently worked to give overall supervision for the entire war effort, even going so far as to insist that specific orders be issued to his commanders in the field, and, on occasion, interfering in military operations in all the far-flung theatres of the war.

Yamada documents eleven major instances where the emperor was deeply involved in supervising the actual conduct of war operations. According to the evidence in this work, Hirohito pressured the High Command to order an early attack on the Philippines, including the fortified Bataan peninsula. He pressed for, and secured, the deployment of army air power in the Guadalcanal campaign. Following Japan's withdrawal from Guadalcanal he demanded a new offensive in New Guinea, which was duly carried out. Unhappy with the navy's conduct of the war, he criticised the withdrawal from the central Solomon Islands and demanded naval battles against the Americans for the losses they had inflicted in the Aleutians. Finally, it was at his insistence that plans were drafted for the recapture of Saipan and, later, for an offensive in the battle of Okinawa.

Yamada's work is an excellent guide to a remarkable historical document, written around the time of Kinoshita Michio's diary but, like Kinoshita, not published until the great 'emperor boom' of 1989—90. This document is the Showa emperor's dokuhakuroku or dictated account of the key events during his first twenty years as emperor. It was taken down in five dictation sessions in the spring of 1946, by close aides.

When the popular literary magazine *Bungei Shunju* conveniently published the dokuhakuroku in December 1990, it created a sensation by enabling readers to get a new and deeper insight into the emperor's character. For the first time since the war, many saw the forgotten fighting generalissimo side to Hirohito—a side that Yamada Akira and other Japanese historians had already documented on the basis of the emperor's 'questions' to his military commanders, and their reports to him on the unfolding war situation.

The first point to consider about the dokuhakuroku, however, is the political intention behind its genesis. The emperor's first person survey of Japan's crises and wars from 1928 to 1945 was composed in order to answer questions that had arisen specifically in connection with the Tokyo war crimes trial. The fear then was that the Americans might bring pressure on the emperor to abdicate, or even to testify as a witness in the forthcoming trials. The second point is that the published document is essentially a shortened version of an original that was copied out in pencil by the liaison officer of the Imperial Household, Terasaki Hidenari.

It has been conjectured by well-informed Japanese scholars such as Awaya Kentaro and Hata Ikuhiko, that Terasaki made an abbreviated English translation of the document and presented it to high officials within SCAP. Evidence in Terasaki's own diary as well as Kinoshita Michio's suggests that Terasaki probably acted with the approval of the Japanese foreign minister, Yoshida Shigeru.

Judging from the large number of copies that the Terasaki version of the dokuhakuroku has sold in Japan and the media attention it has gained, one may say that this single document has attracted more public attention than any of the other new historical materials on Emperor Hirohito. Although many Japanese have commented favourably on the Showa emperor of the dokuhakuroku, many more, from all walks of life, have been shocked by the revelations: the amazing alibis by which he sought to exonerate himself for the defeat, his lack of consideration for the Japanese people, or guilt for the millions of victims of Japanese aggression.

The lack of moral fibre shown by his constant shifting onto others of his own ultimate responsibility for the defeat, and his failure to reflect on his own mistakes, have drawn the most critical comments. Readers have also raised questions about his dismissal of his first prime minister, Tanaka Giichi, in 1929, his decision to sanction the starting of the Pacific War in 1941; and his role, three and a half years later, in Japan's decision to surrender unconditionally to the Allies.

For their part, professional historians have concentrated on the many myths about the emperor and his court advisers, or those whom US Ambassador Joseph Grew used to call the 'moderates' around the throne. One such myth is the notion that Emperor Hirohito was a normal constitutional monarch who, with a few well-publicised (and therefore undeniable) exceptions, never issued commands but merely expressed opinions or put his seal to documents. Another is that during the Pacific War he was a member of the peace camp, trying to surrender before the US began its all-out bombing campaign of the Japanese mainland. The dokuhakuroku has undermined the emperor's false renown as a constitutionalist and pacifist and raised questions about his incredibly belated decision to surrender in August 1945. In these and other ways, it has helped advance the whole debate on his unacknowledged war responsibility, even though much of what it contains is not new to historians.

The emperor of the dokuhakuroku combined a keen sense of himself as an absolute sovereign, with a remarkable capacity to pretend that he was a normal constitutional monarch. He was certainly a political realist with an appetite for the fruits of territorial aggrandisement, and that might have made him susceptible to the rhetoric of hakko ichiu (eight corners of the world under one roof). When he observed in the dokuhakuroku that:

> it does not matter much if an incident occurs in Manchuria because Manchuria is rural; but if something were to happen in the Tientsin-Peking area, Anglo-American intervention would surely worsen and might lead to a clash.

he seems to have been speaking true to character. In the Asian arena he could safely express his expansionist inclinations; and in China's north-eastern provinces in particular he easily rationalised the aggression of his armed forces. But when dealing with the West he preferred caution because he lacked confidence in Japan's ability to win a war against the United States and Britain, and was far more aware than his military commanders of Japan's vulnerability to economic blockade. Essentially, he believed in force but wanted to combine it with its opposite, diplomacy, so that Japan might retain the fruits of its aggression against weaker Asian neighbours.

Equally well-documented are the emperor's frequent disagreements with the military and his condemnations of their recklessness. These disagreements, however, were mainly tactical and not principled. They stemmed from what the emperor imagined the United States or Britain would do in response to any particular act of Japanese aggrandisement. Although the military's rise to power in the 1930s created situations in which the emperor's orders were sometimes disobeyed, rifts between him and his military should not be exaggerated. Moreover, the military never had enough power to establish a dictatorship and could only operate through the authority of the emperor. As historian Yoshida Yutaka has observed, the military's rise to power during this period was also a process in which Emperor Hirohito strengthened his voice and projected his will in the policy making process.

Two other aspects of the emperor's world-view can be gathered from the dokuhakuroku. One was his sense of Japan as a 'have-not' nation (vying with the Anglo-American powers who were intent on keeping it in a subordinate international position within the Washington treaty system). Another element appears to have been a low regard for party government at home. Needless to say, these too were features that the emperor shared with the militarists; and both are exemplified in his defiant introduction to the dokuhakuroku. This particular monologue appears as a document attached to Kinoshita Michio's diary, written about the same time as the dokuhakuroku, but it is not reproduced in full in the published and abbreviated (Terasaki Hidenari) version. Here, addressing the origins of the Second World War, is what the emperor says:

> Japan's call for racial equality, advocated by our representatives at the peace conference following World War I, was not approved by the Great Powers. Everywhere in the world discrimination between Yellow and White remained, as in the rejection of immigration to California and the Whites-only policy in Australia. These were sufficient grounds for the indignation of the Japanese people who suffered from having a small, overpopulated territory and a lack of raw materials, yet had considerable ability to develop.

Nor was that all. Despite my visit to England and the efforts I made for mutual friendship, the Anglo-Japanese alliance was abrogated immediately after my visit. As time passed, Great Power pressure on Japan to reduce its armaments grew steadily stronger. We were forced to return Tsingtao. In China anti-Japanese education, which drew on the sympathy of the Great Powers for the weaker party, had very deep roots. For these reasons Japan-China relations could only continue to worsen. Moreover, our political ability to deal with these unfavorable international conditions showed signs of gradual debilitation as a result of the corruption of the political parties. The feeling spread among the nation's masses that entrusting politics to the party politicians was endangering the future of the state. The selfless spirit of the nation cries out in such times of national crisis.

Because the military stood up under such circumstances, bearing the frustrations of the nation, it was extremely difficult to check the spirited young men who formed its core, even though they acted recklessly without regard to means. For their reckless behavior appeared to exhibit some common ground with the patriotic action of breaking the deadlock of the state.

Having rationalised Japan's war of aggression as a just war of defence against white Western imperialism and Chinese resistance, the emperor launches into a discussion of his first political crisis: the assassination, in June 1928, of the Manchurian warlord Chang Tso-lin by staff officers of his Kwantung Army, and his subsequent scolding (in effect, firing) of his prime minister, the Seiyu-kai party president, General Tanaka Giichi, for his alleged mishandling of the incident. His intention is to introduce at the outset his main defence: namely, that he was a 'normal constitutional monarch', who ratified military faits accomplis but was unable to interfere in cabinet decisions.

If the dokuhakuroku raised many different aspects of the emperor's war responsibility, other new documents published in recent years have helped to carry that discussion into the post-Second World War period. On three different occasions the Showa emperor considered abdicating as a way of acknowledging his responsibility for Japan's war dead (as opposed to the Asian and Western victims of its aggression). The first was right after the surrender; the second was around the time of the reading of the final verdict in the Tokyo War Crimes Trial in November 1948; and the third was right after Japan signed the San Francisco Peace Treaty and regained its independence in 1951. Throughout that seven year period, the question of abdication was at once a war responsibility issue and an issue of protecting the imperial institution itself, on the ideological plane, from the dangerous idea of political accountability to which the emperor's prewar and wartime activites had exposed it.

In 1980 Tokyo University Press brought out the previously unpublished post-war diaries of Kido Koichi, covering the period December 15th, 1945, to the end of 1948, together with various Kido interviews, interrogations, memorandums and letters. Kido, who had been sentenced to life imprisonment as a 'Class A' war criminal by the Tokyo War Crimes Tribunal in November 1948, also gave thirty depositions to the Tribunal's International Prosecution Section between December 21st, 1945 and March 15th, 1946. And in 1987 this entire record was also published by the leading authority of the Tokyo Trials,

Awaya Kentaro, and others. In Awaya's commentary on Kido one finds new documentary evidence of Kido's strong feelings on the war responsibility issue and how he tried to get the emperor to act on the third and last occasion when he considered abdicating. Having served the emperor as Privy Seal and close confidant between June 1940 and November 1945, Kido knew what he was talking about when, from Sugamo prison on October 17th, 1951, he sent the emperor the following secret messege:

> I had left the same word when I bid farewell to His Majesty [December 1945]. No matter how one looks at it, the Emperor bears responsibility for losing the war. Therefore, once you have thoroughly carried out the Pots-dam Proclamation—in other words, when a peace treaty has been signed—I think it is most proper for you to take responsibility and abdicate for the sake of your imperial ancestors and for the nation.... By doing this, the bereaved families of those who died and were wounded in the war, those who were not repatriated and the families of the war criminals will some-how feel requited. I think that should make a very important contribution to national unity centered on the Imperial House. However, if you do not do this, then the end result will be that the Imperial Family alone will not have taken responsibility and an unclear mood will remain which, I fear, might leave an eternal scar.

Emperor Hirohito could never bring himself to abdicate. Nor could he adjust easily to the spirit of the new peace constitution which, although it stripped him of all political powers, had been largely established for his bene-fit. The conservative party politician and diplomatic historian Ashida Hitoshi served as foreign minister in the first socialist cabinet of Katayama Tetsu in 1947 and was prime minister in his own cabinet in 1948. His seven volume diary, published in 1986, has shed important light on the imperial institution during the entire occupation period. Ashida confirms the emperor's unabated (and unconstitutional) political activism and his inability to desist from interfering directly in domestic and foreign policy affairs. In an entry of July 22nd, 1947, Ashida describes how the emperor urged him to 'align' with the United States in the Cold War with the Soviet Union and pressured him to continue the practice of making informal reports to the throne on diplomatic problems, even though such reports violated the new constitution.

By 1947 the Cold War had started to affect Japan, accelerating a reverse course in US occupation policy and creating new opportunities for the emperor to project his views into the policy-making process. As the interna-tional situation worsened, the emperor began to act more forcefully in the old mould, not only insisting that the government make unofficial reports to the throne (naiso), which it did, but secretly operating behind the scenes to ensure that the Ashida government cooperated with Washington against the Soviet Union. Ashida even records that on March 10th, 1948, the emperor importuned him to take action against the Japanese Communist Party, though any such action would have been illegal under the new constitution. By re-establishing the practice of naiso, and in other ways, Emperor Hirohito continued to act not as a 'symbol' but as a political monarch.

Finally, new light has also been shed on the emperor's role in the establishment of the Shidehara Kijuro cabinet (October 1945 to April 1946), and how that cabinet colluded with MacArthur's GHQ to defend him on the issue of his responsibility for the defeat and for having indulged Japan's military cliques in their rise to power. Tsugita Daizabiro nikki, the short diary of Tsugita Daizaburo, chief cabinet secretary in the Shidehara government, brings alive the world of early post-surrender Japan with its millions of unemployed, demobilised soldiers, looming food shortages, mushrooming popular movements, and rising criticisms of those responsible for the great defeat.

Tsugita wrote from the viewpoint of a professional bureaucrat and politician who believed in the twin myths of the Showa emperor as a constitutional monarchist and a pacifist who had brought the war to an end. The following diary entry of October 26th, 1945, suggests that from a very early point in the occupation General MacArthur was predisposed to exonerate the emperor of all war crimes charges, without even bothering to investigate the available evidence.

> Around 6 o'Clock [Army] Lt. General Haraguchi [Hatsutaro] called on me. He said that he had met [Brigadier General Bonner F.] Fellers of MacArthur's headquarters and was told that the problem of the Emperor's responsibility for the attack on Pearl Harbor is the 'most important and critical' issue on the American side. The topic came up of how to deal with it. Both MacArthur and Fellers have very warm feelings toward His Majesty. Haraguchi has no doubt that they are thinking of how to solve this problem without causing trouble for the Emperor. However, American public opinion is very strong; there is also a proposal from the Soviet Union; and it seems that it is not so easy for MacArthur to do as he pleases. In any case, he said that we must have prepared and ready a general explanation [i.e. defense for the Emperor]. Regarding this matter, I think that since the Meiji Emperor, the Emperor of Japan has approved all matters reported to him by the Government or the Imperial Headquarters and never once has he exercised a 'veto.' But at the time of the ending of the war, the Cabinet ministers and the staff officers of the Imperial Headquarters could not reach agreement. So, at the prime minister's request, the Emperor made a decision. One can say that this is almost the only instance in which the Emperor's will was reflected directly in government. I think it is most appropriate to explain this fact honestly.

Ten days earlier, on October 16th, 1945, Washington had instructed MacArthur to 'proceed immediately to assemble all available evidence of Hirohito's participation in and responsibility for Japanese violations of international law'. From Tsugita's comments, it would seem that MacArthur responded to Washington's order by alerting the Shidehara cabinet to prepare a general defence of the emperor. Worried about how the United States would proceed on the issue of punishing war criminals, the Shidehara cabinet for the remainder of its existence worked closely with MacArthur's GHQ to protect the emperor from the Tokyo Tribunal. A statement it adopted on November 5th, 1945, to guide government officials in answering questions 'On matters of war responsibility' laid out the official line thereafter: all war responsibility (by which they meant responsibility for having lost the war) lay with the Government and the military High Command, while the emperor bore no responsibility whatever.

Meanwhile, MacArthur's efforts to solve the problem of the emperor's war responsibility without causing trouble for the Emperor' were neither entirely successful, nor salutary for the Japanese people. The very logic of the reforms entailed the smashing of emperor ideology by promoting a broad interpretation of war responsibility in all areas of Japanese national life. So, while MacArthur was attacking the social basis of the emperor system, extending the pursuit of war responsibility even to school teachers who had indoctrinated the Japanese nation with militarism and ultranationalism, he was also moving in the opposite direction where the emperor himself was concerned. By shielding the emperor from the scrutiny of the war crimes investigators, and later discouraging his abdication, MacArthur abetted the Japanese conservatives in preventing the Japanese people from coming to grips with their own past aggression.

With the publication of the dokuhakuroku and other documents, the veil that was drawn over the Showa Emperor's war responsibility and his failure to abdicate has been pulled back. New debate on the role of the palace groups in the period of fascism and war has also been stimulated. The prevailing views in the West of the emperor as a pacifist standing outside the political process, and the palace 'as a break on extremism throughout its prewar existence', have never corresponded to reality and are now sure to be revised in the light of the new material.

This will also bring the Japanese people back into the debate on war responsibility from which they were largely excluded during the occupation period. Since the death of Hirohito, a post-Cold War evolution has got underway in which issues of war responsibility and monarchy have once again become part of a necessary Japanese dialogue with the past. For historians, the danger in this debate is that because of documents like the dokuhakuroku, which focus solely on the emperor as an individual in the decision-making process, we are apt to lose sight of the elusive prewar emperor system itself; and what it reveals about the deeper structures of Japanese state and society: its triangulation with power, class and cultural themes.

Further Reading:

- Edited by Ito Takashi & Hirose Junko—*Makino Nobuaki nikki* (Tokyo, 1990)
- Yamada Akira—*Showa tenno no senso shido* (Tokyo, 1990)
- John W. Dover—*Empire & Aftermath* (Harvard, 1979)
- Saturo Ienaga—*The Pacific War* (New York, 1978)
- Nakamura Masanori—*The Making of the Symbol Emperor System* (New York, 1992)

NO

Stephen S. Large

Emperor Hirohito and Shōwa Japan

Conclusion ...

The Emperor's War Responsibility

Had the Emperor [Hirohito] been tried, it would have been logical for the IMTFE [International Military Tribunal, Far East] to convict and sentence him for formally sanctioning nearly every act of Japanese aggression and war in the 1931–1945 period, including, for example, the participation of Japanese army units from Korea in the Manchurian incident; the Japanese invasion of Jehol in 1933; the escalation of war with China in 1938; Japanese operations at Changkufeng in 1938; and the fateful decision for war which led to Japan's attack on Pearl Harbor in 1941. In addition, he sanctioned other Japanese initiatives which contributed in different ways to war: Japan's withdrawal from the League of Nations in 1933; Japan's entry into the Axis Alliance in 1940; and Japan's southern advance into French Indochina in 1940 and 1941.

For such critics of the Emperor as David Bergamini and Inoue Kiyoshi, his formal sanctions were emblematic of his deeper participation in a Japanese conspiracy to wage war. The strong implication is that he was as bloodthirsty as Kaiser Wilhelm II who, following the battle of Tannenberg in September 1914, 'proposed to kill 90,000 Russian prisoners of war by driving them onto the barren spit of land in the Baltic Sea known as the Kurische Nehrung, and letting them starve to death'.

The intense passions pervading this interpretation are readily understandable when we recall the carnage wrought by Japan in the Emperor's name. Yet, this interpretation is untenable. It ignores ... that he personally opposed, and tried to use his influence privately at court to prevent, the acts of aggression that he ultimately sanctioned as representing the formal imperial will. He 'was absolutely consistent in using his personal influence to induce caution and to moderate, and even to obstruct, the accumulating, snowballing impetus towards war'. In retrospect, his only major success was the part he played at court in assisting the Hamaguchi cabinet on behalf of the London Naval Treaty in 1930.

Still, concerning the Emperor's war responsibility, Ishida Takeshi writes,

> since under the Meiji Constitution only the Emperor, as the supreme commander of the Imperial Army, was empowered to control the army, the

emperor cannot be absolved of responsibility for Japan's invasion of China in the 1930s and other Asian countries in World War II, though it is true that these actions were planned by the militarists.

Similarly, Ō numa Yasuaki concedes that the Emperor opposed war but agrees that he was accountable for war because the war crimes tribunal 'regarded as criminal not only positive acts but also "disregard" of the "legal duty" to prevent breaches of the laws of war...'. That the Emperor was accountable, not for acts of commission in conspiring to wage war, but for acts of omission in failing to prevent it, is therefore the central issue in considering his war responsibility. Could he have done more, should he have tried to do more, to oppose war?

For the historian, because of the methodological problems it poses, this question is as difficult to answer as it is necessary to ask. Not to ask it would imply a determinist view in which history is invariably governed by impersonal forces and structures over which individuals have little or no control; pushed to an extreme, the responsibility which individuals share for historical outcomes would be ignored.

On the other hand, to ask it implies a voluntarist view that individuals invariably matter more than impersonal forces and structures in the making of history. This assumption runs the two fold risk of over-simplifying the complexities of historical causation and making too much of individual responsibility for historical outcomes. Furthermore, it often leads to over-reliance on indirect and inconclusive evidence in making dubious counterfactual claims about what might have happened had individuals acted differently.

Clearly, an approach is needed which addresses the intricate interaction of impersonal forces, structures and individuals in shaping historical events and processes. Here, 'the problem that then confronts us has at its center the network of dependence within which scope for individual decisions opens to the individual, and which at the same time sets limits to his possible decisions'. [I] have considered this problem in probing how the Emperor perceived his political role, how he acted upon his perceptions, and with what consequences, while also exploring why his personal intentions for peace were so much at variance with the effects of his war-sanctioning.

More particularly,...this [selection emphasizes] the combination of 'external' and 'internal constraints'... that defined the political 'opportunities' available to the Emperor and his 'abilities' to respond to them when confronted by the issue of war in early Shō wa history. These constraints were both positive and negative: positive, in that some plainly obstructed action, and negative, in that some comprised 'an absence, such as lack of resources, strength, skill, or knowledge, that, equally, prevents a potential option from being realized'....

The formidable 'external constraints' on the Emperor make it unreasonable to hold that he could have done more to oppose war or that had he done more, war could have been averted. By way of a brief recapitulation, first, it was always clear that 'The emperor was to be neither a political partisan nor a policy maker. He was to ratify decisions produced by governmental leaders with the Imperial Seal'. He did not attend meetings of the cabinet or the liaison conferences, where decisions were made. Only when Japan's leaders competed in the process of 'working through the court' to declare the imperial will was he given opportunities to influence policy-making. Although he certainly was manipulated, especially by the military, he was no robot, for he exerted influence as he advised, encouraged, and warned. But his influence for peace was ignored, leaving him to confer automatically ritual sanction in the imperial conference on decisions reached elsewhere by others beforehand, as he was expected to do. Throughout prewar and wartime Shō wa, 'Far from being his personal decision-making powers, therefore, the Emperor's prerogatives were the source of authority for rule by others'.

Second, the military, which set the pace in developing a 'national defense state' and in determining Japanese foreign policy, not only ignored his opposition to war, it often presented him and the government with the *fait accompli* of war, only perfunctorily reported to him its strategic plans and operations, and frequently withheld information from him.

This last point bears directly on a question that is often asked: how much did the Emperor know about the military's policies and projects? What he could have done about what he knew is a more important issue, but that aside, we are left to speculate concerning the information at his disposal.... But did he know about such other infamous operations as the biological warfare experiments on prisoners of war that were carried out by the army's Unit 731 in Manchuria?

Probably not. It is true that Unit 731 was established, as an 'epidemic and water supply unit', under the authority of the imperial seal. However, the imperial seal was used to authorize a great many wartime activities of which the Emperor was unaware and it has not been established that he knew of the Unit's true purpose, which is unlikely, given the army's consistent deceitfulness in dealing with him. As Gavan McCormack writes, in an otherwise critical assessment of his career, 'The peculiar tragedy of Hirohito's life was to have been born and raised at the center of a web of deceit', which he continued to experience, and complain about, throughout the early Shō wa period.

Third, the Emperor's advisers constrained him in significant ways and on occasion, they, too, deliberately deceived him, as when, in 1931, Prince Saionji told the foreign minister, 'It is not necessary to lie but tell the Emperor things that will please him in order to ease his mind'. Moreover, on other occasions when he wanted to convene an imperial conference with the intention of speaking out against war, his advisers opposed the idea and thereby negated whatever imperial influence for peace he might have applied.

In 1939, Harada Kumao told the new prime minister, Hiranuma,

> It is regrettable to know that no knowledge of His Majesty's intelligence and virtues is being transmitted to the people.... For instance, in politics, it is the wish of the Emperor to respect and guard strictly the spirit of the Constitution, but this cannot be told to the people.... The Emperor's ideas are not at all evident either in politics or diplomacy....

Harada continued,

> If one should explain that it is the Emperor's desire to conduct a com-
> pletely constitutional government, it is said that Saionji, Makino, or other
> immediate officials do what they please behind the scenes by using the
> name of the Emperor. As a result, the spirit of the Constitution is ignored
> and matters are conducted in such a way that the Emperor's wishes cannot
> be conveyed to the people.

For all Harada's regret, he and other members of the court circle were mostly
to blame for failing to communicate the Emperor's political wishes to the
public and insofar as their fear of violence caused them to keep him out of
controversial situations, the violent incidents of the early 1930s on the part of
Shōwa Restoration extremists constituted a fourth, and very significant,
'external constraint' on the court, including the Emperor.

Fear of violent reprisals from the imperial way faction partly explains
why he failed to follow through on his pledge to 'cleanse the army' following
the suppression of the February 1936 rebellion. Similar fears of a possible
coup also figured in his sanction of the decision for war in 1941. Throughout
the prewar years of Shōwa, fear of 'riding a boat against the rapids', not only
of army power but also of war-inspired popular nationalism, traumatized, and
effectively neutralized, the Emperor and his advisers.

Finally, the most important 'external constraint' on the Emperor was the
contradictory nature of the Meiji constitution. At best, 'Every constitutional
monarchy has an element of ambiguity. In most cases the authority of the
monarchy has been eroded in stages over time, so the limits of its power are
not entirely clear.' This was true of Britain, too. For instance, Harold Nicolson
writes of King George V that though he was determined to 'act strictly in
accordance with his duties and responsibilities as a Constitutional Monarch',
he 'was often driven by the winds and tides of events into these zones of
uncertainty, and was obliged to determine, with little more than the stars to
guide him, which was the true constitutional course to pursue'.

What made the Meiji constitution especially ambiguous was its provisions
for both absolute and limited monarchy, to the point where, in 1932, the American political scientist, Kenneth Colegrove, justifiably preferred to call the Japanese system not a constitutional monarchy but a 'constitutional autocracy'.
The Emperor's contradictory powers gave rise to an acute symbolic dissonance
whereby the people saw him as an absolute monarch while Japan's political
elites paid lipservice to the idea that he was a constitutional monarch. Until,
that is, this latter perception was buried once and for all in prewar Shōwa by
the 'Minobe incident' [attack on Minobe for having suggested that the emperor
was an organ of the state] of 1935. Thereafter, imperial absolutism became
national orthodoxy, not so that the Emperor would actually rule but so that the
power of others who ruled in his name would be unassailable.

The confused and uncertain powers which the constitution ascribed to
him forced the Shōwa Emperor to improvise in opposing the military and
war. To be sure, article LV, which established the principle of ministerial

responsibility, entitled him to expect that ministers of state would pay heed to his advice, warning, and encouragement in many areas of national policy. But whether they would do so was never guaranteed and in any case, where his relations with the military were concerned, article XI mattered more because it gave him the right of supreme command. It is this article which prompts the view that he should have been held accountable for failing to control the military, and in particular, the army and navy chief of staff offices.

Yet whether article XI ensured his control of the military was questionable. It, and article XII, which enabled the Emperor to determine the organization and peace standing of the armed forces, were originally meant 'to prevent cabinet intervention in affairs related to military strategy and operations; also to prohibit Diet [government] interference in determining the military strength needed for national defense. They were not framed to provide an institutional base for the Emperor's direction of military affairs'.

Regardless of its original purpose, article XI conceivably could still have been used by the Emperor to try and control the military. However, this would have been extremely difficult because 'there was absolutely no provision holding the supreme command responsible to the Tennō for its decisions or vice versa'. To recall Masuda Tomoko's similar point about article XI, 'there was no clear definition regarding either the scope of the right of supreme command or the person responsible for exercising it'. Thus, the Shōwa Emperor did not know how far he could go in using his supreme command prerogative to control the military. He evidently thought that the chiefs of staff should be responsible to him in the same way as ministers of state were responsible to him for their politics. But his concept of ministerial responsibility clashed with their political irresponsibility as the chiefs of staff repeatedly usurped his authority.

What does such usurpation signify when it comes to assessing the 'emperor system' in prewar Shōwa Japan? Many Japanese, and a minority of Western, historians have typically 'subsumed all aspects of the modern Japanese state and society under the category of "emperor system", or *tennōsei*, seeing it as the capstone' of power. But 'The construct of the emperor-system state ... is of little utility in terms of detailed historical inquiry, for it exaggerates the unity, strength, and rigidity of the Japanese state from 1890 to the nation's defeat'.

Given the prevalence of 'elite pluralism' and all of the political divisions, ... which made prewar Japan anything but totalitarian, if the 'emperor system' means anything, its distinguishing feature was is amorphousness. Takeyama Michio captures this reality when he writes, 'The history of the early Shōwa era demonstrates the absence of control. The government and the military were divided ..., the emperor-system had become nominal and the insubordination of the military had usurped the Emperor's authority'....

In sum, the combination of 'external constraints' mentioned above make it doubtful that the Emperor could have done more to prevent war. But again, should he have tried to do more, and if so, why did he not do more, to prevent it? It is in pondering this problem that the 'internal constraints' discussed [earlier], which arose from his personality, temperament, political style and political beliefs, are important.

The rigid upbringing of the emperors in the Heian period was 'hardly designed to encourage the development of a vigorous personality, let alone any determination to challenge the political status quo'. Nor had much changed by the Tokugawa period when 'The training of imperial children bred in them habits of docility and rigidly patterned behavior'. Since rigid courtly precedents of protocol and ritual still obtained during his childhood, it is not surprising that his upbringing left the Shōwa Emperor a passive person who always was inclined to 'play by the rules', as when he performed Shintō rites whose underlying myths he personally rejected, or sanctioned war, despite his private hopes for peace.

This early conditioning to be passive was a long-term 'internal constraint' on his 'ability' to oppose war. Another was his scientific, rational world view as a marine biologist who was most at ease in his laboratory and when collecting specimens in Sagami Bay or elsewhere in Japan. Believing in the 'geometry' and orderly evolution of politics and government, which to him seemed comparable to the ordered and evolutionary patterns of the natural world, he was not the sort of man who could face, and deal effectively with, the reality of violence in domestic political life and foreign policy. His reliance on logical argument, and what Honjō Shigeru observed as his scholarly, almost pedantic, manner, made little impact on military men who subscribed to the different rationality of strategic ends and means and who were set on war.

It should be remembered, however, that although he was a naturalist who respected the sanctity of life, as when he once despaired that an officer had given him a pair of cranes which had been shot for his pleasure, he was not a pacifist. Despite his instinctive preference for international cooperation, the Showa Emperor was himself a nationalist whose abiding concern with national security ultimately made him susceptible to the argument in late 1941 that, encircled, Japan had to go to war to save itself and its overseas possessions.

[I have] also speculated that there were aspects of the Emperor's political style, including in particular his indirection and understatement, which rendered him more passive than assertive in expressing his opposition to war. It was suggested that these tendencies may have reflected certain general features of the political culture of the Japanese aristocracy....

Another feature of aristocratic political culture in Japan which possibly impinged on the Emperor's 'ability' to oppose war is the ancient Chinese emphasis, translated into Japan, on the normative 'non-assertion' of monarchy. Herschel Webb quotes Han Fei Tzu as having written in the third century BC: 'The sceptre should not be shown. For its inner nature is non-assertion'. The sage-king merely 'remains empty' and relies on his ministers to govern: 'If the ruler has to exert any special skill of his own, it means that affairs are not going right'. Webb comments that in Japan, 'The *ideal* of non-assertion remained influential'.

To the extent that it influenced the Shōwa court, then this ideal helps to explain the Emperor's passive political style. And insofar as the Shōwa court was influenced by the ancient Japanese tradition in which emperors primarily used their religious authority to legitimize the secular power and policies of others, this tradition, too, informed his scrupulous sanctioning of policies, including those that led to aggression and war....

Perhaps the Emperor unconsciously used his constitutional scruples to disguise his inability to stand up to the military. Be that as it may, a major theme in this study has been the importance he consistently attached to upholding the example of Emperor Meiji as a constitutional monarch. The late Edwin Reischauer wrote in 1975, 'Since the present Emperor has always been a conscientious Constitutional monarch, it really is not proper to inquire what his own particular views may have been, even under the old system'. However, precisely because the Emperor so diligently operated as a constitutional monarch, it is absolutely essential 'to inquire what his own particular views may have been', if we wish to understand how, more than any other, this 'internal constraint' led him to tie his own hands politically even while others tied them.

...[T]he Shōwa Emperor was one of the 'very few' sovereigns who, for reasons of political conviction, made it a point to operate strictly as a limited monarch .... Sugiura Shigetake encouraged him to respect the principles of constitutional monarchy in emulation of Meiji. Later, after observing for himself the theory and practice of constitutional monarchy in Britain during his tour of Europe in 1921, the then Crown Prince 'conceived his own role as that of a constitutional monarch in the British mould, automatically sanctioning any bill approved by the cabinet', with King George V as his model.

This stance was in turn greatly reinforced by Saionji and his circle of constitutional monarchists who advised him during the Taisho regency and thereafter, well into the 1930s. Under their influence, he especially 'refrained from exercising the prerogative of supreme command ... Deferring to parliamentary democracy based on constitutional government, he did not take the initiative'. Finally, through these advisers, and directly when Minobe Tatsukichi lectured at the palace, Minobe further strengthened the Emperor's resolve to function as a constitutional monarch with limited powers. The Emperor may not have followed Minobe's constitutional interpretation in every detail. But he firmly embraced Minobe's concept of the emperor as an 'organ' of the state.

He thus insisted on the rule of law, the principle of ministerial responsibility, and the need at all costs to avoid what he often referred to as 'the bane of despotism'. There is no question that 'In his own interpretation of the Constitution, the Emperor at all times acted constitutionally and it would have been out of character and contrary to his convictions about the rule of law to do otherwise'.

At times, in crisis situations, he acted and spoke as if he saw the possibility of using the absolute powers ascribed to him in the Meiji constitution to defend constitutional government, as when he reacted strongly to the exceptional political crisis of the February 1936 army insurrection. Furthermore, it will be recalled that during the Changkufeng crisis, he declared to the war minister and the army chief of staff, 'you may not move one soldier *without my command*'. And, when reflecting on the decision for war in 1941, he said in

1946, 'If at the time *I had suppressed* the advocacy of war' the public would have been incensed and a coup might have taken place. These statements suggest a more assertive model of imperial action.

Nevertheless, he deliberately rejected this model and instead virtually 'absolutized' the model of constitutional monarchy as he understood it. Thus, after dismissing Tanaka Giichi in 1929, and after helping to suppress the 1936 army rebellion, he worried that he had gone too far as a constitutional monarch. If anything, his determination to uphold his limited powers grew all the more as other elites sought to exploit his absolute powers in declaring the imperial will.... After Japan's defeat, Prince Konoe regretted that the Emperor had not boldly challenged the military:

> Out of reserve, the Emperor seldom expresses his own views. Prince Saionji and Count Makino taught His Majesty not to take the initiative, in adherence to the British-style constitutions, but the Japanese Constitution exists on the premise of the Emperor's personal administration.

The Emperor, Konoe complained, should have asserted his prerogative of supreme command to control the military. He concluded, 'If the Emperor merely gives encouragement or advice as in England, military affairs and political diplomacy cannot advance in unison'.

Konoe had exposed the contradictory nature of Japan's 'constitutional autocracy' but his criticism of the Emperor was self-serving. Konoe himself blocked the Emperor when he wanted to take the initiative: for example, when he told the Emperor not to speak at the crucial imperial conference of 11 January 1938, which ratified the decision to 'annihilate' the enemy in China. In fact, knowing of the Emperor's constitutional scruples, Konoe deliberately used the principle, that a constitutional monarch should not interfere with government policy, to prevent him from openly opposing all-out war in China. Kido, too, neutralized the Emperor politically in this way. When testifying on trial after the war, he said, 'I used to counsel the Emperor to approve [policy], trusting the government in accordance with constitutional government'....

The Shōwa Emperor ... 'was actually downright stubborn in his observance of the Constitution'. Accordingly, he refused on 14 January 1938 to see the army chief of staff, Prince Kan'in, even though he knew that Kan'in shared his own opposition to the Konoe cabinet's pro-war stance on China. Of Kan'in's intentions, he said, 'I judged that this might surely be a plan to overturn what had already been determined [by the government] and I refused to see him'.

The same consideration convinced him that he had no choice as a constitutional monarch but to sanction the decision for war in 1941. There is thus a certain validity in Kamishima Jiro's remark. 'It is probably correct to say that he conducted himself generally in accordance with the "organ theory"' and that 'on that account, the war broke out' in December 1941. Ironically, however, his sanction served perfectly the interests of the militarists and it mattered little that he sanctioned war thinking that this was required of him as a constitutional monarch while to them he sanctioned it as an absolute monarch who, a god himself, spoke for the gods in commanding the destiny of imperial Japan.

After Japan attacked Pearl Harbor the Emperor, as 'manifest deity', was used by the government to sponsor Japan's 'holy war' and encourage the people in hard times. Yet his own constitutionalism still led him to support General Tōjō Hideki's leadership even after the war went badly for Japan and a 'peace party' had emerged, for he believed that it would be improper for a constitutional monarch to depose a prime minister, as he had once deposed Tanaka. And when he intervened to end the war in August 1945, he did so only at the request of the prime minister, after the government had reached a complete impasse in debating whether to carry on with a lost cause. His intervention was critical in ending the war but even at that point, 'the Emperor was only the instrument and not the prime mover, of Japan's momentous decision' to surrender.

Looking back on the prewar years of Shōwa,

> Should the Emperor have betrayed his own principles of Constitutional monarchy, which also served to preserve the Imperial institution by putting it, at least publicly, above politics? Should he have taken an inflexible stand, and suffered the consequences, including the probable assassination of his most trusted advisers, and his own captivity, or at least the loss of what freedom he had to influence politics?

The Emperor's consistent and principled adherence to constitutional monarchy was his strongest point and in modern times it would be strange indeed to criticize any sovereign for not acting in effect despotically. Also, if it takes a despotic intervention to avert the crisis of war, the crisis has probably already passed the point of no return in any case. All the same, however, in view of the terrible consequences of war fought in the Emperor's name, there is a strong case that, whatever the risks, he ought to have subordinated his constitutional principles to expediency, on the chance that a dramatic refusal to sanction war might have caused those who favored war to think twice.

The last chance to intervene with any hope of success was in the early stages of the Sino-Japanese War when there existed the potential, however slim, for mobilizing the caution of the army general staff to challenge the belligerent policy of Prime Minister Konoe and the generals who supported it. That the chance was missed made this arguably the darkest episode in the Emperor's career.

By late 1941, it was simply too late to intervene for peace with the United States and its allies, given that there was too much of a broad consensus on the part of military and civilian leaders that Western sanctions made war absolutely necessary. A failed imperial intervention for peace in 1941 might have ennobled him in the tradition of fallen heroes, which Ivan Morris has characterized as 'the nobility of failure' in Japanese history. But few men and women in history are cut out to be heroes and the Shōwa Emperor was not one of them.

The Emperor sanctioned war, but to conclude, this study confirms that 'Hirohito was neither the bloodthristy tyrant that David Bergamini has described, nor the reckless reactionary depicted by Inoue Kiyoshi'. Nor was he Edward Behr's devious sovereign who turned a blind eye to aggression while cleverly contriving to let others take responsibility for war. Rather, he exemplified what is more commonly found in history, major figures who, politically, were 'mediocre rather than great'. In the last analysis, the Shōwa Emperor was the unwilling symbol, not the maker, of chaos and catastrophe.

POSTSCRIPT

Should Japanese Emperor Hirohito Have Been Held Responsible for Japan's World War II Actions?

Many people today feel that the Japanese have never accepted responsibility for World War II. First, they refused to acknowledge the commission of numerous atrocities in China, which included horrific medical experiments performed on prisoners of war, and the notorious "Rape of Nanking," in which thousands of innocent Chinese civilians were brutally killed by the Japanese armed forces. Later, they denied using Korean and other Asian women as sex slaves for their military personnel, until the evidence was too overwhelming to ignore. Negative accounts of Japanese troop behavior during the war seldom made their way into their history books or movie houses. Some have stated that one reason the Japanese may have difficulty in accepting responsibility today is that they were never required to do so earlier. And today, with most Japanese citizens having no direct contact with the war, it is unlikely they can be convinced that their country's armed forces committed atrocities and that the father of their present emperor may have been responsible for them. For more information about this subject, see Gavan McCormack, "Japan's Uncomfortable Past," *History Today* (May, 1998).

One of the earliest works critical of Hirohito and Japan was David Bergamini's *Japan's Imperial Conspiracy*, 2 vols. (William Morrow, 1971), written by one who suffered internment by the Japanese during the war. This was followed by Edward Behr's *Hirohito: Behind the Myth* (Villard, 1980), which provided the impetus for the BBC/PBS film mentioned in the introduction. Hirohito also had his defenders, among them: Charles D. Sheldon, "Japanese Aggression and the Emperor, 1931–1941, from Contemporary Diaries," *Modern Asian Studies* (vol. 10, no. 1, 1976); and Jerrold M. Packard, *Sons of Heaven: A Portrait of the Japanese Monarchy* (Charles Scribner's Sons, 1987); and Edwin P. Hoyt, *Hirohito: The Emperor and the Man* (Bergin & Garvey, 1992).

Most of the recent books on Hirohito tend to be more condemning than exculpatory. This may be due to the loss of influence of those older historians who supported the American-directed post-war Japanese settlement and its concomitant exoneration of Hirohito. Some of the leading critical accounts are Herbert Bix, *Hirohito and the Making of Modern Japan* (HarperCollins, 2000); Daikichi Irokawa, *The Age of Hirohito: In Search of Modern Japan* (The Free Press, 1995); John W. Dower, *Embracing Defeat: Japan in the Wake of World War II* (W.W. Norton, 1999); and Richard B. Frank, *Downfall: The End of the Imperial Japanese Empire* (Random House, 1999).

More surprising than the opposing sides taken by various historians regarding the question raised by this issue, is the number of historians who have written books about twentieth-century Japan that cover the World War II era and are notoriously silent about the question of Hirohito's responsibility. In some of these works, his existence during the war is barely acknowledged.

ISSUE 12

Was Stalin Responsible for the Cold War?

YES: John Lewis Gaddis, from *We Now Know: Rethinking Cold War History* (Clarendon Press, 1997)

NO: Martin J. Sherwin, from "The Atomic Bomb and the Origins of the Cold War," in Melvyn P. Leffler and David S. Painter, eds., *Origins of the Cold War: An International History* (Routledge, 1994)

ISSUE SUMMARY

YES: Historian John Lewis Gaddis states that after more than a half a century of cold war scholarship, Joseph Stalin still deserves most of the responsibility for the onset of the cold war.

NO: Historian Martin J. Sherwin counters that the origins of the cold war can be found in the World War II diplomacy involving the use of the atomic bomb, and he places much of the blame for the cold war on the shoulders of Franklin D. Roosevelt, Harry S. Truman, and Winston Churchill.

It is hard to imagine that the cold war is over when it played such a pivotal role in world affairs for parts of five decades. But the disintegration of the Soviet Empire has ushered in a new era in strategic diplomacy. What shape this new international relations era will take has yet to be determined, but it is unlikely that it will influence our lives in the same manner as the cold war. It is now the job of historians to compose a reassessment of the cold war, which would cover questions of causes, effects, and responsibility.

The historiography of the cold war seemed to begin simultaneously with the onset of tensions between the democratic and communist worlds. With the question of responsibility looming large, the debate among historians seemed to center around two distinct groups of scholars. The first group, commonly referred to as the orthodox or traditional school, held the Soviet Union responsible for the cold war. Because some of the school's proponents were themselves participants (some were even policymakers) in the events of the era, it was easy for them to see Soviet culpability in the broken promises and duplicitous actions, which seemed to highlight the early cold war years. And as the Soviet Empire cast its menacing shadow over Eastern Europe, it became increasingly apparent to the traditionalists that Joseph Stalin could not be trusted. Also, the volatile nature of the postwar world—especially the vulnerability of the newly emerging nations of the postimperialist era—created tempting morsels for the "Russian Bear." A new policy, "containment," was created to control the voracious Soviet appetite. It would last for almost half a century and would lead to many crises, wars, and conflicts, which marked the cold war. Behind all of this loomed the towering figure of Stalin and, to a lesser degree, the men who succeeded him.

A new school of thought was created that opposed the cold war views of the traditionalists. Members of this school of thought became known as the revisionists, and they began to view the cold war from an entirely different perspective. From this would come a new set of assumptions, including (1) the postwar weakness of the Soviet Union, which prevented the Soviets from being the threat to world peace that many felt they were, (2) the obsession of free-world leaders in viewing any world problem as being Soviet-created, (3) the view that, after a careful examination of World War II diplomacy, many of the actions of the Western Allies, including the use of the atomic bomb, induced Soviet leaders to feel threatened and to react accordingly. Thus, much of the responsibility for the cold war, according to the revisionists, must be laid at the feet of the West and its leaders.

Subsequently, much of cold war historiography was dominated by this traditionalist/revisionist dichotomy. And, as the historical profession became more influenced by a conflict-oriented mode rather than a consensus-centered mode, the revisionists began to gain momentum in the crisis-laden 1960s and 1970s. The Vietnam War helped to trigger this response, as many began to see the mistakes of the cold war being played out again and again. There were no longer any "sacred cows" of the traditionalist variety.

The sudden decline of world communism seemed to usher in an aura of cold war justification. After all, in the eyes of many, the West had won; the enemy had been vanquished, and the end of the struggle seemed to have a ring of vindication to it. But the scars of the past were too deep to hide, and the critical examination of cold war politics continued.

New sources of information, especially those from the formerly secret Soviet archives, were opened up in order to assist historians in their search for answers. What was discovered was revelatory, but it changed few minds. Traditionalists and revisionists contined to hold the same opinions that they held a generation ago.

One historian, John Lewis Gaddis, author of the first selection, named this recent reexamination the "New Cold War." Having been involved in cold war historiography for most of its existence, he drew the conclusion that the Soviet Union and Stalin in particular still bear most of the responsibility for the cold war. Historians such as Gar Alperovitz, Gabriel Kolko, Martin J. Sherwin, and others continued to push the revisionist agenda, that the United States and its allies were responsible for the cold war, and Sherwin represents their viewpoint in his selection.

John Lewis Gaddis

 **YES**

We Now Know:
Rethinking Cold War History

[Joseph] Stalin appears to have relished his role, along with [Franklin D.] Roosevelt and [Winston] Churchill, as one of the wartime Big Three. Such evidence as has surfaced from Soviet archives suggests that he received reassuring reports about Washington's intentions: "Roosevelt is more friendly to us than any other prominent American," Ambassador Litvinov commented in June 1943, "and it is quite obvious that he wishes to cooperate with us." Whoever was in the White House, Litvinov's successor Andrei Gromyko predicted a year later, the Soviet Union and the United States would "manage to find common issues for the solution of ... problems emerging in the future and of interest to both countries." Even if Stalin's long-range thinking about security did clash with that of his Anglo-American allies, common military purposes provided the strongest possible inducements to smooth over such differences. It is worth asking why this *practice* of wartime cooperation did not become a *habit* that would extend into the postwar era.

The principal reason, it now appears, was Stalin's insistence on equating security with territory. Western diplomats had been surprised, upon arriving in Moscow soon after the German attack in the summer of 1941, to find the Soviet leader already demanding a postwar settlement that would retain what his pact with Hitler had yielded: the Baltic states, together with portions of Finland, Poland, and Romania. Stalin showed no sense of shame or even embarrassment about this, no awareness that the *methods* by which he had obtained these concessions could conceivably render them illegitimate in the eyes of anyone else. When it came to territorial aspirations, he made no distinction between adversaries and allies: what one had provided the other was expected to endorse....

On the surface, this strategy succeeded. After strong initial objections, Roosevelt and Churchill did eventually acknowledge the Soviet Union's right to the expanded borders it claimed; they also made it clear that they would not oppose the installation of "friendly" governments in adjoining states. This meant accepting a Soviet sphere of influence from the Baltic to the Adriatic, a concession not easily reconciled with the Atlantic Charter. But the authors of that document saw no feasible way to avoid that outcome: military necessity required continued Soviet cooperation against the Germans. Nor were they themselves prepared to relinquish spheres of influence in Western Europe and the Mediterranean, the Middle East, Latin America, and East Asia. Self-determination was a sufficiently malleable concept that each of the Big Three could have endorsed, without sleepless nights, what the Soviet government had said about the Atlantic Charter: "practical application of these principles will necessarily adapt itself to the circumstances, needs, and historic peculiarities of particular countries."

That, though, was precisely the problem. For unlike Stalin, Roosevelt and Churchill would have to defend their decisions before domestic constituencies. The *manner* in which Soviet influence expanded was therefore, for them, of no small significance. Stalin showed little understanding of this. Having no experience himself with democratic procedures, he dismissed requests that he respect democratic proprieties. "[S]ome propaganda work should be done," he advised Roosevelt at the Tehran conference after the president had hinted that the American public would welcome a plebiscite in the Baltic States. "It is all nonsense!" Stalin complained to [Soviet Foreign Minister V. M.] Molotov. "[Roosevelt] is their military leader and commander in chief. Who would dare object to him?" When at Yalta F.D.R. stressed the need for the first Polish election to be as pure as "Caesar's wife," Stalin responded with a joke: "They said that about her, but in fact she had her sins." Molotov warned his boss, on that occasion, that the Americans' insistence on free elections elsewhere in Eastern Europe was "going too far." "Don't worry," he recalls Stalin as replying, "work it out. We can deal with it in our own way later. The point is the correlation of forces."

The Soviet leader was, in one sense, right. Military strength would determine what happened in that part of the world, not the enunciation of lofty principles. But unilateral methods carried long-term costs Stalin did not foresee: the most significant of these was to ruin whatever prospects existed for a Soviet sphere of influence the East Europeans themselves might have accepted. This possibility was not as far-fetched as it would later seem.... [Stalin] would, after all, approve such a compromise as the basis for a permanent settlement with Finland. He would initially allow free elections in Hungary, Czechoslovakia, and the Soviet occupation zone in Germany. He may even have *anticipated an enthusiastic response* as he took over Eastern Europe. "He was, I think, surprised and hurt," [W. Averell] Harriman [one of Roosevelt's closest advisors] recalled, "when the Red Army was not welcomed in all the neighboring countries as an army of liberation." "We still had our hopes," [Nikita] Khrushchev remembered, that "after the catastrophe of World War II, Europe too might become Soviet. Everyone would take the path from capitalism to socialism." It could be that there was another form of romanticism at work here, quite apart from Stalin's affinity for fellow authoritarians: that he was unrealistic enough to expect ideological solidarity and gratitude for liberation to override old fears of Russian expansionism as well as remaining manifestations of nationalism among the Soviet Union's neighbors, perhaps as easily as he himself had overridden the latter—or so it then appeared—within the multinational empire that was the Soviet Union itself.

If the Red Army could have been welcomed in Poland and the rest of the countries it liberated with the same enthusiasm American, British, and Free

French forces encountered when they landed in Italy and France in 1943 and 1944, then some kind of Czech–Finnish compromise might have been feasible. Whatever Stalin's expectations, though, this did not happen. That non-event, in turn, removed any possibility of a division of Europe all members of the Grand Alliance could have endorsed. It ensured that an American sphere of influence would arise there largely by consent, but that its Soviet counterpart could sustain itself only by coercion. The resulting asymmetry would account, more than anything else, for the origins, escalation, and ultimate outcome of the Cold War.

◦

... It has long been clear that, in addition to having had an authoritarian vision, Stalin also had an imperial one, which he proceeded to implement in at least as single-minded a way [as the American]. No comparably influential builder of empire came close to wielding power for so long, or with such striking results, on the Western side.

It was, of course, a matter of some awkwardness that Stalin came out of a revolutionary movement that had vowed to smash, not just tsarist imperialism, but all forms of imperialism throughout the world. The Soviet leader constructed his own logic, though, and throughout his career he devoted a surprising amount of attention to showing how a revolution and an empire might coexist....

Stalin's fusion of Marxist internationalism with tsarist imperialism could only reinforce his tendency, in place well before World War II, to equate the advance of world revolution with the expanding influence of the Soviet state. He applied that linkage quite impartially: a major benefit of the 1939 pact with Hitler had been that it regained territories lost as a result of the Bolshevik Revolution and the World War I settlement. But Stalin's conflation of imperialism with ideology also explains the importance he attached, following the German attack in 1941, to having his new Anglo-American allies confirm these arrangements. He had similar goals in East Asia when he insisted on bringing the Soviet Union back to the position Russia had occupied in Manchuria prior to the Russo-Japanese War: this he finally achieved at the 1945 Yalta Conference in return for promising to enter the war against Japan. "My task as minister of foreign affairs was to expand the borders of our Fatherland," Molotov recalled proudly many years later. "And it seems that Stalin and I coped with this task quite well."...

◦

From the West's standpoint, the critical question was how far Moscow's influence would extend *beyond* whatever Soviet frontiers turned out to be at the end of the war. Stalin had suggested to Milovan Djilas that the Soviet Union would impose its own social system as far as its armies could reach, but he was also very cautious. Keenly aware of the military power the United States and its allies had accumulated, Stalin was determined to do nothing that might involve the USSR in another devastating war until it had recovered sufficiently to be certain of winning it. "I do not wish to begin the Third World War over the Trieste question," he explained to disappointed Yugoslavs, whom he ordered to evacuate that territory in June 1945. Five years later, he would justify his decision not to intervene in the Korean War on the grounds that "the Second World War ended not long ago, and we are not ready for the Third World War." Just how far the expansion of Soviet influence would proceed depended, therefore, upon a careful balancing of opportunities against risks....

Who or what was it, though, that set the limits? Did Stalin have a fixed list of countries he thought it necessary to dominate? Was he prepared to stop in the face of resistance within those countries to "squeezing out the capitalist order"? Or would expansion cease only when confronted with opposition from the remaining capitalist states, so that further advances risked war at a time when the Soviet Union was ill-prepared for it?

Stalin had been very precise about where he wanted Soviet boundaries changed; he was much less so on how far Moscow's sphere of influence was to extend. He insisted on having "friendly" countries around the periphery of the USSR, but he failed to specify how many would have to meet this standard. He called during the war for dismembering Germany, but by the end of it was denying that he had ever done so: that country would be temporarily divided, he told leading German communists in June 1945, and they themselves would eventually bring about its reunification. He never gave up on the idea of an eventual world revolution, but he expected this to result—as his comments to the Germans suggested—from an expansion of influence emanating from the Soviet Union itself. "[F]or the Kremlin," a well-placed spymaster recalled, "the mission of communism was primarily to consolidate the might of the Soviet state. Only military strength and domination of the countries on our borders could ensure us a superpower role."

But Stalin provided no indication—surely because he himself did not know—of how rapidly, or under what circumstances, this process would take place. He was certainly prepared to stop in the face of resistance from the West: at no point was he willing to challenge the Americans or even the British where they made their interests clear.... He quickly backed down when confronted with Anglo-American objections to his ambitions in Iran in the spring of 1946, as he did later that year after demanding Soviet bases in the Turkish Straits. This pattern of advance followed by retreat had shown up in the purges of the 1930s, which Stalin halted when the external threat from Germany became too great to ignore, and it would reappear with the Berlin Blockade and the Korean War, both situations in which the Soviet Union would show great caution after provoking an unexpectedly strong American response.

What all of this suggests, though, is not that Stalin had limited ambitions, only that he had no timetable for achieving them. Molotov retrospectively confirmed this: "Our ideology stands for offensive operations when possible, and if not, we wait." Given this combination of appetite with aversion to risk, one cannot help but wonder what would have happened had the West tried containment earlier. To the extent that it bears partial responsibility for the coming of the Cold War, the historian Vojtech Mastny has argued, that responsibility lies in its failure to do just that....

Stalin's policy, then, was one of imperial expansion and consolidation differing from that of earlier empires only in the determination with which he pursued it, in the instruments of coercion with which he maintained it, and in the ostensibly anti-imperial justifications he put forward in support of it. It is a testimony to his skill, if not to his morality, that he was able to achieve so many of his imperial ambitions at a time when the tides of history were running against the idea of imperial domination—as colonial offices in London, Paris, Lisbon, and The Hague were finding out—and when his own country was recovering from one of the most brutal invasions in recorded history. The fact that Stalin was able to *expand* his empire when others were contracting and while the Soviet Union was as weak as it was requires explanation. Why did opposition to this process, within and outside Europe, take so long to develop?

One reason was that the colossal sacrifices the Soviet Union had made during the war against the Axis had, in effect, "purified" its reputation: the USSR and its leader had "earned" the right to throw their weight around, or so it seemed. Western governments found it difficult to switch quickly from viewing the Soviet Union as a glorious wartime ally to portraying it as a new and dangerous adversary. President Harry S. Truman and his future Secretary of State Dean Acheson—neither of them sympathetic in the slightest to communism—nontheless tended to give the Soviet Union the benefit of the doubt well into the early postwar era....

Resistance to Stalin's imperialism also developed slowly because Marxism-Leninism at the time had such widespread appeal. It is difficult now to recapture the admiration revolutionaries outside the Soviet Union felt for that country before they came to know it well.... Because the Bolsheviks themselves had overcome one empire and had made a career of condemning others, it would take decades for people who were struggling to overthrow British, French, Dutch, or Portuguese colonialism to see that there could also be such a thing as Soviet imperialism. European communists—notably the Yugoslavs—saw this much earlier, but even to most of them it had not been apparent at the end of the war.

Still another explanation for the initial lack of resistance to Soviet expansionism was the fact that its repressive character did not become immediately apparent to all who were subjected to it....

One has the impression that Stalin and the Eastern Europeans got to know one another only gradually. The Kremlin leader was slow to recognize that Soviet authority would not be welcomed everywhere beyond Soviet borders; but as he did come to see this he became all the more determined to impose it everywhere. The Eastern Europeans were slow to recognize how confining incorporation within a Soviet sphere was going to be; but as they did come to see this they became all the more determined to resist it, even if only by withholding, in a passive but sullen manner, the consent any regime needs to establish itself by means other than coercion. Stalin's efforts to consolidate his empire therefore made it at once more repressive and less secure.

Meanwhile, an alternative vision of postwar Europe was emerging from the other great empire that established itself in the wake of World War II, that of the United States, and this too gave Stalin grounds for concern....

⚜

What is there new to say about the old question of responsibility for the Cold War? Who actually started it? Could it have been averted? Here I think the "new" history is bringing us back to an old answer: that *as long as Stalin was running the Soviet Union a cold war was unavoidable.*

History is always the product of determined *and* contingent events: it is up to historians to find the proper balance between them. The Cold War could hardly have happened if there had not been a United States and a Soviet Union, if both had not emerged victorious from World War II, if they had not had conflicting visions of how to organize the postwar world. But these long-term trends did not in themselves *ensure* such a contest, because there is always room for the unexpected to undo what might appear to be inevitable. *Nothing* is ever completely predetermined, as real triceratops and other dinosaurs discovered 65 million years ago when the most recent large asteroid or comet or whatever it was hit the earth and wiped them out.

Individuals, not asteroids, more often personify contingency in history. Who can specify in advance—or unravel afterwards—the particular intersection of genetics, environment, and culture that makes each person unique? Who can foresee what weird conjunctions of design and circumstance may cause a very few individuals to rise so high as to shape great events, and so come to the attention of historians? Such people may set their sights on getting to the top, but an assassin, or a bacillus, or even a carelessly driven taxicab can always be lurking along the way. How entire countries fall into the hands of malevolent geniuses like Hitler and Stalin remains as unfathomable in the "new" Cold War history as in the "old."

Once leaders like these do gain power, however, certain things become highly probable. It is only to be expected that in an authoritarian state the chief authoritarian's personality will weigh much more heavily than those of democratic leaders, who have to share power. And whether because of social alienation, technological innovation, or economic desperation, the first half of the twentieth century was particularly susceptible to great authoritarians and all that resulted from their ascendancy. It is hardly possible to imagine Nazi Germany or the world war it caused without Hitler. I find it increasingly difficult, given what we know now, to imagine the Soviet Union or the Cold War without Stalin.

For the more we learn, the less sense it makes to distinguish Stalin's foreign policies from his domestic practices or even his personal behavior. Scientists have shown the natural world to be filled with examples of what they call "self-similarity across scale": patterns that persist whether one views them microscopically, macroscopically, or anywhere in between. Stalin was like that: he functioned in much the same manner whether operating within the international system, within his alliances, within his country, within his party, within his personal entourage, or even within his family. The Soviet leader waged cold wars on all of these fronts. The Cold War *we* came to know was only one of many from *his* point of view.

Nor did Stalin's influence diminish as quickly as that of most dictators after their deaths. He built a *system* sufficiently durable to survive not only his own demise but his successors' fitful and half-hearted efforts at "de-Staliniza-tion." They were themselves its creatures, and they continued to work within it because they knew no other method of governing. Not until [Mikhail] Gor-bachev was a Soviet leader fully prepared to dismantle Stalin's structural leg-acy. It tells us a lot that as it disappeared, so too did the Cold War and ultimately the Soviet Union itself.

This argument by no means absolves the United States and its allies of a considerable responsibility for how the Cold War was fought—hardly a sur-prising conclusion since they in fact won it. Nor is it to deny the feckless stu-pidity with which the Americans fell into peripheral conflicts like Vietnam, or their exorbitant expenditures on unusable weaponry: these certainly caused the Cold War to cost much more in money and lives than it otherwise might have. Nor is it to claim moral superiority for western statesmen. None was as bad as Stalin—or Mao—but the Cold War left no leader uncorrupted: the wield-ing of great power, even in the best of times, rarely does.

It is the case, though, that if one applies the always useful test of counter-factual history—drop a key variable and speculate as to what difference this might have made—Stalin's centrality to the origins of the Cold War becomes quite clear. For all of their importance, one could have removed Roosevelt, Churchill, Truman, Bevin, Marshall, or Acheson, and a cold war would still have probably followed the world war. If one could have eliminated Stalin, alterna-tive paths become quite conceivable. For with the possible exception of Mao, no twentieth-century leader imprinted himself upon his country as thoroughly and with such lasting effect as Stalin did. And given his personal propensity for cold wars—a tendency firmly rooted long before he had even heard of Harry Truman—once Stalin wound up at the top in Moscow and once it was clear his state would survive the war, then it looks equally clear that there was going to be a Cold War whatever the west did. Who then was responsible? The answer, I think, is authoritarianism in general, and Stalin in particular.

NO

Martin J. Sherwin

The Atomic Bomb and the Origins of the Cold War

During the Second World War the atomic bomb was seen and valued as a potential rather than an actual instrument of policy. Responsible officials believed that its impact on diplomacy had to await its development and, perhaps, even a demonstration of its power. As Henry L. Stimson, the Secretary of War, observed in his memoirs: "The bomb as a merely probable weapon had seemed a weak reed on which to rely, but the bomb as a colossal reality was very different." That policymakers considered this difference before Hiroshima has been well documented, but whether they based wartime diplomatic policies upon an anticipated successful demonstration of the bomb's power remains a source of controversy. Two questions delineate the issues in this debate. First, did the development of the atomic bomb affect the way American policymakers conducted diplomacy with the Soviet Union? Second, did diplomatic considerations related to the Soviet Union influence the decision to use the atomic bomb against Japan?

These important questions relating the atomic bomb to American diplomacy, and ultimately to the origins of the Cold War, have been addressed almost exclusively to the formulation of policy during the early months of the Truman administration. As a result, two anterior questions of equal importance, questions with implications for those already posed, have been overlooked. Did diplomatic considerations related to Soviet postwar behavior influence the formulation of [Franklin D.] Roosevelt's atomic energy policies? What effect did the atomic legacy Truman inherited have on the diplomatic and atomic energy policies of his administration?

Although Roosevelt left no definitive statement assigning a postwar role to the atomic bomb, his expectations for its potential diplomatic value can be recalled from the existing record. An analysis of the policies he chose from among the alternatives he faced suggests that the potential diplomatic value of the bomb began to shape his atomic energy policies as early as 1943. He may have been cautious about counting on the bomb as a reality during the war, but he nevertheless consistently chose policy alternatives that would promote the postwar diplomatic potential of the bomb if the predictions of scientists proved true. These policies were based on the assumption that the bomb could be used effectively to secure postwar diplomatic aims; and this assumption was carried over from the Roosevelt to the Truman administration.

From Martin J. Sherwin, "The Atomic Bomb and the Origins of the Cold War," in Melvyn P. Leffler and David S. Painter, eds., *Origins of the Cold War: An International History* (Routledge, 1994). Copyright © 1994 by Martin J. Sherwin. Originally published in *American Historical Review*, no. 78 (October 1973). Reprinted and abridged by permission of the author. Notes omitted.

Despite general agreement that the bomb would be an extraordinarily important diplomatic factor after the war, those closely associated with its development did not agree on how to use it most effectively as an instrument of diplomacy. Convinced that wartime atomic energy policies would have postwar diplomatic consequences, several scientists advised Roosevelt to adopt policies aimed at achieving a postwar international control system. [Winston] Churchill, on the other hand, urged the President to maintain the Anglo-American atomic monopoly as a diplomatic counter against the postwar ambitions of other nations—particularly against the Soviet Union. Roosevelt fashioned his atomic energy policies from the choices he made between these conflicting recommendations. In 1943 he rejected the counsel of his science advisers and began to consider the diplomatic component of atomic energy policy in consultation with Churchill alone. This decisionmaking procedure and Roosevelt's untimely death have left his motives ambiguous. Nevertheless it is clear that he pursued policies consistent with Churchill's monopolistic, anti-Soviet views.

The findings of this [selection] thus raise serious questions concerning generalizations historians have commonly made about Roosevelt's diplomacy: that it was consistent with his public reputation for cooperation and conciliation; that he was naive with respect to postwar Soviet behavior; that, like [Woodrow] Wilson, he believed in collective security as an effective guarantor of national safety; and that he made every possible effort to ensure that the Soviet Union and its allies would continue to function as postwar partners. Although this [selection] does not dispute the view that Roosevelt desired amicable postwar relations with the Soviet Union, or even that he worked hard to achieve them, it does suggest that historians have exaggerated his confidence in (and perhaps his commitment to) such an outcome. His most secret and among his most important long-range decisions—those responsible for prescribing a diplomatic role for the atomic bomb—reflected his lack of confidence. Finally, in light of this [selection's] conclusions, the widely held assumption that Truman's attitude toward the atomic bomb was substantially different from Roosevelt's must also be revised.

Like the grand alliance itself, the Anglo-American atomic energy partnership was forged by the war and its exigencies. The threat of a German atomic bomb precipitated a hasty marriage of convenience between British research and American resources. When scientists in Britain proposed a theory that explained how an atomic bomb might quickly be built, policymakers had to assume that German scientists were building one. "If such an explosive were made," Vannevar Bush, the director of the Office of Scientific Research and Development, told Roosevelt in July 1941, "it would be thousands of times more powerful than existing explosives, and its use might be determining." Roosevelt assumed nothing less. Even before the atomic energy project was fully organized he assigned it the highest priority.

The high stakes at issue during the war did not prevent officials in Great Britain or the United States from considering the postwar implications of their atomic energy decisions. As early as 1941, during the debate over whether to join the United States in an atomic energy partnership, members of the British government's atomic energy committee argued that the matter "was so important for the future that work should proceed in Britain." Weighing the obvious difficulties of proceeding alone against the possible advantages of working with the United States, Sir John Anderson, then Lord President of the Council and the minister responsible for atomic energy research, advocated the partnership. As he explained to Churchill, by working closely with the Americans British scientists would be able "to take up the work again [after the war], not where we left off, but where the combined effort had by then brought it."

As early as October 1942 Roosevelt's science advisers exhibited a similar concern with the potential postwar value of atomic energy. After conducting a full-scale review of the atomic energy project, James B. Conant, the president of Harvard University and Bush's deputy, recommended discontinuing the Anglo-American partnership "as far as development and manufacture is concerned." What prompted Conant's recommendations, however, was his suspicion—soon to be shared by other senior atomic energy administrators—that the British were rather more concerned with information for postwar industrial purposes than for wartime use. What right did the British have to the fruits of American labor? "We were doing nine-tenths of the work," Stimson told Roosevelt in October. Early in January 1943 the British were officially informed that the rules governing the Anglo-American atomic energy partnership had been altered on "orders from the top."

By approving the policy of "restricted interchange" Roosevelt undermined a major incentive for British cooperation. It is not surprising, therefore, that Churchill took up the matter directly with the President and with Harry Hopkins, "Roosevelt's own, personal Foreign Office."

Conant and Bush understood the implications of Churchill's intervention and sought to counter its effect. Information on manufacturing an atomic bomb, Conant noted, was a "military secret which is in a totally different class from anything the world has ever seen if the potentialities of this project are realised." Though British and American atomic energy policies might coincide during the war, Conant and Bush expected them to conflict afterward.

The controversy over the policy of "restricted interchange" of atomic energy information shifted attention to postwar diplomatic considerations. The central issue was clearly drawn. The atomic energy policy of the United States was related to the very fabric of Anglo-American postwar relations and, as Churchill would insist, to postwar relations between each of them and the Soviet Union. The specter of Soviet postwar military power played a major role in shaping the Prime Minister's attitude toward atomic energy policies in 1943.

Churchill could cite numerous reasons for this determination to acquire an independent atomic arsenal after the war, but Great Britain's postwar military-diplomatic position with respect to the Soviet Union invariably led the list. When Bush and Stimson visited London in July, Churchill told them quite frankly that he was "vitally interested in the possession of all [atomic energy] information because this will be necessary for Britain's independence in the future as well as for success during the war." Nor was Churchill evasive about his reasoning: "It would never do to have Germany or Russia win the race for something which might be used for international blackmail," he stated bluntly and then pointed out that "Russia might be in a position to accomplish this result unless we worked together." Convinced that the British attitude toward the bomb would undermine any possibility of postwar cooperation with the Soviet Union, Bush and Conant vigorously continued to oppose any revival of the Anglo-American atomic energy partnership.

On July 20, however, Roosevelt chose to accept a recommendation from Hopkins to restore full partnership, and he ordered Bush to "renew, in an inclusive manner, the full exchange of information with the British." At the Quebec Conference, the President and the Prime Minister agreed that the British would share the atomic bomb. The Quebec Agreement revived the principle of an Anglo-American atomic energy partnership, albeit the British were reinstated as junior rather than equal partners.

The debate that preceded the Quebec Agreement is noteworthy for another reason; it led to a new relationship between Roosevelt and his atomic energy advisers. After August 1943 the President did not consult with them about the diplomatic aspects of atomic energy policy. Though he responded politely when they offered their views, he acted decisively only in consultation with Churchill. Bush and Conant appear to have lost a large measure of their influence because they had used it to oppose Churchill's position. What they did not suspect was the extent to which the President had come to share the Prime Minister's view.

Roosevelt was perfectly comfortable with the concept Churchill advocated—that military power was a prerequisite to successful postwar diplomacy. As early as August 1941, during the Atlantic Conference, Roosevelt had rejected the idea that an "effective international organization" could be relied upon to keep the peace: an Anglo-American international police force would be far more effective, he told Churchill. By the spring of 1942 the concept had broadened: the two "policemen" became four, and the idea was added that every other nation would be totally disarmed. "The Four Policemen" would have "to build up a reservoir of force so powerful that no aggressor would dare to challenge it," Roosevelt told Author Sweetser, an ardent internationalist. Violators first would be quarantined, and, if they persisted in their disruptive activities, bombed at the rate of a city a day until they agreed to behave. A year later, at the Tehran Conference, Roosevelt again discussed his idea, this time with Stalin. As Robert A. Divine has noted: "Roosevelt's concept of big power domination remained the central idea in his approach to international organization throughout World War II."

Precisely how Roosevelt expected to integrate the atomic bomb into his plans for keeping the peace in the postwar world is not clear. However, against the background of his atomic energy policy decisions of 1943 and his peace-keeping concepts, his actions in 1944 suggest that he intended to take full advantage of the bomb's potential as a postwar instrument of Anglo-American diplomacy. If Roosevelt thought the bomb could be used to create a more peaceful world order, he seems to have considered the threat of its power more effective than any opportunities it offered for international cooperation. If Roosevelt was less worried than Churchill about Soviet postwar ambitions, he was no less determined than the Prime Minister to avoid any commitments to the Soviets for the international control of atomic energy. There could still be four policemen, but only two of them would have the bomb.

The atomic energy policies Roosevelt pursued during the remainder of his life reinforce this interpretation of his ideas for the postwar period. The following three questions offer a useful framework for analyzing his intentions. Did Roosevelt make any additional agreements with Churchill that would further support the view that he intended to maintain an Anglo-American monopoly after the war? Did Roosevelt demonstrate any interest in the international control of atomic energy? Was Roosevelt aware that an effort to maintain an Anglo-American monopoly of the atomic bomb might lead to a postwar atomic arms race with the Soviet Union?

The alternatives placed before Roosevelt posed a difficult dilemma. On the one hand, he could continue to exclude the Soviet government from any official information about the development of the bomb, a policy that would probably strengthen America's postwar military-diplomatic position. But such a policy would also encourage Soviet mistrust of Anglo-American intentions and was bound to make postwar cooperation more difficult. On the other hand, Roosevelt could use the atomic bomb project as an instrument of cooperation by informing Stalin of the American government's intention of cooperating in the development of a plan for the international control of atomic weapons, an objective that might never be achieved.

Either choice involved serious risks. Roosevelt had to balance the diplomatic advantages of being well ahead of the Soviet Union in atomic energy production after the war against the advantages of initiating wartime negotiations for postwar cooperation. The issue here, it must be emphasized, is not whether international control was likely to be successful, but rather whether Roosevelt demonstrated any serious interest in laying the groundwork for such apolicy.

Roosevelt knew at this time, moreover, that the Soviets were finding out on their own about the development of the atomic bomb. Security personnel had reported an active Communist cell in the Radiation Laboratory at the University of California. Their reports indicated that at least one scientist at Berkeley was selling information to Russian agents. "They [Soviet agents] are already getting information about vital secrets and sending them to Russia," Stimson told the President on September 9, 1943. If Roosevelt was indeed worried to death about the effect the atomic bomb could have on Soviet-American postwar relations, he took no action to remove the potential danger, nor did he make any effort to explore the possibility of encouraging Soviet postwar cooperation on this problem.

Had Roosevelt avoided all postwar atomic energy commitments, his lack of support for international control could have been interpreted as an attempt to reserve his opinion on the best course to follow. But he had made commitments in 1943 supporting Churchill's monopolistic, anti-Soviet position, and he continued to make others in 1944. On June 13, for example, Roosevelt and Churchill signed an Agreement and Declaration of Trust, specifying that the United States and Great Britain would cooperate in seeking to control available supplies of uranium and thorium ore both during and after the war. This commitment, taken against the background of Roosevelt's peacekeeping ideas and his other commitments, suggests that the President's attitude toward the international control of atomic energy was similar to the Prime Minister's.

Churchill rejected the assumption that international control of atomic energy could be used as a cornerstone for constructing a peaceful world order. An atomic monopoly would be a significant diplomatic advantage in postwar diplomacy, and Churchill did not believe that anything useful could be gained by surrendering this advantage. The argument that a new weapon created a unique opportunity to refashion international affairs ignored every lesson Churchill read into history. "You can be quite sure," he would write in a memorandum less than a year later, "that any power that gets hold of the secret will try to make the article and this touches the existence of human society. This matter is out of all relation to anything else that exists in the world, and I could not think of participating in any disclosure to third or fourth parties at the present time."

When Roosevelt and Churchill met at Hyde Park in September 1944 following the second wartime conference at Quebec, they signed an *aide-mémoire* on atomic energy. The agreement bears the markings of Churchill's attitude toward the atomic bomb. It contained an explicit rejection of any wartime efforts toward international control: "The suggestion that the world should be informed regarding tube alloys [the atomic bomb], with a view to an international agreement regarding its control and use, is not accepted. The matter should continue to be regarded as of the utmost secrecy." The *aide-mémoire* then revealed the full extent of Roosevelt's agreement with Churchill's point of view. "Full collaboration between the United States and the British Government in developing tube alloys for military and commercial purposes," it noted, "should continue after the defeat of Japan unless and until terminated by joint agreement." Finally the *aide-mémoire* offers some insight into Roosevelt's intentions for the military use of the weapon in the war: "When a bomb is finally available, it might perhaps, after mature consideration, be used against the Japanese, who should be warned that this bombardment will be repeated until they surrender."

Within the context of the complex problem of the origins of the Cold War the Hyde Park meeting is far more important than historians of the war generally have recognized. Overshadowed by the Second Quebec Conference on one side and by the drama of Yalta on the other, its significance often has been overlooked. But the agreements reached in September 1944 reflect a set of attitudes, aims, and assumptions that guided the relationship between the atomic bomb and American diplomacy during the Roosevelt administration and, through the transfer of its atomic legacy, during the Truman administration as well. Two alternatives had been recognized long before Roosevelt and Churchill met in 1944 at Hyde Park: the bomb could have been used to initiate a diplomatic effort to work out a system for its international control, or it could remain isolated during the war from any cooperative initiatives and held in reserve should cooperation fail. Roosevelt consistently favored the latter alternative. An insight into his reasoning is found in a memorandum Bush wrote following a conversation with Roosevelt several days after the Hyde Park meeting: "The President evidently thought he could join with Churchill in bringing about a US-UK post-war agreement on this subject [the atomic bomb] by which it would be held closely and presumably to control the peace of the world." By 1944 Roosevelt's earlier musings about the Four Policemen had faded into the background. But the idea behind it, the concept of controlling the peace of the world by amass-ing overwhelming military power, appears to have remained a prominent fea-ture of his postwar plans.

◈

Harry S. Truman inherited a set of military and diplomatic atomic energy pol-icies that included partially formulated intentions, several commitments to Churchill, and the assumption that the bomb would be a legitimate weapon to be used against Japan. But no policy was definitely settled. According to the Quebec Agreement the President had the option of deciding the future of the commercial aspects of the atomic energy partnership according to his own estimate of what was fair. Although the policy of "utmost secrecy" had been confirmed at Hyde Park the previous September, Roosevelt had not informed his atomic energy advisers about the *aide-mémoire* he and Churchill signed. Although the assumption that the bomb would be used in the war was shared by those privy to its development, assumptions formulated early in the war were not necessarily valid at its conclusion. Yet Truman was bound to the past by his own uncertain position and by the prestige of his predecessor. Since Roosevelt had refused to open negotiations with the Soviet government for the international control of atomic energy, and since he had never expressed any objection to the wartime use of the bomb, it would have required consid-erable political courage and confidence for Truman to alter those policies. Moreover it would have required the encouragement of his advisers, for under the circumstances the most serious constraint of the new President's choices was his dependence upon advice. So Truman's atomic legacy, while it included several options, did not necessarily entail complete freedom to choose from among all the possible alternatives.

"I think it is very important that I should have a talk with you as soon as possible on a highly secret matter," Stimson wrote to Truman on April 24. It has "such a bearing on our present foreign relations and has such an impor-tant effect upon all my thinking in this field that I think you ought to know about it without further delay." Stimson had been preparing to brief Truman on the atomic bomb for almost ten days, but in the preceding twenty-four hours he had been seized by a sense of urgency. Relations with the Soviet Union had declined precipitously. The State Department had been urging Tru-man to get tough with the Russians. He had. Twenty-four hours earlier the President met with the Soviet Foreign Minister, V. M. Molotov, and "with rather brutal frankness" accused his government of breaking the Yalta Agree-ment. Molotov was furious. "I have never been talked to like that in my life," he told the President before leaving.

With a memorandum on the "political aspects of the S-1 [atomic bomb's] performance" in hand, Stimson went to the White House on April 25. The document he carried was the distillation of numerous decisions already taken, each one the product of attitudes that developed along with the new weapon. The Secretary of War himself was not entirely aware of how various forces had shaped these decisions: the recommendations of Bush and Conant, the policies Roosevelt had followed, the uncertainties inherent in the wartime alliance, the oppressive concern for secrecy, and his own inclination to consider long-range implications. It was a curious document. Though its language revealed Stimson's sensitivity to the historic significance of the atomic bomb, he did not question the wisdom of using it against Japan. Nor did he suggest any concrete steps for developing a postwar policy. His objective was to inform Truman of the salient problems: the possibility of an atomic arms race, the danger of atomic war, and the necessity for international control if the United Nations Organization was to work. "If the problem of the proper use of this weapon can be solved," he wrote, "we would have the opportunity to bring the world into a pattern in which the peace of the world and our civilizations can be saved." To cope with this difficult challenge Stimson suggested the "establishment of a select committee" to consider the postwar problems inherent in the development of the bomb.

What emerges from a careful reading of Stimson's diary, his memorandum of April 25 to Truman, a summary by [Major General Leslie R.] Groves of the meeting, and Truman's recollections is an argument for overall caution in American diplomatic relations with the Soviet Union: it was an argument against any showdown. Since the atomic bomb was potentially the most dangerous issue facing the postwar world and since the most desirable resolution of the problem was some form of international control, Soviet cooperation had to be secured. It was imprudent, Stimson suggested, to pursue a policy that would preclude the possibility of international cooperation on atomic energy matters after the war ended. Truman's overall impression of Stimson's argument was that the Secretary of War was "at least as much concerned with the role of the atomic bomb in the shaping of history as in its capacity to shorten the war." These were indeed Stimson's dual concerns on April 25, and he could see no conflict between them.

Despite the profound consequences Stimson attributed to the development of the new weapon, he had not suggested that Truman reconsider its use against Japan. Nor had he thought to mention the possibility that chances of securing Soviet postwar cooperation might be diminished if Stalin did not receive a commitment to international control prior to an attack. Until the bomb's "actual certainty [was] fixed," Stimson considered any prior approach to Stalin as premature. As the uncertainties of impending peace became more apparent and worrisome, Stimson, Truman, and the Secretary of State-designate, James F. Byrnes, began to think of the bomb as something of a diplomatic panacea for their postwar problems. Byrnes had told Truman in April that the bomb "might well put us in a position to dictate our own terms at the end of the war." By June, Truman and Stimson were discussing "further *quid pro quos* which should be established in consideration for our taking them [the Soviet Union] into [atomic energy] partnership." Assuming that the bomb's impact on diplomacy would be immediate and extraordinary, they agreed on no less than "the settlement of the Polish, Rumanian, Yugoslavian, and Manchurian problems." But they also concluded that no revelation would be made "to Russia or anyone else until the first bomb had been successfully laid on Japan."

Was an implicit warning to Moscow, then, the principal reason for deciding to use the atomic bomb against Japan? In light of the ambiguity of the available evidence the question defies an unequivocal answer. What can be said with certainty is that Truman, Stimson, Byrnes, and several others involved in the decision consciously considered two effects of a combat demonstration of the bomb's power: first, the impact of the atomic attack on Japan's leaders, who might be persuaded thereby to end the war; and second, the impact of that attack on the Soviet Union's leaders, who might then prove to be more cooperative. But if the assumption that the bomb might bring the war to a rapid conclusion was the principal motive for using the atomic bomb, the expectation that its use would also inhibit Soviet diplomatic ambitions clearly discouraged any inclination to question that assumption.

Thus by the end of the war the most influential and widely accepted attitude toward the bomb was a logical extension of how the weapon was seen and valued earlier—as a potential instrument of diplomacy. Caught between the remnants of war and the uncertainties of peace, policymakers were trapped by the logic of their own unquestioned assumptions. By the summer of 1945 not only the conclusion of the war but the organization of an acceptable peace seemed to depend upon the success of the atomic attacks against Japan. When news of the successful atomic test of July 16 reached the President at the Potsdam Conference, he was visibly elated. Stimson noted that Truman "was tremendously pepped up by it and spoke to me of it again and again when I saw him. He said it gave him an entirely new feeling of confidence." The day after receiving the complete report of the test Truman altered his negotiating style. According to Churchill the President "got to the meeting after having read this report [and] he was a changed man. He told the Russians just where they got on and off and generally bossed the whole meeting." After the plenary session on July 24 Truman "casually mentioned to Stalin" that the United States had "a new weapon of unusual destructive force." In less than three weeks the new weapon's destructive potential was demonstrated to the world. Upon learning of the raid against Hiroshima Truman exclaimed: "This is the greatest thing in history."

As Stimson had expected, as a colossal reality the bomb was very different. But had American diplomacy been altered by it? Those who conducted diplomacy became more confident, more certain that through the accomplishments of American science, technology, and industry the "new world" could be made into one better than the old. But just how the atomic bomb would be used to help accomplish this ideal remained unclear. Three months and one day after Hiroshima was bombed Bush wrote that the whole matter of international relations on atomic energy "is in a thoroughly chaotic condition." The wartime relationship between atomic energy policy and diplomacy had been based upon the simple assumption that the Soviet government would surrender important geographical, political, and ideological objectives in exchange for the neutralization of the new weapon. As a result of policies based on this assumption American diplomacy and prestige suffered grievously: an opportunity to gauge the Soviet Union's response during the war to the international control of atomic energy was missed, and an atomic energy policy for dealing with the Soviet government after the war was ignored. Instead of promoting American postwar aims, wartime atomic energy policies made them more difficult to achieve. As a group of scientists at the University of Chicago's atomic energy laboratory presciently warned the government in June 1945: "It may be difficult to persuade the world that a nation which was capable of secretly preparing and suddenly releasing a weapon as indiscriminate as the [German] rocket bomb and a million times more destructive, is to be trusted in its proclaimed desire of having such weapons abolished by international agreement." This reasoning, however, flowed from alternative assumptions formulated during the closing months of the war by scientists far removed from the wartime policymaking process. Hiroshima and Nagasaki, the culmination of that process, became the symbols of a new American barbarism, reinforcing charges, with dramatic circumstantial evidence, that the policies of the United States contributed to the origins of the Cold War.

POSTSCRIPT

Was Stalin Responsible for the Cold War?

Time, place, perspective—all play a role in historical assessment, and any analysis of responsibility for the cold war supports that statement. The cold war's first chroniclers were participants in postwar global politics, and their views were shaped by their personal experiences. Time provided distance, and the events of the coming decades nurtured a movement toward radical politics, which some have referred to as the "New Left." This paved the way for revisionist interpretations of the cold war's origins.

The use of the atomic bombs against Japan in 1945 created a cloud over cold war historiography. Some historians believe that this use was advocated not only to quickly end the war against Japan, but also to teach the Soviet Union a lesson in United States power politics. What course might the post–World War II era have followed if the West had sought different means to end the war? Many believe that the use of atomic weapons and the start of the cold war are inextricably connected.

Useful sources on cold war historiography should begin with the authors of the two selections. Gaddis's career as a cold war scholar can be traced from his *The United States and the Origins of the War, 1941–1947* (Columbia University Press, 1972) to *We Now Know: Rethinking Cold War History* (Routledge, 1997). Sherwin has extended the scholarship of his original *American Historical Review* article, "The Atomic Bomb and the Origins of the Cold War: U.S. Atomic Energy Policy and Diplomacy 1941–1945" (October 1973) in *A World Destroyed: The Atomic Bomb and the Grand Alliance* (Alfred A. Knopf, 1975).

Other significant works written in the traditionalist vein include Louis Halle, *The Cold War as History* (Harper & Row, 1967); Herbert Feis, *From Trust to Terror: The Onset of the Cold War, 1945–1950* (W. W. Norton, 1970); and Norman Graebner, *Cold War Diplomacy: American Foreign Policy 1945–1960* (Princeton University Press, 1962). Important revisionist works on the origins of the cold war include two books by Gar Alperovitz, *Atomic Diplomacy: Hiroshima and Potsdam* (Penguin Books, 1985) and *The Decision to Use the Bomb and the Architecture of an American Myth* (Alfred A. Knopf, 1995). Also included is Lloyd Gardner, *Architects of Illusion: Men and Ideas in American Foreign Policy, 1941–1949* (University of Chicago Press, 1970).

The many works of George F. Kennan, considered to be containment's prime mover, provide invaluable assistance to the study of this issue, as do the works of Russian diplomats Vyacheslav Molotov and Andrei Gromyko, both of whom were "present at the creation" of the cold war. Two recent cold war anthologies are David Reynolds, ed., *The Origins of the Cold War in Europe: International Perspectives* (Yale University Press, 1994) and Allan Hunter, ed., *Rethinking the Cold War* (Temple University Press, 1998).

On the Internet . . .

Confucian Tradition(s)

Confucian Tradition(s) is a Web site that provides a primer on things Confucian; this site is good for both student and teacher, veteran and novice.

`http://www.clas.ufl.edu/users/gthursby/rel/kongfuzi.htm`

Islam, the Modern World, and the West

Islam, the Modern World, and the West is a Web site divided into four major sections: General Considerations; Islam in the United States; Islam, the Muslim World, and Contemporary Issues; and Islam Today in the Various Regions of the Muslim World.

`http://www.arches.uga.edu/~godlas/islamwest.html`

Rwanda Genocide: Ten Years Later (BBC NEWS)

Includes the story of the "One Hundred Days" in audio and images, the return of survivors, how the West failed to intervene, ceremonies to honor the victims, movies on the subject, and the callenge of deep divisions that remain.

`http://news.bbc.co.uk/1/hi/in_depth/africa/2004/rwanda/`
`default.stm`

The Centre for Peace Studies in the Balkans

Provides a variety of sources of information on that part of Europe formerly called its "powderkeg." Consists of headlines that introduce relevant stories, studies, opinions and commentary, archives, a search engine, and links.

`http://balkanpeace.org/`

Attack on America: Osama bin Laden, al-Qa'ida, and Terrorism

A university-based Web site that provides a variety of links to the following subjects: Osama bin Laden and al-Qa'ida, the Taliban and Afganistan, terrorism research sources and government publications, and additional background on terrorism and the September 11, 2001, attacks.

`http://www.lib.ecu.edu/govdoc/terrorism.html`

Afghan Women's Network—Official Web Site

This extensive site describes awareness workshops being conducted to raise awareness among Afghan women about their legal rights, including the right to vote in parliamentary elections. Also included are conflict resolution training, gender awareness, child rights, a code of conduct for NGOs (Non-Governmental Organizations), and leadership training for women. Many photos.

`http://www.afghanwomensnetwork.org/`

PART 3

The Contemporary World

*A*s the world begins a new millennium, it is difficult to predict what the new century will bring. If some of the problems facing our world today continue to grow in seriousness, it is likely that the beginning of the millennium will not be a peaceful one, as the September 11, 2001, terrorist attacks on the United States seem to indicate.

- Are Chinese Confucianism and Western Capitalism Compatible?
- Does Islamic Revivalism Challenge a Stable World Order?
- Was Ethnic Hatred Primarily Responsible for the Rwandan Genocide of 1994?
- Were Ethnic Leaders Responsible for the Disintegration of Yugoslavia?
- Do the Roots of Modern Terrorism Lie in Political Powerlessness, Economic Hopelessness, and Social Alienation?
- Have Afghan Women Been Liberated From Oppression?

ISSUE 13

Are Chinese Confucianism and Western Capitalism Compatible?

YES: A. T. Nuyen, from "Chinese Philosophy and Western Capitalism," *Asian Philosophy* (March 1999)

NO: Jack Scarborough, from "Comparing Chinese and Western Cultural Roots: Why 'East Is East and...'," *Business Horizons* (November 1998)

ISSUE SUMMARY

YES: Philosophy professor A. T. Nuyen maintains that the basic tenets of classical capitalism are perfectly compatible with the key elements of Chinese philosophy.

NO: Management professor Jack Scarborough contrasts the Western heritage of democracy, rationality, and individualism with Confucian values of harmony, filial loyalty, and legalism. Based on his comparison, Scarborough finds that Chinese Confucianism is incompatible with Western capitalism.

Why do Western nations play such a dominant role in the world economy? Are scientific materialism and aggressive individualism responsible for the West's economic prosperity? And, does the East need to abandon the conservative values of Confucianism and Taoism if it wishes to compete economically in the twenty-first century? There is widespread agreement that capitalism has been a successful economic ideology. What the authors of the following selections disagree about is whether classical capitalism, as articulated more than two hundred years ago, or a more modern form of capitalism should receive the credit. The resolution of this question will help us to understand whether or not Confucianism and capitalism are compatible.

When Scottish economist Adam Smith published *An Inquiry Into the Nature and Causes of the Wealth of Nations* in 1776, the same year as the Declaration of Independence, he inspired the Western economic system that came to be known as capitalism. Smith was profoundly influenced by the ideas of the French physiocrats. As the name suggests, these thinkers supported physiocracy—"the rule of nature"—letting natural laws prevail in human society. Classical capitalism urges a hands-off approach, adopting the French term *laissez-faire* (to leave alone) as the best method of creating economic prosperity. Left unmolested, economic forces will be self-regulating, guided by what Smith called "the invisible hand" of the marketplace. Too much of a product drives prices down, discouraging further production; scarcity increases prices, stimulating production. Supply and demand naturally regulate the economy if government stays out of the process.

Smith encountered the ideas of François Quesnay on a trip to Europe around 1760. Quesnay was a brilliant French physician who originated the ideas of physiocracy after a long and thoughtful investigation into the functioning of the economic system. Smith, who had previously written on morals, turned his attention to what causes "the wealth of nations." Smith would have dedicated his masterpiece to Quesnay had Quesnay not died. Some scholars believe that Quesnay may have been inspired by the Chinese philosophy of wu-wei (literally translated as "no action"), which encourages individuals to allow the Tao to regulate everything with perfect efficiency, benefiting all.

Without pressing this point, A. T. Nuyen traces Quesnay's admiration of Confucius as a model human being and presents Quesnay's view that the Chinese system of government was an appropriate model for European nations to emulate. The emperor might have to enact "despotic laws" aimed at ensuring the smooth functioning of the natural laws regulating the economy. However, these laws would function simply to remove impediments and to allow natural forces to operate freely. Nuyen cites antitrust laws in the United States as a modern application of "legal despotism" in the service of natural laws. For Nuyen, classical capitalism arose from the same virtues that inspired the ancient Chinese philosophical systems of Confucianism and Taoism.

Jack Scarborough, by contrast, uses a couplet from a Rudyard Kipling poem about India and the West—"East is east and west is west and never the twain shall meet"—to explain the "enormous gulf" that he sees as separating Asia from Western capitalist economies. While the East, especially "once-great China," was reduced through imperial repression and Confucian discipline to "unrelenting poverty and hardship," the West went on to nearly conquer the world—first politically and later economically. Scarborough's selection is aimed at communicating the "cultural differences" that must be taken into account if one hopes to do business in China.

Scarborough has in mind present-day capitalism, which presumes an aggressive individualism that would have been equally foreign to both Confucius and Smith. He attributes China's economic weakness in the modern world to centuries of self-imposed isolation as well as to a cultural appreciation of harmony, communal loyalty, and an acknowledgement that nature acts with a superior wisdom.

Nuyen, having demonstrated the compatibility between Chinese philosophy and classical capitalism, counters that the economic gap between the West and Asia cannot be attributed to the "cultural factor." Instead, Nuyen suggests that colonialism and post-colonial ideologies are more likely factors.

A. T. Nuyen  **YES**

Chinese Philosophy and Western Capitalism

As we stand now at the end of the 20th century, many nations in the East are well on their way along the path of economic growth and development. To be sure, the East, with the exception of Japan, still has a great deal of catching up to do before it can become the equal of the West in terms of economic prosperity. Also, progress has been uneven. On this score, economic commentators seem to agree that the nations that have done well are those that have adopted the capitalist model that has served the West well over the last hundred years. For instance, W. J. F. Jennerpoints out that, apart from Japan, "all the East Asian countries that have prospered in recent decades were colonies of either Britain or of Japan for generations before the Second World War", and as such inherited the capitalist structure of the West. Japan itself, Jenner contends, could not have prospered without "external conditions needed for rapid industrial growth", such as Western technology, capital and export markets.

Despite the fact that one can point to many obvious exceptions to Jenner's observations, there is fairly widespread support for his view. Thus, it is often enough said that what is holding back economic progress in the East is the "cultural" factor. Commentators frequently suggest that peoples of the East, particularly the ethnic Chinese, subscribe to values which are not conducive to economic progress, values that place the family and the community above individual interests, and spirituality above material well-being. By contrast, the West is said to subscribe to the kind of individualism and materialism that give its peoples a competitive edge. To do well in the economic arena, the suggestion goes, the East needs to embrace the Western capitalist model wholeheartedly by making fundamental changes in their cultural and philosophical outlook. If Asian, particularly Chinese, values had anything to do with economic success, they would have to be thoroughly cleansed through Western values and beliefs. Pace those commentators who credit the success in many Asian countries to Confucianism, Jenner insists that for Confucianism, or any other Chinese philosophical system, to work, "it needs dynamic, alien, Western institutions and forms of economic organization". Thus, in Jenner's view, only when "alien, Western factors came into play were certain elements within some inherited East Asian value systems able to bring about successful capitalist development". By themselves, such value systems are an obstacle to growth.

From A. T. Nuyen, "Chinese Philosophy and Western Capitalism," *Asian Philosophy*, vol.9, no. 1 (March 1999). Copyright ©1999 by *Asian Philosophy*. Reprinted by permission of Taylor & Francis Ltd., http://www.tandf.co.uk/journals, and the author. Notes omitted.

Behind views such as Jenner's is the supposition that capitalism is wholly a product of the West, that it is inherently an alien system from the point of view of the East, that it does not sit well with the traditions of the East and that the capitalist model cannot be successfully embraced without some violence being done to those traditions. The aim of this [selection] is to challenge such a notion. My thesis is that it is classical capitalism that first set the West on its course towards economic prosperity, and that the fundamental tenets of classical capitalism are perfectly compatible with the key elements of Chinese philosophy. Indeed, as we shall see, many historians of ideas have traced the origins of classical capitalism all the way back to Chinese thought. Setting aside whether anything can be made of the historical link, I shall attempt to show how classical capitalism could have developed from the fundamentals of Chinese philosophy. If I am right, the economic gap between the West and Asia has to be accounted for in terms other than the "cultural" factors, such as, perhaps, colonialism and post-colonialist ideologies.

By classical capitalism I mean an economic system based on unfettered competition, the unrestricted availability of productive technologies, the free movement of labour and other factors of production, and the smooth flow of information within both the producer and consumer groups. It is a system based on what economists call "perfect competition". Such a system would result in commodities being produced at the lowest possible costs and made available to consumers at the lowest possible prices. Under ideal conditions, the system would result in what economists call "Pareto efficiency", a state of affairs in which it is not possible to make someone better off, in the economic sense, without making someone else worse off. It is important to note that anti-competitive behaviour is an obstacle in the attainment of the economic benefits of the system. The most common form of anti-competitive behaviour is monopoly. This could result from the monopolisation of factors of production, or productive technologies, or the distribution of commodities. It is for this reason that anti-competitive behaviour has been outlawed in many capitalist nations. The USA, for instance, enforces its anti-trust law fairly vigorously, albeit with varying degrees of success. The other factor that tends to restrict competition is government intervention through burdensome rules and regulations, and the involvement of the state in the economy itself through state-owned companies. This is why capitalist nations such as the USA tend to make laws aimed at giving all economic agents a free reign and to minimize public ownership (in a process known as "privatisation"). The term "free enterprise", or the French equivalent, namely, laissez-faire, can be used as a name for the capitalist system I have described, provided that by "free" we mean free from anti-competitive forces, not free to engage in restrictive practices, and certainly not free to indulge in any kind of behaviour whatsoever in the pursuit of profit.

Classical capitalism as I have described it has evolved from the works of classical thinkers such as Francois Quesnay and the physiocrats, Bernard Mandeville and Adam Smith. It was Quesnay and his fellow physiocrats who persuaded the French government to overturn the interventionist policy of the mercantalists and to free up the market. It is true that Quesnay supported a governmental system known as "legal despotism", interpreted by some commentators as a model for absolute monarchy and thus might be taken as being against the spirit of free enterprise. However, Quesnay's intention in advocating legal despotism really was to set up the legal framework for free enterprise. The "despotic" laws were meant to ensure the smooth functioning of economic laws which were for the physiocrats, as we shall see later, identical with natural laws. The laws that Quesnay advocated have to be compared with the laws aimed at promoting free enterprise in modern capitalist nations, such as antitrust laws in the USA. It is for this reason that Quesnay is regarded by many commentators as undoubtedly the founder of modern capitalism. For instance, according to Weulerrse, Quesnay's doctrine expresses "the scientific principles of capitalism, pure and simple, of complete capitalism"; it represents "the triumph of the spirit of capitalism". At any rate, Quesnay's advocacy for free enterprise found a powerful support in Adam Smith in whose hands his economic/natural laws became the laws of the "invisible hand". I take for granted that Smith's doctrine of the wealth of nations is directly responsible for the wealth of modern capitalist nations. Given the theoretical connection between Smith and Quesnay, I shall restrict myself to Quesnay.

The brief excursion into economic history above may serve to confirm the impression that the intellectual roots of modern capitalism lie buried wholly in Western soil and that the Eat needs to make drastic internal changes if it is to adapt the alien capitalist model successfully. However, many historians have claimed that, at the philosophical level, Quesnay's ideas came directly from the East, from Chinese philosophy to be more precise. It is not altogether clear whether and to what extent Quesnay was influenced by Chinese thoughts, or whether he borrowed anything from the East. However, it is worth pursuing the historical link before turning to the more straightforward comparative reading of Quesnay and Chinese philosophers. What we do know is that Quesnay himself acknowledged his debt to Chinese philosophy, especially to Confucianism. His book, *Le Despotism de la Chine*, is not a critique of the Chinese system of government; rather, it is a description of a system on which he based his concept of legal despotism, mentioned [earlier]. According to J. J. Clarke, Quesnay

> regarded China as an ideal society that provided a model for Europe to follow, and in discussing Chinese despotism he wrote that 'I have concluded from the reports about China that the Chinese constitution is founded upon wise and irrevocable laws which the Emperor enforces and which he carefully observes himself'.

While the Chinese system of government was for Quesnay a model that Europe should follow, Confucius himself was for him a model of the perfect person. According to one historian, Quesnay modelled himself on Confucius, so much so that his disciples called him "The Confucius of Europe": "His manuscript for *Le Despotism de la Chine* contains a few pages on the life of Confucius which were deleted from the published version, but which provide a disarmingly close approximation to an autobiographical assessment and statement of personal purpose". In the manuscript, Quesnay expressed his admiration for Confucius's "grave, modest and serious air", his "most profound knowledge" and his "intent of spreading his doctrine and working for the reformation of men". Above all, Quesnay admired Confucius for the fact that by "his gravity, his modesty, his sweetness and his frugality, by his scorn of terrestrial pleasures, and by a continual vigilance on his own conduct, he was himself an example of the precepts he advanced in his writings and his discourses ..."

Given what we know about Quesnay's respect and admiration for Confucius as a person, it is not surprising that historians go on to speculate that Quesnay freely made use of Confucius's philosophy and derived from it many useful ideas. What is evident is that he interpreted that philosophy as advocating the observance of the laws of nature and the adoption of nature's guiding principle, having in mind no doubt the notion of the tao. As Quesnay saw it, nature's guiding principle, in the philosophy of Confucius, is a force that commands "the respect, the fear [and] the recognition" in all of us, a force that "knows all, ... even the most secret recesses of the heart ...". Furthermore, this force of nature, if allowed to operate unhindered, will result in the best for all, including human beings. From this it is but a small step to the conclusion that Quesnay either borrowed or was influenced by this view of Chinese philosophy, given his own doctrine that in economic affairs, it is best to follow the laws of nature, a doctrine for which Pierre-Samuel du Pont de Nemours aptly coined the term "physiocracy" in 1767, meaning literally "the rule of nature". It is certainly true that Quesnay thought that the laws of nature should not be interfered with, that nature should be left alone to operate, that in the economic sphere, we should let nature be, laissez-faire. Interestingly, one historian has speculated that the term "laissez-faire" is the French translation of the Chinese wu-wei: "Both lawmaker and law had to recognize the principle of ... natural order, and in doing so conform to the Chinese ideal of wu-wei, which has ever inspired their theories of government".

It may be said that the historical evidence above is consistent with the thesis that Quesnay was influenced by Chinese philosophy as it is with a quite different thesis, namely, that Quesnay merely saw a parallel between his own doctrine and what he took to be the philosophy of Confucius. It is not my intention in this [selection] to settle this issue. My interest is confined to the question of whether capitalism is really so alien to the East that the East could not assimilate it without making some profound changes in its fundamental beliefs. However we interpret the historical evidence connecting physiocracy with Confucianism, or Quesnay with Confucius, the fact remains that the historical discussion above opens up the possibility for arguing that Chinese philosophy, and in particular Confucianism, provides a hospitable background for, rather than thwarting, the development of the kind of capitalism that has brought economic prosperity to the West. If the argument is successful then, as pointed out above, we have to look elsewhere for an explanation as to why such development failed to take place early enough in the East, thus resulting in the current economic gap between the East and the West. With this in mind, we can now take a closer look at Quesnay's doctrine of free enterprise, or the physiocrats' idea of laissez-faire, in order to see whether it could have grown out of Chinese philosophy.

From Quesnay's writings, it is clear that he saw the world as a self-regulating machine governed by a set of immutable laws ordained by God, its Creator. He also saw that the economy and its economic agents were part of that world and subject to the same laws. The economic part of the world in turn could be seen as a whole consisting of interdependent parts, such as production, consumption, exchange, etc. That part of the world, the economy, would function well if its component parts were to function in harmony with each other. As is well-known, Quesnay constructed the Tableau economique to model the interdependencies in the economy, thus allowing a greater understanding, better prediction and more effective regulation of economic activities. The key to it all is the harmony of the various component parts comprising the whole, a harmony that depends on the balancing of the oppositional forces exercised by the component parts. As Quesnay puts it in the essay "Hommes", in the case of the state, good government depends on "the balance of the bodies of the state, each restrained in turn by the other". What is true about the state is also true about the economy, indeed true generally. Thus, the general aim in human affairs is to achieve and maintain the "balance of bodies" comprising the whole. Since the whole is a self-regulating mechanism governed by natural laws, this is the same as saying that we should aim at restoring the natural order. Indeed, being a self-regulating mechanism, the economy possesses self-adjusting forces that tend to return it to the natural order and so in the usual course of events, the best policy turns out to be one of letting such forces operate unhindered, of letting nature be, of laissez-faire. Intervention is necessary only to restore the natural order.

Breaking down the component parts of the economy, we get to the ultimate economic unit, the individual person. The person too is a natural entity subject to natural laws. Quesnay knew this only too well, being a medical practitioner, a renown surgeon, for most of his life. Since the aim of the economy is, as Quesnay put it, the "perpetual reproduction of those goods necessary for the subsistence, conservation and convenience of men", it is important to understand the nature of "men". Influenced by the rationalist philosophy of Descartes, Quesnay saw the individual person as a rational creature who, naturally endowed with the capacity to reason, knew what he or she wanted and knew the best way to obtain it. It follows that the best economic policy is to allow the individual the freedom to pursue his or her own interests. However, it would be wrong to say that Quesnay advocated economic individualism. For Quesnay, the pursuit of self interest was never an end in itself; it was rather the means towards the goal of social harmony, and ultimately the harmony of the whole of nature. It is natural to let people engage in activities aimed at the satisfaction of natural needs and wants. To let people be, laissez-faire, is to follow the rule of nature, to be physiocratic. Self-interested economic activity should be permitted and assisted to take place unhindered, enterprise at the individual level should be free, only because it would lead to a good outcome at the social level, and a good society in turn would result in the well-being of the world. As is well-known, this doctrine is foreshadowed by Mandeville's Fable of the Bees and later received theoretical backing in Adam Smith, who turned it into the doctrine of the "invisible hand".

I have outlined the fundamental tenets of classical capitalism, or laissez-faire capitalism, as formulated by its founder, Francois Quesnay. By the time of Adam Smith, the economy of Western Europe, particularly that of Great Britain, had begun to reorganize itself along the lines of free enterprise, aided along in the process by Enlightenment ideas that emphasise personal freedom. In the case of France, the transition was facilitated by the presence of physiocrats in the government itself. Indeed, a well-known promoter of physiocracy, Anne Robert Turgot, became a finance minister of Louis XVI. The foundation stone was set for the economic prosperity of Western Europe. Why similar developments did not take place in Asia is a matter I happily leave to the historians. My purpose here is to show that it is not because the laissez-faire doctrine is philosophically alien to the East. Indeed, as pointed out [earlier], some historians even claim that Western thinkers responsible for the laissez-faire doctrine were influenced by Chinese philosophy—Turgot himself was described by Martin Bernal as a "promoter of Chinese economic ideas". Whatever can be made of this historical claim, we can certainly show that the fundamental tenets of classical capitalism could have grown out of Chinese philosophy, out of Confucianism in particular. I turn now to this task.

That the world is governed by a universal and natural force is a fundamental belief in Chinese philosophy. It is a part of most Chinese philosophical systems. This force is the tao. While Taoism and Confucianism draw different implications from the belief in the tao, both subscribe to the view that the tao is a creative force causally responsible for the existence of the world. The process of creation is described in the well-known chapter 42 of the Tao Te Ching. The tao is not only a creative force; it is also a regulative principle that maintains its own creation. Indeed, the tao permeates all aspects of the world and so can properly be equated with nature itself. Thus, the tao is God, nature and natural laws rolled into one. Where the laws of the tao operate unhindered, there is established the natural order and there is harmony. Where there are acts in defiance of the laws of the tao, the natural order is upset and there is chaos. Thus, for there to be harmony, all actions must comply with the laws of the tao, or with the rule of nature. To act in accordance with the tao is to let nature rule, to subscribe to physiocracy in the literal sense. Clearly then, the Chinese cosmology translates easily into the physiocratic belief in a natural order which regulates all aspects of life, including all human experiences.

As we saw [earlier], the French physiocrats considered the society and all the social units within it down to the individual persons as parts of the natural order subject to the same rule of nature. However, unlike other animals, humans have the capacity to reason and so can choose to act in ways that are contrary to the rule of nature. This gives rise to the physiocratic belief that the harmony of the world rests squarely on the individual person, that to establish the order of nature we have to start with the individual person. This idea could have grown out of Chinese philosophy. In both Taoism and Confucianism, the natural law, or the law of the tao, should be observed by all component parts of the natural whole, by all societies, groups of individuals, families and finally the individual people themselves. Given that the individual person has the power of choice, on his or her shoulders alone rests the responsibility to realise the law of the tao. Thus, as recorded in the Analects, Confucius said that "It is man that can make the Way [Tao] great, and not the Way that can make man great". This is echoed in the last few lines of chapter 25 of the Tao Te Ching: "Man models himself on earth, Earth on heaven, Heaven on the way, And the way on that which is naturally so". Clearly then, the focus of Chinese philosophy is on the individual, no less than is the case in physiocracy or in the Western tradition generally. If we understand "individualism" in this sense, there is no reason to think that Quesnay's "economic individualism" is alien to the Chinese tradition.

If it rests on the individual to "make the Way great" then, it follows, the individual should be left alone, if not encouraged, to do so. To interfere with the individual in his or her natural pursuits, particularly in the pursuits to secure the goods "necessary for their subsistence, conservation and convenience" (to borrow Quesnay's words), is to interfere with the way of nature itself. Thus, not only that the individual should let nature be if he or she is to follow the tao, or to "model himself on the earth", the government too should follow the tao by letting the individuals be. To let be is to take no action, or rather to do by not doing, wu-wei. This policy can be found advocated in many diverse philosophical systems. It is, as we would expect, most prominent in Taoism. Thus,

> The way never acts yet nothing is left undone. Should lords and princes be able to hold fast to it, The myriad creatures will be transformed of their own accord.

> —(Tao Te Ching, chapter 37)

Wu-wei is the way of the tao. For lords and princes to follow the way of the tao is for them to take no action, to let the people be. Lords and princes can "win the empire by not being meddlesome", and when they are "not meddlesome ... the people prosper of themselves" (Tao Te Ching, chapter 57). This policy is endorsed by Confucius, who praised Shun for governing his empire well by taking "no [unnatural] action". Even the Legalists, who were well-known for their advocacy of a strong government, subscribed to the policy of wu-wei. As Wing-Tsit Chan puts it, the "Taoist ideal of taking no action (wu-wei) had a strong appeal to the Legalists because if laws worked effectively at all times, there would be no need for any actual government". Given the widespread philosophical support for the idea that "people prosper of themselves" if the government lets them be, it is surely perverse to suggest that any economic doctrine that advocates letting people be to pursue their economic interests, or laissez-faire, is alien to the East.

It may be said that the Chinese doctrine of wu-wei encourages passivity which is contrary to the qualities of drive and determination required for economic success. However, it should be noted that translating "wu-wei" as "taking no action" or "doing nothing" is highly misleading. Even within Taoism, wuwei does not mean total passivity. Taking no action is not an end in itself but rather a means to achieving something positive. Thus, chapter 10 of the Tao Te Ching speaks of not "resorting to action" in order to "govern the state", and chapter 51 speaks of taking no action to "give(s) [the myriad creatures] life", to "benefit(s) them". That positive things result from the non-action of the tao is due to its te, its "mysterious virtue", or "its "Dark Potency" as A. C. Graham has put it. It is true, though, that the Taoists, particularly Chuang Tzu, believe in the potency of the tao, and believe that nature will have its own way in the end and does not need much from humans to assert its own order. The Confucianists, by contrast, attribute to humans a greater capacity for departing from the order of nature. For them, wu-wei amounts to taking action to emulate the no-action way of nature itself. For this reason, some commentators describe the Confucian policy as wei-wu-wei, active inaction, rather than simply wu-wei. What this means is that the individual should be vigilant to correct his or her behaviour, and the government should take action to help the individual "make the way great". Clearly then, wu-wei does not translate into a lack of drive and determination. On the contrary, it entails the utmost determination to embrace the tao, and requires the constant drive to improve oneself by following the way of nature. The same thing applies to the state. Wu-wei does not mean inaction on the part of the government. Since humans have the capacity to act contrary to nature, to let nature be, wu-wei, is to intervene to keep recalcitrant humans in line. If restrictive behaviour in economic affairs is contrary to the way of nature then wu-wei calls for a positive action against it. Quesnay's advocacy for "despotic laws" to preserve and restore the natural order could have grown out of the Chinese doctrine of wu-wei. As we saw earlier, some historians are convinced that it did. Whether laissez-faire was in fact the physiocrats' translation of wu-wei, it could easily have been.

It may be said further that many different economic systems could have grown out of the Chinese metaphysics of the tao. What remains to be shown is how such metaphysics could have engendered classical capitalism described earlier. The key feature of classical capitalism is competition. However, this is not to be taken as a destructive relationship in which each economic agent is out to dominate others, to drive them out of business. Rather, it is a mutually dependent relationship in which each economic unit acts to check and to balance the actions of all other units. For instance, prices are kept at the lowest possible level because the action of raising the price by any one producer will be neutralised by the actions of other producers who will take the advantage of selling more of their own products by undercutting their rivals. Classical capitalism is a system of checks and balances, resulting in a state of equilibrium among the opposing forces. This is what Quesnay had in mind when he spoke of the "balance of the bodies". Such balance exists in nature. This is why, for Quesnay, there should be the same natural checks and balances in the economy. To let it be, laissez-faire, is to let the natural checks and balances operate to produce harmony, or equilibrium. Could this doctrine have grown out of Chinese philosophy? The answer is, once again, yes. It could have grown out of many Chinese philosophical systems, but more specifically, out of the Confucian doctrine of chung yung.

As Chung-ying Cheng has pointed out, the idea of harmony is embraced by all the major schools of Chinese philosophy. This idea is encapsulated in the I Ching diagram of yin and yang forming a harmonious unity. The harmony in any unity rests on the balance of the forces exercised by the component parts, or the "bodies" of the whole. There is harmony if the force of one "body" is balanced by that of another. There is harmony in nature because

> ... Something and Nothing produce each other; The difficult and the easy complement each other; The long and the short off-set each other;

> —(Tao Te Ching, chapter 2)

The idea of harmony as the balance of oppositional forces is also endorsed in the book of Chung yung. For instance, taking a person's psychology as a unified whole, Chung yung declares that when the "passions awaken and each and all attain due measure and degree, that is harmony". There is harmony in nature because "the seasons succeed each other and the sun and the moon appear with the alternations of night and day". The human society is capable of attaining harmony insofar as its laws "form the same system" with the laws of nature. Harmony in society will be attained if laws are enacted to preserve the balance of opposing forces. This means in turn to keep to the middle path, the mean, between the extremes. Mapping all this onto the economy, we can draw the conclusion that economic harmony will be attained if the opposing forces in theeconomy arekept inabalance, if no oneeconomicunitisallowed to dominate the others. Thus, only a competitive economic system is consistent with the Chinese idea of harmony. A system consisting of monopolies, state or private, lacks the checks and balances necessary for harmony. Such a system may be stable in the sense of producing a technical equilibrium with predictable and non-fluctuating outputs and prices, but it is not harmonious and is contrary to the order of nature, contrary to the tao. The Chinese notion of harmony entails that the state should make laws to ensure the balance of economic forces, laws that prevent anti-competitive behaviour, laws that strengthen the mutual dependencies of all economic units on each other. Such laws would be continuous with the laws of nature, the laws by which "the seasons succeed each other and the sun and the moon appear with the alternations of day and night".

I have argued that laissez-faire or free-enterprise capitalism is not alien to the Chinese way of thinking insofar as that way is informed by philosophical beliefs in the way of nature. What is certainly alien is an economic system that is driven by greed, ruthless individualism and the desire for absolute power. What is alien is a system of cut-throat competition without checks and balances, a system that allows extremes to develop rather than stays in the middle path, a system that encourages monstrous monopolies having the power to take over the laws of the market, to upset the order of nature. To be sure, the popular image of capitalism is closer to cut-throat competition than to free-enterprise in the classical sense. However, it is doubtful that the former has had anything to do with the economic prosperity of the West. If this is alien to the East then it is a reason to celebrate, not a cause of despair. Indeed, future historians could well attribute the economic crisis occurring in Asia at the end of the 20th century to Asia's attempt to embrace the greed-is-good mentality of cut-throat competition. I have argued that Asia need not sacrifice its philosophical soul at the altar of economic progress. On the contrary, if I am right in my reading of Chinese philosophy and if classical thinkers such as Quesnay and Smith are right about the causes of the wealth of nations, now that Asia has regained its power to determine its own destiny, economic prosperity depends on Asia's returning to its philosophical roots, maintaining the path of chung yung and embracing the way of the tao.

Comparing Chinese and Western Cultural Roots: Why "East Is East and ..."

"Oh, East is East, and West is West, and never the twain shall meet."

—Rudyard Kipling, The Ballad of East and West (1889)

Well, we meet now. As China accelerates into its inevitable place among the world's most important states and markets, the world is paying close attention. And as Westerners scrutinize China's pronouncements and actions, they become more aware of the great differences in how we think, what we believe, and how we behave. Although Kipling's familiar words applied to India, the thought expressed applies at least as well to China. Some might expect to see some convergence as trade, travel, and education bring us closer. But an enormous gulf remains because these differences have very deep and substantial roots that have produced highly divergent value systems.

The attitudes and behavior of a cohesive or otherwise unified group of people are shaped by the prevailing value system that defines for them what is good and bad, acceptable and unacceptable, desirable and undesirable, important and unimportant. We call this collectively shared value system that establishes behavioral norms a "culture": an artifact of a common experience and history, the dominant religion, political, social, and economic conditions, geographic, climatic, and topographic factors, and resource endowments. The ability to resist the tendency to judge another culture according to one's own values—the trap of ethnocentrism—can be strengthened by an understanding of how those differences came to be.

A brief review of the more salient differences between China and the West, as seen through Western eyes, is a good place to begin. Students of this topic, particularly those interested in Chinese ways of business and management practices, are familiar with such notions as "face," guanxi, and guo qing. "Face" generally is a matter of maintaining one's public dignity and standing. For the Chinese, there are two components of face: lien and mianzi. The former concerns one's reputation for integrity and morality; the latter is prestige attached to professional reputation, knowledge, wealth, and success.

A large component of lien is people's ability to live up to their obligations within the framework of Confucian hierarchy, social harmony, and strict behavioral ritual (li). The surest way to lose face is to act in a way that causes another to lose it. To avoid such uncivilized, disharmonious behavior, the Chinese practice a form of indirect speech that, to Westerners, seems overly modest and even self-effacing. The practice is sometimes so extreme as to appear disingenuous or even deliberately deceitful, as in overly optimistic promises and commitments. Another by-product of face-saving (or harmony-preserving) behavior is shaming, the ploy of getting one's way in negotiation by appealing to one's counterpart's obligation to conform to li. A common example is related to the Confucian ideal of the doting, overly solicitous parent and the resulting asymmetrical relationship of obligation whereby the parent expects much less from the child than the parent gives. A Chinese negotiator might attempt to portray a counterpart representing a large, accomplished company or developed country in the role of parent. Thus, an ostensibly weaker or technologically less advanced Chinese firm or governmental body assumes the role of the needy child to extract asymmetrical concessions.

Guanxi is the now well-known custom of relying on a network of fully committed personal relationships when conducting business or other affairs. A by-product is the need for go-betweens to establish a new business relationship. Another is that, unlike in Japan, personal loyalties and commitments take precedence over all others except family—including company ties. These asymmetrical relationships also favor the weaker party and must be cultivated assiduously. The obligations embodied in Confucian values and guanxi take the place of laws and contracts relied upon by Westerners to regulate business relationships.

Guo qing is a 2,000-year-old term meaning that China is special and the way things are done there are unique and, presumably, superior. This implies that outsiders (long considered barbarians) must learn these ways and adapt if they are to become functional in China. Such an attitude is to be expected from a people who constitute the world's oldest culture, the Middle Kingdom, and who lived for thousands of years largely in self-imposed isolation but who, nevertheless, accomplished much artistically, scientifically, and socially. Fan Xing sums up the observations and views of many with [a] comparison of common traits [in Table 1].

Table 1

Chinese	American
Intuitive	Rational
Aesthetic	Scientific
Introverted	Extroverted
Self-restrained	Aggressive
Dependent	Independent
Procrastinating	Active
Implicit	Explicit
Synthetic	Analytical
Patient	Impatient
Group-oriented	Individualistic
Desire for eternity (i.e., continuity)	Eager to change

Hence, the Chinese lean toward a more holistic, systemic, nonlinear, fatalistic world view. Their attitude toward time is more relaxed; they tend to be humble and modest; and their culture is one of high-context communication and collectivism....

Chinese and Western Cultural Roots Compared

... Confucian disdain for science and commerce has been an enormous constraint on economic development. Nevertheless, according to Paul Kennedy's 1987 *The Rise and Fall of the Great Powers*, in the Middle Ages the Chinese invented paper, printing by movable type, gunpowder, a mechanical clock, and the magnetic compass. And they were producing more iron than Great Britain did in the early years of the Industrial Revolution. With the exception of iron, used for arms, these technological advances were developed by Taoist alchemy, primarily for religious and ceremonial purposes.

Chinese ships were trading as far as the Indian Ocean a century before the Portuguese rounded the Cape of Good Hope. However, as the Ming dynasty sought to reestablish the ancient order after the Mongols were finally subdued at the end of the fourteenth century, the Mandarins put an end to foreign adventures and turned inward once again. In keeping with its relative isolation and highly ethnocentric self-concept as the Middle Kingdom, China has a strong tradition of xenophobia. Westerners have long been called yang gui zi, or "foreign devils" (gui lao in Cantonese). Even China's cultural progeny, the Japanese, are called "devils of the Eastern Sea." When Western adventurers, priests, and merchants finally arrived in some force in the nineteenth century, they were confined to a few coastal enclaves, and the Mandarins limited intercourse to the minimum necessary to sustain a tidy stream of tax revenue from trade.

This reaction to the West stands in stark contrast to Japan's. Once finally opened to the West after the Meiji Restoration in 1868, the Japanese aggressively sought Western expertise in industry, technology, and administration—a practice that still continues. One consequence was that relatively tiny Japan was able to invade and occupy much of China in the 1930s, the first nation to do so successfully since the Mongols.

As is typical of agrarian, subsistence economies, the large and extended family—essential to eke out an existence from the land—was and remains the primary social and economic unit. The ultimate source of security and refuge, the family was responsible for the debts and conduct of its members. Individual wrongdoing caused great loss of face (lien) for the entire family. The Confucian emphasis on social harmony was intended largely to maintain the family's central role and extend its organization to society as a whole. Many Chinese still feel very strong ties to their home villages, including those now living in urban, industrial environments. Typical Chinese enterprises remain relatively small, with simple functional structures built around the founding family.

Europeans had a very different experience that would be replicated in North America. A much more heterogeneous people, they are comprised of numerous indigenous tribes and many others that made their way into Europe primarily from Central Asia. Europe's topography and extensive river systems allowed great internal mobility, and its location and many ports made it a crossroads between Asia and Africa. Temperate climate and ample arable land supported surplus agriculture, which enabled the early development of towns and the attendant specialization of labor that impelled acceleration of trade and foreign exploration. These adventures made Europeans aware of new products and brought riches that stimulated still more exploration and, ultimately, mercantilism. Thus was made possible the accumulation of wealth that financed the artistic, technological, and political advances of the Renaissance. After the fall of the Roman Empire, there was no monolithic, centralized authority capable of enforcing an inward focus, as the imperial Mandarins did in China. The Roman's extensive financial, legal, and transportational infrastructure supported internal intercourse and opened the door to the external world.

Government

In the sixth century B.C., when the Greeks were contemplating protection of individual rights and the rule of law as the best means for rendering order and peace from chaos and oppression, Confucius was pondering the same problem. But although his intentions were equally benign, his solution was quite different. He concluded that social harmony would best be served not by a system of citizens' rights protected by law, but by a rigidly hierarchical system of reciprocal duties and highly regulated and ritualized behavior built around the principle of filial loyalty. This was the origin of guanxi, li, and face. Taught and perpetuated by the family, Confucianism established and enforced behavioral norms. Confucius believed leaders should earn their authority through a demonstration of learning, wisdom, and the virtues of humanity—benevolence, righteousness, propriety, and trustworthiness—in the way a good father commanded the respect of his children. In return, people would owe their leaders total loyalty and support. Analogous relationships could be established throughout society in a hierarchical cascade, thereby rendering it peaceful, harmonious, and productive.

Confucius believed leadership was too important to leave the accidents of heredity; the opportunity to lead should be open to all so that the most meritorious would rise to the top. He believed people were essentially good and that they required only education in the ways of a harmonious society. Education, then—including setting a proper example—was the most fundamental responsibility of leadership. Wisdom, along with character, was an important measure of merit. This is why knowledge and accomplishment are a major source of face (mianzi).

Leaders were expected to conduct themselves with placid reserve, modesty, and self-restraint, much like the Greek stoic ideal. The people had the right to question leaders who failed these tests, but not to question the fundamental order of society. However, no consideration was given to individual rights or due process. Rule was a matter of personality and preparation, not law.

Eventually, Confucius's views came to permeate China's culture and constitute the essence of its value system and that of all East Asia. One institution that did not adopt Confucian thinking, at least with respect to merit being the primary qualification for power, were the imperial dynasties that ruled China until Sun Yat-Sen's nationalist revolution in the early twentieth century. Nevertheless, the governmental structure that evolved was clearly Confucian, an elaborate bureaucracy replete with ministries, many hierarchical layers extending down to the local level, and a professional civil service with its own examination system and training academy (many centuries before Max Weber introduced merit-based bureaucracy to the West). It was much more elaborate than the Romans' administrative structure and more similar to that of the medieval Church. Portuguese traders labeled the top bureaucrats Mandarins, from the Latin mandare, "to command." Confucius's views were traditional and conservative, and the Confucian bureaucracy did what bureaucracies do best: preserve them.

Within the context of imperial rivalries and internal and external strife, the administrative decisions of the Mandarins have controlled day-to-day life in China for more than 2,000 years. Even under the most benign of rulers, Confucianism was applied as a kind of state orthodoxy. Under its rubric, China's highly centralized rule routinely confiscated and redistributed wealth, established state monopolies, price controls, and collective land ownership, and conscripted unwilling soldiers and forced labor (used in building the Great Wall).

Confucius saw commerce as a pursuit of low status, an attitude that would persist in China except for the small entrepreneurial class that emerged around the European enclaves in the late nineteenth century. These entrepreneurs became the "Overseas Chinese," the foundation of expatriate communities in Hong Kong, Singapore, Vietnam, and elsewhere after the communist victory in 1949. Of course, the long-standing, statist tradition had made China fertile ground for communism, which differed from the state orthodoxy more in name than in substance.

Many manmade hardships combined with frequent natural disasters made life miserable for the ordinary Chinese. According to LaTourette, average life expectancy remained below 30 years of age even as China entered the twentieth century. The depredations of Mao, including his purges and artificial famines (when, for example, during the "Great Leap Forward" every village was to manufacture steel regardless of the consequences of fields left untended) were but a recent example.

A stream of thought that emerged concurrently with Confucianism was legalism, offering a very different prescription for maintaining order. Unlike Confucius, the legalists held that people were inherently bad and that a firm hand was needed to keep them in line. They believed that the primary responsibility of government (the king, and later the emperor) toward its subjects was to maximize their martial skills to help preserve and expand the state. Indeed, legalism was instrumental in first unifying the empire in the third century B.C. Although it soon dissipated as a philosophical discipline, the precedent it set cast China's emperors from that point forward with a much harder edge than Confucius would have envisioned or preferred.

The Romans applied Greek ideals to a large empire. Whereas Greek democracy, limited to the city-state and the upper class, took the form of a simple plebiscite or referendum, the Roman solution was representative democracy. The Romans elaborated and expanded the protection of law to more classes of citizens and developed the notion of checks and balances. All this may have come to naught after the Empire fell but for the towns that emerged during the Pax Romana, created by surplus agriculture and its hand-maiden, specialized labor. The vitality of trade centered in these towns even-tually produced sufficient wealth to finance the revival of classical art, science, and thinking known as the Renaissance and the great period of Euro-pean exploration and empire-building. The ensuring Enlightenment refined classical political ideas, generated new ones (such as the social contract and the right of all people to own private property), and produced the philosophi-cal rationale and impetus that led to the institutional arrangements governing Western democracies today.

It is an interesting coincidence that the sixth century B.C. witnessed the origins of the divergent value systems of East and West: Confucius's harmony and filial loyalty combined with legalism and Taoist fatalism on one hand, and Greek democracy, rationality, and individualism on the other. Thence-forth, imperial repression continued in once-great China, abetted by Confu-cian discipline, Taoist passivity, Buddhist introspection, and unrelenting poverty and hardship. But the West would go on to nearly conquer the world, at least for a time, first politically and then economically.

Cosmology

Taoism (pronounced "dowism") filled a spiritual void in the pragmatic Con-fucian world. It advocated simplicity, detachment from the concerns of everyday life, and harmony with nature as the means of establishing social unity and harmony. Like other agrarian societies perpetually struggling to eke out an existence and accustomed to frequent hardship, the Chinese felt dependent upon and subservient to nature and sought the protection of their ancestors. (In Chinese art, one never sees flower arrangements or a still life of fruit in a bowl representing an attempt to improve on nature.) Natu-ral disasters were believed to be an expression of nature's wrath over human misdeeds.

According to the Tao (the "Way") taken from the ancient I. Ching, people must seek harmony with nature and accommodate its whims. This cosmology is embodied in the notion of yin and yang, the arrangement of nature into opposing but complementary and oscillating forces such as day and night, high and low tide, male and female. Time has no beginning or end; it does not lapse or expire; it is cyclical rather than linear. Time and phenomena simply happen; hence, they are to be sensed or experienced, not conserved or mea-sured. Everything is related to everything else—what Trompenaars called a dif-fuse view of the world rather than a specific or compartmentalized view. A perception of interrelatedness promotes holistic thinking and a systemic view.

Cyclical patterns of yin and yang, like a spinning gyroscope, create a sense of stability, whereas a more linear path trails off into the unknowable.

The application of accumulated wisdom and intuition rather than rationality is the normal way of thinking for the traditional Confucianist. The scientific method would be an alien and dangerous notion because, in the Taoist world view, it would tend to polarize rather than harmonize. Excessive knowledge was thought to make people ungovernable. The fatalism inherent in Taoist cosmology renders superfluous any search for cause-and-effect relationships—the essence of scientific inquiry. Moreover, science would be tantamount to tampering with nature and its natural rhythms. It would also present the risk of departure from the tradition and stability dear to Confucian bureaucrats. Many of China's technological advances were driven not by a search for understanding but by the efforts of Taoist priests to achieve immortality on earth—efforts the Confucianists considered frivolous and superstitious.

The contrast between Chinese and Western cosmology is stark. For the Westerner, there is no greater truth than what can be objectively measured and tested. The opposite of that shown to be true must be false. In other words, Western logic cannot accommodate the simultaneous validity of contradictory circumstances embodied in the Tao. Westerners tend to think in logical, linear patterns. For the Chinese, intuition, emotion, and the need to maintain harmonious relationships constitute truth; objective information is less important. Westerners assume they can employ and shape nature to their own ends. It is difficult to imagine the Chinese deciding, as did the medieval Dutch, that it was not only desirable but quite possible to push back the North Sea, reclaim much of its bottom, and convert it to cities and fertile farmland.

All of this, of course, traces back to a very different cosmological view with roots in ancient Greece. Aristotle thought that by observation and experimentation, man could begin to understand how nature worked. Once that understanding began to accumulate, it was quite natural for the Greeks and their heirs to find ways to employ this knowledge. Early success gave Westerners confidence that they could harness nature and its resources rather than submit to it.

Religion and Ethical Standards

By Western standards, China is a secular society; most Chinese do not "belong" to a faith in the sense of being a Christian, a Jew, or a Muslim. Little thought is given to supreme beings, other than venerated ancestors, or to such matters as holiness or life after death. There is a dearth of universal ethical principles or moral absolutes other than maintaining the security and well-being of the family and living up to one's Confucian obligations. These remain the primary normative prescriptions for correct behavior. Because maintaining social harmony and order is the highest ideal, minimization of conflict is essential and absolutes are seen as sources of conflict.

Like the ancient Greeks, Confucius advocated a "golden mean," a moderation and balance in all things. But unlike the Greeks, Confucius and his followers believed this meant being reasonable rather than relying on reason.

They held no relentless quest for the "truth," which many Westerners search for in the spiritual realm as diligently as they do in the scientific. Such a search would be futile, for when and where the yang prevails, its opposite yin will follow, and so on.

Behavior that maintained one's system of relationships was expected, rather than adherence to abstract principles. The "right" decision was the one that best served the present circumstances, not some code of temporal or religious law. Ethics were largely relative or situational, particularistic rather than universal. In any given circumstances, one might invoke Confucius, Buddha, the Tao, a venerated ancestor, or an animistic spirit, depending on whatever seemed to provide the most appropriate guidance. Europeans found this lack of "principle" barbarian. On the other hand, the Chinese considered barbarian the Europeans' aggressive, disharmonious behavior and ignorance of li.

Confucianism makes no pretense as a religion. Rather, it is a system of values that govern interpersonal behavior with an eye toward building a civil society. It does not speak to humanity's relationship with any supreme being. Taoism and Buddhism are more concerned with obtaining release from worldly cares and woe than with holiness or heavenly aspirations. The asceticism and mendicancy of Buddhist monks is not consistent with Confucian humanism and its ideals of hard work, order, and propriety. Celibacy attacks the bedrock of the Chinese society, the family.

Nevertheless, even as Buddhism declined in its home on the Indian subcontinent, it spread rapidly throughout East Asia. Buddha's first principle, that life is pain, certainly rang true with the vast majority of Chinese, who lived largely miserable lives. His prescription for escape into a state of enlightenment had great appeal. Accordingly, the more inclusive Mahayana form of Buddhism was more welcome in China because it held that a good Buddhist in any walk of life could reach an enlightened state, nirvana, and freedom from the needs and desires that made life so painful. In contrast, the more rigorous Theravada form held the pursuit of enlightenment to be a full-time pursuit and thus possible only for cloistered monks. In practice, the Chinese tended to set aside the search for enlightenment and settled for abiding by the behavioral standards embodied in Buddha's prescriptive "Eightfold Path"—standards that were consistent with those of Confucius. Buddhism's most significant impact on the Chinese value system lay in teaching that life is in a state of constant flux and a sorrow-free life of serenity and peace means accepting rather than resisting change. Any sense of individuality, self, ego, or soul was made transient and meaningless by this flux. Thus, Buddhism served to amplify the importance of Confucian behavioral norms and collectivism and Taoist receptivity to change.

Chinese religion has evolved in ways that support and advance the maintenance of social harmony. In contrast, Judaism and Christianity (and Islam as well) prescribe behavioral and ethical standards intended to allow the faithful an opportunity to please and prove their worthiness to their Creator and Supreme Being. While banning behavior detrimental to maintaining a civil society (though perhaps one not quite as well-mannered as China's), these religions also prescribe how the Supreme Being should be worshipped and require followers to hold certain beliefs, make certain expressions of faith, and participate in various rituals.

Secular authorities in the West, particularly the Romans building on the precedent set by the ancient Greeks, extended ecclesiastical law into a natural law that dealt with practices, abstract principles, and beliefs beyond the spiritual domain. From natural law, greatly elaborated during the Enlightenment, were derived such notions as liberty, justice, equity, fairness, the binding contact, and, ultimately, the social contract between people and their governments. These important social and political virtues, binding governments as well as citizens, acquired the force of principle as important to many—and perhaps more so to some—as the tenets of sacred scripture. Though Westerners might disagree on what is "fair" in any set of circumstances, few would argue against the worth of "fairness."

The Chinese, like most human beings, will recognize the evil of a wanton crime, but they will have trouble responding to the invocation of abstractions such as "fair trade." What is fair to the Chinese is whatever works, whatever action or manner of speech is necessary to execute a transaction satisfactorily for both parties. Westerners are taught to place the principle of honesty above the nicety of harmony; for them, constructive criticism is the "right" thing to do, even if painful. For the Chinese, this threat to harmony is antisocial. Likewise, most Westerners would be appalled that a manager could be so unprincipled as to show favoritism in hiring a relative. A Chinese would be equally appalled by any reluctance to do so.

Managerial Implications

The Chinese are not necessarily better or worse than Westerners, only different. As we have seen, this is the result of a very different set of traditions, not of inherent flaws in the Asian or national character or even of communism. An appreciation of these actual attitudinal and behavioral differences is obviously of great interest to those who would negotiate with the Chinese, teach or learn from them, do business in China, or find themselves working with them in any capacity. Table 2 encapsulates some of these differences and the ways in which they may affect working relationships....

The Chinese mind is accustomed to coping comfortably with dichotomies and accepting both poles as valid. Such bipolar conundrums as effectiveness and efficiency, high quality and low cost, short-term and long-term, profit and growth, stability and progress, may come easier to the Chinese. They intuit a holistic and mutually complementary, dependent, or symbiotic relationship among all things. Accordingly, they may be better strategic thinkers than Westerners because they can come to terms with the attendant multiplicity of variables and mental trade-offs, recognize and adapt to what "nature" gives them (recall the strategic lessons of the Vietnam War), be comfortable with flux, and stay less encumbered by the urge to find the "truth" before acting.

Table 2

A Summary of Western and Chinese Cultural Differences and the Implications for Management

Comparing pertinent features of the history of the West with that of China, we can make the following distinctions:

The West	China
Individual rights	Individual duty and collective obligations
Rule by law	Rule by personality and imperial authority
The collective right to grant, question, and reject political authority	Unquestioning submission to hereditary authority backed by force
Political and ethnic pluralism	Monolithic power and homogeneity
Cultural interaction	Cultural isolation
Sufficient resources to support early urbanization, specialization of labor, and large-scale trade	An agrarian, subsistence economy and endless hardship, both natural and imposed
An external orientation	An internal orientation
Physical and social mobility	Permanence in situ
Reliance on reason and the scientific method	Reliance on precedent, intuition, and wisdom
An aggressive, active approach to nature, technology, and progress	Passive, fatalistic submission

Another manifestation of holistic thinking is the Chinese sense that the relationship among the parties to a business transaction is part of that transaction, not preliminary to it. When you want to get beyond the social niceties and relationship-building and get down to business, you must step back and recognize that the social interaction is an essential part of the process. All Chinese seek to cement such relationships into their guanxi networks, building a system of reciprocal, mutual obligation and dependency (renqing).

The Chinese will respect and appreciate a Westerner's knowledge of their culture. However, it is probably better to act with good manners and a sincere respect for Chinese culture than as an expert if, as a result, one comes across as self-assured to the point of arrogance. Remember that, like the Japanese, the Chinese tend to think of themselves as so unique that foreigners cannot comprehend them and their ways completely. It is probably wise to accept that proposition and, accordingly, be open-minded and meticulously well-mannered, listen more and speak less, learn at least as much as you try to teach, and avoid any form of aggressiveness, arrogance, individual competitiveness, self-promotion, or ostentation.

It is worth repeating here that interpersonal relationships, rather than the content and practice of business, are affected most by these cultural differences. Your domestic success can be replicated in China if you learn and adapt to Chinese ways of building and maintaining relationships. You can introduce Western practices successfully, but you must first build trust. This is best done by demonstrating your sincerity in working for some common good that accrues to your Chinese counterparts, to their enterprise, and to the Chinese people.

POSTSCRIPT

Are Chinese Confucianism and Western Capitalism Compatible?

Both Confucianism and capitalism can be confusing concepts. For further insight into the former, see Issue 12 of *Taking Sides: Clashing Views on Controversial Issues in World History, Volume I*. This issue discusses the role of Confucianism in shaping the warrior code of the Japanese samurai. Along with Shinto and Zen Buddhism, Confucian values contributed to the formation of the Japanese worldview. Any good translation of *The Analects* will introduce the teachings of Confucius, a Chinese master from the sixth century B.C.E., and allow him to speak for himself. A very complete resource for Chinese thought in general is *Sources of Chinese Tradition*, 2 vols., compiled by William Theodore de Bary and Irene Bloom (Columbia University Press, 1999). The first volume extends from earliest times to 1600 C.E.

Capitalism can be equally daunting. Issue 1 in this volume provides a context for the modern world with its look at the role of capitalism in launching the Industrial Revolution. Smith's classic *The Wealth of Nations* is available from the University of Chicago Press (1976) and also in a Modern Library edition (Random House, 1994). A good, straightforward introduction to the field of economics is *Economics Explained* by Robert Heilbruner and Lester Thurow (Simon & Schuster, 1998). This book describes the influence of Quesnay on Smith as well as the key components of classical capitalism in simple, engaging prose. A good backup source for terms is John Black, *Oxford Dictionary of Economics* (Oxford University Press, 1997).

For greater depth, see "The Physiocrats: Six Lectures on the French Economistes of the 18th Century," originally delivered at the London School of Economics in 1897 and reprinted by Augustus M. Kelley publishers in 1989. Elizabeth Fox-Genovese's *The Origins of Physiocracy* (Cornell University Press, 1976) provides a modern historical account of the works of Quesnay and his unacknowledged collaborator Victor Riqueti, marquis de Mirabeau. Gianni Vaggi's *The Economics of François Quesnay* (Duke University Press, 1987) offers a reconsideration of Quesnay's theories in the light of contemporary economic theory. *François Quesnay* (1694–1774), Mark Blaug, ed. (Edward Elgar Publishing Limited, 1991), is Volume II of the Pioneers in Economics series, which presents "critical appraisals of influential economists." And, finally, Quesnay's *Tableau Economique*, Marguerite Kuczynski and Ronald L. Meek, eds. (Augustus M. Kelley Publishers, 1972), explores the history of the several editions of Quesnay's conceptual construct—the tableau economique—which lays out the ideas on which classical capitalism is constructed.

ISSUE 14

Does Islamic Revivalism Challenge a Stable World Order?

YES: John L. Esposito, from *The Islamic Threat: Myth or Reality?* 2nd ed. (Oxford University Press, 1995)

NO: Sharif Shuja, from "Islam and the West: From Discord to Understanding," *Contemporary Review* (May 2001)

ISSUE SUMMARY

YES: Professor of Middle Eastern studies John L. Esposito sees the Iranian Revolution against Western-inspired modernization and Egypt's "holy war" against Israel as examples of the Islamic quest for a more authentic society and culture, which challenges a stable world order.

NO: Professor of international relations Sharif Shuja identifies the rise of Islamic movements as resistance to Western domination rather than as a threat to the West as such and traces Western fears of a monolithic Islamic entity to the errors of an "Orientalist" mindset.

For many Westerners the adjective *Islamic* seems to be linked inexorably with either *fundamentalist* or *terrorist*. Particularly since the Islamic revolution of 1978–1979 in Iran, images of Western hostages and calls for a *jihad*, or holy war, have created a climate of fear and mistrust between the West and Islam. Are the two on a collision course, rooted in history and driven by an absolute incompatibility of beliefs and lifestyles? Or can Islam play a role in a stable world order that affirms Islam's own tradition while accommodating secularism and pluralism? The two selections that follow acknowledge the flash points and conclude by placing the emphasis at different places.

Because Islam sees itself as the fulfillment of both Judaism and Christianity—as the final word of God for human beings—it has from the beginning sought to spread its truth throughout the world. In the tradition of jihad, those who died in the attempt to bring Islam to nonbelievers were ensured a place in Paradise. Early successes came during Europe's so-called Dark Ages. Muslim learning and culture were more advanced, and it was only natural for conquering armies to assume that their religion enjoyed a comparable superiority. Unlike Christianity, Islam gained secular power within the founder Muhammad's lifetime (c. 570–632), and the rulers that followed him, known as caliphs, combined secular and religious power. There could be no conflict between church and state because the church and the state were one.

For many Muslims in the modern world, the political and military domination of the West has brought a secularism that is repugnant to all they hold sacred. It seems to them that Westerners—with their lack of respect for traditional authority, their emancipated and exploited women, and their shallow and materialistic values—have won. Becoming modern is generally equated with embracing the consumer culture and values of the West. The question seems to be whether or not Islamic countries can modernize without giving up their core values and embracing those of the West.

Both of the following selections point out that people in the West must begin by understanding the history and idea systems of modern Islam, whose believers constitute one-fifth of the world's population. In the first selection, John L. Esposito notes that the clout provided by oil has brought the Islamic Middle East into the world economy and given it the power to be a significant player in either supporting or destabilizing a peaceful world order. Believing that Islam has superseded both Judaism and Christianity calls Muslims to impose the law of God on all the world. In the search for an authentic Islamic culture, Esposito concludes, Muslims present a strong challenge to the political and cultural values of the West.

In the second selection, Sharif Shuja acknowledges the points of potential conflict between Islam and the West. However, he insists that the rise of Islamic movements signals resistance to Western domination and control over Muslim territories and resources and does not necessarily pose a threat to the West as such. He describes the Westernization that colonized more than two-thirds of the Muslim world during the first half of the twentieth century as one major globalizing force. There is now under way another globalizing force, which he calls the demographic Islamization of the Western world, represented by dramatic increases in the Muslim populations of Europe and the United States. Shuja counters Samuel P. Huntington's contention that the Islamic threat has been going on for 1300 years. What is wrong with Huntington's thesis, according to Shuja, is the depiction of Islamic countries as "part of a wider pan-Islamic movement, united in their hostility to the West and the United States." This kind of phobia can arise out of an "Orientalist" mindset that glosses over the diversity within Islam. Shuja sees Islamic revivalism as a successor to failed nationalist programs that in their own way tried to chart a third alternative between the undesirable poles of capitalism and communism. The best way to reduce extremism, Shuja contends, is through gradual democratisation. He points to hopeful signs, such as the voices of moderate Muslims who joined a worldwide outcry against the Islamicist regime in Afghanistan that decided to blow up centuries-old statues of the Buddha during the early months of 2001.

John L. Esposito  **YES**

The Islamic Threat: Myth or Reality?

Are Islam and the West on an inevitable collision course? Are Islamic fundamentalists medieval fanatics? Are Islam and democracy incompatible? Is Islamic fundamentalism a threat to stability in the Muslim world and to American interests in the region? These are critical questions for our times that come from a history of mutual distrust and condemnation.

From the Ayatollah Khomeini to Saddam Hussein, for more than a decade the vision of Islamic fundamentalism or militant Islam as a threat to the West has gripped the imaginations of Western governments and the media. Khomeini's denunciation of America as the "Great Satan," chants of "Death to America," the condemnation of Salman Rushdie and his *Satanic Verses*, and Saddam Hussein's call for a jihad against foreign infidels have reinforced images of Islam as a militant, expansionist religion, rabidly anti-American and intent upon war with the West.

Despite many common theological roots and beliefs, throughout history Muslim-Christian relations have often been overshadowed by conflict as the armies and missionaries of Islam and Christendom have struggled for power and for souls. This confrontation has involved such events as the defeat of the early Byzantine (eastern Roman) empire by Islam in the seventh century; the fierce battles and polemics of the Crusades during the eleventh and twelfth centuries; the expulsion of the Moors from Spain and the Inquisition; the Ottoman threat to Europe; European (Christian) colonial expansion and domination in the eighteenth and nineteenth centuries; the political and cultural challenge of the superpowers (America and the Soviet Union) in the latter half of the twentieth century; the creation of the state of Israel; the competition of Christian and Muslim missionaries for converts in Africa today; and the contemporary reassertion of Islam in politics.

"Islamic fundamentalism" has often been regarded as a major threat to the regional stability of the Middle East and to Western interests in the broader Muslim world. The Iranian Revolution, attacks on Western embassies, hijackings and hostage taking, and violent acts by groups with names like the Army of God (Jund Allah), Holy War (al-Jihad), the Party of God (Hizbullah), and Salvation from Hell have all signaled a militant Islam on a collision course with the West. Uprisings in the Muslim republics of the Soviet Union, in Kosovo in Yugoslavia, in Indian Kashmir, in Sinkiang in China, and on the West Bank and in Gaza, and more recently, Saddam Hussein's attempted annexation of Kuwait, have reinforced images of an expansive and potentially explosive Islam in global politics.

With the triumph of the democratization movement in Eastern Europe and the breakup of the Soviet empire, Islam constitutes the most pervasive and powerful transnational force in the world, with one billion adherents spread out across the globe. Muslims are a majority in some forty-five countries ranging from Africa to Southeast Asia, and they exist in growing and significant numbers in the United States, the Soviet Union, and Europe. For a Western world long accustomed to a global vision and foreign policy predicated upon superpower rivalry for global influence if not dominance—a U.S.-Soviet conflict often portrayed as a struggle between good and evil, capitalism and communism—it is all too tempting to identify another global ideological menace to fill the "threat vacuum" created by the demise of communism.

However diverse in reality, the existence of Islam as a worldwide religion and ideological force embracing one fifth of the world's population, and its continued vitality and power in a Muslim world stretching from Africa to Southeast Asia, will continue to raise the specter of an Islamic threat....

As Western leaders attempt to forge the New World Order, transnational Islam may increasingly come to be regarded as the new global monolithic enemy of the West: "To some Americans, searching for a new enemy against whom to test our mettle and power, after the death of communism, Islam is the preferred antagonist. But, to declare Islam an enemy of the United States is to declare a second Cold War that is unlikely to end in the same resounding victory as the first." Fear of the Green Menace (green being the color of Islam) may well replace that of the Red Menace of world communism.

Islam and Islamic movements constitute a religious and ideological alternative or challenge and in some instances a potential danger to Christianity and the West. However, distinguishing between a religious or ideological alternative or challenge and a direct political threat requires walking the fine line between myth and reality, between the unity of Islam and the diversity of its multiple and complex manifestations in the world today, between the violent actions of the few and the legitimate aspirations and policies of the many. Unfortunately, American policymakers, like the media, have too often proved surprisingly myopic, viewing the Muslim world and Islamic movements as a monolith and seeing them solely in terms of extremism and terrorism. While this is understandable in light of events in Iran and Lebanon and the Gulf crisis of 1990-91, it fails to do justice to the complex realities of the Muslim world and can undermine relations between the West and Islam....

The Islamic Resurgence

Islam reemerged as a potent global force in Muslim politics during the 1970s and 1980s. The scope of the Islamic resurgence has been worldwide, embracing much of the Muslim world from the Sudan to Indonesia. Heads of Muslim governments as well as opposition groups increasingly appealed to religion for legitimacy and to mobilize popular support. Islamic activists have held cabinet-level positions in Jordan, the Sudan, Iran, Malaysia, and Pakistan. Islamic organizations constitute the leading opposition parties and organizations in Egypt, Tunisia, Algeria, Morocco, the West Bank and Gaza, and Indonesia. Where permitted, they have participated in elections and served in parliament and in city government. Islam has been a significant ingredient in nationalist struggles and resistance movements in Afghanistan, the Muslim republics of the former Soviet Central Asia, and Kashmir, and in the communal politics of Lebanon, India, Thailand, China, and the Philippines.

Islamically oriented governments have been counted among America's staunchest allies (Saudi Arabia and Pakistan) and most vitriolic enemies (Libya and Iran). Islamic activist organizations have run the spectrum from those who work within the system—such as the Muslim Brotherhoods in Egypt, Jordan, and the Sudan—to radical revolutionaries like Egypt's Society of Muslims (known more popularly as Takfir wal-Hijra, Excommunication and Flight) and al-Jihad (Holy War), or Lebanon's Hizbullah (Party of God) and Islamic Jihad, which have resorted to violence in their attempts to overthrow prevailing political systems.

Yet to speak of a contemporary Islamic revival can be deceptive, if this implies that Islam had somehow disappeared or been absent from the Muslim world. It is more correct to view Islamic revivalism as having led to a higher profile of Islam in Muslim politics and society. Thus what had previously seemed to be an increasingly marginalized force in Muslim public life reemerged in the seventies—often dramatically—as a vibrant sociopolitical reality. Islam's resurgence in Muslim politics reflected a growing religious revivalism in both personal and public life that would sweep across much of the Muslim world and have a substantial impact on the West in world politics.

The indices of an Islamic reawakening in personal life are many: increased attention to religious observances (mosque attendance, prayer, fasting), proliferation of religious programming and publications, more emphasis upon Islamic dress and values, the revitalization of Sufism (mysticism). This broader-based renewal has also been accompanied by Islam's reassertion in public life: an increase in Islamically oriented governments, organizations, laws, banks, social welfare services, and educational institutions. Both governments and opposition movements have turned to Islam to enhance their authority and muster popular support. Governmental use of Islam has been illustrated by a great spectrum of leaders in the Middle East and Asia: Libya's Muammar Qaddafi, Sudan's Gaafar Muhammad Nimeiri, Egypt's Anwar Sadat, Iran's Ayatollah Khomeini, Pakistan's Zia ul-Haq, Bangladesh's Muhammad Ershad, Malaysia's Muhammad Mahathir. Most rulers and governments, including more secular states such as Turkey and Tunisia, becoming aware of the potential strength of Islam, have shown increased sensitivity to and anxiety about Islamic issues. The Iranian Revolution of 1978–79 focused attention on "Islamic fundamentalism" and with it the spread and vitality of political Islam in other parts of the Muslim world. However, the contemporary revival has its origins and roots in the late sixties and early seventies, when events in such disparate areas as Egypt and Libya as well as Pakistan and Malaysia contributed to experiences of crisis and failure, as well as power and success, which served as catalysts for a more visible reassertion of Islam in both public and private life.

The Experience of Failure and the Quest for Identity

Several conflicts (e.g., the 1967 Arab–Israeli war, Chinese–Malay riots in Malaysia in 1969, the Pakistan–Bangladesh civil war of 1971, and the Lebanese civil war of the midseventies) illustrate the breadth and diversity of these turning points or catalysts for change. For many in the Arab and broader Muslim world, 1967 proved to be a year of catastrophe as well as a historic turning point. Israel's quick and decisive defeat of Arab forces in what was remembered as the Six-Day War, the Israeli capture and occupation of the Golan Heights, Sinai, Gaza, the West Bank, and East Jerusalem, constituted a devastating blow to Arab/Muslim pride, identity, and self-esteem. Most important, the loss of Jerusalem, the third holiest city of Islam, assured that Palestine and the liberation of Jerusalem would not be regarded as a regional (Arab) issue but rather as an Islamic cause throughout the Muslim world. The defense of Israel is dear to many Jews throughout the world. Likewise, for Muslims who retain a sense of membership in a transnational community of believers (the *ummah*), Palestine and the liberation of Jerusalem are strongly seen as issues of Islamic solidarity. As anyone who works in the Muslim world can attest, Israeli control of the West Bank, Gaza, and Jerusalem as well as U.S.–Israeli relations are topics of concern and bitter debate among Muslims from Nigeria and the Sudan to Pakistan and Malaysia, as well as among the Muslims of Europe and the United States.

The aftermath of the 1967 war, remembered in Arab literature as the "disaster," witnessed a sense of disillusionment and soul-searching that gripped both Western-oriented secular elites as well as the more Islamically committed, striking at their sense of pride, identity, and history. Where had they gone wrong? Both the secular and the Islamically oriented sectors of society now questioned the effectiveness of nationalist ideologies, Western models of development, and Western allies who had persisted in supporting Israel. Despite several decades of independence and modernization, Arab forces (consisting of the combined military might of Egypt, Jordan, and Syria) had proved impotent. A common critique of the military, political, and sociocultural failures of Western-oriented development and a quest for a more authentic society and culture emerged—an Arab identity less dependent upon the West and rooted more indigenously in an Arab/Islamic heritage and values. Examples from Malaysia, Pakistan, and Lebanon reflect the turmoil and soul-searching that occurred in many parts of the Muslim world....

From Failure to Success

During the seventies Islamic politics seemed to explode on the scene, as events in the Middle East (the Egyptian–Israeli war and the Arab oil embargo of 1973, as well as the Iranian Revolution of 1978–79) shocked many into recognition of a powerful new force that threatened Western interests. Heads of state and opposition movements appealed to Islam to enhance their legitimacy and popular support; Islamic organizations and institutions proliferated. In 1973 Egypt's Anwar Sadat initiated a "holy war" against Israel. In contrast to the 1967 Arab–Israeli war which was fought by Gamal Abdel Nasser in the name of Arab nationalism/socialism, this war was fought under the banner of Islam. Sadat generously employed Islamic symbols and history to rally his forces. Despite their loss of the war, the relative success of Egyptian forces led many Muslims to regard it as a moral victory, since most had believed that a U.S.-backed Israel could not be beaten.

Military vindication in the Middle East was accompanied by economic muscle, the power of the Arab oil boycott. For the first time since the dawn of colonialism, the West had to contend with and acknowledge, however begrudgingly, its dependence on the Middle East. For many in the Muslim world the new wealth, success, and power of the oil-rich countries seemed to indicate a return of the power of Islam to a community whose centuries-long political and cultural ascendence had been shattered by European colonialism and, despite independence, by second-class status in a superpower-dominated world. A number of factors enhanced the Islamic character of oil power. Most of the oil wealth was located in the Arab heartland, where Muhammad had received the revelation of the Quran and established the first Islamic community-state. The largest deposits were found in Saudi Arabia, a self-styled Islamic state which had asserted its role as keeper of the holy cities of Mecca and Medina, protector of the annual pilgrimage (*hajj*), and leader and benefactor of the Islamic world. The House of Saud used its oil wealth to establish numerous international Islamic organizations, promote the preaching and spread of Islam, support Islamic causes, and subsidize Islamic activities undertaken by Muslim governments.

No event demonstrated more dramatically the power of a resurgent Islam than the Iranian Revolution of 1978–79. For many in the West and the Muslim world, the unthinkable became a reality. The powerful, modernizing, and Western-oriented regime of the Shah came crashing down. This was an oil-rich Iran whose wealth had been used to build the best-equipped military in the Middle East (next to Israel's) and to support an ambitious modernization program, the Shah's White Revolution. Assisted by Western-trained elites and advisers, the Shah had governed a state which the United States regarded as its most stable ally in the Muslim world. The fact that a revolution against him and against the West was effectively mounted in the name of Islam, organizing disparate groups and relying upon the mullah–mosque network for support, generated euphoria among many in the Muslim world and convinced Islamic activists that these were lessons for success to be emulated. Strength and victory would belong to those who pursued change in the name of Islam, whatever the odds and however formidable the regime.

For many in the broader Muslim world, the successes of the seventies resonated with an idealized perception of early Islam, the Islamic paradigm to be found in the time of the Prophet Muhammad, the Golden Age of Islam. Muhammad's successful union of disparate tribal forces under the banner of Islam, his creation of an Islamic state and society in which social justice prevailed, and the extraordinary early expansion of Islam were primal events to be remembered and, as the example of the Iranian Revolution seemingly verified, to be successfully emulated by those who adhered to Islam. Herein lies the initial attraction of the Iranian Revolution for many Muslims, Sunni and Shii alike. Iran provided the first example of a modern Islamic revolution, a revolt against impiety, oppression, and injustice. The call of the Ayatollah Khomeini for an Islamic revolution struck a chord among many who identified with his message of anti-imperialism, his condemnation of failed, unjust, and oppressive regimes, and his vision of a morally just society.

By contrast, the West stood incredulous before this challenge to the Shah's "enlightened" development of his seemingly backward nation, and the resurrection of an anachronistic, irrational medieval force that threatened to hurtle modern Iran back to the Middle Ages. Nothing symbolized this belief more than the black-robed, bearded mullahs and the dour countenance of their leader, the Ayatollah Khomeini, who dominated the media, reinforcing in Western minds the irrational nature of the entire movement.

The Ideological Worldview of Islamic Revivalism

At the heart of the revivalist worldview is the belief that the Muslim world is in a state of decline. Its cause is departure from the straight path of Islam; its cure, a return to Islam in personal and public life which will ensure the restoration of Islamic identity, values, and power. For Islamic political activists Islam is a total or comprehensive way of life as stipulated in the Quran, God's revelation, mirrored in the example of Muhammad and the nature of the first Muslim community-state, and embodied in the comprehensive nature of the Sharia, God's revealed law. Thus the revitalization of Muslim governments and societies requires the reimplementation of Islamic law, the blueprint for an Islamically guided and socially just state and society.

While Westernization and secularization of society are condemned, modernization as such is not. Science and technology are accepted, but the pace, direction, and extent of change are to be subordinated to Islamic belief and values in order to guard against the penetration of Western values and excessive dependence on them.

Radical movements go beyond these principles and often operate according to two basic assumptions. They assume that Islam and the West are locked in an ongoing battle, dating back to the early days of Islam, which is heavily influenced by the legacy of the Crusades and European colonialism, and which today is the product of a Judaeo-Christian conspiracy. This conspiracy is the result of superpower neocolonialism and the power of Zionism. The West (Britain, France, and especially the United States) is blamed for its support of un-Islamic or unjust regimes (Egypt, Iran, Lebanon) and also for its biased support for Israel in the face of Palestinian displacement. Violence against such governments and their representatives as well as Western multinationals is legitimate self-defense.

Second, these radical movements assume that Islam is not simply an ideological alternative for Muslim societies but a theological and political imperative. Since Islam is God's command, implementation must be immediate, not gradual, and the obligation to do so is incumbent on all true Muslims. Therefore individuals and governments who hesitate, remain apolitical, or resist are no longer to be regarded as Muslim. They are atheists or unbelievers, enemies of God against whom all true Muslims must wage jihad (holy war)....

As some dream of the creation of a New World Order, and many millions in North Africa, the Middle East, Central Asia, and southern and Southeast Asia aspire to greater political liberalization and democratization, the continued vitality of Islam and Islamic movements need not be a threat but a challenge. For many Muslims, Islamic revivalism is a social rather than a political movement whose goal is a more Islamically minded and oriented society, but not necessarily the creation of an Islamic state. For others, the establishment of an Islamic order requires the creation of an Islamic state. In either case, Islam and most Islamic movements are not necessarily anti-Western, anti-American, or anti-democratic. While they are a challenge to the outdated assumptions of the established order and to autocratic regimes, they do not necessarily threaten American interests. Our challenge is to better understand the history and realities of the Muslim world. Recognizing the diversity and many faces of Islam counters our image of a unified Islamic threat. It lessens the risk of creating self-fulfilling prophecies about the battle of the West against a radical Islam. Guided by our stated ideals and goals of freedom and self-determination, the West has an ideal vantage point for appreciating the aspirations of many in the Muslim world as they seek to define new paths for their future.

Islam and the West:
From Discord to Understanding

The spread of Islam has had an impact on the globalisation of culture. Islam has spread not only as a religion but has also helped to give birth to languages which are spoken by many more non-Muslims than Muslims. Kiswahili in Africa is today the most important indigenous language to have emerged out of Africa—but its origins lie in the interaction between Islam and African culture. Islam and the Arabic language have bequeathed the Arabic alphabet for languages like Farsi, Urdu, Old Hausa and others. The Arabs have given the world the so-called Arabic numerals through which the twentieth century has computerised the human experience. Today the Quran (Koran) is the most widely read book in its original language in human history. Muslims are expected to read the Quran in the original Arabic and not a translation that may change the intended meaning. The Bible is the most widely read book in translation.

As the twenty-first century begins, almost one out of every five human beings is a Muslim. In the course of the 21st century a quarter of the human race will probably be Muslim. The new demographic presence of Islam within the Western world is indicative that Islamisation is now a major globalising force.

Perspectives on Islamisation/Westernisation

In the second half of the twentieth century both Muslim migration to the West and conversions to Islam within the West consolidated a new Islamic presence. In Europe as a whole, there are now 20 million Muslims, eight million of whom are in Western Europe. These figures exclude the Muslims of the Republic of Turkey, who number some 50 million. There are new mosques from Munich to Marseilles.

Also as a manifestation of the demographic Islamisation of the Western world, there are now over a thousand mosques and Islamic centres in the United States alone. And the country has professional associations for Muslim engineers, Muslim social scientists and Muslim educators. There are some six million American muslims—and the number is rising impressively. Indeed, the American society in general is now coping with this issue, which creates cultural tensions between Islam and the West, as some observers have noted.

From Sharif Shuja, "Islam and the West: From Discord to Understanding," *Contemporary Review*, vol. 278, no. 1624 (May 2001). Copyright © 2001 by *Contemporary Review*. Reprinted by permission of The Contemporary Review Company Limited.

Currently Islam is the fastest growing religion in Central Asia. After the collapse of the U.S.S.R., all five states of Central Asia—Kazakhastan, Kyrghystan, Uzbekistan, Turkemenistan and Tajikistan—made an official place for Islam as the dominant religion. In France, Islam is becoming the second most important religion numerically after Catholicism. In Britain, Muslims have been demanding state subsidies for Muslim denominational schools. In Germany it has been belatedly realised that the importation of Turkish workers in the 1970s was also an invitation to the muezzin and the minaret to establish themselves in German cities. Australia has discovered that it is a neighbour to the largest Muslim country in the world in terms of population (Indonesia). There are new mosques, Islamic schools and Quranic centres from Brisbane to Perth.

Westernisation, on the other hand, is also a major globalising force. In the first half of the twentieth century, the West had colonised more than two-thirds of the Muslim world, from Africa to Asia. The first half of the twentieth century also witnessed the collapse of the Ottoman Empire and the complete de-Islamisation of the European state-system. The aftermath included the abolition of the caliphate as the symbolic centre of Islamic authority. The ummah (Islamic community) became more fragmented than ever and became even more receptive to Western cultural penetration. Other forces which facilitated the cultural Westernisation of the Muslim world included the replacement of Islamic and Quranic schools with Western style schools; the increasing use of European languages in major Muslim countries; and the impact of the Western media upon the distribution of news, information and entertainment. In other words, the West has in turn spread not only its technology and market ideology but also its languages (especially English, French and Spanish), its educational systems, consumer culture, including the dress code for men world-wide, and its mass media. The net result has indeed been a form of globalisation of aspects of Western culture. But at what cost?

In almost every liberal country in the West, crime is escalating, violence sometimes quadrupling, street mugging is on the rise, and the culture of the fortress city is developing. Suicide is now the second leading cause of death among American adolescents, the causes including the decline of family values and a more general national malaise. By comparison, suicide is a rare form of violence in the Muslim world.

There are scholars who feel that there is another way of looking at globalisation—and that is to focus on the three techno-systemic revolutions of all human history. There was first the agricultural revolution which started before Islamic and Western civilisations and transformed the relationship between man and plants. Millennia later there was the industrial revolution for which Islamic science helped to prepare the ground but which was essentially led by the West. This transformed the relationship between man and all material resources.

And now there is the emerging information revolution which leaves the West both triumphant and vulnerable—but is also leaving Islam marginalised. This is the revolution which is transforming the relationship between man and knowledge itself. But the question arises: can the Muslim world enter the positive sphere of globalisation without risking the negative aspects of Westernisation?

One of the remarkable things about the twentieth century is that it combined the cultural Westernisation of the Muslim world, on the one hand, and the more recent demographic Islamisation in the Western world, on the other. The foundations for the cultural Westernisation of the Muslim world were laid mainly in the first half of the twentieth century. The foundations for the demographic Islamisation in the Western world were laid in the second half of the twentieth century. The cultural Westernisation of Muslims contributed to the brain drain of Muslim professionals and experts from their homes in Muslim countries to jobs and educational institutions in North America and Europe. It is in this sense that the cultural Westernisation of the Muslim world in the first half of the twentieth century was part of the preparation for the demographic Islamisation in the West in the last fifty years.

Islamic Revivalism in Context

There are scholars and policy makers in the West who are concerned with recent Islamic revivalism and face tensions about how Islam is to be treated in Western textbooks and the media, especially as Islam becomes a more integral part of Western society. As one observer (Ali Mazrui) put it:

> Judaism, Christianity and Islam are the three Abrahamic creeds of world history. In the twentieth century the Western world has often been described as a 'Judeo-Christian civilisation', thus linking the West to two of those Abrahamic faiths. But if in countries like the US Muslims will soon outnumber Jews, is Islam becoming the second most important Abrahamic religion after Christianity? Numerically Islam may overshadow Judaism in much of the West, regardless of future immigration policies.

The question has therefore arisen about how Islam is to be treated in Western classrooms. In the Muslim world, 'education has become substantially Westernised. Is it now the turn of education in the West to become partly Islamised?' Can the Western world enter the positive sphere of globalisation and draw on the traditional wisdom of cultures such as Islam which point towards a more integrated society with drastically decreased levels of crime and violence?

The rise of Islamic movements in different parts of the world, aimed at resisting Western domination and control over Muslim territories and resources, Muslim cultures and communities, has provoked a new wave of aggressive emotions against the religion and its practitioners. That it is resistance to Western domination and control—and not some threat to the West as such—which is taking place within the Muslim world is a reality that is concealed from the general public. What Islamic movements are opposed to is the annexation and occupation of their lands as in the case of Palestine and Lebanon, the usurpation of their rights over their own natural resources as in the case of the Gulf Sheikhdoms, and the denigration of their religion as often happens in the Western media, sometimes abetted by local elites and writers.

Salman Rushdie's *The Satanic Verses* is a case in point. The results were terrifying. A holy man called for the author's death. Thousands were engaged in riots, dozens were killed, and normally brave defenders of free expression hunkered down or bent with the wind. Undoubtedly, the book is offensive to many Muslims. But books are published, plays are written and movies produced throughout the year that are deemed offensive by some group or other. And civilised people have learned not to murder the librarian or bomb the theatre to express their distaste. In this case, the intolerant reach of the Ayatollah has touched us all. Islamic groups and some individuals have expressed strong resentment and anger over Rushdie, the publisher of the book and Western media, and demanded the immediate ban of this book. Broadly speaking, they see their struggle as part of the still unfulfilled quest for self-determination and for genuine sovereignty. Such Muslim resistance is portrayed as an 'Islamic threat' by some Western academics, including Samuel P. Huntington. Conflict between Western and Islamic civilisations, Huntington in his article 'The Clash of Civilizations' points out, 'has been going on for 1300 years. The Gulf War is only the most recent important example'. His argument has been the centre of controversy for the last decade.

At the turn of the Western millennium, it is crucial to consider whether Islam is a monolithic force; whether the clash between Islam and the West is inevitable; and whether the so-called Islamic civilisation poses a credible threat to the West.

Huntington depicts the Islamic countries as part of a wider pan-Islamic movement, united in their hostility to the West and the United States. So convinced is Huntington of the 'kin-country' syndrome that even the Gulf War of 1990 becomes clear evidence of the brewing clash between Islam and the West.

The depiction of Islam and the Islamic countries as a monolithic entity may reflect the errors of the Orientalist mind-set, which refuses to understand the diversity within Islam for the convenience of a simple explanation. The assumed identity, through segregation and confinement of the Islamic civilisation, is a product of the Western imagination and sustains a deep phobia because the simple explanation, ironically, renders Islam both 'unknown' and mysterious.

It is orientalist scholarship that has invested Islam both with internal unity and an external political ambition. Orientalists have reconstructed Islam as a political religion despite the fact that there is little in original Islamic sources on how to form states or run governments. It also produced a particular reading of the 'orient' that was at odds with reality. Edward Said, in his article 'Orientalism Reconsidered' argued that 'designations like Islam and the Arabs … represented interests, claims, projects, ambitions, and rhetorics that were not only in violent disagreement, but were in situation of open warfare'. These diversions, however, were quickly glossed over and the myth that the Islamic countries possessed a fundamental unity of purpose that transcended national boundaries became the accepted consensus. The myth has, so far, refused to adapt itself to reason.

If the notion of a political and monolithic Islam should be taken with some scepticism, it is still true that a fundamentalist movement has emerged with the specific political task of reforming Muslim societies. This, however, is essentially a reaction to Westernisation, though not modernisation, and constitutes an attempt to check a perceived social drift and weakening of morals. In the West, modernisation is synonymous with Westernisation, but Muslim 'fundamentalists' clearly dissociate the two. This discordant understanding of modernisation has given Western analysts the impression that a rejection of Westernisation is the equivalent of a battle-cry against the West.

It should also be mentioned that the fundamentalist movement, most active in the Shi'ite countries of Iran, Iraq and Lebanon, is diverse and a minority movement in most Islamic countries. Even assuming Islamic fundamentalism would spread significantly, it is not inevitable that it will inexorably lead to a clash with the West. After all, the West, and particularly the United States, has maintained a very special relationship with Saudi Arabia, one of the most fundamentalist Arab States.

Therefore, even if we grant that Islam forms a united movement in comparison to Western culture, it is not certain whether the Islamic civilisations will constitute a true adversary to the West. However, it would be helpful if commentators in the West recognised that the pursuit of modernisation need not be accompanied by Westernisation, and that a rejection of Westernisation is not an inevitable call to do battle with the West.

It is helpful here to recognise that Islamic revivalism is in many ways the successor to failed nationalist programmes and offers an Islamic alternative or solution, a third way distinct from capitalism and communism. Islamists argue that Islam is not just a collection of beliefs and ritual actions, but rather a comprehensive ideology embracing public as well as personal life. It is important to understand that Islamic activism in some countries is a cause of concern but not for alarm. It is not a challenge to any civilisation. Like radicals throughout history, Islamic radicals become moderate once accommodated and incorporated into the socio-political mainstream. If they do not, they perish or become sociologically irrelevant cults. Therefore, extremism can best be reduced through gradual democratisation, a process and a system of governance which the West is not actively encouraging in the Muslim world, and particularly not in the Middle East.

So far the reality is that Islamic revivalism is neither a product of the Iranian revolution nor a result of Libyan extremist policies. The depth of frustration and anger is a reaction against European colonial rule, support for unpopular regimes and the internal weaknesses of the Muslim governments. Although some scholars argue that the present awakening in the Muslim world is a response to the decline of power and the loss of divine favour, in fact, the current revolt is a product of the weak economies of the Muslim countries, illiteracy and high unemployment, especially among the younger generation. The lack of political institutions, absence of democracies and good governments in the Muslim world is also an immediate cause of extremism. In this context, the Muslim demands for change are no different from the demands in Eastern Europe.

In many Muslim countries the secular nationalists and Islamists are united in the common cause of popular democracy. They are demanding the right to gain legitimate power with ballots rather than bullets. These forces are also cooperating with each other to topple monarchies, military dictators and authoritarian governments. They blamed their governments for their countries' backwardness and failure to achieve economic self-sufficiency and development. In addition to these internal reasons, there are also some external factors which push the Islamists to struggle for the rights and protection of Muslims which are under the siege of oppressive rule. Muslims are worried about the people of Palestine and they cannot ignore the inhuman massacres of Muslims in Bosnia, Chechnya and Kashmir. Such experiences tend to make Muslims think that the West is against them.

This author believes that the conflicts in Bosnia, Chechnya and Kashmir are political in nature. Others could say that the current conflict is either directly based on religious differences or at least involves an element of religion which contributes to the conflict. Military means, however, is not a solution. Devising appropriate mechanisms for their resolution continues to require the application of scientific method, rational inquiry and balanced argument. Because you dislike war does not mean you should not study it. And because we don't like the behaviour of politicians does not mean we can ignore them.

The Road Ahead

We should start from the premise that there is a need for all members of our global village to work towards harmony, cohesion and a peaceful world. We need to emphasise that the expressed goal of all religions is to achieve peace in the world. Conflict often arises in the way in which representatives of religions interpret these principles and the way they should be applied.

In this context one needs to be clear about the teachings of Islam. Some analysts in the West take the view that the rapidly growing Muslim population in Europe and the United States, and Islamic revivalism generally, are potential threats to Western culture. The study of Islam demonstrates that this is not a violent doctrine. Islam, like other world religions, is a faith of peace and social justice. In fact, Islam is as universalist as Christianity, and offers generous consolation when it comes to finding purpose and guiding the soul in a confusing world. It does not turn to fundamentalist militancy, because it has always been a tolerant religion and dislikes extremism and killing. Islam does not encourage terrorism and threatening behaviour. These violent concepts do not originate in Islam as a faith. Those groups who practise terror under the flag of Islam are a small minority, rejected by the great majority of Muslims. In relation to aggressive attitudes, the key message to Western scholars is to oppose the extremist Muslims but not blame all Islam.

Today's tensions would lead to tomorrow's aspirations. What we need now is the culture of peace that would help broaden cross-cultural understanding between Islam and the West. With proper knowledge of the culture of the Arab and Muslim worlds, this understanding would help foster tolerance and resolve conflict. We need to 'sustain a diversity of cultures, not a diversity of imagined clashes and conflicts.'

Now that the Muslim world, through Pakistan, has an 'Islamic nuclear bomb', Muslim leadership matters more than ever. There is every likelihood of other Muslim nations joining Pakistan in the near future. The West should not ignore the danger. The world will become an even more dangerous and unstable place.

President [Bill] Clinton predicted that the events of 1998 (when Pakistan/India exploded nuclear devices) were a foretaste of things to come, that this is the way that the wars of the future will be fought. He may be right. But the response of the Muslim world will depend on whether the militancy model prevails, or that of moderation. Therefore, the need for the West to understand Islam and to actively encourage moderation and democratisation in the Muslim world has again arisen.

Indeed, extremism can best be reduced through gradual democratisation. Efforts should be directed to expedite the transition to democracy in the Muslim world. They should be made to feel that the West is on their side, particularly if the movements that precisely champion the values of democracy arise there.

The New Millennium brings fresh challenges and opportunities in relations between Islam and the West. Religious leaders now must re-establish the will to implement the true essence of their religion and to find those factors which provide common ground with other religions. It is then required for them to initiate dialogue with other religious leaders with the purpose of finding commonalities and joining forces in setting standards for dealing with the wider issues of cultural diversity. It is pointed out that governments must have a strong interest in supporting such moves. Moderate Muslims showed a good example of this recently when they joined in worldwide protests against the action of the Islamicist regime in Afganistan's decision to blow up statues of the Buddha.

This process has to be on-going because as conditions in our world change, so does the need to find new responses. Now we are thinking in terms of 'cultural diversity'. The message is that people are not all the same, but that their differences are of mutual interest; their societies and cultures are often historically interdependent in surprising ways; and that seeking to understand one another is an intrinsically enlightening process whose fruits are material, political and cultural.

POSTSCRIPT

Does Islamic Revivalism Challenge a Stable World Order?

Understanding how Islam sees itself and its place in the world might make us fearful or hopeful. If Islam cannot accommodate to Western, secular values, as Esposito points out, does it challenge a stable world order? Shuja is more hopeful, believing that through a process of political maturation Islamic states may become more fully integrated into an increasingly globalized world civilization. One key is a fuller understanding among Western nations of the goals of Islamic revivalism. Furthermore, the West must understand its own image in the Muslim world and not expect a commitment to secularism that would appear to Muslims as blasphemy. Whether deeper dialogue will bring Islam and the West closer together or push them further apart is not yet clear.

A fascinating survey of how people have perceived God from the time of Abraham to the present can be found in Karen Armstrong, *A History of God* (Ballantine Books, 1993). Since Judaism exists in its own right and is the foundation for both Christianity and Islam, this "4000-year quest" provides insight into key similarities and points of difference. Any good text on world religions will provide an introduction to Islam; particularly accessible is Huston Smith, *Illustrated World's Religions: A Guide to Our Wisdom Traditions* (Harper San Francisco, 1994), which is also available on videocassette. Students who have not read the Qur'an might like to explore these scriptures, which are available in English translation in paperback.

The dilemma of becoming modern without becoming Western is addressed by Bernard Lewis in "The West and the Middle East," *Foreign Affairs* (January/February 1997). Other books by Lewis include *Islam and the West* (Oxford University Press, 1993) and *The Middle East: A Brief History of the Last 2,000 Years* (Scribner, 1995).

Director of Columbia University's Middle East Institute Richard Bulliet has written an account of Islam's success among people who live far from the political center, such as those in Iran. In *Islam: The View From the Edge* (Columbia University Press, 1994), Bulliet argues that the origins of today's Islamic resurgence are to be found in the eleventh century. Other books of note are *Orientalism* by Edward Said (Pantheon, 1978) and *Islam and the Cultural Accommodation to Social Change* by Bassam Tibi (Westview Press, 1991). In Francis Fukuyama's influential book *The End of History and the Last Man* (Free Press, 1992), the chapter entitled "The Worldwide Liberal Revolution" considers Islam as an alternative to liberalism and communism.

ISSUE 15

Was Ethnic Hatred Responsible for the Rwandan Genocide of 1994?

YES: Alison Des Forges, from "The Ideology of Genocide," *Issue: A Journal of Opinion* (1995)

NO: René Lemarchand, from "Rwanda: The Rationality of Genocide," *Issue: A Journal of Opinion* (1995)

ISSUE SUMMARY

YES: Alison Des Forges states that ethnic hatred between Hutus and Tutsis in Rwanda was primarily responsible for the Rwandan genocide of 1994.

NO: René Lemarchand admits that ethnic rivalries played a role in the catastrophe, but the ability of the Hutus to engage in "planned annihilation" free of any local or international restraint was a more important factor.

On April 6, 1994, Rwanda's President Juvenal Habyarimana and Burundi's President Cyprien Ntaryamira were killed when their plane was shot down near the Kingali, Rwanda airport. Both men were working to bring peace to their countries, which had been ripped apart by ethnic rivalries and resultant violence that had plagued their countries and the entire central African Lake District for decades. It was thought that extremists in Rwanda, who did not want these peace negotiations to succeed, were responsible for this act.

In the three months that followed, 800,000 Tutsis were slaughtered by the Hutu-dominated Rwandan government while the world's nations stood by and did nothing to stop it. What circumstances made this blatant act of genocide possible?

Throughout the twentieth century, Rwanda experienced periods of ethnic violence involving the rival Hutu and Tutsi tribes. The former, native to the region, represented more than 80 percent of the country's people, while the latter, who emigrated to the area from another part of Africa centuries ago, numbered 15 percent. This violence began during the colonial period when first the Germans, and then the Belgians, favored the Tutsi over the

Hutu during their colonial rule; the latter even used the Tutsi to enforce their colonial rule. This created resentment among the Hutu who waited for an opportunity to assert their majority power. This occurred in the 1960s when many European countries pulled out of Africa.

In 1961–1962, when the Belgians withdrew from the area and the two nations of Rwanda and Burundi were formed, massacres of the Tutsi ensued. Peace was finally restored when General Juvenal Habyarimana, a Hutu, seized power and restored a semblance of order to the country in 1973. Under his rule, which would last for more than 20 years, Hutus were given preferential treatment in practically all aspects of Rwandan life. This was opposed by Tutsi exiles in the region, who ultimately formed the Rwanda Patriotic Front (RPT) to defend Tutsi rights in the country. Both sides waged war throughout the 1980s.

In 1990, under pressure from Western nations, Habyarimana agreed in principle to establish a true democratic government based on ethnic rights, which led to peace and stability in the area. When his plane was shot down on April 6, 1994, many thought peace was close at hand. In fact, his assassination is blamed on extremists from his own party who did not want the peace plan to succeed. The slaughter of Tutsis—and moderate Hutus who spoke against it—began immediately and lasted until July. While the world watched and its nations did nothing, more than three-quarters of a million people were slaughtered, most by machete-wielding paramilitary troops. Many women who survived the ordeal told stories of wholesale rape that ultimately resulted in pregnancies and children that no one wanted. Furthermore, these deeds exacerbated Africa's AIDS crisis due to its wholesale perpetration of unsafe sex.

What factors created the Rwandan Genocide of 1994? According to Alison Des Forges, the long-standing differences between Hutu and Tutsi created in the Hutu extremists an "ideology of genocide," which they used to maintain their political control over the country by annihilating their Tutsi rivals. René Lemarchand states a more important factor was the Hutu's ability to launch a genocidal campaign free of any local or international restraint.

Alison Des Forges

 **YES**

The Ideology Of Genocide

Mobilizing thousands of Rwandans to slaughter tens of thousands of others required effective organization. Far from the "Failed State" syndrome that appears to plague some parts of Africa, Rwanda was too successful as a state. Extremists used its administrative apparatus, its military, and its party organizations to carry out a "cottage-industry" genocide that reached out to all levels of the population and produced between five hundred thousand and one million victims. Those with state power used their authority to force action from those reluctant to kill. They also offered attractive incentives to people who are very poor, giving license to loot and promising them the land and businesses of the victims. In some cases, local officials even decided ahead of time the disposition of the most attractive items of movable property. Everyone knew who had a refrigerator, a plush sofa, a radio, and assailants were guaranteed their rewards before attacking. But even with the powerful levers of threat and bribe, officials could not have succeeded so well had people not been prepared to hate and fear the Tutsi. Extremists who were ready to use slaughter to hold on to political power constructed an ideology of genocide from a faulty history that had long been accepted by both Hutu and Tutsi. Like the identity cards that had guaranteed privileges to the Tutsi during the colonial period and then served to identify them as victims for the genocide, the history that had once legimated their rule was ultimately turned against them to justify their massacre.

Before the arrival of the Europeans, the ruling elite had a sense of its own superiority. (Has there ever been an elite that did not?) In the late eighteenth and early nineteenth centuries, when Rwanda was located in regions best suited for pastoralism, members of the elite prided themselves on their knowledge about and control of cattle and looked down on cultivators lacking in both. Later in the nineteenth century, the central state expanded into regions dominated by cultivators and the elite increasingly made alliances with local leaders, whether *abahinza*, persons with ritual importance, or *abakuru*, heads of important lineage groups. In the same period, the ruler Rwabugiri took into his service significant numbers of men from outside the elite in order to increase his control over the old aristocratic lineages. Keeping pace with these political changes, aristocrats adjusted their attitudes to stress military skills and scorned masses who fell short in martial ability and experience.

From *Issue: A Journal of Opinion*, vol. xxiii/2, January 20, 1995, pp. 44-47. Copyright © 1995 by African Studies Association Secretariat. Reprinted by permission.

This sense of superiority appears to have been linked to the aristocrats' sense of what they owned and what they could do than to any emphasis on racial characteristics. Indeed, the elite that we now call Tutsi encompassed a number of competing lineages who had arrived in Rwanda at different times over a period of centuries and who had different interests as well as varied backgrounds. In the same way, the masses that are now known as Hutu included both peoples long resident within Rwanda and those who had just arrived from Zaire or Uganda. Given the complex variables in the situation, the categories of Hutu and Tutsi remained flexible and individuals could and did move from one to the other.

While the Tutsi sense of superiority to Hutu appears more elitism than racism, the attitudes of both groups towards the Twa were clearly racist. They scorned this small part of the population, in recent times less than one percent of the total, and refused not just intermarriage but even the normal courtesies of sharing food and drink with them.

When the Europeans arrived at the start of the twentieth century, they brought their own kind of racism, which would have enormous impact upon Rwandan ideas and practices. They assumed their own superiority and valued others in relation to their perceived nearness—physically and geographically—to themselves. Translating their racism into the African context, they formulated the "hamitic hypothesis," according to which "white Africans" from the northeast had brought civilization to the rest of the benighted continent. Colonialists found the Tutsi of Rwanda the ideal Hamites: tall, elegant, narrow-featured. Tutsi even wore togas, surely proof of a remote connection with Roman colonies of North Africa. Determined to validate their own prejudices, Europeans explained as unfortunate aberrations those Tutsi who did not conform to their image of what a Tutsi should look like, that is, like a dark-skinned European. They paid little attention to the distinctions among "Hutu" of different regions and origins. Accustomed to viewing Tutsi and Hutu as homogeneous groups, they ascribed stereotyped intellectual and moral qualities to the people of each category. With little hesitation, they decided that the Tutsi were more intelligent—and perhaps more devious—and so born to rule, while the Hutu, dumb but good-natured, could never be other than productive, loyal subjects. They put these ideas into practice by limiting posts in the administration, as well as the higher education needed for these jobs, to Tutsi. And to ensure that only Tutsi had access to these benefits, they instituted a system of population registration, labeling each person at birth as Hutu, Tutsi or Twa.

The Tutsi, politically astute by training not by birth, readily understood the prejudices of the Europeans and exploited them fully to their own benefit. Not only did they use European backing to extend and intensify their control over the Hutu— whose faults they exaggerated to the gullible Europeans—they also joined with the Europeans to create the ideological justification for this exploitation.

In a great and unsung collaborative enterprise over a period of decades, Europeans and Rwandan intellectuals created a history of Rwanda that fit European assumptions and accorded with Tutsi interests. The Europeans provided a theoretical, teleological framework and the Rwandans provided the supporting data to describe the progress of Rwanda to the height of its power at the end of the nineteenth century. The first and most "primitive" inhabitants were the Twa, the hunters and gatherers. Next the trusty Hutu lumbered upon the scene to cut the forests and create some fledging political organizations. Then in swooped the conquering Tutsi from Ethiopia, a minority that subjugated the far more numerous mass through their martial skill and superior intelligence—and, some said, through offering the grant of their cattle. The final and still uncompleted chapter in this steady climb upward, was, of course, the arrival of that even lighter-skinned and more clever minority, still fewer in numbers but more powerful in organization, the Europeans, who established their control over all the others. The determined onward thrust of the narrative allowed for no pauses or deviations from this simple and substantially distorted account of the growth of the nation. Ignoring the fundamentally "Hutu" nature of much of the ritual and many of the institutions of the central state, and neglecting the role played by leading Hutu in the late nineteenth and early twentieth centuries, these mutually-supportive historians created a mythic history to buttress a colonial social order. The Europeans who participated in this enterprise included administrators, scholars and missionaries. The Rwandans were chiefs, poets, and historians attached to the court, although the most outstanding of them, Alexis Kagame, was also identified with the church. The sophisticated and convincing canon they produced, backed as it was by extensive data, served as the accepted description of the Rwandan past until Jan Vansina challenged some of its basic assumptions in 1962.

The joint product was shaped in Rwanda and packaged in Europe, and then delivered back into the school-rooms of Rwanda by European or European-educated teachers. In addition, the results of the collaborative enterprise were accepted by intellectuals in the circles around the court, even those without European-style schooling—and integrated into their oral histories. It was not surprising that Tutsi were pleased with this version of history. But even the majority of Hutu swallowed this distorted account of the past, so great was their respect for European-style education. Thus people of both groups learned to think of the Tutsi as winners and the Hutu as losers in every great contest of the Rwandan past.

Faulty history was complicated by inadequate anthropology: the categories "Bantu" and "Ethiopoid," drawn from terms purporting to describe language groups, were applied to Hutu and Tutsi. reinforcing the idea that they were two distinct and internally coherent groups of people who had originated in different parts of Africa.

Extremist Tutsi, encouraged by European admiration and influenced by the amalgam of myth and pseudoanthropology, moved from elitism to racism. They transformed the dividing line between themselves and Hutu into the same kind of line that had once separated them and the Hutu from the Twa. The majority of Tutsi apparently did not accept this racism and continued to interact with Hutu much as they had in the past. But the formulation of the extreme position altered the terms of discourse and opened the way to a corresponding and equally virulent formulation on the part of extremist Hutu.

When Hutu overthrew the Tutsi in a revolution beginning in 1959, they did not question the basic elements of the myth—the arrival of a Tutsi minority and its subjugation of the Hutu majority. Although in the years immediately after, Rwandan and foreign scholars began presenting a different version of the past, one in which the Hutu played a more important role in shaping the growth of the state, these new ideas did not make their way into either political discourse or popular consciousness. Indeed, some politicians continued to stress the completeness of Tutsi control as a way to heighten feeling against them and to increase solidarity among the Hutu. They did not openly subscribe to the idea of Tutsi superiority as such, but by offering no explanation of how a small number could have conquered a much larger population, they perpetuated the belief that the Tutsi had capacities greater than those of the Hutu.

Ordinary people, who had no way to evaluate how truthfully the distant past was presented, did have their own experience to draw on, the experience of the colonial period. They knew that in that time Tutsi domination had been repressive, so they not surprisingly concluded that Tutsi control in earlier periods had been similarly intense.

In the early days of the revolution, Hutu had attacked mostly Tutsi who had some link with official power; they had left their ordinary Tutsi neighbors in peace. Then in the early 1960's Tutsi refugee groups, who had fled into exile at the start of the revolution, launched a series of attacks into Rwanda. After each, Hutu attacked Tutsi who still lived within the country, steadily widening the circle of victims until even Tutsi who had had no connection with previous power-holders were at risk. Local politicians and officials were responsible for this gradual enlarging of the pool of potential victims, whom they accused of aiding the invaders. They whipped up feeling against Tutsi to increase their own power, to consolidate the community behind them in unifying it against the minority. They profited from encouraging attacks on the Tutsi both directly, by showing they were strong enough to get people killed, and indirectly, by confiscating and then redistributing the property of victims who had been killed or driven away.

Then after more than twenty years of inaction, the refugee community attacked Rwanda on October 1, 1990, President Juvenal Habyarimana and his supporters saw the chance to exploit the invasion to consolidate Habyarimana's power base, which had been slipping after his long years in power. Like authorities in the 1960's, they attempted to do this by targeting Tutsi within the country as "accomplices" of the invading Rwandan Patriotic Front (RPF). They had at hand all the elements needed to construct an ideology of hate against the minority:

- the identification of all Tutsi with those who once ruled, an identification developed during the attacks of the 1960's;
- the link, real for a few but supposed for all, with the RPF who had invaded the country;
- the belief that in the past Tutsi had ruled repressively and that, through the RPF, they intended to re-establish the same exploitative regime;

- the belief that Tutsi were a separate and alien people, not part of the "Bantu" group, but from somewhere outside Rwanda and hence with no right to live in Rwanda;
- the conviction that the Tutsi had been able in the past to subjugate far larger numbers of Hutu because of superior intelligence or deviousness and still possessed the capacity to do so.

From the early days after the invasion, the extremists began to exploit these elements. According to one Rwandan army officer he was directed almost immediately after the invasion to spread the word throughout northeastern Rwanda that the RPF had attacked to restore the Tutsi monarch. Over the months that followed two other elements were added to transform the ideology of hate into the ideology of genocide:

- the belief that previous measures to end Tutsi control, killing some and driving away others—had failed and that the only way to ensure they would never take power again was to eliminate them completely; and
- the fear that Tutsi themselves intended to slaughter vast numbers of Hutu and would so do unless the Hutu struck first.

The moment when hatred became a determination to extirpate no doubt occurred at different times for different people, but certainly was widespread among the Habyarimana circle by November 1992. At the end of that month, Leon Mugesera, a Canadian-educated linguist who was a favorite of Habyarimana, delivered an inflammatory speech in northwestern Rwanda urging the Hutu to unite to send all the Tutsi back where they came from, that is, to Ethiopia, by "the river route," by killing them and throwing them in the rivers that eventually feed into the Nile. This solution, appealing in its simplicity and completeness, was never challenged, far less disavowed, by Habyarimana or others of his MRND party.

But some months before Habyarimana had been obliged to open up his single-party state to other parties and had enlarged his government to include representatives of opposition groups. The Minister of Justice, Stanislas Mbonampeka, represented the Liberal Party, a party then opposed to Habyarimana. He issued a warrant for the arrest of Mugesera, but was unable to carry out the warrant because Mugesera fled to a military camp where he remained hidden until he escaped from the country. (He turned up eventually in Canada where he is at the time of present writing.)

There is no better indication of the spread of the cancer of genocidal ideas than the positions of Mbonampeka. Ready to arrest Mugesera for incitement to violence in December 1992, he had himself been won to the merits of genocide by the spring of 1994. At the meeting of the United Nations Human Rights Commission held in Geneva, in late May 1994, Mbonampeka appeared as part of the Rwandan government delegation to defend its actions. At that time, he told a small group of participants in the meeting, including the writer, that the killing taking place in Rwanda was "normal." After the RPF victory, Mbonampeka fled to Zaire where, in November 1994, he was named to the rump government, once again, as Minister of Justice.

As the war continued and the RPF gained ground both militarily and through its diplomacy, the ideology of genocide was taken up by growing numbers of people. Two events were key in pushing many to this extreme position. First, the Arusha accords signed in August 1994 consolidated so many RPF gains that they seemed proof to many that once again the Tutsi were to be the winners. Second, in October 1993, Melchior Ndadaye, the recently elected President of Burundi and a Hutu, was assassinated by officers of the Tutsi-dominated army. The violence, and the suddenness by which the apparently successful transition to majority Hutu rule in Burundi was disrupted, demonstrated to many in Rwanda that no Tutsi could be trusted. It was then easy to argue that Tutsi/RPF in Rwanda, like Tutsi in Burundi, would inevitably overturn any power-sharing arrangement.

By April, the ideology was fully developed. When President Habyarimana's plane was shot down, those who assumed control of the government had no trouble integrating the assassination into the already-existing framework. Who was actually responsible was irrelevant to the use they could make of the killing. Without hesitation or doubt, they proclaimed that the RFP, with usual Tutsi deviousness and ruthlessness, had struck down the national leader who had wanted to make peace with them. Well prepared by exposure to the ideology of hate, most Hutu believed them. This assassination provided yet another reason to hate and fear the Tutsi.

A theme which had been present from the early days of the revolution but which had only limited importance in the ideology of genocide was the extent to which Tutsi had depended on outside support for their success. Most Hutu recognized that the support of the colonialists had been a fundamental element of the Tutsi repression, but they placed little stress upon this, particularly once the Belgian administration had switched its support to them. After the 1990 invasion, the Habyarimana government did exploit the link between the RPF and Ugandan President Museveni and attempted to discredit the RPF as the tool of a foreign government. A substantial number of RPF leaders had served in the army that brought Museveni to power, many of the troops who fIrst invaded Rwanda had deserted from the Ugandan army, and Uganda had served as a channel for RPF supplies. The Rwandan government even charged that the RPF invasion was the start of a campaign to re-establish a grand Tutsi empire of the Great Lakes region. (Within this argument, Museveni was described as Tutsi, an exaggeration of the fact that apparently one of his grandmothers was Tutsi.)

In more recent propaganda efforts, the Belgians, the United Nations and the Americans have displaced the Ugandans as prime supporters of the RPF. A pamphlet entitled "Le Peuple Rwandais Accuse...", circulated since September 1994 over the signature of then Minister of Justice Agnès Ntamabyaliro, names these outsiders as responsible for backing the RPF success. This pamphlet seems to represent a slight modification in the ideology of hate concerning Tutsi. No longer are they strong enough to conquer the Hutu masses alone; now, they must instead use their skills to attract the foreign support that then allows them to triumph. In other respects, this pamphlet continues the old themes and even states explicitly that the Tutsi were guilty of genocide against the Hutu, surely the most extraordinary of the distortions yet introduced into the description of events in the region. The assertion now heard among leaders of the rump government is that the Tutsi themselves were guilty of genocide and that if there were in fact a Hutu genocide of the Tutsi, it was justified by the need for defense against the Tutsi plan. This latest addition to the ideology of genocide suggests that the killing is far from over.

In late October 1994, a varied group of Rwandans met at a seminar sponsored by the Fondation pour le Progrès de l'Homme to discuss how to rebuild the country. Given its location in Kigali, the seminar did not attract any representatives from Rwandans who were in exile in surrounding countries, but it did include Hutu and Tutsi with very different interests and point of view from within Rwanda. One day of discussion was devoted to the theme of "History," giving the participants ample opportunity to voice their versions of the past. At the end, all agreed that the history of Rwanda must be rewritten. Indeed; provided it is done not by attempting to "unwrite" the faulty version of the past, but rather by preserving it, examining its distortions, understanding them and—one hopes—learning from them.

NO

René Lemarchand

Rwanda: The Rationality of Genocide

The image of Rwanda conveyed by the media is that of a society gone amok. How else to explain the collective insanity that led to the butchering of half a million civilians, men, women and children? As much as the scale of the killings, the visual impact of the atrocities numbs the mind and makes the quest for rational motives singularly irrelevant. Tribal savagery suggests itself as the most plausible subtext for the scenes of apocalypse captured by television crews and photojournalists.

Ironically, just as "tribalism" is being reaffirmed by the media as the bane of the continent, Rwanda's descent into hell makes it a society not unlike others in Europe and Asia where genocide has been intrinsic to their recent historical experience. Seen in the broader context of 20th century genocides, the Rwanda tragedy underscores the universality—one might say the normality—of African phenomena. The logic that set in motion the infernal machine of the Rwanda killings is no less "rational" than that which presided over the extermination of millions of human beings in Hitler's Germany or Pol Pot's Cambodia. The implication, lucidly stated by Helen Fein in a recent publication of the Institute for the Study of Genocide, is worth bearing in mind: "Genocide is preventable because it is usually a rational act: that is, the perpetrators calculate the likelihood of success, given their values and objectives".

The Rwanda genocide is neither reducible to a tribal meltdown rooted in atavistic hatreds nor to a spontaneous outburst of blind fury set off by the shooting down of the presidential plane on April 6, as officials of the Habyarimana regime have repeatedly claimed. However widespread, both views are travesties of reality. What they mask is the political manipulation that lies behind the systematic massacre of civilian populations. Planned annihilation, not the sudden eruption of long-simmering hatreds, is the key to the tragedy of Rwanda.

It is not my intention to dispose of one myth by promulgating another, the fantasy of a pre-colonial society where Hutu and Tutsi lived in an eternally blissful harmony. That Rwandan society was one of the most centralized and rigidly stratified anywhere in Africa cannot be denied, any more than the use of force in the conquest of peripheral Hutu kingdoms. But this does not mean that conflict was necessarily more intense or frequent between Hutu

From *Issue: A Journal of Opinion*, vol. xxiii/2, December 1994, pp. 8-11. Copyright © 1994 by African Studies Association Secretariat. Reprinted by permission. Notes omitted.

and Tutsi than between Tutsi and Tutsi. Much of the historical evidence suggests precisely the opposite.

The Legacy of Revolution

While there is general agreement among Rwanda specialists that the roots of conflict lie in the transformation of ethnic identities that has accompanied the advent of colonial rule, the chain of events leading to the killings begins with the Hutu revolution of 1959–62—a revolution, I might add, which would have quickly fizzled had it not been for the sustained political, moral, and logistical assistance which the Catholic Church and the *tutelle* authorities provided the insurgents. The result was a radical shift of power from Tutsi to Hutu and the exodus of thousands of Tutsi families to neighboring territories.

Few would have imagined that thirty years later the sons of the refugee diaspora in Uganda would form the nucleus of a Tutsi-dominated politico-military organization, the Rwanda Patriotic Front (RPF), that would successfully fight its way into the capital city and defeat an army three times its size.

Fewer still could have anticipated the price of their victory. On the eve of the October 1, 1990 invasion, no one within the RPF had the slightest idea of the scale of the cataclysm they were about to unleash. The assumption, fed through rumor and self-induced optimism, was that the Habyarimana regime was a pushover, and would quickly collapse in the wake of the invasion. While grossly overestimating the strength of the internal opposition, the RPF did not anticipate the massive military support that President Juvénal Habyarimana was about to receive from the French. Nor did they foresee the catalytic effect of the invasion on Hutu solidarities, and the growing determination of hard-liners within the government to manipulate ethnic hatreds for political advantage. The perceptions that the RPF leaders had of themselves—at of liberators, dedicated to the overthrow of a thoroughly corrupt and oppressive dictatorship—turned out to be sadly out of sync with the image that a great many Hutu had of their would-be "liberators."

Counter-revolutionaries as Hamites

Different levels of meaning can be read into the invasion of Rwanda by the RPF, each corresponding to a distinctive set of actors. What the French saw as an intolerable anglo-saxon threat to their *chasse gardée*—"the Fashoda syndrome"—the hard-liners in the Habyanmana camp did not hesitate to denounce as a brazen attempt by externally supported counter-revolutionaries to turn the clock back to the pre-revolutionary era, when Tutsi hegemony was the order of the day.

The "Hamitic" frame of reference added yet another ominous dimension to the counter-revolutionary image projected by the invaders. This is where the legacy of missionary historiography, evolving from speculation about cultural affinities between Hamites and Coptic Christianity to politicized dogma about the Ethiopian origins of the Tutsi, now referred to as "féodo-Hamites", contributed a distinctively racist edge to the discourse of Hutu politicians. Already the ideological stock-in-trade of Hutu revolutionaries in the fifties (who saw in "Hamitization" a Tutsi plot to exclude them from positions of responsibility), official references to the Hamitic peril gained renewed salience in the wake of the invasion. Thus Leon Mugesera, the Hutu "boss" from Gisenyi, who, in a much quoted statement, urged his followers to send the Tutsi back to their country of origins, Ethiopia, through the quickest route, via the Akanyaru river (known to have disgorged countless Tutsi corpses into Lake Victoria).

What emerges from the urgings of a Leon Mugesera, and the incitements to violence distilled by "Radio Libre des Mille Collines," the extremist outlet, is an image of the Tutsi as both alien and clever, not unlike the image of the Jew in Nazi propaganda. His alienness disqualifies him as a member of the national community; his cleverness turns him into a permanent threat to the unsuspecting Hutu. Nothing short of physical liquidation can properly deal with such danger.

The Regional Dimension of Hutu Rule: North vs. South

Acceptance of the Hamitic myth by Hutu politicians was not limited to any particular region or locality, yet it was among the northern Hutu that it found its most receptive echo. The reason, in part, is historical. Unlike the Hutu of the southern and central regions, their northern kinsmen were incorporated rather late into the fold of the monarchy, and with considerable assistance from the German Schutztruppe. To this day, the northerners, also known as Kiga, form a distinctive subculture. Their contacts with the Tutsi monarchy, and Tutsi culture in general, were few and far between; very few northerners married Tutsi women; for their awareness of a pre- Tutsi past, inhabited by kinglets (*abahinza*) and lineage heads (*kaburi b'imiryango*), landowners (*abakonde*) and clients (*abagererwa*), sorcerers and prophetesses, there is no equivalent among southern Hutu. No wonder the thrust of their "revolutionary" efforts in the 1950s aimed at turning the clock back to the golden age of pre-Tutsi days.

Nor is it too surprising if the army coup that brought Habyarimana to power in 1973 had as its key political objective to take power away from the southern Hutu (led by the late President Grégoire Kayibanda) and place it firmly into northern hands. And to make sure that power and privilege would remain a monopoly of the north, what was more natural, in Habyarimana's mind, than to order the massacre of anywhere from 40 to 50 incarcerated Hutu politicians from the central and southern regions, thus eliminating at one fell swoop his regional enemies, the "révolutionnaires de la première heure"? (From this deed Habyarimana derived an additional benefit, when, some years later he turned against Major Théoneste Lizinde, at the time his chief of security and now a key RPF personality, and accused him of having personally engineered the assassination of the southern politicians in Ruhengeri!).

It was this critically important regional dimension in the distribution of power that inspired in the minds of the northerners a nightmarish vision of the RPF as a potential ally of Hutu politicians from the south. To the image of the Hamite as an essentially alien and predatory creature was added the frightening possibility that they might join hands with the Hutu opposition and undo everything that had been accomplished since the 1973 coup.

Since June 1991, when the legitimacy of multi-party democracy was finally recognized, the ruling Mouvement National pour la Révolution et le Développement (MNRD) had to reckon with several opposition groups, most notably the ethnically-mixed Parti Liberal (PL), the Parti Social Démocrate (PSD), and the Mouvement Démocratique Républicain (MDR). All three parties could conceivably be viewed as potential allies of the RPF, but because of its substantial support among the Hutu masses of Butare and Gitarama, in the south, and because of its unique pedigree, traceable to the historic, southern-led Parti de l'Emancipation du Peuple Hutu (Parmehutu), the spearhead of the Hutu revolution until dissolved by Habyarimana in 1973, the MDR became the object of intense suspicion by northerners. This perhaps explains their determined and largely successful efforts to split it down the middle. The result was a growing rift between moderates and hard-liners (the latter also known as "Hutu power"), the former led by Faustin Twagiramungu (now Prime Minister), the latter by Dismas Nsengiyaremye, Frodouald Karamira and Donat Murego. That all three were once among Habyarimana's bitterest opponents, only to emerge as his staunchest supporters, is illustrative of how appropriate rewards, or thinly veiled threats, could bring about spectacular shifts of loyalty.

The Scuttling of Arusha

Whether as counter-revolutionary threat, vector of Hamitic hegemony or potential ally of the Hutu opposition, the RPF, in the minds of the Habyarimana clique, had to be destroyed as a political force. This meant the rejection of any kind of political compromise with the RPF, including ad hoc alliances with its representatives during the transition to multiparty democracy.

Yet the concept of compromise was at the very heart of the Arusha accords, signed on August 4, 1993, after a year of off-and-on negotiations. In the power-sharing arrangement hammered out at Arusha the RPF would have a total of five cabinet seats out of a total of 21, and eleven seats in the transitional national assembly out of a total of 70, putting it on par with the ruling MNRD. Compromise, likewise, was the name of the game in the restructuring of the armed forces: 40 per cent of the troops and 50 per cent of the officer corps would consist of RPF elements. Agreement of sorts was also reached on the repatriation of refugees, the demobilization of troops and on multiparty elections 22 months after the signature of the accords.

By instigating ethnic violence on a substantial scale the MNRD, assisted by its faithful ally, the crypto-fascist, rabidly anti-Tutsi Coalition pour la Défense de la République (CDR), knew that they could effectively derail the peace process. The killing of some 300 Tutsi in the Gisenyi prefecture in February 1993 was designed to do just that. It is surely not a matter of coincidence that the killings occurred shortly after the signature of one of the key power-sharing agreements (technically known as "protocol of agreement with the RPF on the sharing of power within the context of a broadly based transitional government") on January 9, 1993.

The wanton killing of Tutsi civilians thus became the quickest and most "rational" way of eliminating all basis for compromise with the RPF: the reassertion of Hutu solidarities would soon transcend regional differences and make it virtually unthinkable for Hutu and Tutsi to agree on anything.

The pattern was set long before the Arusha talks got under way. In the weeks immediately following the October 1990 invasion an estimated 300 Tutsi were massacred in cold blood in Kibilira. Then in retaliation for the RPF raid on Ruhengeri, in January 1991, came the physical elimination of at least a thousand Bugogwe cattle herders and their families, a Tutsi subgroup. In 1992 hundreds of Tutsi were killed in the Bugesera region when government-sponsored rumors warned the Hutu that they were about to be massacred by the RPF and their civilian collaborators.

The persistent indifference of the international community in the face of organized murder, coupled with France's rising levels of military assistance to the murderers, were powerful inducements for the regime to further strengthen its organizational capacities. By 1992 the institutional apparatus of genocide was already in place. It involved four distinctive levels of activity or sets of actors: (a) the akazu ("little house" in Kinyarwanda), that is the core group, consisting of Habyarimana's immediate entourage, i.e. his wife (Agathe), his three brothers-in-law (Protée Zigiranyirazo, Seraphin Rwabukumba and Elie Sagatwa), and a sprinkling of trusted advisers (most notably Joseph Nzirorera, Laurent Serubuga and Ildephonse Gashumba); (b) the rural organizers, numbering anywhere from two to three hundred, drawn from the communal and prefectoral cadres (préfets, sous-préfets, conseilleurs communaux, etc,); (c) the militias (interhamwe), estimated at 30,000, forming the ground-level operatives in charge of doing the actual killing; (d) the presidential guard, recruited exclusively among northerners, and trained with a view to providing auxiliary slaughterhouse support to civilian death squads. Thus came into being an organizational structure ideally suited to the task at hand.

Ndadaye's Assassination

With the assassination of President Melchior Ndadaye of Burundi on October 21, 1993, genocide came to be seen increasingly by MNRD politicians as the only rational option, and compromise, along the lines of Arusha, as synonymous with political suicide. As the first Hutu president in the history of Burundi, Ndadaye's election brought to a close 28 years of Tutsi hegemony. His death at the hands of an all- Tutsi army carried an immediate and powerful demonstration effect to the Hutu of Rwanda. As ethnic violence swept across the country, causing some 200,000 panic-stricken Hutu to seek refuge in Rwanda, the message conveyed by Ndadaye's assassination came through clear and loud: "Never trust the Tutsi!"

With Ndadaye's death vanished what few glimmers of hope remained that Arusha might provide a viable formula for a political compromise with the RPF. Though formally committed to implement the accords, Habyarimana was fast losing his grip on the situation. Meanwhile, and as if to further bolster the posture of MNRD hard-liners, tens of thousands of Hutu refugees from Burundi, and highly politicized by the events there, were now available for political mobilization precisely where they were most needed, in the south-central regions, seen by the akazu as the least "reliable."

Compounding the divisive effects of Ndadaye's assassination, the selection of candidates to the transitional organs of government unleashed a frenzy of competition for the spoils of office both within and among parties. Some opposition parties, such as the Parti Liberal (PL), or the Parti Social Démocrate (PSD), found themselves overnight in the throes of bitter ethnic struggles; others seemed almost to disintegrate in factional squabbles between extremists and moderates. Political assassinations sometimes disposed of both, in tit-for-tat fashion.

Nonetheless, orchestrating a transition that would meet the expectations of "Hutu power" (the phrase that came to designate the extremist fringe among opposition parties) and effectively reduce the influence of RPF elements in government seemed utterly illusory as long as Arusha provided the basic constitutional frame of reference for institutionalizing a compromise.

The Shooting Down of the Presidential Plane: A Rational Plot?

This is where the shooting down of Habyarimana's plane, on April 6, seems entirely consistent with the overall strategy of MNRD extremists. Despite the absence of solid evidence in support of an akazu-sponsored plot, it is easy to see the logic that might have prompted such a move. Not only did Habyarimana's death remove once and for all the specter of Arusha (even at the cost of losing in the process a key member of the "akazu," Elie Sagatwa), but by making it unmistakably clear that "it was the RPF that did it" the same extremists could now point to their "dastardly crime" as a moral justification for genocide. Who actually fIred the missile that brought down Habyarimana's plane may never be known, any more than who ordered the missile to be fired. But if the circumstantial evidence is any index, there is every reason to view the shooting of the plane as an eminently rational act from the standpoint of the immediate goals of Hutu extremists.

In Kigali the killing of opposition figures, Hutu and Tutsi, began moments after the crash, on the basis of pre-established lists. Two categories of potential allies of RPF were targeted: (a) moderate (as distinct from "Hutu power") Hutu politicians from the south/central regions, most of them affiliated to the Mouvement Démocratique Républicain (MDR), and (b) opposition leaders (Hutu and Tutsi) identified with the Parti Liberal (PL) or Parti Social Démocrate (PSD). So far from being selected on the basis of ethnic criteria, the victims were generally seen as animated by a sense of compromise and conciliation towards the RPF, in short as potential traitors. Those two categories were disposed of in a matter of hours. Doing away with Tutsi civilians proved a more difficult undertaking, yet the scale and swiftness of the carnage leaves no doubt the efficiency of the machete-wielding death squads. If we are to believe the testimony of eye witnesses, there was a macabre rationality to the methods employed by the killers: as one survivor told this writer, "where large numbers of people had to be killed, as happened where dozens or hundreds had sought refuge in churches, the death squads went about it methodically: phase one involved breaking the ankles so as to prevent the victims from running away; once the victims were immobilized, they worked on the wrists and arms, to prevent them from fighting back; the killers could then turn to the last phase, using clubs, sticks and machetes to break the skulls and necks." Horribly "rational" as well was the systematic slaughter of infants: after all, many of the RPF soldiers were toddlers when their parents fled their homeland during the 1959 revolution; why make the same mistake twice?

That a carnage of this magnitude could have been going on day after day, week after week, without interference from the international community speaks volumes for its lack of resolve in dealing with massive human rights violations. That they could literally get away with murder must have been a major consideration in the minds of the organizers of the killings. Given the extent of French backing, military, logistical, political and economic, they correctly assumed that they could act with impunity. They knew that the Fashoda syndrome would work to their advantage; they knew that the French Embassy would look the other way each time it was confronted with irrefutable evidence of massive human rights violations; and they knew, when the circumstances required, how to capitalize upon the close ties of friendship between President Mitterrand's son, Jean-Christophe, and his "buddy," Juvénal Habyarimana.

It is difficult to believe that the French were not aware of the potential for genocide created by the systematic manipulation of ethnic identities, by the mob killings of Tutsi over a period of years, and by the incitements to violence broadcast by Radio Mille Collines. If so it defies Cartesian logic to comprehend how the self-styled "patrie des droits de l'homme" could shove under the rug such massive human rights violations in the name of the threats posed to its higher geopolitical interests by the Trojan horse of Anglo-Saxon imperialism. It only took a logic of calculated risks for the authors of the genocide to grasp the implications of this paradox. The lesson to be drawn is nowhere more clearly articulated than by Helen Fein: "Abusive powers will continue to abuse as long as it works: the movement to change the taken-far-granted assumption that sovereignty implies indifference to our neighbors' crimes (like respect for family implied by overlooking child abuse next door) is still to emerge from gestation in images of mass flight, chaos, blood and death."

POSTSCRIPT

Was Ethnic Hatred Responsible for the Rwandan Genocide of 1994?

The Holocaust, in which 6 million Jews were murdered by Nazi Germany, was supposed to have taught valuable lessons to the world—namely that it did happen, and could happen again if steps were not taken to prevent it. In 1948, the United Nations (UN) defined and condemned genocide, and many expected that lessons were indeed learned and genocidal acts would never again occur. Fifty years later, political annihilation in Cambodia, "ethnic cleansing" in the former Yugoslavia, and the slaughter in Rwanda have proven the folly of such thinking. Why did we fail—again?

A lesson we should have learned from Rwanda is that words are important, but actions are better suited to prevent acts of genocide. In the case of Rwanda, no one—the UN, the United States, European nations, African nations—stepped forward until it was too late. A myriad of world leaders, including U.S. President William Clinton and UN Secretary Kofi Annan, have expressed remorse for what they didn't do in regard to the Rwandan genocide. Have lessons finally been learned? We'll have to wait for that answer.

The literature regarding the Rwandan genocide is substantial and cannot be repeated here. A few important sources are Bill Berkeley, *The Graves Are not Yet Full: Race, Tribe, and Power in the Heart of Africa* (Basic Books, 2001); Alison Des Forges, *Leave None to Tell the Story: Genocide in Rwanda* (Human Rights Watch, 1999); Alain Destexhe, *Rwanda and Genocide in the Twentieth Century* (New York University Press, 1999); Philip Gourevitch, *We Wish to Inform You That Tomorrow We Will Be Killed with Our Families: Stories from Rwanda* (Farrar, Straus, and Giroux, 1998); Fergal Keane, *Season of Blood: A Rwanda Journey* (Viking, 1995); Mahmood Mamdami, *When Victims Became Killers: Colonial, Nativism, and the Genocide in Rwanda* (Princeton University Press, 2001); Linda Melvern, *A People Betrayed: The Role of the West in Rwanda's Genocide* (Zed Books, 2000); and Gerard Prunier, *The Rwanda Crisis: History of a Genocide* (Columbia University Press, 1995).

Finally, an important source on the subject of genocide in the modern era is Samantha Power, *A Problem from Hell: America in the Age of Genocide* (Basic Books, 2002), with chapters devoted to each of the era's major acts of genocide.

ISSUE 16

Were Ethnic Leaders Responsible for the Disintegration of Yugoslavia?

YES: Warren Zimmermann, from *Origins of a Catastrophe* (Times Books, 1996)

NO: Steven Majstorovic, from "Ancient Hatreds or Elite Manipulation? Memory and Politics in the Former Yugoslavia," *World Affairs* (Spring 1997)

ISSUE SUMMARY

YES: Career diplomat Warren Zimmermann, the United States' last ambassador to Yugoslavia, argues that the republic's ethnic leaders, especially Slobodan Milosevic, bear primary responsibility for the nation's demise.

NO: Political science professor Steven Majstorovic contends that while manipulation by elite ethnic leaders played a role in the death of Yugoslavia, the fragile ethnic divisions, formed by memory and myth, also played an important role in the country's demise.

It is not often that the world can witness the death of a country, but that is precisely what many say we witnessed in the 1990s with the passing of Yugoslavia. In a graduated series of events, various areas broke from the Yugoslav republic until only Serbia and Montenegro remained. This was only the latest move in the complex and confusing game of Balkan politics.

Because of its volatile history, the Balkans were once referred to as Europe's "powder keg." The area's history began when the Balkans were settled by the southern branch of the Slavic family tree a millennium ago. During Europe's medieval period, Serbs, Croats, and Bosnians established ethnic kingdoms, which were soon overrun and conquered by the forces of the Ottoman Empire, which maintained control over part of the area for almost 500 years. When Ottoman power began to erode in the eighteenth and nineteenth centuries, one result was a gradual loss of Turkish control over their Balkan lands. The Ottomans were replaced by the Austrian Hapsburg Empire, one of their traditional rivals. While many of the Slavic citizens preferred a

Christian-based rule to a Muslim one, some would only be satisfied with independence accomplished along ethnic lines.

Balkan opposition to Hapsburg hegemony manifested itself in June 1914, when the heir to the Hapsburg Empire was assassinated by a Serbian nationalist group. This event proved to be the immediate cause of World War I, as Europe's nations blundered into a costly conflict. (For background information on World War I and its causes, see Issue 8 in this volume.)

At the war's conclusion, the victorious Allies decided that the solution to the Balkan quagmire was a federal republic comprising the disparate ethnic and religious groups, many of whom had been there for a thousand years. Thus, Serbs, Croats, Slovenes, Bosnians, Herzegovenians, Montenegrins, Ottomans, Macedonians, and Albanians were asked to live together in the new nation of Yugoslavia.

The nation's initial period of establishment was brief, as World War II brought Nazi occupation to Yugoslavia. Complicating things further was the fact that while most "Yugoslavs" fought against the German occupation, others (Croats and Bosnian-Herzegovinians) actually collaborated with the Nazis, resulting in numerous atrocities. The main victims would be the Jews and the Serbs, many of whom were massacred by the Croat Ustashas and their Nazi cohorts. The Serbs would not forget this.

After the war, Yugoslavia once again became a federal republic, with separate states established in Slovenia, Croatia, Bosnia-Herzegovina, Serbia, Montenegro, and Macedonia. Its leader was Josip Broz (Tito), a World War II hero to many, whose leadership held the republic together until his death in 1980. The gradual decline of Yugoslavia began in the 1980s; by 1995 it had virtually disintegrated.

The problems that brought about Yugoslavia's disintegration are many. The ancient ethnic rivalries and conflicts were extremely difficult to overcome. Complicating matters were the religious differences, with Eastern Christian Orthodoxy, Roman Catholicism, and Islam claiming the allegiance of the area's peoples. And of course there is the history—who did what to whom and when they did it—which has influenced the myths and realities of the Balkan landscape.

Contemporary leaders of Yugoslavia during the post–Tito era represented neither ideology nor country, but ethnic constituencies. They acted on the latter's behalf in their own quest for power. To what extent are these leaders personally responsible for Yugoslavia's demise? Or, was the country eventually doomed to failure by ethno-religious-historical forces beyond anyone's control?

Two responses regarding who and what was responsible for the demise of Yugoslavia are expressed by Warren Zimmermann and Steven Majstorovic in the following selections. Zimmermann holds the former Yugoslavia's ethnic leaders primarily responsible for the country's demise. Majstorovic accepts that "elite manipulation" played a role in Yugoslavia's demise, but he states that the "ancient hatreds" that have become embedded in the Balkan psyches are difficult to ignore as factors.

Warren Zimmermann

 **YES**

Origins of a Catastrophe

Preface

This is a story with villains—villains guilty of destroying the multiethnic state of Yugoslavia, of provoking three wars, and of throwing some twenty million people into a distress unknown since the Second World War. How could this tragedy have happened to a country that by most standards was more prosperous and more open than any other in Eastern Europe? My thesis is that the Yugoslav catastrophe was not mainly the result of ancient ethnic or religious hostilities, nor of the collapse of communism at the end of the cold war, nor even of the failures of the Western countries. Those factors undeniably made things worse. But Yugoslavia's death and the violence that followed resulted from the conscious actions of nationalist leaders who coopted, intimidated, circumvented, or eliminated all opposition to their demagogic designs. Yugoslavia was destroyed from the top down.

This [selection] is primarily about those destroyers. As American ambassador between 1989 and 1992, I saw them frequently and came to know them well. Speaking with me before their faces had become familiar to Western television viewers, they hadn't yet learned the full panoply of defenses against questions from foreigners. They described their plans, sometimes honestly, sometimes deceitfully, but always passionately and with a cynical disregard for playing by any set of rules. This record of their words and actions provides evidence for a coroner's report on the death of Yugoslavia....

The prime agent of Yugoslavia's destruction was Slobodan Milošević, president of Serbia. Milošević claimed to defend Yugoslavia even as he spun plans to turn it into a Serb-dominated dictatorship. His initial objective was to establish Serbian rule over the whole country. When Slovenia and Croatia blocked this aim by deciding to secede, the Serbian leader fell back on an alternative strategy. He would bring all of Yugoslavia's Serbs, who lived in five of its six republics, under the authority of Serbia, that is, of himself.

Milošević initiated this strategy in Croatia, using the Yugoslav army to seal off Serbian areas from the reach of Croatian authority. His plan in Bosnia was even bolder—to establish by force a Serbian state on two-thirds of the territory of a republic in which Serbs weren't even a plurality, much less a majority. In league with Radovan Karadžić, the Bosnian Serb leader with whom he later broke, Milošević was responsible for the deaths of tens of thousands of Bosnians and for the creation of the largest refugee population in Europe since the Second World War.

Franjo Tudjman, elected president of Croatia in 1990, also played a leading role in the destruction of Yugoslavia. A fanatic Croatian nationalist, Tudjman hated Yugoslavia and its multiethnic values. He wanted a Croatian state for Croatians, and he was unwilling to guarantee equal rights to the 12 percent of Croatia's citizens who were Serbs. Tudjman's arrogance in declaring independence without adequate provisions for minority rights gave Milošević and the Yugoslav army a pretext for their war of aggression in Croatia in 1991. And Tudjman's greed in seeking to annex Croatian areas of Bosnia prolonged the war and increased the casualties in that ill-starred republic.

Slovenian nationalism was different from the Serbian or Croatian sort. With a nearly homogeneous population and a location in the westernmost part of Yugoslavia, Slovenia was more democratically inclined and more economically developed than any other republic in Yugoslavia. The Slovenes wanted to be free of the poverty and intrigue of the rest of Yugoslavia. They particularly detested Milošević, charging him with making Yugoslavia uninhabitable for non-Serbs. Under the presidency of Milan Kucan—a conflicted figure buffeted toward secession by the winds of Slovenian politics—Slovenia unilaterally declared its independence on June 25, 1991. The predictable result, irresponsibly disregarded by Kučan and the other Slovene leaders, was to bring war closer to Croatia and Bosnia....

Decline...

A law graduate of Belgrade University, Milošević began his career as a communist apparatchik with an authoritarian personality already noticed by schoolmates. He was too young and too junior to have been close to [Josip Broz] Tito, but he was old enough (thirty-eight when Tito died) to have prospered in the Titoist system. I never saw in him the personal animus against Tito that many other Serbs felt. In fact, on my first visit to his office I noticed a large painting of Tito behind his desk; significantly, he took it down in 1991, the year Yugoslavia fell apart.

As he cultivated a nationalist persona, Milošević dropped the external aspects of his communist formation. He purged himself of the wooden language that makes communists the world over such hapless communicators. He dropped all references to communism. And he renamed the League of Communists of Serbia the Serbian Socialist Party.

In two ways, however, Milošević failed to break the ties. The first was his continued reliance on communist techniques of control over his party, the Serbian police, the media, and the economic sector. The second was his highly visible wife, Mirjana Marković, a Belgrade University professor and frequent author of turgid Leninist essays in glossy Serbian magazines. Marković flaunted her communism; in fact, she cofounded a communist party in 1990. She was thought to have the influence of a Lady Macbeth over her husband, particularly with regard to his frequent abrupt dismissals of hitherto trusted subordinates. Liberal Serbs described her variously as flaky, crafty, amoral, or vicious.

Whatever his real views of Tito, Milošević was nevertheless the vessel for the Serbian claim that Tito had denied Serbs the role to which destiny had entitled them. The charge may have been partly true, but it was certainly exaggerated. Serbs were a major element of Tito's partisan army during World War II, including its first two elite units, and played a prominent role in the Yugoslav army and police afterward. At his death, however, Tito left Yugoslavia so decentralized that no ethnic group—and certainly not the Serbs—could possibly dominate it. Given Serbian messianism, it became inevitable that a Serbian nationalist would rise up to redress the imagined wrongs dealt his nation. It was a tragedy for Serbia, its neighbors, and Europe as a whole that this nationalist turned out to be Slobodan Milošević....

Milošević deploys his arguments with force and apparent conviction. They're always internally consistent, even when based on fallacies or delusions. "You see, Mr. Zimmermann," he would say, "only we Serbs really believe in Yugoslavia. We're not trying to secede like the Croats and Slovenes, we're not tied to a foreign country like the Albanians in Kosovo, and we're not trying to create an Islamic state like the Muslims in Bosnia. They all fought against you in World War II. We were your allies." ...

In my view, Milošević is an opportunist rather than an ideologue, a man driven by power rather than nationalism. In the late 1980s he was a communist official in search of a legitimation less disreputable than communism, an alternative philosophy to help him consolidate his hold on Serbia, and a myth that would excite and energize Serbs behind him. He calculated that the way to achieve and maintain power in Serbia was to seize the nationalist pot that Serbian intellectuals were brewing and bring it to a boil.

I don't see Milošević as the same kind of ethnic exclusivist as Croatia's President Franjo Tudjman, who dislikes Serbs, or Bosnian Serb politician Radovan Karadžić, who hates everybody who isn't a Serb. Milošević felt no discomfort in bragging to me, no matter how fraudulently, about Serbia as a multiethnic paradise. Nor, I'm sure, did it disturb his conscience to move ruthlessly against Serbian nationalists like Karadžić when they got in his way. He has made a compact with nationalism as a way to bring him power. He can't break the compact without causing political damage to himself, but it has a utilitarian rather than an emotional value for him.

I can't recall ever seeing a cooler politician under pressure than Slobodan Milošević. In March 1991 he lunched with me and six other Western ambassadors. The meeting came during one of the most explosive crises of his political career. The week before, he had weathered the largest street demonstration ever mounted against his rule, had lost a bid to overthrow the leaderships of Slovenia and Croatia, and was in the process of trying to destroy the presidency of Yugoslavia.

He had come to our lunch from a four-hour meeting with hostile Belgrade University students. Yet he looked and acted as if nothing gave him greater pleasure than to sit down for a long conversation with us. He addressed all our questions with equanimity, asserting with good humor that the Kosovo Albanians were the most pampered minority in Europe, that street demonstrations (which had brought him to power) were wrong, and that Serbia had the freest media and the freest election system in Yugoslavia.

As I pondered the surreal quality of Milošević's remarks, I couldn't help admiring his imperturbability. I went back to the embassy and wrote a facetious cable saying that I had finally penetrated the mystery of the man. There were really two Milošević's. Milošević One was hard-line, authoritarian, belligerent, bent on chaos, and wedded to the use of force to create a Greater Serbia. Personally, he was apoplectic, he hated Westerners, and he spoke in Serbian. Milošević Two was polite, affable, cooperative, and always looking for reasonable solutions to Yugoslavia's problems. He was calm, he liked to reminisce about his banking days in New York, and he spoke good English.

I did note that Milošević One and Milošević Two had several traits in common: they disliked Albanians, they were strong in the defense of Serbian interests, and they seemed to believe that the world was ganging up against Serbia. Milošević Two, I wrote, would often be summoned to repair the horrendous damage caused to Serbia's reputation by Milošević One, who would be sent back to the locker room. There his handlers would salve his wounds and get him ready for the next round. The one sure thing, I concluded, was that Milošević One would always be back.

The strategy of this schizoid figure was based on the fact that Serbs were spread among five of Yugoslavia's six republics. Slovenia was the only exception. At the foundation of Yugoslavia after World War I, Serbia's chief interest was that all these Serbs live in a single state. Before Tito, Serbia had dominated that state. Now, after Tito, Milošević wanted to restore that dominance. His chief obstacle in the late 1980s was Slovenia, ironically the only republic without large numbers of Serbs. The Slovenes were the first to challenge the unity of Yugoslavia.

Milošević, no supporter of Yugoslav unity except as a vehicle for Serbian influence, wrapped himself in the mantle of unity as he sharpened his duel with the Slovenes. His concept of unity was Serbian nationalism buttressed by communist methods of control. It tolerated neither democracy nor power-sharing with other national groups. Because it was unacceptable to all Yugoslavs who wanted real unity or real democracy, or both, it was bound to be divisive. In fact, Milošević's pursuit of a narrow Serbian agenda made him the major wrecker of Yugoslavia....

Departures

On May 12, 1992, the State Department announced that I was being recalled to Washington in protest against the Serbian aggression in Bosnia....

The days before our departure and the weeks after gave us time for introspection about a country where we had lived six years and that had affected us deeply. How was it possible that such attractive people, on whom the gods of nature and fortune had smiled, could have plowed their way straight to hell? Shortly before we left Belgrade, I tried to answer that question in a cable entitled "Who Killed Yugoslavia?" It was intended as an analysis of the fatal elements in Yugoslavia's distant and recent past, laced with some nostalgia for what had been lost. I used as a framework the old English folk song "Who Killed Cock Robin?" a tale of murder complete with witnesses, grave-diggers, and mourners, but nobody to save the victim or bring him back to life....

With the perspective of years, of the Bosnian war, and of many gross misrepresentations of Yugoslavia's collapse, it's important to eliminate some of the reasons often cited. First, Yugoslavia was not destroyed by ancient Balkan hatreds. This doesn't mean that the Balkans don't see the with violence. The First World War was touched off by the assassination in Sarajevo of an Austrian archduke by a Bosnian Serb; the Second was for Yugoslavia not only a liberation war but a civil war with over half a million Yugoslav deaths.

But is Yugoslavia so unique? Europe, taken as a whole, has endured two civil wars in this century, involving sixty million deaths, including the genocidal annihilation of six million European Jews. Placid England suffered in the fifteenth century the Wars of the Roses, which moved Charles Dickens to remark: "When men continually fight against their own countrymen, they are always observed to be more unnaturally cruel and filled with rage than they are against any other enemy." The English lived through an even bloodier period in the seventeenth century: a king was executed and many of the people of Ireland massacred by Cromwell's forces. France had its wars of religion in the sixteenth century and its blood-drenched revolution in the eighteenth. Nor has the United States been immune from domestic conflict. More Americans died in our civil war than in any foreign war we have ever fought.

Balkan genes aren't abnormally savage. Bosnia enjoyed long periods of tranquility as a multiethnic community. Serbs and Croats, the most antagonistic of adversaries today, had never fought each other before the twentieth century. The millennium they spent as neighbors was marked more by mutual indifference than by mutual hostility. Serbs, though demonized by many as incorrigibly xenophobic, don't fit that stereotype. Milovan Djilas's son Aleksa, author of a brilliant history of nationalism in Yugoslavia, points out that, with all the manipulative tools at Milošević's disposal, it still took him four years to arouse the Serbian population and that, even then, thousands of Serbs fled the country to avoid fighting in Croatia.

The Yugoslav wars can't be explained by theories of inevitable ethnic hatreds, even when such explanations conveniently excuse outsiders from the responsibilities of intervening. There was plenty of racial and historical tinder available in Yugoslavia. But the conflagrations didn't break out through spontaneous combustion. Pyromaniacs were required.

Second, religion wasn't at the heart of Yugoslavia's demise. The Yugoslav wars were primarily ethnic, not religious, wars. The major proponents of destructive nationalism weren't driven by religious faith. Franjo Tudjman had been a communist most of his life; he converted to Catholicism when he turned to nationalist activities. Milošević, a lifelong communist, never, as far as I know, entered a Serbian Orthodox church except for blatant political purposes. I recall a visit he made for electoral reasons to a Serbian monastery on Mt. Athos in northern Greece. Not even the official photographs could disguise the disconcerted and uncomfortable look on his face. Even Bosnia was largely a secular society; a 1985 survey found that only 17 percent of its people considered themselves believers.

None of this absolves the Serbian and Croatian churches. There were many religious people in Yugoslavia, particularly among rural folk. The Serbian Orthodox Church and the Catholic Church in Croatia were willing accomplices of the political leaders in coopting their parishioners for racist designs. These two churches were national churches, in effect arms of their respective states when it came to ethnic matters. They played a disgraceful role by exacerbating racial tensions when they could have urged their faithful toward Christian healing.

With regard to Bosnia, both the Serbian and Croatian regimes felt the need to impute fanatic religiosity to the Muslims in order to satanize them. But the portrayal was false. The Bosnia I knew was probably the most secular Muslim society in the world. The growing number of Muslim adherents today is a consequence of the war, not one of its root causes.

Third, Yugoslavia was not a victim of communism or even of its demise. Yugoslavs didn't live under the Soviet yoke, unlike their neighbors in the Warsaw Pact, for whom communism was an alien and evil implant. Gorbachev's withdrawal from Eastern Europe liberated whole countries but had little direct effect on Yugoslavia, whose communism, whatever its defects, was homegrown. In Eastern Europe the fault line was between communism and Western-style democracy; in Yugoslavia it was between ethnic groups. Tito's relative liberalism within the European communist world coopted many people for the Yugoslav party who would have been Western-oriented dissidents in Czechoslovakia or Poland.

In Yugoslavia the dissidents were for the most part nationalists, not liberals, and they marched to domestic drummers beating out racist, not Western, themes. Communists in Yugoslavia wore black hats or white hats, depending on whether they were nationalists or not. The most rabid nationalists, like Milošević or Tudjman, were or had been communists. So had many antinationalist, democratic figures, like Drnovšek, Gligorov, Tupurkovski, and many courageous journalists and human rights activists. In most of Eastern Europe, the word "communist" explained a good deal about a person; in Yugoslavia it explained next to nothing.

Fourth, Yugoslavia wasn't destroyed by foreign intervention or the lack of it. General Kadijević, in his paranoid account of the end of Yugoslavia, blames the United States, Germany, and the European Community, acting in collusion with traitors in Slovenia, Croatia, and Kosovo. Foreign countries did make serious mistakes in Yugoslavia, but they didn't destroy it. The failure to do more to support Prime Minister Marković, the lack of a forceful Western reaction to the shelling of Dubrovnik, and the European Community's premature decision to recognize the independence of Yugoslavia's republics were all mistakes, but not fatal ones. Whatever inducements or penalties the West might have devised, they wouldn't have been enough to suppress the nationalistic rage that was overwhelming the country. The war in Bosnia was another matter; there the West could have saved the situation and didn't. But the murder of Yugoslavia was a crime of domestic violence.

The victim itself had congenital defects. Yugoslavia was a state, but not a nation. Few felt much loyalty to Yugoslavia itself. Tito sought to encourage fealty by guaranteeing ethnic autonomy rather than by trying to create an ethnic melting pot. Political energy was directed more toward gaining a better position in Yugoslavia for one's ethnic group than toward preserving the viability of the state. Nobody wanted to be a member of a minority; nobody expected minorities automatically to be protected. Vladimir Gligorov, son of the wise president of Macedonia and a perceptive scholar, captured this feeling when he asked ironically, "Why should I be a minority in your state when you can be a minority in mine?"

These character traits damaged, but didn't doom, Yugoslavia. The country didn't commit suicide. As the court of history pursues its investigation of the death of Yugoslavia, I can imagine the following indictments: Slovenia for selfishness toward its fellow Yugoslavs; Tudjman's Croatia for insensitivity toward its Serbian population and greed toward its Bosnian neighbors; the Yugoslav army for ideological rigidity and arrogance, culminating in war crimes; Radovan Karadžić for attacking the principle of tolerance in Yugoslavia's most ethnically mixed republic; and—most of all—Slobodan Milošević for devising and pursuing a strategy that led directly to the breakup of the country and to the deaths of over a hundred thousand of its citizens. Nationalism was the arrow that killed Yugoslavia. Milošević was the principal bowman.

The Serbian leader made Yugoslavia intolerable for anybody who wasn't a Serb. He is hated among Albanians, Slovenes, Croats, Muslims, Macedonians, and Hungarians. And he has brought his own people into poverty and despair. The potentially prosperous and influential Serbia on which he expatiated in our last meeting in April 1992 is now an economic and civil shambles. Much of its youth and middle class—the foundation of democratic construction—has fled to the west. Milošević's dream of "all Serbs in one state" is a nightmare today; Serbs are now scattered among four states—"Yugoslavia" (Serbia and Montenegro), Bosnia, Croatia, and Macedonia. In seeking to dominate Yugoslavia, Milošević destroyed it. In seeking to tear out the pieces where Serbs lived, he wrecked, for a generation or more, the future of all Serbs.

NO

Steven Majstorovic

Ancient Hatreds or Elite Manipulation? Memory and Politics in the Former Yugoslavia

Any optimism generated by the Dayton peace accords in late 1995 was substantially eroded by events during the spring and summer of 1996. These events marked a protracted and tragic endgame in the former Yugoslavia. The flight from Sarajevo by Bosnian Serbs in February and March 1996 was the first indication of things to come. During the summer, refugees who tried to return to their former homes were harassed and attacked by paramilitary gangs. The early focus was on the behavior of the Bosnian Serbs, but now it is apparent that a policy of ethnic apartheid is being pursued by all sides in Bosnia....

The complexity of the Yugoslav conflict illustrates that the genesis of the war and the issues of ethnonational identity that fed the flames of conflict are far from being understood in any way that reflects some set of shared perspectives among scholars and pundits. For example, the exodus from Sarajevo by the Serbs in February and March 1996 seems to defy logic and rationality. One analytic perspective contends that the war is a product of "ancient hatreds" rooted in primordial identity and consequently any national group that falls under the political control of another is in mortal danger. The experience of some Serbs who left Sarajevo certainly reinforces this contention, as they ran a gauntlet of hostile Bosnian Muslims, supposedly bent on revenge. An opposing perspective views the war as the product of elite manipulation and fearmongering by ethnic entrepreneurs who fanned the flames of hatred for their own purposes and who manipulated ethnonational identity issues that are themselves just a product of an "invented tradition." Analysts who adhere to the second perspective suggested that Serbs should take hold of their senses, accept the guarantees of the Bosnian-Croat Federation, ignore their leader's warnings, and stay in Sarajevo. Despite assurances, however, the Serbs who stayed in Sarajevo have been continually threatened. Bosnian Prime Minister Hasan Muratovic promised that the violence against Serbs in Sarajevo would be stopped. But unfortunately, most of the Serbs in Sarajevo now want to leave, including many who were loyal to the Bosnian government during the war.

Clearly, the Yugoslav conflict is an almost ideal laboratory for addressing some of the central questions that scholars of nationalism and ethnicity pose.

From Steven Majstorovic, "Ancient Hatreds or Elite Manipulation? Memory and Politics in the Former Yugoslavia," *World Affairs,* vol. 159, no. 4 (Spring 1997). Copyright © 1997 by The American Peace Society. Reprinted by permission of *World Affairs*. Notes omitted.

Those who espouse a primordialist conception of national identity have ample evidence to support their position, while the constructionists also have abundant data that support their contention that national identity is essentially an artificial and modern phenomenon that is often at the mercy of ambitious leaders who manipulate and instrumentalize ethnonational identity.

This [selection] argues that prevailing analyses of ethnic conflict in the former Yugoslavia that focus either on a notion of ancient, primordial hatreds rooted in centuries-old identities, or on the premise that ethnic identity in the Balkans is a modern social construction that has been instrumentalized by political elites, miss the essential nature of the ongoing struggle. Historical memory constrains the options that leaders exercise in conflict creation and in peacemaking. Ethnic identity in the former Yugoslavia, however, has also been and will continue [to] be somewhat flexible and politically adaptive but only within a framework that does not threaten the constraints imposed by myth and memory. The constraints on masses and elites imposed by historical experience are particularly applicable for the Serbs, somewhat less so for the Croats, and even less so for the Bosnian Muslims. The Balkan conflict has both premodern, primordial characteristics and modern, constructed/instrumentalized elements in which ancient antagonisms (sometimes hatreds) and modern politics have both contributed appreciably to the tragedy, and an overemphasis on either perspective misrepresents the nature of ethnic conflict and politics in the former Yugoslavia....

Memory and Myth in Serbian, Croatian, and Bosnian Muslim Ethnonational Identity

When the term "Balkan politics" is conjured up, a mental picture that many people might have is one of incessant conflict, ethnic tinderboxes, and terrorist plots. This stereotypical view of Balkan politics is not wholly inaccurate. The Balkans have historically been a crossroads for conquest and occupation. The area that is now Yugoslavia was settled by the migration of Slavic tribes during the sixth century. Those tribes were independent until the beginning of the twelfth century, when the Croatians yielded to Hungarian political dominance, and until the beginning of the fifteenth century when the Serbians were defeated by the Ottoman Turks. External rule from Austria, Hungary, Italy, or Turkey lasted until the beginning of the twentieth century, although in a series of revolts the Serbs had formed an independent state by the middle of the nineteenth century.

In addition to being distinguished from each other by self-defined differences in tribal custom and culture, the South Slavs were further differentiated by the split in the Christian church. As a consequence, the Croats and Slovenes identified with Roman Catholicism, while the Serbs were under the jurisdiction of Byzantium and had formed by the thirteenth century an independent Serbian Orthodox Church. This division between East and West was reinforced when the Eastern Orthodox Serbs fell under Turkish rule, while the Croats and Slovenes answered to Rome and Hungary, and eventually to the

Austro-Hungarian Empire. Thus, when the South Slavs were brought into a common state in 1918, the stage for ethnonational conflict had been set by a thousand years of history.

Serbian identity can best be understood as a combination of three historical experiences: the memory of the Battle of Kosovo in 1389 and the subsequent five hundred years of servitude and resistance against the Ottoman Turks; the successful revolts against the Turks early in the nineteenth century that culminated in an independent Serbian state by the middle of the century; and the role of the Serbs as allies of the West in two World Wars.

By the fourteenth century, the Serbs under Tsar Dusan had grown into a medieval empire that spanned the Balkans from the Adriatic to Western Bulgaria and to most of Albania and some areas in northern Greece. After his death in 1355, centralized power started to ebb, and various Serb nobles started to unravel the system set up by Dusan. In 1371, however, Prince Lazar came to power and a temporary recentralization of control was established. This short period ended at Kosovo Polje (The Field of Blackbirds) on 28 June 1389.

The battle between the Serb forces of Prince Lazar and the Ottoman Turks was at the time perceived as either a pyrrhic victory for the Turks or indecisive. The Serbian state survived for another seventy years before finally succumbing to Ottoman rule. However, the cataclysmic nature of a battle in which Prince Lazar and his son were beheaded, the Turkish Sultan Murad disemboweled by the Serbian knight Milos Obilic, and in which there were horrific losses on both sides (over 100,000 deaths in an eight-to-ten-hour battle) created a myth-making apparatus that has shaped Serbian consciousness to this day.

The battle decimated the Serb nobility and cost the Ottomans dearly. Almost immediately, Serbian poets, priests, and peasants started to propagate the notion of Christian martyrdom by the Serbian people, Prince Lazar, and Milos Oblic. The primordialization of the event had all the elements of a passion play played out in real life. Interestingly enough, the perspective of the Ottoman Turks only reinforces the Serbian myths:

> Yet this Ottoman view in some ways mirrors traditional Serbian views. Both the Ottoman and Serbian accounts emphasize the battle's cataclysmic nature. Both traditions have martyrdom as a theme.

Added to this vision shared between the Serbs and the Turks, the battle itself is routinely listed in historical surveys as one of the most important events in history. The result of all this valorization is an identity marker that is so rooted in real historical events that it is almost impossible for Serbs to escape its ubiquitous presence in Serbian identity.

Also a part of the Kosovo myth is the tale of migration by Serbs from Kosovo, the failed attempts to migrate back over a period of centuries, and the final triumphant return to Kosovo in 1912. Taken together, these events, which were kept alive by the Serbian Orthodox church in the liturgy and by traveling troubadours who annually embellished the story in an ever-growing epic poem ("The Kosovo Cycle"), suggest that even the horrible events in Bosnia may have been less destructive than the potential for catastrophe in the Serbian province of Kosovo that is today 90 percent Albanian.

The memory of an independent state that was relinquished to form the Kingdom of South Slavs is also a critical part of Serb identity. The theme of successful revolt and emancipation dominates the mythicizing of the Balkan Wars. Finally, the Serbian role in World War I and World War II completes the picture. Serbs suffered enormous losses in both wars and continually stress their part in the Allied victories, comparing their role to Croat, Bosnian Muslim, and Albanian collaboration. In particular, the role of General Draza Mihailovich and the Chetnik resistance in World War II is highlighted, as archival evidence has suggested a reassessment of [Josip Broz] Tito and the role of the partisans.

Surprisingly, Serbs do not consider the genocidal policies of the Croatian Ustasha state and their Bosnian Muslim allies during World War II as an important element of Serbian identity. Instead, the events are often used as a way to stereotype all Croatians and Muslims by both Serb masses and elites. In particular, the Ustasha- and Muslim-led genocide of Serbs in Croatia and Bosnia in World War II has been the key to understanding Bosnian Serb and Croatian Serb propaganda and military mobilization strategies against Croats and Muslims in the contemporary period. Both Rodovan Karadzic and Ratko Mladic, the Bosnian Serb military leader, have used the events of World War II to successfully demonize Croats and Muslims in the eyes of the Serbs.

Croatian identity also has a memory of a medieval kingdom, but one that peacefully gave up its sovereignty to the Hungarian crown in 1102. The project of identity primordialization by the Croats has been to present events since 1102 as evidence for the continuity of a Croatian state in waiting. The keys to this continuity are peasant uprisings, a succession of Croatian kings, advances in Croatian culture and learning that depict Croatia as a part of a Western European culture that is distinct from the Serbs, and the unbroken reality of Croatian national consciousness that goes back to the seventh century. What is often ignored by Serbs is that it was the efforts of Croat intellectuals and church leaders in the nineteenth century that first broached the idea of a single South Slav state.

Croatian identity is also tied to the Catholic church and its role in resisting Serbian dominance in the interwar period. The issue of Serbian dominance is hotly debated between Serbs and Croats. While Croats refer to Serbian dominance, Serbs refer to Croat obstructionism. The debate has no resolution, but by 1938 Croatia did win considerable autonomy from Belgrade and was, effectively, a state within a state.

Another part of the Croatian primordialization project is to address the events of World War II by minimizing the Ustasha aspect and emphasizing the role of the Croats in the partisan resistance led by Tito. This interpretation, however, is also open for debate between Croats and Serbs, since most sources that address Tito's partisan movement make it clear that an overwhelming majority of the partisans were Serbs, and that many Croatians did not join until Tito, a Croat, offered a pardon at the end of 1943 to anyone who joined the partisans, although Tito's action did alienate many Serb partisans. It should also be noted that many Serb renegade units participated in revenge massacres against Croatian and Muslim civilians toward the end of World War II. These killings numbered in the thousands and are remembered by Croats and Muslims who insist that the slaughter was mutual and that the world has tended to ignore Croatian and Muslim victims of World War II.

Croatian identity is also reinforced by the failure of the Croatian Republic to separate from Yugoslavia during what is called the Croatian Crises or Croatian Spring of 1968–72. The crises started out as an attempt to liberalize the economic and political system. But the movement was eventually taken over by nationalist elements who pushed for Croatian independence. An alarmed Tito brutally ended the movement and purged the Croatian party of liberals. He then did the same thing to the Serbian party to effect some semblance of ethnic symmetry. Unfortunately, many of the liberals who were purged in both the Serbian and Croatian Communist parties were the type of leaders who might have been effective in heading off the level of conflict in the Yugoslav conflict of 1991–95. But it is from the experience of 1968–72 that many Croatians today stereotype Serbs as conservative Communists while Croats see themselves as liberal democrats in the Western tradition. It was also during the period of the Croatian Crises that Franjo Tudjman became a staunch nationalist who started to write revisionist tracts about what he labeled the myth of the number of Serbian deaths in World War II.

The next element in the continual primordialization of Croatian identity will become the successful secession from Yugoslavia in 1991, Croatian suffering at the hands of the Serbs, and the German-led recognition by the world community. Pronouncements from Zagreb seem to support this view, although it is still too early for any complete evaluation.

Until the Bosnian war and the siege of Sarajevo began in 1992, Bosnian Muslim identity was essentially a tug of war between Serbian, Croatian, and Bosnian Muslim interpretations of history. The Serb perspective is that the Muslims are Islamicized Slavs who were mostly Serbs. The Croat view is that these same Slavs were Catholic Croats. Some Bosnian Muslims, however, claim that they are descended from the Bogomils, who were a heretic Manechean sect. Moreover, many Muslim intellectuals during the nineteenth century started to claim that the Bogomils were really Turks from Anatolia and that the "only thing Slavic about the Bosnian Muslims is their language, which they absorbed from the indigenous population." There are also perspectives that contend that the Bogomils were much more than a sect and that contemporary Bosnian Serbs are not really Serbs but an offshoot of the Vlachs, a sheep-herding people related to the Rumanians.

Muslim ethnic identity got a boost in 1971 when they were officially declared a nationality by the Tito regime. He thought that this declaration might end the warring claims for Muslim identity by the Serbs and Croats. Tito's rationale was that the creation of Bosnia-Hercegovina as a republic at the end of World War II had outlived its usefulness as a buffer between the Croats and the Serbs and that some other policy was necessary.

There are many recent works that present the history of Bosnia as generally one of interethnic harmony and cooperation. But it is [Robert J.] Donia and [John V. A.] Fine's thorough research that, despite their contentions, highlights very ancient roots of the conflict in Bosnia. They present a rich chronology of Bosnian life from antiquity to the present tragedy. Their most important contribution is the thorough and impressive debunking of the incessant claims of Croatian and Serbian chauvinists. Serb nationalists produce evidence that most Bosnian Muslims are Orthodox Serbs who were forcibly converted to Islam by the Ottoman Turks, while Croat nationalists argue that Bosnian Muslims are by blood the "truest" and "purest" of Catholic Croats who were led astray by the Turks.

The conversion to Islam in Bosnia was characterized by a very complex process. Bosnian Muslims were once Slavic Christians who were neither Serbs nor Croats but had a distinct Bosnian identity and belonged to a Bosnian church that ostensibly bowed toward Rome, a fact that Croats seize upon to make their claims. But the rites of this church closely followed the Eastern Orthodox model, which Serbs contend establishes Serbian identity. But what is most evident is that the Bosnian church was never well established, there were few priests, and the Bosnian Slavic peasants maintained only a tenuous tie to Christianity. Thus, with the Ottoman penetration into Bosnia in the fifteenth century, these peasants began a gradual conversion to Islam in a pragmatic decisionmaking process that took between one and two centuries. Moreover, the contention by some modern Bosnian Muslim scholars that Muslim identity was never Christian but instead sprang from the Bogomils, a sect that rejected Christianity and its rituals, is also refuted by evidence that the Bogomils in Bosnia were very few in number and were never influential in the development of Bosnian history.

Eventually, Muslims adapted to the erosion of Ottoman hegemony, the nineteenth century influence of the Austro-Hungarian empire, the Balkan Wars and World War I, the first Yugoslavia in which Serbs predominated, World War II, the Tito period in which the Muslims finally gained official status as a nation in Bosnia, and the final degeneration into civil war. During this period, the Muslims often exhibited a predilection for compromise and pragmatism, especially after the fall of the Ottoman empire, as the Muslims formed political parties and interest groups whose purpose was to tread the narrow balance point between blatant Croat and Serb attempts to capture their loyalty. Throughout the period, the tolerant, cooperative, and multicultural nature of Bosnian society is stressed by Bosnian Muslim nationalists. But a closer examination reveals that Bosnian society was somewhat less tolerant and harmonious than some would contend.

The constructionist and instrumentalist perspectives suggest that Croat and Serb ethnic consciousness did not exist in Bosnia prior to the nineteenth century and that the often mentioned notion that the current war is based on "ancient hatreds" is false. But history presents a more complex picture. It is clear that the development of medieval Bosnia did not occur in isolation and was closely connected to events in Serbia and Croatia. Also, the Ottoman millet system identified ethnic groups by religion instead of ethnicity. Consequently, it is often mistakenly assumed that since the Turks used a non-ethnic marker to identify Croats and Serbs, a pre-nineteenth-century Croat and Bosnian ethnicity did not exist. But Serbian settlers started moving into Bosnia by the early fifteenth century to escape Ottoman expansion into Kosovo, the Serbian heartland. After some initial migration of Croats out of Bosnia, the Franciscan order successfully helped to maintain a Croat presence in the area of western Bosnia known as Hercegovina. Furthermore, the Austrians offered Serbs land to act as a military buffer against the Turks, and by the seventeenth century Serbs occupied the Krajina in Croatia and adjacent areas in Bosnia. Croat and Serb consciousness was well established and was not simply a construction of nineteenth-century nationalism.

In the social system built by the Ottomans, the Muslim converts were landowners and freeholders, and the overwhelming majority of peasants, who were taxed heavily and lived as second-class citizens, were Serbs, along with a number of Croats. The peasants, especially the Serbs, who lived in this Jim Crow system chafed at the inequities and started to revolt by the nineteenth century. Of particular interest to a contemporary understanding of ethnic frictions is that, as the Ottoman empire eroded and was forced to make concessions to subject populations, it was in Bosnia where the local Muslim landlords were the most reactionary and hostile to any changes that threatened their paramountcy.

If the above-recounted issues are not evidence of "ancient hatreds," then at least there was fertile ground in Bosnia for ancient antagonisms. When it came to manipulating public opinion, Milosevic in Serbia and Tudjman in Croatia are often cited as architects of the war in Bosnia. However, Bosnian President Alija Izetbegovic should not be left off the hook. His role in the war, his rather radical political views, and his reneging on the Lisbon Agreement of 1992 that would have maintained a multiethnic Bosnia need to be examined closely. Still, it is clear from the evidence that despite the protestations of extremist Serbs and Croats, the reality of a Muslim national identity is undeniable. The notion of a Bosnia in multiethnic harmony before the current struggle is an insupportable myth that could be maintained only by a centralized Communist system. When Tito died and the system collapsed, history started to catch up rather quickly.

It should be apparent that at this point Muslim identity is still in the process of primordialization. The sieges of Sarajevo and Mostar and the killing fields of Srebrenica will be the building blocks as Kosovo was for the Serbs. Instead of historical records and oral history, the Bosnian Muslims will have access to videotapes, and Benedict Anderson's notion of the printing press as a vehicle for the imaging of identity has evolved to NPR and PBS. The Bosnian Muslims are quickly moving from being Yugoslavs to Bosnian Muslims, and women wearing veils have started to appear in villages and even on the streets of Sarajevo. Moreover, the flirtation with Islamic forces from the Middle East, particularly Iran, has been recently documented.

In contrast to Muslim identity, Serbian identity is rooted in a centuries-old primordialization project. Despite Milosevic's manipulation of the Serbian media and elections, the force of elite manipulation in an instrumentalist fashion is not as significant as one would think for Serbian identity today because Milosevic, or any democratic alternative to him, would be constrained by history from stepping too far outside the successful Kosovo-inspired primordialization of identity. There are even arguments that in the case of the Serbs it is the elites who have been shaped by the memories and the myths of the masses. The Serbs, more than the Croats or Muslims, are shackled by their view of history and may not be able to escape what they see as an apocalyptic destiny, a destiny that unfortunately combines national paranoia with a sense of a messianic mission to defend Christianity from the mounting forces of Islam.

The Croatian model represents an ethnic identity that is still in the process of primordialization, which is committed to reinforce the notion of a thousand-year history. This project is augmented by a heavy dose of instrumentalism as President Tudjman and his supporters on the Right try to hold onto the power and privileges that they enjoyed during the Communist era. An example of this effort is the release of the new Croatian currency during May 1994. The new currency is called the "Kuna" and refers to a forest marten. The only memory of this currency dates back to the Ustasha regime, and Jews and Serbs in Croatia have protested in vain. Croatian historians, some quite reluctantly, have scrambled to discover or perhaps imagine instances where marten skins have been used in trade within Croatia during the past thousand years. Some isolated instances have been discovered and so the process of primordialization continues.

Moreover, the Croats, as they did during the 1960s, have recently declared that Croat is a separate language from Serbian and have introduced numerous words that go back to Slavic anachronisms from the past. Differences in dialect between Serbian, Croatian, and Bosnian are probably less pronounced, according to most linguists, than between American and British English. But the process of identity differentiation through language policy is in high gear. In reaction, the Serbs and the Bosnian Muslims have also jumped on the bandwagon, and perhaps in five hundred years there will be three different languages created from the current Serbo-Croation.

The Muslims are in some sense the most free to pursue their own vision of an ethnic identity. Without a Kosovo or a thousand-year state to guide them, they are in a Big Bang period of imagining their place in the world. The process of primordialization occurs under the watchful eye of the world, and the instrumental policies of the government in Sarajevo are profoundly tied to this process. Primordialist, constructivist, and instrumentalist categories have collapsed upon each other in Sarajevo, and the Bosnian Muslims have the luxury of picking and choosing, although there is growing evidence that their role as absolute victim is starting to come under question as more recent evidence has started to point toward a more symmetrical structure of suffering in the current conflict. Choices for the Croats are more limited but still possible.

The Serbs are fanatically committed to a mythic identity that may not allow choices, even if they desire them. Moreover, the Serbs have already started to mythicize the expulsion of 250,000 civilians from the Krajina region of Croatia, an expulsion that the United States refrained from labeling "ethnic cleansing." The Serbs have also started to focus on the slaughter of Serbs in the Srebrenica area before the Bosnian Serb army atrocities of July 1995 as new fodder for their continued vision of martyrdom. If the Serbs cannot break out of a primordialization process that has exhausted itself, then the outlook for the Balkans is very bleak indeed, and the post-Dayton events of 1996 may be the harbinger of tragedy when the NATO forces leave Bosnia.

The complexity of the ethnic conflict in the former Yugoslavia has illustrated the difficulty of mono-causal analyses. Despite the penchant in postmodern analysis for stressing the decentered person who can change identities like clothing, ethnonational identity often predisposes people to dispense with rational decisionmaking and instead embrace a policy of radical ethnic altruism in which lives are sacrificed. And although the examination of elite behavior is part and parcel of the methodology of social scientists, this methodology falls short when historically rooted conflicts are examined. In the dark street of available data, it is elite behavior that is lit by the lamp at the end of the street. But it is the rest of the street in which the richness and cultural thickness of memory, myth, and shared experience lurks in shadows. The data in these shadows are often difficult to measure empirically. We must, however, seriously consider their validity lest we ignore them at great cost to future peacemaking and conflict resolution.

POSTSCRIPT

Were Ethnic Leaders Responsible for the Disintegration of Yugoslavia?

The biggest loss caused by the disintegration of Yugoslavia is to the country's people. They are the ones who have been driven from their homes, placed in "detention centers," beaten, humiliated, raped, and brutally murdered in frighteningly high numbers. The actual number of the displaced, humiliated, tortured, and dead is hard to come by, given the fluid and anarchic nature of the Yugoslavian battleground. Most chilling has been the use of the term ethnic cleansing to describe the "Balkan killing fields," conjuring up memories of the Nazi Holocaust. In support of such indictments, charges of genocide and "crimes against humanity" have been leveled against many former Yugoslavs, both participants in the crimes and the leaders who may have ordered or permitted them. Several Yugoslav political and military leaders, including former president Slobodan Milosevic, have been presently brought to trial for war crimes committed in Bosnia-Herzegovina and Kosovo.

After years of neglect by the outside world, it is ironic that it took the demise of Yugoslavia to bring the country the attention it deserved. Many books on the subject have been written recently, and some writers have attempted to look at this crisis through the eyes of its victims, such as Roger Cohen in *Hearts Grow Brutal: Sagas of Sarajevo* (Random House, 1998). Laura Silber and Allan Little's *Yugoslavia: Death of a Nation* (Penguin Books, 1997) gives a blow-by-blow account of Yugoslavia's death and is a concise, chronological account of the last 10 years of its life. Some works have examined the genocide factor; a useful anthology on this subject is Thomas Cushman and Stjepan Mestrovic, eds., *This Time We Knew: Western Responses to Genocide in Bosnia* (New York University Press, 1998). For those who need some historical background on Yugoslavia's past, see John R. Lampe, *Yugoslavia as History: Twice There Was a Country* (Cambridge University Press, 1996).

For information on Kosovo, the Balkans' latest casualty, see Tim Judah, *Kosovo: War and Revenge* (Yale University Press, 2000) and William J. Buckley, ed., *Kosovo: Contending Voices on Balkan Interventions* (William B. Eerdmans Publishing, 2000). For an account of the war from a military/diplomatic perspective, consult Ivo H. Daalder and Michael E. O'Hanlon, *Winning Ugly: NATO's War to Save Kosovo* (Brookings Institute, 2000).

Whether the trial of Slobodan Milosevic and others on charges of war crimes and crimes against humanity will bring relief to the Balkans remains to be seen. The troubled 1000-year history of the area indicates that any settlement will be neither quick nor acceptable to all concerned parties.

ISSUE 17

Do the Roots of Modern Terrorism Lie in Political Powerlessness, Economic Hopelessness, and Social Alienation?

YES: Anatol Lieven, from "Strategy for Terror," *Prospect* (October 2001)

NO: Mark Juergensmeyer, from "Terror in the Name of God," *Current History* (November 2001)

ISSUE SUMMARY

YES: World policy analyst Anatol Lieven states that dated United States cold war policies and despair-inducing political, economic, and social conditions have contributed to the rise of radical Islamists, some of whom were responsible for the September 11, 2001, attacks.

NO: International relations specialist Mark Juergensmeyer contends that the roots of the September 11, 2001, attacks lie in the radical views of the terrorists, especially the symbolism of cosmic war and the battle between good and evil.

What is the relationship between modern terrorist acts (such as the sarin gas attack initiated by Aum Shinrikyo in Tokyo, Timothy McVeigh's assault on the Murragh Federal Building in Oklahoma City, the actions of Afghanistan's Taliban and the wider al Qaeda network) and the religions (Buddhism, militant Christianity, and revivalist Islam) invoked to justify terrorist acts? Do the roots of all of these acts lie in feelings of despair, alienation, and powerlessness? Is the ancient pull of religion as a force in an increasingly secular world simply reasserting itself? This issue traces the roots of twenty-first-century terrorism by exploring the intellectual and cultural environments that produce it.

When Osama bin Laden spoke about the "humiliation and disgrace" suffered by Islam for "more than 80 years," he was evoking a bitter past that culminated in the occupation of Constantinople in 1918 and the subsequent carving up of the Ottoman Empire by European powers into what we call the modern Middle East. The countries created, the frontiers drawn, and even the system of independent secular states, based on national citizenship, were

European creations and quite foreign to the Islamic worldview that had prevailed since the time of the prophet Muhammad in the seventh century. At that time Islam unified a people who lived in many geographical areas. It is hardly surprising, then, that residents of the modern Middle East would find the imposition of secular states, based not on religion or on tribal identity, to be confusing at best.

As the inheritor of Western world dominance, the United States is seen by many in the Muslim world as playing a similar game—propping up corrupt leaders who serve its own purposes, while allowing disparities in wealth and power between the haves and the have-nots to increase. With the collapse of the Soviet Union in 1989, the Muslim Middle East, bereft of outside allies, was forced to create indigenous bases from which to oppose what it views as the latest foreign hegemon, the United States.

To many in the Middle East, modernization has meant the importation of corrupt Western values and a decadent Western lifestyle. Communism and democracy seem to have been eclipsed by a global market, larger and more powerful than any nation-state and responsible to neither law nor moral ideal. For some the only hope seems to lie in a return to an idealized version of the early, pure form of Islam, which existed at the time of the prophet Muhammad. Wahhabism, a strict, eighteenth-century movement that sought to purify and renew Islam, was embraced first by the rulers of Saudi Arabia and has also inspired such extremist reformers as the Taliban in Afghanistan and the Muslim Brotherhood in Egypt.

Moderate, mainstream Islam has rules governing warfare that are quite similar to the so-called "just war" theory articulated by the Christian theologian Augustine in the fifth century. War may be undertaken only under specific circumstances (in defense of the faith or to right a great wrong), noncombatants should be protected, and prisoners must be fairly treated. There is nothing in the Qur'an to justify steering airplanes into skyscrapers. Nonetheless, the impulse behind these acts has received intense and emotional support from a surprising variety of sources.

In a world that seems godless to many, the globalization of Western popular culture and the unresponsiveness of national governments have led some to take matters into their own hands. Afghanistan, the battleground for control of the vast oil and gas reserves of Central Asia, is merely the latest focus in an ongoing struggle between tribal and global impulses. Can aggressive, violent forms of religion thrive when people are basically content with their lot? As we discuss in Issue 14 of this volume, Islamic revivalism does not necessarily represent a threat to a stable world order. What motivates people to participate in terrorist acts is the major question posed by this issue.

In the following selections, Anatol Lieven faults despair-inducing economic, social, and political conditions in the Middle East for facilitating the rise of radical Islamists, some of whom carried out the September 11th attacks. Mark Juergensmeyer counters that the roots of the attacks lie in the radical religious views of the terrorists, especially their use of the powerful symbolism of cosmic war—the battle between good and evil.

Anatol Lieven  **YES**

Strategy for Terror

The US has been the target of a very serious act of war, conducted by a formidably cruel, brave, fanatical and well-organised enemy with a terrifying capacity for both savagery and self-sacrifice. At the time of writing, a few hours after the attacks, the casualty figures are not known, but it is clear that this has been by far the worst terrorist attack in history and the worst attack of any kind ever directed against the American mainland.

On the assumption that the perpetrators are identified and traced to some physical space a ferocious military response will be necessary. Not to do this would be to betray the victims and display weakness. However, successful war requires both a capacity for ruthlessness and an intelligent political strategy, including the attraction and conciliation of essential allies. So what we also desperately need is a fundamental reassessment of many of the attitudes which have guided American policies since the end of the cold war. In some areas at least, we may get this. For while war produces strongly emotional responses, it can also provoke stark clarity of thought and a radical re-ordering of previous priorities.

Such new thinking is essential, not only on the part of the US, but also of Britain and other American allies. This is not just because the US will expect our full support in hunting down and destroying the perpetrators of this atrocity. It is also because our own cities are under the same threat, and the extent of this threat may be determined by what actions and policies America now pursues. We therefore have to work with the US to shape common strategies.

The attack has underlined the irrelevance of America's dominant security priorities, which are still rooted in cold war attitudes and structures. This is true of three areas: first, the attempt to cast Russia and China as major threats to vital US interests. Second, the strategy of National Missile Defence (NMD) and the militarisation of space. And third, policy towards Israel and its occupation of the West Bank and Gaza—since this attack originated in the Muslim world and was clearly motivated by hatred of Israel and of US support for Israel.

Very much against its will, America is now effectively at war alongside Israel. That gives it the right, and, perhaps, the possibility of finally controlling some of its ally's more outrageous actions. But while some Americans in private are already placing the blame for what has happened on blind US support for Israel, the short-term tendency will be to back Israel to the hilt in whatever action it now takes. This temptation will of course be increased by the ugly popular celebrations of "victory" in parts of the Arab world.

A hardline response from the US is appropriate in the short-term. More-over it would be wrong to execute any significant policy shifts that could be construed as a victory for the terrorists. But if the US response results in too much pressure on the governments of Pakistan and other fragile states (in the case of Pakistan, by forcing the Taleban to hand over Osama bin Laden) these states may collapse—with radical Islamists left to pick up the pieces. This is where American allies need to play a part. Above all, a new US policy needs to be shaped by three linked realisations. First, that since the end of the cold war, there has come into being the basis of a unified world system in which the world's other leading states are partners, not enemies, and in which all these states are under threat from similar forces. In other words, there really is the makings of an "international community"—or would be, if the US could stop acting as if it alone constituted this community. The community is based on shared adherence to western-led modernity. The only categorical opponents of this modernisation project are indeed religious maniacs—who are not to be found in Moscow or Beijing. Second, that with the exception of certain middle eastern states, the real threat to the world order comes not from states, but from below: from alienated populations. And third, since the US cannot occupy and police the Muslim world in the struggle against Muslim terrorism, it is essential to have the co-operation of leading Muslim states. This is some-thing which was already emphasised by the aftermath of the attacks on Khobar Towers and the USS Cole.

The reordering of policy towards Israel is a slender hope, at least in the short term. But when it comes to NMD and policy towards Russia and China, a shift is more likely.

The failure, until now, to move away from the cold war has its roots not only in various forms of inherited bigotry, but also in very strong interests within the US security establishment. This establishment was a product of the cold war, and it needs a cold war-type enemy: huge, identifiable, and, most importantly, armed with either high-tech conventional arms or with old-style nuclear missiles. Hence the endless insistence on the danger of a restoration of the Soviet Union.

Russia is no longer strong enough to fulfil that role, so China has been widely promoted as a replacement. But a pathological loathing of Russia remains in important parts of the US establishment and, until last week at least, some bizarre arguments were still made concerning Russia.

Thus the leaders of the only institute in Washington explicitly devoted to the study of the Caucasus and central Asia has been arguing for an Ameri-can reconciliation with the Taleban as part of a new strategy of driving Rus-sian influence out of the region. In other words, these people wanted to revive American policies of the 1980s—with which some of them were closely associ-ated—of support for the Afghan Mujahedin; despite the fact that the Soviet glo-bal threat has disappeared, Russia is not in occupation of Afghanistan, and this past American policy has helped to produce Osama bin Laden and the safe haven given to him by the Taleban. Such people have sought to deny the presence of international Muslim radicals in Chechnya—though the latter have a website which publicises its victories and casualties, and despite the fact that

Osama bin Laden's aides have spoken publicly of sending volunteers and supplies to Chechnya. Hopefully, we will now be hearing less of such stupidity.

Concerning NMD, no more argument should be necessary. For years now, both critics and allies of the US, plus other states, have been arguing that the real threat to the American mainland comes not from ballistic missiles, but from terrorism; that a ballistic missile defence system would therefore be a form of Maginot Line which our enemies would simply outflank. After all, if a missile had been fired at the US last week, the country responsible would have been obliterated by an American counter-strike hours later. Given the nature of the actual attack, we may never be exactly sure which group or combination of groups was responsible and, therefore, of how and where to retaliate. More than five years after the bomb attack on the US barracks at Khobar Towers in Saudi Arabia in 1996, which killed 19 US servicemen, American intelligence analysts are still at odds over whether the perpetrators were agents of Osama bin Laden, of Saddam Hussein, or Iran—and if so which Iranian-backed group—or even of some combination between them. One reason for this failure has been the attitude of the Saudi authorities and intelligence services, who for their own security reasons have refused to seriously investigate an Iranian role. An even less helpful stance was taken by the Yemeni authorities after the attack on the USS Cole.

One way of combating the kind of attacks we saw is of course better security in the US; but this will not necessarily prevent a terrorist attack, as long as that terrorist is prepared to die. In the end, the key to fighting this war successfully has to be good intelligence—and given the difficulty that American agents have of penetrating the world of the Islamist extremists, for such intelligence the west desperately needs Arab and Muslim allies. The Saudis in particular will have to be persuaded to drop the decades-old strategy begun by Saudi Arabia's founder, Kind Ibn Saud, according to which the House of Saud has turned a blind eye to Saudi-based radicalism beyond the borders of the kingdom, as long as the radicals do not cause trouble within Saudi Arabia itself.

The help of leading Muslim states will also be essential if there is to be an invasion and occupation of some part of the Muslim world. For, in their different ways, the US bombardment of targets in Sudan and Afghanistan, and the aftermath of the Nato bombardment of Yugoslavia, have shown the inadequacy of long-range bombardment when it comes to destroying enemies on the ground, who are dispersed and hidden in a friendly civilian population.

Unfortunately, over the past ten years, US Muslim allies have been severely undermined by Israeli policies and American refusal to act against those policies while continuing massively to help Israel with financial and military aid. This primarily refers to the failure quickly and honestly to honour the Oslo agreement, the continuation of Jewish settlement in the occupied territories and the failure of the west in general to offer generous financial aid to Palestinian refugees. This has been in defiance of UN resolutions, of the wishes of almost all other US allies, including all allies in the middle east—and of America's professed principles and the rules it insists on elsewhere. The result of this has been the collapse of the peace process and renewed mass protest and terror—including, for the first time, by Israeli Arab citizens.

Israel and its US backers have stuck with policies which were necessary at a time of threats to Israel's existence; the threats came not only from its Arab neighbours, but indirectly from their superpower backer, the Soviet Union. Over the past generation, this has changed—but basic American policies do not appear to have changed in any way. With American military backing, Israel crushingly defeated its Arab neighbours and forced two of them to make peace. By far the largest, Egypt, became an American client state. The Soviet Union collapsed, not only crippling the remaining radical Arab states militarily, but releasing an immense flood of Soviet Jewish emigrants to Israel. This established Jewish demographic superiority (within Israel's pre-1967 borders) beyond challenge. Due to this link, but more importantly because of a common threat from Islamist extremism, Russia has actually become in many ways a de facto ally of Israel (at least when it comes to intelligence sharing).

Saddam Hussein's invasion of Kuwait in 1990 united most of the Arab world behind the west's response. A key part of the price the US had to pay for putting this broad anti-Saddam coalition together was to promise its Arab allies to push Israel towards a just peace with the Palestinians. Largely as a result of the American failure to do this, US Arab allies have been reduced to what a Jordanian ex-minister described to me as "shell regimes." This pro-western figure—he was a senior fellow at an American think tank at the time—said that the repeated humiliations of the Arab world by Israel had destroyed the domestic prestige of his own and other Arab elites seen as pro-American, and hollowed out the entire state system. "The only reason we are still standing is because no one is strong enough yet to push us over."

It is not only unyielding American policy towards Israel which has undermined its diplomacy in much of the Muslim world—there has also been a failure to exploit opportunities. Sections of the Iranian regime remain bitterly hostile to the US—but they are far more hostile to Iraq and the Taleban, who just happen to be America's own greatest enemies in the region. In 1998, after Taleban massacres of Iranian diplomats and Afghan Shias, Iran nearly went to war with Afghanistan. Up to now, this has not been made the basis for any new American strategy with regard to Iran—partly because so few US analysts have even noticed it. A chance to gain a new ally in the fight against Sunni terrorism has been lost. Instead, the US is risking new action in the Persian Gulf in the face of Iraqi, Afghan and Iranian hostility, with Iran armed by Russia—despite the fact that all these states loathe and fear each other. American policy in the region is officially described as "dual containment" (of Iraq and Iran). Up until last week at least, it was more like quadruple containment (of Iraq, Iran, Russia and Afghanistan), in obedience to policies laid down by a profoundly ignorant US Congress, under the sway of domestic lobbies.

To blame Muslim-based terrorism on Israel would be unfair and inadequate, for a whole set of reasons. The humiliation of the Arab and Muslim worlds by Israel is so infuriating to them, in part because it is only the last in a long history of defeats starting in the 17th century and extending far into the 20th—overwhelmingly at the hands of the Christian or western worlds. It is of course true that the west has often played a disgraceful role—at least in the 20th century, when it repeatedly betrayed its own professed ideals in its behaviour towards Muslim peoples. However, the key reason for these defeats has been the prolonged decline of the Muslim world relative to the west—defeats which were already producing radical Muslim responses (whether in Sufi or Wahabi guise) in the last decades of the 18th century. The key reason for this decline has been the multiple failures of development and progress within the Muslim world.

It is the pathologies produced by these failures, as well as the appearance of Israel and the US as objects of hatred, which have produced the phenomenon of modern Muslim extremist. Though they have found their most widespread and powerful expressions in the Muslim world, these pathologies are not restricted to that world. They are to be found wherever proud people, with strong but in part irrational traditions, feel defeated or radically unsettled by aspects of western-dominated modernity....

The danger to world order comes not from the ruling elites, who are increasingly integrated into the global market order (even in China, Russia and India), but from the excluded: those numerous social and ethnic groups who, for whatever reasons of culture, history or geography, are unable to take part in the world banquet—or who have declined in status, even if they have benefited economically. After all, the great European political pathologies of the 20th century did not have their roots in underdevelopment as such; rather they stemmed from the effects of uneven development and cultural change on deeply conservative societies.

Many of these excluded groups and individuals are simply pitiable, far too weak and miserable to threaten anyone. Others, however, have proud cultural traditions which make it very difficult for them to accept second-class status. Their strong fighting traditions give them a distinct edge in certain kinds of warfare, in organised crime and in the areas where the two intersect. Such groups give hostile states the chance to hit at the west without exposing their hands directly and thereby suffering retaliation.

Of course, such alienated groups form a relatively small minority of the world's population. The greater part of humanity has benefited to a greater or lesser extent from economic growth and "globalisation" in recent decades. But those who have not—or think they have not—are still too numerous. They can certainly not be mastered by the high-tech fighter aircraft, heavy battle tanks and enormous aircraft carriers on which the post-cold war US military remains determined to spend so much money.

This then is the dark side of the global village—the ability of that village's alienated minorities to hit out at their perceived oppressors over huge distances. Because the Muslim world was the oldest and grandest rival of the west and its greatest "victim," because "fundamentalist" Islam provides a singularly tough and yet flexible ideological framework for modern extremism, and because of the role of Israel and the US as a focus on hatred, it is in the Muslim world that these pathologies have assumed their greatest and more dangerous forms.

It would be wrong to copy Samuel Huntington and posit one single Muslim cultural-political world united in difference from and hostility to the west. The Muslim world is immensely varied, both in its own cultures and in its attitudes to the west. In the largest Muslim state by far—Indonesia—radical Islam as yet plays a rather limited role. But, sadly, one thing which does unite most Muslim countries is relative political and socio-economic failure.

With the exception of some of the oil-endowed Gulf states and—to a limited degree—Turkey and Malaysia, every single Muslim country has failed to enter the developed world, whether in its western or east Asian variant. Almost all are menaced by rapid, and in some cases, virtually uncontrolled population growth, flooding inadequate labour markets with unemployable and embittered young men. Almost all are failing to educate or use their female populations, in some cases disgracefully so. Afghanistan has collapsed altogether, becoming a murderous theocracy and international menace. Others are threatened with this fate. The behaviour of elites and state services across most of the region presents a deeply depressing picture. Most importantly, this has been true of regimes across the political spectrum, from authoritarian traditional monarchies and western-backed semi-democracies through anti-western radical nationalist and military regimes to ex-communist ones in the former Soviet Union.

It is not surprising in these circumstances that many people in the region have fallen back on revolutionary Islam as a last resort when everything else has failed, and on belief in a supposedly "Koranic" or Shariah system. As a result of this, the Muslim world finds itself in a profoundly peripheral position vis-à-vis the western-dominated world. At the same time (unlike Africa or Latin America) it retains a deeply-felt—and assiduously cultivated—collective memory of the Islamic sphere as a great cultural, economic and political metropolis in its own right.

So in attacking America, Muslim terrorists would certainly not only be attacking Israel's key backer, but also the central symbol of their own failure. And anti-American Arab nationalism is—in the classical fashion of all nationalisms—an ideology which is capable of sucking up and drawing strength from a whole set of other, unconnected resentments, including bitter resentment of the corruption and oppression of the Arabs' own regimes. Israeli and American behaviour has provided a dangerous focus for this.

The Chinese have some of the same historically-based feelings and, in the past, this contributed to the appalling pathologies of Maoism; but China has the largest population on earth, with one of the world's fastest growing economies. Economic success has been the hallmark of the other Chinese states, Taiwan, Singapore and Hong Kong. Indeed the Chinese diaspora has been one of the most economically successful groups in world history. China is a genuinely powerful, relatively orderly state under a nationalist and authoritarian, but rational and pragmatic leadership. It has become a successful participant in the western-defined modernisation project. The position of the Muslim world is very different.

I gained certain insights into the roots of Muslim extremism during my work as a stringer for *The Times* in Pakistan and Afghanistan in the late 1980s

—not only through meeting some precursors of the Taleban among the Afghan Mujahedin, but among radical groups in Pakistan. I especially remember a long conversation with some young members of a "fundamentalist" group in Lahore. None were from the bottom of society. They came from that classical breeding group of fascistic and religious extremism, the struggling lower middle class and upper peasantry.

They were under threat not only of sinking into the immiserated, semi-employed proletariat—with the Hira Mandi, or prostitutes' quarter, as the possible destiny of their womenfolk—but of being able to escape and rise only through entry into the junior ranks of organised crime, especially heroin smuggling. Given the state of the Pakistani economy, legitimate economic opportunities were few. Their traditional communities and cultures were being undermined by urbanisation and "atomisation." The semi-western, semi-modern new culture being thrust on them was of the most repulsive kind, especially concerning the treatment of women—a mixture of western licentiousness with local brutality, crudity and chauvinism.

In these depressing circumstances, adherence to a radical Islamist network provides a sense of cultural security, a new community and some degree of social support—modest, but still better than anything the state can provide. Poverty is recast as religious simplicity and austerity. Perhaps, even more importantly, belief provides a measure of pride: a reason to keep a stiff back amidst continual humiliations and temptations. In the blaring, stinking, violent world of the modern "third world" Muslim city, the architecture and aesthetic mood of the mosque is (like the Catholic churches in central America described by Graham Greene in *The Lawless Roads*) the only oasis, not only of beauty but of an ordered and coherent culture and guide to living. Of course this is true ten times over for a young male inhabitant of an Afghan, Chechen or Palestinian refugee camp.

NO

Mark Juergensmeyer

Terror in the Name of God

Perhaps the first question that came to mind on September 11 when the horrific images of the aerial assaults on the World Trade Center and the Pentagon were conveyed around the world was: Why would anyone want to do such a thing? As the twin towers crumbled in clouds of dust and the identities and motives of the perpetrators began to emerge, a second question arose: Why would anyone want to do such a thing in the name of God?

These are the questions that have arisen frequently in the post–cold war world. Religion seems to be connected with violence everywhere—from the World Trade Center bombings to suicide attacks in Israel and the Palestinian Authority; assassinations in India, Israel, Egypt, and Algeria; nerve gas in the Tokyo subways; unending battles in Northern Ireland; abortion-clinic killings in Florida; and the bombing of Oklahoma City's federal building.

What does religion have to with this virtually global rise of religious violence? In one sense, very little. If the activists involved in the World Trade Center bombing are associated with Osama bin Laden's al Qaeda, they are a small network at the extreme end of a subculture of dissatisfied Muslims who are in turn a small minority within the world of Islam. Osama bin Laden is no more representative of Islam than Timothy McVeigh is of Christianity, or Japan's Skoko Asahara is of Buddhism.

Still, one cannot deny that the ideals and ideas of these vicious activists are permeated with religion. The authority of religion has given bin Laden's cadres what they believe is the moral standing to employ violence in their assault on the very symbol of global economic power. It has also provided the metaphor of cosmic war, an image of spiritual struggle that every religion has within its repository of symbols: the fight between good and bad, truth and evil. In this sense, the attack on the World Trade Center was very religious. It was meant to be catastrophic, an act of biblical proportions.

What is striking about the World Trade Center assault and many other recent acts of religious terrorism is that they have no obvious military goal. These are acts meant for television. They are a kind of perverse performance of power meant to ennoble the perpetrators' views of the world and to draw us into their notions of cosmic war.

The recent attacks in New York City and Washington, D.C.—although unusual in the scale of the assault—are remarkably similar to many other acts of religious terrorism around the world. In my recent comparative study of religious terrorism, *Terror in the Mind of God,* I have found a strikingly familiar

From Mark Juergensmeyer, "Terror in the Name of God," *Current History,* vol. 100, no. 649 (November 2001). Copyright © 2001 by Current History, Inc. Reprinted by permission.

pattern. In each case, concepts of cosmic war are accompanied by strong claims of moral justification and an enduring absolutism that transforms worldly struggles into sacred battles. It is not so much that religion has become politicized but that politics has become religionized. Worldly struggles have been lifted onto the high proscenium of sacred battle.

This is what makes religious terrorism so difficult to combat. Its enemies have become satanized: one cannot negotiate with them or easily compromise. The rewards for those who fight for the cause are transtemporal, and the time lines of their struggles are vast. Most social and political struggles look for conclusions within the lifetimes of their participants, but religious struggles can take generations to succeed. When I pointed out to political leaders of the Hamas movement in the Palestinian Authority that Israel's military force was such that a Palestinian military effort could never succeed, I was told that "Palestine was occupied before, for two hundred years." The Hamas official assured me that he and his Palestinian comrades "can wait again—at least that long," for the struggles of God can endure for eons. Ultimately, however, Hamas members "knew" they would succeed.

In such battles, waged in divine time and with heaven's rewards, there is no need to compromise one's goals. No need, also, to contend with society's laws and limitations when one is obeying a higher authority. In spirtualizing violence, religion gives terrorism a remarkable power.

Ironically, the reverse is also true: terrorism can give religion power as well. Although sporadic acts of terrorism do not lead to the establishment of new religious states, they make the political potency of religious ideology impossible to ignore. Terrorism not only gives individuals the illusion of empowerment, it also gives religious organizations and ideas a public attention and importance that they have not enjoyed for many years. In modern America and Europe it has given religion a prominence in public life that it has not held since before the Enlightenment over two centuries ago.

Empowering Religion

The radical religious movements that have emerged from cultures of violence around the world have three elements in common. First, they reject the compromises with liberal values and secular institutions that most mainstream religion has made, be it Christian, Muslim, Jewish, Hindu, Sikh, or Buddhist. Second, radical religious movements refuse to observe the boundaries that secular society has set around religion—keeping it private rather than allowing it to intrude into public spaces. And third, these radical movements try to create a new form of religiosity that rejects what they regard as weak, modern substitutes for the more vibrant and demanding forms of religion that they imagine to be essential to their religions' origins.

One of the men accused of bombing the World Trade Center in 1993 told me in a prison interview that the critical moment in his religious life came when he realized that he could not compromise his Islamic integrity with the easy vices offered by modern society. The convicted terrorist, Mahmud Abou-halima, claimed that the early part of his life was spent running away from himself. Although involved in radical Egyptian Islamic movements since his college years in Alexandria, he felt there was no place where he could settle down. He told me that the low point came when he was in Germany, trying to live the way that he imagined Europeans and Americans did: a life where the superficial comforts of sex and inebriates masked an internal emptiness and despair. Abouhalima said his return to Islam as the center of his life carried with it a renewed sense of obligation to make Islamic society truly Islamic—to "struggle against oppression and injustice" wherever it existed. What was now constant, Abouhalima said, was his family and his faith. Islam was both a "rock and a pillar of mercy." But it was not the Islam of liberal, modern Muslims—they, he felt, had compromised the tough and disciplined life the faith demanded.

In Abouhalima's case, he wanted his religion to be hard, not soft like the humiliating, mindnumbing comforts of secular modernity. Activists such as Abouhalima—and Osama bin Laden—imagine themselves defenders of ancient faiths. But in fact they have created new forms of religiosity: like many present-day religious leaders they have used the language of traditional religion to build bulwarks around aspects of modernity that have threatened them, and to suggest ways out of the mindless humiliation of modern life. Vital to their image of religion, however, was that it be perceived as ancient.

The need for religion—a "hard" religion as Abouhalima called it—was a response to the soft treachery they had observed in the new societies around them. The modern secular world that Abouhalima and the others inhabited was a chaotic and violent sea for which religion offered an anchor in a harbor of calm. At some deep and almost transcendent level of their consciousnesses, they sensed their lives slipping out of control, and they felt both responsible for the disarray and a victim of it. To be abandoned by religion in such a world would mean a loss of their own individual locations and identities. In fashioning a "traditional religion" of their own making, they exposed their concerns not so much with their religious, ethnic, or national communities, but with their own personal, perilous selves.

Assaults on Secularism

These intimate concerns have been prompted by the perceived failures of public institutions. As the French sociologist Pierre Bourdieu has observed, social structures never have a disembodied reality; they are always negotiated by individuals in their own strategies for maintaining self-identity and success in life. Such institutions are legitimized by the "symbolic capital" they accrue through the collective trust of many individuals. When that symbolic capital is devalued, when political and religious institutions undergo what German philosopher Jurgen Habermas has called a "crisis of legitimacy," the devaluation of authority is experienced not only as a political problem but as an intensely personal one, as a loss of agency.

This sense of a personal loss of power in the face of chaotic political and religious authorities is common, and I believe critical to Osama bin Laden's al Qaeda group and most other movements for Christian, Muslim, Jewish, Sikh,

Buddhist, and Hindu nationalism around the world. The syndrome begins with the perception that the public world has gone awry, and the suspicion that behind this social confusion lies a great spiritual and moral conflict, a cosmic battle between the forces of order and chaos, good and evil. Such a conflict is understandably violent, a violence that is often felt by the victimized activist as powerlessness, either individually or in association with others of his gender, race, or ethnicity. The government—already delegitimized—is perceived to be in league with the forces of chaos and evil.

One of the reasons why secular government is easily labeled as the enemy of religion is that to some degree it is. By its nature, the secular state is opposed to the idea that religion should have a role in public life. From the time that modern secular nationalism emerged in the eighteenth century as a product of the European Englightenment's political values, it did so with a distinctly antireligious, or at least anticlerical, posture. The ideas of John Locke about the origins of a civil community and the "social contract" theories of Jean Jacques Rousseau required very little commitment to religious belief. Although they allowed for a divine order that made the rights of humans possible, their ideas had the effect of taking religion—at least church religion—out of public life. At the time, religious "Enemies of the Enlightenment"—as the historian Darrin McMahon describes them in a new book with this title—protested religion's public demise. But their views were submerged in a wave of approval for a new view of social order in which secular nationalism was thought to be virtually a natural law, universally applicable and morally right.

Post-Enlightenment modernity proclaimed the death of religion. Modernity signaled not only the demise of the church's institutional authority and clerical control, but also the loosening of religion's ideological and intellectual grip on society. Scientific reasoning and the moral claims of the secular social contract replaced theology and the church as the bases for truth and social identity. The result of religion's devaluation has been a "general crisis of religious belief," as Bourdieu has put it.

In countering this disintegration, resurgent religious activists have proclaimed the death of secularism. They have dismissed the efforts of secular culture and its forms of nationalism to replace religion. They have challenged the idea that secular society and the modern nation-state are able to provide the moral fiber that unites national communities or give the ideological strength to sustain states buffeted by ethical, economic, and military failures. Their message has been easy to believe and has been widely received because the failures of the secular state have been so real.

Antiglobalism

The moral leadership of the secular state was increasingly challenged in the last decade of the twentieth century following the end of the cold war and the rise of a global economy. The cold war provided contesting models of moral politics—communism and democracy—that were replaced with a global market that weakened national sovereignty and was conspicuously devoid of political ideals. The global economy became controlled by transnational businesses accountable to no single governmental authority and with no clear ideological or moral standards of behavior. But while both Christian and Enlightenment values were left behind, transnational commerce transported aspects of Westernized popular culture to the rest of the world. American and European music, videos, and films were beamed across national boundaries, where they threatened to obliterate local and traditional forms of artistic expression.

Added to this social confusion were convulsive shifts in political power that followed the breakup of the Soviet Union and the collapse of Asian economies at the end of the twentieth century. The public sense of insecurity that came in the wake of these cataclysmic global changes was felt not only in the societies of those nations that were economically devastated by them—especially countries in the former Soviet Union—but also in economically stronger industrialized societies. The United States, for example, saw a remarkable degree of disaffection with its political leaders and witnessed the rise of right-wing religious movements that fed on the public's perception of the inherent immorality of government.

Is the rise of religious terrorism related to these global changes? We know that some groups associated with violence in industrialized societies have had an antimodernist political agenda. At the extreme end of this religious rejection in the United States were members of the American anti-abortion group Defensive Action; the Christian militia and Christian Identity movement; and isolated groups such as the Branch Davidian sect in Waco, Texas. Similar attitudes toward secular government emerged in Israel—the religious nationalist ideology of the Kach party was an extreme example—and in Japan with the Aum Shinrikyo movement. Like the United States, contentious groups within these countries were disillusioned about the ability of secular leaders to guide their countries' destinies. They identified government as the enemy.

The global shifts that have given rise to antimodernist movements have also affected less-developed nations. India's Jawaharlal Nehru, Egypt's Gamal Abdel Nasser, and Iran's Riza Shah Pahlavi once were committed to creating versions of America—or a kind of cross between America and the Soviet Union—in their own countries. But new generations of leaders no longer believed in the Westernized visions of Nehru, Nasser, or the Shah. Rather, they were eager to complete the process of decolonization and build new, indigenous nationalisms.

When activists in Algeria who demonstrated against the crackdown against the Islamic Salvation Front in 1991 proclaimed that they were continuing the war of liberation against French colonialism, they had the ideological rather than political reach of European influence in mind. Religious activists such as the Algerian leaders; the Ayatollah Khomeini in Iran; Sheikh Ahmen Yassin in the Palestinian Authority; Maulana Abu al-Ala Mawdudi in Pakistan; Sayyid Qutb and his disciple, Sheik Omar Abdul Rahman, in Egypt; L. K. Advani in India; and Sant Jarnail Singh Bhindranwale in India's Punjab have asserted the legitimacy of a postcolonial national identity based on traditional culture.

The result of this disaffection with the values of the modern West has been what I described in my earlier book, The New Cold War?, as a "loss of faith" in the ideological form of that culture, secular nationalism. Although a few years ago it would have been a startling notion, the idea has now become virtually common-place that secular nationalism—the idea that the nation is rooted in a secular com-pact rather than religious or ethnic identity—is in crisis. In many parts of the world it is seen as an alien cultural construction, one closely linked with what has been called the "project of modernity." In such cases, religious alternatives to sec-ular ideologies have had extraordinary appeal.

This uncertainty about what constitutes a valid basis for national iden-tity is a political form of post-modernism. In Iran it has resulted in the rejec-tion of a modern Western political regime and the creation of a successful religious state. Increasingly, even secular scholars in the West have recognized that religious ideologies might offer an alternative to modernity in the politi-cal sphere. Yet, what lies beyond modernity is not necessarily a new form of political order, religious or not. In nations formerly under Soviet control, for example, the specter of the future beyond the socialist form of modernity has been one of cultural anarchism.

The al Qaeda network associated with Osama bin Laden takes religious violence to yet another level. The implicit attack on global economic and political systems that are leveled by religious nationalists from Algeria to Indonesia are made explicit: America is the enemy. Moreover, it is a war waged not on a national plane but a transnational one. Their agenda is not for any specific form of religious nation-state but an inchoate vision of a global rule of religious law. Rather than religious nationalists, transnational activists like bin Laden are guerrilla antiglobalists.

Postmodern Terror

Bin Laden and his vicious acts have a credibility in some quarters of the world because of the uncertainties of this moment of global history. Both violence and religion historically have appeared when authority is in question, since they are both ways of challenging and replacing authority. One gains its power from force, and the other from its claims to ultimate order. The combi-nation of the two in acts of religious terrorism has been a potent assertion indeed.

Regardless of whether the perpetrators consciously intended them to be political acts, all public acts of violence have political consequences. Insofar as they are attempts to reshape the public order, they are examples of what the sociologist Jose Casanova has called the increasing "deprivatization" of reli-gion. In various parts of the world where defenders of religion have attempted to reclaim the center of public attention and authority, religious terrorism is often the violent face of these attempts.

The postmodern religious rebels such as those who rally to the side of Osama bin Laden have therefore been neither anomalies nor anachronisms. From Algeria to Idaho, their small but potent groups of violent activists have represented masses of supporters, and they have exemplified currents of thinking and cultures of commitment that have risen to counter the prevailing modernism—the ideology of individualism and skepticism—that in the past three centuries emerged from the European Enlightenment and spread throughout the world. They have come to hate secular governments with an almost transcendent passion. They have dreamed of revolutionary changes that would establish a godly social order in the rubble of what the citizens of most secular societies have regarded as modern, egalitarian democracies. Their enemies have seemed to most people to be both benign and banal: symbols of prosperity and authority such as the World Trade Center. The logic of this kind of militant religiosity has therefore been difficult for many people to comprehend. Yet its challenge has been profound, for it has contained a fundamental critique of the world's post-Enlightenment secular culture and politics.

Acts of religious terrorism have thus been attempts to purchase public recognition of the legitimacy of religious world views with the currency of violence. Since religious authority can provide a ready-made replacement for secular leadership, it is no surprise that when secular authority has been deemed to be morally insufficient, the challenges to its legitimacy and the attempts to gain support for its rivals have been based in religion. When the proponents of religion have asserted their claims to be the moral force undergirding public order, they sometimes have done so with the kind of power that a confused society can graphically recognize: the force of terror.

POSTSCRIPT

Do the Roots of Modern Terrorism Lie in Political Powerlessness, Economic Hopelessness, and Social Alienation?

The two arguments represented in this issue seem intertwined. The religious goals and motivations of those who are responsible for the September 11th attacks in the United States have been clearly stated; at the same time, the recruitment of terrorists from the young, disillusioned male population in the Islamic world cannot be denied. The answer to the question of what lies at the roots of modern terrorism depends on which of the two forces plays a more important role in creating modern terrorism.

Answers to the questions raised in this issue extend beyond the boundaries of academic debate; the future of the Middle East as we know it may be at stake. If the religious radicalism of the terrorists was primarily responsible for the September 11th attacks, the present attempt to eradicate them will not permanently solve the current crisis. However, if the environmentally-induced terrorist argument is correct, amelioration of the conditions that create a fertile ground for terrorism could remove the need for its desperate tactics.

Needless to say, the literature on terrorism is vast and diverse. The following recommendations include sources from the past that have proven to be all too prophetic as well as contemporary sources that deepen our understanding of both sides of this issue.

Originally published in 1989 David Fromkin's *A Peace to End All Peace: The Fall of the Ottoman Empire and the Creation of the Modern Middle East* (Henry Holt & Company, 2001) provides a readable, scholarly account of the creation of the modern Middle East in the years following World War I. Two articles by Middle East scholar Bernard Lewis provide supplementary material that brings the situation up-to-date. See "The Roots of Muslim Rage," *The Atlantic Monthly* (September 1990) and "The Revolt of Islam," *The New Yorker* (November 19, 2001).

Works that provide a useful introduction to the religious nature of Middle Eastern society include Judith Miller, *God Has Ninety-Nine Names: Reporting From a Militant Middle East* (Simon & Schuster, 1997). This book investigates militant Islamic movements in ten countries with an emphasis on Islamic diversity. Also see Karen Armstrong's *The Battle for God* (Ballantine Books, 2000), which considers historical and modern fundamentalist movements in Judaism, Christianity, and Islam. Juergensmeyer's *Terror in the Mind of God: The Global Rise of Religious Violence* (University of California Press, 2001) explores the relationship between religious fundamentalism and violence. An article by Walter Laqueur, "The New Face of Terrorism," *The Wash-*

ington Quarterly (Autumn 1998) examines how religious fundamentalism has changed the nature of modern terrorism.

For the environmentally induced terrorism argument, consult Benjamin R. Barber, *Jihad vs. McWorld: How Globalism and Tribalism Are Shaping the World* (Ballantine Books, 1996), which considers the dialectical nature of these two forces, as each creates the other. Barber also wrote an article entitled "Jihad vs. McWorld," *The Atlantic Monthly* (March 1992) that encapsulizes the arguments in his book. Finally, Ahmed Rashid's *Taliban: Militant Islam, Oil and Fundamentalism in Central Asia* (Yale University Press, 2001), written by a Pakistani journalist well experienced in current Middle Eastern affairs, explores the role of the Taliban in the current crisis.

ISSUE 18

Have Afghan Women Been Liberated From Oppression?

YES: Sima Wali, from "Afghan Women: Recovering, Rebuilding," *Carnegie Council on Ethics & International Affairs* (October 2002)

NO: Noy Thrupkaew, from "What Do Afghan Women Want?" *The American Prospect* (August 26, 2002)

ISSUE SUMMARY

YES: International Afghan advocate for refugee women Sima Wali documents the pivotal roles Afghan women have played in rebuilding their communities, praises their courage in denouncing warlords, and calls for their full participation in the newly formed constitutional government.

NO: Journalist Noy Thrupkaew argues that dissension among women's groups in Afghanistan and the high profile of the Western-backed Revolutionary Association of the Women of Afghanistan (RAWA) are hampering progress; a more unified and moderate approach is needed.

The modern history of Afghanistan began in 1979, with the Soviet invasion and subsequent occupation. The powerful jihad that ultimately expelled the Soviets also fortified indigenous tribal codes that treat women as property and encouraged the fundamentalism that brought the Taliban to power in 1996. During the 1990s, Western journalists began reporting on the draconian measures decreed by the Taliban that barred women from education, health care, work, and freedom of movement. In this oppressive environment, RAWA (Revolutionary Association of the Women of Afghanistan) opened clandestine schools and hospitals for Afghan women and girls, provided international journalists with secret film footage of Taliban atrocities (including public executions of women for adultery), and offered ferociously anti-fundamentalist rhetoric that was repeated in news media around the world.

Likening the situation of rigid separation of the sexes in Afghanistan to rigid separation of the races in South Africa, human rights organizations in the West began to use the term "gender apartheid" to describe the plight of Afghan women.

Following the September 11, 2001 attacks, the United States launched a bombing campaign targeting Taliban and Al-Qaeda bases in Afghanistan. After the Taliban regime fell, the United Nations held peace talks in Bonn, Germany, that brought various political parties together in conversation and sketched out the parameters of an interim government with Hamid Karzai, a unifying political figure, as president. In January 2002, interim President Karzai signed a Declaration of Essential Rights of Afghan Women, which guaranteed legal equality between women and men, equal protection under the law, equal rights to both education and political participation, and the freedoms of movement, speech, and dress (to wear or not wear the burqa or any form of head covering). The following June a loya jirga, or grand assembly, met to elect a transitional goverment; women delegates participated.

Months of intense negotiations led to a constitution that was agreed to in January 2004 by a *loya jirga* of regional representatives. Karzai, president of the transitional government, signed the constitution later that month. In 12 chapters and 161 articles, the Afghan constitution mandates a strong presidency and provides for upper and lower legislative houses, secures equal legal rights for women and men, and establishes Islam as the country's sacred religion, but guarantees protection for other faiths. Women have been guaranteed a percentage of the seats in both upper and lower legislative houses. On October 9, 2004, the first presidential election was held in Afghanistan, with extraordinarily high turnout, including large numbers of women who stood in line for hours. Although Karzai was elected in a landslide, Massouda Jalal, a female physician, was also a candidate for president. She gave campaign speeches inside mosques and rallies in villages where women still needed their husband's permission to register to vote. Many women, in fact, were instructed by their husbands how to vote. In preparation for parliamentary elections on September 18, 2005, a census—the first since 1979—was conducted in spring 2005. The lower house will have 249 seats, with provinces sharing them on the basis of population, very much like the U.S. House of Representatives.

There are clear signs of hope. Roads and schools have been rebuilt, and women will have a voice in the government. The first woman-managed radio station in Kabul came on the air November 13, 2001, with the words, "The Taliban are gone," and Voice of Afghan Women recently received the first Reflections of Hope Award from Oklahoma City, on the tenth anniversary of the bombing of the Murrah Federal Building. But, the Taliban are resurgent, people do not feel safe, narcotic trafficking and the flow of arms continue unabated, and warlordism and violence against women persist. In the villages far from the capital city of Kabul, women are not allowed to speak with men outside their immediate families, and fathers can still force their daughters into arranged marriages, even treating them as commodities to settle debts. Once married, a woman has no protection from an abusive husband. If a woman runs away from her husband (threatening his honor and dignity), she can be beaten or even jailed and prosecuted. A woman who is kidnapped or raped brings shame upon her household and, typically, will not be accepted back. An increasing number opt for suicide. Throughout Afghanistan, maternal and infant mortality ratios are the highest in the world, 300,000 children die each year from preventable diseases, and 85 percent of women are illiterate. Clearly, some Afghan women have been liberated from oppression, but others have not.

Sima Wali  **YES**

Afghan Women: Recovering, Rebuilding

The United States' foreign policy in Afghanistan has a long history of misguided plans and misplaced trust—a fact that has contributed to the destruction of the social and physical infrastructure of Afghan society. Afghans contend that after having fought as U.S. allies against the Soviet Union—with the price of more than two million dead—the United States swiftly walked away at the end of that bloody, twenty-three-year conflict. The toll of the war on Afghan society reflected in current statistics is so staggering as to be practically unimaginable: 12 million women living in abject poverty, 1 million people handicapped from land mine explosions, an average life expectancy of forty years (lower for women), a mortality rate of 25.7 percent for children under five years old, and an illiteracy rate of 64 percent. These horrific indicators place Afghanistan among the most destitute countries in the world in terms of human development.

In 1996 the Taliban walked into this breach, immediately issuing edicts banning Afghan women from the public domain. The harshness of the terms of segregation evoked comparisons with South Africa's apartheid regime—leading human rights organizations in the West to call it "gender apartheid." Women were prohibited from working outside their homes, attending school, or appearing in public without a close male relative. They were forced to ride on "women only" public buses, were forbidden to wear brightly colored clothes, and had to have the windows in their houses painted so that they could not be seen from outside. Initially, they could only be treated by female doctors; later, they could be examined—but not seen or touched—by male doctors, in the presence of a male relative. The standard punishment for theft and adultery was public stoning, or even execution; yet a woman had no right to petition a court directly.

These ultraconservative policies and the hardships they imposed are by now quite well known—thanks in part to work done before the war in Afghanistan by women's groups in the United States. In 1998, for example, an alliance of women's rights groups protested the U.S. oil company Unocal's collaboration with the Taliban regime in a project to build a natural gas pipeline through Afghanistan. This grassroots campaign, much like the 1980s anti-apartheid movement for South Africa, publicized the plight of Afghan women and provided a new set of interlocutors in U.S. foreign policy. In essence, the message of this movement was that the conditions of life for Afghan women symbolized the total devastation of Afghan society.

From *Ethics & International Affairs*, vol. 16, issue 2, October 2002, pp. 15–20. Copyright © 2001 by Carnegie Council on Ethics & International Affairs. Reprinted by permission. Notes omitted.

The Status Of Women

From the beginning of the war, the status of women denied even the most basic human rights under the Taliban regime was a significant part of the moral justification for the antiterrorism campaign in Afghanistan. The Taliban's introduction of draconian measures against Afghan women left them exceedingly poor, unhealthy, and uneducated. In Afghan society, women constitute the most underprivileged group: the vast majority of the 22 million Afghans who rely on international assistance for survival have been women. Globally, they represent the most extreme example of what is known as the "feminization of poverty": for years their health care and nutritional needs have been ignored; their labor has gone unrecognized and unpaid; they have lacked access to education; they have been denied land ownership or inheritance rights; and they have had no decision-making power in the community. That is, they have had none of the resources they would need to escape the cycle of poverty.

Contributing to this near-total lack of capabilities women in particular have to adequately take care of themselves and their families is the fact that the Afghan crisis is currently the most serious and complex human emergency in the world. There are 1.1 million internally displaced people in Afghanistan and almost 3.6 million living in neighboring countries. The majority of them are women. Because of the disproportionate death toll in men during the war against the Soviet Union, it is women who are now charged with taking care of the approximately one million orphaned children, the elderly, and the handicapped—though they are, themselves, traumatized, malnourished, and undersupported.

How can the status of women in Afghanistan improve given these daunting challenges? The first thing to realize is that despite these appalling statistics, Afghan women are resources for development, not just victims. I can testify to their resilience and courage and to the contributions they have made in the past two decades of war. While men took up arms, Afghan women and their male supporters were busy rebuilding their communities by providing critically needed human services. Thus the success of rapid development schemes hinges on the formal rehabilitation and active protection of women's equal status in Afghan society.

The implications of gender inequality for the future of Afghanistan are significant given that women represent more than half of the population. Without their participation in political and economic life, it will be impossible for the country to develop and integrate successfully into a global society. What is needed to start the process is an up-to-date, accurate analysis of gender inequality. Reliable basic data—such as the percentage of women in the total population, family size, the number of households headed by women—and human development indicators for health, education, and income were last published in 1996.

Only after the appropriate data is collected can the government create responsible policies for gender mainstreaming—that is, for alleviating the segregation of women and their effective social, economic, and political marginalization. Women must be integrated into all sectors of Afghan society, including public life as paid government employees. For gender inequality to be addressed seriously, women need to participate more proportionately in government (currently, they hold only 11 percent of seats in the loya jirga council). They should also hold posts in all ministries, not just in the Ministry of Women's Affairs.

The War On Terrorism And Its Aftermath

Following a long lapse in U.S. interest in Afghanistan, this war-ravaged nation stood at the epicenter of world attention almost immediately after the September 11 attacks on U.S. soil. Afghanistan, which had been denied the credit it was due for having helped free the world of communism, now grabbed headlines for all the wrong reasons. Suddenly made famous as the homeland of the Taliban and host to Osama bin Laden and his mercenaries, Afghanistan was excoriated as a country that waged war against its women. The Western world did not need any more justifications than these to launch its offensive. For the first time in world history, a major war was being linked—however tenuously—to the freedom of women.

Initially, the people of Afghanistan—and women in particular—welcomed U.S. and international forces, publicly rejoicing in the streets of Kabul. As the euphoria wore off, however, the burqa-clad women were increasingly unwilling to emerge from their shroud-like coverings, alleging a lack of security, rampant rape, ethnic witch-hunting campaigns against the Pashtun tribe, generalized violence, and widespread abuse by various factions of the Northern Alliance forces. Women in refugee camps spoke of becoming the targets of recently disarmed men—whose new weapons were harassment and rape. Without the protection of security forces, refugee and internally displaced women from neighboring countries who had fled the war fear returning to their home areas in Afghanistan, while others fear leaving their homes to participate in public life as teachers, health workers, entrepreneurs, and government officials.

Given these dangers, women demonstrated remarkable courage during the recent loya jirga—the council that met in Kabul June 10–16 to elect a transitional government by articulating their long-held grievances against warlords and their armed supporters. Giving testimony was not without its risks, particularly for those who came from outside Kabul and whose safe return to their provinces and respectful treatment by local warlords could not be assured. As the campaign to bring down al-Qaeda progressed, both Afghan women and men had to be wary of the increased power of these warlords, whom the U.S.-led forces hoped to win over to the war on terrorism through gifts of weapons and money. Indeed, Afghan women cite this empowerment of warlords as one of the gravest threats to the establishment and the maintenance of a secure environment. For these reasons, multinational peacekeeping forces must be expanded beyond Kabul to provide security for women and all Afghans, and to train Afghan security forces which should themselves accept women recruits.

In addition to serious questions about basic security for women, there are deep socioeconomic issues for all Afghans such as the lack of adequate employment, education, income, and housing—coupled with a new nepotism among certain forces in power. Under these circumstances, the needs of Afghan women have once again been deferred. However, as the cases of intimidation against Sima Samar, the former minister of women's affairs, and other female loya jirga delegates indicate, women's issues concern everyone—not just women. Samar was alleged to have said that she did not believe in sharia (Islamic law), and was charged in court with blasphemy. Warlords invoked the allegation to threaten her repeatedly, and it became the basis for the Supreme Court chief justice's claim that she was not fit to hold a government office. It took the intervention of then-Chairman Karzai to abolish all charges against her and subsequently reassign her to head the Human Rights Commission. By undermining the legitimate representation of all Afghan people, gender-inspired threats to current or former government officials directly imperil the prospects for Afghanistan's success in building a state governed by the rule of law and the respect for human rights.

It is thus important that international nongovernmental organizations and other interlocutors pressure national governments to place conditionalities on reconstruction aid that are predicated on gender sensitivity. As soon as the transitional government gains access to the funds promised but as yet unreleased—at the International Conference for Reconstruction Assistance to Afghanistan in Tokyo last January, the international community will give its first attention to rebuilding political institutions and physical infrastructure, and to making provisions for security forces. Only a fraction of the funds may be used to address the social and civil institutions ravaged by the war. It is here, then, that the international community should reorient some of its priorities toward these latter institutions, and thereby show its commitment to helping build a peaceful, tolerant, and democratic Afghan society.

Looking Ahead

The era when states might commit grave human rights abuses against their own citizens with impunity is past. The U.S. public has, as a result of September 11, broad access to images of and news stories about human beings who are experiencing inordinate suffering. Will they reach out to help? That depends. First, Americans should reconsider the origins of the war in Afghanistan, and come to terms with the United States' own role in it. Second—and consequentially—they should understand that events in Afghanistan directly affect their lives in the United States.

As tragic as the attacks on September 11 were, one of their unintended outcomes was to produce renewed thinking about the need to address the inhumane conditions to which the Afghan people have long been subject. The most striking aspect of this effect is that rhetoric decrying the indecency and criminality of Taliban treatment of Afghan women actually passed from rhetoric to action. This may have simply been a by-product of the U.S.-led war on terrorism, but it should not distract us from accepting and building on these opportunities for the Afghan people and, especially, for Afghan women.

NO

Noy Thrupkaew

What Do Afghan Women Want?

The unveiling took place amid the giddy whirl of a $1,000 ticket, all-star production of Eve Ensler's *The Vagina Monologues* on Feb. 10, 2001. Raucous merriment had come and gone: Ensler conducted a chorus of ecstatically groaning celebrities, Glenn Close urged the audience to reclaim the c-word by yelling it at the top of its lungs. Then Oprah Winfrey recited Ensler's latest monologue, "Under the *Burqa*," and a hush fell over the crowd as Oprah exhorted its members to "imagine a huge dark piece of cloth / hung over your entire body / like you were a shameful statue." As the piece wound to a close, a figure in a *burqa* ascended to the stage. Oprah turned and lifted the head-to-toe shroud.

Voila! There stood Zoya, a young representative of the Revolutionary Association of the Women of Afghanistan (RAWA), the group of 2,000 Afghan women who had seized the West's imagination with ferociously anti-fundamentalist rhetoric, secret footage of Taliban atrocities and clandestine schools and hospitals for Afghan girls and women. Center stage, Zoya delivered a fiery speech about the oppression of Afghan women and RAWA's ongoing resistance to the Taliban regime. Eighteen thousand people leaped to their feet, and New York City's Madison Square Garden rang with cheers.

RAWA has always had a flair for the dramatic, and this appearance was no exception. It was pure, delicious theater: the stark words, the ominous, oppressive *burqa* and the "hey presto" transformation of suffering into strength with the flick of a hem. The unveiling also captured part of RAWA's appeal to American feminists, as it let the audience appreciate the friction between the image of silenced Afghan women and the brand of outspoken feminism that RAWA espouses.

Although the Pakistan- and Afghanistan-based group was founded in Kabul in 1977, RAWA didn't receive worldwide recognition until U.S. feminist campaigns for Afghan women's rights hit their stride in the late 1990s. After September 11, the attention only intensified. Hundreds of articles and two books chronicled RAWA's struggle, the group's *burqa*-clad members spoke across the United States and, at one point, a flashing banner reading "Welcome, Oprah viewers!" greeted visitors to RAWA's Web site.

But is a group that is inspirational in the United States effective in Afghanistan? With its confrontational, no-holds-barred language and allegiance to a secular society, RAWA reflects much of the Western feminist community's own values—

a fact that has earned RAWA strong support in the West but few friends in a strongly Muslim country weary of political battles and bloodshed. Similarly, part of RAWA's allure, for Ensler at least, has been its militant, radical, "uncompromising" nature, as Ensler told Salon.com in November 2001. But this quality has a dark side. RAWA has denounced numerous other Afghan women's groups as insufficientlly critical of fundamentalism. It has also publicly attacked prominent Afghan women activists—some of whom have in turn raised questions about RAWA's own political connections. As a result, Afghan women's nongovernmental organizations and Afghan feminist expatriates have expressed concern about a radical, lone-wolf organization garnering so much Western attention. In Afghanistan's slow, painful shift from war to nation building, they say, perhaps the country needs stronger support for voices of coalition building rather than for those advocating solitary revolution.

◈

To understand the nature of RAWA's partnership with Western feminists, it helps to return to the starting point for U.S. feminist activism on Afghan women's rights: the Feminist Majority's "Campaign to Stop Gender Apartheid in Afghanistan." Although the campaign has come under fire for a few alleged missteps—some critics have charged it with focusing too much on the *burqa* as a symbol of victimhood—the Feminist Majority's project has earned widespread praise for mobilizing grass-roots support and scoring significant U.S. political victories for Afghan women's rights.

After the Taliban militia seized control of Afghanistan in 1996, the Feminist Majority's staff began noticing "one-inch Associated Press clips that women couldn't go out unattended, couldn't gather, wear noisy shoes, white socks," according to Eleanor Smeal, the Feminist Majority's executive director. Shocked by these reports and by news that the Taliban had denied countless women access to work, health care and education, Feminist Majority staff consulted with the U.S. State Department and Afghan women activists in the United States before launching their campaign in 1997. Through a series of petitions, protests, celebrity fundraisers and political negotiations, the Feminist Majority played a significant role in the 1998 refusal by the United Nations and the United States to grant formal recognition to the Taliban. Its next pressure campaign helped push U.S. energy company Unocal out of a $3 billion venture to put a pipeline through Afghanistan, which would have provided the Taliban with $100 million in royalties. Within three years of launching the campaign, the Feminist Majority and its allies had also improved U.S. refugee policy toward Afghanistan, set up support for Afghan schools for girls and pushed through increases in emergency aid.

RAWA was only one of about 240 U.S. and Afghan women's groups the Feminist Majority contacted over the course of its campaign. But when the Feminist Majority invited RAWA to its Feminist Expo 2000, the campaign helped catapult the Afghan group into the spotlight. Dispatches from the exposition, a conference of 7,000 feminists from around the world, invariably mentioned the RAWA delegates' powerful speeches and passionate conviction. RAWA had officially caught the eye of the feminist world.

Ensler, too, played a vital role in bringing RAWA to the U.S. public's attention. After seeing RAWA's Pakistan-based orphanages and schools, where little girls were "being brought up as revolutionaries," Ensler became "completely smitten by [RAWA]" and decided to help, she told Salon.com. "V-Day," Ensler's worldwide campaign to eradicate violence against women through performances of The Vagina Monologues, awarded RAWA $120,000 in 2001 and a similar grant in 2002.

Nothing, however, drew attention to the plight of Afghan women like the aftermath of September 11. The Feminist Majority and RAWA were soon deluged with calls from the media. Smeal was quoted in countless articles; RAWA was so overwhelmed that members had to decline interview requests. RAWA's secret footage of public hangings and shootings, captured on video cameras hidden under its members' *burqas*, aired over and over on Saira Shah's *Beneath the Veil* documentary, which was in heavy rotation on CNN. Oprah viewers sent more digital cameras than RAWA could use, while poems from Western women imagining themselves under the *burqa* choked the group's Web site. The site also featured numerous songs, including one about RAWA's martyred founder written by the women's rock band Star Vomit. In short, RAWA became "the darling of the media and the feminists," recalls Illinois State University women's studies director Valentine M. Moghadam.

September 11 brought both the Feminist Majority and RAWA new momentum. The Feminist Majority purchased *Ms. Magazine* and published a special insert on its Afghanistan campaign to introduce itself to *Ms.* readers. Along with coalition partners Equality Now, the National Organization for Women and Ensler, the project, renamed the Campaign to Help Afghan Women and Girls, pushed for an expansion of security forces beyond Kabul and an increase in funding to the interim government and women-led NGOs. RAWA continued to raise funds for its schools and hospitals and went on speaking tours around the world. Both organizations were busy but productive, blessed with a resurgence of public interest and largely positive media attention. And then came the letter.

✦❀✦

On April 20, 2002, a U.S.-based RAWA supporter posted an open letter to *Ms.* on RAWA's listserv. It would later appear all over the Internet—on Middle Eastern studies' listservs and feminist online communities. Written by Elizabeth Miller from Cincinnati, the letter called Ms. Magazine the "mouthpiece of hegemonic, U.S.-centric, ego driven, corporate feminism." Miller proceeded to take the Feminist Majority to task for failing to mention the work of RAWA in its *Ms. Magazine* insert; it also charged the organization with ignoring the atrocities Afghan women suffered under the current U.S. allies in Afghanistan, the Northern Alliance. Even worse, the letter continued, was the Feminist Majority's support for the work of Sima Samar, then Afghanistan's interim minister of women's affairs. Miller claimed that Samar was "a member of the leadership council of one of the most notorious fundamentalist factions Hezb-e Wahdat [the Islamic Unity Party of Afghanistan]."

Asked about the letter, Smeal chuckles, then sighs. "The idea [behind the insert] was to introduce us by one of our campaigns," she says. Part of the insert's role was to tell "the pre-September 11, U.S. feminist story behind the campaign," according to Jennifer Jackman, the Feminist Majority's director of research. That story necessarily highlighted the unsung work of UN feminists, the two women appointed to the interim Afghan government and Afghan expatriate activist Sima Wali. The omission of RAWA was not political, Smeal insists. "We felt everyone knew RAWA," she said.

As for the letter's allegation that the Feminist Majority had not spoken out against the Northern Alliance, Smeal's own words to the media discount that. "The Northern Alliance is better than the Taliban toward women, but they are still not good," Smeal told me shortly after September 11. "We have to think beyond wartime, and we can't call some crowd 'freedom fighters' if they're not."

But the allegation against Samar was the most disturbing and difficult to dismiss. Human Rights Watch has charged Hezb-e Wahdat, a largely Hazara group, with taking part in reprisals against Pashtun civilians in northern Afghanistan. Some probing, however, finds little evidence that Samar has anything to do with Hezb-e Wahdat. Rather, what comes to light is a pattern of RAWA-led smear campaigns against other Afghan women who rise to prominence.

A strongly outspoken advocate for women's rights and a former RAWA member herself, Samar seems an unlikely member of Hezb-e Wahdat, although she is Hazara. Samar is renowned for her nonprofit group Shuhada, which operates hospitals and schools for girls throughout Pakistan and Afghanistan. In light of her women's work, the allegation of Samar's affiliation with a fundamentalist group is "baseless," says Jackman, especially considering the recent ultraconservative attacks that effectively prevented Samar from being reappointed to her position as women's affairs minister.

The Hezb-e Wahdat allegation surfaced throughout RAWA's interviews with the press, and also in a series of e-mails that a RAWA supporter named Sarah Kamal sent to Afghan expatriate activist Zieba Shorish-Shamley and the International Centre for Human Rights and Democratic Development, a Canadian organization that planned to award Samar a human-rights award in 2001. (The e-mails also included attacks against Fatana Gailani, executive director of the Afghanistan Women's Council and a four-time humanitarian-aid award winner for her work on behalf of Afghan refugees.) After conducting an investigation, the president of the organization wrote a letter dismissing the charges and lauding Samar's humanitarian work. Backed by Amnesty International research, the Canadian group found that Samar had set up schools and hospitals in Hazarajat, a Hezb-e-Wahdat-controlled area, and it concluded that "it would have been inevitable for Dr. Samar to be in touch with leaders of this party to facilitate her work. Contact with party officials is a common feature of humanitarian activity throughout Afghanistan but does not amount to taking up the membership of the party." Bolstered by references from organizations including the UN and the U.S.-based Afghan Refugee Information Network, the jury panel granted Samar the award.

As for Shorish-Shamley, she says she was initially supportive of RAWA but that her feelings changed when she saw the "vicious" nature of the accusations against Samar and Gailani. Shorish-Shamley shared an e-mail that she said RAWA wrote to Samar:

> While our beloved land is being reduced for more than a decade to a pulp in the filthy claws of a handful of fundamentalist executioners ... and RAWA, as the sole anti-fundamentalists organization, is at a tough strife with the insane Taliban and Jehadi gangs, it sounds really illogical to discuss the 'fighting with each other' but we are committed to expose it, for you are no longer 'ours,' as it is long ago you have aligned yourself to the rank of the most traitorous enemies of our people. We, thereby, treat you as a leader of the fundamentalists' party; alas it is as a part of our struggle against fundamentalism.

After continuing on for eight more vitriolic pages ("... persons like Sima Samar enjoy the favor of the fundamentalist slaughterers") the letter ends with an absurdly polite postscript: "As I was busy with many other preoccupations, sorry that it took time to reply [to] your letter."

⟨⊙⟩

Not surprisingly, RAWA's letter offensives and the distrustful atmosphere in Afghanistan have fueled rumors about the group's own political ties. Azadi Afghan Radio has reported that RAWA is "alleged to be run by men who belong to the former Afghan Maoist (pro-Chinese Shohla Communist Party) group." Other rumors include RAWA's alleged connection to Pakistani intelligence or Mujahideen-e Khalq, a group the U.S. State Department deemed a terrorist organization in 1999. RAWA member Saba denies all accusations, saying, "When women ... are leading a movement, it is difficult for people to tolerate. They think politics is only something for men."

The allegations haven't slowed RAWA down much. As the only Afghan feminist organization with significant Western support, media access and an Internet presence, RAWA has remained productive and resilient. Nor have RAWA's accusers chosen tactics likely to scorch the earth. The Azadi Afghan Radio, which has ties to the Northern Alliance, was careful to praise RAWA's "courage," and it advised Western supporters to speak to Afghans and NGOs about RAWA before making up their minds about the group. Afghan expatriate activists Wali and Shorish-Shamley have fielded many complaints from Afghan NGOs about RAWA, but both women were initially reluctant to air the grievances they heard.

Many of RAWA's Western backers, in turn, remain unfazed by rumors of unsavory political connections. Ensler has denied RAWA's alleged Maoist ties, telling Salon.com, "I may not be the most thorough investigator—that's why

I'm not a journalist." Nonetheless, she said in the same interview, "I've become RAWA's greatest defender."

The Feminist Majority, however, was none too pleased with RAWA's role in lobbing accusations at other groups. "We really have problems with groups attacking each other," says Jackman. "There needs to be solidarity among women's organizations." The Feminist Majority has refuted RAWA's attacks, but not as a matter of "public debate" because "we have not wanted to engage in debate other than over what strategies are most effective. It's not our role to be passing judgment on groups," Jackman says.

Now that the Feminist Majority is focusing on nation building rather than on fighting the Taliban's oppression of women, RAWA has ceased in any case to represent the strategy in greatest demand. "They're not involved in the [push for] security, women's participation, reconstruction, working with a lot of different groups," says Jackman. Some Afghan and Afghan-expatriate feminists put a finer point on this concern. The ability to work with others, build coalitions and use tactics that are in keeping with the more moderate "Afghan norm," says Wali, are all crucial skills for making the transition from resistance to reconstruction—and they are skills that RAWA seems to lack.

Navigating the factionalism and distrust of post-war Afghanistan would be a challenge for any political group, but the ground is clearly most fertile for one that is moderate and inclusive. Civil war, drought and interference from neighboring states have contributed to an atmosphere of mutual suspicion among Afghans, according to Neamat Nojumi, a Central and South Asian specialist and former *mujahideen* unit commander in the Soviet-Afghan war who is currently a United States Agency for International Development consultant. After years of Soviet occupation and wars among factions with extreme agendas, intimations of Maoist, Marxist or any overtly political agenda are terrifying for many Afghans, he says.

In this fragile environment, RAWA's perceived strengths—the uncompromising, radically feminist quality that Ensler recognizes as that of a "kindred spirit"—seem more like liabilities. As Ensler's quote attests, for many Western feminists, RAWA reflects a familiar yet glorified self-image: the fiery words, the clenched fists and protest signs, the type of guerilla feminism that seems unflinchingly brave. But to many Afghan women, RAWA's tactics look altogether too dangerous. Says Sayed Sahibzada, an Afghan United Nations Development Programme officer who has worked with more than 40 Afghan women-led NGOs, "I have not heard one group that goes along with RAWA. They say, 'If there is a RAWA participant [in a training], we are not going to participate.'" New York City's large Afghan-American population is similarly conflicted about the group. Masuda Sultan of Women for Afghan Women lauds RAWA's "long and committed history" of bravery. But she notes that "most Afghan women don't feel that RAWA represents them," because of the group's revolutionary rhetoric and alleged ties to Maoism.

RAWA has done little to build bridges. In addition to the campaign against Samar and Gailani, it has often shunned other women's groups. RAWA member Saba took issue with all the prominent Afghan and Afghan-American women I mentioned, saying that they had been part of the Northern Alliance, or the Soviet regime, or hadn't taken a strong stand against fundamentalism. This stance hasn't won over many Afghans: One activist calls RAWA the "Tali-babes" because of its fiercely judgmental attitude.

But to effectively counter RAWA's perceived intolerance, opposing feminist groups need to build coalitions themselves. "I'm not trying to bring [RAWA] down. We have to work across political boundaries and viewpoints," says Wali. "They are one of the diverse voices of Afghan women." But RAWA's radical language and tactics, along with the strategies of some Western feminists—such as Ensler, who brought *The Vagina Monologues* to Pakistan and Afghanistan—"backfire on people like us," says Wali. "We are trying to influence the men, many of whom still have Taliban ideology, and they say, 'You are part of these extremists.' It's not time yet. We can't do something extreme and leave Afghan women to deal with it. [RAWA has] a very Westernized radical approach. They are revolutionary. The Afghan people are saying we don't need a revolution, we need a democracy."

Afghanistan may be closer now than ever to a day when voices such as RAWA's won't seem dangerously radical. But in the meantime, Western feminists need to support, fund and take their cues from the other "moderate ... diverse voices of Afghan women," and keep the pressure on their own governments, says Wali. This is something that even RAWA fan Ensler is beginning to do by working with Samar and by contributing to other groups. The Feminist Majority has nurtured connections with Samar's Shuhada group, which kept open numerous clinics, hospitals and schools in the central part of Afghanistan despite the Taliban's restrictions, as well as with the Pakistan-based Afghan Women's Resource Center, among many other Afghan NGOs.

In their own way, these Afghan groups are themselves "revolutionary," says Jackman. "This is a place where giving a girl a book and a pencil is revolutionary." Equally revolutionary is the dedication "to sharing the same agenda," adds Jackman. Even women who were formerly "arch rivals" are working together, says Wali, and their willingness to reach across ethnic and political divides is an important step toward forging trust in the strife-torn country. "There are so many non-partisan Afghan community organizers and leaders," says Wali, "but no one hears them because they are trying to mend society. RAWA has a place in that society, but we need to sit down together—especially with the dissenting, far-fetched voices—and realize that we have a common agenda....We are waging a jihad of social justice and peace. We need to transcend our differences and work together—that is the key to rebuilding Afghanistan."

POSTSCRIPT

Have Afghan Women Been Liberated From Oppression?

Afghanistan has been eclipsed by Iraq as the focus for international media attention. Even when a story is reported from inside Afghanistan, however, it almost always reflects life in the capital city of Kabul. President Hamid Karzai lives and works in a heavily fortified area in Kabul and rarely ventures outside the capital. For most women (and men) in Afghanistan, village life proceeds as it always has. A good place to begin exploring this issue might be with the Amnesty International Report *Afghanistan: Women Under Attack*. Published in May 2005, the report compiled by Nazia Hussein reflects interviews she conducted with women across the country. It details the persistence of feudal customs, in which men treat women as property with no fear of punishment or social disapproval. Afghan women, the report concludes, are murdered, raped, and imprisoned with impunity.

Women for Afghan Women, Sunita Mehta, ed., (Palgrave Macmillan, 2002) is a collection of essays, poems, and photographs from the organization named in the title. An introduction by Sima Wali, author of the "Yes" side of this issue, defines the Afghan people as historically and ethnically distinct from both Arabs and Iranians, describes the languages they speak—chiefly Dari and Pashto—and strongly asserts their lack of connection with Osama bin Laden and Al-Qaeda. Essays dispel the stereotype of Afghan men as "women-haters" and explore both the *loya jirga* and United Nations policies as they affect Afghan women. Cheryl Benard's *Veiled Courage: Inside the Afghan Women's Resistance* (Broadway Books, 2002) explores the resistance of Afghan women to oppression. She provides a history of RAWA (Revolutionary Association of the Women of Afghanistan), beginning with its founding in the late 1970s by a charismatic woman known as Meena, who was killed by Pakistani police with ties to the Afghan secret police. Her courageous leadership continues to inspire RAWA members today, especially the 11 elected women who comprise leadership. RAWA members serve as role models for others who face demoralizing conditions and engage both supporters and challengers in dialogue. Resisting the current project of nation building that accepts ethnic identity as the most important factor, RAWA seeks to alter the culture of female inferiority by altering patterns of male socialization and ideals of masculinity.

My Forbidden Face: Growing Up Under the Taliban, a Young Woman's Story by Latifa (Talk Miramax, 2002) offers a true account of Kabul life from 1996–2001, by a young author using a pseudonym. Educated during the Soviet occupation and ready to begin her university education as a journalist in 1996, "Latifa" describes how her life was "confiscated" by the Taliban. Her narrative concludes as the American bombing begins in October 2001: "... who speaks for Afghanistan? I don't know anymore." *Prisoners of Hope: The Story of Our Captivity and Freedom in Afghanistan* (Doubleday, 2002), by Dayna Curry and Heather Mercer, describes the imprisonment, trial by the Taliban, and rescue by U.S. Special Forces of two Christian missionaries from Waco, Texas. And *Behind the Burqa: Our Life in Afghanistan and How We Escaped to Freedom* by "Sulima" and "Hala" as told to Batya Swift Yasgur (John Wiley & Sons, 2002), is the story of two sisters, 16 years apart in age. "Sulima," the elder, fled the Communist regime in 1979 and "Hala," the younger, fled persecution by the Taliban in 1997. Both were working to educate women. Finally, the first novel in English about Afghanistan is *The Kite Runner* (Penguin, 2003) by Khaled Hosseini, a physician now living in the United States. It is especially helpful in illustrating the power of tribal differences (majority Pashtun and minority Hazara) as well as sectarian ones (majority Sunni and minority Shi'a). It evokes life before the Soviet invasion and confronts the repressive Taliban regime as well.

Is the Influence of the European Union in World Affairs Increasing?

YES: Mitchell P. Smith, from "Soft Power Rising," *World Literature Today* (January/February 2006)

NO: Efstathios T. Fakiolas, from "The European Union's Problems of Cohesion," *New Zealand International Review* (March/April 2007)

ISSUE SUMMARY

YES: Political science and international studies professor Mitchell P. Smith argues that the European Union excels in the use of soft power to achieve desired outcomes at minimal cost, by avoiding the use of military force and sharing the burden of enforcement with others.

NO: Efstathios T. Fakiolas, Strategy and SouthEast European Affairs Analyst, contends that Europe's failure to achieve European "Union-hood" seriously hampers its effectiveness in the global community.

T he European Union (EU) is celebrating its fiftieth anniversary in 2007. From the early common market forged by the European Coal and Steel Community in 1951, through the 1957 Treaty of Rome that created the European Economic Community, to the so-called Maastricht Treaty that created the European Union in May 1993, Europe has been on a path toward great cohesiveness. Almost a half billion people, from 27 member nations, share unfettered economic and commercial exchange. Thirteen of the 27 member nations share a common currency, the Euro, as do four nations not currently members of the EU—Andorra, the Holy See, Monaco, and San Marino. There is a flag, with a circle of 12 gold stars against a deep blue background, and an anthem, based on "Ode to Joy" from Beethoven's Ninth Symphony.

Some of the member nations—Bulgaria, Estonia, Finland, Latvia, Lithuania, Romania, and Slovenia—might not fit the traditional image of Europe. And three unequivocally European nations—Iceland, Norway, and Switzerland—are not members of the EU and have no wish to be. There is no common language or shared media. In fact, the European Parliament in Brussels, Belgium, conducts its business in 20 official languages and can seem distant and impersonal. A proposed constitution, drafted by former French President Valerie Giscard d'Estang and 104 colleagues comprising a Convention on Europe's Future, although signed amid great celebration in Rome in 2004 by all member nations and three candidate countries, has failed to be ratified. When France and the Netherlands voted no, the ratification process was effectively brought to a standstill.

There is significant tension over the question of how much of a federation Europe should be. At the same time, there is a strong commitment to shared values among citizens of the European Union, which favors diplomacy and internationalism to resolve global disputes and is formally committed to peace, opposition to the death penalty, and support of climate initiatives to resist or reverse global warming. There is also substantial opposition to what is often perceived as hegemony on the part of the United States. In the current flash points in Iraq and Iran, Europe favors talking and holding out carrots rather than brandishing sticks.

This issue focuses on the contrast between hard and soft power. Clearly, the United States is the master of hard power, with its military might and sophisticated weapons systems. Europe trades in soft power, defined by Joseph Nye as the ability to get others to follow, through attraction rather than coercion. The "yes" side argues that Europe's soft power is on the rise. The "no" side cites Europe's lack of cohesion and "union-al" identity as serious barriers to its influence on the world stage.

YES

Mitchell P. Smith

Soft Power Rising: Romantic Europe in the Service of Practical Europe

Few successful international organizations can claim romantic as well as practical origins. In fact, the European Union (EU) is unique in its blending of (1) romantic aspirations for transcendence of the ills of the nation-state in the aftermath of two world wars and (2) practical objectives of enhancing the political stability and economic prosperity of its members.

The preamble to the Treaty of Rome that created the European Economic Community in 1957 embodies both elements of the European integration project. The romantic dimension finds expression in the call for "ever closer union among the peoples of Europe," and reference to the pooling of resources "to preserve and strengthen peace and liberty." Elsewhere in the preamble, the quest for removal of obstacles to "steady expansion, balanced trade, and fair competition" and "the progressive abolition of restrictions on international trade" gives voice to practical Europe. A half-century later, have practical considerations overwhelmed the romantic, or has the romantic longing for unity proven an obstacle to practical achievement? Arguably, as the European Union seeks a renewed sense of purpose and direction after conjuring a single currency and expanding to twenty-five member states, concrete objectives are attainable only as long as the romantic notion of constructing a better world finds resonance on the European continent and beyond.

The contemporary juxtaposition of a United States that appears to have shed the romance and idealism of its founding and the apogee of Europe's romantic dimension have prompted widespread interest in the EU as a meaningful global entity. Several recent accounts emerging from this tension portray the European Union as an anti-America: an increasingly unified world of low inequality, concern for the cohesiveness of society, respect for the environment, and commitment to a peaceful world order and resolution of conflicts through engagement and diplomacy. This romantic Europe is a magnetic pole of attraction, both to aspiring member states (the region of aspirants stretches increasingly further eastward, initially into the central European states of Poland, the Czech Republic, and Hungary, and now to Ukraine and Georgia as well as northward to the Baltics and southward to the Balkans) and to poorer countries outside the European continent that seek a reliable provider of development assistance and access to important markets.

From *World Literature Today*, January–February 2006, pp. 20–23. Copyright © 2006 by World Literature Today. Reprinted by permission.

More cynical observers—hard-headed realists in the language of international-relations theory, such as Robert Kagan, who in his much-debated 2002 *Policy Review* article contrasted Europe's weakness with America's strength—suggest that this postconflict semi-utopia is possible only with the military security provided by the United States. For these analysts, Europe must be judged by its practical self, and, from this perspective, it is a troubled entity. The large European Union economies—especially Germany and Italy, but France as well—characterized by sluggish growth, population aging, and persistent mass unemployment, appear to be spent forces relative to the dynamism of the United States. The European Union has proven ineffectual in responding to recent episodes of conflict and instability on the European continent. Such a Europe offers little as a model for emerging capitalist democracies and remains inconsequential as a global actor.

The coexistence of triumph and failure in the European Union during the past two years has added to the ambiguity of Europe's trajectory and to the apparent tension between the romantic and the practical. At midnight on April 1, 2004, fireworks lit the skies across central and eastern European capitals as countries from the former Soviet bloc (along with Malta and Greek Cyprus) celebrated their official accession to the European Union. With the expansion to twenty-five members, the European Union became a single market in goods, services, and capital for 455 million citizens, consumers, and businesspeople. Referendums on joining the EU were endorsed with enthusiasm by central and eastern European publics. As the world's largest market for goods and services, the EU appeared to be on the rise as a border-free region with a single currency of increasing heft in the international economy.

The proposed EU constitution—negotiated in 2002–3 and ultimately signed and sealed in December 2004—promised to codify the stunning achievements of the EU and create a foundation for effective decision making in a body of twenty-five members and more. Once in effect in 2006, the constitution would create the framework for more powerful global projection of the EU's voice. The organization sought to accomplish this by codifying the aspirations of the European Union and especially by increasing the continuity of the leadership of EU institutions and creating a single ministry for European Union foreign affairs.

As the first ten EU member states ratified the constitutional treaty, the EU appeared in spring 2005 to be well on the way to fulfilling its potential as a global power. Then, the fragility of the entire apparatus was ostensibly revealed by the French electorate's rejection of the constitution and an even more resounding "no" from a Dutch citizenry historically supportive of the integration project. More profound than the "no" votes themselves was the sense of uncertainty that emerged across Europe. Directionlessness prevailed. In Italy, a government minister (granted, from a right-wing populist party) called for abandonment of the European currency, the euro, and the return of the historically flimsy Italian lira. Confidence in the euro slipped, and EU political leaders expressed uncertainty about how to proceed. "Crisis" became a mantra.

In fact, Europe's current malaise preceded the French and Dutch referendum results. Given the size of the single European market and the large share of the EU in global trade, the EU has established parity with the United States in its ability to set the terms of global economic exchange. Speaking with one voice in the World Trade Organization, the EU is a pivotal actor in the setting of the global trade agenda and establishment of rules governing international finance and trade in goods and services. Building on this accomplishment and the introduction of the euro in 1999, leaders of EU member states meeting at a summit in Lisbon in 2000 articulated the lofty goal of becoming "the world's most dynamic, knowledge-based economy" by the end of the decade. Surpassing the dynamism of the U.S. economy was the aim. Progress toward this objective has proven elusive, however. Efforts to develop new mechanisms for job creation and intensified investment have yielded few results. The course of the Lisbon project bears little resemblance to the earlier project of establishing a single European market by 1992. In that endeavor—beginning in the mid-1980s, when the Europeans set their sights on a rising Japan as well as the United States, and so brilliantly crafted under the leadership of European Commission president Jacques Delors, a former French finance minister—the goals and means to the single market were firmly established, as were the costs of not acting. A decade later, the Lisbon objectives were nebulous and the means to attain them unclear and contested. In fact, between 2000 and 2006, the EU has by most measures lost ground relative to the United States. More than midway through the decade, the Europeans find themselves farther from their goal than when they began their quest for economic supremacy.

Nevertheless, there is a looming gap in global leadership that the EU, at least in part, may be positioned to fill. A United States mired in Iraq faces intense international unpopularity, if not outright hostility. This unpopularity is not limited to French impatience with American hyper-puissance but in fact emanates from numerous corners, ranging from those antagonized by pronounced American unilateralism and antiglobalization activists around the world to actors in developing countries opposed to U.S. overconsumption of global resources. The ability of the United States to set the agenda for global affairs, and the extent to which people across the globe look to the United States for leadership in solving international problems, appears to be waning in the opening years of the twenty-first century.

Critics of U.S. foreign policy warn that policymakers have lost sight of the crucial significance of "soft" power. As articulated by international-relations scholar Joseph Nye, soft power is the ability to get others to follow, by virtue of attraction rather than coercion. Soft power enables the possessor to achieve desired outcomes at minimal cost by avoiding the use of military force and sharing the burden of enforcement with allies. Whereas hard power remains relatively concentrated (with annual U.S. military expenditures exceeding those for all EU member states combined), there has been a geographical diffusion of other forms of power. This is especially true of economic power, which is increasingly shared not only by the EU and the United States but also by China and such rising regional economic powers as Brazil, South Africa, and India. In this environment, the EU, as a leader in global humanitarian aid and development assistance, appears ascendant in the global hierarchy by virtue of its soft power. If the romantic longing to knit nations and peoples together in peace and prosperity represents a European vision, soft power is a means to its realization.

Romantic Europe, it seems, is bearing fruit in the form of increased attraction as a locus of global problem solving and a system of values and institutions worthy of emulation.

The most compelling evidence of EU soft-power ascendance is the transformation undertaken by numerous governments in response to the lure of EU membership. The foremost examples are in eastern and central Europe, where dramatic transitions toward democracy and market economies occurred in the space of a decade The behavior of other governments, including Turkey and Ukraine, with a combined population of more than 100 million, also has been altered by the attraction of eventual EU membership. Furthermore, the new member states have extended outward the geographical embrace of the European integration project. The Slovenian government has become a leading advocate for Croatian membership in the EU. Poland champions the Ukrainian cause. The European Union has been a touchstone for Ukraine in the aftermath of the Orange Revolution, helping define the path toward more efficient and less corrupt administration, reforming relations between state and society, and pursuing Ukrainian membership in the World Trade Organization.

Indeed, in his February 2005 speech before the European Parliament, Ukrainian president Viktor Yuschenko announced that "the new president and government of Ukraine have clearly defined the ingredients and forms for future decisions. These are the norms and standards of the European Union, its legislation, legal, political, economic, and social culture. European integration is the most effective and, in fact, the only programme of reforms for contemporary Ukraine."

Although its ultimate place in Europe remains highly contested, the Turkish government, under pressure from the EU institutions in which it seeks full participation, has during the past five years adopted an impressive array of reforms. Most significant of these is a serious effort to curtail the powers of the Turkish military. The National Security Council, formerly a vehicle for the military's exercise of power over the executive, has been transformed into an advisory body with a civilian majority. Parliament has been granted greater powers of oversight over the defense budget. The government even has pursued corruption charges against senior officers, a departure from the untouchable status of the officer corps in the recent past. In a set of constitutional reforms passed in 2001, Turkey abolished the death penalty except in times of war and for terrorist crimes, eased conditions for the broadcast and publication of materials in the Kurdish language, and broadened rights of political parties, trade unions, and other intermediary associations. The EU has been a catalyst for revival of the Turkish government's privatization program in the face of a reluctant state bureaucracy, entailing the withdrawal of government ownership from a wide range of state economic enterprises in industries from telecommunications to cigarettes, steel, and cement and from seaports to thermal-power plants. The EU continues to press Ankara for additional reforms in the areas of women's rights and the rights of non-Muslim minorities.

Consonant with its rising soft power, the EU has captured a certain moral authority yielded by the United States. The conflict in Chechnya illustrates this point. Although the Russian government was by many accounts responsible for widespread human-rights abuses in its war in Chechnya, U.S. criticism of Russia was muted in the face of the Russian government's claim to be fighting the global war on terror alongside the United States. The EU, in contrast, submitted draft resolutions condemning Russian human-rights abuses in Chechnya to the UN Human Rights Commission in 2002, 2003, and 2004. The European Parliament was vocal in its criticism of the Russian human-rights violations. The credibility of EU institutions was elevated by virtue of their central role as advocates for the rights of Russian minorities in the Baltic states prior to their accession to the EU in 2004. Moreover, the European Union is now taking a leading role in the reconstruction of Chechnya following a decade of war. This includes such citizen initiatives as the French-based student group Etudes sans Frontieres, modeled after the Paris-based Medecins sans Frontieres, which has brought a small group of students from the University of Grozny to study in the French university system.

In the realm of humanitarian aid, the EU and its member states are by far the global leaders. Assailed for its inability to wield hard power in Bosnia and Kosovo, the EU led the humanitarian relief effort. In recent months the EU has devoted substantial resources to famine relief in Ethiopia and Eritrea, drought relief in Afghanistan, natural-disaster preparation in the central Asian republics, food aid in Niger and Mali, and promotion of regional economic integration in the Common Market for Eastern and Southern Africa. U.S. development and humanitarian aid has fallen steadily as a share of gross domestic product for more than four decades (to less than one-tenth of 1 percent, far lower than the poorest of the older fifteen EU member states, Greece and Portugal); levels in EU member states remain closer to those sustained by the United States at the peak of its soft power in the 1960s. The European Union seeks to reach an aid level of 0.56 percent of GDP by 2010. EU member states lead the effort on behalf of global poverty alleviation. Many development economists insist that aid does not foster autonomous economic growth; nevertheless, as the U.S. military learned in Indonesia in the wake of the 2004 tsunami, deployment of national resources for benign aims generates enhanced esteem around the globe.

Consistent with its predilection for the exercise of soft power, a Europe that rivals the United States economically wishes to equal the United States as a diplomatic power, even while leaving U.S. military supremacy uncontested. Iran offers a first test of whether this will be possible. The European Union, with the British, French, and German governments acting in the name of the entire organization, has led the way in nuclear diplomacy in Iran. Iran has resisted EU inducements, moving forward with its nuclear program, and the outcome remains undetermined. However, it is clear that, for the Iranian government, the EU is the only possible interlocutor. The United States hulks in the background, casting a shadow over negotiations with periodic threats to use force if necessary; with the United States mired in Iraq, such threats bear little credibility.

So how do we assess the rising soft power of the European Union in comparison, say, with the supreme military power of the United States? Above all, it must be kept in mind that in terms of trade, flows of capital, and international rule-making, the United States-EU relationship is the most densely interdependent on the globe. The United States and EU, in other words, are in fact more partners than rivals. An economically weak European Union is not in the interest of the United States, nor is it helpful for the global economy. The same may be said for a diplomatically weak EU. Pressing global problems cannot be resolved without international leadership, and mounting evidence indicates the United States can no longer lead alone.

How should we conceptualize soft power? Does it have a long half-life? Is it as easily created as destroyed? Experience suggests that, because soft power is largely a product of how others perceive the motives of a nation's policies, a concept closely related to trust, soft power tends to reproduce itself. Soft power begets soft power, just as mistrust begets misperception and further mistrust. In contrast, the U.S. experience in Iraq suggests that hard power, when used without a patina of soft power, can degrade if it does not swiftly produce the desired result. Prophets of international politics have incorrectly predicted the demise of military power as a source of international influence in the past. But soft power has long been a necessary complement to hard power, a dimension of power that enhances and renders more durable hard-power resources. Are we perhaps witnessing a growing disjuncture in the distribution of hard- and soft-power resources?

Ultimately, the EU's soft-power ascendance does not mean the EU will achieve all its economic and diplomatic objectives in the coming decade. Scholars generally agree that in order to enhance its global role, the EU will need to balance its stock of soft power with a modicum of hard power—something it has attempted to do through creation of a 60,000-strong European Rapid Reaction Force designed to address tasks of peacekeeping and emergency intervention on the European continent and beyond. The EU also must transcend its current malaise wrought of uncertainty and internal conflict and develop a renewed sense of purpose. Sustaining soft power demands resources; reviving economic growth is not a simple matter for countries with adverse ratios of active to retired persons and heavy public-pension burdens. Plans to increase global development aid will meet popular resistance without an improvement in domestic economic conditions. In the wake of the negative referendum outcomes in France and the Netherlands, European publics seem reluctant to countenance membership enlargement beyond Bulgaria and Romania, both slated for membership next year. If Turkey is rebuffed in the wake of heroic efforts to secure democracy, the EU pole may lose some of its magnetic pull.

In other words, practical achievements in European integration and the romantic longing for unity are interdependent. In the absence of sufficient material resources, the yearning for deeper union will falter; without a vibrant romantic Europe, the EU will struggle to transcend its internal languor. Similarly, only the vitality of romantic Europe can ensure the continued accumulation of soft power by the European Union and kindle the promise of a more influential EU in the world. A European Union with burgeoning soft-power resources would hardly emerge as a global hegemon. However, such an EU may well be an essential purveyor of global stability as the wedge between concentrated hard-power and diffuse soft-power resources deepens.

Efstathios T. Fakiolas  **NO**

The European Union's Problems of Cohesion

The end of the war in 1945 left Germany entirely humiliated and Britain's and France's erstwhile mastery in world politics in ruins. Yet, while throughout Europe proper democracies might be counted only on the fingers of one hand, a course of building an Iron Curtain partitioning the continent into two rival camps was set in train. This occurred because most of Europe's governments and peoples had been dragged into the vortex of the Second World War. And they had war because as Robert Schuman, one of the founding fathers of today's European Union, put it: 'Europe was not united'.

However, the experience of decline, along with the direct threat posed by the Soviet Union and its Central and East European satellites, stimulated elites in Western Europe to set off, under the guidance of the United States, a process of integration by establishing the European Coal and Steel Community in 1952 and the European Economic Community in 1958. Nearly fifty years later, the process of enlarging and deepening integration in Europe, coupled with the end of the Cold War and the collapse of the Soviet Union and Yugoslavia, has led not only to the creation of a European common market and monetary union with a single currency but also to the incorporation of eight Central and East European countries (Hungary, Czech Republic, Poland, Slovakia, Slovenia, Lithuania, Latvia, Estonia) into the European Union. Today, most of Europe's peoples (450 million out of more than 820 million) and countries (25 out of 48, including the five so-called 'Lilliputians': Andorra, Monaco, Liechtenstein, Holy See and San Marino), stretching from the Atlantic coasts of Portugal and Ireland to the outer borders of mainland Russia and Turkey, are full members of a common economic and political space, of an increasingly integrated Union marked out by inter-governmental bargains and supranational dynamics in which, closing ranks as Europeans, they enjoy security and prosperity. What is more, in their collective capacity as a Union, they are able to perform a leading, though not yet determining, role in world politics.

Secondary Status

Notwithstanding the European Union's global economic power, to date Europe has not restored its erstwhile hegemony on the world stage. It is still being

From *New Zealand Review*, vol. 32, issue 2, March–April 2007, pp. 19–23. Copyright © 2007 by New Zealand Institute of International Affairs. Reprinted by permission.

relegated to the rank of a great power plagued by 'capability-expectations gap' weaknesses. This owes much to what Henry Kissinger points out: 'United Europe will continue as a Great Power; divided into national states, it will slide into secondary status.' A case in point, in that regard, has been the US-led war in Iraq, which has left Europe bitterly divided and its prestige severely raped. Incompatible leadership and national pursuits undeniably bear much of the blame for this development. The roots of the division, one might venture, lie in what Valery Giscard d'Estaing—the influential former French President, who chaired the Convention on the Future of Europe, which on 18 July 2003 submitted to the EU member-states the 'Draft Treaty Establishing a Constitution for Europe'—asserts: 'you can't build a society purely on interests; you need a sense of belonging'.

In reality, contrary to Giscard d'Estaing's view, in terms of international distinctiveness and European commonality a shared sense of belonging to Europe among EU elites and publics exists, and with every passing day it grows. But the sense of belonging to the same 'European family' is technocratic, based on functional utility and common foundations of Europe's national identities and virtues, rather than sentimental, grounded on community attachment and allegiance. This sense in itself can hardly serve as a powerful intellectual and cultural force for much closer integration, as a constructive belief tool of binding and underpinning a full-fledged Union. At the core of the problem, therefore, is the question of the conceptualisation of an evolving EU identity. Something more is needed than a mere feeling of externally and internally recognisable legal-institutional identification and political and economic togetherness.

Loosened Ties

Indeed, the war in Iraq has resulted in loosening the ties of the European Union. Early in 2003, on the one hand, France took the lead, backed as it was by Germany and Russia, to campaign against the war and ultimately succeeded in building up a blocking coalition in the Security Council, which denied US plans the legitimacy of a UN resolution. On the other, the leaders of five member states (United Kingdom, Italy, Spain, Portugal and Denmark) and three then candidate countries (Poland, Hungary and Czech Republic) of the European Union issued a public statement laying down the reasons for their determination to help Washington in its efforts to overthrow Saddam Hussein. To this was added a declaration of a similar commitment of support by governments of ten states of the former Soviet bloc, of which seven were accession or potential candidate countries (Estonia, Latvia, Lithuania, Slovakia, Slovenia, Romania, Bulgaria, Albania, Croatia, and Macedonia).

Despite the opposition of the French-German axis and Russia, the United States succeeded in forming a coalition of the willing, rallying forces from 35 countries round the flag. Of those states, six originated from the EU-15 and thirteen from the EU-25, while nine were European but not EU member-states. Against France and Germany, three out of the five great powers of the EU-15, that is United Kingdom, Italy and Spain, supported the Bush administration's moves. To a certain degree, it was the decision of the eight Central and East European states out of the ten new member states of the European Union to throw in their lot with the United States that tipped the scales against those member-states who were pledged to stand up to American designs. Hence, no matter how marginal in number and in terms of population and economic might, the majority of the European Union and Europe sided with Washington in waging war on Iraq. This in turn set the stage for a dramatic split between two polar opposites, the 'old' and the 'new' Europes, as Donald Rumsfeld, the then US Secretary of Defense, characteristically labelled them. Natural as it was, this division led to the paralysis of EU foreign policy, thereby preventing it from playing a constructive, if any, resolution part in the conflict.

United Opposition

Interestingly, the division of Europe over Iraq has had to do with its governments, not with its peoples. Unlike their leadership, the overwhelming majority of European citizens were united in their peace-loving attitude. This fact was not merely under-appreciated. More important still, it eroded the European public support for the war. On 15 February 2003, massive anti-war demonstrations swept most European capitals. Of the five largest peace protests, three were held in London, Madrid and Rome, the capitals of the United States' staunchest EU allies. In light of the growing gap between European political leaderships and publics, it is not by chance that Giscard d'Estaing named this day as the birthday of European consciousness, while Romano Prodi, the then President of the European Commission, was said to have declared that the governments of the EU countries had no choice but to follow their peoples.

It is true that the Central and East European member states of the European Union have found themselves in confusion with regard to the shape the Union they have recently joined should finally take. This basically relates to a split inside the European Union itself between those who advocate that European integration should go wider without expropriating more power from national governments and those who favour much stronger federalist impulses. At the same time, the Central and East European newcomers are determined not simply to preserve national sovereignties and identities retrieved after decades of Soviet rule but also to establish their right not to be treated as second-class fellows of the club. As they are convinced that Washington has historically been the most reliable defender of liberal democracy, they deem the anti-hegemonic actions of Paris and Berlin as biased against the United States. This may result in the eruption of an irreversible rift between the European Union and the United States and, by extension, in the breakdown of the trans-Atlantic security regime. From this angle, they appear to distrust French President Jacques Chirac, who has both warned them against their quite benevolent attitude towards the United States over the use of force in Iraq and berated them for pursuing an influence that their capabilities barely warrant.

Core Axis

All in all, the opinion widely held at that time that European countries were once more as deadly divided as they had so often been in the past is a matter of taste and ephemeral impression, not of real substance. Notwithstanding several rivalries caused by specific national interests and the circumstances of the time, the French-German axis or strategic partnership remains the cornerstone of EU politics, though without being the predominant force within the Union. Nothing proceeds in the latter without prior consultation and agreement between France and Germany. Unless these two countries reach a compromise and take the lead in advancing new policies, the European Union is most often driven into stagnation. Attempts at isolating or breaking up this partnership are doomed to failure. Thoughts of bringing London, Madrid and Rome together into an alternative leadership coalition intended to line up with the Central and East European newcomers in a US-leaning 'new' European bloc have been, if not shattered with the recent fall of the pro-American Jose Maria Aznar government in Spain, relegated to the realm of planning and rhetoric.

Rather, the consensus on the need for unity and solidarity has been restored in the European Union. In December 2003 EU heads of government decided to put Giscard d'Estaing's constitutional treaty to a ratification process. This treaty was expected both to forge the commonality among the member states and to enhance European Union's international standing, democratic accountability, functional coherence and policy effectiveness. Recent resounding French and Dutch No votes have cast doubts on whether the EU Constitution has any hope of being implemented, but it is notable that among the first member-states to ratify it were Lithuania, Hungary, and Slovenia. The Central and East European newcomers appreciate the positive effects of accession and see themselves as integral parts of the Union. They realise they must work with the European Union, which represents a dynamic process of integration over which they have a unique privilege of say and possibility of control. It is no coincidence that Slovenia has since the first days of 2007 become the thirteenth member-state of the European Monetary Union, while Estonia, Lithuania, Poland, Hungary and the Czech Republic are intent on meeting the criteria and joining the Euro-zone by 2010 at latest.

Full Circle

Despite controversies and numerous setbacks, to come full circle, the European Union has within the span of half a century evolved into a growing and increasingly integrated union of nation-states. A clear sign of the attractiveness of EU membership is the fact that two South-east European countries, Bulgaria and Romania, joined the Union in January 2007, three more have been conferred the status of candidacy (Croatia, Macedonia, Turkey) and four have been formally placed as potential candidates in queue (Albania, Montenegro, Bosnia-Herzegovina and Serbia with Kosovo). Today, the European Union has first-tier great power attributes and a considerable pool of human and material resources; as well as supranational administrative capabilities, and an acquis communautaire detailed in about 80,000 pages of regulations, directives, and decisions covering almost everything from monetary affairs and the environment through safety rules in workplaces to foreign, security, and defence policy. Still, it aspires to carve out its own sphere of influence through particular region-building and boundary-drawing policies in South-east Europe and the Mediterranean. Last but not least, it proves able to transform border conflicts and, thereby, provide security within and outside its region.

All this progress is boosting the dynamics of EU integration, above all mirrored in the fact that the political, economic, and social future of Europe and most European states is being affected more by decisions taken in Brussels than in the capitals of the great European or non-European powers of our day. Europe's security, growth, and development are all the more dependent on the fate of the European Union. The result is that the European Union's institutional and legal apparatus of ruling, along with its firm commitment to democratic decision-making procedures, confer on its citizens a broader if somewhat loose sense of belonging to a common European grouping. Put differently, EU institutions, law, norms, policies, and funding mechanisms serve as a solid, functional basis for constituting and reproducing a legal, political entity and an ensuing notion of togetherness, where not only international and domestic politics and economics are closely linked to the European Union's fortunes but also the status of membership is synonymous with the privilege of being part of Europe.

Shared Memories

The sense of belonging originates in shared historical memories of lasting national divisions and murderous wars, a heritage of common civilisation in the areas of classic music and arts, and a common tradition of respect for human and democratic values. It denotes a mutual awareness of the fact that national interests are becoming all the more functionally inter-related, and that without further political and defence integration the European Union will hardly be able to play for high stakes to the benefit of its people and the world's peace. Also, it points to a widespread conviction that European distinctiveness in itself is denoted by the European Union's ethnic diversity, cultural heterogeneity and linguistic pluralism. But does this sense entail a predisposition of EU citizens to feel, think and behave as having a solely EU identity at the European level regardless of nationality, language, religious conviction, local loyalties, ideology, and party affiliation?

No one doubts that, say, the Euro and European citizenship are powerful cements of the sense of belonging between EU citizens. However, few people have convincingly argued that these elements can reshape national beliefs and value orientations of each member state's society in a way that will produce and foster popular identification with the European Union. They can hardly act alone as identity symbols destined to create the self-image of a post-national community and an ideal of 'union-alist' consciousness, and thereby to inculcate in the European Union's elites and peoples the idea of European 'Union-hood'.

National Sense

Nationhood, nationalism, and statehood remain alive across Europe. For EU citizens they are the primary sources not merely of authority and legitimacy but also of felt identity. Inasmuch as it does little to construct a standard of European 'Union-hood' and 'Union-al-ism' and substitute them for 'nation-hood' and 'national-ism', the sense of belonging is not powerful enough to keep the European Union on the path towards further integration. It proves to be a sufficient but not the necessary cement of an evolving EU identity.

The problem is that it is not clear yet what the European Union means to its leadership and peoples. Despite the stunning success of its expansion to the east, the Union still needs to discover its purpose and inject new breath to the European project of integration. Does the European Union aim at building an inter-governmental, a supranational or a post-national Union? The mistake that some integrationsists often commit is to identify the future of the European Union exclusively with the creation of a traditional federal state. Having in mind the case of the United States, they suggest that the EU countries should dissolve their national structures and build federal bodies. Yet they overlook the fact that the United States, or Italy and Germany, were formed through violence or civil strife, and that in general the federal state is a product of the historical development of the nation state, and reflects nothing less than a different conception of national identity, statehood, and sovereignty.

Peaceful Process

By contrast, the process of EU integration can in no way fall into line with a linear or pre-ordained course towards taking the shape and substance of a full-fledged European federation. Rather, it has resulted in the construction of several post-state institutions through the transfer of authority from the national to the supranational level, but without eliminating the legacy of the nation state's machinery of ruling and legitimacy at all. More important still, EU integration has been launched and so far carried on by peaceful means and mutually beneficial compromises, not through war and coercion. In effect, EU identity could be normally conceived as 'union-al' rather than purely inter-governmental or supranational. It is not merely intertwined with such commonly held values in Europe as liberty, the rule of law, justice, respect for human rights, tolerance, moderation and non-discrimination as to sex, race, religion and nationality. It is also tied to the European Union's integration dialectic of inter-governmentalism and supranationalism. Therefore, EU leadership and citizens need to look for their felt identity in European 'Union-hood' and 'Union-al-ism.'

What is badly lacking, in short, is a predominant frame of reference for the Union. It is this shortage that pushes European citizens apart. Ideally, the frame could be made of a legitimising ideology, a discourse, symbols, and images, all designed to establish the historical time, depict the political and cultural space of the Union and articulate a vision of common mission. This is the necessary cement for the European Union's elites to tie its institutions together with its citizens into an integrated 'union-hood.' But that frame is striking by its absence. Alongside it goes the lack of a resolute leadership able to devise a 'union-ally' tailor-made model of democratic governance. With all those elements of identity construction missing, EU public opinion is unlikely to be swayed. That is the primary lesson to learn from the rejection of the EU Constitution in France and the

Netherlands. The European Union must win the hearts and minds of its peoples. On that count, it displays a poor record. This is the Achilles heel of European integration. The idea of European 'Unionhood' and 'Union-al-ism' still remains to be constructed and deployed. This is the critical arena in which the future of the European Union will be decided in its long march towards fuller union.

POSTSCRIPT

Is the Influence of the European Union in World Affairs Increasing?

Robert Kagan, in a much-quoted 2002 *Policy Review* article, contended that Europe has the luxury of its peace-loving, environmentally conscious society only because the United States and its military might are standing watch over the world. Kagan fleshes out this thesis in *Paradise and Power: America and Europe in the New World Order* (Alfred A. Knopf, 2003). America is like the sheriff in the movie "High Noon," according to Kagan, forced to face the outlaw alone, because the townspeople don't see the outlaw as a direct threat to themselves.

A book much more supportive of the EU is *Protecting Our Environment: Lessons from the European Union* by Janet R. Hunter and Zachary A. Smith (SUNY Albany, 2005), which praises the EU for including sustainability in its core objectives and integrating environmental and economic policies. The authors conclude that "international environmental regimes"—transnational systems of norms, rules, and structures that guide environmental action—will be necessary to solve worldwide environmental problems and, using case studies, find the EU a good model to follow.

Ever Closer Union: An Introduction to European Integration, 3rd edition, by Desmond Dinan (Lynne Rienner, 2005), offers a neutral and balanced view of the European Union that includes an excellent introduction, a map and list of abbreviations and acronyms, plus three sections of text: History, Institutions, and Policies. A short, general introduction may be found in the American Chamber of Commerce's *The EU Made Simple* (Amcham EU, 2006). Every nation gets a thumbnail profile, and there is a concise Who's Who in the European Union. *Statistical Yearbook of the EU Region* is available for free download at http://europa.eu.int/comm/eurostat/ and students should enjoy Captain Euro at http://www.captaineuro.com. Adam Andros, only child of a European ambassador and a professor of paleontology took on the identity of Captain Euro, after an event perpetrated by Dr. D. Vider.

The EU faces some compelling challenges. One concerns the question of the geographical limits of Europe. Turkey, now a candidate country, lies mostly in Asia. Its largest city, Istanbul, straddles the Bosporus Strait, giving it one foot in Europe and another in Asia. However, Ankara, its capital city, is fully outside Europe. Its membership would push the limits of the EU all the way to the borders of Iran and Iraq. Further, its population of 70 million rivals Germany's in size and is 99.8 percent Muslim. The former Pope John Paul II lobbied strenuously and unsuccessfully for over 2 years for acknowledgement of Europe's "Christian roots." Most Europeans are comfortable with Turkey's secular government. However, its accession to the EU will rest in part on substantially improved respect for the rights of non-Muslim communities as well as on Turkey's recognition of Cyprus, an EU member.

A more philosophical question asks whether there will ever be a United States of Europe. How strong a federation will be possible, how much pooling of sovereignty? France and Germany, historic enemies, now form a core of the European Union, and continent-wide war is now unthinkable—a clear gain. But, how deep is European identity? Is Europe a source of emotional attachment for most Europeans? A recent survey in the French daily *Le Figaro* found that 71 percent of French respondents took some pride in their European identity. But, for countries that remain peripheral, such as Britain, Europe may remain "a convenience rather than a concept," in the words of German Ministry official Karsten Vogt.

The Erasmus Program has brought 1.5 million Europeans to study for a year in a university outside their own country. The film "L'Auberge Espagnole" (The Spanish Inn) chronicles this jumbling of cultures and explorations of all kinds, as students develop new identities during their year of mingling.

ISSUE 20

Should the United States Pursue a Policy of Liberal Imperialism in the Twenty-First Century?

YES: Max Boot, from "Liberal Imperialism," *American Heritage* (June/July 2002)

NO: Immanuel Wallerstein, from "The Eagle Has Crash Landed," *Foreign Policy* (July/August 2002)

ISSUE SUMMARY

YES: Foreign policy author and commentator Max Boot argues that the United States should continue its policy of liberal imperialism in the twenty-first century because it represents the best alternative to insure permanent world peace.

NO: Author and professor Immanuel Wallerstein argues that U.S. foreign policy has created major problems and that the United States should cease aggressive actions, preventing further damage at home and abroad.

World War II brought an end to the age of imperialism. In its aftermath, colonial empires became sovereign, independent states and took their places in the newly formed United Nations. This process proceeded unevenly, and in some areas, nation-building could only be accomplished with aid and assistance from the United States. Sometimes military interventions occurred in order to protect the area from outside forces. Often, these interventions were not wanted by the emergent nations.

The Cold War between the free and communist worlds that accompanied imperialism's demise created a competition for spheres of influence. As each side sought to extend its control into these newly formed states, there were inevitable armed conflicts, such as U.S. military actions in Korea and Vietnam. The latter was a particularly contentious episode as thousands of Americans lost their lives fighting for a cause that many Americans had lost faith in. As a result, U.S. presidents became more cautious about committing troops to future overseas conflicts.

U.S. policy began to change with the rise to power of a group that would be known as the "neo-cons" (New Conservatives). Beginning in the 1980s during the Reagan years, they argued for the right of the United States to use force, if necessary, to extend its influence around the world, protect our international interests, and promote world peace.

Few such attempts were made in the Reagan and Clinton years, but the election of George W. Bush in 2000 brought a new group of neo-cons to policy-making positions. People such as Paul Wolfowitz, Elliott Abrams, and Richard Perle began to speak in defense of unilateral U.S. action to promote American interests in the world. The 9/11/2001 terrorist attack gave their words a sense of urgency. If states and leaders threatened U.S. interests, they had to be removed.

In 2001, a U.S. military campaign began in Afghanistan to oust the Taliban regime, which had been aiding and abetting Al-Qaeda–based terrorists. In a relatively short time, the Taliban fell, and the world witnessed the beginnings of a democratic government in Afghanistan. Following this success, President Bush set his sights on a bigger target—Saddam Hussein and his murderous regime in Iraq. Accusing him of building weapons of mass destruction and harboring terrorists, the United States led a war in Iraq with some allied assistance.

The military part of the campaign was successful: Hussein was removed from power, tried, and executed by a new Iraqi government. However, the battle for the minds and hearts of the Iraqi people has produced few tangible desired results, and the American people seem to have lost faith in this mission in the same manner that they did in Vietnam a generation ago. President Bush's plummeting approval rating and his party's loss of control of both houses of Congress in the 2006 elections chronicle this rising discontent.

Should the United States continue its policy of "liberal imperialism" and nation-building throughout the world? Here, Max Boot calls this obligation one the United States should meet. Immanuel Wallerstein argues that this policy has already failed and should be abandoned before it does any more damage to our nation and the world.

YES

Liberal Imperialism

In late January 2002 Hamid Karzai, the newly installed leader of Afghanistan, visited Washington and New York. He received a standing ovation at the President's State of the Union address, and glowing press attention, in no small part because of his gentle demeanor and splendid attire. But he did not receive what he had come for, an enlarged U.S. peacekeeping presence in his war-torn country. President Bush turned him down cold, offering him economic aid, military aid, anything but what he really wanted: U.S. troops to patrol his country and bring peace to his people. America was not going to engage in "nation building," Bush declared.

This should have come as no surprise. To large segments of the Republican foreign policy establishment and the military, nation building became anathema in the 1990s, thanks to the debacle in Somalia so powerfully depicted in Black Hawk Down. During the 2000 presidential campaign, Condoleezza Rice, now Bush's national security adviser, complained that our troops had no business escorting children to kindergarten, a reference to the American peacekeeping role in Bosnia and Kosovo. Yet U.S. attempts at nation building—otherwise known as imperialism—long predate the Clinton administration.

The most successful examples are, of course, post-World War II Germany, Italy, and Japan. The U.S. Army helped transform three militaristic dictatorships into pillars of liberal democracy—one of the most important developments of the twentieth century. Critics of nation building argue that those examples aren't relevant to today's world, that Germany, Italy, and Japan were advanced industrialized nations that had some experience with the rule of law and democratic institutions. And besides, the United States made a very large, very long-term commitment to those countries, a commitment justified by their importance to the world, but one that can not be so urgent in small Third World countries like Afghanistan and Haiti.

Fair enough. Let's leave Germany, Italy, and Japan aside, and look at the U.S. peacekeeping record in what is now known as the Third World. Between the Spanish-American War and the Great Depression, the United States embarked on an ambitious attempt at "progressive" imperialism in the Caribbean, Central America, and the Pacific. Successive administrations, from McKinley to Wilson, were emboldened to act by a variety of concerns. There were strategic reasons (keeping foreign powers out of areas deemed vital to American interests, such as

From *American Heritage*, June/July 2002, pp. 62–68. Copyright © 2002 by American Heritage, Inc. Reprinted by permission.

the Panama Canal Zone) and economic ones (expanding opportunities for American businesses in promising markets, such as China). Above all, there was the pull of "The White Man's Burden," the title of a famous poem written in 1899 by Rudyard Kipling in an attempt to persuade Washington to annex the Philippine islands.

The United States did annex the Philippines. It also occupied a number of territories that remain part of the United States to this day, under various legal guises: Samoa, Guam, Hawaii, Puerto Rico, and the Virgin Islands. A number of other places were occupied temporarily: in addition to the Philippines, the Panama Canal Zone, Haiti, the Dominican Republic, Nicaragua, and the Mexican city of Veracruz, the shortest occupation being that of Veracruz (seven months) and the longest that of the Canal Zone (almost a century). In the process the United States developed a set of colonial administrators and soldiers who would not have been out of place on a veranda in New Delhi or Nairobi. Men like Leonard Wood, the dashing former Army surgeon and Rough Rider, who went on to administer Cuba and the Philippines; Charles Magoon, a stolid Nebraska lawyer who ran the Panama Canal Zone and then Cuba during the second U.S. occupation (1906–09); and Smedley Butler, the "Fighting Quaker," a Marine who won two Congressional Medals of Honor in a career that took him from Nicaragua to China.

They were tough, colorful, resourceful operators who used methods not found in any training manual. There is, for example, the story of how the Haitian-U.S. Treaty of 1915, which gave a legal gloss to an American occupation that would last 19 years, came into being. For years Marines told one another that when Major Butler was sent over to the presidential palace to obtain the signature of President Philippe Sudre Dartiguenave, the president, not wanting to sign, hid in his bathroom. Butler simply commandeered a ladder and climbed up through the bathroom window to present the treaty and a pen to the startled Dartiguenave. "Sign here," the major commanded, and the president did. Whether or not this "gorgeous legend" (as one Marine called it) is actually true, it gives an accurate flavor of how U.S. rule was consolidated.

Most of these occupations followed a pattern. The United States was usually drawn in by political unrest and a threat to its foreign financial interests; Washington often feared that if it did not act, some other power would. The United States would then occupy the capital, and its armed forces, usually a handful of Marines, fan out over the countryside to establish order. Often there was some guerrilla resistance, but it was usually put down quickly by a small number of American troops, who had more sophisticated weaponry and (even more important) better training than their adversaries. In Haiti in 1915, 2,000 Marines pacified a country of two million people, at a cost of only three dead Americans. The longest and most arduous American colonial campaign was waged in the Philippines. It took 70,000 soldiers four years and more than 4,000 American casualties to consolidate American control over the islands.

Having established its rule, the United States would set up a constabulary, a quasi-military police force led by Americans and made up of local enlisted men. Then the Americans worked with local officials to administer a variety of public services, from vaccinations to schools to tax collection. American officials, though often resented, usually proved more efficient and less venal than their native predecessors.

A priority was improving public health, partly out of altruism and partly out of a desire to keep U.S. troops healthy in a tropical clime. The pattern was set in Cuba, where Walter Reed, an Army doctor, proved that yellow fever was spread by a particular variety of mosquito. A mosquito-eradication campaign undertaken at gunpoint drastically reduced the incidence of malaria and yellow fever, which had been ravaging the island for centuries. In Veracruz in 1914 the Army general Frederick Funston cleaned up the water supply, improved sewage, and even imported 2,500 garbage cans from the United States. The death rate among city residents plummeted.

American imperialists usually moved much more quickly than their European counterparts to transfer power to democratically elected local rulers. In 1907, under U.S. rule, the Philippines became the first Asian state to establish a national legislature. In 1935 the archipelago became a domestically autonomous commonwealth headed by President Manuel Quezon, a former insurrectionist who once complained of the difficulty of fostering nationalism under this particular colonial regime: "Damn the Americans" Why don't they tyrannize us more?" (Total independence came in 1946, after Filipinos had fought side by side with GIs against the Japanese.)

In many of the countries the United States occupied, holding fair elections became a top priority, because once a democratically elected government was installed, the Americans felt they could withdraw. In 1925 the Coolidge administration refused to recognize the results of a stolen election in Nicaragua and the following year sent in the Marines, even though the strongman who had stuffed the ballot boxes, Gen. Emiliano Chamorro Vargas, was ardently pro-American. The United States went on to administer two elections in Nicaragua, in 1928 and 1932, that even the losers acknowledged were the fairest in the country's history. "The interventions by U.S. Marines in Haiti, Nicaragua, the Dominican Republic and elsewhere in those years," writes the Harvard political scientist Samuel Huntington, "often bore striking resemblances to the interventions by Federal marshals in the conduct of elections in the American South in the 1960s: registering voters, protecting against electoral violence, ensuring a free vote and an honest count."

That is certainly not the popular impression. The interventions in Central America and the Caribbean have become infamous as "gunboat diplomacy" and as "banana wars" undertaken at the behest of powerful Wall Street interests. Smedley Butler helped solidify this myth when, after his retirement from the Marine Corps, he became an ardent isolationist and anti-imperialist. He spent the 1930s denouncing his own career, claiming he had been "a racketeer for capitalism" and a "high-class muscle man for Big Business."

In fact, in the early years of the twentieth century, the United States was least likely to intervene in those nations (such as Argentina and Costa Rica) where American investors held the biggest stakes. The longest occupations were undertaken in precisely those countries—Nicaragua, Haiti, the Dominican Republic—where the United States had the smallest economic stakes. Moreover, two of the most interventionist Presidents in U.S. history, Theodore Roosevelt and Woodrow Wilson, were united in their contempt for what TR called "malefactors of great wealth." Wilson was probably the most imperialist President of all, and his interventions had a decidedly idealistic tinge. His goal, as he proclaimed at the start of his administration, was "to teach the South American republics to elect good men."

How well did the United States achieve this aim? The record is mixed. Its greatest success (outside those territories that remain under the Stars and Stripes to this day) was in the Philippines, which was (no coincidence) the site of one of its longest occupations. Among the institutions Americans bequeathed to the Filipinos were public schools, a free press, an independent judiciary, a modem bureaucracy, democratic government, and separation of church and state. Unlike the Dutch in the East Indies, the British in Malaya, or the French in Indochina, the Americans left virtually no legacy of economic exploitation; Congress was so concerned about protecting the Filipinos that it barred large landholdings by American individuals or corporations. The U.S. legacy was also a lasting one: The Philippines have been for the most part free and democratic save for the 1972–86 period, when Ferdinand Marcos ruled by fiat. That's more than most other Asian countries can say.

The U.S. legacy in the Caribbean and Central America was more fleeting. It is not true, as some critics later charged, that the United States deliberately installed dictators such as Duvalier, Bautista, and Somoza. The governments left in power by American troops were usually democratic and decent. But they were also too weak to survive on their own. In the past the United States might have intervened to support democratically elected regimes. In the 1930s, however, President Franklin Delano Roosevelt renounced the interventionist policies of his predecessors, stretching back to the days of his cousin Theodore and beyond. Henceforth, FDR said, U.S. relations with Latin America would be governed by the Good Neighbor policy, which meant in essence that Washington would work with whoever came to power, no matter how.

The U.S. ambassador to Managua, Arthur Bliss Lane, was shocked and upset when Anastasio ("Tacho") Somoza, the commander of the Nicaraguan National Guard, murdered the former rebel leader Augusto Sandino and deposed the democratically elected president (who was also his uncle), Dr. Juan Bautista Sacasa. Lane wanted to intervene, as the United States had in the past, but Roosevelt refused. Of Somoza, FDR famously (if perhaps apocryphally) said, "He may be a son of a bitch, but he's our son of a bitch." But make no mistake: Somoza did not attain power because of U.S. support; he attained power because of its indifference. The same might be said of François Duvalier in Haiti, Rafael Trujillo in the Dominican Republic, and other dictators who took over after U.S. withdrawal.

Although its effects often wore off, U.S. rule looks pretty good by comparison with what came before and after in most countries. Haiti offers a particularly dramatic example. Prior to the U.S. occupation in 1915, seven presidents were overthrown in seven years. After the last U.S. Marines left, in 1934, the country lapsed back into instability, until, in 1957, the black nationalist Papa Doc Duvalier assumed power. He and "Baby Doc," his son Jean Claude, ruled continuously until 1986, presiding over a reign of terror undertaken by their savage secret police, the Tontons Macoutes. After Baby Doc's overthrow it was back to chaos, leavened only by despotism. In 1994 the United States was driven to intervene once again to oust a military junta and restore to power President Jean Bertrand Aristide. But no matter who's in charge, the Haitian people continue to suffer horrifying levels of poverty, crime, disease, and violence; their country is the poorest in the Western Hemisphere, and one of the poorest on earth.

By contrast, the almost two decades of American occupation stand out as an oasis of prosperity and stability. While not exactly democratic (the United States ruled for a time through an appointed president, Louis-Eustache-Antoine-François Borno) the American occupation was undertaken with minimal force. There were fewer than 800 Marines in the country, and life was freer than just about any time before or since. The Americans made no attempt to exploit Haiti economically; in fact, the U.S. authorities actively discouraged large American companies from setting up shop, for fear that they would take advantage of the people. The American administrators ran this government fairly and efficiently, and by the time they left they could tick off a long list of achievements: 1,000 miles of roads and 210 bridges constructed, 9 major airfields, 1,250 miles of telephone lines, 82 miles of irrigation canals, 11 modern hospitals, 147 rural clinics, and on and on.

Unfortunately, most of the physical manifestations of the American empire—roads, hospitals, telephone systems—began to crumble not long after the Marines pulled out. This should be no surprise; it has been true whenever more technologically advanced imperialists leave a less sophisticated area, whether they be the Romans pulling out of Britain or the British out of India. The two most lasting legacies of American interventions in the Caribbean may be a resentment of the Yanquis, now perhaps fading, and a love of baseball, still passionately felt.

That does not mean, however, that U.S. occupation is entirely futile. American troops can stop the killing, end the chaos, create a breathing space, establish the rule of law. What the inhabitants do then is up to them. If the American goal is to re-create Ohio in Kosovo or Haiti, then the occupiers are doomed to disappointment. But if the goals are more modest, American rule can serve the interests of occupiers and occupied alike. Put another way, nation building is generally too ambitious a task, but state building is not; the apparatus of a functioning state can be developed much more quickly than a national consciousness.

Most successful examples of state building start by imposing the rule of law—as the United States did in the Philippines, and Britain in India—as a prerequisite for economic development and the eventual emergence of democracy. Merely holding an election and leaving will likely achieve little, as the United States discovered in Haiti in 1994. For American occupation to have a meaningful impact, it should be fairly lengthy; if Americans are intent on a quick "exit strategy," they might as well stay home.

History teaches another important lesson: that occupation duty sometimes leads troops into committing what are today called human rights abuses. It's easy to exaggerate the extent of these excesses. Brian Linn's recent history *The Philippine War, 1899–1902* suggests that the conduct of U.S. soldiers from 1899 to 1902 was not nearly as reprehensible as everyone from Mark Twain to New Left historians of the 1960s would have us believe.

But whenever a small number of occupation troops are placed in the midst of millions of potentially hostile foreigners, some unpleasant episodes are likely to occur. During the U.S. occupation of the Dominican Republic (1916–24), a Marine captain named Charles F. Merkel became notorious as the Tiger of Seibo; he personally tortured one prisoner by slashing him with a knife, pouring salt and orange juice into the wounds, and then cutting off the man's ears. Merkel killed himself in jail after, rumor had it, a visit from two Marine officers who left him a gun with a single bullet in it. When word of such abuses reached the United States, it caused a public uproar. In the 1920 election the Republican presidential candidate Warren G. Harding sought black votes by denouncing the "rape" of Hispaniola perpetrated by a Democratic administration. This kind of criticism is not so different from the questions raised today about U.S. treatment of Taliban prisoners.

American troops must take great care to avoid heinous conduct, not only for moral reasons but also for practical ones. If imperialists are provoked into too many grisly reprisals—as the French were in Algeria, or the Americans in Vietnam—support for their enterprise back home is likely to evaporate. And it is also much harder to win the "hearts and minds" of uncommitted civilians if you are routinely torturing or killing their relatives. Some criticism of their conduct notwithstanding, this is a danger that U.S. troops have largely avoided in Afghanistan with the discriminating use of "smart" weapons.

It is not just civilians who risk getting killed in nation building; so do U.S. troops. The most notorious recent example is the Battle of Mogadishu on October 3–4, 1993, which left 18 Americans dead, 82 injured, and 1 captured. The Rangers and Delta Force commandos who took part in this all-night fire fight did not feel defeated afterward; they were prepared to get on with the job of freeing Somalia's people from the rule of warlords. But the Clinton administration decided it could not tolerate casualties and pulled out. This is the worst possible outcome because it sent a message of irresolution that emboldened America's enemies, most notably Osama bin Laden, to step up their attacks against various U.S. targets.

It is inevitable that any nation bent on imperialism will encounter setbacks. The British army suffered major defeats with thousands of casualties in the First Anglo-Afghan War (1838–42) and the Anglo-Zulu War (1879). This did not appreciably dampen British determination to defend and extend their empire. If Americans cannot adopt a similarly tough-minded attitude, they have no business undertaking nation building. This is not to suggest that America should sacrifice thousands of young men for ephemeral goals but that policymakers need to recognize that all military operations run certain risks, and the United States should not flee at the first casualty. More important, Washington should not design these operations (as with the occupation of Haiti in 1994) with the primary goal of producing no casualties. That is a recipe for ineffectuality.

Given the costs, moral and material, what is the case for undertaking imperialism at all? It's not so different today from 100 years ago. There's the economic argument: The United States can add areas like Central Asia and the Balkans to the world free-trade system. (They might seem like economic basket cases today, but so, a few decades ago, did Taiwan and South Korea. Both have prospered under U.S. military protection.) There is also the idealistic argument: The United States has a duty to save people from starvation and ethnic cleansing. This is a direct descendant of the "white man's burden," except today it's not limited to whites or to men but extends to everyone in the West. If these were the only reasons for America to undertake nation building, then it would be a hard sell, as indeed it was for large segments of the public in the 1990s. But since September 11, 2001, another argument for imperialism has come to the fore: self-interest.

We can only wonder what might have happened if after the Soviets were driven out in the early 1990s, the United States had helped build up Afghanistan into a viable state. It might not have become the home of the Taliban and Al Qaeda, and the World Trade Center might still be standing.

This is only speculation, of course. But in the Balkans we can already see a payoff to nation building undertaken by the United States and its allies. The violence that claimed some 300,000 lives in the Wars of Yugoslavian Succession is over. Kosovo, Macedonia, Croatia, Serbia, Slovenia, and Bosnia live in a state of uneasy peace under the eyes of Western troops. Aside from saving lives, there's another reason for the United States to take satisfaction in this outcome. Islamic extremists, who migrated to the Balkans in the early 1990s to help their fellow Muslims in Kosovo and Bosnia resist Serb oppression, have been denied a toehold in the region. NATO troops have been able to arrest and deport a number of terrorist suspects in Albania and Bosnia before they could blow up American installations. If U.S. troops had never intervened in the first place, it is likely that the Balkans would have turned into another Afghanistan, a refuge for terrorists, and this one located near the heart of Europe. Similar action may be necessary to drain other potential swamps that breed crime and violence.

Any call for a renewed campaign of nation building by Western states is likely to run into an obvious objection: Didn't imperialism go out of style decades ago, when European administrators were chased out of one colony after another? True enough. Europeans found that the cost of ruling Third World countries whose young men were fired up by nationalist doctrines was too high to pay. Then, too, in the wake of the Holocaust, the racist assumptions that had justified a small number of whites ruling over millions of nonwhite people lost their intellectual respectability. The British withdrew more or less gracefully from most of their empire, while the French fought to keep Vietnam and Algeria and suffered humiliating defeats. If the Europeans, with their long tradition of colonialism, have found the price of empire too high, what chance is there that Americans, whose country was born in a revolt against empire, will replace the colonial administrators of old?

Not much. The kind of imperial missions the United States is likely to undertake today are very different. The Europeans fought to subjugate "natives";

Americans will fight to bring them democracy and the rule of Law. (No one wants to put Afghanistan or Bosnia permanently under the Stars and Stripes.) European rule was justified by racial prejudices; American interventions are justified by human-rights doctrines accepted (at least in principle) by all signatories of the U.N.'s Universal Declaration of Human Rights. European expeditions were unilateral; American missions are usually blessed with international approval, whether from the U.N., NATO, or simply an ad hoc coalition.

This is not to suggest that American attempts at nation building are destined to be easy or painless. Dealing with local warlords is a difficult task that, if mishandled, can lead to disaster, as in Lebanon in 1983 or Somalia in 1993. But it is important to note that these days the bulk of ordinary people are likely to support, at least in the beginning, an American peacekeeping presence in their country. From Kosovo to Afghanistan, GIs are seen as liberators, not oppressors. Most inhabitants of these war-torn lands want American troops to stay as long as possible. The question is whether policy-makers in Washington will heed their pleas for help and launch another period of "liberal imperialism."

Immanuel Wallerstein

 **NO**

The Eagle Has Crash Landed

$\mathbf{T}$he United States in decline? Few people today would believe this assertion. The only ones who do are the U.S. hawks, who argue vociferously for policies to reverse the decline. This belief that the end of U.S. hegemony has already begun does not follow from the vulnerability that became apparent to all on September 11, 2001. In fact, the United States has been fading as a global power since the 1970s, and the U.S. response to the terrorist attacks has merely accelerated this decline. To understand why the so-called Pax Americana is on the wane requires examining the geopolitics of the 20th century, particularly of the century's final three decades. This exercise uncovers a simple and inescapable conclusion: The economic, political, and military factors that contributed to U.S. hegemony are the same factors that will inexorably produce the coming U.S. decline.

Intro to Hegemony

The rise of the United States to global hegemony was a long process that began in earnest with the world recession of 1873. At that time, the United States and Germany began to acquire an increasing share of global markets, mainly at the expense of the steadily receding British economy. Both nations had recently acquired a stable political base—the United States by successfully terminating the Civil War and Germany by achieving unification and defeating France in the Franco-Prussian War. From 1873 to 1914, the United States and Germany became the principal producers in certain leading sectors: steel and later automobiles for the United States and industrial chemicals for Germany.

The history books record that World War I broke out in 1914 and ended in 1918 and that World War II lasted from 1939 to 1945. However, it makes more sense to consider the two as a single, continuous "30 years' war" between the United States and Germany, with truces and local conflicts scattered in between. The competition for hegemonic succession took an ideological turn in 1933, when the Nazis came to power in Germany and began their quest to transcend the global system altogether, seeking not hegemony within the current system but rather a form of global empire. Recall the Nazi slogan *ein tausendjähriges Reich* (a thousand-year empire). In turn, the United States assumed the role of advocate of centrist world liberalism—recall former U.S. President Franklin D. Roosevelt's "four freedoms" (freedom of speech, of worship, from want, and

From *Foreign Policy*, July/August 2002, pp. 60–68. Copyright © 2002 by the Carnegie Endowment for International Peace. Reprinted with permission. www.foreignpolicy.com

from fear)—and entered into a strategic alliance with the Soviet Union, making possible the defeat of Germany and its allies.

World War II resulted in enormous destruction of infrastructure and populations throughout Eurasia, from the Atlantic to the Pacific oceans, with almost no country left unscathed. The only major industrial power in the world to emerge intact—and even greatly strengthened from an economic perspective—was the United States, which moved swiftly to consolidate its position.

But the aspiring hegemon faced some practical political obstacles. During the war, the Allied powers had agreed on the establishment of the United Nations, composed primarily of countries that had been in the coalition against the Axis powers. The organization's critical feature was the Security Council, the only structure that could authorize the use of force. Since the U.N. Charter gave the right of veto to five powers—including the United States and the Soviet Union—the council was rendered largely toothless in practice. So it was not the founding of the United Nations in April 1945 that determined the geopolitical constraints of the second half of the 20th century but rather the Yalta meeting between Roosevelt, British Prime Minister Winston Churchill, and Soviet leader Joseph Stalin two months earlier.

The formal accords at Yalta were less important than the informal, unspoken agreements, which one can only assess by observing the behavior of the United States and the Soviet Union in the years that followed. When the war ended in Europe on May 8, 1945, Soviet and Western (that is, U.S., British, and French) troops were located in particular places—essentially, along a line in the center of Europe that came to be called the Oder-Neisse Line. Aside from a few minor adjustments, they stayed there. In hindsight, Yalta signified the agreement of both sides that they could stay there and that neither side would use force to push the other out. This tacit accord applied to Asia as well, as evinced by U.S. occupation of Japan and the division of Korea. Politically, therefore, Yalta was an agreement on the status quo in which the Soviet Union controlled about one third of the world and the United States the rest.

Washington also faced more serious military challenges. The Soviet Union had the world's largest land forces, while the U.S. government was under domestic pressure to downsize its army, particularly by ending the draft. The United States therefore decided to assert its military strength not via land forces but through a monopoly of nuclear weapons (plus an air force capable of deploying them). This monopoly soon disappeared: By 1949, the Soviet Union had developed nuclear weapons as well. Ever since, the United States has been reduced to trying to prevent the acquisition of nuclear weapons (and chemical and biological weapons) by additional powers, an effort that, in the 21st century, does not seem terribly successful.

Until 1991, the United States and the Soviet Union coexisted in the "balance of terror" of the Cold War. This status quo was tested seriously only three times: the Berlin blockade of 1948–49, the Korean War in 1950–53, and the Cuban missile crisis of 1962. The result in each case was restoration of the status quo. Moreover, note how each time the Soviet Union faced a political crisis among its satellite regimes—East Germany in 1953, Hungary in 1956, Czechoslovakia in 1968, and Poland in 1981—the United States engaged in little more than propaganda exercises, allowing the Soviet Union to proceed largely as it deemed fit.

Of course, this passivity did not extend to the economic arena. The United States capitalized on the Cold War ambiance to launch massive economic reconstruction efforts, first in Western Europe and then in Japan (as well as in South Korea and Taiwan). The rationale was obvious: What was the point of having such overwhelming productive superiority if the rest of the world could not muster effective demand? Furthermore, economic reconstruction helped create clientelistic obligations on the part of the nations receiving U.S. aid; this sense of obligation fostered willingness to enter into military alliances and, even more important, into political subservience.

Finally, one should not underestimate the ideological and cultural component of U.S. hegemony. The immediate post-1945 period may have been the historical high point for the popularity of communist ideology. We easily forget today the large votes for Communist parties in free elections in countries such as Belgium, France, Italy, Czechoslovakia, and Finland, not to mention the support Communist parties gathered in Asia—in Vietnam, India, and Japan—and throughout Latin America. And that still leaves out areas such as China, Greece, and Iran, where free elections remained absent or constrained but where Communist parties enjoyed widespread appeal. In response, the United States sustained a massive anticommunist ideological offensive. In retrospect, this initiative appears largely successful: Washington brandished its role as the leader of the "free world" at least as effectively as the Soviet Union brandished its position as the leader of the "progressive" and "anti-imperialist" camp.

One, Two, Many Vietnams

The United States' success as a hegemonic power in the postwar period created the conditions of the nation's hegemonic demise. This process is captured in four symbols: the war in Vietnam, the revolutions of 1968, the fall of the Berlin Wall in 1989, and the terrorist attacks of September 2001. Each symbol built upon the prior one, culminating in the situation in which the United States currently finds itself—a lone superpower that lacks true power, a world leader nobody follows and few respect, and a nation drifting dangerously amidst a global chaos it cannot control.

What was the Vietnam War? First and foremost, it was the effort of the Vietnamese people to end colonial rule and establish their own state. The Vietnamese fought the French, the Japanese, and the Americans, and in the end the Vietnamese won—quite an achievement, actually. Geopolitically, however, the war represented a rejection of the Yalta status quo by populations then labeled as Third World. Vietnam became such a powerful symbol because Washington was foolish enough to invest its full military might in the struggle, but the United States still lost. True, the United States didn't deploy nuclear weapons (a decision certain myopic groups on the right have long reproached), but such use would have shattered the Yalta accords and might have produced a nuclear holocaust—an outcome the United States simply could not risk.

But Vietnam was not merely a military defeat or a blight on U.S. prestige. The war dealt a major blow to the United States' ability to remain the world's dominant economic power. The conflict was extremely expensive and more or less used up the U.S. gold reserves that had been so plentiful since 1945. Moreover, the United States incurred these costs just as Western Europe and Japan experienced major economic upswings. These conditions ended U.S. preeminence in the global economy. Since the late 1960s, members of this triad have been nearly economic equals, each doing better than the others for certain periods but none moving far ahead.

When the revolutions of 1968 broke out around the world, support for the Vietnamese became a major rhetorical component. "One, two, many Vietnams" and "Ho, Ho, Ho Chi Minh" were chanted in many a street, not least in the United States. But the 1968ers did not merely condemn U.S. hegemony. They condemned Soviet collusion with the United States, they condemned Yalta, and they used or adapted the language of the Chinese cultural revolutionaries who divided the world into two camps—the two superpowers and the rest of the world.

The denunciation of Soviet collusion led logically to the denunciation of those national forces closely allied with the Soviet Union, which meant in most cases the traditional Communist parties. But the 1968 revolutionaries also lashed out against other components of the Old Left—national liberation movements in the Third World, social-democratic movements in Western Europe, and New Deal Democrats in the United States—accusing them, too, of collusion with what the revolutionaries generically termed "U.S. imperialism."

The attack on Soviet collusion with Washington plus the attack on the Old Left further weakened the legitimacy of the Yalta arrangements on which the United States had fashioned the world order. It also undermined the position of centrist liberalism as the lone, legitimate global ideology. The direct political consequences of the world revolutions of 1968 were minimal, but the geopolitical and intellectual repercussions were enormous and irrevocable. Centrist liberalism tumbled from the throne it had occupied since the European revolutions of 1848 and that had enabled it to co-opt conservatives and radicals alike. These ideologies returned and once again represented a real gamut of choices. Conservatives would again become conservatives, and radicals, radicals. The centrist liberals did not disappear, but they were cut down to size. And in the process, the official U.S. ideological position—antifascist, anticommunist, anticolonialist—seemed thin and unconvincing to a growing portion of the world's populations.

The Powerless Superpower

The onset of international economic stagnation in the 1970s had two important consequences for U.S. power. First, stagnation resulted in the collapse of "developmentalism"—the notion that every nation could catch up economically if the state took appropriate action—which was the principal ideological claim of the Old Left movements then in power. One after another, these regimes faced internal disorder, declining standards of living, increasing debt dependency on international financial institutions, and eroding credibility. What had seemed in the 1960s to be the successful navigation of Third World decolonization by the United States—minimizing disruption and maximizing the smooth transfer of power to regimes that were developmentalist but scarcely revolutionary— gave way to disintegrating order, simmering discontents, and unchanneled radical temperaments. When the United States tried to intervene, it failed. In 1983, U.S. President Ronald Reagan sent troops to Lebanon to restore order. The troops were in effect forced out. He compensated by invading Grenada, a country without troops. President George H.W. Bush invaded Panama, another country without troops. But after he intervened in Somalia to restore order, the United States was in effect forced out, somewhat ignominiously. Since there was little the U.S. government could actually do to reverse the trend of declining hegemony, it chose simply to ignore this trend—a policy that prevailed from the withdrawal from Vietnam until September 11, 2001.

Meanwhile, true conservatives began to assume control of key states and interstate institutions. The neoliberal offensive of the 1980s was marked by the Thatcher and Reagan regimes and the emergence of the International Monetary Fund (IMF) as a key actor on the world scene. Where once (for more than a century) conservative forces had attempted to portray themselves as wiser liberals, now centrist liberals were compelled to argue that they were more effective conservatives. The conservative programs were clear. Domestically, conservatives tried to enact policies that would reduce the cost of labor, minimize environmental constraints on producers, and cut back on state welfare benefits. Actual successes were modest, so conservatives then moved vigorously into the international arena. The gatherings of the World Economic Forum in Davos provided a meeting ground for elites and the media. The IMF provided a club for finance ministers and central bankers. And the United States pushed for the creation of the World Trade Organization to enforce free commercial flows across the world's frontiers.

While the United States wasn't watching, the Soviet Union was collapsing. Yes, Ronald Reagan had dubbed the Soviet Union an "evil empire" and had used the rhetorical bombast of calling for the destruction of the Berlin Wall, but the United States didn't really mean it and certainly was not responsible for the Soviet Union's downfall. In truth, the Soviet Union and its East European imperial zone collapsed because of popular disillusionment with the Old Left in combination with Soviet leader Mikhail Gorbachev's efforts to save his regime by liquidating Yalta and instituting internal liberalization (perestroika plus glasnost). Gorbachev succeeded in liquidating Yalta but not in saving the Soviet Union (although he almost did, be it said).

The United States was stunned and puzzled by the sudden collapse, uncertain how to handle the consequences. The collapse of communism in effect signified the collapse of liberalism, removing the only ideological justification behind U.S. hegemony, a justification tacitly supported by liberalism's ostensible ideological opponent. This loss of legitimacy led directly to the Iraqi invasion of Kuwait, which Iraqi leader Saddam Hussein would never have dared had the Yalta arrangements remained in place. In retrospect, U.S. efforts in the Gulf War accomplished a truce at basically the same line of departure.

But can a hegemonic power be satisfied with a tie in a war with a middling regional power? Saddam demonstrated that one could pick a fight with the United States and get away with it. Even more than the defeat in Vietnam, Saddam's brash challenge has eaten at the innards of the U.S. right, in particular those known as the hawks, which explains the fervor of their current desire to invade Iraq and destroy its regime.

Between the Gulf War and September 11, 2001, the two major arenas of world conflict were the Balkans and the Middle East. The United States has played a major diplomatic role in both regions. Looking back, how different would the results have been had the United States assumed a completely isolationist position? In the Balkans, an economically successful multinational state (Yugoslavia) broke down, essentially into its component parts. Over 10 years, most of the resulting states have engaged in a process of ethnification, experiencing fairly brutal violence, widespread human rights violations, and outright wars. Outside intervention—in which the United States figured most prominently—brought about a truce and ended the most egregious violence, but this intervention in no way reversed the ethnification, which is now consolidated and somewhat legitimated. Would these conflicts have ended differently without U.S. involvement? The violence might have continued longer, but the basic results would probably not have been too different. The picture is even grimmer in the Middle East, where, if anything, U.S. engagement has been deeper and its failures more spectacular. In the Balkans and the Middle East alike, the United States has failed to exert its hegemonic clout effectively, not for want of will or effort but for want of real power.

The Hawks Undone

Then came September 11—the shock and the reaction. Under fire from U.S. legislators, the Central Intelligence Agency (CIA) now claims it had warned the Bush administration of possible threats. But despite the CIA's focus on al Qaeda and the agency's intelligence expertise, it could not foresee (and therefore, prevent) the execution of the terrorist strikes. Or so would argue CIA Director George Tenet. This testimony can hardly comfort the U.S. government or the American people. Whatever else historians may decide, the attacks of September 11, 2001, posed a major challenge to U.S. power. The persons responsible did not represent a major military power. They were members of a nonstate force, with a high degree of determination, some money, a band of dedicated followers, and a strong base in one weak state. In short, militarily, they were nothing. Yet they succeeded in a bold attack on U.S. soil.

George W. Bush came to power very critical of the Clinton administration's handling of world affairs. Bush and his advisors did not admit—but were undoubtedly aware—that Clinton's path had been the path of every U.S. president since Gerald Ford, including that of Ronald Reagan and George H.W. Bush. It had even been the path of the current Bush administration before September 11. One only needs to look at how Bush handled the downing of the U.S. plane off China in April 2001 to see that prudence had been the name of the game.

Following the terrorist attacks, Bush changed course, declaring war on terrorism, assuring the American people that "the outcome is certain" and informing the world that "you are either with us or against us." Long frustrated by even the most conservative U.S. administrations, the hawks finally came to dominate American policy. Their position is clear: The United States wields overwhelming military power, and even though countless foreign leaders consider it unwise for Washington to flex its military muscles, these same leaders cannot and will not do anything if the United States simply imposes its will on the rest. The hawks believe the United States should act as an imperial power for two reasons: First, the United States can get away with it. And second, if Washington doesn't exert its force, the United States will become increasingly marginalized.

Today, this hawkish position has three expressions: the military assault in Afghanistan, the de facto support for the Israeli attempt to liquidate the Palestinian Authority, and the invasion of Iraq, which is reportedly in the military preparation stage. Less than one year after the September 2001 terrorist attacks, it is perhaps too early to assess what such strategies will accomplish. Thus far, these schemes have led to the overthrow of the Taliban in Afghanistan (without the complete dismantling of al Qaeda or the capture of its top leadership); enormous destruction in Palestine (without rendering Palestinian leader Yasir Arafat "irrelevant," as Israeli Prime Minister Ariel Sharon said he is); and heavy opposition from U.S. allies in Europe and the Middle East to plans for an invasion of Iraq.

The hawks' reading of recent events emphasizes that opposition to U.S. actions, while serious, has remained largely verbal. Neither Western Europe nor Russia nor China nor Saudi Arabia has seemed ready to break ties in serious ways with the United States. In other words, hawks believe, Washington has indeed gotten away with it. The hawks assume a similar outcome will occur when the U.S. military actually invades Iraq and after that, when the United States exercises its authority elsewhere in the world, be it in Iran, North Korea, Colombia, or perhaps Indonesia. Ironically, the hawk reading has largely become the reading of the international left, which has been screaming about U.S. policies—mainly because they fear that the chances of U.S. success are high.

But hawk interpretations are wrong and will only contribute to the United States' decline, transforming a gradual descent into a much more rapid and turbulent fall. Specifically, hawk approaches will fail for military, economic, and ideological reasons.

Undoubtedly, the military remains the United States' strongest card; in fact, it is the only card. Today, the United States wields the most formidable military apparatus in the world. And if claims of new, unmatched military technologies are to be believed, the U.S. military edge over the rest of the world is considerably greater today than it was just a decade ago. But does that mean, then, that the United States can invade Iraq, conquer it rapidly, and install a friendly and stable regime? Unlikely. Bear in mind that of the three serious wars the U.S. military has fought since 1945 (Korea, Vietnam, and the Gulf War), one ended in defeat and two in draws—not exactly a glorious record.

Saddam Hussein's army is not that of the Taliban, and his internal military control is far more coherent. A U.S. invasion would necessarily involve a serious land force, one that would have to fight its way to Baghdad and would likely suffer significant casualties. Such a force would also need staging grounds, and Saudi Arabia has made clear that it will not serve in this capacity. Would Kuwait or Turkey help out? Perhaps, if Washington calls in all its chips. Meanwhile, Saddam can be expected to deploy all weapons at his disposal, and it is precisely the U.S. government that keeps fretting over how nasty those weapons might be. The United States may twist the arms of regimes in the region, but popular sentiment clearly views the whole affair as reflecting a deep anti-Arab bias in the United States. Can such a conflict be won? The British General Staff has apparently already informed Prime Minister Tony Blair that it does not believe so.

And there is always the matter of "second fronts." Following the Gulf War, U.S. armed forces sought to prepare for the possibility of two simultaneous regional wars. After a while, the Pentagon quietly abandoned the idea as impractical and costly. But who can be sure that no potential U.S. enemies would strike when the United States appears bogged down in Iraq?

Consider, too, the question of U.S. popular tolerance of nonvictories. Americans hover between a patriotic fervor that lends support to all wartime presidents and a deep isolationist urge. Since 1945, patriotism has hit a wall whenever the death toll has risen. Why should today's reaction differ? And even if the hawks (who are almost all civilians) feel impervious to public opinion, U.S. Army generals, burnt by Vietnam, do not.

And what about the economic front? In the 1980s, countless American analysts became hysterical over the Japanese economic miracle. They calmed down in the 1990s, given Japan's well-publicized financial difficulties. Yet after overstating how quickly Japan was moving forward, U.S. authorities now seem to be complacent, confident that Japan lags far behind. These days, Washington seems more inclined to lecture Japanese policymakers about what they are doing wrong.

Such triumphalism hardly appears warranted. Consider the following April 20, 2002, *New York Times* report: "A Japanese laboratory has built the world's fastest computer, a machine so powerful that it matches the raw processing power of the 20 fastest American computers combined and far outstrips the previous leader, an I.B.M.-built machine. The achievement . . . is evidence that a technology race that most American engineers thought they were winning handily is far from over." The analysis goes on to note that there are "contrasting scientific and technological priorities" in the two countries. The Japanese machine is built to analyze climatic change, but U.S. machines are designed to simulate weapons. This contrast embodies the oldest story in the history of hegemonic powers. The dominant power concentrates (to its detriment) on the military; the candidate for successor concentrates on the economy. The latter has always paid off, handsomely. It did for the United States. Why should it not pay off for Japan as well, perhaps in alliance with China?

Finally, there is the ideological sphere. Right now, the U.S. economy seems relatively weak, even more so considering the exorbitant military expenses associated with hawk strategies. Moreover, Washington remains politically isolated; virtually no one (save Israel) thinks the hawk position makes sense or is worth encouraging. Other nations are afraid or unwilling to stand up to Washington directly, but even their foot-dragging is hurting the United States.

Yet the U.S. response amounts to little more than arrogant arm-twisting. Arrogance has its own negatives. Calling in chips means leaving fewer chips for next time, and surly acquiescence breeds increasing resentment. Over the last 200 years, the United States acquired a considerable amount of ideological credit. But these days, the United States is running through this credit even faster than it ran through its gold surplus in the 1960s.

The United States faces two possibilities during the next 10 years: It can follow the hawks' path, with negative consequences for all but especially for itself. Or it can realize that the negatives are too great. Simon Tisdall of the *Guardian* recently argued that even disregarding international public opinion, "the U.S. is not able to fight a successful Iraqi war by itself without incurring immense damage, not least in terms of its economic interests and its energy supply. Mr. Bush is reduced to talking tough and looking ineffectual." And if the United States still invades Iraq and is then forced to withdraw it will look even more ineffectual.

President Bush's options appear extremely limited, and there is little doubt that the United States will continue to decline as a decisive force in world affairs over the next decade. The real question is not whether U.S. hegemony is waning but whether the United States can devise a way to descend gracefully, with minimum damage to the world, and to itself.

POSTSCRIPT

Should the United States Pursue a Policy of Liberal Imperialism in the Twenty-First Century?

Liberal imperialism has attracted the attention of many scholars and policymakers eager to contribute to the debate on its merits. Scottish historian Niall Ferguson has argued persuasively that the United States is obligated to assume the mantle of world leadership as the free world's best hope. In "A World without Power," *Foreign Policy* (July–August 2004), he provides a strong case for such a course of action. *Collapse: The Rise and Fall of the American Empire* (Penguin Books, 2005) provides more information on the subject. Max Boot's *The Savage Wars of Peace: Small Wars and the Rise of American Power* (Basic Books, 2003) provides historical and contemporary examples to support his arguments in support of liberal imperialism.

This policy also has its critics. In "The Compulsive Empire," *Foreign Policy* (July/August 2003), Robert Jarvis argues that U.S. liberal imperialism is both dangerous and counterproductive. In "Imperial Amnesia," *Foreign Policy* (July/August 2004), John Judis reports striking similarities between American interventions in Mexico and the Philippines, almost a century ago, and the current one in Iraq. In *The Paradox of American Power: Why the World's Only Superpower Can't Go It Alone* (Oxford University Press, 2002), foreign policy expert Joseph J. Nye builds a case for multilateral actions, not unilateral ones, when force is needed to guarantee world peace.

Any attempt to predict the future role of liberal imperialism in the world would be speculative in nature; however, there are trends that could be used to offer some useful information. Support in the United States for the Iraq War is rapidly declining as the death toll increases and the new Iraqi government seems helpless in controlling the nation's affairs. Furthermore, rather than limiting the worldwide terrorist threat, many believe that our presence seems to have increased it.

In November 2008, the American people will elect a new president. That election will determine the future course of U.S. foreign policy and the effects it will have on the world.

Contributors to This Volume

EDITORS

JOSEPH R. MITCHELL is a history instructor at Howard Community College in Columbia, Maryland, and a popular regional speaker. He is currently co-authoring a book on the history of the planned city of Columbia, Maryland, to be published by The History Press in late 2006. He received an MA in history from Loyola College in Maryland and an MS in African American history from Morgan State University, also in Maryland. He is the principal co-editor of *The Holocaust: Readings and Interpretations* McGraw-Hill/Dushkin, 2001).

HELEN BUSS MITCHELL is a professor of philosophy and director of the women's studies program at Howard Community College in Columbia, Maryland. She is the author of *Roots of Wisdom*, 4th ed., available in Spanish and Chinese in 2006, and *Readings from the Roots of Wisdom*, 3rd ed. (Wadsworth/Thomson Learning). She is also the creator, writer, and host of a philosophy telecourse *For the Love of Wisdom*, which has been distributed nationally by PBS and Dallas TeleLearning. She has earned numerous degrees, including a PhD in Intellectual and Women's history from the University of Maryland.

AUTHORS

DEREK ALDCROFT is research professor in economic history at Manchester Metropolitan University, London, and the author of *Europe in the International Economy, 1500–2000* (Edward Elgar Publishers, 2003).

W. G. BEASLEY is emeritus professor of the history of the Far East at the University of London. He is the author of many works on Japan, including *The Rise of Modern Japan* (St. Martin's Press, 1995).

V. R. BERGHAHN is professor of history at Brown University. He is the author of fifteen books, including the forthcoming *German Big Business and Europe, 1918–1992.*

HERBERT BIX is professor of history at Binghamton University and the author of *Hirohito and the Making of Modern Japan* (Perennial Books, 2001).

MAX BOOT is Senior Fellow in National Security Studies at the Council of Foreign Relations in New York.

CHRISTOPHER R. BROWNING is professor of history at the University of North Carolina, Chapel Hill. A leading Holocaust historian, his most recent book is *Nazi Policy, Jewish Workers, German Killers* (Cambridge University Press, 2000).

PAUL A. COHEN is professor of Asian studies and history at Wellesley College in Massachusetts. He is the author of *Discovering History in China: American Historical Writing on the Recent Chinese Past* (Columbia University Press, 1984).

LANCE E. DAVIS is a professor at the California Institute of Technology. He is the coauthor of *In Pursuit of Leviathan: Institutions, Productivity, and Profits in American Whaling, 1818–1906* (University of Chicago Press, 1997).

ALISON DES FORGES a board member and researcher at the Human Rights Watch, is the author of *Leave None to Tell the Story: Genocide in Rwanda* (Human Rights Watch, 1999).

HASIA R. DINER is professor of history at New York University. Her research interests include American Jewish history, immigration-ethnic history, and women's history.

JOHN L. ESPOSITO is a professor of Middle Eastern studies. His publications include *Islam and Democracy* (Oxford University Press, 1996).

EFSTATHIOS T. FAKIOLAS, a graduate of the department of war studies, King's College, London, is Strategy and SouthEast European Affairs Analyst in the Department of Strategic Planning, ATEbank (Agricultural Bank of Greece).

JOHN LEWIS GADDIS is Robert Lovett Professor of History at Yale University. He has contributed extensively to cold war historiography with at least six major works on the subject.

DANIEL JONAH GOLDHAGEN is a professor of government and social studies at Harvard University. He has written articles and reviews on subjects related to the Holocaust.

ANDREW GORDON is a professor of history at Harvard University and the author of *A History of Modern Japan: From Tokugawa Times to the Present* (Oxford University Press, 2003).

HENRIETTA HARRISON is a lecturer in Chinese at the University of Leeds in England. She is the author of *The Making of Republican China: Political Ceremonies and Symbols in China, 1861–1911* (Oxford University Press, 2000).

ROBERT A. HUTTENBACK was a professor of history at the University of California at Santa Barbara, where he was chancellor from 1977 to 1986.

MARK JUERGENSMEYER is professor of sociology and director of global and international studies at the University of California at Santa Barbara. He is the author of *Terror in the Mind of God: The Global Rise of Religious Violence* (University of California Press, 2000).

CHRISTINE KINEALY is a fellow of the University of Liverpool, where she lectures on Irish and British history. She is the author of *A Death-Dealing Famine: The Great Hunger in Ireland* (Pluto Press, 1997).

PETER KROPOTKIN (1842–1921) was a Russian revolutionary who wrote his autobiography entitled *Memoirs of a Revolutionist* in 1899.

STEPHEN S. LARGE is lecturer in modern Japanese studies and reader in modern Japanese history at the University of Cambridge in England. He is the author of *Emperors of the Rising Sun: Three Biographies* (Kodansha International, 1997).

RENÉ LEMARCHAND is professor emeritus at the University of Florida and has written about and worked extensively in Southern Africa.

ANATOL LIEVEN is a senior associate at the Carnegie Endowment for International Peace. His latest book is *Chechnya: Tombstone of Russian Power* (Yale University Press, 1998).

JOHN M. MacKENZIE is a professor of imperial history at Lancaster University in England. He is the editor of *Imperialism and Popular Culture* (Manchester University Press, 1986).

STEVEN MAJSTOROVIC is an assistant professor of political science at the University of Wisconsin, Eau Claire. He has written and lectured extensively on modern European politics.

MARK MAZOWER a professor of history at Birbeck College, University of London, and Columbia University, is the author of *Dark Continent: Europe's Twentieth Century* (Vintage, 1998).

FRANÇOISE NAVAILH is a Russian film historian at the University of Paris. She teaches Russian language and is aÿspecialist in Russian cinema.

A. T. NUYEN is a member of the department of philosophy at the University of Queensland in Brisbane, Australia.

LESLEY A. RIMMEL is associate professor in the department of history, School of International Studies, at the Oklahoma State University in Stillwater, Oklahoma.

JACK SCARBOROUGH is a management educator at Barry University in Florida and a retired U.S. Coast Guard commander.

SIMON SCHAMA is a professor of art and art history at Columbia University. He is the author of *The Embarrassment of Riches: An Interpretation of Dutch Culture During the Golden Age* (Alfred A. Knopf, 1987).

JOAN W. SCOTT is a professor of social science at Princeton University's Institute for Advanced Study. She is the author of *Gender and the Politics of History* (Columbia University Press, 1988).

MARTIN J. SHERWIN is the Walter S. Dickson Professor History at Tufts University. He is the author of *A World Destroyed: The Atomic Bomb and the Grand Alliance* (Random House, 1977).

EDWARD SHORTER directs the history of medicine program at the University of Toronto. He is the author of *From the Mind Into the Body* (Free Press, 1996).

SHARIF SHUJA is adjunct assistant professor of international relations at Bond University in Australia. He has contributed numerous articles to professional journals that specialize in Asian affairs.

MITCHELL P. SMITH is associate professor of political science and international and area studies and codirector of the European Union Center at the University of Oklahoma. His latest book is *States of Liberalization: Redefining the Public Sector in Integrated Europe* (State University of New York Press, 2005).

RICHARD STITES is a professor of history at Georgetown University. He is the author of *Revolutionary Dreams* (Oxford University Press, 1989) and *Russian Popular Culture* (Cambridge University Press, 1992).

LOUISE A. TILLY is an assistant professor of history and director of the women's studies program at the University of Washington. She is the author of numerous articles on social history.

SIMA WALI is president of Refugee Women in Development and vice president and treasurer of the Sisterhood Is Global Institute. A native of Afghanistan, she is an international advocate for the rights of refugee and internally displaced women.

IMMANUEL WALLERSTEIN is a senior research scholar at Yale University and author of, most recently, *The End of the World as We Know It: Social Science for the Twenty-First Century* (University of Minnesota Press, 1999).

PETER WETZLER is professor of Japanese business, politics, and language at the East Asia Institute of the Ludwigshafen School of Business Administration in Germany. He has published works on Japanese history both in English and German.

SAMUEL R. WILLIAMSON, JR. is professor of history at the University of the South. He is the author of *Austria-Hungary and the Origins of the First World War* (St. Martin's Press, 1991).

WARREN ZIMMERMANN served as the last U.S. ambassador to Yugoslavia, and, after retirement from the Foreign Service, is now a professor of international diplomacy at Columbia University.

Index